FLEDGLING EAGLES

FLEDGLING EAGLES

Christopher Shores

WITH JOHN FOREMAN, CHRISTIAN-JACQUES EHRENGARDT,
HEINRICH WEISS AND BJORN OLSEN

GRUB STREET · LONDON

Published by
Grub Street
The Basement
10 Chivalry Rd
London SW11 1HT

Copyright © 1991 Grub Street, London
Text copyright © Christopher Shores

Reprinted 1998

Maps by Jeff Jefford

British Library Cataloguing-in-Publication Data
Shores, Christopher, *1937–*
    Fledgling eagles: the complete account of air operations during
    the phoney war and Norwegian Campaign 1940.
    I. Title.
    940.5421481

ISBN 0 948817 42 9

Edited by John Davies

Typeset by Maron Graphics, Wembley

Printed and bound in Great Britain by
Biddles Ltd, Guildford and King's Lynn

———

CONTENTS

INTRODUCTION AND ACKNOWLEDGEMENTS

As with most of the campaign histories with which I have been involved, this one has been 'in the making' for something over 20 years. Elements from the research undertaken have provided the basis for various other articles and publications over the years, but here the whole story is brought together for the first time.

Firstly, I would like to express my personal thanks to my patient and long-suffering co-authors, who have had a long wait to see the fruits of their labours. Secondly, a particular debt of gratitude goes to my old friend and colleague, that great naval/air historian David Brown, now Head of Naval Historical Branch, but a young Sea Venom navigator when I first knew him! His help and guidance with the operations of the carrier-based Skua squadrons off the Norwegian coast was absolutely vital.

Help and encouragement over the years has also come from other regular members of our 'team' – notably Brian Cull, Russell Guest and Winfried Bock.

At the time of going to press, the exciting news of the discovery of a huge new 'cache' of information on Luftwaffe fighter claims had reached us. Indeed, we had just enough time to see the first examples of this in the comprehensive victory claims list at the end of Dr Jochen Prien's third volume of his excellent history of Jagdgeschwader 53. Where large-scale rewriting was not required, we were able to incorporate some of the new information regarding this unit. However, it is now clear to us that much new or additional information in this regard is coming to light from this source which will impinge not only on this volume, but also on the earlier titles in this series covering Malta and the Balkans. It will therefore be the intention in due course to publish a slim addendum incorporating the further information relevant to all four books.

In conclusion thanks are expressed to Bjorn Hafsten, who provided additional data on the Luftwaffe in Norway at proof-reading stage; to Flt Lt Andrew Thomas and Knut Arveng for the supply of some excellent photos, and to Wg Cdr 'Jeff' Jefford for preparing the maps. Thanks also to Johann Illner and the late Josef Fözö for details of their own activities in 1940.

Christopher Shores
29 October 1991

MAP 1: THE WEST WALL AND MAGINOT LINE

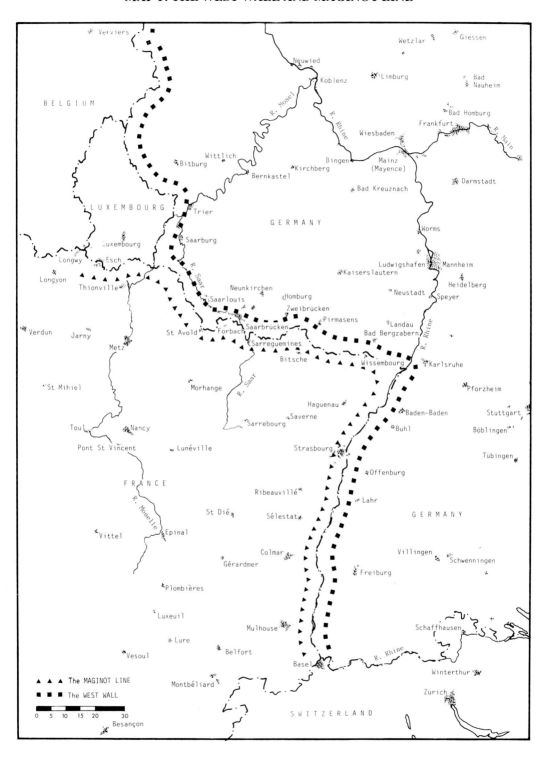

▲ ▲ ▲ The MAGINOT LINE
■ ■ ■ The WEST WALL

0 5 10 15 20   30

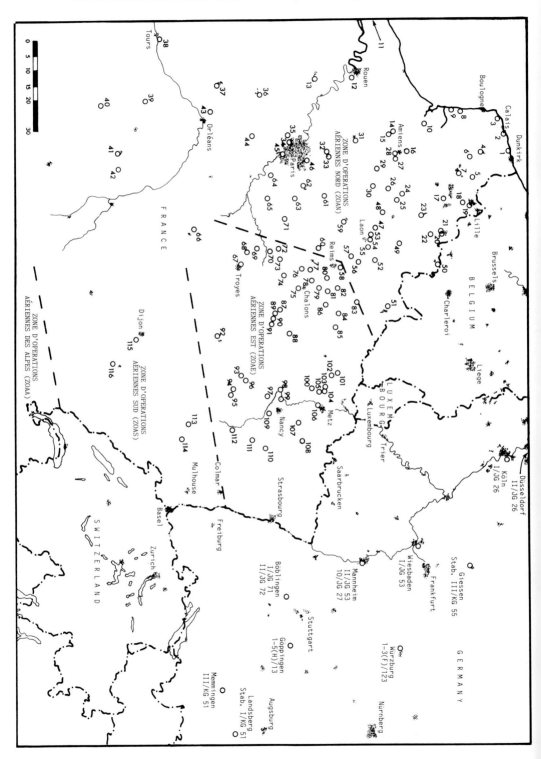

KEY

1	Dunkirk/Mardyck	59	Soissons/Saconin
2	Calais/Marck	60	Le Plessis/Belleville
3	Calais/St-Inglevert	61	Betz/Bouillancy
4	St-Omer/Wizernes	62	Meaux/Esbly
5	Merville	63	Coulommiers
6	Norrent Fontes	64	Melun/Villaroche
7	Béthune/Labuissière	65	Nangis
8	Le Touquet	66	Auxerre/Branches
9	Berck	67	Troyes/Barberey
10	Abbeville/Drucat	68	Echemines
11	Le Havre/Octeville	69	Romilly
12	Rouen/Boos	70	Anglure/Vouarces
13	Evreux/Fauville	71	La Ferté-Gaucher
14	Poix	72	Sézanne
15	Moyencourt	73	Connantre
16	Bertangles	74	Sommesous
17	Vitry-en-Artois	75	Chalons/Ecury-sur-Coole
18	Lille/Ronchin	76	Villeneuve/Vertus
19	Lille/Seclin	77	Plivot
20	Valenciennes	78	Condé/Vraux
21	Denain/Prouvy	79	Mourmelon-le-Grand
22	Vertain/Le Quesnoy	80	Wez-Thuisy
23	Cambrai/Niergnies	81	Auberives
24	Flamicourt	82	Bétheniville
25	Mons-en-Chaussée	83	Attigny
26	Rosières-en-Santerre	84	Challerange
27	Amiens/Glisy	85	Chatel-Chéhéry
28	Amiens/Mont Joie	86	Suippes
29	Montdidier	87	Vitry-le-Francois/Vauxclerc
30	Roye/Amy	88	Vassincourt/Bar-le-Duc
31	Beauvais/Tillé	89	Orconte
32	Persan/Beaumont	90	Perthes
33	Cantilly-lès-Aigles	91	St Dizier
34	Paris/Villacoublay	92	Chaumont/Semoutiers
35	Paris/Buc	93	Neufchâteau
36	Chartres	94	Vittel
37	Châteaudun	95	Auzainvilliers
38	Tours	96	Martigny-lès-Gerbonveaux
39	Romorantin/Pruniers	97	Toul/Ochey
40	Châteauroux/Deols	98	Toul/Croix-de-Metz
41	Bourges	99	Velaine-en-Haye
42	Avord	100	Cambley
43	Orléans/Bricy	101	Senon/Spincourt
44	Etampes/Mondesir	102	Etain/Rouvres
45	Paris/Orly	103	Etain/Buzy
46	Paris/Le Bourget	104	Conflans/Doncourt
47	La Fère/Courbes	105	Mars-la-Tour
48	St-Simon/Clastres	106	Metz/Frescaty
49	Villers-lès-Guise	107	Delme/Essey
50	Maubeuge/Elesmes	108	Morhange
51	Mézières/Tournes/Belval	109	Nancy/Azelot
52	Clermont-lès-Fermes	110	Herbeviller
53	Laon/Couvrons	111	Xaffévillers
54	Laon/Chambry	112	Epinal/Dogneville
55	Laon/Athies/Athies-sur-Laon	113	Luxeuil/St-Sauveur
56	Amifontaine	114	Lure/Malbouhans
57	Jouvincourt/Berry-au-Bac	115	Di jon/Longevic
58	Reims/Courcy	116	Dole/Taveaux

MAP 3: THE NORTH SEA TRIANGLE

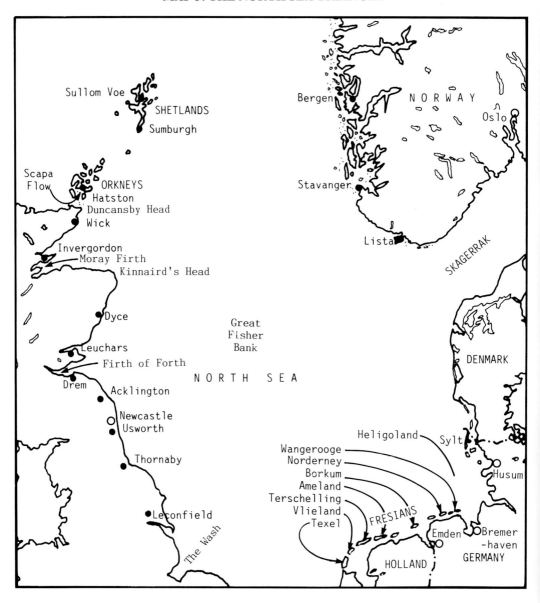

PART ONE

Chapter 1

BACKGROUND TO THE AIR WAR

The period between the Anglo-French declaration of war on Germany on 3 September 1939, following that nation's invasion of Poland, and the start of the major German Spring offensive on 10 May 1940, has gone down in history as the 'Phoney War'. It was indeed an odd period of wary preparation, of speculation and of complacency. Following the 'Blitzkrieg' in Poland, it was often referred to satirically as the 'Sitzkrieg', since both sides appeared to sit back and do little.

The events of great moment that transpired during 1940 have conspired to overshadow this early period to a great extent, so that today the geographical areas of conflict, the make-up and disposition of the opposing forces, and the duties they undertook have tended to slip into the backwaters of history, and be lost to the sight of most who have an interest in the air war. Yet during these early months the war in the air was by no means always 'phoney', many savage engagements taking place. Indeed it was a period when several of the major theories of the air forces involved were first put to the test and their strengths or weaknesses discovered.

The team of researchers who have prepared this study have gathered together the first complete picture of the air war over Western and Northern Europe (not just France) during this period, coupled with the strategic and tactical situations behind it. It is their hope and intention to set before the reader a concise and clear picture of events, containing much that is new and of interest.

The situation in September 1939 can scarcely be described as a sudden leap from peace to war. The road to general conflict had been a cumulative one, each act of aggression or of international tension fuelled and followed by the next. In Europe Hitler's occupation of Czechoslovakia had already caused a general mobilization during 1938, while Italy's annexation of Albania had passed with less notice. The long and bloody civil war in Spain had been over for only some six months, while in the Far East China had been fighting desperately for survival against the armies of Imperial Japan for over two years. Unnoted in the West, an undeclared war of considerable proportions was just reaching its climax on the borders of Manchuria and Mongolia, fought between Japan and the Soviet Union. Here the forces employed in terms of armour and air power far outstripped those operating in Spain; indeed not until May 1940 were these actions to be matched in intensity and magnitude.

Following the fall of France and the Low Countries in early summer 1940, the main focus of aerial operations for both the Royal Air Force and the Luftwaffe by day became centred over south-eastern England, north-west France and

Belgium. This remained as an area of great importance and much in the public eye for the next four years until after the Normandy invasion had been launched and had made substantial headway.

In 1939 the scenario was totally different. France was an ally of Britain, so there was no question of major activity in the air space dividing the two countries, while Belgium, Holland and Denmark were still neutral, as was Norway further to the north. This left two widely separated areas over which all major actions were to take place. The first of these was above the normal frontier between France and Germany, an area which an inspection of Map 1 shows to be not so large as might be expected. To the north lie the boundaries of Belgium and Luxembourg, while to the south are Switzerland and Italy. Only the line from Saarbrücken to Mulhouse, via Karlsruhe and Strasbourg forms a direct joint with German territory. Here are the oft-disputed provinces of Alsace and Lorraine, where Germanic names are as common among the populace as are those specifically Gallic ones, and where both languages are commonly spoken. Here also was the vaunted Maginot Line, and facing it Germany's Westwall. These were great permanent fortifications which it was surmised would prevent any advance in either direction unless one or other of the adversaries was prepared once more to infringe the sovereignty of the neutrals to north or south.

It was in this area that the Armeé de l'Air and the Royal Air Force contingents, the Air Component and the Advanced Air Striking Force (AASF), would meet the Luftwaffe on frequent occasions, and where most initial Allied dispositions would concentrate.

Far away to the north and west, a separate war was to be launched between the Luftwaffe and the RAF, its axis based on the line from the north German coastlines on the North Sea and Baltic — the German Bight — to Scotland and Northern England. This area, roughly triangular in shape, will conveniently be referred to by the name coined for it by the Germans — the North Sea Triangle. The German Bight at this time provided Germany's only access to the sea, and it was here that the Kriegsmarine was based, with its modern capital ships, its destroyers and cruisers, and its flotillas of U-Boats.

Across the North Sea, situated to the north of Scotland, was the main base of the British Home Fleet at Scapa Flow. Substantial numbers of airfields were situated in Scotland and the north of England for the defence of Scapa Flow and of the industrial heartlands of the North and Midlands against attacks from northern Europe. Initially the opposing naval bases were to provide the main focus for attacks by the bombing forces of the opposing combatants.

Comparative Aerial Strengths

It is appropriate in the first instance to consider the strength, dispositions and equipment of the air forces involved, beginning with that of the German Luftwaffe, which was in September 1939 undoubtedly the most prepared of the three.

The greater part of the Luftwaffe's operational strength was grouped into four Luftflotten (Air Fleets) on an area basis:

Luftflotte 1	East	Luftflotte 3	West
Luftflotte 2	North-West	Luftflotte 4	East

Additionally there was an autonomous Luftwaffe Lehrdivision which was

COMPARATIVE STRENGTHS: SEPTEMBER 1939

Aircraft type	Luftwaffe			Armée de l'Air	Royal Air Force
	West	East	Total		
Bombers	274 (250 Serv)*	897 (825 Serv)	1,171 (1,075 Serv)	359 App	480
Dive-bombers	34 (32 Serv)	315 (295 Serv)	349 (327 Serv)	—	—
Ground-attack Aircraft	—	39 (39 Serv)	39 (39 Serv)	—	—
Single-engined Fighters	600 (587 Serv)	459 (428 Serv)	1,059 (1,015 Serv)	439	549 est
Twin-engined Fighters	—	102 (90 Serv)	102 (90 Serv)	68	105 est
Long-range Reconnaissance	136 (122 Serv)	181 (159 Serv)	317 (281 Serv)	163	30 est
Close-range Reconnaissance & Army Co-op	95 (67 Serv)	144 (109 Serv)	239 (176 Serv)	345+	96 est
Coastal (including flyingboats & floatplanes)	133 (124 Serv)	56 (51 Serv)	189 (175 Serv)	—	171
Transport	12 (10 Serv)	533 (496 Serv)	545 (506 Serv)	30	—
Sub Total	1,289 (1,192 Serv)	2,726 (2,492 Serv)	4,010 (3,684 Serv)	Aeronavale	Fleet Air Arm
Naval Bombers	—	—	—	108	141
Naval Fighters/Fighter/Dive-Bombers	—	—	—	42	18
Shipborne Floatplanes	—	—	—	—	15
Long-range Flyingboats	—	—	—	30 app	—
Short-range Flyingboats & Floatplanes	—	—	—	150 app	80 est
Sub Total				330 app	254 est
TOTALS	1,284 (1,192 Serv)	2,726 (2,492 Serv)	4,010 (3,684 Serv)	1,734 app	1,730 app

For this purpose, Seaflieger and Trägergruppe 186 aircraft are treated as being part of the Luftwaffe

Not including Armée de l'Air & Aeronavale units in Madagascar, Syria, Indo-China, or in the South Pacific

Totals do not include 21 reserve squadrons of Bomber Command which were employed only for operational training, although two became operational later; nor does it include 435 RAF aircraft based overseas

* Serv = Servicable

equipped with Staffeln of all major service types; this was an operational test organisation, staffed by experienced personnel and entrusted with the testing and development of new techniques under operational conditions. There was also a self-sufficient unit, Luftwaffenkommando Ostpreussen, based in East Prussia, deployed along the Polish "Corridor". In September 1939 both these units were operating under the control of Luftflotte 1.

Additional to the above forces were the army co-operation and tactical reconnaissance units of the Heeresfliegerverbände; the coastal units of the Seefliegerverbände, and a sizeable air transport force. The first of these was divided into three Heeresgruppen, one in the west (four Staffeln of Do 17Ps,

Heinkel He 111Hs of KG 1 at Giessen, winter 1939/40. *(ECPA)*

seven Staffeln of Hs 126s and one of He 45s and 46s); and two in the east — Heeresgruppe Nord and Sud. The Seefliegerverbände included coastal reconnaissance, bombing and minelaying units equipped with flyingboats and floatplanes, which were based on the Baltic and North Sea coasts, 11 Staffeln in the west and five in the east. There was also a composite group, Trägergruppe 186, intended for carrier-based operations when a new aircraft carrier which was under construction (*Graf Zeppelin*) was completed. In the meantime the single Staffel of dive-bombers was attached to Lutflotte 1, while the two fighter Staffeln operated in Luftflotte 2, all land-based. Finally there was the transport force; 7 Fliegerdivision was the paratroop and airlanding force, with five Gruppen of Ju 52/3m aircraft, five paratroop battalions and elements of an airlanding infantry regiment. A further seven Gruppen provided a general transport service throughout Germany. There were altogether some 650 transport aircraft on strength, with further civil airliners that could be impressed for service if required.

On the outbreak of war Luftflotten 1 and 4 were at once engaged in the campaign in Poland, thus offering no immediate threat to the British and French when they became involved. Initial operations over the Franco-German border would be undertaken by units of Luftflotte 3, while activity over the German Bight and North Sea would be the province of Luftflotte 2 and the Seefliegerverbände. Within a few days of the initial attack on Poland the Luftflotten involved were reinforced from the west. Luftflotte 2 despatched Kampfgeschwader 27 to Luftflotte 1, together with 2/KG 54 and 5/KG 28, while Stab, I and II/KG 55 were sent to Luftflotte 4. This meant that effectively the whole dive-bomber force and the major part of the medium bomber strength was deployed in the east, leaving only reconnaisance and fighter units, together with a minimal bombing force to provide a holding defence in the west.

At this time the Luftwaffe was approaching completion of a programme of re-equipment of its units with the most modern products available from the German aircraft industry, but this programme was by no means finished. Among the elite Stukagruppen, all had re-equipped with Junkers Ju 87B aircraft (or the basically-similar R version, modified for long-range operations). The only unit still flying the older Henschel Hs 123A single-seat biplane dive-bomber was II(Schlacht)/LG 2, an operational test unit investigating ground attack — as

Main Luftwaffe Seeflieger floatplanes at the outbreak of the war were the Heinkel He 59 biplane (left foreground and right background) and He 115 monoplane (centre background). *(ECPA)*

opposed to dive-bombing — techniques; even this unit was scheduled to receive Ju 87Bs at an early date, although in the event this re-equipment was never to take place.

Amongst the medium bomber units, all early versions of the standard Heinkel He 111 had been replaced in front line Gruppen by the improved H and P models, but for those Kampfgruppen equipped with bombing variants of the Dornier Do 17, modernization had not progressed quite so far. Although the current Do 17Z version was now the predominant type, quite substantial numbers of the older, more lightly-armed Do 17M were still in service, together with a few even earlier Do 17Es. The Do 17P equipped the majority of the long-range reconnaissance Staffeln. The best bomber yet to appear in Germany, the

Junkers Ju 88A, was only just entering service, a single Staffel (1/KG 25) having been formed with these aircraft just before the outbreak of war.

For army co-operation and short-range tactical reconnaissance duties, the Henschel Hs 126A predominated, although a few Staffeln still had on hand small numbers of the earlier biplane Heinkel He 45 and monoplane He 46 types. Transport aircraft were almost exclusively Junkers Ju 52/3m trimotors, to which were added a small handful of experimental types and impressed civil airliners. Water-based types included six Staffeln of He 60 single-engined biplane float-planes, five of Dornier Do 18 twin-engined flyingboats, four of Heinkel He 59 twin-engined biplane floatplanes, one of Heinkel He 115 twin-engined mono-plane floatplanes, and a few Arado Ar 196 single-engined monoplane float-planes, intended for catapult launching from battleships and cruisers. The He 115Bs were intended to supplant the He 59s at early date, while the Ar 196As were to do likewise to the He 60s.

Messerschmitt Bf 109Es at dispersal at the outbreak of war. *(ECPA)*

The fighter force had all-but completed its modernization so far as the Jagdgruppen were concerned, but had barely started in respect of the Zerstörer-gruppen. 14 Gruppen and two Staffeln were fully-equipped with early models of the Messerschmitt Bf 109E — probably the most effective fighter anywhere in the world at the time — while one more Gruppe and one Staffel were partially equipped with this type. Only two night-flying Staffeln and the single Marine Jagdgruppe still retained the earlier versions of the fighter (the latter unit whilst awaiting a deck-landing conversion of the Bf 109E). A further pair of night-fighter Staffeln still flew the old Arado Ar 68E biplane.

The situation amongst the Zerstörergruppen was very different. Only three Gruppen had so far received the powerful new twin-engined Messerschmitt Bf 110C heavy fighter for which these units had been formed. Six further Gruppen still retained Bf 109D fighters of substantially lower performance and armament than either the Bf 110C or the Bf 109E, and one had been equipped with the latter type in the interim. All were awaiting re-equipment with the twin-engined aircraft, but in the meantime were being employed on normal fighter duties, for which all but two received a temporary designation, together with the title Jagdgruppe. These were as follows:

Normal Designation	Temporary Designation	Aircraft
II/ZG 1	JGr 101	Bf 109E
I/ZG 2	JGr 102	Bf 109D
I/ZG 26	—	Bf 109D
II/ZG 26	—	Bf 109D
III/ZG 26	JGr 126	Bf 109D
I/ZG 52	JGr 152	Bf 109D
II/ZG 76	JGr 176	Bf 109D

The activities of these latter units were to give rise to some misleading early assessments of German fighter performance, since they were frequently engaged both over Poland and in Western Europe. The Bf 109D was of similar performance to the French Morane 406, but was outperformed by both the other main Anglo-French types it might meet — the Curtiss H-75A Hawk and the Hawker Hurricane I. It was also inferior in armament to all but the early models of the H-75A, with only four 7.9mm machine guns, one in each wing and two above the engine in the nose. The Bf 109E on the other hand, was superior in performance — and later in armament — to all these initial opponents. However the E-1 models in service at the start of the war were armed like the C and D versions, only with four 7.9mm machine guns. This armament was manifestly inadequate for a modern fighter, and subsequent models would have the wing guns replaced with 20mm MG FF cannons. It would be some weeks before cannon-equipped models became available for normal issue to front line units, and initially even the splendid 'Emil' lagged behind most Allied fighters at least in terms of armament.

Over Poland the Bf 109E was to play no large part, being retained mainly for the defence of Luftwaffe bases. Air superiority was left to the Zerstörergruppen, which operated the earlier Bf 109s and their new Bf 110s. Reports from Poland noted that during that campaign the Polish fighter pilots considered the Bf 110 to be a much more formidable opponent than the Bf 109; this was the reason for that conclusion. Indeed during the Polish fighting 94 victories were to be claimed by Bf 110 pilots, while only 13 were credited to those flying Bf 109s. By a strange coincidence however, by far the most successful individual pilot in Poland was Hpt Hannes Gentzen of JGr 102, who claimed no less than seven of the Bf 109 successes.

An Order of Battle for the Luftwaffe units in the west at the start of September 1939, including those Headquarters (Oberbefehlshaber der Luftwaffe) units which might operate there begins on page 16. To provide a full picture of Luftwaffe strength, a similar Order of Battle for the forces in the east, which initially would be fully involved elsewhere, is reproduced on pages 19-24.

It is probably useful at this stage to consider the comparative rank designations and the abbreviations generally used for these in so far as they relate to the commanders and aircrew of the three air forces involved. These may be found on page 47.

LUFTWAFFE ORDER OF BATTLE — WEST

Unit	Base	Commander	Aircraft on Strength/ Serviceable	Type
OBERBEFEHLSHABER DER LUFTWAFFE				
FA/ObdL				
8(F)/LG 2	Berlin-Werder	Maj Keienburg	12/11	Do 17P
10(F)/LG 2	Kiel-Holtenau	Maj Wolff	12/10	Do 18
1 Westa/ObdL	Berlin Gatow	Reg Rat Dr Kopp	8/8	He 111J
Ln Abtlg 100	Köthen	Maj Pusch	12/10	Ju 52
			6/6	He 111H
LUFTFLOTTE 2	Braunschweig	Gen d Flieger Felmy		
		Oberst Wühlisch — Chief of Staff		
Direct Command				
1(F)/122	Goslar	Hpt Wappenhaus	12/10	Do 17P
2(F)/122	Münster		11/10	He 111H
Wekustaffel 26	Braunschweig	Oblt von Rotberg	6/6	Do 17P
3 Fliegerdivision	Münster	GenMaj Putzier		
Kampfgeschwader 54		Oberst Lackner		
Stabstaffel	Fritzlar	Hpt Graf von Still fried und Rattonitz	6/6	He 111P
I/KG 54	Fritzlar	Maj Höhne	33/30	He 111P
II/KG 28	Gütersloh	Maj Koester	35/34	He 111P
1/KG 25	Jever	Hpt Pohle	12/12	Ju 88A
4 Fliegerdivision	Braunschweig	Gen d Flieger Keller		
I/KG 26	Lübeck-Blankensee	Maj Loebel	36/32	He 111H
Luftgaukommando XI	Hannover	GenLt Wolff		
II/JG 77	Nordholz	Maj Schumacher	33/33	Bf109E
5 & 6(J)/TrGr186	Kiel-Holtenau	Maj Hagen	23/23	Bf 109B/E
Zerstörergeschwader 26	Varel	Oberst von Döring		
Stabsschwarm	Varel		3/1	Bf 109D
I/ZG 26	Varel	Hpt Kaschka	43/39	Bf 109D
JGr 126	Neumünster	Hpt Schalk	46/41	Bf 109D
Luftgaukommando VI	Münster	GenMaj A.Schmidt		
Jagdgeschwader 26	Odendorf	Oberst von Schleich		
Stabsschwarm	Odendorf		3/2	Bf 109E
I/JG 26	Odendorf	Maj Handrick	44/43	Bf 109E
II/JG 26	Bönninghardt	Hpt Knüppel	38/38	Bf 109E
11(NJ)/LG 2	Köln-Ostheim	Oblt Bascilla	9/9	Bf 109D

I/JG 52	Bonn-Hangelar	Hpt von Pfeil und Ellguth	48/38	Bf 109E
II/ZG 26	Werl	Maj Vollbracht	48/45	Bf 109D
LUFTFLOTTE 3	Roth by Nürnberg	Gen d Flieger Sperrle GenMaj Ritter von Pohl — Chief of Staff		
Direct Command				
1(F)/123	Ansbach		12/11	Do 17P
2(F)/123	Würzburg	Hpt von Normann	12/12	Do 17P
Wekustaffel 51	Roth	Oblt Nissen	6/6	He 111J
5 Fliegerdivision	Gersthofen, near Augsburg	GenMaj Ritter von Greim		
JGr 152	Biblis	Hpt Lessman	48/45	Bf 109D
Kampfgeschwader 51		Oberst Dr Fisser		
Stabsstaffel	Landberg		9/9	He 111H
I/KG 51	Memmingen	Obstlt Korte	36/34	He 111H
III/KG 51	Memmingen	Oberst Stoeckl	36/33	He 111H
6 Fliegerdivision	Frankfurt/Main	GenMaj Dessloch		
Kampfgeschwader 53		Oberst Stahl		
Stabsstaffel	Schwäbisch Hall	Hpt Wittmann	6/6	He 111H
II/KG 53	Schwäbisch Hall	Obstlt Kohlbach	32/30	He 111H
III/KG 53	Giebelstadt	Maj von Braun	33/32	He 111H
III/StG 51	Wertheim	Maj von Klitzing	3/3	Do 17P
			31/29	Ju 87B
JGr 176	Gablingen	Hpt Schmidt-Coste	50/42	Bf 109D
Luftgaukommando VII	München	GenLt Zenetti		
I/JG 51	Eutingen	Hpt von Berg	46/32	Bf 109E
I/JG 71	Fürstenfeldbruck	Maj Kramer	34/34	Bf 109D
10/JG 72	Böblingen	Oblt Fözö	17/11	Ar 68
11/JG 72	Böblingen	Hpt von Kornatzki	16/11	Ar 68
Luftgaukommando XII	Wiesbaden	GenMaj Dr Weissmann		
Jagdgeschwader 53		GenMaj Klein		
Stabsschwarm	Wiesbaden-Erbenheim		3/3	Bf 109E
I/JG 53	Kirchberg	Hpt von Janson	46/38	Bf 109E
II/JG 53	Mannheim-Dandhofen	Hpt Frhr von Maltzahn	44/38	Bf 109E
Luftgaukommando XIII	Nürnberg	GenMaj Heilingbrunner		
I/JG 70	Herzogenaurach	Maj Kithil	50/21	Bf 109D

General der Flieger Berlin   GenMaj Ritter
  beim ObdM   Oberst Roth - Chief of Staff

F d LUFT WEST   Jever   GenMaj Bruch

Küstenflieger-				
gruppe 106	Norderney	Obstlt Jordan		
1/KüFlGr 106	Norderney	Hpt von Schrötter	10/10	He 60
2/KüFlGr 106	Norderney	Obstlt Bischoff	12/12	Do 18
3/KüFlGr 106	Borkum	Maj Horn	10/10	He 59
3/KüFlGr 706	Norderney	Hpt Stein	12/12	He 59

Küstenflieger-				
gruppe 306	Hörnum	Obstlt von Helleben		
2/KüFlGr 306	Hörnum	Hpt von Roth	12/11	Do 18
2/KüFlGr 506	Hörnum	Hpt Hartwig	12/11	Do 18
2/KüFlGr 606	Hörnum	Hpt von Laue	12/9	Do 18

Küstenflieger-				
gruppe 406	List	Maj Minner		
1/KüFlGr 406	List	Hpt Wiesand	8/8	He 115
2/KüFlGr 406	List	Maj Bartels	12/10	Do 18
3/KüFlGr 406	List	Hpt Bergemann	9/9	He 59
1/BöFlSt 196	Wilhelmshaven	Maj Lessing	12/12	He 60

General der Luftwaffe beim ObdH
          Berlin   GenMaj Bogatsch
                 Oberst Drum - Chief of Staff

HEERESGRUPPE 'C' (KOLUFT)
          Frankfurt   GenMaj Bieneck

Heeresgruppe C

1(F)/22	Frankfurt-Rebstock		12/10	Do 17P
XXX Armee-Korps 4(H)/12	near Rheinberg		12/7	He 46
V ArmeeKorps				
3(H)/13	Villingen		12/8	Hs 126

5 Armee   Mayen   Oberst Krüger

5 Armee 2(F)/22	Bonn-Hangelar		12/8	Do 17P
VI ArmeeKorps				
2(H)/12	Rüdesheim		12/10	Hs 126
GenKomm Eifel				
1(H)/12	Wengerohr		12/11	Hs 126

1 Armee   Kreuznach   Oberst Sperrling

1 Armee 3(F)/22	Koblenz-Karthausen		12/10	Do 17P

LUFTWAFFE ORDER OF BATTLE — WEST (Continued)

IX ArmeeKorps				
1(H)/13	Worms		11/11	Hs 126
XII ArmeeKorps				
4(H)/22	Hoppstädten		12/8	Hs 126
GenKomm				
Saarpfalz 1(H)/23	Pferdsfeld		12/8	Hs 126
7 Armee	Calw	Oberst Kieffer		
7Armee				
7(F)/LG 2	Deckenpfronn		12/11	Do 17P
GenKomm				
Oberrhein	Huchenfeld/			
2(H)/13	Malmsheim		12/4	Hs 126

LUFTWAFFE ORDER OF BATTLE — EAST

Unit	Base	Commander	Aircraft on Strength/ Serviceable	Type
LUFTFLOTTE 1	Stettin-Henningsholm	Gen d Flieger Kesselring		
Direct Command				
1(F)/121	Stargard-Klützow	Oblt Klinkicht	12/10	Do 17P/F
3(F)/121	Stargard-Klützow		12/7	Do 17P/F
Wekustaffel 1	Stargard	Oblt Woyna	3/3	He 111J
1 Fliegerdivision	Schönfeld/Crössinsee	GenLt Grauert		
Kampfgeschwader 1		GenMaj Kessler		
Stabsstaffel	Kolberg		9/9	He 111H
I/KG 1	Kolberg	Oberstlt Krauss	38/34	He 111E
I/KG 152	Pinnow-Plathe	Maj Kosch	37/34	He 111H
Kampfgeschwader 26		GenMaj Sieburg		
Stabsstaffel	Gabbert		6/5	He 111H
II/KG 26	Gabbert	Maj von Busse	35/31	He 111H
I/KG 53	Schönfeld-Crössinsee	Maj von Mahnert	31/31	He 111H
Kampfgeschwader 27		Oberst Behrendt		
Stabsstaffel	Werneuchen		6/5	He 111P
I/KG 27	Werneuchen	Oberstlt Graumnitz	35/31	He 111P
II/KG 27	Neuhardenberg	Maj de Salengre Drabbe	36/32	He 111P
III/KG 27	Königsberg/ Neumark	Maj Nielsen	36/33	He 111P
II/StG 2	Stolp-Reitz	Hpt Schmidt	3/3	Do 17P
			35/34	Ju 87B
III/StG 2	Stolp-West	Hpt Ott	3/3	Do 17P
			36/34	Ju 87B
IV(St)/LG 1	Stolp-Reitz	Hpt Kögel	3/3	Do 17P
			39/37	Ju 87B

Unit	Base	Commander	Strength	Aircraft
4(St)/TrGr 186	Stolp-West	Hpt Blattner	12/12	Ju 87B
I/ZG 1	Mühlen I	Maj Huth	34/27	Bf 110C
I(J)/LG 2	Malzkow (1 Staffel)	Hpt Trübenbach	42/33	Bf 109E
	Lottin (2 & 3 Staffeln)			
2(F)/121	Schönfeld/Crössinsee	Maj Wenz	11/10	Do 17P/F
JGr 101	Lichtenau	Maj Reichardt	48/48	Bf 109E
Lutwaffenkomman-	Königsberg-Ballith	GenLt Wimmer		
do Ostpreussen				
Kampfgeschwader 3		Oberst von Chamier-Glisczinski		
Stabsstaffel	Elbing		9/7	Do 17Z
II/KG 3	Heiligenbeil	Maj Munske	38/36	Do 17Z
III/KG 3	Heiligenbeil	Oberstlt Neuhüttler	39/30	Do 17Z
I/StG 1	Elbing	Hpt Hozzel	3/2	Do17P
			38/38	Ju 87B
1(F)/120	Neuhausen	Maj Schub	12/11	Do 17P
Luftwaffen-				
Lehrdivision	Gut Wickbold/Jesau	GenMaj Förster		
Lehrgeschwader 1		Oberst Dr Knauss		
Stabsstaffel	Neuhausen		9/8	He 111H
II/LG 1	Powunden	Maj Dobratz	39/34	He 111H
III/LG 1	Prowehren	Maj Bormann	39/32	He 111H
Kampfgeschwader 2		Oberst Fink		
Stabsstaffel	Jesau		9/9	Do 17Z
I/KG 2	Gerdauen	Maj Krahl	36/33	Do 17M
II/KG 2	Schippenbeil	Oberstlt Weitkus	39/37	Do 17Z
I(Z)/LG 1	Jesau	Maj Grabmann	33/32	Bf 110C
4(F)/121	Jesau	Hpt Kerber	12/11	Do 17P/F
Luftgaukommando	Königsberg/			
I	Ostpreussen	GenMaj Musshoff		
I/JG 1	Gutenfeld	Maj Woldenga	46/46	Bf 109E
I/JG 21	Gutenfeld	Hpt Mettig	39/37	Bf 109D
Luftgaukommando				
III	Berlin	GenLt Weise		
Jagdgeschwader 2		Oberstlt von Massow		
Stabsschwarm	Döberitz		3/3	Bf 109E
I/JG 2	Döberitz	Maj Vieck	41/40	Bf 109E
10(N)/JG 2	Straussberg	Hpt Blumensaat	9/9	Bf 109D
Luftgaukommando				
IV	Dresden	GenMaj Mayer		
Jagdgeschwader 3		Oberstlt Ibel		
Stabsschwarm	Zerbst		3/3	Bf 109E
I/JG 3	Brandis	Maj von Houwald	44/38	Bf 109E

Unit	Location	Commander	Strength	Aircraft
I/JG 20	Sptottau	Maj Lehmann	37/36	Bf 109E
LUFTFLOTTE 4	Reihenbach/ Schlesien	Gen d Flieger Löhr		
Direct Command				
3(F)/123	Schweidnitz	Hpt Liebe-Piderit	12/12	Do 17P
Wekustaffel 76	Schweidnitz	Reg Rat Dr Dubois	3/3	He IIIJ
2 Fliegerdivision	Grottkau/Schlesien	GenMaj Loerzer		
Kampfgeschwader 4		Oberst Fiebig		
Stabsstaffel	Oels		6/6	He 111P
I/KG 4	Langenau	Oberstlt Maier	27/27	He 111P
II/KG 4	Oels	Maj Erdmann	30/30	He 111P
III/KG 4	Langenau	Maj Evers	33/32	He 111P
Kampfgeschwader 76		Oberst Schultheiss		
Stabsstaffel	Breslau-Schöngarten		9/9	Do 17Z
I/KG 76	Breslau Schöngarten	Oberstlt Fröhlich	36/36	Do 17Z
III/KG 76	Rosenborn	Oberstlt Zach	39/39	Do 17Z
Kampfgeschwader 77		Oberst Seywald		
Stabsstaffel	Grottkau		9/9	Do 17E/F
I/KG 77	Brieg	Maj Balck	37/37	Do 17E
II/KG 77	Grottkau	Oberstlt Augustin	39/39	Do 17E
III/KG 77	Brieg	Oberst von Stutterheim	38/34	Do 17E
I/StG 2	Nieder-Ellguth	Maj Dinort	3/3	Do 17P
			38/37	Ju 87B
I/ZG 76	Ohlau	Hpt Reinecke	35/31	Bf 110C
3(F)/122	Woisselsdorf	Maj Schneider	12/10	Do 17P
Fliegerführer z b V	Oppeln	GenMaj von Richthofen		
Stukageschwader 77		Oberst Schwartzkopf		
Stabsschwarm	Neudorf		3/3	Ju 87B
I/StG 77	Ottmuth	Hpt von Dalwigk	3/3	Do 17P
			39/34	Ju 87B
II/StG77	Neudorff	Hpt von Schönborn	3/3	Do 17P
			39/38	Ju 87B
I/StG 76	Nieder-Ellguth	Hpt Siegel	3/3	Do 17P
			36/28	Ju 87B

JGr 102	Gross-Stein	Hpt Gentzen	45/45	Bf 109D
Lehrgeschwader 2		Oberstlt Baier		
Stabsschwarm (J)	Nieder-Ellguth		3/2	Bf 109E
II(Schlacht)/LG 2	Altsiedel	Maj Spielvogel	39/39	Hs 123
1(F)/124	Schlosswalden	Oblt Stockhausen	11/10	Do 17P

Luftgaukommando				
VIII	Breslau	GenMaj Waber		
I/JG 76	Ottmütz	Hpt von Müller-Rienzburg	51/45	Bf 109E
I/JG 77	Juliusburg-Nord	Hpt Janke	48/43	Bf 109E

Luftgaukommando **XVII**	Vienna	Gen d Flak Hirschauer	
No Flying Units under Command			

En route from Luftflotte 2 to join Luftflotte 4

Kampfgeschwader 55		GenMaj Sussmann		
Stabsstaffel			6/6	He 111P
I/KG 55		Maj Heyna	33/25	He 111P
II/KG 55		Oberstlt Lachemair	29/25	He 111P

F d Luft Ost	Dievenow/Pommern	GenMaj Coeler	

Küstenfliegergruppe **506**	Pillau/Ostpreussen	Oberstlt von Wild		
1/KüFlGr 506	Pillau/Ostpreussen	Hpt Busch	12/10	He 60
3/KüFlGr 506	Pillau/Ostpreussen	Hpt Fehling	10/9	He 59

Küstenfliegergruppe **706**	Kamp/Pommern	Oberstlt Edert		
1/KüFlGr 706	Nest/Pommern	Maj Kaiser	12/11	He 60
1/KüFlGr 306	Nest/Pommern	Hpt Heyn	12/11	He 60
5/BoFlSt 196	Kiel-Holtenau	Hpt Wibel	10/10	He 60

HEERESGRUPPE NORD (KOLUFT)	Bad Polzin	GenMaj Krocker	

Heeresgruppe Nord				
2(F)/11	Bad Polzin		12/12	Do 17P
3 Armee	Mohrungen	Oberst Zock		
3 Armee 3(F)/10	Wiesenhof		12/9	Do 17P
XXI ArmeeKorps				
1(H)/10	Oschen	Maj von Frantzius	11/10	Hs 126
I ArmeeKorps				
2(H)/10	Ganshorn	Oberstlt Thiet	12/12	Hs 126
4 Armee	Jastrow	Oberst Keiper		
4 Armee 3(F)/11		Maj von Berchem	12/10	Do 17P

II ArmeeKorps					
	3(H)/21		Maj Reichardt	12/12	Hs 126
III ArmeeKorps					
	2(H)/21		Hpt Fischer-See	11/6	Hs 126
XIX ArmeeKorps, att. 3 PzDiv					
	9(H)/LG1	Scholastivkovo, near Preuss. Friedland	Hpt Börner	12/12	Hs 126

HEERESGRUPPE SÜD (KOLUFT)

		Neisse	GenMaj Julius Schulz		

Heeresgruppe Süd

	4(F)/11	Neisse	Hpt Kirchbach	12/11	Do 17P
VII ArmeeKorps					
	4(H)/31	Schwieben	Hpt Nagel	12/10	He 45/46

8 Armee   Breslau   Oberst von Gerlach

8 Armee	1(H)/21	Mirkau	Hpt Warnet	12/12	Hs 126
X ArmeeKorps					
	4(H)/23	Juliusburg-Süd	Maj Filips	12/12	He 46/45
XIII ArmeeKorps					
	5(H)/13	Juliusburg-Süd	Maj Pinnow	12/11	He 46/45

10 Armee   Oppeln   Oberstlt Lohmann

10 Armee	3(F)/31	Stubendorf	Hpt Borsikow	12/7	Do 17P
IV ArmeeKorps			Maj von		
	1(H)/41	Stubendorf	Winterfeld	12/5	Hs 126
XI ArmeeKorps					
	4(H)/21	Gross-Lassewitz	Oblt Cucuel	12/6	He 46/45
XIV ArmeeKorps					
	3(H)/12	Kreutzberg-Süd	Oblt Raabe	12/8	Hs 126/He 46
4 PzDiv					
	4(H)/13	Kreutzberg-Süd	Oblt Schloer	12/9	Hs 126/He 46
XV ArmeeKorps					
	1(H)11	Grünwiese	Hpt Haufer	12/10	Hs 126/He 46
XVI ArmeeKorps					
	2(H)/41	Gross-Lassewitz	Hpt Haack	12/11	Hs 126
3 leiDiv			Hpt Meyer-		
	3(H)/41	Stubendorf	Sach	12/6	Hs 126/He 46
1 PzDiv					
	2(H)/23	Gross-Lassweitz	Maj Stein	12/9	Hs 126/He 46

OBERBEFEHLSHABER DER LUFTWAFFE

7 Fliegerdivision	Wahlstatt	GenMaj Student		
A St FlDiv 7	Liegnitz	Oblt Sähloff (Equipment not known)		
Kampfgeschwader				
z b V1		Oberstlt Morzik		
Stabsschwarm	Liegnitz		3/3	Ju 52
I/KGzbV 1	Schönfeld-Seifersdorf	Maj Witt	53/53	Ju 52
II/KGzbV 1	Schönfeld-Seifersdorf	Oberstlt Drewes	53/53	Ju 52
III/KGzbV 1	Aslau	Hpt Zeidler	53/52	Ju 52
IV/KGzbV 1	Liegnitz uber Lüben	Maj Janzen	53/53	Ju 52
KGrzbV 9	Aslau	Maj Christ	53/53	Ju 52

Luftgaustäben zbV für Versorgungs- und Transportaufgaben zur Verfügung

Kampfgeschwader				
z b V 2		Oberst Conrad		
Stabsschwarm	Küpper-Sagan		3/3	Ju 52
I/KGzbV 2	Sorau	Hpt von Hornstein	52/52	Ju 52
II/KGzbV 2	Freiwaldau	Oberstlt Stoltenhoff	53/53	Ju 52
III/KGzbV 2	Freiwaldau	Maj Neudörffer	52/52	Ju 52
IV/KGzbV 2	Breslau-Gandau	Oberstlt Alefeld	53/53	Ju 52
Kampfgeschwader				
z b V 172		Maj von Gablenz		
Stabsschwarm	Berlin-Tempelhof		?/?	Ju 52
II/KGzbV 172	Berlin-Tempelhof	Hpt Krause	26/16	Ju 52
III/KGzbV 172	Berlin-Tempelhof	Maj Babekuhl	26/0	Ju 52

The Armeé de l'Air

Let us now turn to the French. The Armeé de l'Air and the small Aeronavale (air arm of the French Navy) were already fully established forces in 1939, and relatively few new units were to be added to the existing establishment during the ensuing eight months. The greatest difference between the French and German forces was the extent to which the equipment of the former had lapsed into obsolescence, and had not been replaced by more appropriate types. The situation was at its worst amongst the bomber units, for of an otherwise impressive strength of 34 Groupes de Bombardment in Metropolitan France and North-West Africa, only one solitary unit had begun re-equipment with modern Loire et Olivier LeO 451 medium bombers. The rest flew a heterogeneous collection of elderly types, none of them capable of operating by day with any realistic hope of survival (much less of success) when faced by determined fighter opposition. The most numerous and modern of these aircraft were Bloch MB 210s, backed by smaller numbers of Amiot 143s and Potez 540s of similar vintage. There were two groupes of heavy four-engined Farman F 222s, which were also definitely long in the tooth, together with a number of even older types — Bloch MB 200s, LeO 206s and LeO 257Bis.

The reconnaissance units were somewhat better off. The long-range strategic

CHANGES IN IDENTITY OF LUFTWAFFE UNITS, SEPTEMBER 1939 — OCTOBER 1940

Sep.	Oct.	Nov.	Dec.	Jan.	Feb.	Mar.	Apr.	May	Jun.	Jul.	Aug.	Sept.	Oct.
1939				**1940**									
I/JG 1										III/JG 27			
I/JG 20										III/JG 51			
I/JG 21										III/JG 54			
I/KG 25	I/KG 30												
I/JG 70					I/JG 54								
I/JG 71	II/JG 51												
I/JG 76										II/JG 54			
I/JG 77										IV/JG 51			
JGr 101						II/ZG 1				III/ZG 76			
JGr 176						II/ZG 76							
JGr 152			I/ZG 52										
JGr 126					III/ZG 26								
JGr 102					I/ZG 2				II/ZG 2				
I(Schw Jagd)/LG 1	V(Z)/LG 1												
4(St)/TrGr 186								I/ZG 1	ErpGr 210				
5(J)/TrGr 186 } 6(J)/TrGr 186 }		II(J)/TrGr 186								III/JG 77			
4(J)/TrGr 186									ErpGr 210				
	LG 1									III/StG 1			I/NJG 3
10(N)/JG 2								IV(N)/JG 2		II/NJG 1			
10(N)/JG 26 } 11(N)/LG 2 }							Z/KG 30						I/NJG 2

Loire et Olivier 451 bomber of GB I/12; this unit received its first examples of this aircraft in September 1939.

force included 12 groupes, four of which had Potez 637 aircraft, and six had Bloch MB 131s. These were both twin-engined aircraft similar in concept to the Dornier Do 17 and Bristol Blenheim. While the performance of the latter type was not particularly high, both aircraft were of more modern design than the vast majority of the bombers. The 60 escadrilles of army co-operation tactical reconnaissance aircraft (equivalent to a strength of some 30 groupes) were basically reserve units and were, without exception, equipped with obsolescent single-engined types — many of them biplanes — the least elderly of which were of Mureaux design.

The fighter force was in slightly better shape. The main fighter was the Morane MS 406, which while slightly dated, was of approximately equal standard to the Bf 109D, and was certainly of more recent design and construction than any of the bomber and reconnaissance types except the Potez 637s and the few LeO 451s. 11 Groupes de Chasse were available with these aircraft, plus one more which was based in North Africa. While more modern products from the French industry were awaited, supplies of Curtiss H-75A Hawk fighters had been acquired from the United States of America. These equipped four groupes, and were undoubtedly the best fighters available to the French at this time, although they were outclassed in all respects bar manoeuvreability by the new German Bf 109E.

A further five groupes still retained the older Dewoitine D 510 fighters, while two night-fighter groupes flew the fighter version of the twin-engined Potez 63, the Po 631. Six reserve escadrilles were equipped with older second-line types such as Dewoitine D 371 and D 501, Bleriot-Spad S 510 and Nieuport NiD 622.

The Aeronavale possessed three fighter escadrilles, all equipped with obsolescent types, the most modern of which were Dewoitine D 510s, together with a number of escadrilles of flyingboats, floatplanes, torpedo-bombers and dive-bombers, all of some vintage. Indeed the Navy was very nearly equipped with a different type of aircraft in every escadrille — a spotter's paradise, but a quartermaster's nightmare!

New equipment was on order almost across the board, but was proving to be slow in coming off the production lines. For the fighters, the excellent Dewoitine D 520 was awaited, backed by the rather less impressive Bloch MB 151 and 152 series. To boost home production more Curtiss H-75As had been ordered,

Morane 406 of GC II/3, flown by the unit's second-in-command.

together with the newer H-81A (P-40 Tomahawk). Dutch-built Koolhoven FK 58 fighters were also being purchased as a stop-gap. The bombers were to be replaced by growing numbers of LeO 451s, supplemented by Amiot 351s, and by Martin 167Fs and Douglas DB-7Fs from America — the latter both fast and heavily-armed twin-engined attack bombers. Several bomber groupes were due for conversion into Groupes d'Assault, after re-equipment with Breguet Br 693 and 695 ground attack aircraft. For longer-term delivery, heavy four-engined Consolidated 32 (forerunner of the B-24 Liberator) aircraft were also on order to replace the Farman F 222s.

The strategic reconnaissance units were eventually to receive the excellent Bloch MB 174, but in the meantime quantities of a developed version of the Potez 63, the Po 63-11, had been ordered to serve both with these units and with the army co-operation escadrilles. The Aeronavale was to receive more

Potez 63-11 reconnaissance aircraft.

modern fighters, and was also to form a substantial dive-bomber force to be equipped with home-produced Loire-Nieuport LN 411s, and American-built Vought V-156Fs. A number of Curtiss SBC-4 Helldiver biplane dive-bombers had also been ordered.

ARMÉE DE L'AIR AND AERONAVALE — 3 September, 1939

ORDER OF BATTLE

At the start of September the majority of Armée de l'Air units were dispersed from their permanent peacetime bases to their operational landing grounds. Where such moves had recently taken place, the peacetime base is indicated in brackets.

Unit	Commander	Base	Type
ESCADRES DE CHASSE			
Escadre de Chasse 1 (Etampes)			
GC I/1	Cdt Pallier	Chantilly	D 510
GC II/1	Cdt Robillon	Buc	D 510
Escadre de Chasse 2 (Chartres)			
GC I/2	Cdt Daru	Beauvais-Tillé	MS 406
GC II/2	Cdt Michel	Clermont-Les Fermes	MS 406
Esc 5/2	Cne Escudier	Clermont-Les Fermes	Po 631
Escadre de Chasse 3 (Dijon)			
GC I/3	Cdt Thibaudet	Velaine-en-Haye	MS 406
GC II/3	Cdt Morlat	Fayence	MS 406
GC III/3	Cne Le Bideau	Salon-de-Provence	MS 406
Escadre de Chasse 4 (Reims)			
GC I/4	Cdt Heurtaux	Wez-Thuisy	H-75A
GC II/4	Cdt Borne	Xaffévillers	H-75A
Escadre de Chasse 5 (Reims)			
GC I/5	Cdt Murtin	Suippes	H-75A
GC II/5	Cdt Hugues	Toul	H-75A
Escadre de Chasse 6 (Chartres)			
GC I/6	Cdt Tricaud	Blida, Algeria	MS 406
GC II/6	Cdt Fantanet	Anglure	MS 406
GC III/6	Cne de Place	Villacoublay	MS 406
Escadre de Chasse 7 (Dijon)			
GC I/7	Cdt de Pas	Biskra, Algeria	MS 406
GC II/7	Cdt Durieux	Luxeuil	MS 406
GC III/7	Cdt Crémont	Ambérieu	MS 406
Escadre de Chasse 8 (Marignane)			
GC I/8	Cdt Collin	Hyères	D 501, 510
GC II/8	Cdt Gibon-Guilhem	Marignane	Po 631
Escadre de Chasse 9			
GC I/9	Cdt Rousseau-Dumarcet	Tunis	MS 406
Escadre de Chasse du Nuit (Etampes)			
GCN I/13	Cne Treillard	Meaux-Villenoy	Po 631
GCN II/13	Cne Pouyade	Le Plessis-Bellerville	Po 631

ARMÉE DE L'AIR AND AERONAVALE — 3 September, 1939

ORDER OF BATTLE (Continued)

Escadrilles Regional de Chasse

I/561	Cdt Ronzet	Rouen-Boos	D 501, Ni-D 622, 629
II/561	Cdt Risacher	Calais & Villacoublay	SPAD 510, Ni-D 622
562	Cdt Viguier	Lyon-Bron	D 501, Ni-D 622

North African reserve and auxilliary units not included in totals

Groupe de Chasse Autonome 5	D510

Escadrilles Regional de Chasse

571	Ni-D 622
572	Ni-D 622
573	Ni-D 622
574	D 371

ESCADRES DE BOMBARDMENT

Escadre de Bombardment 11 (Toulouse)

GB I/11	Mas de Rue	MB 210
GB II/11	Mas de Rue	MB 210

Escadre de Bombardment 12 (Reims)

GB I/12	Auzainvilliers	MB 210
GB II/12	Damblain	MB 210

Escadre de Bombardment 15 (Avord)

GB I/15	Avord	F 222
GB II/15	Avord	F 222

Escadre de Bombardment 19 (Bordeaux)

GB I/19	Kalaa-Djerda, Tunisia	MB 210
GB II/19	Kalaa-Djerda, Tunisia	MB 210

Escadre de Bombardment 21 (Bordeaux)

GB I/21	Laon-Chambry	MB 210
GB II/21	Athies-sous-Laon	MB 210

Escadre de Bombardment 23 (Toulouse)

GB I/23	Istres	MB 210
GB II/23	Istres	MB 210

Escadre de Bombardment 25 (Tunis)

GB I/25	Tunis	MB 200
GB II/25	Tunis	LeO 257bis

Escadre de Bombardment 31 (Tours)

GB I/31	Connantre	MB 200, LeO 451
GB II/31	Marigny-le-Grand	MB 200

Escadre de Bombardment 32 (Chateaurose)

GB I/32	Dijon	MB 200
GB II/32	Chissey	MB 200

Escadre de Bombardment 34 (Le Bourget)

GB I/34	Abbeville	Am 143

GB II/34	Poix	Am 143
Escadre 35 (Lyon)		
GB II/35	Pontarlier	Am 143
Escadre de Bombardment 38 (Metz)		
GB I/38	Setif, Tunisia	Am 143
GB II/38	Setif, Tunisia	Am 143
Escadre 39		
GB I/39	Rayak, Syria	MB 200
Escadre de Bombardment 51 (Tours)		
GB I/51	La Perthe	MB 210
GB II/51	Troyes-Barberey	MB 210
Escadre de Bombardment 54 (Le Bourget)		
GB I/54	Peronne — Mons en Chaussée	Po 633, ANF 115
GB II/54	Montdidier	Po 540
Escadre 61		
GB II/61	Blida, Algeria	MB 200
Escadre de Chasse 62 (North Africa)		
GB I/62		(LeO 206)*
GB II/62		(LeO 206)*
Escadre de Bombardment 63		
GB I/63	Marrakesch, Morocco	Po 540
GB II/63	Setif, Tunisia	Am 143

ESCADRES DE RECONNAISSANCE

Escadre de Reconnaissance 22 (Orleans)		
GR I/22	Chatel-Chehery	MB 131
GR II/22	Etain-Rouvres	MB 131
Escadre de Reconnaissance 33 (Nancy)		
GR I/33	St. Dizier	Po 637, Po 542
GR II/33	Soissons-Saconin	Po 637, Po 542
Escadre 35 (Lyon)		
GR I/35	Lons le Saunier	MB 131
Escadre de Reconnaissance 36 (Pau)		
GR I/36	Vitry-en-Artois	Po 540
GR 11/36	La Malmaison	Po 540
Escadre 39		
GR II/39	Rayak, Syria	Po 29
Escadre de Reconnaissance 52 (Nancy)		
GR I/52	Chaumont-Semoutiers	Po 637, Po 542
GR II/52	Herberviller	Po 637, Po 542
Escadre de Reconnaissance (Lyon)		
GR I/55	Orange-Plan de Dieu	MB 131

* The LeO 206 was completely obsolete and was in the process of being withdrawn at the outbreak of war.

GR II/55	Lure-Malbouhans	MB 131

Escadre 61

GR I/61	Blida, Algeria	MB 131

Groupe de Reconnaissance Autonome (Mourmelon)

14eme G.A.R.
  (GR I/14)
	Martigny-les-
	  Gerbonveaux
		MB 131

TRANSPORT

Groupement de l'Infanterie de l'Air

1/601	Alger	Po 650
2/601	Alger	Po 650

Section Aèriènne de Transport

SAT 1	Etampes	Wibault trimotor
SAT 5	,,	,,
SAT 8	,,	,,
SAT 9	,,	,,

Groupe de Marche du Service Geographique des Armees

GMSGA	Orly	Po 540

GROUPES AÈRIÈNNES D'OBSERVATION

1 Armée

GAO 502	Attigny	ANF 115
GAO 503	Meaulte	ANF 115, Po 25
GAO 504	Chartres	Po 390, LeO C 30
GAO 505	Plivot	Po 390, MB 200, Po 25
GAO 544	Bourges	Bre 270

II Armée

GAO 507	Chalons- Champforgueil	ANF 115
GAO 510	Rennes	Po 390, Po 25
GAO 518	Bordeaux	Bre 270, Po 25
GAO 2/520	Luxeuil-La Chapelle	ANF 115, LeO C30

III Armée

GAO 1/506	Conflans	ANF 117, Po 540
GAO 2/506	Etain-Buzy	ANF 117
GAO 1/508	Sarrebourg-Buhl	Bre 270, Po 25
GAO 2/508	Mars La Tour	Bre 270, Po 25
GAO 1/551	Attigny	ANF 117, ANF 113, Po 25
GAO 3/551	Stenay-Wisseppe	ANF 117

ARMÉE DE L'AIR AND AERONAVALE — 3 September, 1939

ORDER OF BATTLE (Continued)

IV Armée

GAO 509	Tours	Bre 270
GAO 1/520	Delme	ANF 115, Po 25

V Armée

GAO 512	Limoges	Po 390, Po 25
GAO 517	Nancy (or Toulouse)	Po 390, LeO C 30
GAO 548	Fayence	ANF 115
GAO 553	Sarrebourg-Buhl	ANF 115, Po 540

VI Armée & Armée des Alpes

GAO 1/514	Tallard	ANF 117, Po 25, LeO C 30
GAO 2/514	Challes-les-Eaux	ANF 115

VIII Armée

GAO 501	Lille-Flers	ANF 115
GAO 513	Montbeliard	Po 390, Po 25
GAO 516	Aix-le-Bourget (Savoie)	Bre 270
GAO 543	Belfort-Chaux	Bre 270, Po 25
GAO 552	Mourmelon	ANF 115, Po 540, LeO C 30

IX Armée

GAO 511	Nantes	Po 390, Po 25, Po 540
GAO 545	Auxerre	Bre 270, Po 25
GAO 547	La Malmaison	Bre 270, Po 25
GAO 2/551	Villers-les-Guise	ANF 115
GAO 4/551	Clastres	ANF 117, Po 540, LeO C 30

Not with an Armée

GAO 515	Avignon	ANF 117
GAO 546	Romilly	Bre 270, Po 25
GAO 550	Calvi	Bre 270

Reserve

GAO 581
GAO 582
GAO 1/589

AERONVALE

i) Shipboard Units — aircraft carrier *Bearn*, cruiser and battleship catapults.

Escadrilles de Chasse

AC 1	Lt de V Ferran	Lanvéoc-Poulmic	D 376
AC 2	Lr de V Folliot	Hyères	D 376

HC 1†	St.Mandrier	Loire 210
HC 2†	Lanvéoc-Poulmic	Loire 210

Escadrilles de Bombardment

AB 1	Hyères	V 156F
AB 2	Berck (Abbeville)	Levasseur PL 101

Escadrilles de Torpillage

HB 1	Karouba	Latecoere 298B
HB 2	Karouba	Latecoere 298B

Escadrilles de Surveillance

HS 1,2,3 and 4	Aboard ships	Loire 130
HS 5		Loire 130, GL 811

ii) Coastal Units— floatplanes and flyingboats

Escadrilles de Bombardment

B1	Port Lyautey, Morocco	LeO 257bis
B2	Cherbourg	LeO 257bis
B3	Mediouna, Tunisia	LeO 257bis

Escadrilles de Torpillage

T1	Cherbourg	Latecoere 298A
T2	Lanvéoc-Poulmic	Latecoere 298B
T3	Cherbourg	Latecoere 298B

Escadrilles de l'Exploration (long-range flyingboats)

E1	Lanvéoc-Poulmic	Br 521 Bizerte
E2	Lanvéoc-Poulmic	Br 521 Bizerte
E4	Dakar, West Africa	Latecoere 301, 302
E5	Berre	Br 521 Bizerte
E6	Lanvéoc-Poulmic	Latecoere 523
E7	Karouba	Loire 70
E8	Lanvéoc-Poulmic	Potez-CAMS 141 (1 a/c)
E12‡		Latecoere 522 (1 a/c)

Escadrilles de Surveillance (short-range flyingboats and floatplanes)

1S1	Cherbourg	CAMS 55, Loire 130
1S2	Cherbourg	Latecoere 29-0, GL 812
2S1	Lanvéoc-Poulmic	CAMS 55, GL 812

† Both units disbanded 22 November 1939.
‡ E12 was disbanded at the end of September 1939 and the single aircraft handed to E6. The unit was later reformed with the single LeO 246 flyingboat.

ARMÉE DE L'AIR AND AERONAVALE — 3 September, 1939

ORDER OF BATTLE (Continued)

2S2		CAMS 37
2S4	Lanvéoc-Poulmic	CAMS 37, GL 812
3S1	St. Mandrier, Toulon	GL 812
3S2	Deauville	LeO C 30 autogyro
3S3	Berre	GL 812
3S4	Berre	CAMS 55, NC 470, Short S 82
3S6	Aspretto, Corsica	Levasseur PL 15, GL 812
4S1	Bizerte, Tunisia	CAMS 55
4S2	Bizerte, Tunisia	CAMS 55

The organization of the Armée de l'Air was somewhat more complex than that of either the RAF or the Luftwaffe, being based neither wholly on an area system, nor on a role system. The organization was also to be considerably changed during the months preceding May 1940, and a brief synopsis therefore follows, covering the position in September 1939, and the main changes made.

At the outbreak of war the Armée de l'Air was divided into three Armées Aèriènnes:

1ere Armée Aèriènne — Gal Mouchard; English Channel to Swiss Border.
3eme Armée Aèriènne — Gal Houdemont; South-East France (Italian border).
5eme Armée Aèriènne — Gal Pennes; North Africa.

The Commander in Chief Gal Vuillemin, had his headquarters at 'Point Z', located at St. Jean-les-deux-Jumeaux, some 20 kilometres south-east of Paris.

To control operational flying over the main Western Front area, the ZOAE (Zone d'Operations Aèriènnes Est) was formed on 7 September 1939, followed on 1 October by the ZOAN (Nord) and on 22 October by the ZOAS (Sud). A fourth Zone, the ZOAA (Alpes) was formed on 23 February 1940, replacing the 3eme Armée Aèriènne, and on that same date all three Armées Aèriènnes were disbanded.

For operations the ZOAN and ZOAE came respectively under the control of Groupe d'Armée No 1 (Gal Billotte) and Groupe d'Armée No 2 (Gal Pretelot), while the ZOAS came under the Groupe d'Armée No 3 (Gal Besson). Vuillemin however retained three Divisions Aèriènnes under his direct control for strategic use, one of which was situated within each ZOA, These were:

1ere DAe (Gal Escarden) — ZOAN
3eme DAe (Gal Valin) — ZOAE
6eme DAe (Gal Hebrard) — ZOAS

Each DAe comprised a single strategic groupe de reconnaissance, and a variable number of groupes de chasse and bombardment. The permanent reconnaissance units were:

$$1^{ere} \text{ DAe} - \text{GR II/33}$$
$$3^{eme} \text{ DAe} - \text{GR I/52}$$
$$6^{eme} \text{ DAe} - \text{GR I/33}$$

Vuillemin's immediate subordinate officer was Gal Têtu, Commandant les Forces Aèriènnes de Cooperation du Front Nord-Est. He was responsible for all army co-operation units and the British Air Component, his command being exercised directly over the ZOAs, the commanders of which had numerous army co-operation units under their control.

Each ZOA covered exactly the areas of operation of a number of armies, and to aid each individual army a command known as FA (Forces Aèriènnes) was set up, each with a variable number of GCs, GRs, GBs and GAOs to hand. For instance, ZOAN covered the area of the following armies, and their commensurate FAs:

Iere Armée (Gal Blanchard)	FA 101 (Gal Canonne)
IIeme Armée (Gal Huntziger)	FA 102 (Gal Roques)
VIIeme Armée (Gal Giraud)	FA 107 (Col. Chambe)
IXeme Armée (Gal Corap)	FA 109 (Gal Augereau)

To complicate matters further, the various fighter units came under the control of six Groupements, which were allocated to the various ZAOs:

ZOAN	Gpt 21, 23 and 25
	Gpt Chasse de Nuit
ZOAE	Gpt 22
ZOAS	Gpt 24

The Royal Air Force

The Royal Air Force was well on the way to completing the re-equipment of its existing units with modern types, but was still in the midst of a process of rapid expansion. Thus during the early months of the war — unlike the Armée de l'Air — it was to add many new units to its Order of Battle, particularly within Fighter Command. The main striking arm, Bomber Command, was divided into six groups. Each of the first five of these employed a different type — 1 Group; ten squadrons of Fairey Battle single-engined light bombers, all in the process of moving to France, plus two non-operational units, one of which (57 Squadron) was about to transfer to 22 Army Co-operation Group. Another unit — 18 Squadron — had just similarly transferred; 2 Group had eight squadrons of Bristol Blenheim twin-engined light bombers, two of which were non-operational; 3 Group: nine squadrons of Vickers Wellington heavy bombers (three of which were non-operational training units); 4 Group; eight squadrons of Armstrong-Whitworth Whitley heavy night bombers, six of them operational;

'Backbone' of the AASF was the Fairey Battle. This was an aircraft of 15 Squadron, LS-Y, P2177 (named 'Sylveste'), which is seen here at Conde-Vraux soon after arriving in France. (*V.F. Bingham via A. Thomas*)

5 Group; ten squadrons of Handley-Page Hampden medium bombers (four of which were non-operational training units). 6 Group was an operational training organization in its entirety, including seven squadrons and one flight. These units, with 11 of the non-operational squadrons in the other five groups, were later combined to form Nos 11, 12, 13, 14, 15, 16 and 17 Operational Training Units.

ROYAL AIR FORCE ORDER OF BATTLE

Unit	Base	Commander	Type
BOMBER COMMAND	High Wycombe, Bucks	Air Chief Marshal Sir E.R. Ludlow-Hewitt	
1 Group	Abingdon, Berks	Air Vice-Marshal A.C. Wright	
Operational units all in the process of moving to France to become part of the Advanced Air Striking Force — see below.			
57 Squadron (Group Pool)	Upper Heyford		Blenheim I
98 Squadron (Reserve/ Training)	Hucknall		Battle II
2 Group	Wyton, Hunts	Air Vice-Marshal C.T. MacLean	
21 Squadron	Watton		Blenheim IV
82 Squadron	Watton		Blenheim IV
107 Squadron	Wattisham		Blenheim IV
110 Squadron	Wattisham		Blenheim IV
114 Squadron	Wyton		Blenheim IV
139 Squadron	Wyton		Blenheim IV
90 Squadron (Group Pool)	West Raynham		Blenheim I,IV
101 Squadron (Reserve)	West Raynham		Blenheim IV

3 Group   Mildenhall, Suffolk   Air Vice-Marshal J.E.A. Baldwin

9 Squadron	Honington	Wellington I, IA
37 Squadron	Feltwell	Wellington I, IA
38 Squadron	Marham	Wellington I, IA
115 Squadron	Marham	Wellington I, IA
99 Squadron	Mildenhall	Wellington I
149 Squadron	Mildenhall	Wellington I
214 Squadron (Reserve)	Methwold	Wellington I
215 Squadron (Reserve)	Honington	Harrow II, Wellington I
148 Squadron (Group Pool)	Stradishall	Anson I, Wellington I

4 Group   Linton-on-Ouse, Yorks   Air Vice-Marshal, A. Coningham

10 Squadron	Dishforth	Whitley IV
51 Squadron	Linton-on-Ouse	Whitley II, III
58 Squadron	Linton-on-Ouse	Whitley III
77 Squadron	Driffield	Whitley III, V
102 Squadron	Driffield	Whitley III
78 Squadron (Reserve)	Ternhill	Whitley I, IV, IVA, V
97 Squadron (Group Pool)	Leconfield	Anson I, Whitley II, III
166 Squadron (Group Pool)	Leconfield	Whitley I, III

5 Group   Grantham, Lincs   Air Commodore W.B. Gallaway

44 Squadron	Waddington	Hampden I
50 Squadron	Waddington	Hampden I
49 Squadron	Scampton	Hampden I
83 Squadron	Scampton	Hampden I
61 Squadron	Hemswell	Hampden I
144 Squadron	Hemswell	Hampden I
106 Squadron (Reserve)	Cottesmore	Anson I, Hampden I
185 Squadron (Reserve)	Cottesmore	Hereford I, Hampden I
7 Squadron (Group Pool)	Doncaster	Anson I, Hampden I
76 Squadron (Group Pool)	Finningley	Anson I, Hampden I

6 Group (Training)

35 Squadron	Cranfield	Battle II, Anson I
52 Squadron	Upwood	Battle III, Andon I
63 Squadron	Upwood	Battle II, Anson I

ROYAL AIR FORCE ORDER OF BATTLE (Continued)

75 Squadron	Stradishall		Anson I, Wellington I
104 Squadron	Bassingbourne		Anson I, Blenheim I
108 Squadron	Bicester		Blenheim I
207 Squadron	Cranfield		Anson I, Battle II, III

FIGHTER COMMAND		Air Chief Marshal Sir Hugh C.T. Dowding	
	Stanmore, Middx		
11 Group	Uxbridge, Middx	Air Vice-Marshal E.L. Gossage	
3 Squadron	Croydon	Sqn Ldr H.H. Chapman	Hurricane I
17 Squadron	Croydon	Sqn Ldr C. Walter	Hurricane I
615 Squadron	Croydon	Sqn Ldr A.V. Harvey	Gladiator I, II
32 Squadron	Biggin Hill	Sqn Ldr T.B. Prickman	Hurricane I
79 Squadron	Biggin Hill	Sqn Ldr C.C. McMullen	Hurricane I
601 Squadron	Biggin Hill	Sqn Ldr B.S. Thynne	Blenheim IF
56 Squadron	North Weald	Sqn Ldr E.V. Knowles	Hurricane I
151 Squadron	North Weald	Sqn Ldr E.M. Donaldson	Hurricane I
604 Squadron	North Weald	Sqn Ldr R.A. Budd	Blenheim IF
25 Squadron	Northolt	Sqn Ldr J.R. Hallings-Pott, DSO	Blenheim IF
111 Squadron	Northolt	Sqn Ldr H. Broadhurst	Hurricane I
600 Squadron	Northolt	Sqn Ldr D.deB. Clarke	Blenheim IF
43 Squadron	Tangmere	Sqn Ldr R.E. Bain	Hurricane I
605 Squadron	Tangmere	Sqn Ldr Lord Willoughby de Broke	Gladiator I, II
1 Squadron	Tangmere	Sqn Ldr P.J.H. Halahan	Hurricane I
54 Squadron	Hornchurch	Sqn Ldr H.M. Pearson	Spitfire I
65 Squadron	Hornchurch	Sqn Ldr J. Heber-Percy	Spitfire I
74 Squadron	Hornchurch	Sqn Ldr C.E. Sampson	Spitfire I
501 Squadron	Filton	Sqn Ldr M.V.M. Clube	Hurricane I
24 Squadron (Communications)	Hendon	Wg Cdr D.F. Anderson, DFC, AFC	Various
12 Group	Watnall, Notts	Air Vice-Marshal T.L. Leigh-Mallory	
19 Squadron	Duxford	Sqn Ldr H.I. Cozens	Spitfire I
66 Squadron	Duxford	Sqn Ldr E.J. George	Spitfire I
611 Squadron	Duxford	Sqn Ldr G.L. Pilkington	Spitfire I
29 Squadron	Debden	Sqn Ldr P.S. Gomez	Blenheim IF
85 Squadron	Debden	Sqn Ldr D.F.W. Atcherley	Hurricane I
87 Squadron	Debden	Sqn Ldr W.E. Coope	Hurricane I
46 Squadron	Digby	Sqn Ldr P.R. Barwell, DFC	Hurricane I
73 Squadron	Digby	Sqn Ldr B.W. Knox	Hurricane I
504 Squadron	Digby	Sqn Ldr Sir H.M. Seely, MP	Hurricane I
23 Squadron	Wittering	Sqn Ldr V.B.J. Jackson	Blenheim IF
213 Squadron	Wittering	Sqn Ldr J.H. Edwards-Jones	Hurricane I

610 Squadron (non-operational)	Hooton Park	Sqn Ldr I.R. Parker	Hurricane I
616 Squadron (non-operational)	Doncaster	Sqn Ldr W.K. Beisiegel	Gauntlet II, Battle II, III
13 Group	Newcastle-on-Tyne	Air Vice-Marshal R.E. Saul	
41 Squadron	Catterick	Sqn Ldr G.A.G. Johnston	Spitfire I
609 Squadron (converting)	Catterick	Sqn Ldr G.H. Ambler	Spitfire I
64 Squadron	Church Fenton	Sqn Ldr D. Cooke	Blenheim IF
72 Squadron	Church Fenton	Sqn Ldr R.A. Lees	Spitfire I
602 Squadron	Abbotsinch	Sqn Ldr A.D. Farquhar	Spitfire I
603 Squadron (converting)	Turnhouse	Sqn Ldr E.H. Stevens	Spitfire I
607 Squadron	Usworth	Sqn Ldr L.E. Smith	Gladiator I, II
COASTAL COMMAND	Northwood, Middx	Air Chief Marshal Sir Frederick W. Bowhill	
15 Group	Mount Batten, Plymouth	Air Commodore R.G. Parry	
204 Squadron	Mount Batten	Wg Cdr K.B. Lloyd, AFC	Sunderland I
210 Squadron	Pembroke Dock	Wg Cdr W.J. Daddo-Langlois	Sunderland I
228 Squadron (on the way from the Mediterranean)	Pembroke Dock	Wg Cdr L.K. Barnes	Sunderland I
217 Squadron	Warmwell	Wg Cdr A.P. Revington	Anson I
502 Squadron	Aldergrove	Sqn Ldr L.R. Briggs	Anson I
16 Group	Chatham, Kent	Air Commodore R.L.G. Marix	
42 Squadron	Bircham Newton	Sqn Ldr H. Waring	Vildebeest III, IV
22 Squadron (converting to Beaufort I)	Thorney Island	Sqn Ldr M.V. Ridgeway	Vildebeest III, IV
48 Squadron	Thorney Island	Wg Cdr J.L. Findlay	Anson I
206 Squadron	Bircham Newton	Sqn Ldr N.H. de'Aeth	Anson I
500 Squadron	Detling	Sqn Ldr V.G. Hohler	Anson I
18 Group	Donibristle/Rosyth, Scotland	Air Vice-Marshall C.D. Breese	
220 Squadron	Thornaby	Wg Cdr A.H. Paul, AFC	Anson I, Hudson I
201 Squadron	Sullum Voe, Shetlands	Wg Cdr C.H. Cahill, DFC, AFC	London II
209 Squadron	Invergordon	Wg Cdr C.G. Wigglesworth, AFC	Stranraer
224 Squadron	Leuchars	Wg Cdr E.A. Hodgson	Hudson I
233 Squadron	Leuchars	Wg Cdr W.C.P. Bullock	Anson I, Hudson I

ROYAL AIR FORCE ORDER OF BATTLE (Continued)

240 Squadron	Invergordon	Wg Cdr R.H Carter, OBE, DFC	London II
269 Squadron	Montrose	Wg Cdr F.L. Pearce, DSO, DFC	Anson I
608 Squadron	Thornaby	Sqn Ldr G. Shaw, DFC	Anson I
612 Squadron	Dyce	Sqn Ldr F. Crerar	Hector I, Anson I

22 Army Co-operation Group

	Old Sarum		
2 Squadron	Hawkinge	Wg Cdr A.J.W. Geddes, OBE	Lysander I, II
4 Squadron	Odiham	Sqn Ldr G.P. Charles	Lysander II
13 Squadron	Odiham	Sqn Ldr S.H.C. Gray	Lysander II
16 Squadron	Old Sarum	Sqn Ldr R.E.S. Skelton	Lysander II
26 Squadron	Catterick	Sqn Ldr T.J. Arbuthnot	Lysander II
53 Squadron	Odiham	Sqn Ldr W.B. Murray	Blenheim IV
59 Squadron	Andover	Sqn Ldr J.B. Fyfe, DFC	Blenheim IV
613 Squadron	Ringway	Sqn Ldr E. Rhodes	Lysander I
614 Squadron	Llandow, Cardiff	Sqn Ldr R.E.C. Cadman	Hector I
18 Squadron	Upper Heyford		Blenheim I

(in process of transferring from 1 Group, Bomber Command to 22 Group)

Advanced Air Striking Force

	Reims, France	Air Vice-Marshal P.H.L. Playfair

(Units in the process of arriving from 1 Group, Bomber Command)

75 Wing

15 Squadron (ex Abingdon)	Betheniville	Battle III
40 Squadron (ex Abingdon)	Betheniville	Battle III
88 Squadron (ex Boscombe Down)	Auberive-sur-Suippes	Battle III
218 Squadron (ex Boscombe Down)	Auberive-sur-Suippes	Battle III

76 Wing

12 Squadron (ex Bicester)	Berry-au-Bac	Battle III
142 Squadron (ex Bicester)	Berry-au-Bac	Battle III
105 Squadron (ex Harwell)	Reims/Champagne	Battle III
226 Squadron (ex Harwell)	Reims/Champagne	Battle III

71 Wing

103 Squadron	(ex Benson)	Challerange	Battle III

150 Squadron (ex Benson)   Ecury-sur-Coole   Battle III

FLEET AIR ARM

HMS *Ark Royal*   North Western Approaches, Atlantic

Squadron	Commander	Aircraft
800 Squadron	Lt Cdr G.N. Torry, RN	Skua II, Roc I
803 Squadron	Lt Cdr D.R.F. Campbell, RN	Skua II, Roc I
810 Squadron	Capt N.R.M. Skene, RM	Swordfish I
818 Squadron	Lt Cdr J.E. Fenton, RN	Swordfish I
820 Squadron	Lt Cdr G.B. Hodgkinson, RN	Swordfish I and 1 Walrus
821 Squadron	Lt Cdr G.M. Duncan, RN	Swordfish I

HMS *Courageous*   South Western Approaches, Atlantic

Squadron	Commander	Aircraft
811 Squadron	Lt Cdr R.S. Borrett, RN	Swordfish I
822 Squadron	Lt Cdr P.W. Humphreys, RN	Swordfish I

HMS *Hermes*   South Western Approaches, Atlantic

Squadron	Commander	Aircraft
814 Squadron	Lt Cdr N.S. Luard, RN	Swordfish I

HMS *Furious*   In Dock, Home Fleet
No squadrons allocated

HMS *Glorious*   Mediterranean Fleet, Alexandria

Squadron	Commander	Aircraft
802 Squadron	Lt Cdr J.P.G. Bryant, RN	Sea Gladiator
812 Squadron	Lt Cdr A.S. Bolt, RN	Swordfish I
823 Squadron	Lt Cdr R.D. Watkins, RN	Swordfish I
825 Squadron	Lt Cdr J.W. Hale, RN	Swordfish

HMS *Eagle*   Far East Fleet, Singapore

Squadron	Commander	Aircraft
813 Squadron	Lt Cdr N. Kennedy, RN	Sqordfish
824 Squadron	Lt Cdr A.J. Debenham, RN	Swordfish

1st Battle Squadron, Home Fleet; HMS *Barham*, *Malaya* and *Valiant*

Squadron	Commander	Aircraft
701 Squadron	Lt Cdr W.L.M. Brown, RN	Swordfish I (floatplane)

2nd Battle Squadron, Home Fleet; HMS *Nelson*, *Rodney* and *Resolution*

Squadron	Commander	Aircraft
702 Squadron	Lt Cdr R.A.B. Phillimore, RN	Walrus I, Swordfish I(f/p)

Battlecruiser Squadron, Home Fleet

Squadron	Commander	Aircraft
705 Squadron	Lt P.E. O'Brien, RN	Swordfish I (floatplane)

HMS *Albatros*

Squadron	Commander	Aircraft
710 Squadron	Lt Cdr H.L. Hayes, RN	Walrus I

1st Cruiser Squadron, Mediterranean Fleet

Squadron	Commander	Aircraft
711 Squadron	Lt Cdr A.H.T. Fleming, RN	Walrus I

2nd Cruiser Squadron, Home Fleet

Squadron	Commander	Aircraft
712 Squadron	Lt Cdr G.A. Tilney, RN	Walrus I

3rd Cruiser Squadron, Mediterranean Fleet

Squadron	Commander	Aircraft
713 Squadron	Lt S.J. Hamilton, RN	Seafox I

4th Cruiser Squadron, East Indies Station

Squadron	Commander	Aircraft
714 Squadron	Lt Cdr A.S. Webb, RN	Walrus I

ROYAL AIR FORCE ORDER OF BATTLE (Continued)

5th Cruiser Squadron, China Station
715 Squadron   Lt P.J. Milner-Barry, RN   Walrus I

6th Cruiser Squadron, South African Station
716 Squadron   Lt A.J.T. Roe, RN   Walrus I, Seafox I

8th Cruiser Squadron, American and West Indies Station
718 Squadron   Lt Cdr J.C. Cockburn, RN   Walrus I, Seafox I

New Zealand Division
720 Squadron   Lt Cdr B.E.W. Logan, RN   Walrus I

ROYAL AIR FORCE OVERSEAS

Egypt		**India**	
14 Squadron	Wellesley	5 Squadron	Wapiti
45 Squadron	Blenheim I	20 Squadron	Audax, Lysander
55 Squadron	Blenheim I	27 Squadron	Wapiti
113 Squadron	Blenheim I	28 Squadron	Audax
211 Squadron	Blenheim I	31 Squadron	Valentia
70 Squadron	Valentia	60 Squadron	Blenheim I
216 Squadron	Bombay, Valentia		
33 Squadron	Gladiator I, II	**Ceylon**	
80 Squadron	Gladiator I, II	273 Squadron	Vildebeest, Seal
112 Squadron	Gladiator I,II		
208 Squadron	Lysander		

Sudan		**Singapore**	
47 Squadron	Wellesley	11 Squadron	Blenheim I
223 Squadron	Wellesley, Vincent	34 Squadron	Blenheim I
		39 Squadron	Blenheim I
Palestine		62 Squadron	Blenheim I
6 Squadron	Hardy, Lysander	36 Squadron	Vildebeest II
		100 Squadron	Vildebeest II
Iraq		205 Squadron	Singapore III
30 Squadron	Blenheim I	230 Squadron	Sunderland I
84 Squadron	Blenheim I		

Aden			
8 Squadron	Vincent		
94 Squadron	Sea Gladiator		
203 Squadron	Singapore III		

Fighter Command was divided into three groups, each with responsibility for a different part of the country. In the south was 11 Group, which included ten squadrons of Hawker Hurricanes, four of Bristol Blenheim IF twin-engined fighters, three squadrons of Supermarine Spitfires, one of Gloster Gladiator biplanes and one communications squadron. 12 Group, with responsibility for

Hawker Hurricane I (N2358) of 1 Squadron, seen here being refuelled at Vassincourt late in 1939.

the defence of East Anglia and the South Midlands, had four squadrons of Spitfires, three of Hurricanes, two of Blenheim IFs and one of elderly Gloster Gauntlet biplanes. In Scotland and the north of England was 13 Group, with five Spitfire squadrons and one each of Blenheim IFs and Gladiators. Four more squadrons of Hurricanes were released for service in France on the outbreak of war.

Army Co-operation was the province of a single group – No 22 – equipped with seven squadrons of Westland Lysanders and Hawker Hectors for tactical reconnaissance, and two units of Blenheim IVs for strategic reconnaissance; the group was in the process of being strengthened by the addition of two further squadrons of Blenheim Is (Nos 18 and 57). The force in the United Kingdom was rounded off by Coastal Command, which like Fighter Command comprised three groups, albeit much smaller in content. 15 Group guarded the Western Approaches for which it employed two squadrons of Short Sunderland four-

613 Squadron was still equipped with the elderly Hawker Hector biplane for army co-operation duties. ZR-X, K8116, seen here at Odiham, was to dive-bomb targets in Calais in May 1940. (J. Beedle via A. Thomas)

Vickers Vildebeeste IV torpedo-bomber of 42 Squadron, Coastal Command, seen at Bircham Newton at the outbreak of war. *(RAF Bircham Newton via A. Thomas)*.

engined flyingboats and two of Avro Anson reconnaissance-bombers. 16 Group in the south-east had three squadrons of Ansons and two torpedo-bomber units, one of which was in the process of converting from old Vickers Vildebeest biplanes to modern Bristol Beauforts; the other would follow suite as soon as possible. In the north, north-east and north-west, 18 Group employed nine squadrons for its multifarious duties, including three with Ansons, three newly-equipped with American-built Lockheed Hudson patrol bombers, and three flyingboat units with a variety of Sunderlands and older Short Singapores, Saro Londons and Supermarine Stranraers. 15 Group was about to be reinforced by a third Sunderland squadron (No 228), which was just returning from the Middle East.

In addition to these forces, the RAF possessed a further 35 squadrons which were stationed at various colonial bases. These were as follows:

Egypt —   three fighter, five bomber, two bomber-transport and one army
            co-operation squadron
Sudan —   two bomber squadrons
Palestine — one army co-operation squadron
Iraq —   two bomber squadrons
Malta —   one flyingboat squadron
Aden —   one bomber, one flyingboat and one fighter squadron
India —   two bomber, four army co-operation and one transport squadron
Ceylon —   one general purpose squadron
Singapore — four bomber, two torpedo-bomber and one flyingboat squadron.

The Royal Navy had available seven aircraft carriers in 1939, only one of which — HMS *Ark Royal* — could be considered completely modern. This splendid vessel, with no less than six squadrons aboard, was patrolling in the Atlantic, covering the North-Western Approaches, whilst the South-Western Approaches were covered by HMS *Courageous* with two squadrons, and HMS *Hermes* with one. *Courageous*'s sister ship, HMS *Furious*, was in dock with no squadrons allocated, while the smallest and oldest vessel on charge, HMS *Argus* was in use only for deck landing and other training purposes. The other two carriers were far from home — HMS *Glorious* in the Mediterranean, with her four squadrons temporarily ashore at RNAS Dekheila, near Alexandria in Egypt, while HMS *Eagle* with two squadrons, was in the Far East.

The carrier-based units of the Fleet Air Arm were equipped predominantly with Fairey Swordfish biplane torpedo-bombers, which were also employed for reconnaissance, gunnery spotting and conventional bombing. 12 squadrons of these rather dated aircraft were available. *Glorious* included in her group a single squadron of Gloster Sea Gladiator biplane fighters, while aboard *Ark Royal* were two squadrons of Blackburn Skua two-seat fighter/dive-bomber monoplanes, both supplemented by a trio of Blackburn Rocs. The Roc was an ill-conceived aircraft developed from the Skua; basically the same aircraft, but without the normal forward-firing armament of four .303in machine guns, the Roc had been fitted with a Boulton Paul power-operated turret mounting a quartet of similar guns, located behind the pilot in the space previously allocated to the navigator/air gunner's rear seat. The Roc was not to prove a success.

In October *Furious* would put to sea, heading for the North Atlantic. As she did so, 818 Squadron aboard *Ark Royal* would transfer to this vessel. At the same time a new unit would be formed to complete her air group; this was 816 Squadron, also with Swordfish aircraft, which would initially be commanded by Lt Y. Dalyell-Stead.

In addition to the carrier-based units, the Fleet Air Arm also had available 12 nominal catapult squadrons, all of which were fairly small units which had begun life as Flights. All but one were based around the world, providing aircraft for use on the launching catapults of the Royal Navy's various battleships and cruisers; their equipment included Fairey Swordfish and Seafox floatplanes, or Supermarine Walrus amphibians. The twelfth unit was the recently-formed 710 Squadron, which maintained six of its nine Walrus amphibians on the seaplane carrier HMS *Albatros*.

Ashore this small air force had a further five training squadrons, all numbered in the 700 series, and another 11 would be formed before the end of 1939. The cadres of new operational units would be drawn from these as the need and opportunity arose.

Agreement had long existed with the French that on the outbreak of war a British Expeditionary Force and a substantial RAF complement should be moved to France forthwith. Consequently two distinct elements were prepared by the Royal Air Force for service there. The first of these was the Advanced Air Striking Force, basically intended for strategic operations. This comprised the whole of Bomber Command's 1 Group — the Battle force — to be reinforced in due course by the Blenheims of 2 Group. To support the BEF as the Air Component, would go the whole of 22 (Army Co-operation) Group, together with four Hurricane squadrons and the two ex-1 Group Blenheim I squadrons. The Air Component, commanded by Air Vice-Marshal C.M.B. Blount, was to come under the direction of General Lord Gort, commander of the Expeditionary Force. The AASF initially would remain under Bomber Command control, but in the field would be directed in the first instance by the new commander, Air Vice-Marshal P.H.L. Playfair.

To operate the units to be based in France, a number of Wings were formed, together with supporting supply and repair organizations. The initial unit composition proposed for these Wings so far as the Air Component was concerned, was to be as follows:

50 (Army Co-operation) Wing
4 and 13 Squadrons (Lysanders)
53 Squadron (Blenheim IVs)

51 (Army Co-operation) Wing
2 and 26 Squadrons (Lysanders)
59 Squadron (Blenheim IVs)

60 (Fighter) Wing
1, 73, 85 and 87 Squadrons (Hurricanes)

70 (Bomber) Wing
18 and 57 Squadrons (Blenheim Is)

For the AASF, nine Bomber Wings, numbered 71-72, 74-76, 79 and 81-83 were proposed, the first five each to control two of 1 Group's Battle squadrons, the next four to control two squadrons each of 2 Group's Blenheims. In the event the 2 Group units were never to become a part of the AASF, and remained in England, 79 and 81-83 Wings remaining formations on paper only. However, immediately after the German invasion of Poland — and before the expiry of the Allied ultimata to that nation — the 1 Group units were the first to make the move, the various Wing Headquarters beginning their journeys on 2 September. On arrival only three of the Wings were initially to become operational, 75 and 76 each controlling four squadrons rather than two.

The squadrons also began to move virtually at once, 40, 142, 103 and 105 flying out that same day, followed on 3rd by 12, 15 and 150. The three remaining units had all arrived in France by mid-month.

The Air Component was slower to move however, its arrival being timed more to coincide with that of the BEF. First priority was to provide fighter cover

Still bearing its peacetime unit marking on the tailfin, this Hurricane I of 85 Squadron has recently reached Rouen. Another of the unit's aircraft takes off overhead.

for the disembarkation of this force, and consequently it was the units of 60 Wing which left England first, 1 and 73 Squadrons moving to Le Havre on 9 September, while 85 and 87 Squadrons flew in to Rouen on 10th and 15th respectively. On this latter date a flight of Avro Tutor biplane trainers arrived at Amiens as the first element of the Communications Squadron, but it was to be the 18th before the first of the reconnaissance units − 53 Squadron − was to reach France.

COMPARATIVE RANKS

Luftwaffe		Armée de l'Air		Royal Air Force	
Reichsmarchall				Marshal of the Royal Air Force	
GeneralFeldmarschall	(GenObst)			Air Chief Marshal	(ACM)
GeneralOberst	(GenObst)			Air Chief Marshal	(ACM)
General der Flieger	(Gen d Flg)	General	(G^{al})	Air Marshal	(AM)
GeneralLeutnant	(GenLt)			Air Vice-Marshal	(AVM)
GeneralMajor	(GenMaj)			Air Commodore	(Air Cdr)
Oberst	(Obst)	Colonel	(Col)	Group Captain	(Grp Capt)
Oberstleutnant	(Obstlt)	Lieutenant-Colonel	(Lt Col)	Wing Commander	(Wg Cdr)
Major	(Maj)	Commandant	(Cdt)	Squadron Leader	(Sqn Ldr)
Hauptmann	(Hpt)	Capitaine	(Cne)	Flight Lieutenant	(Flt Lt)
Oberleutnant	(Oblt)	Lieutenant	(Lt)	Flying Officer	(Flg Off)
Leutnant	(Lt)	Sous Lieutenant	(Sous Lt)	Pilot Officer	(Plt Off)
Fahnenjunker	(Fhj)	Aspirant	(Asp)	—	
—		Adjutant Chef	(Adj Chef)	—	
—		Adjutant	(Adj)	Warrant Officer	(Wt Off)
Oberfeldwebel	(Ofw)	Sergeant Chef	(Sgt Chef)	Flight Sergeant	(F/Sgt)
Feldwebel	(Fw)	Sergeant	(Sgt)	Sergeant	(Sgt)
—		Caporal Chef	(Cpl Chef)	—	
Unteroffizier	(Uffz)	Caporal	(Cpl)	Corporal	(Cpl)
Obergefreiter	(Obgf)			Leading Aircraftsman	(LAC)
Gefreiter	(Gef)			Aircraftsman 1st Class	(AC 1)
Flieger	(Flg)			Aircraftsman 2nd Class (AC 2)	
(Funker/Kanonier)				(Signaller or Wireless Operator/Gunner)	
Seeflieger		Aeronavale		Fleet Air Arm	
				Commander	(Cdr)
KapitanLeutnant	(KptLt)	Capitaine de Corvette	(Cne de Corv)	Lieutenant/Commander /Major, RM	(Lt Cdr) (Maj. RM)
Oberleutnant zur See	(Oblt z See)	Lieutenant de Vaisseaux	(Lt de Vas)	Lieutenant/Captain, RM	(Lt/Capt, RM)
Leutnant zur See	(Lt z See)			Sub Lieutenant/Lieutenant RM	(Sub Lt/Lt, RM)
				Midshipman	(Midspmn)
				Petty Officer	(Pty Off)
				Leading Airman	(L/Air)

Chapter 2

FIGHTER BATTLES OVER THE WESTERN FRONT

Messerschmitt Bf 109Es of 1/JG 53 at Wiesbaden on 1 September 1939, awaiting the outcome of the attack on Poland. *(ECPA)*

Before dawn on 1 September 1939 German forces launched their Operation 'Ostmarkflug' against Poland. Despite a spirited resistance by the Poles, the technical superiority of the Luftwaffe and of the Wehrmacht's armoured divisions, coupled with daring concepts of mobile deep penetration warfare, added a new word to the world's vocabulary — 'Blitzkrieg'. In short order the Polish forces were to be outmanoeuvred, outclassed and destroyed.

At once the British and French governments acted upon their treaty obligations to the Poles, serving joint ultimata upon the German government requiring a withdrawal of forces from Poland by 3 September. General mobilization was proclaimed in both countries, and next day the British government introduced an urgent Bill stipulating compulsory military service for all able-bodied men aged 18-41; it was passed at once by the House of Commons.

Following consultations with the French, a final Diplomatic Note was despatched to Adolf Hitler by Neville Chamberlain, the British Prime Minister, at 0900 on 3 September, requiring an undertaking to withdraw from Poland be given by 1100. No reply was received and at 1115 he broadcast to the nation that "No such undertaking had been received, and that consequently this country is at war with Germany." Almost within the hour the air-raid sirens wailed over London — a dramatic effect, but a mistaken one; it had been a false alarm.

Meanwhile the French had served their own final ultimatum at 1230, expiring at 1700; at 1730 they too declared war on Germany, and before the day was out Australia and New Zealand had followed suite. It was to be a few more days before the other great Dominions of the Commonwealth followed the Mother Country, South Africa's declaration coming on 6 September and that from Canada on the 10th.

Fed on a diet of predictions in the Press regarding the efficiency of aerial bombing, and the military might of Germany, the populations of France and Britain quite expected immediate large-scale air raids to commence, and for fighting on the Western Front on the 1914 scale to begin at once. In fact, Adolf Hitler had been genuinely taken by surprise when the Allies had actually carried through their threats. His army and air force were by no means so large as was supposed, and for the moment were almost totally committed in Poland. A holding operation and a game of bluff became the order of the day, for the Germans were in no way ready to meet a major offensive in the West, while sustained Anglo-French air attacks could have proved most embarrassing. Indeed at this stage something over 100 Allied divisions — however ill-equipped and unready — were faced by only 23 German divisions, several of which were considered to be second rate!

To avoid provocation in the air, the OKW, Germany's High Command, at once issued its Directive No 2 on 3 September, specifying that no air attacks against England or France, or against merchant shipping on the high seas were to be made. Only attacks on warships or their bases, or on troop transports which had been unquestionably identified were to be permitted to the Luftwaffe, and then only after the RAF or Armée de l'Air had instituted such attacks. A supplement to this order followed three days later indicating that these restrictions did not apply to coastal units directly supporting merchant shipping in the German Bight and mined areas.

3/9/39

Indeed so unready for war in the West were all combatants, that to the universal surprise of nearly all involved nothing at all happened on the Franco-German border, or in the air overhead, during the initial few days of the war. Over the North Sea Triangle the situation was different however, and to its credit it was the RAF which made the first moves. At 1250 on 3 September, barely an hour and a half after the announcement of the outbreak of war Flg Off A. McPherson lifted Blenheim IV N6215 of 139 Squadron off the runway at Wyton for the first operational sortie of the war — a reconnaissance of the German Fleet at Wilhelmshaven. The aircraft landed safely again at 1650.

That same evening 49, 83 and 144 Squadrons at Scampton were ordered to despatch nine Hampdens to find and bomb the German warships, but in poor visibility and falling darkness they were able to see nothing, and the raid was abandoned. With darkness, ten Whitleys set out to drop propaganda leaflets over Germany — the first of many such sorties to be undertaken under the codename 'Nickel' during the next eight months. Three of these bombers failed to return, and it was initially thought that the first operational losses had been sustained. However all had force-landed in France, one 58 Squadron aircraft

Blenheim IV XD-B, N6216, of 139 Squadron, sister aircraft of N6215 which undertook the RAF's first sortie of the war on 3 September. *(139 Squadron Records via A. Thomas)*

(K8969) being destroyed near Amiens when it crashed.

Despite this quiet and loss-free start to the war in the military sphere, a more sombre note of things to come was heralded before 3 September was out, by news of the sinking by torpedo of the liner *Athenia*. She fell victim to a U-Boat some 200 miles west of the Hebrides, though fortunately it proved possible to rescue most of the passengers, including 311 US citizens. Needless to say, this act did little to enhance the image of Nazi Germany in the eyes of the neutral world.

4/9/39

In the air the 'shooting war' started towards the end of the afternoon of Monday, 4 September. At around 1600 British bombers began leaving their bases for a concerted attack on the German Fleet and its bases. Five Blenheims each from 107, 110 and 139 Squadrons, and six Hampdens each from 49 and 83 Squadrons, were briefed to attack warships in the Schillig Roads, while six Wellingtons from 9 Squadron and eight from 149 Squadron left shortly afterwards on their way to Brünsbüttel.

The three formations made their individual ways to the target areas, and once more the Hampdens were unsuccessful in locating their objectives in the misty conditions prevailing. These also caused the five Blenheims of 139 Squadron to become separated from the rest of their formation; completely lost, they also aborted and returned to base. The other Blenheims continued to Wilhelmshaven however, the aircraft of 110 Squadron led by Flt Lt K.C. Doran approaching at low level shortly before 1800. Doran's bomb aimer set his sights on the cruiser *Admiral Scheer* but his bombs fell about 30 feet short, only one exploding. Sgt Hanne was not on target and swung away, his bombs falling harmlessly into the water. One of the bombs released by Plt Off Ling hit the stern of the vessel destroying its catapult-mounted Arado Ar 196A floatplane, whilst the second landed in the water; both failed to explode. Flg Off H.L. Emden (N6199) attacked, but his aircraft was hit by Flak and went down in the sea in flames near Mellum Platte. The last Blenheim, flown by Sgt Abbott, was forced away from its target by the weight of defensive fire, and he returned without attacking.

It was into this inferno of Flak that 107 Squadron now flew, this formation taking the light cruiser *Emden* (ironically the same name as that of the pilot who had just become the RAF's first operational casualty of the war) as their target; the vessel was anchored near the Wiesbaden Bridge. Flt Lt W.F. Barton led the attack in N6184, but the aircraft was hit by Flak and blew up in the air, only one member of the crew surviving to become a prisoner. Plt Off W.J. Murphey's N6188 was hit in the starboard engine, but he pressed home the attack; whilst his bombs exploded in the water some 12 yards from the cruiser's starboard side, the stricken aircraft crashed straight into the ship, hitting the sick bay on the port side. 11 sailors were killed and 30 wounded. Flg Off H.B. Lightoller's N6189 was shot down before it could attack, crashing on the shore, while Sgt A.S. Prince's N6240 was damaged; as the pilot nursed the aircraft away, it was intercepted north of Bremerhaven by Lt Metz of II/JG 77 in a Bf 109E, and was shot down. Again one member of the crew survived to go into captivity. Plt Off Stephens in the last aircraft had lost touch with his wingmen and turned back without attacking. As the surviving Blenheims headed for home, Flt Lt Doran encountered a Dornier Do 18 flyingboat (M2+LK of 2/KüFlGr 106) north-west of Borkum and made two head-on attacks on this, but failed to inflict any worthwhile damage. The following month Doran was to receive one of the first two DFCs of the war for leading this raid; the other went to Flg Off McPherson of 139 Squadron for undertaking the war's first sortie.

During the raid the Luftwaffe had also suffered its first operational casualty in the West, for as some of the defending fighters were scrambling, one Bf 109D of 2/ZG 26 suffered an engine failure and crashed into the sea near Mellum Platte, Lt Hans Falke being killed.

Even as the Blenheims were enduring their ordeal, the Wellingtons from 9 and 149 Squadrons were making their own attack, their targets being the battle-cruisers *Scharnhorst* and *Gneisenau* (later to become so familiar to Bomber Command crews), which were lying at anchor off Brünsbüttel. At about 1805 three 9 Squadron bombers attacked, claiming to have set one ship on fire, although German records show that no damage was actually caused. In fact one bomber from each formation dropped its bombs into the harbour, the rest sending theirs ineffectually into the open sea. Bf 109Es from II/JG 77 had been scrambled from Nordholz on the approach of the raiders, and these met the bombers near the target. Fw Alfred Held at once shot down one Wellington, while a second was attacked by Fw Hans Troitsch as it was under fire from the Flak defences, and this was also shot down; F/Sgt I. Birley (L4268) and F/Sgt A.J. Turner (L4275) of 9 Squadron both failed to return. Having occurred slightly earlier than Metz's combat with the Blenheim, these were recorded as the first Luftwaffe victories of the war in the West. Flg Off Torrington-Leech, manning one of the gun turrets in the aircraft of the formation leader, Sqn Ldr L.S. Lamb, claimed one of nine attacking fighters shot down. (On 30 October, Lamb and his crew would be killed in a crash).

5/9/39

No account was taken by Bomber Command of this early evidence of the vulnerability of the Wellington to attack by fighters. Indeed all seven losses on the 4th were attributed to Flak, and the statement was made "it seems highly unlikely that either of the two missing aircraft (Wellingtons) was shot down by fighters." While this day's activities led to no immediate escalation of the air war, it did mark the beginning of regular operations. These were resumed early on the morning of 5 September when at 0525 Anson 'B' (K6183) of 206

HM King George VI decorates Flt Lt K.C. Doran with one of the first two DFCs of the war.

Squadron took off for a North Sea patrol with Flg Off L.H. Edwards at the controls. Eight He 115 floatplanes of 1/KüFlGr 106 were involved in similar duties from their base at Norderny on this morning, and one of these, M2+FH, was encountered by the Anson when flying at 300 feet. Edwards at once attempted to get on the tail of the German aircraft, but it turned swiftly and the gunners opened fire, the turret-gunner of the Anson being hit at once. Deprived of his main armament, Edwards attempted to evade but the Heinkel now pursued him vigorously, and after a 15 minute dogfight one of the fuel tanks in the wings of the Anson exploded, and the aircraft crashed into the sea. The German pilot circled until he spotted two men in the water. However, after landing nearby he and his crew were able only to find the pilot, Edwards, who was taken aboard in an injured condition.

Another Anson (K8845 of 233 Squadron) attacked a British submarine in error, but fortunately missed. However, the explosion of the depth charges which had been dropped caught the low-flying aircraft and inflicted such damage that the pilot had to ditch nearby! Later that same day the first Luftwaffe reconnaissance over Britain was undertaken, a single He 111 of 1(F)/ObdL making a sortie to Scapa Flow, where despite heavy anti-aircraft fire, a cruiser and three destroyers were seen under steam. The war at sea also erupted again, British naval forces claiming three German merchant vessels sunk in the Atlantic, while the Cunarder *Bosnia* went down to gunfire from a U-Boat. The day ended with evening patrols over the North Sea, where Hudson 'N' of 224 Squadron flown by Flg Off F.E. Burton engaged Do 18 K6+WK of 2/KüFlGr 506 off the Scottish east coast. After a brief exchange of fire the flyingboat escaped into cloud, having inflicted slight damage on its attacker, and suffered three hits itself. That night the Whitleys of 4 Group were again over Germany, waging the propaganda war.

6/9/39
The 6th saw slightly stronger German activity with the despatch early in the morning of six He 111s of I/KG 26 to the Thames estuary area on the first armed reconnaissance. Nothing was seen, and they returned with their bombs. They were followed by a single Do 17 of Wekusta 26, which flew a long and uninterrupted weather reconnaissance up the length of Britain, from Bicester to Scapa Flow.

A more disturbing event on this date was an illustration of the shortcomings of the British Radio Direction Finding (RDF — later renamed Radar) Chain Home system. Later investigation disclosed that the limitations of the system were still such that an error of 180° — a reciprocal — could take place. However the full facts of this unfortunate affair have not before been published. As the six He 111s of I/KG 26 were undertaking their reconnaissance in force over the Thames Estuary, 56 Squadron at North Weald was ordered to scramble at 0640, two flights of Hurricanes taking off led by the commanding officer, with instructions to patrol between Harwich and Colchester. As the formation headed for its designated patrol area, 'B' Flight was ordered to break away and patrol over Essex. Two more Hurricanes had followed as reserves, and were ordered to patrol over North Weald, but instead these two headed off after the squadron, half a mile behind and 1,000 feet lower. However, the German bombers had turned away and were not seen by the Hurricane pilots. Meanwhile the 56 Squadron formation was then plotted by the RDF Station at Canewdon, which now assumed the main 56 Squadron formation to be the 'hostiles' (the KG 26 plot having faded from the screen) and the following pair of 'spare' Hurricanes to be the intercepting formation. Now tragedy struck, for a flight of Spitfires from 74 Squadron at Hornchurch led by Flt Lt A.G. Malan, had been ordered aloft to intercept, since 56 Squadron's aircraft appeared to have failed to make contact. These saw below them the errant pair of reserve Hurricanes between Gravesend and Ipswich, and three of the Spitfires carried out a perfect 'bounce'. Before the mistake had been realised, they had shot down L1985 in which Plt Off M.L. Hulton-Harrop crashed to his death, while L1980 was hit and slightly damaged, Plt Off F.C. Rose carrying out a force-landing in a field five miles south of Ipswich. The Spitfire pilots were subsequently subjected to a Court Martial, but were fully exonerated. This incident became known hereafter in Fighter Command as the 'Battle of Barking Creek'.

It was not only the RAF which could make such errors however, for the very next day a Do 18 of 2/KüFlGr 606 attacked a U-Boat by mistake, though on this occasion without serious effect. However on return to Hornum this aircraft crashed, all the crew being lost. While patrol activity over the North Sea continued, no further engagements took place for some days, and such losses as there were, were of an accidental nature.

7–8/9/39
On 7 September Hudson N7247 of 224 Squadron (Flg Off H.D. Green and crew) failed to return from a North Sea patrol, the cause of their loss not being ascertained, but probably due to adverse weather conditions into which they had flown. On the next day came the first reports of attacks on U-Boats by RAF aircraft, when two Sunderlands, one from 204 Squadron (L5799) and one from 210 Squadron, both released bombs on one such vessel seen south and west of Lizard Head, Cornwall, without obvious results. The Command provided further demonstration of the rather heavy operational losses it was to suffer during the coming months when Anson K6127 of 206 Squadron was forced to ditch off Calais, and Hudson N7210 of 224 Squadron was damaged beyond repair during a landing crash at Leuchars.

7/9/39
Meanwhile however, the slumbering Western Front was at last showing some signs of life. On 7 September the French Army launched a so-called limited offensive in the Saar, but this was little more than large-scale patrolling which caused the weak German outposts to be withdrawn into the security of the Westwall. "French forces are advancing East of the Maginot Line, and have crossed the German frontier in the direction of Saarbrücken!" trumpeted the British Press, but it was hardly the truth. Two days later the 4th and 5th Armées made small advances into territory abandoned by the Germans south-west of Saarbrücken, while units of 3rd Armée occupied a small salient known as the Warndt Forest. Their stay was short however, and by 4 October they would have withdrawn again.

8/9/39
It was on 8 September that the air forces first clashed on this front, the initial engagement occuring at around 0700. Six Curtiss H-75As of GC II/4 led by Sgt Chef Cruchant, patrolled over the Landau-Saargemünd region, where they were fired on for nearly 30 minutes by the gunners of Festungsflakabteilung 33. They were then attacked by a Schwarm of Bf 109Es (four aircraft) of I/JG 53 led by Oblt Werner Mölders, who had been the top-scoring fighter pilot of the Legion Condor in Spain. The Messerschmitts directed their attack at the leading trio of H-75As, but without success. Turning into them, the French pilots engaged in a brief dogfight, following which the Germans disengaged and dived away to the north-east. Adj Villey and Sgt Chef Casenoble each claimed one shot down, both shared with Sgt Chef Cruchant; it was reported that these fell within the German lines. Several weeks later on 6 October, they would receive official confirmation of these victories, but in the event no such losses were recorded by the Luftwaffe. Oblt Mölders' aircraft had indeed been hit in the engine, and he was obliged to force-land at Birkenfeld. It would seem either that all three pilots fired at this aircraft, or that they incorrectly deduced that the black smoke pouring from the exhausts of the Bf 109s' Daimler-Benz engines as they

accelerated into their dives, denoted engine fires. This would become a common error, which would persist for some years, leading to much overclaiming against the German fighters by all of the air forces pitted against them.

Two combats followed during the afternoon and evening which have in the past been confused with each other. A Potez 637 (No. 52) of GR II/52, flown by Aspirant Halle was attacked by Bf 109s of an unidentified unit during a reconnaissance flight, and came down at Herbevilliers with both engines dead, making a safe force-landing. In the evening a Rotte (pair) of Bf 109Ds from II/JG 52 patrolled at 10,000 feet over the Karlsruhe-Kehl area, sighting a French reconnaissance aircraft described by the fighter pilots as a "high wing monoplane", attempting to machine-gun the Rhine bridge near Kehl. Lt Paul Gutbrod attacked the aircraft as it headed off in a westerly direction, making two passes from astern which caused it to break up in the air and crash near Karlsruhe; the observer baled out, badly wounded, but the pilot fell without a parachute and was killed. This was the first Luftwaffe victory on the Western Front. There seems little doubt that this was an ANF Mureaux 115 (No. 14) from GAO 553, which had been sent off at 1725 from Sarrebourg to reconnoitre the Karlsruhe area to check whether Luftwaffe units were present there. The French reported that this aircraft was shot down by Flak, Sgt Chef Piaccentini and his observer, Lt Davier, both being killed. Clearly however, it had fallen to the fighters rather than Flak; indeed no Flak claim was submitted by the Germans. However, the coincidence of a claim by II/JG 52 and a loss by GR II/52 has proved too tempting for some historians in the past, and Halle's aircraft has been ascribed as Gutbrod's victim, but this does not seem to have been the case, although undoubtedly two victories were reported by the German OKW Report for this day.

There was more action during the night, but in somewhat unusual circumstances. From England six Whitleys of 77 Squadron and six from 102 Squadron undertook leaflet dropping operations over Germany. For both squadrons it was to prove an eventful night, but particularly for 102. One bomber, K8950 'H', flown by Sqn Ldr S.S. Murray, was shot down by Flak over Thuringia, the crew becoming prisoners. At least two more strayed over Belgium on their return flight, violating that country's neutrality. Duty pilots at the Nivelles fighter base were alerted when the incursions were first reported, and shortly afterwards Capt Lucien Boussa of the 5ᵉ Escadrille of Flight Regiment 2 took off in a Fairey Fox biplane, joined by two Fairey Fireflies of the 4ᵉ Escadrille, flown by Daniel Leroy du Vivier and Marcel Michotte. The trio intercepted one Whitley, and Boussa fired a burst in front of its nose in an effort to force it to land. Instead the gunner returned fire, hitting Leroy du Vivier's Firefly, obliging him to make a force-landing forthwith. Another Fox flown by Boussa's No 2, Adj Albert Genot, with Cpl Roger Alaffe as his gunner, had now also got off the ground, and this pursued another bomber, signalling its position by radio. A white Verey light was fired at the bomber, which replied with a red and continued on its way. Genot drew off, and like Boussa fired a burst across the Whitley's bows. This aircraft too returned fire, hitting the Fox in the tail and rear fuselage and setting it on fire. The crew baled out as the stricken aircraft went down to crash on the estate of Count Gaston d'Oultrement at Nouvelles. Genot was wounded in the hand, and Alaffe broke his right shoulder on landing. It would seem that their opponent was Whitley K8951 (Flt Lt Connell), the crew of which reported shooting down a fighter. The bomber was itself damaged in this encounter and went on to crash-land at Lognes, France, the pilot having suffered a slight head wound.

Meanwhile on the ground the news of the interceptions was out, and two more pilots (this time from the 1e Escadrille) Alexis Jottard and Sous Lt Jean Offenberg pulled on flying suits over their pyjamas, taking off in their Fireflies to join in. They soon spotted Whitley DY-J, K8985, flown by Flt Lt W.V.G. Cognan, on its way back from Kiel and Hamburg. They fired a green flare and forced the bomber down to land on their own airfield, where the crew were interned. Several of the Belgian pilots involved, including Boussa, Leroy du Vivier and Offenberg, would later fly with the RAF after the occupation of their own country in 1940.

Meanwhile 77 Squadron aircraft were also making emergency landings all over France. Flt Lt Hallam (K8960) landed at Sommesous with his fuel exhausted, while Flg Off Williams (K8949) came down at Senlis. Flg Off Raphael (K8961) crash-landed at Buc, the bomber striking a parked Dewoitine fighter. It had been quite a costly night for delivering a few leaflets!

9/9/39

With daylight on 9 September the air war over the frontier continued to escalate. A formation of Bloch MB 131s of the 14eme GAR ventured over into German territory in the late morning. One of these (No 92), flown by Sgt. Chef Bouvry and commanded by Cne Fion, the observer, lagged behind due to engine trouble, and was surprised at high altitude over Salzbach by two Bf 109Es of I/JG 53 flown by Ofw Walter Grimmling and Uffz Walter Bezner. The Bloch turned hard to starboard, diving for the frontier, but the two Messerschmitts were already close behind it. Grimmling opened fire at 250 yards, closing to 50 yards, and the starboard engine caught fire. As the aircraft dropped, the German pilots pulled away to avoid crossing the border, and were unable to witness the crash, but Flak gunners confirmed the victory, stating that the

Bloch MB 131 of the 14eme GAR's 2e escadrille at dispersal at Martigny-lès-Gerbonveaux. This unit lost two such aircraft to Bf 109s on 9 September.

Ofw Walter Grimmling (left) is congratulated upon receiving JG 53's first Iron Cross of the war for his victory on 9 September. *(ECPA)*

aircraft was French (Grimmling initially claimed that his opponent was a Blenheim). A little later the same French unit lost a second Bloch (Cne Frebillot observer, Adj Thiebault, pilot), which crashed into No Mans' Land near Mortigny after being attacked over St Ingbert by six Bf 109s; one of the gunners, Caporal Martelliere, died of his wounds two days later; the aircraft was shot down by Oblt Rupp of 1/JG 52.

In the afternoon three Bf 109Ds of JGr 152 encountered French aircraft in the Zweibrücken area at 1445. These were three Bloch MB 200 bombers of the 31eme Escadre, which were flying a reconnaissance sortie over the Saar, the French High Command having ordered that a few such missions be undertaken. The Messerschmitts attacked and Hpt Lessmann shot down No 163, commanded by Cdt Delozanne, CO of GB II/31, which crashed near Saarbrücken with the

Hpt Lessmann's JGr 152 Bf 109D undergoing engine maintenance at Illesheim. *(ECPA)*

loss of the lives of the crew members; Oblt von Bothmer went after No 132, which force-landed in flames in the same area, five men being taken prisoner, including the pilot, Lt Berenger, and the Escadre commander, Lt Col Enselem, who was acting as second pilot.*

During the day H-75As of GC II/4 patrolled over the Wissembourg area, where they were in time to assist a pair of Mureaux from GAO 1/520, which were under attack by Messerschmitts. The Curtiss fighters dived to the aid of the reconnaissance aircraft, and by engaging the German machines enabled them to escape. One of the Mureaux avoided six attacks by performing steep spirals.

One Potez 637 of GR I/52 flown by Cpl Chef Dumas, was attacked by Bf 109s whilst returning from a sortie to Ulm; it was damaged and the gunner was wounded. Three MS 406s from GC I/3, led by Lt Lacombe, made an unauthorised strafing attack on Saarbrücken airfield, setting a hangar on fire, but when they landed Lacombe was to receive a severe reprimand for having attacked a target on German soil! It seems that Bf109Es from 3/JG53 may also have joined this engagement, Lt Wilhelm Hoffmann of this unit also claiming a Bloch 200 at this time.

10/9/39

The following day, Sunday 10 September, marked the beginning of the second week of the war. Nothing happened until the afternoon, when two Mureaux 113 reconnaissance aircraft from GAO 1/506 were 'bounced' over the Saarlautern area by two Bf 109Es from 2/JG 53. The Mureaux were at 4,500 feet, and Oblt Rolf Pingel dived down from 6,000 feet to attack one. He shot this down in flames near Ensdorf at 1430, and the wreck was inspected by German personnel; on the fin it carried the identification marking 'Mureaux 113 No 4'. The crew, Lt Leleu and Sous Lt Moll, were both killed.

In the evening French artillery bombarded St Arnaul airfield near Saarbrücken, two Mureaux 115s of GAO 1/520 providing observation for the gunners; they were escorted by Moranes from GC I/3. At 1825 the two Mureaux were jumped by four Bf 109Es of 1/JG 53; Uffz Heinrich Bezner attacked the first one, diving 1,500 feet to do so. His first attack was not successful, and the

Ofw Grimmling of 1/JG 53 gained his second victory over this GAO 1/520 Mureaux 115 on 10 September, in which Sgt Lahaye and Lt Cappoen crash-landed.

aircraft turned sharply for the safety of its own lines. Bezner attacked again and this time managed to shoot it down in flames just inside French territory at Grosbliederstroff, killing Sgt Tacquart and his observer, Lt Potié. Meanwhile Ofw Grimmling had engaged the second, making two passes and shooting it down into German territory at Auersmacher, south of Saarlautern. Lt Cappoen's crew survived, evaded capture, and reached the French lines safely. The MS 406s had been engaged by four more Bf 109Es meantime, and two of them were slightly damaged.

At around the same time another Schwarm from I/JG 53 reported meeting another reconnaissance aircraft south of Saarlautern, and this was claimed shot down on the French side of the lines by Lt Georg Claus, although in this case his claim was not confirmed; no additional French losses were recorded. During the day Lt Hartmann Grasser of JGr 152 shot down a French captive observation balloon, whilst another of these was brought down by pilots of I/JG 53 during the week. The day also saw the allocation to the Western Front of nine reserve divisions of the Wehrmacht.

11–12/9/39

Following these three active days, a quieter spell ensued. On 11th four Bf 109Es of I/JG 53 and an equal number of H-75As from GC II/5 clashed near Saarbrücken, but without damage to either side. However an ANF Mureaux 117 (No 70) of GAO 3/551 was brought down by Flak between Perl and Apach, the crew (Cne Rossignol and Lt Sueur) being killed. Next day a second Mureaux from this unit fell victim to Flak, crashing near Güdingen in No Mans' Land; on this occasion the crew survived unhurt.

Now it was over the North Sea that activity continued. On 12th a Do 18 from 2/KüFlGr 106 (M2+EK) was obliged to make a force-landing on the sea whilst returning from a reconnaissance flight over the Shetlands-Firth of Forth area with two other flyingboats from this unit. It is possible that the aircraft had been damaged in combat with a Hudson of 224 Squadron, Flg Off Hollington of this unit reporting an inconclusive engagement with a Do 18 on this date. The German crew was rescued by the submarine U-13, while next day the air-sea rescue vessel *Gunther Plüschow* took the abandoned 'boat in tow; at 1220 it capsized and sank near Norderney.

That same afternoon six He 115s from 1/KüFlGr 106 were reconnoitring in the same area, to the east of Norderney, when at 1421 a Fokker T VIIIW of the Dutch Naval Air Service approached from out of the sun. Assuming this to be a hostile intruder, the crew of M2+LH at once attacked, and the Fokker went down to force-land on the sea, where it immediately capsized. The Heinkel landed alongside and picked up all four members of the Dutch crew. At that moment Do 18 M2+LK of 2 Staffel appeared overhead, and assuming that the Heinkel had suffered a force-landing, put down beside it to offer help. In doing so the flyingboat sprang a leak, and unable to take off again, drifted helplessly towards the Dutch island of Ameland, where Lt zur See Horst Rust and his crew were interned.

14–17/9/39

On 9 September the carriers HMS *Ark Royal*, *Courageous* and *Hermes* had sailed into the Atlantic with a screen of destroyers to undertake anti-submarine patrols. During Thursday, 14 September, *Ark Royal* was attacked by U-39, which was sunk by the destroyer escort, but only after near-missing the British vessel with torpedoes. Skuas from 803 Squadron were flown off in the afternoon to protect the ship from further such attacks, and two of these found U-30, commanded by KapitänLeutnant Lemp, on the surface. They dive-bombed the submarine, but both aircraft came down in the sea. Royal Navy records indicate that they were brought down by the explosions of their own bombs, but the Kriegsmarine claimed that they had in fact been shot down by the U-Boat's gunners. U-30 survived the attack and picked up both pilots, though in each case the gunner perished. Three days later HMS *Courageous* was 350 miles west of Land's End when U-29 was able to approach unobserved and sink the carrier with great loss of life, despite the fact that some of her Swordfish were in the air at the time, searching for just such an attack. 518 Royal Navy personnel, 26 members of the Fleet Air Arm and 36 RAF servicing crew were lost. It was then realised that such patrols were far too dangerous for the carriers and they ceased forthwith.

Over the Western Front Bf 109Es of II/JG 53 clashed with MS 406s of GC I/3 in the Saarbrücken area on 15th, but again there was no conclusive result, the Moranes withdrawing westwards. A more definite engagement took place on 17th however, when five I/JG 53 Messerschmitts intercepted a Bloch MB 131 (No 86) from GR I/22 (Sous Lt Capdeville, Lt Leroy, Lt Roussell and Adj Saron) which was undertaking a reconnaissance over the Saarbrücken area. This was shot down over Morsbach by Hpt Dr Erich Mix and Lt Balfanz, none of the crew surviving. Mix had been a fighter pilot during the First World War, with three victories to his credit. During the day however, came the ominous news that Russian troops had invaded Poland along the entire Eastern frontier of the country.

In Western Poland the front was reported to have collapsed under the weight of the Wehrmacht's crushing blows, and Brest-Litovsk had fallen to the invaders. In France this period was marked by the withdrawal of the majority of the French bomber units from the north-western area. Already on 5th the 12ᵉ Escadre had pulled out of the Vosges to Caen-Carpiquet to replace its Bloch MB 210s with LeO 451s. Now all units save those flying Amiot 143s and Farman F 222s were ordered to rear bases for re-equipment.

18/9/39

Monday, 18 September, was again relatively uneventful, a day enlivened only by a strafing attack on German army barracks near Saarburg made by three H-75As from GC II/4 at 1630. A totally different type of operation was taking place over the Atlantic however, where a patrolling Sunderland, 'D' from 204 Squadron, depth-charged a U-Boat without result. Somewhat later however, Sunderland 'E', L5802, from this same unit picked up a radioed 'SOS' from the MV *Kensington Court*, which was approximately 100 miles south of Ireland, and under attack by another U-Boat. The vessel's location was also about 100 miles from the Sunderland, but the pilot Flt Lt J. Barrett, made all speed to the rescue. On arrival the crew saw that the stricken ship's lifeboats had been launched, while overhead another Sunderland from 228 Squadron was already circling. Barrett took over the covering role, hunting for the U-Boat, while the 228 Squadron machine landed and picked up 20 members of the crew. Barrett then also went down to pick up the other 14. He was later awarded the DFC for his part in this rescue.

The following day saw two encounters over the North Sea between opposing patrol aircraft, but both proved indecisive. At 1005 an Anson of 612 Squadron encountered Do 18 8L+EK of 2/KüFlGr 606 some 122 miles east of Wick. In the short combat which followed the Anson made four firing passes, but the Dornier disappeared undamaged into the clouds. An hour later at 1110, an He 115 of 1/KüFlGr 406 fought a Hudson of 224 Squadron south of Mandal, Norway. On this occasion it was the British aircraft that escaped in cloud.

By this time several of the newly-arrived RAF Fairey Battle squadrons had begun undertaking reconnaissance sorties over the Franco-German frontier area, the first such being flown by a trio of 150 Squadron aircraft on 10th; other squadrons were soon being similarly employed. The first RAF engagement with the Luftwaffe over the Western Front involved such aircraft on Wednesday, 20 September — a day on which the relative quiet of the preceding days was replaced by an eruption of quite violent action.

Three Battles from 88 Squadron and six from 218 Squadron were to undertake reconnaissance flights during this day, and it was the former of these formations which ran into trouble. The bombers had taken off at 1000 and by 1147 were to the west of Saarbrücken when three Bf 109Ds of JGr 152 appeared, and at once attacked them. Two Battles were shot down at once by Hpt Lessmann and Oblt Wiggers; K9245 (F/Sgt Page) went down in flames, while Flg Off R.C. Graveley crash-landed K9242, this aircraft immediately catching fire. The lone survivor was K9243 (Flg Off Baker); the gunner in this aircraft, Sgt F. Letchford, claimed one Bf 109 shot down, and this was confirmed by French ground observers, being acclaimed as the first aerial victory of the war for the Royal Air Force. No aircraft was in fact lost by the Luftwaffe, and in official RAF records a footnote was added to the account of this action, "Probably unconfirmed and incorrect." It seems clear that although Letchford shot at a Bf 109, he did not hit it; the aircraft seen falling in flames by both the Battle crew and the French was obviously F/Sgt Page's machine.

A trio of 88 Squadron Fairey Battles over the French countryside. *(IWM)*

Mureaux 115 No 21 of GAO 507 after force-landing following an attack by II/JG 53.

At 1345 Bf 109Es of II/JG 53 intercepted a Mureaux 115 (No 21) of GAO 507, which was shot down by Oblt Schulze-Blanck (who claimed it as a 'Potez'); Lt Bonal and Adj Chef Senne both suffered slight injuries, but force-landed and were rescued by French troops. Meanwhile six H-75As from GC II/5 covered another reconnaissance aircraft over the Apach-Büdingen sector, where three of the fighters acting as high cover were drawn away by a lone Hs 126, which was subsequently thought to have been deliberately luring them into ambush. Suddenly at 1450 a trio of Bf 109Es from 1/JG 53 dived on them, two more Messerschmitts following. Oblt Mölders led his Schwarm out of the sun, closing on the last Curtiss. From a range of 50 yards he shot down the aircraft of Sgt Queguiner who baled out after suffering slight burns; the fighter crashed in flames west of Merzig. A second H-75A was claimed at 1455 by Uffz Freund, and this would appear to have been the aircraft flown by Sgt Pechaud, who force-landed it at St Mihiel after it had been hit by 22 bullets. Lt Brandhuber reported that he saw Freund's victim disappearing in the direction of Beckingen with the right wing on fire. One Messerschmitt of 3/JG 53 was shot down into the lines by Sgt Chef Legrand, Uffz Martin Winkler being wounded; he died on 24 September. The other three Curtisses then joined the combat, Sgt Chef Lachaux and Cne Huvet reporting hits on two of the Messerschmitts, but without seeing any results; Lachaux reported attacking the fighter which had just shot down Queguiner. One Bf 109E was in fact hit and force-landed near Hermeskiel, damaged 50% but with the pilot unhurt. At around this time another Schwarm from 1/JG 53 joined combat with a formation of H-75As, and one was claimed shot down by Hpt von Janson. These would seem to have been aircraft of GC I/5 which reported a fight with Bf 109s Adj Salmand, Adj Genty and Sgt Warnier claiming one probably shot down between them over Vouzon-ville; no loss was actually suffered on either side.

A Potez 637 (No 25) of GR I/33 undertook a reconnaissance over the Pirmasens area, but was engaged by a Flak battery commanded by Wacht-meister Stumm. The aircraft was subjected to a ten second barrage of 37mm shells, following which it fell on German soil near Trier, the observer (Cne Schneider) dying of his injuries. Elsewhere, one of GR II/55's Bloch MB 131s violated Swiss airspace near Montbeliard, where it was shot down by the local AA defences. During the day three observation balloons were claimed

Wachtmeister Stumm poses by the remains of Potez 637 No 25 of GR I/33, shot down by his flak battery near Trier on 20 September.

destroyed by German fighters in the area south of Saarbrücken, one of them by StFw Prestele of I/JG 53.

21–22/9/39

Next day there was a further combat when two French reconnaissance aircraft — a new Potez 63-11 and a Potez 390 (No 50), both of GAO 505 — flew sorties covered by nine Moranes of GC I/3. The Po 390, flown by Sgt Chef Achiantre, was reconnoitring the Rubenheim-Altheim-Hornbach sector, and was attacked south-west of Hornbach by five Bf 109Es of Gruppenstab I/JG 53. The French aircraft was badly damaged in the first pass by Hpt Lothar von Janson, but managed to recross the lines and crashed near a French artillery battery with the observer, Cne Leonard, who had been hit by the first burst, dead aboard. Meanwhile the Messerschmitts had taken on the escorts, and Sous Lt Baize was shot down by Hpt Dr Mix. Baize baled out, but his parachute caught fire and he fell to his death.

On this same date two Blenheims from 110 Squadron at Wattisham undertook a reconnaissance over North Germany. Plt Off R.J. Hill's aircraft reached the Hanover area, but was twice engaged by Luftwaffe fighters. The first such interception was made by a lone Bf 109, which closed to 30 yards, at which range the gunner claimed to have shot it down — although no German loss is in fact recorded. Two more fighters subsequently attacked but were not able to inflict any damage.

During a patrol over the Vitry-le-Francois area by Moranes from GC III/2, Sgt Duclos became completely disorientated. Totally lost, he landed in error at Ensheim, just inside the German frontier, where he was made a prisoner. French artillery batteries were subsequently able to destroy his aircraft, which could be seen from the French lines. His unit enjoyed more success on 22nd however, when its Moranes were again sent out on patrol, this time over the Altheim-Waschbronn area. Here the pilots spotted a Dornier Do 17P of 3(F)/22 flying at 18,000 feet over Zweibrücken with an escort of four fighters. The French pilots possessed a height advantage and at once dived to attack, Adj Romey's fire killing the pilot, Uffz Kurt Seiffert, whereupon the Dornier crashed vertically into the ground west of Neunkirchen in the Saar; one more

Hpt Dr Erich Mix of I/JG 53, who gained several victories during World War I, and who was to serve as a fighter pilot throughout most of the second war. *(ECPA)*

member of the crew was killed but the third man baled out, wounded. So fast had been Romey's attack that the survivor believed the aircraft to have been shot down in error by German Flak. Because the aircraft had fallen on German soil without adequate witnesses, Romey was credited only with a probable.

Dornier Do 17P of 3(F)/22 in flight. *(ECPA)*

While activity in the West had been increasing, the defeat of Poland had swiftly been accomplished, allowing plans to be prepared for the transfer of a substantial part of the Luftflotten which had been involved there to strengthen those facing the British and French. Such transfers were already beginning when on 22 September the Luftwaffe ObdL/Führungsstab Ia issued Order 5292/39 to all four Luftflotten regarding redisposition, as indicated overleaf:

1. REMAINING IN THE EAST

Luftflotte 1	I/KG 2
	1(F)/120
Luftflotte 4	KG 77 (less I Gruppe)
	1(F)/124

2. FOR THE AIR DEFENCE OF BERLIN AND CENTRAL GERMANY

I/JG 2 with 10(NJ)/JG 2
I/JG 3
I/JG 20 (two Staffeln)

3. ALL OTHER UNITS TRANSFERRED TO LUFTFLOTTEN 2 AND 3

The establishment of these Luftflotten was now to include:

a) Luftflotte 1

Fliegerdivisionen	I, IV and X
Reconnaissance	FAG 122 with 1-5 Staffeln; 1(F)/121
Bombers	I/KG 30, KG 26, KG 54, KG 4
	Stab LG 1 and II and III/LG 1
	KG 55, KG 27, KG 1
	LN-Abteilung 100
Dive Bombers	IV(St)/LG 1
	I(St)/TrGr 186
Destroyers	Stab ZG 26 with I and II/ZG 26
	I/ZG 1
Fighters	JGr 101
	II(J)/TrGr 186, I/JG 1, I/JG 26
	II/JG 26, III/JG 26, 10(NJ)/JG 26
	I/JG 21
	I(J)/LG 2, II/JG 77
	JGr 126, I/JG 52

b) Luftflotte 3

Fliegerdivisionen	II, V, VI and zbV
Reconnaissance	FAG 121 with 3(F)/121 and 4(F)/121
Bombers	KG 51, KG 53, Stag and II/KG 2
	KG 76, KG 3, I/KG 77
Dive Bombers	All units except those with Luftflotte 2
Ground Attack	II(Sch)/LG 2
Destroyers	I(Schw J)/LG 1, I/ZG 76
Fighters	JGr 176, JGr 152, JGr 102
	I/JG 51, II/JG 52, I and II/JG 53
	I/JG 54, I/JG 76
	I/JG 77, I/JG 71
	7 and 8/JG 53, 10(NJ)/JG 72

c) Under Control of ObdL

Reconnaissance	FAG/ObdL with 1(F) and 2(F)/ObdL,
	8(F)/LG 2 and 2(F)/121
VII Fliegerdivision	KGzbV 1

A trio of Morane 406s of GC I/3 led by Cne Roger Gerard.

24/9/39

The increase in available strength did not at first make itself felt either over the Western Front or the North Sea, where activities continued much as before. On Sunday, 24 September, as the fourth week of the war commenced, the French fighters suffered their first defeat. Early in the afternoon six Morane 406s from GC I/3 flew cover to a reconnaissance Mureaux in the area west of Saarbrücken. Here they were bounced from above by eight Bf 109Ds of JGr 152, Sgt Jean Garnier's Morane going down in flames near Etting, while a second was hit and force-landed; Garnier failed to survive. The remaining fighters then became involved in a dogfight during which Cne Roger Gerard shot down Lt Kurt Rosenkranz, who had himself shot down one of the first two Moranes to fall;

GC I/3 entertained their victims of 24 September before they were taken to prison camp. Left is Lt Kurt Rosenkranz of JGr 152, alongside his victor, Cne Roger Gerard (right). *(ECPA)*

Pilots of GC I/3 with a black cross trophy cut from one of their victims. Left to right are Sous Lt Salva, Sous Lt Lucien Potier, Cne Bernard Challe, Sgt Chaussat and Sgt Chef Octave.

Gerard was then also obliged to bale out of his stricken fighter. Meanwhile a second Messerschmitt flown by Gefr Hesselbach had been shot down by Adj Antonin Combette, but again he too was shot down and baled out. The two German pilots who had gone down, both crash-landed and became prisoners; they would be repatriated in June 1940. Apart from Rosenkranz's victory, the other three Moranes were claimed by Oblt Werner Schnoor, Lt Lothar Hagen and Ofw Johannes Oertel.

During a second patrol the Messerschmitts of JGr 152 were again successful. Six H-75As of GC II/4 had taken off at 1440 to escort a Po 637 of GR II/52 over the Hornbach-Eppenbronn sector. At 1530 Adj Camille Plubeau spotted six Bf 109s east of Hornbach, and these were at once attacked. Adj Dardaine shot down one Messerschmitt over the French lines, which crashed near Betviller, Oblt Borth, the pilot, being severely injured. Lts Horst Elstermann and Hartmann Grasser then each claimed a Curtiss shot down, Sgt Antoine de la Chapelle baling out of his blazing fighter, coming down safely inside No Mans' Land, while two more H-75As were hit and badly damaged; Adj Henri Dardaine and Lt Gabriel Duperret managed to regain their base in these. Meanwhile Plubeau and Adj Georges Tesseraud had given chase to their attackers, reporting that they had hit them hard and seen fuel leaking from both. Lt Elstermann force-landed near Weilerbach, his Messerschmitt having been hit 13 times, and classified as damaged 40%, while Lt Grasser force-landed near Bingen with 30% damage to his aircraft; neither pilot was hurt. While chasing the Bf 109Ds, the pursuing H-75As suddenly came upon a Schwarm of four Bf 109Es of I/JG 53 over the Pirmasens area, and Adj Plubeau claimed one of these shot down, but no loss was suffered.

For the French strategic reconnaissance units the week beginning 24 September was to be remembered as 'La Semaine Noir' — 'The Black Week' — for it was to see the loss of five Potez 637s with seven killed and two badly wounded amongst the crews. On this date Lt Israel of GR II/33 set out to photograph the Odendorf-Euskirchen area, where he was fired on by Flak. Emerging from a cloud, he encountered two Bf 109s head-on, one of these

Lt Hartmann Grasser of JGr 152 with his Bf 109D after being awarded the Iron Cross 1st Class for his victory on 24 September.

sweeping round onto the tail of the aircraft. Despite his efforts, and those of Adj Robert with the rear gun, the Messerschmitt could not be shaken off. Robert claimed hits on the attacker, but Israel himself was wounded, and Po 637 No 7 was badly damaged. The aircraft escaped into clouds, but after 200 kilometres, one of the engines stopped and Israel had to force-land at Orconte.

Bf 109Es of I/JG 53 intercepted Mureaux 115 No 107 of GAO 1/502, which was being flown on a reconnaissance by Sous Lt Petit. Ofw Kühlmann attacked, his first burst wounding Lt Bernard, the observer/gunner. At this point seven escorting MS 406s of GC I/3 came to the rescue and drove the Messerschmitts off, allowing the damaged Mureaux to regain its base and land. The Germans reported meeting four escorting Moranes and Kühlmann was credited with having shot the Mureaux down — I/JG 53's tenth victory. A further German fighter claim on this date has not been identified in detail, but may relate to Israel's Potez.

25/9/39
On Monday a further big fight took place over the Weissenburg area, where a Po 637 of GR II/52 flown by Lt Tissier was on its way to photograph Bergzabern. On this occasion it had been provided with a close escort of three H-75As from GC II/4, a section of six more from GC I/4 providing high cover. Moranes from GC I/3 were also patrolling in the area. The French aircraft were intercepted by a mixed force of Bf 109s from I/JG 51, II/JG 52 and II/JG 53, and a dogfight began. Initially the three highest-flying H-75As of GC I/4 were bounced at 1205 by a half dozen Bf 109Es from I/JG 51, Hpt Douglas Pitcairn and Uffz Heinz Bär claiming two shot down; two of the Curtiss fighters did indeed crash-land. Meanwhile the third pilot, Sous Lt Pierre Verrey opened fire on one of the Messerschmitts which he described as carrying a "long yellow and black insignia". He reported that the undercarriage of this aircraft dropped down, it lost altitude, and was thought to have crashed near Bienwald. As the Bf 109 went down, its wingman overshot and flew right in front of Verrey's Curtiss, allowing him to get in a good burst at point-blank range. This second aircraft, also credited to Verrey as confirmed, was reported to have crashed near Bienwald as well. In fact he had inflicted 10-15% damage on both

Involved in his first successful combat on 25 September was one of the Luftwaffe's future 'greats'. Fw Heinz Bär, later a Geschwader Kommodore with 220 victories, stands (right) with his Staffel-kapitän, Oblt Douglas Pitcairn, with one of 1/JG 51's Bf 109Es.

Messerschmitts, which were flown by Ofw Oskar Sicking and Fw Josef Oglodek, but both returned.

While this was going on part of the II/JG 53 formation attacked the trio of GC II/4 aircraft, and Cne Pierre Claude, the formation leader, was shot down by Lt Eduard Schröder. It was subsequently reported that Claude had shot down one of his opponents which fell at Surbourg, near Lauterbourg, but had been obliged to bale out of his own aircraft (No 112) when it began to burn. His wingmen reported that two Messerschmitts then opened fire on him, and he was found to be dead on landing, with two bullets through his head. Claude's two wingmen attacked the two Messerschmitts, Sous Lt Georges Baptizet diving behind one amongst clouds and seeing his bullets set the right wing on fire, but as the German was able to escape over Bergzabern, he was credited only with a probable. Adj Tesseraud at the same time claimed a Messerschmitt shot down over Bienwald, which was confirmed, while Baptizet, who had been carried away from the melee while chasing his opponent, returned to the fray. He attacked a single Bf 109 which was circling idly and chased it down to tree-top level, but was forced to let it go when his ammunition ran out. As he had seen hits it was claimed as a probable. Tesseraud opened fire on yet another Bf 109 which escaped over its own lines, and this too was optimistically claimed by the French HQ as a probable, although apparently this was not officially credited to Tesseraud. In fact three of JG 53's Bf 109Es had indeed been hit, Fw Hellge of 6 Staffel being shot down and killed south-east of Bergzabern, while two more aircraft crash-landed in the same area, one damaged 53% and the other 45%; both pilots were slightly wounded.

Four further Bf 109s from 4/JG 52 had attacked Lt Tissier's Potez whilst the escort was so heavily engaged, and this aircraft was shot down by Oblt August-Wilhelm Schumann, force-landing near Sarralbe, where Tissier and his gunner pulled the observer, Sous Lt Amarra, from the wreckage just before it blew up.

Claude's death apparently while parachuting down, deeply shocked the French pilots, and following this incident the Inspection de la Chasse was obliged to publish a special instruction expressly forbidding such action against German pilots, though in their next combat the pilots of GC II/4 were sorely tempted to retaliate. Whether Claude was deliberately shot, or fell into the fire of aircraft already in combat remains a debatable point, as do most such instances.

Reconnaissance was also undertaken from England on 25th, three Blenheim IVs from 107 Squadron operating over Western Germany. One of these flown by the commanding officer, Wg Cdr Basil Embrey, was intercepted over Leer by two Messerchmitts, but escaped despite sustaining damage to a fuel tank and the turret. Meanwhile three Do 17Ps of 2(F)/123 made the first Luftwaffe reconnaissance over France, covering the airfields at Reims, Mourmelon, Chalons-sur-Marne, Vitry, Brienn, Troyes and Sezanne.

26–27/9/39

Another Po 637 was sent out on 26th on a midday reconnaissance to Constance. This aircraft, No 46 of GR I/52, was intercepted by 12 Bf 109Ds of JGr 176. Mortally hit by fire from Lt Güth's Messerschmitt, the Potez dived towards the

Lt Güth of JGr 176 displays one of the rudders from the Potez 637 of GR I/52 which he shot down on 26 September.

70

StFw Ignatz Prestele, Legion Condor veteran, became a predator of French observation balloons during September. *(ECPA)*

ground with the gunner and observer dead, and Adj Brard, the pilot, wounded in the legs. As it fell it was fired on by Flak gunners and hit again, Brard suffering further wounds, this time to his shoulder. The aircraft crashed near Siegmaringen at 1145.

A further Armée de l'Air reconnaissance machine, this time a Bloch MB 131 (No 80) of GR II/55, was caught near Freiburg by six Bf 109s of II/JG 52 and this was also shot down, falling victim to Lt Martin Mund. Although it was initially reported by the French that two members of the crew had been killed, the Germans confirmed that all three survived with wounds as prisoners, including Cne Evano, the commander/observer, and Adj Chef Girard, the pilot. Elsewhere over the frontier area, II/JG 53 reported combat with Curtiss H-75As at 1615, but without obvious results, while StFw Prestele of I/JG 53 again claimed a French balloon shot down west of Merzig.

The Advanced Air Striking Force Battles were now operating regularly by day, usually two squadrons providing the required dozen or so aircraft on a rota basis. On 26th 88 Squadron sent off six aircraft which were joined by a welcome escort of eight French fighters, but no such comforting presence was available to three 103 Squadron machines which went off to the Saarbrücken area shortly after midday on Wednesday, 27th. All was well until they reached the Bitsch area at 1220, but here three fighters — which subsequently proved to be French H-75As — attacked and drove the Battles down to ground level; they then broke away, apparently having realized their mistake. No sooner had they departed then four Bf 109Ds of JGr 152 pounced upon the bombers and proceeded to attack them vigorously. Ogfr Josef Scherm was seen to shoot down Battle K9271 (Flg Off Vipan), which was badly hit and crash-landed near Bitsch when the engine ceased to function; the observer, Sgt Vickers, was badly hurt, dying in hospital next day. The gunner in one of the other Battles managed to get a good burst into Scherm's fighter however, and this crashed at once near Bockweiler, the pilot being killed. The other two Battles escaped.

Six H-75As of GC II/4 were again patrolling over the Hornbach-Waschbronn area a little while after this combat, and here at 1325 three Bf 109Ds of JGr 176 on their first operational sortie over the lines from Gablingen, attempted to attack Sous Lt Baptizet's aircraft. The French pilots reacted swiftly, Sgt de La Chapelle attacking one Messerschmitt which was behind Baptizet and claiming it shot down over Hornbach. The German pilot in fact escaped, and crash-landed his badly shot-up fighter near Bad Homburg, with 50% damage. The other two Messerschmitts turned away south and were pursued by the six French fighters, which caught up with them near Lahr, where another short combat took place; here Baptizet and Adj Tesseraud each shot one down. Uffz Ernst Köpke's aircraft went down in flames to crash near Unterharmersbach, the pilot being killed, while Lt Rinow, who had been wounded, baled out of his badly damaged aircraft near Triberg. After assessing the claims, the French credited two confirmed victories to Baptizet, de La Chapelle and Tesseraud jointly, de La Chapelle's first claim being classed as a probable.

A few hours later at about 1600 nine Bf 109Es of I/JG 53 intercepted Po 637 No 4 of GR II/52 which Adj Chef Saudry was piloting over the Farbach area. The reconnaisance machine was shot down by Lt Karl-Wilhelm Heimbs with the loss of all three members of the crew. A Potez 29 (No 1700) from GAO 2/508 was also attacked by two Bf 109s of I/JG 53 during the day, but managed to escape and land at Thionville in a damaged condition with Lt Lambert, the pilot, and Lt Lequeu, the observer, both slightly wounded.

28/9/39

Early on 28th a pair of Blenheim IVs from 110 Squadron left England for a reconnaissance over the Osnabrück area, setting off at 0740. Neither returned, both N6212 (Wg Cdr I.McL. Cameron) and N6206 (Flg Off D. Strachan) being reported missing. The former Blenheim was shot down over the Osnabrück area by Fw Klaus Faber of I/JG 1, while the latter fell to Lt Helmut Henz of II/JG 77, crashing into the German Bight. The day also marked the first operational sorties by other, French-based, Blenheims of 53 Squadron.

Later in the day three H-75As of GC II/5 intercepted a tactical reconnaissance Henschel Hs 126 escorted by a single Bf 109E of 2/JG 26 over the northern sector of the front. The Curtisses attempted to attack the Henschel, but this made good its escape. Some minutes later the patrol was attacked by the Messerschmitt, Lt Bürschgens, the pilot of this, claiming to have shot down one of the H-75As. He was then shot down himself by Sgt Heme, and crash-landed near Mettbach, eight kilometres from Tünsdorf, having been wounded; the aircraft was 50% damaged. Heme was credited only with a probable, since Bürschgens' crash had not been witnessed. No French loss was actually suffered on this occasion. During the day a Mureaux 115 (No 6) of GAO 553 was reported shot down in flames by Flak in the Götzdorf/Wissembourg area, near Bitsche. Adj Chef George, the pilot, baled out, but died of his wounds while on the way to hospital; the observer Lt Lapadie, was killed. It seems that the aircraft actually fell to a Bf 109D flown by Oblt Vitzthum of JGr 152, crashing near Götzenbruck, south-west of Bitsche, or to Lt Vogel of 4/JG53, who also claimed a Mureaux.

During the day Uffz Georg Pavenzinger of 2/JG 51 became lost and force-landed his Bf 109E, 'Red 9' (WerkNr 3326) near Brumat, where he was taken prisoner. This was the first almost undamaged example of the latest Messerschmitt to fall into Allied hands.

30/9/39

Saturday, 30 September, brought 'La Semaine Noir' to an end — but with the most severe fighting yet experienced over France since the outbreak of war. Late in the morning six Battles of 150 Squadron left Ecury-sur-Coole for a high altitude photographic reconnaissance over the Saarbrücken-Merzig area; one bomber was forced to return early due to engine trouble, but the other five continued, led by Sqn Ldr Macdonald in K9283. At 1200, some 55 minutes after take off, they were attacked by eight Bf 109Es of 2/JG 53, and were slaughtered. The first to go down fell to StFw Ignatz Prestele, a Legion Condor veteran with four victories gained in that war. Within minutes three more had been shot down by Oblt Rolf Peter Pingel (another ex-Legion Condor experte), Uffz Kaiser and Uffz Kornatz. K9387 (Flg Off Corelli), N2028 (Plt Off Poulton), K9484 (Plt Off Saunders) and N2093 (Flt Lt Hyde-Parker) were all lost, most of the Battles falling in flames. During the combat one Bf 109 was also reported to have gone down in flames, but since none were lost the observer must have seen one of the Battles falling. A Messerschmitt was also seen to go down in a steep spiral and this was undoubtedly that flown by Prestele, who dropped out of the fight after his Bf 109 suffered hits in the fuel tank. Pingel's fighter was also slightly damaged, being hit eight times. The combat was not yet over however; the lone survivor, Sqn Ldr Macdonald's aircraft, now headed for home with Uffz Josef Wurmheller 'sitting on his tail'. Wurmheller chased the Battle, determinedly pumping shells and bullets into it and only breaking off combat some 30 kilometres behind the French lines. He returned claiming the Battle destroyed, and so it proved. Macdonald managed to reach base, where he put the crippled K9283 down, but the Battle at once caught fire as it came to rest. The crew were able to escape, but the aircraft was a total loss − the complete formation had been wiped out! Following this disastrous operation further unescorted reconnaissances over the front by the Battle squadrons were cancelled.

During the afternoon a number of hard-fought engagements took place

The five pilots of 2/JG 53 — four of them future 'Experten' — who destroyed a complete formation of 150 Squadron Battles on 30 September. Left to right are Uffz Hans Kornatz, Uffz Josef Wurmheller, Oblt Rolf Pingel (Staffelkapitän), StFw Ignatz Prestele and Uffz Robert Kaiser.

between French and German fighters, some of the details of which are rather confused. It seems likely that the various formations involved, operating over the middle and southern sectors of the front, may well have become engaged with more than one of the opposing formations. Since it has not been possible to resolve with any final degree of certitude just which aircraft were engaged with which, separate accounts of each side's activities are included.

Possibly the first French aircraft to appear were six H-75As of GC II/4, led by Adj Plubeau, which covered a Potez 63 over the Delfeld-Edelbronn area. Twenty minutes into the mission three Bf 109s were seen near Saarbrücken and three more at height over Pirmasens. The Messerschmitts dived straight after the Potez, Asp de La Chapelle going after the leader and Plubeau taking his wingman. Using their great speed from the dive, the Germans escaped, Plubeau claiming hits on one when he saw smoke from the engine.

A little later four Moranes from GC I/3 and three from GC III/3 escorted Potez 637 No 54 of GR II/52 over the Wissembourg area. Above Ensheim at 1450 Bf 109Es, which appear to have been two Schwarme from 3/JG 53, attacked the GC III/3 trio. Although his aircraft was riddled with bullets, Adj Chef Michel Marias was able to claim one of the attackers shot down before crashing near Bischmisheim, unhurt; Lt Patroux was wounded in the right arm and was obliged to force-land in open country south of Güdingen. The German unit submitted claims for a Morane and a Curtiss, credited to Hpt Wolfgang Lippert and Ofw Erich Kühlmann, but Ofw Willibald Hien was fatally wounded during the fight, and crashed near Bischmisheim.

The GC I/3 Moranes failed to make contact with the Messerschmitts, three more of which got through to the Potez, which was hard hit. It seems likely that the attacker was Hpt Günther von Maltzahn of II/JG 53, who claimed one such aircraft shot down during the midday period. Adj Chef Mercy, although wounded, got the aircraft back over French lines where he ordered the observer to bale out − the gunner having already been killed during the fighters' attack. Mercy then managed to accomplish a successful crash-landing, and even managed to rescue the exposed photographic negatives from the flaming wreckage.

On 30 September Adj Chef Michel Marias of GC III/3 (seen here smoking his pipe) was obliged to force-land his damaged Morane 406 — but not before he had shot down one of his attackers from 3/JG 53.

Somewhat later at 1658 a dozen H-75As from GC II/4 were off to escort a pair of Mureaux over the Altenstadt-Schebenhardt area. Two more reconnaissance aircraft — Po637s of GR II/22 — headed for the Siegfried Line, escorted by a patrouille of three GC II/5 H-75As, with two more sections from GC I/5 patrolling overhead. It seems that formations from both I and II/JG 53 were again in the air. Oblt Hubert Kroeck of II Gruppe led one Schwarm in an attack on the Mureaux, firing on one personally, but overshooting it and going to the aid of his Rottenflieger, Uffz Rudolf Schmidt, who was under attack. A trio of GC II/4 Curtisses had dived after the four Messerschmitts, Adj Villey attacking the leader's wingman — obviously Schmidt — while Lt Regis Guieu got the leader in his sights as Kroeck attempted to get on Villey's tail, and opened fire. Kroeck at once broke away, apparently streaming water vapour and black smoke. Villey's target meanwhile had exploded in mid-air over the Hagenau Forest, and Schmidt was killed. Subsequently ground observers reported that they had seen a Bf 109 crashing in flames near Lauterbourg, and this was considered to be the aircraft attacked by Guieu; he was awarded a confirmed victory. This was not the case in fact, for Kroeck returned safely to base, where it seems that he was credited with having shot down the Mureaux he had initially attacked.

The I Gruppe aircraft, led by Hpt Lothar von Janson, had undoubtedly become engaged with the second French formation, and it seems possible that more II Gruppe aircraft were also involved, for the crew of the Potez, their mission completed and on their return flight, subsequently reported seeing 15 Bf 109s attacking their escorts; they thought that they had seen five Messerschmitts and three H-75As falling in flames. I Gruppe claimed two Curtiss and one aircraft identified as a 'Battle', these being credited to von Janson, Lt Hilbradt and Uffz Heinrich Leschert (the 'Battle'), but Lt Karl-Wilhelm Heimbs and Lt Willi Hoffmann were both shot down and killed, falling near Bethingen and at Merzig/St Wendel respectively, whilst Uffz Fritz Uhl baled out over the latter location.

The French fighters had dived to attack the Messerschmitts, and in the dogfight that followed Adj Pierre Genty of GC I/5 claimed two Bf 109s shot down, one during a head-on attack over Silvingen, and one which he attacked from behind over Wehingen-Battingen. Cne Huvet of GC II/5 claimed two more over the same areas, while Sgt Chef Francois Lachaux claimed one north-west of Wehingen. The victories were costly to the French, Sous Lt Restif and Sgt Edouard Lepreux (H-75A No 34) of I/5 both being killed while Lt Hubert Boitelot force-landed his badly damaged aircraft at Toul; Restif's H-75A-1, No 15, crashed in the Bergholtz Forest near Laurstroff. Sgt Magniez of II/5 was also killed, crashing at Weisskirchen, where he was buried by the Germans.

During the afternoon, and possibly mainly in this combat, II/JG 53 submitted five more claims. One of these by Oblt Vollmer was for another Mureaux — possibly during the fight with GC II/4 — whilst Oblt Vogel and Fw Czikowski each claimed fighters identified as Moranes. Of greater difficulty to identify, Oblt Bretnütz claimed another 'Battle', and Oblt Schülze-Blanck a 'Caudron'; the latter was hit and was obliged to force-land on the west bank of the Rhine near Lauterbourg. As the wounded pilot approached the ground, the engine caught fire and his aircraft was classed as 30% damaged. It seems possible that this was the crash reported which led to Guieu's earlier claim subsequently being confirmed.

During these engagements therefore, JG 53 had claimed 13 victories — seven fighters identified as three Moranes and four Curtisses — one Potez 63, two Battles, two Mureaux and one Caudron. They had lost five Messerschmitts and four of their pilots, with a sixth aircraft force-landed. In return, the French had claimed eight Bf 109s shot down and had lost three H-75As and their pilots, with one more force-landed, plus one Potez 637; two Moranes had been hit and damaged, one of these force-landing. It seems that two Mureaux had been shot down, but details are not available, nor is there definite confirmation of this from French records. The identity of the two Battles and the Caudron remain a mystery, and the inconsistencies of this violent afternoon therefore remain partially unresolved. Suffice to say that the fighting had been desperate, and losses on both sides quite severe. So ended 'Black Week', and with it the first month of the war over the Western Front — for the air forces it had clearly been anything but 'phoney'!

With the exception of the Fairey Battle squadrons, the RAF in France had still played little part, but this would soon change. Since arrival there had been considerable movement of units, and during the second half of the month the following changes had taken place:

> 1 and 73 Squadrons to Norrent Fontes
> 85 and 87 Squadrons to Merville
> 88 Squadron to Baconnes
> 103 Squadron to Monthois
> 105 Squadron to Villeneuve-les-Vertes
> 150 Squadron to Ecury-sur-Coole

The month had also seen the arrival of the Air Component's other Blenheim units, 18 and 57 Squadrons with Mark Is arriving at Beauvraignes and Amy respectively. The first two Lysander squadrons, 4 and 13, also arrived towards the end of September, at Mons-en-Chausee.

29/9/39

For the British fighters, the only event of note had occurred on 29th, when Flg Off E.J. Kain of 73 Squadron flew a Hurricane over Calais to demonstrate it to the French artillery, so that they would be able to recognise the type as friendly in the future. As he approached however, the gunners opened fire at the strange aircraft and shot off the propeller. An extremely annoyed young New Zealand pilot succeeded in making a force-landing on a nearby beach!

20–26/9/39

Whilst the fighting over the front line had been 'hotting-up', other areas had not been without their excitement either. Earlier in the month six of 206 Squadron's Ansons had been detached to Carew Cheriton, near Pembroke, to co-operate with 217 Squadron on operations over the Bristol Channel and Irish Sea. Over the former area on 20 September one aircraft attacked a U-Boat near Lundy Island, but without success. Next day, many miles away to the north-east Flg Off Hollington was patrolling off the German coast in his 224 Squadron Hudson when he was attacked by three biplanes identified as Ar 68 fighters; these may have come from one of the Dämerüngsstaffeln based in the area. In any event he was able to escape them and return unscathed. It was over the

North Sea that most action continued to be seen, the next occurring on 25th when an He 115 of 1/KüFlGr 406 encountered three more 224 Squadron Hudsons south-west of Lista. The British aircraft turned away to the west, and were later spotted by two more of the Gruppe's floatplanes, but on each occasion climbed into clouds to avoid combat.

The Home Fleet had now put to sea on a brief sortie in considerable strength, the vessels sailing towards Norway to cover the return to base of a damaged submarine. Included in the flotilla were the battleships *Nelson* and *Rodney*, battlescruisers *Hood* and *Renown*, aircraft carrier *Ark Royal*, and three cruisers, plus a covering force of four more cruisers and six destroyers. In case German warships might put to sea to give battle, elements of Bomber Command were brought to readiness, and at 0850 on 26th 12 Hampdens of 144 Squadron were sent out on an offensive anti-shipping search, but returned five hours later having seen nothing.

Meanwhile however, the Oberkommando der Marine had organized a search for the British ships, 18 Do 18s from 2/KüFlGr 506, 3/KüFlGr 306 and 2/KüFlGr 606 being sent out, followed later by more from 3/KüFlGr 106 and 3/KüFlGr 406. One of these flyingboats spotted the Fleet through cloud at 1045 in the Great Fisher Bank area, and reported its location which was about 250 miles north-east of Heligoland. No defending fighters were in the air, but three Blackburn Skuas of 803 Squadron were launched and drove the Dornier away. About an hour later two more flyingboats from 2/KüFlGr 506 approached and three more 803 Squadron Skuas were launched, Lt S.B. McEwan, Lt C.L.G. Evans and Lt W.A. Robertson attacking K6+YK (pilot Lt zur See Wilhelm Freiherr von Reitzenstein, aircraft commander Lt zur See Ernst Körner). All three British pilots fired, and finally the Dornier was driven down by McEwan and his gunner, Petty Off B.M. Seymour and forced to land on the water. The crew of four were picked up by the destroyer *Somali*, while the second Do 18 escaped unscathed. Somewhat later another flyingboat approached, and this was driven off by three 800 Squadron Skuas.

The Fliegerdivision 10 'anti-shipping' bombers were at once alerted on receipt of the first sighting report, and at 1250 nine He 111s of 1/KG 26 led by Hpt Vetter took off, followed at 1305 by the detachment of four Ju 88As from I/KG 30 under Lt Walter Storp. Expecting just such an attack, the Royal Navy had emptied all the petrol from the tanks of the Skuas so that they would not burn easily, and had stowed them below decks. Any air attack would be met by the Fleet's anti-aircraft defences it had been decided, and the fighters would play no part!

The German bombers arrived overhead in heavy cloud, the Heinkels bombing from low altitude, but in level flight, and missing. The new Ju 88s then appeared and dived on the ships. Lt Storp got a direct hit on HMS *Hood*, but the bomb bounced off the deck without exploding — it was not just the RAF which suffered such problems! Gefreiter Carl Francke dropped two SC 500 bombs aimed at *Ark Royal*, but only obtained a near miss. He returned claiming that he might have hit the carrier. Later in the day further reconnaissance noted two battleships and covering forces heading west, but no carrier. At once the German propaganda machine leapt upon this, announcing that Francke had sunk the *Ark Royal*. As darkness fell a Do 18 again saw the Fleet and reported the carrier present, but nothing was done to stop the story going out to the world's Press. A Do 17 of 4(F)/122 which carried out a reconnaissance over the

Fleet base at Scapa Flow was hit and slightly damaged by British AA, one member of the crew being wounded.

27/9/39

Next morning at 0700 nine He 111s from 1 and 2/KG 26 and two Ju 88s were sent out again on armed reconnaissance. Only the 1/KG 26 formation saw anything, reporting one cruiser, three destroyers and two motor torpedo boats in the Firth of Forth, but no capital ships.

29/9/39

With the Fleet back at its base, the Hampdens of 144 Squadron were again sent out after German shipping at 0650 on Friday, 29 September. Wg Cdr J.C. Cunningham led off five aircraft first, followed ten minutes later by six more led by Sqn Ldr W.H.J. Lindley. This latter formation found the German destroyers *Bruno Heinemann* and *Paul Jacobi* in the German Bight, three aircraft bombing without success. Lindley's bomber was hit by Flak and Sgt Baker, the second pilot, was wounded. Cunningham's formation simply did not return, and it could only be assumed that they had all been shot down. This was indeed the case, for they had been intercepted by Bf 109Ds of I/ZG 26, Hpt Friedrich-Karl Dickore, Uffz Pollack and Uffz Pitsch shooting down one of the bombers each, while Oblt Günther Specht got two. Return fire hit two of the Messerschmitts which force-landed in the sea, but Uffz Haugk and another pilot were rescued by a German patrol vessel, as were two of the RAF aircrew. Aircraft lost were L4134 (Wg Cdr Cunningham), L4126 (Flg Off R.D. Baugham), L4127 (Flg Off N.C. Beck), L4132 (Plt Off R.M. Coste) and L4121 (Flg Off J.T.B. Sadler). Four members of the various crews survived to be picked up and become prisoners, whilst eight bodies were recovered; the other eight were listed as missing.

Elsewhere over the North Sea on this date Hudson 'X', N7250, of 224 Squadron (pilot Flt Lt J.L. Atkinson) was on patrol when it became engaged in a fight with a Do 18, K6+RK of 2/KüFlGr 506. The Hudson crew saw the gunner in the flyingboat throw up his arms and let go of his gun, making them think they had killed him. In fact the Dornier had been hit by just five bullets, and made good its escape without suffering further damage.

30/9/39

The very next day — 30 September — however, 224 Squadron was to lose two of its Hudsons whilst they were engaged on photographic reconnaissance duties. 'V', N7219, flown by Plt Off D.G. Heaton-Nicholls, had Sylt as its target. Here however, the aircraft was shot down by gunners of Marineflakabteilung 264, and fell into the sea 300 yards from the beach. Two men were seen to bale out, but only one could be rescued. Flg Off J.R. Hollington in 'D', N7216, made for Wilhelmshaven, and this aircraft also failed to return, shot down by a Bf 109E flown by Lt Heinz Demes of 4/JG 77.

As night fell to bring September 1939 to a close, Bomber Command Whitleys were once again off over Germany to drop leaflets. One aircraft from 51 Squadron failed to return from a sortie to Berlin, shot down by gunners of Marineflakabt 216 at Borkum, while another from 10 Squadron crashed on return near Bolton when it ran out of fuel, the crew baling out safely.

Chapter 3

FIGHTER COMMAND IS BLOODED

Following the relatively high level of aerial activity over the Western Front during September — despite the absence of the greater part of the Luftwaffe in Poland — October was to be a considerably quieter month. This was occasioned partly by the onset of autumnal weather conditions, and partly by a slackening of Allied reconnaissance activity as it became clear that no early German onslaught was likely. After the initial abortive attack on the British Fleet on 26 September, German activities were again to be directed against this target during the month, bringing the first taste of serious aerial activity to the skies over the United Kingdom.

October was particularly marked however, by a noteable increase in the number of RAF fighter squadrons, as the expansion programme was urgently speeded-up by the onset of war. The first of these was 152 Squadron, formed on the 1st of the month with Gladiators recently released by 603 Squadron at Acklington. Thereafter other units followed fast; on 2nd 263 Squadron was formed at Filton with ex-605 Squadron Gladiators, while on the 4th 219 Squadron formed at Catterick with Blenheim IFs, and next day the similarly-equipped 229 Squadron came into being at Digby. 10th saw three more new units born — 92 Squadron at Tangmere, raised with a nucleus of pilots from 601 Squadron, 141 Squadron at Turnhouse, and 145 Squadron at Croydon; 92 and 145 had Blenheim IFs as initial equipment, while 141 had Gladiators. Ten days later 253 Squadron was formed at Manston with Magisters, while at the end of the month a veritable plethora of new units appeared, the equipment issued demonstrating a growing shortage of fighters of any type with which to equip them. On 30 October 234 and 245 Squadrons at Leconfield, 242 Squadron at Church Fenton, 264 and 266 Squadrons at Sutton Bridge, and 235, 248 and 254 Squadrons were all formed, 236 Squadron joining them next day.

Of these units 234, 245 and 236 all received Blenheims IFs. 242 and 235 received some of these aircraft, but also some Fairey Battles, while 266 received only the latter type. 248 also received some Blenheim IFs, together with a number of Blenheim IVFs, while 254 Squadron was formed entirely with the later model. 235, 236, 248 and 254 Squadrons were all to be Coastal fighter squadrons, and at an early date were to be transferred to Coastal Command. The real novelty however was 264 Squadron, which received the first production examples of the new Boulton-Paul Defiant two-seat turret fighter.

Thus in one month the RAF had grown by 18 squadrons — indeed no further new fighter units were to be formed before the Summer of 1940. However it would be some time before any of the units could be of practical use; for the time being they represented no more than an investment in the future. Of more immediate import was the conversion during the month by 616 Squadron from Gauntlets to Spitfires. One further fighter squadron with a number in the series being employed was also at least earmarked at this time, although the exact date of its formation remains a matter of some conjecture. 247 Squadron would appear to have begun its existence at Acklington by November 1939, but was not to come together as a full unit until well into 1940. Two Gladiator Flights were certainly formed during late 1939 which subsequently merged to become 247. One of these was known initially as the Orkneys Fighter Flight, based at Sumburgh.

It was not only Fighter and Coastal Commands which received all the benefits of expansion at this time, for at the start of October a new Lysander unit began forming in Army Co-operation Command — 225 Squadron — while 614 Squadron started exchanging its old Hectors for Lysanders.

For the Luftwaffe too, October was to bring a number of changes — both operationally and organisationally. As September had drawn to a close the strategic reconnaissance units — FAGs — had been permitted a new freedom to reconnoitre the whole of the North Sea area, this presaging Hitler's Directive No 5, issued on the last day of the month, which allowed the Luftwaffe to attack British and French warships and merchant ships in the North Sea. This soon led to an escalation of activity by the units of Fliegerdivision 10. On 18 October Directive No 7 was to extend this permission to attacks on warships in military harbours.

In North Germany during the first two days of October several new units were established. Stab/JG 77 was set up at Neumünster under Oberst Manteuffel, while Stab/JG 27 was similarly formed at Münster/Handorf under Oberst Max Ibel, taking control of I/JG 1 at Vörden and I(J)/LG 2 at Plantlünne. On 3rd I/JG 27 began forming at Münster/Handorf. Meanwhile JG 77 was renamed 'Jagdgeschwader Nord' in Luftflotte 2, controlling II/JG 77 at Neumünster and JGr 101 at Ütersen. The new 4/TrGr 186 was formed at this time under Hpt Restemeyer, all three Staffeln of Hpt Seeliger's II(J)/TrGr 186 now equipping with Bf 109Es. Stab/JG 3 was formed on 4 October, while on 8th I(Schwere Jagd)/LG 1 was retitled V(Z)/LG 1.

Like the RAF's Fighter Command, the Luftwaffe was still seeking to expand its operational strength, and on 11 October Luftflotte 4 ordered the formation of three new fighter Gruppen, III/JG 2 at Wien-Schwechat, III/JG 52 at Tulin and III/JG 3 at Zwölfaxing. Four days later I/ZG 1 transferred from Luftflotte 1 in the east, moving to Neuhausen ob Eck under Luftflotte 3 direct command.

Amongst the bomber and reconnaissance force there were also some changes. On 1 October a long-range reconnaissance unit, the Fernaufklärungsstaffel/ ObdL was formed at Bremen under Maj Petersen, equipped with Focke-Wulf Fw 200C four-engined aircraft, developed from the Condor airliner; the unit came under the direct control of Stab FAG/ObdL. Luftflotte 4 issued an order on 9 October for the formation of four new bomber Gruppen as follows:

> II/KG 51 to form at Breslau on 1 December 1939
> III/KG 54 to form at Pilsen on 1 January 1940
> III/KG 55 to form at Crakow on 1 December 1939
> III/KG 76 to form at Wels on 1 January 1940

Next day FAG/ObdL was reformed as follows:

Stab FAG/ObdL	formed from old Stab
1(F)/ObdL	unchanged
2(F)/ObdL	ex- (2(F)/121
3(F)/ObdL	ex- 8(F)/LG 2
4(F)/ObdL	new unit

Later in the month on 16th, KG 1 was transferred to IV FlgKps in Luftflotte 2, the Stab and II Gruppe moving to Fassberg, while I/KG 1 went to Lüneberg and Stab and I/KG 4 to Giessen. Next day III/LG 1 moved to Jever, leaving I FlgKps and becoming part of X Fliegerkorps (which had been expanded out of the old Fliegerdivision 10). At the same time within this latter formation, 2 and 3/KG 26 moved to Westerland/Sylt from the mainland. These moves strengthened the power of the anti-shipping forces considerably, while the fighter re-organisation improved the effectiveness of the air defences of the Kriegsmarine bases, and of the bombers' own base areas. Several Küstenflieger units also made minor base changes at this time.

On a command level Fliegerdivision zbV became VIII Fliegerkorps on 3 October (a new Stab/StG 2 being formed within this FlgKps on 11th). Next day the Luftwaffe-Lehrdivision was disbanded, the Stab becoming the Gen zbV b Luftflotte 1. On the 11th Fliegerdivision 3 became the Gen zbV in Luftflotte 4.

___

1/10/39

Operationally the month appeared to get off to a better start for the Allies when on 1st an unexpected success came to the reconnaissance units of the Armée de l'Air. Returning from a photo-reconnaissance over the German lines on this date, the pilot of a Potez 637 of GR I/52, Adj Chef Fevrier, was advised by his air gunner, Caporal Chef Dumas, that he had spotted an He 111. Fevrier at once attacked this aircraft with his front guns, then flew alongside to allow Dumas to rake their opponent with fire from his flexible gun. Their audacious attack appeared to have achieved immediate success, the big bomber being reported to have burst into flames and crashed near Karlsruhe; no Luftwaffe loss appears to have been recorded for this date however and no confirmation that such an aircraft was shot down has proved possible.

The Allies were not to go unscathed however; just before 1000 on this same day a Blenheim (N6231) of 139 Squadron had taken off from its base at Wyton in England, flown by Flg Off A.C. MacLachlan to undertake a reconnaissance over North-West Germany. It was intercepted over Paderborn by Oblt Walter Adolph of I/JG 1, and shot down in flames; two members of the crew survived to become prisoners. A few minutes after MacLachlan had taken off, he was followed by another of the unit's Blenheims, this one flown by Flg Off A. McPherson. The latter was also intercepted, and was attacked by three Bf 109s, but was able to escape after his aircraft had been hit twice. A Bomber Command 'Nickel' operation that night led to the loss of a 10 Squadron Whitley (K9018) from Dishforth which failed to return; Flt Lt J.W. Allsop's crew were last heard from over the North Sea during their flight home.

The early days of October saw the arrival of further Air Component squadrons in France. The Lysanders of 2 Squadron arrived at Abbeville, whilst

___

those of 26 Squadron settled at the nearby satellite field at Drucat. 59 Squadron with Blenheim IVs moved from Andover to Poix to undertake longer-range reconnaissances, and here it was joined on 12th by the similarly-equipped 53 Squadron, which moved over from Plivot. The Lysanders of 2, 4 and 13 Squadrons were to undertake some short-range tactical photographic sorties over the front during the month, but when no German offensive had begun by the end of October, they ceased these activities and concentrated on training. 4 Squadron moved to Monchy-Lagache early in the month, while later the more recently-arrived 2 Squadron transferred to join 26 Squadron at Drucat. These were to be the last moves for some considerable time for the Lysander units, which settled in to prepare for the winter.

Lysander II RM-B, L4773, of 26 Squadron shortly after arrival in France. This aircraft would be lost in action on 19 May 1940. *(via A.J. Brookes/A. Thomas)*

4/10/39

After the active start to the month, the Western Front was relatively quiet as French troops withdrew from the frontier territory which they had occupied with such a fanfare of publicity during the previous month, when the Poles had still been resisting. The sole further engagement at this time occurred on 4 October when Curtiss H-75As from GC II/4 on an afternoon patrol south-west of Pirmasens, encountered a Henschel Hs 126 army co-operation aircraft of 4(H)/22. Adj Chef Cruchant attacked this, but reported that it appeared to be exceptionally well-flown, and its great manoeuvreability prevented him from being able to claim a confirmed victory. He was awarded a probable, but damage had in fact been negligible, though Oblt Heinz Pape and Uffz Willy Bodien both sustained slight wounds. Meanwhile on 3rd Potez 637 No 39 of GR I/52 had been shot down over Strasbourg by German Flak; the crew were unhurt. Two days later a new Potez 63.11 of the 14eme GAR also fell victim to Flak in the Nancy area, but on this occasion came down in French territory with the crew safe. On this same date Lt Klaus Hilbradt of I/JG 53 collided with another of the unit's aircraft flown by Lt Richardt. Both pilots were killed in the crash which followed.

The rudder of LeO 451 No 6, one of the first such bombers to enter service with GB I/31. It was shot down on 6 October by Lt Hans Berthel of I/JG 52, crashing near Euskirchen.

6/10/39

On Friday 6th one of GB I/31's few LeO 451 bombers (No 6) was despatched on a lone strategic reconnaissance deep into Germany, the crew being accompanied by a Lt Col observer, demonstrating the importance attached to this sortie. The bomber suffered icing problems in the carburettors, and at around 1350 was intercepted by a pair of Bf 109Es from I/JG 52, which made two attacks; it was also hit by fire from Flakabteilung 84's guns, and with all members of the crew wounded, Cne Paul Aouach attempted to nurse his damaged aircraft to the safety of the Belgian frontier. The damage inflicted had been too severe however, and it crashed a few miles short, near Euskirchen, the crew becoming prisoners. The victory was subsequently credited to Lt Hans Berthel of I/JG 52, the latter subsequently visiting his victims in hospital. Immediately thereafter GB I/31 was withdrawn to complete full conversion to the LeO 451 from its remaining MB 210s.

During the course of this day a second success was claimed by the Luftwaffe when JGr 152 shot down Potez 637 No 27 of GR II/33 west of Bad Godesberg. It seems that Lt Horst Elstermann was the successful pilot on this occasion. One of the Bf 109s which had force-landed in France during late September had by now been made airworthy, but was crashed on this date while under test by the Armée de l'Air.

Meanwhile October was seeing more persistent appearances by the Luftwaffe over the British Isles, although it was to be some days before Fighter Command could come to grips with the intruders.

5/10/39

On 5th an He 111P from 2(F)/122 reconnoitred the Moray Firth, but was driven off by three Spitfires from 72 Squadron. On this occasion the fighters did not get close enough to open fire, and no claims could be submitted. In the south 4 October had been a day of high winds, providing some of the fighter squadrons with unexpected opportunities to practice their aerial gunnery when a large number of barrage balloons broke their cables in the London area. The Hurricanes of 111 Squadron enjoyed the main job of disposing of these, shooting down 11 before the day was over.

8/10/39

Two Do 18 flyingboats of 2/KüFlGr 406 were engaged in inconclusive encounters with Hudsons of Coastal Command in the Egersund area on 4th, but four days later there was a more decisive engagement between these opposing patrol aircraft. That morning (8th) three Hudsons from 224 Squadron, 'U' N7217 (Flt Lt A.L. Walmersley), 'M' N7215 (Flg Off F.E. Burton) and 'Q' N7264 (Sgt Cargill) were on a North Sea patrol when they encountered Do 18 M7+ UK of 2/KüFlGr 506 in the area of the Skagerrak. They attacked at once and the Dornier was forced down on the sea, where Lt zur See Hornkuhl and his crew were later rescued from the wreck of their aircraft by the Danish ship *Teddy*. This was the first victory of the war for British-based aircraft of the RAF. That same morning Hpt Winterer of 4/JGr 101 reported intercepting a Hudson north-west of List in his Bf 109B at around 0600. He attacked and claimed that the starboard engine was set on fire before the aircraft disappeared into cloud over the Danish coast. No British record of such an engagement has been found.

Lt zur See Hornkuhl's Do 18 (M7+UK) of 2/KüFlGr 506, forced down by Hudsons of 224 Squadron on 8 October. This was the first victory of the war for British-based RAF aircraft. *(IWM)*

9/10/39

With the increased striking power of X FlgKps now available, the Luftwaffe was anxious to have further opportunities to attack the British Home Fleet. Consequently the battlecruiser *Gneisenau*, cruiser *Köln*, and nine destroyers put to sea in an attempt to lure the British out of harbour. In the early hours of 9 October three 3/KüFlGr 406 Do 18s spotted three British cruisers and two destroyers in the Egersund area, and X FlgKps was at once alerted. 127 He 111s from Stab, I and II/KG 26, II and III/LG 1 were sent out, together with 21 Ju 88s of I/KG 30, while KG 1 was called to readiness as first reserve.

Despite the numbers employed, only four Ju 88s and a few Heinkels were able to find the ships in conditions of extremely bad visibility, and bombing was ineffective. I/KG 30 claimed ten hits on the cruisers, but these could not be confirmed. Despite lack of opposition, it was to prove an expensive mission. One of I/KG 30's Ju 88s, a 3 Staffel aircraft flown by Oblt Konrad Kahl, was hit by AA fire from the ships and crashed into the sea near Kamp, two of the crew being killed; the other two had baled out and survived. Two He 111s of II/KG 26 force-landed in Denmark due to fuel shortage, while one from II/LG 1 crashed near Ludwigslust with the loss of Lt Waldemar Lutz and his crew: a I/KG 26 machine also crashed, but in this crash the crew were unhurt. Amongst the Küstenflieger, Do 18 S4+FK of 2/KüFlGr 406 force-landed off the Norwegian coast and the crew of Oblt zur See Franz Töpper were interned after they had destroyed their aircraft, while S4+JK from the same unit force-landed some distance from Heligoland. He 59 P5+HL of 3/KüFlGr 706 crashed into the sea near Sylt, Oblt zur See Joachim Sander and crew perishing.

10/10/39

Following this unimpressive performance, another lull descended over the North Sea Triangle, coinciding with a resurgence of incidents over the Franco-German border. Here on 10 October six Moranes from GC I/3 escorted a lone Mureaux over Sarreguemines, but the latter returned early due to engine trouble. Cne Pape then saw a single Hs 126 over Ersching, and led his Moranes down to attack. It proved extremely manoeuvrable, making violent evasive turns. Despite this, Pape got in a shot which he observed had severed the support strut to one of the high-mounted wings. The Henschel disappeared over Walsheim and convinced that the aircraft could not fly with this strut missing, the French H.Q. credited Pape with a confirmed victory! No German loss was actually recorded.

Towards evening a lone Amiot 143 of GB II/38 took off on a leaflet-dropping sortie to Mannheim. When flying at considerable altitude the aircraft was intercepted by a Bf 109E of II/JG 53, but escaped undamaged.

11-15/10/39

Next day, Wednesday 11th, the German fighters were more successful. A single Mureaux 115 of GAO 553 had been ordered to reconnoitre the Rhine bridges at Lauterborg and Strasbourg under the cover of eight H-75As. Unfortunately for the reconnaissance crew, no fighters appeared at the rendezvous, and they bravely but inadvisedly proceeded alone. The little monoplane was intercepted near Lauterborg at about 1700 by Lt Eckhardt Priebe of I/JG 77, who shot it down. One member of the crew, Lt Hautiere, was killed, while Asp Laluée was wounded and became a prisoner.

An Hs 126 of 1(H)/23 was attacked west of Zweibrücken by French fighters, but escaped after the observer, Oblt Fritz Möller, had been slightly wounded. A reconnaissance Do 17P from 1(F)/123 crashed during a sortie near Kerzenheim next day, Lt de Res Albert Kohler and his crew being killed.

A special reconnaissance effort was now required by the RAF, and to aid in this three Blenheim IVs from 114 Squadron flew from Wyton to Villeneuve on 12th. Next morning a Blenheim I, L1138 of 57 Squadron, left Amy at 1140 flown by Wg Cdr H.M.A. Day, to reconnoitre the Hamm-Hanover-Soest region. Day headed out over the Saar, radioing that the sky was clear of cloud, and that Flg Off C. Norman who was to follow him an hour later should take a route to the south to avoid fighters. Meanwhile at 1235 two of the 114 Squadron aircraft took off on similar duty, followed a few minutes later by Norman in L1147. The latter headed well to the south, going in over the Black Forest to Munich, and from there northwards to Bremen, finally coming out over the North Sea.

Day's warning had been well-advised, for at around 1400 his Blenheim was intercepted near Birkenfeld by a pair of Bf 109Es from II/JG 53, and shot down in flames by Ofw Ernst Vollmer. As the bomber started going down, one wing buckled and the crew all baled out, but both the observer and gunner had the misfortune to open their parachutes too soon, the silk being consumed by the flames from the aircraft and both fell to their deaths. Day survived to become a prisoner.

Forty-five minutes later the 114 Squadron pair were also in trouble, being intercepted by a Schwarm from I/JG 52 over the Idar-Oberstein area where N6160 (Plt Off K.G.S. Thompson) was shot down by Oblt Kurt Kirchner. Flt Lt Harrison in N6232 managed to escape the attentions of the fighters and the Flak, returning safely. Norman meanwhile, in the 57 Squadron Blenheim I, completed his long sortie, but crash-landed at Harpenden, Hertfordshire, out of fuel.

During the day a Potez 63 was also claimed shot down in the Idar-Oberstein area by Festungsflakabteilung 32, but this was probably a double claim against the 114 Squadron Blenheim — certainly no French aircraft was lost on this date. Next day Po 637s were definitely over the area, two of these suffering

This Amiot 143 of GB I/34 was brought down by Flak near Mayence (Mainz) during the night of 14/15 October; the crew all became prisoners.

interception, but on this occasion escaping without loss. Aircraft No 32 from GR I/52, flown by Adj Chef Fevrier, and No 55 from GR II/55, were each attacked over Karlsruhe by three Bf 109s, but got away; the crews identified their attackers as 'He 112s' on this occasion.

By night the Allies continued to rain leaflets on the heads of the unsuspecting populace below, but these activities remained occasionally expensive as the efficient Flak defences took their toll. On 14 October four of 77 Squadron's Whitleys were detached to Villeneuve in France, to shorten the distance on such sorties, but during the night of 15/16th while on a mission to Frankfurt, K8947 (Flg Off R. Williams) was shot down, the pilot being killed and the other four members of the crew taken prisoner. That same night an Amiot 143 of GB I/34 was similarly lost to Flak south of Mayence, all five members of the crew surviving as prisoners in this case.

During 15th GR II/22 had undertaken its first sortie with one of the new Potez 63.11 aircraft, with the commander of the 3rd Escadrille, Cne Quenet aboard. As the aircraft flew up the Moselle valley, it was struck by Flak as it passed over Serrig, and it crashed, the crew becoming prisoners.

16/10/39

The strategic reconnaissance aircraft — both British and French this time — had a bad day on 16 October. Flg Off Casey took off at 1100 in Blenheim I L1141 of 57 Squadron for a sortie over the Wesel-Bocholt railway, but was intercepted over the Lingen/Ems area by Lt Hans-Volkurt Rosenboom of I/JG 1. The Blenheim was shot down in flames near Furstenau, north-west of Osnabruck, although this time the crew baled out safely to become prisoners.

Po 637 No 42 of GR II/52 was intercepted over Kaiserlautern by five Bf 109Es of 8/JG 53, the German pilots reporting the attack but not observing any crash. The Potez went down in flames with Cne Belèze and Lt Pinzon du Sel dead; Sgt Chef Vergé survived with severe injuries to become a prisoner. A second Po 637 (No 17), this time from GR I/33, was shot down by 20mm Flak near Darmstadt when on a sortie to Mayence. This also fell in flames, and again only one man — the observer, Lt Laemmel — survived, although he too was badly hurt. A second GR II/22 Po 63.11 was hit by Flak over the front, the pilot getting

Cne Quenet (centre) and his crew pose for their German captors with their new Potez 63-11 (No 53) with which GR II/22 had just been re-equipped. The aircraft had been hit by Flak over the Moselle valley.

it back to French territory before crashing at Chatel-Chehery, where it was a complete write-off; the crew were unhurt. Finally a Mureaux 115 of GAO 1/520 was attacked and damaged — but by French fighters! Lt Ducase was wounded.

It was at this stage that the "shooting war" at last came to Fighter Command squadrons in the United Kingdom. The war was by now six weeks old, and so far no RAF fighter pilot had yet fired his guns in anger! In 13 Group's area there had been some redeployment in the most threatened Northern zone. On 7 October 602 Squadron had moved to Grangemouth, and then on 13th to Drem, while on 9th 607 Squadron had moved its Gladiators to Acklington on the north-east coast, where it joined the Spitfires of 609 Squadron and the very new 152 Squadron, which had just begun forming.

Over the next three days Coastal Command was again to suffer a considerable number of operational losses, not caused by hostile action. In this period two Sunderlands of 204 Squadron, two Ansons and a Hudson were all destroyed, the crew of one of the Sunderlands all losing their lives.

Following the issue of Directive No 7, the Germans were now seeking to attack the Home Fleet at its bases, following the lack of success on the high seas, but it was not the Luftwaffe which struck the first blow here. During the night of 13/14 October submarine *U-47* crept submerged into Scapa Flow, her captain, Kaptlt Günther Prien, sending a well-aimed salvo of torpedoes into the battleship *Royal Oak* before escaping unscathed. The big vessel went down at once, taking with her over 800 sailors to their deaths.

16/10/39

Two days later, early on Monday, 16 October, an He 111 of Stab/KG 26 flew a reconnaissance over the Firth of Forth, where a battlecruiser presumed to be HMS *Hood*, was seen entering the Firth. A trio of Spitfires from 602 Squadron were scrambled from Drem, Sqn Ldr A.D. Farqhar (K9962), Flt Lt A.V.R. 'Sandy' Johnston (L1004) and Flg Off Ferguson (K9969) chasing the intruder in cloud, but losing it after opening fire and appearing to have inflicted some damage. They then landed to refuel at the Coastal Command airfield at Leuchars.

In Germany on receipt of the report by the Heinkel crew, I/KG 30 was ordered to attack with 15 Ju 88s under the leadership of the Gruppenkommandeur, Hpt Pohle. Pohle was ordered to attack *Hood* only if the vessel was not already in dock, since no casualties to civilians must be caused. The bombers set out at 1100 (Central European Time), arriving over the Firth some three hours later. The British radar station in the area had suffered a prime failure, and not until the bombers were actually seen overhead were fighters scrambled to intercept. By this time reinforcements were to hand, 16 Gladiators of 607 Squadron having flown up to Drem from Acklington via Usworth, during the morning.

Pohle saw at once that *Hood* was in fact already in dock, but that several cruisers and destroyers were in the Firth, and it was these latter which were attacked. As Pohle went into a dive, the cabin roof was blown off, but he was able to plant a heavy SC 500 bomb onto the cruiser *Southampton*. The bomb went through three decks without exploding, out through the side of the ship, and sank a launch moored alongside. At that stage he was attacked by three

Spitfires, and the port engine was hit at once. Pohle turned out to sea, but a second attack wounded two members of the crew; a third attack wounded the observer and put the starboard engine out of action. Pohle managed to put the stricken bomber down in the Firth near Crail, but only he survived, being rescued by a trawler and taken to hospital. After Pohle had attacked, Lt Horst von Riesen bombed the destroyer *Mohawk*, upon which eight men were killed and 17 wounded. 20 minutes later this Ju 88 was also pursued by a Spitfire and one engine was put out of action. Von Riesen managed to keep the aircraft in the air, just above the sea, and successfully completed the long flight back to Westerland, where the aircraft crashed, suffering 45% damage.

From Turnhouse three more Spitfires from 602 Squadron had been scrambled, while those refuelling at Leuchars were got into the air after the incoming bombers had roared directly over the airfield. Flt Lt G. Pinkerton saw one bomber heading east, and led his section in a line-astern attack on it, he and his No 2 attacking as it came out of cloud. The bomber slowed down, turned to port and dived towards the sea. Flg Off P.A. Webb, who reported seeing two bombers — which like Pinkerton, he identified as He 111s — also attacked until his ammunition was expended, seeing the starboard engine smoking badly, and the speed falling away. Pinkerton then attacked for a second time, and the bomber crashed into the sea.

The other section from this squadron also saw a single bomber as they returned from Leuchars, Sqn Ldr Farquhar claiming hits on this, believing that they had crippled it. They then saw another Spitfire finish it off, and may well have attacked the same aircraft as Pinkerton, or alternatively one subsequently shot down by 603 Squadron. There seems little doubt however, that Pinkerton had been responsible for bringing down Pohle's Ju 88.

Meanwhile numerous 603 Squadron Spitfires were in the air; Red Section (Flt Lt A. Gifford; Plt Off C. Robertson; Flg Off H.K. Macdonald) were off at 1430, followed at 1435 by Yellow Section (Flt Lt G.L. Denholm; Plt Off J.S. Morton; Plt Off G.K. Gilroy). Ten minutes later six more Spitfires followed, and then single aircraft at 1540 and 1600. Denholm's section engaged three bombers over Dalkeith, but these broke formation and fled into clouds, one of the rear gunners managing to put one bullet into Plt Off Gilroy's Spitfire, L1048. Gifford's section attacked a bomber, identified by them as 'possibly an He 111', to the east of Dalkeith, and this was believed to have been one of the aircraft previously attacked by Yellow Section. This aircraft went into the sea off Port Seton, where three of the four crewmen were picked up and made prisoner.

Spitfire of 603 Squadron at Lossiemouth. *(R.D. Gosling via A. Thomas)*

This seems certainly to have been the second Ju 88 lost by I/KG 30, a 1 Staffel aircraft flown by Oblt Siegfried Storp. The gunner was lost, but the other three members of the crew survived as prisoners.

The six aircraft taking off at 1445 saw nothing, apart from Flg Off J.C. Boulter who had become detached; he attacked a bomber which he saw going east from Aberdour without apparent result. The two aircraft which took off more than an hour later intercepted an He 111 over Rosyth at low level and chased it out to sea, breaking off as it headed away with the starboard engine stopped and the rear gunner no longer firing. The Gladiators also flew a number of patrols during the afternoon, but saw nothing. Next morning they flew back to their base at Acklington.

17/10/39

The attacks on the bases at Rosyth and Scapa Flow by the Luftwaffe and Kriegsmarine had by now convinced the Admiralty that these were too danger-ous for continued occupation for the time being, and that night the Home Fleet steamed for the west coast. Thus when four Ju 88s led by the new Kommandeur of I/KG 30, Hpt Fritz Doench, and 13 He 111s of I/KG 26 arrived over Scapa Flow next morning, it was to find the birds flown, and they were able only to attack a blockship. One Ju 88 was shot down by the anti-aircraft defences, crashing on Hoy Island where it burnt out. One member of Oblt Walter Fläming's crew survived. At Lübeck-Blankensee an He 111 of I/KG 26 had crashed as it took off for the raid, three members of the crew being killed. During the raid an intrepid Fleet Air Arm pilot made a single-handed inter-ception of the Heinkels in a Sea Gladiator. Struck by a murderous cross-fire, the little biplane was shot down at once.

607 Squadron's Gladiators had only just got back to Acklington when a section from 'B' Flight was scrambled at 1240 to seek German seaplanes that had been reported off the coast. Flt Lt John Sample, Flg Off G.D. Craig and Plt Off W.H.R. Whitley headed out to sea, where at 1330 they intercepted a Do 18 flyingboat some 25 miles from the coast. This was 8L+DK from 2/KüFlGr 606, flown by Oblt z See Siegfried Saloga, which they attacked individually from astern. The Dornier was not shot down at once, struggling eastwards for about 35 miles before crashing into the sea. The crew were rescued by a British trawler and made prisoner.

Meanwhile a section of Spitfires from 41 Squadron at Catterick (Flg Off H.P. Blatchford; F/Sgt Shipman; Sgt Harris) whilst on a North Sea patrol intercepted an He 111H-1 of 2(F)/122 — F6+PK (WNr 2728) which they shot down, the aircraft crashing into the sea 20 miles off Whitby. The crew tried to get into their dinghy, but only two made it, the pilot, Lt Joachim Kretschmer, and one other being drowned. Another Heinkel from the (F)Staffel/ObdL returned from a reconnaissance to Liverpool with engine damage.

21/10/39

Luftwaffe aircraft next appeared on 21 October, three Ju 88s from I/KG 30 which had taken off at 1235, attacking a convoy sighted off the Yorkshire coast near Flamborough Head, by a reconnaissance aircraft. They were driven off by anti-aircraft fire and no damage was inflicted on the ships. Following the attack a force of nine He 115 floatplanes from 1/KüFlGr 406 was sent out after the same target.

An He 115, this one 8L+AH of 1/KüFlGr 906, is typical of those from 1/KüFlGr 406 which were intercepted by Hurricanes and Spitfires on 21 October. *(ECPA)*

This area had recently been reinforced by Fighter Command, 72 Squadron having moved from Church Fenton to Leconfield, situated to the north of Hull, on 14th, while the Hurricanes of 46 Squadron had moved from Digby to the forward satellite airfield at North Coates on the Lincolnshire coast, on temporary detachment. Both units were ordered to patrol on this afternoon, and at 1415 'A' Flight of 72 Squadron took off followed at 1430 by two more Spitfires flown by Flg Offs D.F.B. Sheen and T.A.F. Elsdon, to patrol over the convoy which was ten miles offshore from Spurn Head. At the same time six Hurricanes of 'A' Flight, 46 Squadron, took off with similar instructions.

72 Squadron's 'A' Flight saw nothing, but soon after Sheen and Elsdon — Blue Section — had settled down to their patrol they saw approaching a loose formation which they identified as comprising 14 He 115s; then turned towards these. As soon as the Küstenflieger saw the Spitfires, they turned away north, but were speedily overhauled, the two fighter pilots expending all their ammunition on the last three Heinkels, two of which were claimed probably destroyed as the formation broke up.

The 46 Squadron Hurricanes were by now over Spurn Head at 5,000 feet when at 1455 they were urgently ordered to intercept 12 floatplanes reported to be approaching from the south-west at 1,000 feet, some five miles distant. The six fighters, flown by Sqn Ldr P.R. Barwell, Plt Off P.J. Frost, F/Sgt E. Shackley (Red Section) and Plt Off R.M.J. Cowles, Plt Off R.P. Plummer, Plt Off P.W. Lefevre (Yellow Section) at once turned in an easterly direction at full speed, losing height. They arrived in the reported area 25 miles east of Spurn Head at 1502, where Barwell sighted the German formation. At this point the two 72 Squadron Spitfire pilots noted the approach of the six Hurricanes, broke off the action and flew home. As the Hurricanes closed in the Heinkels turned away east in an effort to escape, but were caught with ease. The flight gained height, positioned themselves up-sun, and in line-astern came down on eight or nine floatplanes in ragged formation, some 30 miles east of Withernsea.

Barwell attacked one at high speed, coming up abreast of another as he fired. He just had time to see the starboard engine burst into flames as he dived under its tail, about 30 yards from it. Looking back, he saw it attempt to land on the water, but crash as its starboard wing folded back and began to break off. The other members of his section, Frost and Shackley, attacked the Heinkel which Barwell had come up alongside, and saw this crash with its port engine on fire; this was credited to Frost.

At this stage the German formation broke up completely as each pilot sought his own salvation. Barwell noticed one floatplane diving away southwards, and giving chase, fired all the rest of his ammunition at it from 300 yards. F/Sgt Shackley, joined by Plt Offs Cowles and Plummer from the second section, then took up the attack, but from rather long range. Barwell ordered them to close up and then repeat their attack, which they did; Plummer opened fire, upon which the aircraft crashed into the water and turned over on its back. Meanwhile Frost and Plt Off Lefevre, the third pilot of the second section, had engaged in a rather lengthy chase after another Heinkel. After several attacks in and out of cloud, the aircraft suddenly went down and landed on the water with both engines stopped.

Following the successful conclusion of their various combats, the Hurricane pilots headed back for Digby to refuel, landing at 1535. Little return fire had been noticed from the floatplanes, which had clearly taken a severe beating. Next morning an Intelligence report was received that not more than five Heinkels had returned to base, and credits were therefore given for seven destroyed — five by 46 Squadron and two by 72 Squadron. This was an over-estimate, occasioned by the belief that the initial formation had been at least 12 strong, whereas only nine aircraft had been involved. Five had indeed been all that had returned to base, but only four had actually been lost:

S4+DH   Oblt z See Peinemann (three crew killed)
S4+EH   Oblt z See Schlicht   (Schlicht and one other P.O.W.; one killed)
S4+GH   Oblt z See Reimann   (three crew P.O.W.)
S4+YH   Oblt z See Lenz   (Lenz and one other were interned; one killed)

It seems probable that all were shot down by the Hurricanes, though two were undoubtedly severely damaged by the Spitfires first.

22/10/39

The very next day a further engagement took place. At 1435 Red Section of 603 Squadron was scrambled to intercept a raider reported over a convoy off St Abb's Head. Flt Lt Gifford, Plt Off Robertson and Plt Off Morton soon saw a lone He 111 four miles offshore and gave chase as it headed out to sea; this was a reconnaissance aircraft of 1(F)/122 commanded by Oblt Gustav-Adolf Awater. They caught it, and after an exchange of fire it turned back towards the coast, apparently to try and force-land, but came down in the sea seven miles out. Three members of the crew were seen to get into a dinghy (the fourth had been killed), whereupon the Spitfires guided the destroyer *Gurkha* to pick them up. Return fire had been accurate, Morton's Spitfire (L1049) getting a bullet in the sump, while Robertson's L1050 had one through one of the flaps.

26–27/10/39

On 26 October a reconnaissance Do 17P of 4(F)/122 suffered an engine failure whilst on a sortie to the English East coast. Uffz Wendt, the pilot, force-landed at Gröningen in Holland, where he and his crew were interned. In May 1940 they would be handed over to British troops and would spend the rest of the war in prison camps in Canada. The following day 46 Squadron was again engaged, but in much less satisfactory circumstances. On this occasion patrolling Hurricanes shot down a Coastal Command Anson, N5204 of 608 Squadron, which was on a convoy patrol. The aircraft crashed into the sea near the Humber lightship, one of the crew being picked up by HMS *Stork*; Flt Lt G.W. Garnett was dead however, and of the pilot, Plt Off A.D. Baird, no trace was found.

28/10/39

While the RAF fighter squadrons in France had so far achieved no victories — indeed, seen no action − those in the north of Britain were enjoying mounting success, although so far every raider shot down had fallen into the sea. This situation changed on 28 October, when Red Section of 603 Squadron was again sent off, this time at 0915, together with a section of two Spitfires from 602 Squadron, which followed at 1020. The fighters climbed to 14,000 feet over the Firth of Forth, spotting anti-aircraft shell bursts below. 602 Squadron's section, led by Flt Lt A.A. McKellar (soon to become one of the RAF's most successful fighter pilots) attacked first, followed by the 603 Squadron trio (Flt Lt Gifford, Plt Off Robertson and Plt Off Gilroy). The bomber, an He 111 from Stab/KG 26, 1H+JA flown by Lt Rolf Niehoff, was badly hit and after circling around a bus at low level, made a good crash-landing in open country near Kidlaw, six miles south of Haddington, under the gaze of the excited passengers. The aircraft was found to be absolutely riddled with bullets, which had killed two of the crew and wounded the pilot; only the observer remained unhurt in the landing which had caused remarkably little additional damage to the aircraft.

At 1045 602 Squadron's Yellow Section was also scrambled to investigate an unidentified aircraft three miles east of May Island. Flt Lt Hodge spotted the intruder and put his section into line-astern, going into the attack. He had already opened fire when he realised that it was an Anson, and at once broke away. The unfortunate recipient of the assault was an aircraft of 612 Squadron (N5274), which was written-off in the subsequent force-landing; one member of the crew was wounded.

It may have been noticed that, despite the growing number of successes, the British fighters frequently seemed to be making heavy weather of bringing down relatively easy opponents. Due to generally poor levels of aerial gunnery in Fighter Command, the guns of the Command's aircraft had been set to provide a fairly wide pattern of fire on a target at an average range of 400 yards. With .303in guns this was really too long a range for effective damage to be inflicted, and hence the need on several occasions for repeated attacks by several aircraft. The theory was that the 'shotgun effect' allowed mediocre shots a good chance of getting some hits at least. After fighter-versus-fighter combat experience in France, the squadrons there began synchronising their guns all to converge at one spot 250 yards in front of the fighter. This allowed a great weight of fire to strike one small area and resulted in much more immediate and dramatic damage being inflicted — but only when the pilot was a good enough shot to bring his sights to bear on the target. By early summer 1940 this 'spot harmonisation' had become standard in Fighter Command, but throughout most of the 'Phoney War' period it was to be the exception rather than the rule.

Elsewhere the second half of October had been generally fairly quiet — mainly due to adverse weather conditions. Leaflet raids continued, but more losses were suffered. During the night of 25/26th Whitley N1358 (Plt Off P.E.W. Walker) of 77 Squadron failed to return from a sortie over Wilhelmshaven, Bremen and Hamburg. Contact was lost after a radio 'fix' had been given when the aircraft was 70 miles from home on the return flight, and it was presumed down in the sea. Three nights later another Whitley (K8984), this time from 51 Squadron, suffered an engine failure while on a 'Nickel' sortie, the crew baling out over England; K9008, another of this unit's aircraft, force-landed in France at Triercourt where it was written off.

The RAF in France had been undertaking some re-organization in the light of recent experience. The casualties suffered by the Battles during September made it obvious that the AASF bombers would require fighter escort when serious operations began, whilst in the meantime air defence of their bases would not come amiss. Consequently on 10 October 1 and 73 Squadrons were transferred from the Air Component to this force, leaving 60(F) Wing on 15th. 1 Squadron physically moved to Vassincourt better to perform its new duties. Plans were afoot to bring the Component's fighter element back to strength, and 61(F) Wing began forming to control two Gladiator squadrons, 607 and 615, which it was intended would be despatched from England at an early date.

The Blenheim reconnaissance squadrons were suffering some problems during October due to waterlogging of their airfields, 18 and 57 Squadrons moving to Meharicourt and Rosieres respectively during the month. 70 Wing, under the control of which they came, was temporarily reinforced, by the Blenheim IVs of 53 Squadron, which moved to Poix on loan from 50 Wing.

A Whitley V of Bomber Command departs for a leaflet raid over Germany. *(IWM)*

20–21/10/39

Weather continued consistently to restrict operations over the Western Front throughout the latter part of October, and little occurred to enliven events, save on 20th when an over-zealous patrouille of Curtiss H-75As from GC II/5 attacked a Hurricane of 73 Squadron — fortunately without inflicting any damage. Next day a German light Flak unit claimed a Mureaux shot down, and this is believed to have been an aircraft of GAO 2/514 which was brought down over Mechern, the crew being wounded.

23–24/10/39

One of the German reconnaissance aircraft, an Hs 126B-1 of 1(H)/23, on a sortie south-west of Zweibrücken on 23rd, was hit by French DCA, Uffz Erich Diebel being wounded. Next day another such aircraft from 4(H)/22 was also hit, and this one crashed at Hoppstädten due to the damage suffered, the observer, Ofw Kurt Lachs, being killed.

30/10/39

A sudden improvement in the weather on 30th brought a resurgence of activity which ended the month with a flurry. At 1000 on this Sunday morning two 57 Squadron Blenheim Is set out to photograph Westwall installations between Essen and the Belgian/Dutch frontiers. L1246 (Sgt Farmer) was intercepted by a pair of Bf 109s, which attacked from behind and below, hitting the Blenheim twice. Farmer managed to shake them off in a dive to 200 feet, and brought the aircraft back to Orly, where one undercarriage leg collapsed on landing.

Further reconnaissance had noted a heavy concentration of aircraft on North German airfields, and a convoy of some 20-30 vessels, each estimated to be of over 2,000 tons displacement, forming up in the area of the German river estuaries. In consequence six Blenheim IVs from 139 Squadron were despatched from England by 2 Group at 1026, to reconnoitre the area. As soon as these crossed the coast they were beset by Flak and fighters. Flg Off Pepper's aircraft was hit by both, and he returned with the gunner wounded, as did Sgt Price whose Blenheim was damaged by Flak; a third Blenheim, flown by Flg Off McPherson, also suffered Flak damage. 'E' N6234 (Plt Off W.G. McCracken) was caught west of Heligoland by Bf 109Es of II/JG 77 and was shot down into the sea by Fw Erwin Sawallisch.

In the early afternoon another three Blenheim Is were sent off, this time by 18 Squadron from its forward airfield at Metz. Two headed for West Germany while Flt Lt A.A. Dilnot in L6694 retraced 57 Squadron's route over the Westwall south of Dreiländereck. It seems that he flew too far north and passed over the Moselle valley, where his aircraft was intercepted and became the first victory for the new III/JG 53, which had just become operational under its new Kommandeur, Hpt Werner Mölders, who had been posted in from I/JG 53. Mölders noted in his diary:

"I took off with the Gruppenschwarm and three Schwarme of 9 Staffel to patrol against enemy reconnaissance aircraft in the Bitburg-Merzig area. At 1112 (?1412) I noticed Flak activity near Trier. I approached to within 50 metres of the enemy aircraft without being seen, and saw the British roundel very clearly. I opened fire and closed to the shortest possible range without any return fire from the rear gunner, and the left engine gave out a thick white cloud of smoke. It changed very quickly to black. When I pulled up beside it, the

Hpt Werner Mölders, German top-scorer in Spain, quickly became the most successful Luftwaffe pilot on the Western Front also. *(via J. Foreman)*

aircraft burned completely. I observed a parachute, but it seemed to kindle. The Blenheim crashed on Oberemmler Burg, near Klüsserath, on the Mosel River. All the crew were killed."

One of the other aircraft, Flg Off D.F. Elliott's L1415 had made for the Hamm-Hanover region, falling foul of a pair of Bf 109Es from I/JG 21 near Quackenbrück, where it was shot down by Lt Heinz Lange (later a Ritter-kreuzträger with 70 victories).

The Armée de l'Air lost a Potez 63-11, this one an aircraft of GR II/52, which crash-landed in French territory after being hit by Flak; the crew were unhurt. At last on this date the British fighters in France were engaged operationally. At 1430 three Hurricanes from 1 Squadron were ordered off to intercept three aircraft at high altitude. Climbing hard, they finally caught one of these, a Do 17P of 2(F)/123, at 18,000 feet. This was engaged by Plt Off P.W.O. 'Boy' Mould in L1842, the Dornier crashing ten miles west of Toul where Hpt Balduin von Normann and his crew were all killed.

During the day French fighters were also active, Cne Reyne of GC I/5 in an H-75A shooting down an Hs 126B of 1(H)/13 over Rehlingen while Cne Destaillac of this unit was credited with a Bf 109 probably destroyed over the same area. Another Hs 126 of 4(H)/23 was brought down over Bergzabern by three Moranes of GC III/2 flown by Adj Moret, S/Lt Bardin and Lt Lechat. Both Henschels had been engaged in spotting for artillery, and both crash-landed in German territory with the crews unhurt.

31/10/39

Next day — the last of the month — ten Hurricanes of 73 Squadron patrolled over the area between Bouzonville and Saarguemines. Flak gunners opened fire on them near Saarbrücken and managed to hit Sgt H.G. Phillips' aircraft; with his engine badly damaged he had no alternative but to bale out at once.

French anti-aircraft gunners (DCA) were also in action, shooting down an

First RAF victory in France was gained over a reconnaissance Do 17P of 2(F)/123 by Plt Off P.W.O. 'Boy' Mould of 1 Squadron on 30 October. *(IWM)*

Hs 126B of 4(H)/22, which crashed in the frontier area with the observer dead. This aircraft may also have been attacked by S/Lt Plubeau of GC II/4, who also submitted a claim for an Hs 126 on this date over Offenburg. Whilst on a reconnaissance over Trier a Potez 637 (No 5) of GR II/33 was attacked by two Bf 109s, and one member of the crew, Sgt Chef Moreau was badly wounded when a bullet perforated his lung. Adj Guerin landed with all haste at the nearest airfield at Nancy in order that the wounded man might be removed to hospital as quickly as possible.

Like 1 Squadron, 73 had moved base following the transfer to the AASF, and now was at Rouvres. From here it had undertaken its first scrambles only to find that the Hurricanes were frequently attacked by French Moranes and Curtisses which mistook them for Bf 109s. This problem was partially solved by the expedient of painting red, white and blue stripes on the rudders of the aircraft, similar to those carried on French aircraft, but in reverse order.

Reorganisation of the Luftwaffe units involved in operations over the North Sea continued during the latter part of the month, starting with the issue on 21st of an ObdL/Führungsstab Order, 5334/39, which placed X Fliegerkorps under direct ObdL command. At midnight on 25th there occurred a complete reorganisation and renumbering of the Seeflieger units, as follows:

New Designation	Unit Code/Aircraft	Old Designation
Stab/KüFlGr 106	M2+	Stab/KüFlGr 106
1/KüFlGr 106	He 115	1/KüFlGr 106
2/KüFlGr 106	Do 18	2/KüFlGr 106
3/KüFlGr 106	He 59	3/KüFlGr 106
Stab/KüFlGr 406	K6+	Stab/KüFlGr 306
1/KüFlGr 406	Do 18	2/KüFlGr 506
2/KüFlGr 406	Do 18	2/KüFlGr 406
3/KüFlGr 406	Do 18	2/KüFlGr 306

New Designation	Unit Code/Aircraft	Old Designation
2/KüFlGr 906	Do 18	2/KüFlGr 606
Stab/KüFlGr 506	S4+	Stab/KüFlGr 406
1/KüFlGr 506	He 115	1/KüFlGr 406
2/KüFlGr 506	He 115	New unit
3/KüFlGr 506	He 115	3/KüFlGr 406
3/KüFlGr 906	He 59	3/KüFlGr 706
Stab/KüFlGr 806	M7+	Stab/KüFlGr 506
1/KüFlGr 806	He 111J	1/KüFlGr 506
3/KüFlGr 806	He 111J	1/KüFlGr 306
Stab/KüFlGr 906	8L+	Stab/KüFlGr 706
1/KüFlGr 906	He 59	1/KüFlGr 706

On the same day VIII Fliegerkorps came under the direct control of Luftflotte 2, and transferred its Stab HQ to Schloss Dyck/Grevenbroich. At the end of the month JG 77 took control of the following units:

Stab/JG 77	Odendorf
II/JG 77	Dünstekoven
JGr 152	Odendorf
JGr 101	Ütersen

RAF Coastal Command was also modernising during October, both 220 and 233 Squadrons beginning to exchange their Ansons for Hudsons, and both were to commence operations with their new aircraft before the end of the month. The initial aid from the Dominions was also received by this command. Aircrews of the RAAF's 10 Squadron had arrived in England to collect Sunderland flying-boats, which has been ordered by the Australian government. This latter body decided during October to offer the unit for service in the United Kingdom, despatching the rest of the squadron's personnel to bring it up to full strength.

Chapter 4

AUTUMNAL ACTIVITIES

November was to see further expansion and unit movement within the Luftwaffe, commencing on the first day of the month with the formal establishment of III/JG 53, II/JG 51 and KüFlGr 606. This latter unit was to have an establishment of three Staffeln, all to be equipped with Dornier Do 17Z bombers. The following dispositions took place during the month:

2nd: the following units were transferred to the control of JG 2:

> I/JG 2   at Frankfurt-Rebstock
> I/JG 77 at Frankfurt-Rebstock
> I/JG 76 at Frankfurt-Main

10th: Lehrgeschwader 1, with I and II/LG 1, joined I Fliegerkorps.
12th: Stab/JG 1 was formed at Jever under Oberstlt Carl Schumacher, with:

> II(J)/TrGr 186 at Nordholz
> JGr 101 at Ütersen
> 10(N)/JG 26 at Jever

15th: II/JG 51 moved to Eutingen.
18th: in VIII Fliegerkorps, Stab/StG 1 was set up from Stab/LG 2. On the same date a special unit which had been testing radio navigational aids, Luftnachrichten-Abteilung 100 became a part of a new KGr 100 for special bomber operations. Although equipped with Do 17s, it was scheduled for early re-equipment with He 111s.
25th: Stab/JG 51 was formed.

While October had proved to be a relatively quiet month over the Western Front and a busy one over the North Sea, November was to be the opposite. With the Home Fleet gone from Scapa Flow there was, for the time being, little to occasion further ventures by X Fliegerkorps in this area. In France the position was considerably different, as the return to the west of many of the units from Poland allowed a considerable increase in Luftwaffe reconnaissance flights, coupled with some more aggressive fighter patrolling.

2/11/39
The month began with the first victory for one of the RAF squadrons of the Air Component. The Hurricanes of 87 Squadron were now frequently involved

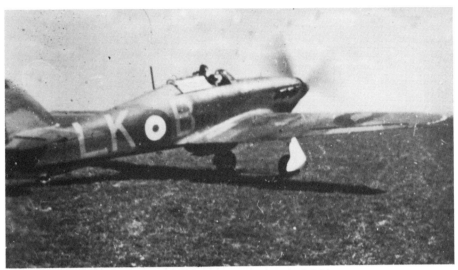

Hurricane of 87 Squadron, Air Component, RAF, on a French airfield.

in interception scrambles after the elusive recce planes, for which purpose the unit had moved to Lille-Seclin; however the pilots found that more often than not they could not even sight their prey. 2 November proved to be an exception however; at 1030 five Hurricanes were ordered off, led by Flt Lt R. Voase-Jeff in L1614. Several sightings were made, and Voase-Jeff gave chase to an He 111 H-2 (WNr 5650) of 2(F)/122 from Münster. He kept after it for 20 minutes, finally sending it crashing down at Stables, near Hazebrook. One member of Oblt Wilhelm Ohmsen's crew had been killed and another wounded, but the other two were unhurt, and were taken prisoner.

Other Hurricanes were scrambled at 1145, Plt Offs W. D. David and Mackworth intercepting another He 111 from the same unit. This one put up a fierce fight, shooting down Mackworth's Hurricane, which was hit in the fuel and oil lines and force-landed at Seclin; David's aircraft was also slightly damaged. Although the British pilots believed that it had force-landed in Belgium, in fact the aircraft returned to Münster-Handorf suffering 30% damage.

The wreckage of F6+EK, the He 111H of 2(F)/122 shot down by Flt Lt Robert Voase-Jeff of 87 Squadron on 2 November, is stripped down for removal.

Flt Lt Voase-Jeff becomes the first member of the RAF to be awarded a French Croix de Guerre for his action on 2 November. He is presented with this medal by Gènèral Vuillemin of the Armée de l'Air.

5/11/39

On the afternoon of Saturday, 5 November, GR II/33 sent Potez 637 No 3 on a reconnaissance over the Trier area. Adj Bernard, the pilot, was flying at about 21,000 feet when the aircraft was intercepted by a Schwarm of I/JG 53 Bf 109Es. Desperately he hauled the Potez around and attempted to flee, but the Messerschmitt pilots, led by Oblt Hans-Karl Mayer in 'Weisse 1', closed in at once in the face of sustained defensive fire from the gunner, Adj Robert. Mayer attacked first without obvious result, Lt Carnier then taking his place. Following his attack a fine stream of vapour was seen emerging from the aircraft and when Mayer attacked again a bright flame appeared between the fuselage and one engine. Moments later the undercarriage dropped into the 'down' position and the Potez fell towards the ground in flames. The pilot and observer were already dead, but Robert managed to bale out before the aircraft crashed near Saarburg at 1515. He had been badly wounded, and finally succumbed on 23 May 1941 following a long hospitalization.

6/11/39

Next day, Sunday 6th, was to see the biggest engagement of the air war over France so far. First however, at 1030 three Blenheims from 57 Squadron and three more from 18 Squadron were despatched on reconnaissances over Germany. In the Frankfurt area L1145 (Plt Off A.D. Morton) of 57 Squadron was intercepted by Lt Max Stotz of I/JG 76, and was shot down in flames; all the crew were killed. Over the Metz area a little later a Mureaux 117, No 107 of GAO 2/506, was surprised by patrolling Bf 109Es of III/JG 53 south-west of

Hpt Hannes Gentzen (right), Luftwaffe top-scorer of the Polish Campaign, claimed his first victory over the Western Front on 6 November, but lost eight aircraft and four pilots from his JGr 102 to Curtiss H-75As of GC II/5. *(ECPA)*

Merzig where it was very badly damaged by Lt Jakob Stoll's fire; Adj Chef Rupert and Lt Gossart managed to get the aircraft back over French territory before baling out near Plappeville. That afternoon another Mureaux, this time No 66 of GAO I/506, was intercepted, again by pilots of 8/JG 53; Uffz Eduard Koslowski attacked and the observer, Lt Schmidt, was killed, while the wounded pilot, Adj Chef Gillat, got it back over Vigny before baling out.

During the early afternoon the sky began to fill with aircraft. From Lachen/ Speyerdorff a large formation of 27 Bf 109Ds from JGr 102 (I/ZG 2) took off for a patrol over the front, led by no less a pilot than Hpt Hannes Gentzen, the Luftwaffe's top-scorer during the Polish Campaign in September. This formation encountered nine Curtiss H-75As of GC II/5 which were escorting a Potez 63 of GR II/22 on a mission to photograph the Sarre. The French fighters had taken off at 1400, led by Lt Houze, and had crossed the lines at about 16,000 feet. North of Metz they spotted 20 Messerschmitts at the same level and seven more 2,000 feet higher. The sun was in the German's favour, so the French pilots made a climbing turn to port to gain height, but at that moment the Germans attacked, and the engagement quickly broke up into a series of individual combats.

Sgt. Salès chased one Messerschmitt to low level before shooting it down, the pilot baling out at about 500 feet near Hunnenberg. Salès then saw another Curtiss in trouble with two Bf 109s, and shot one of the latter down into a wood on the edge of the Sarre near Eincheville. Sgt. Legrand shot down one which

Lt. Pierre Houzé crash-landed his Curtiss H-75A at Toul on return, damaged by Hpt Gentzen's fire. This was the sole French casualty in his highly-successful engagement.

exploded on the bank of the Moselle river near Antilly, and at this same moment another was brought down by Asp Lefol near Anzeling. Sgt Chef de Montgolfier and Sgt Bouhy hit two more, which they reported went down and crash-landed at Ittersdorf, but these were not confirmed. Sgt Chef Tremolet chased another, firing from short range, and it dived inverted, streaming smoke and fuel. Three more were last seen heading for the ground after Adj Dugoujon, Asp Lefol and Sgt Legrand had fired at them. Lt Houzé meanwhile, after several inconclusive fights, found himself hard-pressed by six Bf 109s. His main assailant was Hpt Gentzen himself, and after several bursts of fire had hit the H-75A, Houzé was able to disengage and crash-land on Toul airfield with his engine dead and oil pressure at zero.

The Curtisses had conclusively demonstrated their superiority to the D model of the Bf 109 however, and initial claims were submitted for five confirmed and five probables (Sgt Salès and Sgt Legrand each two confirmed, Asp Lefol one and one probable, Sgt Chef Tremolet, Sgt Chef de Montgolfier, Adj Dugoujon and Sgt Bouhy one probable each. Final credits were set at four confirmed and four probables, one of Legrand's claims being downgraded, and two of the other probables disallowed. This final assessment was if anything on the conservative side. Four Messerschmitts had fallen in the French lines including those flown by two Staffelkapitäne; Oblt Josef Kellner-Steinmetz crashed near Hunnenberg and Oblt Waldemar von Roon north-east of Metz, the former being killed and the latter subsequently dying of his wounds. Lt Günther Voigt baled out south-west of Saarlouis and Fw Fritz Giehl 20 miles north-east of Metz, both becoming prisoners. Four more badly damaged aircraft had force-landed in German territory, one of the pilots — Uffz Hans Hennings — being wounded. Hennings's Bf 109D was a total write-off (70%), and was probably the aircraft attacked by Tremolet. The only success had been Gentzen's victory over Houze. That evening Gentzen was ordered to Berlin to report on the reasons for this, the greatest defeat suffered by the Luftwaffe fighter force in the war so far. Subsequently a few days later the Gruppe was transferred to Bonn/Hangelar airfield and placed under the operational control of JG 77.

Meanwhile Plt Off P.V. Ayerst of 73 Squadron had been scrambled after an

Sgt René Tremolet leaves his H-75A-1 No 57 after the combat of 6 November.

intruding reconnaissance aircraft. He had just spotted and given chase to an He 111, when he was himself set upon and chased by nine Bf 109s — possibly part of the JGr 102 formation — and these put ten bullets through the tailplane of his Hurricane before he was able to escape and land at Nancy. During the evening an He 111 of Stab/KG 51 and one 9 Staffel aircraft undertook the first Luftwaffe leaflet raid over France.

7/11/39
The spell of good weather which had allowed this increased activity continued next day, when the Luftwaffe soon began taking its revenge for the debacle of the 6th. Soon after midday six Blenheim Is drawn equally from 18 and 57 Squadrons once again set out over Germany, but again one failed to return. Over the mouth of the Wupper river 57 Squadron's L1325 (Plt Off H.R. Bewley) was intercepted by Lt Joachim Müncheberg of III/JG 26, the Blenheim crashing into the Rhine at 1343. On this occasion the crew were able to bale out, all surviving as prisoners of war.

The successful French pilots head in to report; left to right, Sgt Edouard Salès, Asp Georges Lefol, Sous Lt Angiolini, Adj Georges Gras and Lt Pierre Houzé.

Potez 637 No 26 of GR I/33, attached temporarily to the 14 ᵉᵐᵉ GAR, was shot down on 7 November by Bf 109Es of III/JG 53.

Two hours later three Potez 637s of GR I/33, attached to the 14ᵉᵐᵉ GAR, set off on a mission over the Sarre valley once more, under the cover of six escorting Morane 406s of GC I/2. A Schwarm of Bf 109Es from 7/JG 53 were flying a frontier patrol led by Hpt Wolf-Dietrich Wilcke, and at 1545 were able to 'bounce' the French formation. While one Rotte held off the Moranes, Wilcke and his Rottenflieger, Fw Franz Gawlick, went after the reconnaissance aircraft, shooting down one each. Potez No 18 crashed at Mercilly with all the crew dead (Adj Trevis, Cne Hocqueviller, Sgt Waryn) while No 26 came down at Louvigny with Sgt Chef Strub dead, the other two members of the crew both being slightly wounded. The third Potez managed to escape unscathed.

A third Potez, this one a Po 63-11 (No 31) from GR II/22 (Adj Chef Lemoine, pilot; Cne Cadoux, observer; Adj Chef Marie, gunner) was attacked over Volklingen by six more Bf 109s of III/JG 53. Badly damaged, the aircraft managed to get back to its own airfield at Metz-Frescaty, where it crashed; Cadoux had been killed by a bullet in the head, but the other members of the crew were safe. Lt Jakob Stoll was credited with shooting down this aircraft. During the day Sgt Salès of GC II/5 intercepted a Do 17P of 3(F)/22 south of Bleskastel and shot it down, the aircraft crashing between St Ingbert and Hassel, Ofw Hans Wagnere and his crew all being killed. That night a Bloch MB 200 heavy bomber of GB I/31 (No 162) undertook a reconnaissance to Koblenz, but was illuminated by searchlights of 2/Res Scheinwerferabt 299. Apparently blinded by the light, Lt Bertaux crashed near Brühl with the loss of the whole crew.

2–4/11/39

While the blood-letting over France was underway, operations over the North Sea had been on a limited scale. On 2nd a Saro London flyingboat crew from 201 Squadron had spotted the merchant vessel *City of Flint*, the prize of the German battlecruiser *Deutschland*, in Norwegian territorial waters on its way to Germany. Two days later another London, this one from 204 Squadron (K9686,

Flt Lt J.H.M. Sinclair) failed to return from a North Sea patrol. Searches by four other Londons and two Sunderlands found nothing; 204 Squadron had just arrived at Sullom Voe from Mount Batten.

7/11/39

During the morning of 7 November several air actions took place, beginning with an unsuccessful bombing attack on a British warship by He 115s of 1/KüFlGr 106. Three Hudsons from 220 Squadron were on patrol north of Texel, and two of these, 'H' (Flt Lt Sheahan) and 'A' (Sgt Scotney) engaged He 115 M2+HH returning from the raid. There was an exchange of fire and the Heinkel disappeared into cloud. A few minutes later Flg Off Parker in 'G' also encountered one — possibly the same aircraft. Again shots were exchanged and the Hudson was hit eight times, while the floatplane suffered damage to one of its floats.

Late that afternoon two He 111s of Stab/KG 26 undertook reconnaissances along the English east coast, but as one landed in the dark at Westerland on conclusion of its sortie, it came into collision with a Bf 109D of JGr 101, both aircraft being written off.

That evening Anson K6190 of 206 Squadron (Plt Off Henderson) sighted a Do 18 of 1/KüFlGr 406 near Grimsby. A short, inconclusive fight followed, before the flyingboat disappeared in cloud. Next day however (8th) the British squadron enjoyed more success. Two more Ansons from the unit's Bircham Newton flight were off on patrol when Plt Off Greenhill in K6195 encountered He 115 M2+FH of 1/KüFlGr 106 at 1100 near the island of Texel. He attacked with his fixed front gun, experiencing fire from the German rear gunner as he did so; his shooting was excellent and the big floatplane crashed into the sea, Lt zur See Bruno Boettger and his crew being killed.

Forty minutes later Plt Off R.H. Harper in K6190 spotted a Do 18, 8L+BK of 2/KüFlGr 906. The flyingboat was flying so low and so slowly that he thought it was actually on the water, and he began by bombing the aircraft, inflicting slight damage. He then attacked with the front gun, achieving a few hits, but at that point a second Do 18 came to the aid of the first. After another exchange of fire Harper was forced to break off the engagement as he had exhausted his ammunition.

10/11/39

Two days later on Thursday, 10th, the Command was again able to achieve a success when Flt Lt Sheahan and Sgt Scotney of 220 Squadron were once more patrolling in their Hudsons, this time with Sheahan flying 'A' and Scotney in 'H'. Off the Yorkshire coast near Scarborough they encountered Do 18 K6+DL of 3/KüFlGr 406, and both attacked, finally forcing the 'boat to come down on the water, where it capsized. Oblt z See Wilhelm Lütjens, the pilot, lost his life but the rest of the crew were rescued by Dutch ships. Meanwhile Scotney had turned the controls of his Hudson over to the second pilot, Sgt Calver. No sooner was Calver fully in control than another 3/406 Do 18 appeared. It was attacked and hit, retreating into cloud.

8/11/39

To return to the Western Front, engagements here were also continuing. At

0945 on 8th Hurricanes of 73 Squadron were sent off after an approaching reconnaissance aircraft. From the ground watchers saw a Do 17P at 17,000 feet being pursued by a single Hurricane which was gradually gaining. The Dornier moved into the sun, obscuring their view of it, but the fighter was seen to be hit by a burst of French anti-aircraft fire which was trailing the German aircraft, and it fell away smoking. Then down came the Dornier, an aircraft of 1(F)/123 flown by Oblt Hans Kutter, and crashed near Lubey, north-west of Metz, all the crew being killed. Flg Off Kain had hit it before his own aircraft was struck, and had thereby gained his first victory. The pilot of a second Hurricane (L1959), Plt Off R.F. 'Dickie' Martin, had fainted at 21,000 feet — possibly from oxygen starvation — and had been obliged to force-land at Esch airfield in Luxembourg, where he was interned.

During the day ten H-75As of GC II/4 were in the air to escort a Potez when at 1415 a lone Do 17P from 1(F)/22 flown by Oblt Hans Blankemeier and escorted by two Bf 109s was seen at 25,000 feet. S/Lt Plubeau reached the German aircraft first whereupon the Messerschmitts, showing a curious lack of fighting spirit, turned away. Plubeau was able to cause severe damage to the Dornier, following which the crew — one of whom had been wounded — baled out. The aircraft then blew up, the wreckage falling to the north-east of Bitsche. Meanwhile Sgt de La Chapelle engaged the fleeing escort fighters without success. Of the Dornier's crew, the wounded man landed in German territory, one of the others came down on the French side of the lines and became a prisoner, and the third was killed.

Five Moranes of GC III/2 were on patrol over the Woerth-Hagenau area when Cne Kerangueven spotted several Bf 109s to the north-west. A brief engagement ensued and Sgt Barbey crashed in German territory, badly wounded. The rest of the formation returned to report that he had been shot down by three Messerschmitts and had baled out, but no Luftwaffe claims were submitted.

10/11/39

Two days later on 10 November Plt Off Dunn of 87 Squadron chased a Luftwaffe reconnaissance aircraft, but followed it too far and ran out of fuel; he was obliged to force-land in Belgium where he too was interned. He had in fact inflicted severe damage on his quarrie, a Do 17P of 4(F)/121. During its return flight to Stuttgart it crashed on the Stuttgart-Ulm autobahn near Echterdingen, Oblt Horst Martinköwitz and his crew all being killed. Dunn was later to be joined in Belgium by Flg Off Glyde and Sqn Ldr Coope, also from 87 Squadron, both of whom were forced to come down in this neutral country's territory on 14th in L1628 and L1813. All three pilots managed to escape on 27th, getting across the frontier to return to their unit.

During the night of 10/11th five Whitleys from 77 Squadron in England flew a 'Nickel' raid over Southern Germany. One returned early, but a second, N1364 (Sqn Ldr J.A.B. Begg) crashed at Bouxelles, south of Nancy, the crew being killed. Worsening weather now brought a lull in activity which lasted for several days. Indeed already on 11th the climatic conditions had taken a heavier toll than the fighting. At 1110 that morning three Blenheims of 114 Squadron departed from Wyton on a photo-reconnaissance sortie over Heligoland. They flew into severe storm conditions, from which only one aircraft re-appeared. Of N6145 (Plt Off B.A. Martyn) and N6150 (Flt Lt R.E. Mills) there was no news, and it was assumed that they had collided in heavy cloud and turbulence.

Newly-arrived Gloster Gladiator of 615 Squadron in France. *(via A. Thomas)*

The RAF in France was now becoming more organised, and was reinforced on 15th when 16 Gladiators of 615 Squadron, together with a similar number from 607 Squadron, arrived at Merville from Croydon to join the Air Component. Ground personnel were carried in a miscellaneous collection of transports comprising four Ensigns, four DH 86s, two Scyllas, a Magister, an Avro 10 and a Fokker airliner. Soon after settling in, the Gladiators joined the Hurricanes of 85 and 87 Squadrons on patrols.

Further wings were now being formed; in the Component, 52 (Nucleus) Wing was formed under Sqn Ldr A.H. Hutton DFC, who was posted in from 53 Squadron. Subsequently 53 and 59 Squadrons were released from 50 and 51 Wings to join this new unit, which was attached directly to BEF Headquarters. Following this move however, neither unit was to fly any further operational sorties throughout the winter, undertaking instead a programme of training. Indeed with the exception of 18 and 57 Squadrons and the fighter units, no Air Component units were currently undertaking operations of any sort — a situation which was to last for some months. The position was barely more active within the AASF, where 1 and 73 Squadrons now came under 67 (F) Wing, which had its headquarters at Neuville under Wg Cdr C. Walter.

Other moves and changes were also afoot, in England as well as France. From the start of the war it had been clear that the RAF was deficient in photographic reconnaissance provision, and the early vulnerability of the Blenheims and Battles in this role merely highlighted the situation. Even before the war a certain amount of clandestine PR work had been undertaken on behalf of the Air Ministry by a civilian, one Sidney Cotton, flying a Lockheed transport aircraft. With the outbreak of war, Cotton was incorporated into the RAF to form a special and very highly secret reconnaissance flight at Heston, equipped with Hudsons and Lockheed 12As. At the start of November this unit received a designation intended to mislead — 2 Camouflage Unit. This was not entirely inappropriate, for some of Cotton's Hudsons did in fact carry the most bizarre experimental camouflage schemes. Subsequently the flight was provided with a few — a very few — specially modified Spitfires, fitted with cameras but with all guns removed to allow extra fuel to be carried, and these were soon flying extremely valuable long-range, high altitude reconnaissances over Germany, relying on height and speed for protection against interception.

On 5 November an offshoot of the Heston unit, the Special Survey Flight, flew to France, arriving at Seclin with one Hudson and one Lockheed 12A. A few days later N3071, a Spitfire PR 1A, painted pale green overall, also reached Seclin from where on 18th the first sortie was flown by Flg Off Maurice 'Shorty' Longbottom, Aachen being the target. Bad weather caused the pilot to abort the mission and return early.

Another new arrival at this time was a communications detachment from 24 Squadron with two DH Rapides which set up at Le Bourget, while on 6 December the Air Component Communication Squadron would be numbered 81 Squadron, now with a strength of 18 Avro Tutors, two Blenheims and two Lysanders. In England, shortage of anti-submarine patrol aircraft led to the formation at Hooten Park of 3 Coastal Patrol Flight, this unit beginning operations with nine Tiger Moths under the control of 206 Squadron at the end of November. At Hendon, the nucleus of 62 (F) Wing began gathering; it was intended that this unit should go out to the Air Component in France in due course, and two more Hurricane squadrons — 46 and 501 — were earmarked for it. In the event 46 Squadron was to be diverted to a somewhat different location, as will be related later. Finally the AASF moved 74 Wing headquarters from Challerange to Tours-sur-Marne, 103 Squadron moving from the former airfield to Plivot.

In the Orkneys continued Luftwaffe reconnaissance had resulted in the formation of a new Fleet Air Arm fighter squadron. At Hatston a number of Sea Gladiators were held in reserve while at Donibristle in Scotland was the training squadron, No 769, with a number of these aircraft. At the end of November four Sea Gladiators were despatched to Hatston, led by Capt R.J. Partridge, one of the Navy's rare Royal Marine pilots, to form the nucleus of a unit. Next day this officially became 804 Squadron under Lt Cdr J.L. Cockburn, while at Wick six more Sea Gladiators were taken from storage and put into service, flying over to Hatston to bring the squadron up to strength.

The French too were making a number of changes at this time, and radically

The first Spitfire in France; the overall pale green PR IA, N3071, detached to Seclin by the Special Survey Flight, prepares to take off for its first sortie on 18 November, Flg Off 'Shorty' Longhorn at the controls. Note the 24 Squadron DH Rapide in the background.

altering their tactical command system, the escadres giving way to the new system of Zones d'Operations Aèriènne insofar as the fighter and reconnaissance units were concerned. On 21 November a Zone d'Operations Aèriènne Nord (ZOAN) and a ZOAE (Est) were established on the Longwy-Belfort axis, for air defence purposes. Attached to these for operational purposes were Groupements de Chasse 22, 23 and 24, the two Hurricane squadrons of the AASF, and the Potez 631 multi-engined fighters of Escadrille 5/2 from GC II/2.

The programme of re-equipment was also at last beginning to gain a little momentum. Supplies of Bloch MB 151 and 152 fighters had been available for some weeks, but delays in modifications to equipment, fitting of gunsights, etc. had slowed introduction to service. The first few MB 152s had been issued to GC I/1 at Buc during October, and by early November, 26 of these were on hand. GC II/1 similarly re-equipped during November, its D 510s going to the Aeronavale at Orly to form a new fighter escadrille, AC 3.

The earlier and less-effective MB 151s were issued to the Escadrilles Regional de Chasse to replace their elderly equipment, and to be followed by MB 152s when available. 1 and 2/561 at Rouen-Boos now became Groupe Aèrièn Regional de Chasse I/561 with the new aircraft, although in January 1940 this unit became GC II/10. 1/562 at Lyon-Bron was expanded temporarily into a Groupe by the subsequent inclusion of Potez 631-equipped ECN 5/13 (which had itself been formed from 2/562 in September), but in January this escadrille became GC III/9. Finally 3 and 4/561 became GARC II/561 at Havre-Octeville, exchanging their 21 Spad S 510s and 12 Ni D 622s for MB 151s early in December; this unit was renamed GC III/10 in January.

At Marignane GC I/8 exchanged D 510s for MB 152s towards the end of the year, while GC II/8, which had converted briefly to Potez 631s for naval co-operation duties, re-converted to the Bloch fighter at this time also. The Potez then went to replace the elderly Dewoitines in Aeronavale escadrilles AC 1 and 2.

Several groupes de chasse had included a few Po 631s on strength at the start of the war for aerial control purposes, but these had now been gathered into a single unit, forming a fifth escadrille in GC II/2 (noted above). During November three Po 631s were detached to each of GC III/2 and I/4 for practice in co-operation with the single-seaters, but were back within ten days. In January 1940 the unit was removed from GC II/2, and became an autonomous entity in Groupement de Chasse 23 as Escadrille de Chasse Multiplace de Jour 1/16. More good news for the fighters was forthcoming in December, when early in that month GC I/3 moved to Cannes to exchange its Moranes for the first Dewoitine 520s.

Amongst the other units, re-equipment of the reconnaissance escadrilles was going ahead fast, although the bomber re-equipment programe only got under-way during early December. In October the Bloch MB 131 units had each received half a dozen Potez 63-11s, 14eme GAR (later known as GR I/14) being the first to receive these followed by GR I/22, II/22, II/55, I/36, II/36 (the two latter units exchanging the older obsolete Po 540s for the new aircraft), I/35 and I/55 in that order. During November similar quantities of Po 63-11s began reinforcing the Po 637-equipped units; it was planned to withdraw the latter for training, but as they proved to be both faster and more manoeuvreable than the Po 63-11, this move was resisted strongly by the crews. During the same month the first GAOs also began re-equipping with Po 63-11s, 501, 502, 505, 4/551,

552 and 546 being the first units involved. No Bloch MB 174s were yet available for any of the reconnaissance units.

Of the bomber groupes, GB I and II/12 had moved to Orleans-Bricy, where both units had commenced conversion to the LeO 451. Four more escadres were to receive these aircraft, and it was planned that all should be operational by the end of February 1940, but deliveries were falling well behind schedule. Units involved were GB I and II/11 at Mas de Rue, GB I and II/23 at Le Vallon, GB I and II/31 at Lezignan and GB I and II/32 at Orange-Plan de Dieu.

The Po 540-equipped GB I and II/54 had moved to Salon, where re-equipment with Breguet Br 691s had commenced at once, but again deliveries were slow and Po 633s, taken over from export orders, were to be issued to these units in December, and to GB I and II/51 the following month, on which to undertake assault training, until sufficient of the new aircraft were available. No Br 693s would appear before April.

GB I and II/19 and GB I and II/32 had all moved to North Africa to await deliveries to Morocco of the Douglas DB-7F. These too were slow in coming however, and none would arrive before January 1940. First deliveries of the Martin 167F were just beginning to reach North Africa around the end of November, allowing GB I and II/62 and I and II/63, which were already based there, to begin re-equipment before the end of the year. For GB I and II/21 and I and II/34 the wait was to be even longer for the Amiot 351/354 series; none of these bombers would be to hand before spring.

The Aeronavale received one somewhat unusual reinforcement at this time in the form of three ex-civil Farman 233-4 aircraft, derivatives of the Armée de l'Air's F 222 heavy bombers. One of these long-ranging aircraft, F-AQJM 'Camille Flammarion', had already been employed for reconnaissance, searching for the German warships *Graf Spee* and *Admiral Scheer* in the North Atlantic. On 22 November Escadrille B 5 was formed at Orly under Cdt Dalliere with the three available examples of this type, undertaking many such sorties. The other two aircraft were F-ARIN 'Jules Verne' and F-ARQA 'Le Verrier'.

13/11/39

Despite the bad weather which prevented activity of note over the Franco-German border, the North Sea Triangle was far from quiet. On Sunday, 13 November, 13 Ju 88s from I/KG 30 were launched on a raid against military installations in the Shetland Islands, two of the bombers attacking the flyingboat base at Sullom Voe. During this attack bombs fell on British soil for the first time in the war, but no damage was done. The Ju 88s left at speed, followed by a concentrated barrage of anti-aircraft fire from both ships and land-based gunners.

Early that same morning several aircraft from the Küstenfliegergruppen undertook reconnaissances along the east coast of England, particularly off East Anglia. At 1015 Blue Section of 'B' Flight, 56 Squadron, was scrambled, and at 1040 Flt Lt I.S. Soden, Plt Off Illingworth and Plt Off P.D. Down saw Do 18 K6+AK of 6/KüFlGr 406 to the east of Harwich, flying at 2,000 feet. Soden attacked first and got two bursts at the flyingboat before it went into cloud. It was seen again a few seconds later, and Illingworth was able to attack, following which Soden again fired from 300 yards, seeing pieces of the wing fly off. The aircraft was last seen heading away east, left wing low, at about 200 feet. The Hurricanes' fire had been reasonably accurate, the Dornier taking about 60 hits, one member of the crew being wounded.

Reconnaissance Do 17s appeared over Scapa Flow on 16th and Rosyth on 17th, but no interceptions could be made, although the latter aircraft — from 1(F)/122 — was slightly damaged by AA fire. Gunners in Lancashire, Cheshire and North Wales all failed to hit a Wekusta 26 He 111 however, when this overflew the area on weather reconnaissance.

14/11/39
Next day Saro London K5912 of 210 Squadron ditched in the North Sea during a patrol, Flg Off Middleton and his crew being rescued by the destroyer HMS *Imperial*, which then sank the flyingboat.

16–17/11/39
The toll taken by the weather remained high; on 16th a Blenheim from 57 Squadron (L1180, Sgt Gilmore) became lost on reconnaissance over Germany and force-landed in Belgium where it was interned, while on 17th a dozen He 111H-2s from I and III/KG 51 took advantage of heavy cloud to undertake a leaflet-dropping sortie over France during the morning. I Gruppe was briefed to cover the Nantes-Brest area, but in high winds two aircraft failed to return, Lt Helmut Domke and his crew of 3 Staffel crashing near Salzburg, while Oblt Klaus Pfordese of 1 Staffel came down near Murcia in Northern Italy — both blown hundreds of miles off course, and totally lost. Only one man from the latter aircraft survived. III Gruppe had drawn the Marseille-Bordeaux area as their target, but suffered similar problems. Hpt Gerhard Plischke, a pilot of an 8 Staffel aircraft, force-landed at Unterlillach, just over the Austro-Italian frontier, the pilot being killed and one other member of the crew injured. A Do 17P of 2(F)/123 also force-landed near Bolzano in Italy, but Lt Werner Vrancken and his crew survived to return to Germany unhurt. This was the first occasion on which German bombers had been lost on such operations, but only two days later another occurred. On 19th He 111P-2s from 2/KG 27 undertook a mission to the Amiens/Lille/Arras area, from which one bomber failed to return; it was believed to have crashed into the North Sea, Oblt Horst Rosenthal and his crew failing to return.

18/11/39
Meanwhile the Küstenflieger were again out on 18 November, reporting a number of unusual engagements. At about 0930 He 115 M2+FH of 1/KüFlGr 106 sighted an unidentified aircraft off Ijmuiden. This closed fast and was soon seen to be a Fokker D.XXI fighter of the Royal Netherlands Army Air Force. The German pilot at once turned sharply away from the coastline and the Dutch pilot allowed the floatplane to depart unhindered. A few minutes later the same crew saw a twin-engined aircraft off Terschelling which they took to be French. The Heinkel headed away northwards but the stranger followed, making three firing passes during which one of the aircraft's floats was hit.

At around 1015 two more He 115s from the same Staffel saw another Dutch aircraft which was identified as a Fokker G-1a, flying to the west of Den Helder. It seems likely that this was in fact the same aircraft which had just attacked the first Heinkel. The fighter turned after the two floatplanes and attacked M2+DH, but after an exchange of fire it swung away and flew towards the Dutch coast.

20/11/39

Dutch airspace was again violated on 20 November, but this time from the east. A Bf 109E of I/JG 21 got lost whilst on a frontier patrol, and strayed over the border near Roermond where the pilot, Lt Rexin, attempted to land on a road. However, he crashed into a building and was killed.

Early in the afternoon of 20th several reconnaissance Do 17s appeared over the British Isles, both over Scotland and in the area of the south-east coast. It appears that one crew of a Do 17F of 1(F)/ObdL (T5+LH) became disorientated and wandered inland, passing over Hornchurch airfield at 1217. Yellow Section of 74 Squadron was at once scrambled to give chase as the aircraft — which was identified as an He 111 — headed away east followed by AA bursts. Flg Off W.E.G. Measures, Plt Off R.G. Temple-Harris and Sgt Flinders caught the aircraft 15 miles east of Southend at an altitude of 27,000 feet at 1245, and executed a classic No 1 attack, closing from 400 to 300 yards before the bomber went into cloud. The Spitfire pilots did not claim to have shot the aircraft down — still identified as a Heinkel — but next day came a report that two survivors, both wounded, had been found at sea in their dinghy by a British warship, and the victory was credited to them. In fact the German pilot, Lt Gerhard Rickertsen, had come down in the sea about 20 miles east of Orfordness, he and both members of his crew being rescued, though two of them had been wounded. About two hours after this engagement had taken place, a trio of Hurricanes from 56 Squadron intercepted a seaplane 20 miles east of Felixstowe — almost certainly an He 115 — and attacked until this disappeared into cloud. That night the Luftwaffe launched its first offensive mining operation, three He 59s of 3/KüFlGr 906 from Norderney laying mines by parachute in the Thames Estuary and off Harwich.

21/11/39

Next day two Do 17Ps from 3(F)/122 were sent off from Goslar on another Channel reconnaissance, and one of these again fell foul of Fighter Command. Flg Off J.W.E. Davies and F/Sgt F.S. Brown of 79 Squadron were scrambled in their Hurricanes from Biggin Hill to patrol over Hawkinge. They were instructed to orbit at 1053, and then vectored onto an intruder, which they intercepted at 1055. Davies attacked first and the Dornier turned away, diving. Both pilots then made three independent attacks from above and to one side, after which the reconnaissance machine spun down into cloud leaving a white trail. It appeared again, momentarily, still spinning and in an inverted position, and was subsequently awarded to the pair as destroyed; it did indeed fail to return. No return fire had been experienced, but the pilots reported that they found the recently-issued new incendiary ammunition (De Wilde) showed up errors in their deflection shooting and made it possible to correct these.

On the other side of the Channel Flt Lt R.H.A. Lee was sent out by 85 Squadron in France on a search patrol off the French coast in the Boulogne area. Here he sighted an He 111, one of a pair from Stab/KG 4 on a reconnaissance, and this he shot down in flames at once. The bomber (WNr 1567) crashed into the sea ten miles north of Cap Griz Nez, where Oblt Gerhard Schieckel and his crew were all killed. The 21st also saw a brief and inconclusive brush between Hudson 'G' of 220 Squadron and a Do 18 from 2/KüFlGr 106; Flg Off Parker claimed hits on the Dornier before it escaped in cloud, but no damage was actually inflicted.

21 November was also the day on which the new Zones d'Operations Aèriènnes were established; it heralded a renewal of activity over the Western Front as the skies cleared and a spell of better weather commenced. Over the Saarbrücken area at 1100, 9 Staffel of III/JG 53 reported engaging in combat with Moranes and Curtisses, making no claims although two Bf 109Es suffered damage of varying seriousness. Their opponents may have been six H-75As of GC II/5, which had taken off to inaugurate a new 'patrouille a priori' (equivalent to the U.S. Navy's Combat Air Patrol). The pilots reported clashing with seven Bf 109s over Metz, these escaping by diving to the ground. Despite a furious dogfight, no claims could be made, and the only result was the belly-landing of Sgt Chef de Montgolfier's Curtiss at Nancy-Esse.

At about the same time two other patrols from GC II/5 encountered Bf 109s escorting a Do 17P of 3(F)/22 from Koblenz flown by Oblt Werner Thiel, over the Pont-à-Mousson area. Sgt Salès and Lt Tremolet shot the Dornier down near Morhange, and it crashed to the north-east of Eincheville; two members of the crew survived and were made prisoners. Two more Bf 109Es of III/JG 53 force-landed at Wiesbaden during the day, but not as a result of combat damage.

At 1505 six GC II/4 H-75As were patrolling at high level over the French lines when two Bf 109s were seen. The French pilots were able to surprise the Messerschmitts, Adj Villey shooting down one which fell at once in flames, crashing between Ludwigwinkel and Sturzelbronn, to the north-east of Bitsche. The other H-75As then attacked the wingman, Sgt Chef Casenoble getting in a good burst which hit the oil coolers and caused a stream of white smoke to pour from the aircraft. This was also reported to have fallen in flames over the Hirtenweider-Pirmasens area, no parachute being seen; this was credited to Casenoble and Sgt Saillard jointly. The Messerschmitts were from I/JG 52, the pilots of which thought they had been attacked by Moranes. The Gruppenkommandeur, Hpt Dietrich Graf von Pfeil, baled out, but was badly burned; he would not fly again.

This Do 17P of 3(F)/22 (4N+EL) was shot down by pilots of GC II/5 on 21 November. The fuselage is being moved to the Place de la Concorde in Paris, where it was put on display. *(via C-J. Ehrengardt)*

His Rottenflieger, Lt Christoph Geller, crash-landed near Hainfeld, south-west of Edenkoben, with his aircraft 60% damaged. Graf von Pfeil's place at the head of I/JG 52 would be taken by Hpt Siegfried von Eschwege.

The day also saw the debut of the Bf 110 over this front, a Staffel of these aircraft from V(Z)/LG 1 escorting a reconnaissance aircraft to the west of Reims. Patrouilles of Moranes from GC I/2 and Curtisses from GC II/5 were engaged, but no losses to either side ensued. Three Moranes from GC III/7 attempted to intercept a reconnaissance aircraft identified as a Junkers, but this escaped when the guns of the French fighters jammed due to frost at high altitude.

22/11/39

The aircraft of the Fernaufklärungsstaffeln appeared over France in force again on Tuesday, 22 November, but defending fighters were quick to react. The first contact over the Franco-Belgium border occurred when a single Morane of GC III/7 flown by S/Lt Delarue intercepted an He 111 from 3(F)/121 which the French pilot incorrectly identified as a Ju 88. Again the French fighter suffered from guns freezing; the Heinkel was on a factory test flight, and the pilot at once pulled his aircraft round and into Belgian airspace where the fighter could not follow. The aircraft later crashed at Dielkirchen, south of Bad Kreuznach, where Ofw Helmuth Gräber and Ober Prüfmeister Otto Schulz were killed; the reason for the crash is uncertain.

Four more MS 406s from GC II/7 flown by Adj Chef Valentin, Sous Lts Gauthier and Gruyelle, and Sgt Chef Lamblin, then saw a Do 17P from 4(F)/121 approaching, returning from a sortie to the Belfort-Montbeliard area. This was pursued to Moos, near Baden-Baden, where it force-landed in flames, all three members of Oblt Helmut Böttcher's crew being wounded. Far to the west Moranes from GC II/2 intercepted another reconnaissance aircraft over the Laon area, and attacked. It was however not a hostile, but a Bloch MB 131 of GR I/36 returning from a reconnaissance over Germany. The badly damaged Bloch landed at Le Fère-Courbes with two members of the crew dead.

Because of recent losses, the Luftwaffe sought to give some fighter protection,

Ofw Erwin Kley of I/JG 2 claimed a victory against the H-75As of GC II/4 on 22 November. *(ECPA)*

A senior French officer contemplates the damage caused to Adj Camille Plubeau's H-75A No 169 during an engagement between GC II/4 and Bf 109Es of I/JG on 22 November.

and the next two Dorniers were supported indirectly by Bf 109Es from 3 Staffel of I/JG 2, which made a Freiejagd (free chase) sweep over the area ahead of the reconnaissance aircraft. Over the Phalsbourg region they were able to surprise some H-75As of GC II/4, and No 95, flown by Sgt Saillard, was shot down at once, the pilot being killed, while Adj Camille Plubeau was wounded and crash-landed No 169 in French territory. These two aircraft were claimed by Lt Helmut Wick and Ofw Erwin Kley. Within a year Wick was to have become the Luftwaffe's top-scoring fighter pilot.

Six Moranes from GC I/3, six from II/6 and nine from III/7 took off to escort a single Potez 63-11 over the Warndt forest (mainly the duty of the I/3 aircraft) and five ANF Les Mureaux 115s over the St Avold-Forbach area (II/6) and the Saareguemines-Rimling area (III/7), these missions going out around midday.

At 1440 the top cover of I/3 was engaged by six Bf 109Es of I/JG 76 over the Nornberg-Bitsche area, these hitting Sgt Bellefin's aircraft hard. Adj Havet fired at one at point-blank range over Sarreguemines, but GC II/6 then joined in the combat, S/Lt Cuffaut and Sgt de Bremind d'Ars being credited with two Bf 109s shot down, shared with the six I/3 pilots (Lacombe, Havet, Vinchon, Thierry, Combette and Bellefin). Two 1 Staffel Messerschmitts force-landed, Lt Heinz Schultz coming down in a field near Puttelange in 'White 11' (WNr 1251), while Fw Karl Hier brought 'White 14' (WNr 1304) down near Goesdorf, both pilots becoming prisoners.

Meanwhile the GC III/7 aircraft had become engaged with two Schwarme of Bf 109Es from I/JG 51, and a long combat was fought. Oblt Hermann-Friedrich Joppien shot down one Morane, Sgt Guillaume carrying out a crash-landing with his aircraft in flames near Heillecourt, where the fighter burnt out. Other Moranes then attacked Joppien, whose Messerschmitt was struck by fire from Sgt Chef Jacquin's guns and he was obliged to break away. His undercarriage had been damaged and as a result the aircraft turned over on landing, though Joppien was unhurt; Jacquin claimed one Messerschmitt damaged. Meanwhile Ofw Herfried Kloimüller had become disoriented and landed his Bf 109E 'Weisse 1' (Werk Nr 1304) on the French airfield at Strasbourg-Neuhof,

'Weisse 11' of I/JG 76 is prepared for display in the Champs Elysees in Paris after being shot down on 22 November by Morane 406s.

where he was made a prisoner. The 'gift' of a brand new example of the latest German fighter was a most welcome one, and the aircraft was at once prepared for a full testing and evaluation programme.

Before the remaining GC III/7 Moranes were able to return to base, three of them were surprised by the Stabsschwarm of I/JG 53; Adj Littolf force-landed No 165 at Azelot, riddled with bullets, while Lt Lancrenon crash-landed No 182 near Houdemont. One of these fighters was claimed by Lt Claus, the other by Hpt Dr Mix, who made at least one claim during this engagement. One of GC II/6's Moranes was also hit, but by French DCA. The undercarriage was damaged but the pilot successfully force-landed at Freybouse, near Gros Tenquin. During the day another Bf 109E of 2/JG 77 was shot down over the Belgian frontier near Sedan by anti-aircraft fire, crashing at Haraucourt where Uffz Edric was killed. A second Messerschmitt from 2/JG 52 crashed in French territory due to oxygen shortage, the pilot of this (Uffz Hellwig) also being killed, while two more such aircraft from I/JG 54 crash-landed near Offenburg when they ran out of fuel, both suffering 50% damage.

German Flak caused severe damage to a further French aircraft when Po 637 No 14 of GR II/3 was hit during a reconnaissance sortie, Lt Sagan carrying out a successful crash-landing at Nevers. Finally two H-75A pilots of GC I/4 spotted a lone He 111 flying at 23,000 feet over Calais heading for the English coast. Lts Weis and Hirschauer gave chase, but as the Curtisses were only marginally faster, it was some time before they could get into firing range. Seeing the pursuers, the Heinkel pilot turned away north, but after being fired on by both fighters, the crew were seen to bale out and the aircraft came down near Gravelines. It was reported that Air Component Hurricanes had also engaged in this combat, although the identity of the pilots involved has not been discovered. The Heinkel, 5J+FA of Stab/KG 4 from Quakenbruch, force-landed at Wevelgem in Belgium after all the crew except the pilot had baled out. The latter, Lt Franz Wichartz reported that he had been attacked by both French and British fighters. The Belgians recorded that the aircraft had suffered little additional damage during the landing. It seems however, that the three

117

crewmen who had baled out all failed to survive. It had certainly been the busiest day yet for the French fighter pilots, who had flown a record 203 sorties.

23/11/39

23 November was to be a similarly busy day as Do 17s and He 111s from a variety of units were sent out in considerable numbers on widespread airfield reconnaissances. At 1000 one Do 17P from 3(F)/22 was seen over Rouvres heading for Verdun; Flg Off E.J. Kain, the young New Zealand pilot with 73 Squadron took off and shot it down, the Dornier crashing at Conflans while Fw Siegfried Dressler's crew baled out to become prisoners. Half an hour later another aircraft from 4(F)/122 (F6+HM) was seen heading towards Commercy at 20,000 feet, and three 1 Squadron Hurricanes were scrambled after this. The aircraft was spotted when anti-aircraft shells burst near it, and all three Hurricanes attacked (Flg Off J.I. Kilmartin, Flg Off C.D. Palmer, Sgt F.J. Soper), forcing the Dornier down. Two of the crew baled out, and thinking that it was finished, Flg Off Palmer flew alongside in L1925. The pilot, Uffz Arno Frankenberger was a man of spirit however, and quite prepared to carry on the fight. Throttling back, he caused the Hurricane to overshoot; he then left his controls to man the free machine gun in the nose, and opening fire, hit the engine of the fighter. This stopped running and Palmer was obliged to make a force-landing. The Do 17 was then successfully crash-landed near Moiremont, west of Verdun, and the pilot taken prisoner. The pilots of 1 Squadron were eager to meet and entertain their gallant opponent.

A little over an hour later three more of the unit's Hurricanes led by Flt Lt G.H.F. Plinston, were scrambled to 20,000 feet between Metz and Verdun. Here an He 111 from 2(F)/122 (F6+FK) was seen returning from the Lille-Arras-Valenciennes area. They cut across the aircraft's escape route, and shot it down over the Saarbrücken area. Sgt A.V. Clowes made the last attack that finally brought the bomber down, but as he broke away half a dozen French fighters arrived to join the combat. In his haste to get at the enemy, one of the

Flg Off Edgar 'Cobber' Kain of 73 Squadron examines the wreckage of the Do 17P.

Adj Chef Pierre Le Gloan of GC III/6 gained his first victory on 23 November. He would later become one of the top-scoring Armée de l'Air pilots of the war.

pilots allowed his aircraft to collide with the tail of Clowes' Hurricane (L1842), and the latter as a result crashed on landing with a badly damaged rudder. Although these have been identified as Moranes in the past, they were in fact H-75As of GC II/5, the pilots of which reported seeing the Heinkel under attack by four Hurricanes — indeed, they named the fourth as Flg Off Orton of 73 Squadron. The French pilots all claimed a share in the destruction of the Heinkel, and this was credited to the three 1 Squadron pilots, to Flg Off Orton, and to Adj Audrain, Sgt Bouhy, and Adj de Montgolfier. The bomber had fallen near Königsmacher on the east bank of the Moselle, near Thionville, where all the crew, save one gunner who had been killed, were made prisoner.

At 1400 Sqn Ldr 'Bull' Halahan and Flg Off M.H. 'Hilly' Brown of 1 Squadron patrolled over the Verdun-Metz region at 20,000 feet, and once again AA bursts were seen, indicating the presence of another Do 17P. Both attacked this aircraft of 4(F)/122 from astern and it went down in flames, outside Haumont-les-Lachoussee, near Longuyon, Ofw Baptist Schapp and his crew all being lost. This was also claimed shot down by French DCA gunners, and was witnessed falling by the crew of a Mureaux of GAO II/506, who saw it crash at Haumont le Chaussee with Hurricanes "on its heels". Both RAF and Luftwaffe records consider the Dornier to have fallen to the fighters. Moranes of GC III/6 flown by Adj Chef Pierre Le Gloan and Sous Lt Martin were responsible for shooting down yet another Do 17P, this one from 5(F)/122, which fell at Bras-sur-Meuse, Lt Kurt Behnke's crew baling out to become prisoners. Meanwhile Lt Bissoudre and Sgt Tourne of GC II/3 chased another lone Do 17P of 1(F)/123 over the Saone river as it was reconnoitring airfields in the Dijon area at 0935; Bissoudre was able to catch up with it south-west of Baume-les-Doubs. Seeing that he was close to the Swiss frontier, Fw Leo Knoch put the Dornier down on its belly at La Chaus de Fronds, he and his crew escaping across the border to be interned. A Do 17Z from Stab/KG2 on a similar mission over Mourmelon and Suippes was attacked by H-75As of GC I/5 and was believed to have been hit by Cne Jean Accart, but managed to escape. It was then caught by Hurricanes of 73

Four pilots of 1 Squadron consider a 7.9mm German aircraft gunner's machine gun taken from one of the Do 17s shot down on 23 November. Left to right are Flg Off Paul Richey, Sqn Ldr P.J.H. 'Bull' Halahan, Sgt A.V. 'Taffy' Clowes and Flt Lt P.R. 'Johnny' Walker.

Squadron to the south of Conflans, where it was shot down in flames by Flg Off J.E. Scoular and Sgt J. Winn. The French authorities reported that it had crashed at Saucy-le-Haut; Oblt Winter and his crew of three were all killed. An eighth bomber — this time an He 111H of Stab/KG53, flown by Oblt Friedrich-Wilhelm Franke — was intercepted by Flg Off N. 'Fanny' Orton of 73 Squadron whilst over the Toul-Nancy-Metz area, and this too was shot down, force-landing south of Boulay on the Moselle near Metz, with two of the crew dead; Franke and the other survivor became prisoners.

It seems that one other claim for an He 111 was made in the area during the day by Sgt C.N.S. Campbell of 73 Squadron, but no details are available. The only Allied loss occurred when Lt Col Mioche, an officer on the staff of the Armeé de l'Air's Groupement de Chasse 23 at Laon-Chambry, attempted to intercept one of the reconnaissance Dorniers over Verneuil-le-Petit in an H-75A. A well-aimed burst of fire from the rear gunner killed him outright.

Possibly the He 111H of Stab/KG 53 shot down by Flg Off N. Orton of 73 Squadron on 23 November. *(IWM)*

Over the Verdun area on this date the Bf 110s of V(Z)/LG 1 reportedly engaged in their first successful combat in the West. Lt Werner Methfessel, one of the more successful pilots of the Polish campaign, who had gained four victories there, claimed one Morane shot down, while his Röttenflieger, an unidentified Uffz, claimed hits on the engine of another (which he identified as a Spitfire); he reported seeing this going down trailing smoke. No French losses have actually been found — unless the victim was Mioche, his opponent wrongly identified as a Do 17.

22–23/11/39

Over the North Sea limited engagements had continued. During 22 November six He 111s of 2/KG 26 went out in the early afternoon to strike at warships and other vessels reported off the Scottish coast. The attack was unsuccessful, but the bombers then proceeded to Lerwick where Saro London L7042 of 201 Squadron was bombed and badly damaged. The flyingboat was subsequently scuttled in deep water. That night 17 He 59s from 3/KüFlGr 906 and 3/KüFlGr 106, and eight He 115s of 1/KüFlGr 106 undertook another mining operation. One parachute mine was spotted by British observers as it fell into the sea off Shoeburyness on the Essex bank of the Thames Estuary, and this was later recovered by Royal Navy divers — the first German aerial mine to be secured for examination.

Next day the battlecruisers *Scharnhorst* and *Gneisenau* attempted to break out into the North Atlantic, in support of which eight He 111s of FAG 122 flew reconnaissances over the British Fleet bases in the Clyde, Moray Firth, Shetlands and at Rosyth and Scapa Flow. Sqn Ldr D.F.W. Atcherley and Flt Lt R.L. Lorrimer of 85 Squadron in France intercepted one 1(F)/122 aircraft over the eastern end of the English Channel as it headed south, and damaged it before it escaped into cloud with a wounded air gunner; the Heinkel had suffered 40% damage.

25/11/39

More attacks on shipping followed on 25th, when 18 He 111s and 21 Ju 88s from I/KG 26 and I/KG 30 were sent out. Only 11 Heinkels found targets, but their bombs all fell into the sea. Ships' AA damaged one aircraft, which landed at Westerland 40% damaged. During the month the first magnetic mine had been laid in British waters by floatplanes and flyingboats of the Küstenfliegergruppen, and by U-Boats. These proved a fearful problem at first, and it was three months before 'degaussing' equipment would be devised and fitted to ships. During this period a quarter of a million tons of precious shipping was lost to this scourge. Bomber Command aircraft instituted nightly patrols over the seaplane bases on Sylt in an effort to prevent their taking off to continue their mining activities, while a strike was organized by Fighter Command.

26–28/11/39

The first attempt to hit the seaplanes at their home base was made on 26 November, when nine Blenheim IFs of 25 Squadron set off at 1115 to attack Borkum. One returned early, and the rest failed to find their target in bad weather conditions, returning to Northolt. Undismayed, a repeat raid was organized for 28th, this time six aircraft from 25 Squadron and six from 601 Squadron refuelling at Bircham Newton on the Norfolk coast, from where they

601 Squadron Blenheim I*F* BQ-E, seen at Manston a few weeks after the Borkum raid of late November. *(via A. Thomas)*

departed at 1405. They arrived over Borkum at 1525, Sqn Ldr J.R. Hallings-Pott leading the 25 Squadron aircraft down to strafe one aircraft on a slipway on one side of the island, and then three more on another slipway on the opposite side. The 601 Squadron flight, led by Flt Lt C.H. Bull, followed them down to repeat the attack. All 12 aircraft then set course for home, landing safely at Debden at 1755, where they reported having shot-up five seaplanes, a gun post and various other targets. Their attack had in actuality achieved very little; one elderly Ju W34/See floatplane was hit twice and an He 59 of 3/KüFlGr 106 once.

29/11/39

At 0825 on 29th three Hurricanes of 111 Squadron, which had moved from Northolt to Acklington during October, were scrambled after an intruding reconnaissance aircraft. Sqn Ldr Harry Broadhurst was vectored onto a 'bandit' off the coast, and finding an He 111 of Stab/KG 26, shot it down at once.

For KüFlGr 406, 29 November was a disastrous day, five of the unit's flying-boats being lost during another series of minelaying sorties. 6K+DK, a Do 18G of 2 Staffel, was shot down by a Hudson 50 miles off the Norwegian coast, south of Egersund. It probably fell victim to a 224 Squadron aircraft, 'A', N7218, flown by Sgt Cargill; this aircraft itself suffered damage during a fight with a Do 18, causing Cargill to break away and head for base before the result of his crew's return fire could be observed, and no claim was submitted. Lt zur See Ulrich Burk and his crew were rescued from the sea by a Norwegian ship, and were interned. A second flyingboat, 6K+KH — a Do 18D of 1 Staffel — was also damaged in combat with a Hudson (apparently from 220 Squadron), and this too came down in the sea, force-landing south of Egersund also. Fw de Reserve Hans Glimkermann taxied the aircraft to Lista on the Norwegian coast, where he and his crew were also interned. This fate also awaited Fw de Res Ferdinand Belghaus's crew when they force-landed 6K+FH at Mandal with a damaged engine; this was another 1 Staffel machine. Oblt zur See Manfred Kinzel of 2 Staffel force-landed 6K+GK in the Faroes when the aircraft ran out of fuel, this crew being interned by the Danish authorities. A third 2 Staffel aircraft, 6K+FK, crashed in the coastal dunes whilst attempting to land at Hornum in bad visibility, Lt zur See Jurgan Lorey's crew all being killed.

It seems likely that one of these aircraft had been engaged with a London

One of 240 Squadron's elderly Saro London flyingboats that were much in evidence during November.

flyingboat of 240 Squadron. The elderly K5263, flown by Flt Lt McConnel, was twice attacked by a Do 18, the crew returning fire on each occasion, following which the German aircraft flew off on a zig-zag course; possibly this was 6K+ FH.

30/11/39
Finally, at dawn next day two more Do 18s (WNrs 0722 and 0842), both of 2/KüFlGr 106, collided whilst taking off from Norderney, both suffering 40% damage. Following these latest losses the General der Luftwaffe/beim ObdM protested strongly against the mining operations, which he considered to be proving unreasonably costly. During the day Luftwaffe reconnaissance aircraft were again over the Scottish east coast. An He 111 of Wekusta 26 was engaged briefly by Spitfires of 602 Squadron but escaped in cloud without damage.

Chapter 5

SLAUGHTER OF THE BOMBERS

If November had been a month of action over the Western Front, then December was certainly the month of the bomber. As autumn hastened into a peculiarly hard winter, activities over the Franco-German border reduced markedly. Efforts were made during the month to improve the equipment of the AASF's bomber arm, following the disastrous showing of the Battles three months earlier. On 1 December 139 Squadron was despatched from Wyton by 2 Group to the airfield at Betheniville, as part of the AASF. It was followed a few days later by 114 Squadron, which moved from the same base to Vraux. At the same time 15 and 40 Squadrons were withdrawn from France, flying to Wyton where their Battles were handed in and training on Blenheim IVs commenced. 12 Squadron changed airfields during the month, moving to Amifontaine.

The Air Component, which also undertook a number of re-arrangements during the month, received a visit from HM King George VI, who inspected

HM King George VI visits the Air Component and inspects detachments from several squadrons. In the foreground are a trio of Hurricanes from 85 Squadron, flanked by three more from 87 Squadron, while facing them are a pair of 615 Squadron Gladiators and a Blenheim IV. *(IWM)*

Gladiators of 607 Squadron at Vitry, winter 1939/40 *(via A. Thomas)*

several of the squadrons including the fighters. 26 Squadron moved its Lysanders to La Triquerie during the first week of December, while on 12th and 13th the recently-arrived 607 and 615 Squadrons both moved to Vitry where they became the operational element of 61 (Fighter) Wing. 85 Squadron was detached to Le Touquet on 19th, but spent an uneventful few days there, returning to Lille-Seclin on the last day of the year.

In Germany during the early part of the month there had been some movement of fighter units again. On 1st JG 77 was re-organised to control:

	Stab/JG77	at Bonn-Hangelar	
I/JG77	at Gütersloh	JGr 102	at Düsseldorf
II/JG 77	at Gütersloh	JGr 152	at Düsseldorf
I(J)/LG 2	at Gymnich		

3/12/39

At the same time fighting had flared over the North Sea Triangle, where Bomber Command took an active part in the anti-shipping war for the first time since September. The War Cabinet in London was anxious to obtain a sinking of a German capital ship, and with this in mind a stepping-up of such activities was prepared. During November several Wellington squadrons undertook practice anti-warship attacks in Belfast Lough, Northern Ireland, and the first actual operation was launched on 3 December. At 0705 on the morning of this day two dozen Wellingtons from 38 (three aircraft), 115 (nine aircraft) and 149 (12 aircraft) Squadrons took off for an armed reconnaissance over the Heligoland area, led by Wg Cdr Kellett of 38 Squadron. Over England they formed up into three 'battle formations' of eight aircraft each, and headed out over the East Anglian coast. To the north of Heligoland they turned southwards, approaching the target area at 1145, and seeing ships at anchor.

The presence of the bombers had already been plotted on the first operational 'Freya' radar set, which was located on Heligoland, and four Bf 109Ds of I/ZG 26 were scrambled to intercept, led by Hpt Dickore. They were too late to catch the bombers before they completed their bomb run, the Wellingtons bombing from 10,000 feet, claiming hits on a cruiser and a trawler, and reporting that a minesweeper was sunk. Actually trawler M1407 — formerly *Johann Schulte* — was hit, and subsequently sank. Considerable Flak was encountered from batteries on the island, and from the warships at anchor, but this failed to inflict

Crews of 149 Squadron go out to their Wellington IAs for the 3 December sortie against German warships. *(IWM)*

any serious damage. Indeed one stick of bombs landed around one battery, damaging it.

As the bombers flew out of range of the gunners, the Bf 109Ds attacked, one pair coming in from above, and one from below. These were successfully fought off by the gunners, several of whom were now ensconced in Boulton-Paul power-operated turrets, which were a feature of the recently-delivered Wellington Ia. Two of the bombers were slightly damaged, one by Oblt Günther Specht, who was himself shot down by Cpl Copley, the rear gunner in Sgt Odoire's 'Z', N2880, of 38 Squadron. One of the bullets from Specht's guns actually lodged in the seat buckle of Copley's harness without injuring him. Specht ditched his stricken fighter in the sea, from where he was rescued. However he had suffered facial wounds which would result in the loss of his left eye; he was credited with one Wellington shot down. Actually N2880 returned

Wellington Ia of 38 Squadron in flight.

Oblt Günther Specht of I/ZG 26, who was shot down and lost one eye; he fell victim to the rear gunner of a 38 Squadron Wellington on 3 December.

to base where on landing it spun off the runway due to a bullet-ripped tyre to one of the main undercarriage legs; 29 bullet holes were later counted in the Wellington.

The three remaining Messerschmitts were by now low on fuel, and broke away to return to Jever. Meanwhile eight of I/ZG 26's new Bf 110Cs had taken off from this base, as had four Bf 109Ds from 10(N)/JG 26, four Bf 109Ds of JGr 101 from Neumünster and eight Bf 109Es from II(J)/TrGr 186 at Nordholz, but all were too late to make any further interceptions.

This action of 3 December engendered in RAF Bomber Command a false optimism. The theory that tight formations of bombers could fight off interception by day by using the combined mutually-supporting fire of their defences, appeared proven. In fact they had met the lower-performing earlier version of the Bf 109, equipped only with rifle-calibre machine gun armament, and indeed with only half the number of these guns compared with their British counterparts, the eight-gun Hurricanes and Spitfires. How the new turret-armed Wellington would stand up against Bf 109Es or Bf 110s with cannon armament was yet to be demonstrated.

6/12/39

Bad weather prevented most activity until Tuesday, 6 December. At 0925 on the morning of that day Anson K6189 (VX-R) of 206 Squadron set off on a North Sea patrol with Plt Off J.H. Grimes at the controls. The aircraft reached the Frisian Islands where it was intercepted by a Bf 110 of 2/ZG 26, 70 miles north of Texel. In the ensuing fight one or other of the pilots apparently made an error of judgement, for the two aircraft collided in mid-air to the west of Texel, both crashing into the sea with the loss of all aboard; the Bf 110 crew were Ofw Franz Hoffman and Uffz Wilhelm Fuchs. Coastal Command Hudsons were also out on patrol, two of these being reported in action. Sgt Potter of 224 Squadron in 'W' N7262 reported making six attacks on a Do 18 flyingboat, finally leaving it with fuel streaming from the starboard engine. Sgt Culver of 220 Squadron in 'A' reported attacking a Do 26, which appeared to be hit. The German gunners returned fire vigorously however, and the Hudson was considerably damaged by bullet strikes to the nose. It seems likely that both Hudsons had encountered the same Do 18, 8L+NL of 1/KüFlGr 406, which returned with 15% damage. Another Do 18, 8L+FK of 2/KüFlGr 906 was reportedly attacked in error by a Bf 110 of I/ZG 76, and force-landed with 40% damage.

Later in the day eight reconnaissance He 111Hs from FAG 122 set off to fly sorties over the Moray Firth and Firth of Forth, but two 1 Staffel aircraft were lost, Lt Heinz Schierholz's WNr 2709 crashing shortly after take-off from Ütersen, while Fw Hans Petersen's WNr 3154 went into the North Sea. Neither of the crews survived.

Despite recent heavy losses, a fourth major mine-laying operation was launched during the night of 6/7th, 18 He 59s and He 115s from 3/KüFlGr 106, 3/KüFlGr 506 and 3/KüFlGr 906 taking part. On this occasion four of the float-planes were lost, including two He 59s of 3/106 and two He 115s of 3/506. Oblt zur See Bernhard Bock's He 59 M2+VL (WNr 1986) crashed on take-off, only one man surviving with injuries. M2+0L (WNr 1974) with Oblt zur See Giesbert Clemens at the controls, crashed whilst attempting to land at Borkum on return from the sortie, all the crew being killed. Fw Fritz-Georg Freese's He 115 S4+ BL (WNr 1899) also crashed on take-off, two members of the crew losing their lives, while Oblt zur See Emil Wodke's S4+EL (WNr 2081) hit the radar mast of Chain Home Station West Beckham on the Norfolk coast and crashed on the beach at Sheringham; again all the crew died.

7/12/39

This was the harbinger of more intense action next day (7th), when at 0800 seven He 111s of I/KG 26 were sent out to attack a convoy off the Scottish coastline which had been spotted by further 1(F)/122 aircraft during an earlier sortie. A few minutes after midday plots on the British radar warned of the bombers' approach. 72 Squadron had arrived at Drem airfield during November to reinforce the Auxilliary Air Force units, and at 1208 this squadron's 'B' Flight was ordered to patrol over Montrose at 2,000 feet. Two minutes later 603 Squadron's Blue Section, which was up on patrol over Arbroath, was warned of seven hostile aircraft approaching south-east of Montrose, heading in that direction, while at 1212 the five more Spitfires from 72 Squadron got into the air and headed for the same location. Both squadrons found the bombers — the seven Heinkels were flying in two 'vic' formations of four and three, one follow-ing directly behind the other at a distance of 600 yards. Flg Off J.L.G. Cunning-ham led the 603 Squadron section into the attack on the second formation, at which the bombers immediately lost altitude until they were only some 50 feet above the sea, heading east. A second attack brought trails of black smoke from some aircraft, but no other result. Plt Off B.J.G. Carbury made a head-on attack on the left-hand aircraft of the first formation, but again achieved no definite results. The section was credited with three damaged, the third by Plt Off 'Ras' Berry.

72 Squadron also attacked at almost the same time, Flg Off Henstock leading Green Section to attack the first four, while Flg Off Sheen and F/Sgt J. Steere as Blue Section, attacked the rear three. Flg Off T.A.F. Elsdon, one of the members of Green Section, repeatedly attacked the leading formation until all his ammunition was exhausted, but with no better result than 603 Squadron had achieved — the 'scatter' harmonisation of the British fighters' guns was proving as ineffective as ever! Return fire struck Sheen's aircraft, wounding him twice in the leg, while one of the earphones in his helmet was shattered by a bullet. He attacked again despite this, but fuel flowing from the punctured petrol tanks of his aircraft forced him to break away and land at Leuchars, from where he was removed to hospital. The rest of 'B' Flight landed at Drem at 1247, having seen none of the Heinkels crash. Intelligence later reported however, that two had failed to reach their base. Indeed two of I/KG 26's Heinkels did fail to return from the raid, though as victims of which attacks cannot now be ascertained. Lt Adalbert Lüneburg's aircraft and that of Fw Alfred Fick both crashed into the sea east of Bell Rock, all eight crew members being lost.

Following these recent actions on either side of the North Sea, both the RAF and the Luftwaffe sought to reinforce their Fleet base areas. On 7 December the Hurricanes of 111 Squadron moved north to Drem from Acklington, while on 11th II/JG 77 moved from Gütersloh to join JG 1; 4 and 6 Staffeln went to Jever and 5 Staffel to Wangerooge. On the same day however I/ZG 26 was transferred from JG 1 to the control of Stab/ZG 26, only 1 Staffel remaining at Jever whilst awaiting the arrival there of I/ZG 76. This experienced Bf 110 unit, already with many combats in Poland to its credit, began moving in from Bonninghardt on 16th and 17th. Meanwhile a second 'Freya' unit was moved to Wangerooge as Ln Regiment (Ver) Köthen, under Lt Wendland, to improve coverage of the German Bight area. During the night of 7/8th, 12 He 59s and ten He 115s were again out mine-laying, on this occasion four more He 59s being lost or badly damaged in accidents, although this time only one crew suffered casualties, one man being killed and the other three all injured. GenMaj Köhler now reported that the mining activities were proving a very heavy drain both on personnel and equipment, and a halt was called. Apparently in response to the earlier mining operations, eight Whitleys from 77 and 102 Squadrons now raided the seaplane bases on Borkum and Sylt by night, without particular effect.

At this same time the scope of attack for the bombers of X Fliegerkorps was widened to include:

1. Ships with enemy flags.
2. Ships with neutral flags under the protection of an enemy convoy.
3. Ships which fired on German aircraft.
4. Ships where the name and place of origin were obscured.

KG 26 was now ordered to concentrate the attacks of its He 111s on merchant shipping while the Ju 88s of KG 30 would concentrate on warships.

12–13/12/39

Following a further lull over the North Sea which lasted nearly a week, the crew of Whitley N1375, piloted by Sgt MacArthur of 102 Squadron, spotted two German aircraft whilst on patrol over the Frisians on 12th. The gunners fired at one, but no hits were seen. Next day, Tuesday 13 December, a trio of Hudsons from 224 Squadron were on patrol in the area when two Do 18s of 3/KüFlGr 406 — part of a force of 12 such aircraft on warship escort — were engaged. Flt Lt Wright in 'J' N7765, Plt Off T.K. Hurley in 'N' N7222 and Sgt Cargill in 'W' N7262, attacked and claimed that they had silenced both rear gunners and damaged the fuel tanks of both flyingboats, much black smoke being seen. Dorniers K6+GK and K6+CL received 14 and 20 hits respectively in this fight, from which all three Hudsons returned undamaged.

14/12/39

Reconnaissance information reported German naval vessels at sea on 14th and at once 12 Wellingtons of 99 Squadron were readied for action. At 1100 they were finally ordered off to search the Heligoland Bight area, actually getting into the air about 45 minutes later. The bombers flew in four 'vics, one behind the other as follows:

	+ N2958 (Sqn Ldr A. McKee)	
+ N2870 (Plt Off H.L. Lewis)		+ N2887 (Flg Off J.P. Dyer)
	+ N2913 (Flt Lt J.F.B. Brough)	
+ N2911 (F/Sgt W.H. Downey)		+ N2886 (F/Sgt J.E.K. Healey)
	+ N2912 (Sqn Ldr R.G.E. Catt)	
+ N2999 (F/Sgt R.J. Williams)		+ N2914 (Flg Off A.F. Smith)
	+ N2957 (Flt Lt E.L. Hetherington)	
+ N2956 (Flg Off J.A.H. Cooper)		+ N2986 (Sgt R.H.J. Brace)

The commanding officer, Wg Cdr J.F. Griffiths, DFC, directed the raid from Sqn Ldr McKee's aircraft.

As the Wellingtons approached the Dutch coast at about 1300 they turned northwards towards Heligoland, flying parallel with the shoreline. Light rain showers forced them to fly at about 500 feet for visibility, a German patrol boat then being spotted which was thought might be an early-warning station. At 1355 the formation changed course and flew towards the Jade Estuary at about

Wg Cdr J.F. Griffiths, DFC (centre) with Cpls Pettit (left) and Bickerstaff, in front of a 99 Squadron Wellington following the action of 14 December.

200 feet, where on arrival at 1425 several warships were seen in the Schillig Roads. They had found the light cruiser *Nürnberg* with an escort of destroyers and motor-torpedo boats, which were incorrectly identified as a battleship, a cruiser and escorting destroyers, steaming south. To avoid overflying the vessels before the crews were ready to bomb, the squadron turned north, then swung through 260° to approach from the rear, a manoeuvre which kept the Wellingtons over the Jade Basin for some considerable time, allowing Bf 109Es from 5/JG 77 to scramble at 1430, with four Bf 110s of 2/ZG 26. A little later more Bf 109Es of II(J)/TrGr 186 followed, but these were not to make contact with the raiders.

As the bombers turned onto their bombing run the destroyers opened up a furious barrage of Flak, and at 1434 the leading 'vic' had the vessels dead ahead. Two minutes later the first three Bf 109Es approached from the direction of Wangerooge and at once opened fire on the rear pair of bombers from behind and below, shooting down N2956 and N2986, the No 2 and 3 aircraft of the last section. As the Messerschmitts climbed away, one was hit by return fire and dived into the sea (WNr 1371), Lt Friedrich Braukmeier being killed.

The Messerschmitt pilots then attacked the left side of the formation, shooting down N2911 and N2870. A third pass at the right side hit N2957 (now the back marker) and brought down N2886. At 1456 Cpl A. Bickerstaff, the rear gunner in the leading Wellington, was able to put a burst directly into the pilot's cockpit area of a Bf 110, which had appeared above and behind the bomber at very close range. He reported that it hung momentarily, burst into flames on the starboard wing between engine and fuselage, and then went down vertically into the sea in a mass of flames. It seems that he had hit Hpt Werner Restemeyer's Bf 110 (WNr 1809) which was indeed damaged 40% (the pilot being wounded), but got back to its airfield. Bickerstaff had probably seen one of the stricken Wellingtons crashing. At this stage the crews in the third section reported seeing first one, and then a second twin-engined fighter go flaming down into the sea, until four fires could be seen on the water. It was then noticed that the No 2 and 3 aircraft of the last section, the left hand aircraft of the second section and the left hand aircraft of the leading section were all missing — clearly it had been Wellingtons that the third section crews had seen falling in flames, not fighters! At that stage the right-hand aircraft of the second section was also seen to go down amid heavy Flak bursts and streams of tracer.

The seven survivors gave up the attempt to attack, and headed home for Newmarket with their bombs still aboard. (The fact that they were not jettisoned even at such a moment of peril illustrates the extent to which peacetime thinking was still predominant!) Flt Lt Hetherington's aircraft, the leader of the ill-fated last 'vic', had been damaged, and he did jettison his bombs in the sea before crossing the coast, going down to crash in a field near Newmarket racecourse shortly afterwards. The pilot was killed and most of the crew injured.

Bomber Command's interrogation of the survivors led to a complete mis-reading of the events that had occurred. Sgt Brace in N2986 was said to have gone down in flames before the fighters attacked, while Plt Off Lewis's N2870 was thought to have been struck by Flak, turned and crashed into the following N2911 of F/Sgt Downey as a result, causing both to fall in flames. Flg Off Cooper in N2956 had last been seen heading for the German coast with the under-carriage down, while F/Sgt Healey's N2886 was considered to have been shot

Ground crew of 4/JG 77 rush to greet the return of a successful pilot to Wangerooge.

down by Flak. Wellington gunners claimed two Bf 109s and a Bf 110 shot down, and another Bf 109 probable. Reported Air Vice-Marshal Bottomley, SASO, Bomber Command: "It is by no means certain that enemy fighters did, in fact, succeed in shooting down any of the Wellingtons." Such is the power of wishful thinking that the British thought that, despite heavy losses to Flak, they had scored another victory over the fighters!

Nothing could have been further from the truth! Naval Flak claimed none of the credit for a victory which went to II/JG 77. This Gruppe's high-performing Bf 109E-1s, although still not cannon-armed aircraft, were apparently responsible for all the casualties, seven Wellingtons being claimed shot down by Hpt Alfred von Loijewski (two), Lt Edgar Struckmann, Lt Heinz Halbach, Fw Erwin Sawallisch (two) and Uffz Herbert Kutscha. Apart from the loss of Braukmeier and the damage to Restemeyer's Bf 110, five more of 5 Staffel's Bf 109Es had been hit and had suffered 5-10% damage in each case, though none of the pilots had been hit. One of the TrGr 186 Messerschmitts had also crashed while taking off, and had been damaged 30%. A German patrol boat picked up two dead RAF crewmen and a great deal of wreckage.

17/12/39
The incorrect assessment of the effectiveness of the German fighters' attack by the British was to have disastrous consequences four days later, when a repeat raid by a larger formation of Wellingtons was to be sent out. In the meantime however, German aircraft again appeared over the English North Sea coast in some numbers on 17 December. Three Stab/KG 26 He 111s undertook an early morning reconnaissance, followed half an hour later by 20 more of these bombers from I Gruppe. No fighter interception took place, and the raiders returned to base having bombed and sunk the motorship *Serenity* (487 tons) off Whitby, the trawlers *Compaganus* and *Isabella Greig*, and the steamer *Zelos* (227 tons) off May Island, and the trawler *Pearl* off the Outer Dowsing lightship. On return one He 111H-2 crashed on fire at Hornum/Sylt, one member of the crew being killed.

At 1310 11 more Heinkels, this time from 6/KG 26, took off for a similar patrol, and these at last were to meet British interception — though on an extremely limited scale. A single Hurricane of 46 Squadron, which unit had recently moved to Acklington to replace 111 Squadron, was on patrol when the pilot Flt Lt C.R.D. Stewart sighted one of the He 111s off the coast. He attacked, but the bomber at once escaped in clouds after one of the gunners had put a single bullet into his aircraft.

To reduce the activity of Luftwaffe coastal aircraft, since these were still actively engaged in laying the deadly magnetic mines around the coasts of Britain, six Whitleys of 10 Squadron went out by night on 17th to attack seaplane bases in the Frisian Islands and enforce the blackout. One of these reported an inconclusive combat with a pair of He 111s, which disappeared in cloud.

18/12/39
Next night more Whitleys from 102 Squadron were to bomb Borkum and Norderney Islands, repeating these raids on 20th, when Sylt was also attacked. On this last occasion night fighter patrols from 10(N)/JG 26 attempted to intercept the seven bombers involved, but without success.

Following the recent level of activity, the strength of the composite Jagdge-

This Whitley V, DY-R, N1380, of 102 Squadron is believed to have been the first RAF aircraft deliberately to have dropped bombs on German soil. *(Real Photos via A. Thomas)*

schwader 1 was now quite formidable. Oberstleutnant Carl Schumacher now had under his command I/ZG 76 (Hpt Reinecke) with Bf 110Cs, 10(N)/JG 26 (Oblt Johannes Steinhoff) with Bf 109Ds, both these units being at Jever; the greater part of II/JG 77 (Hpt Harry von Bülow) with Bf 109E-1s at Wangerooge; II/TrGr 186 (Hpt Seeliger) with Bf 109E-1s at Nordholz; and JGr 101 (Hpt Reichardt) with Bf 109Ds and Es at Neumünster.

It was into this veritable hornets' nest that Bomber Command was to blunder on Sunday 18 December, the resultant clash proving to be the biggest, and without doubt the most important and well-known of the 'Phoney War' period. Following the apparently successful armed-reconnaissance of 3rd, and that of 14th, a similar operation was now put in hand. As on 3rd, 24 bombers were to be involved, and once more the formation was to be led by Wg Cdr Kellett.

At 1000 GMT therefore, nine Wellingtons from 9 Squadron, accompanied by three from 38 Squadron, plus six from 37 Squadron and six from 149 Squadron took off, forming up into four 'battle flights' each of six aircraft over King's Lynn, and then setting off across the North Sea towards the Heligoland area. (See pages 148-49 and Diagram opposite for list of aircraft involved, and their fates.) Some two thirds of the way to the target N2984, one of the 149 Squadron machines, suffered propeller trouble and Flt Lt Dugwit was forced to turn for home. Since strict radio silence was being observed, his No 2 peeled off after him on a purely 'follow-my-leader' basis, leaving 22 bombers to proceed.

By this date no less than three operational test 'Freya' sets had been set up in the area, on the islands of Heligoland, Wangerooge and Borkum — a sad shock for the British had they known of this at the time, for they were still fondly of the illusion that only they possessed the advantage of radio location (as it was then known) for air defence purposes at this stage of the war. It was the Wangerooge 'Freya' that first gave warning of the bombers' approach, this initial plot appearing at 1123 (1323 CET) as the formation was still well to the north-west, heading steadily on a north-easterly course in the direction of

Map of Route of British bombers, 'Battle of Heligoland Bight', 18 December 1939

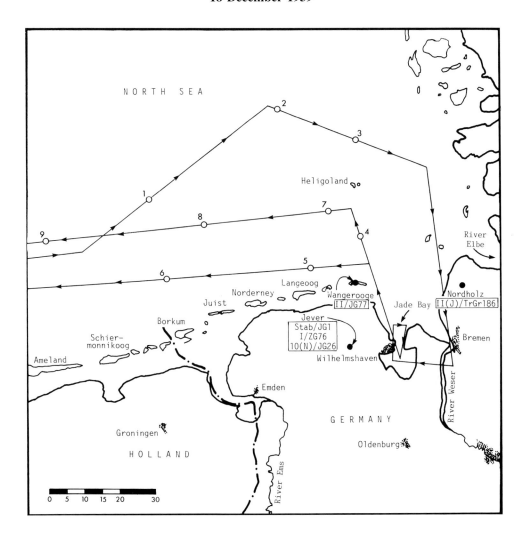

Key

1. Wellingtons picked up on Wangerooge 'Freya', 1323 Central European Time (1123 Greenwick Mean Time).
2. Wellingtons picked up on Heligoland 'Freya', 1343 C.E.T.
3. Wellingtons again picked up on Heligoland 'Freya', 1356 C.E.T.
4. First interception by fighters of 10(N)/JG 26 and Rotte from II/JG 77, 1430-1435; 7 victories claimed – 4 not confirmed.
5. Wellingtons of Southern flight attacked by Gollob's Schwarm of 3/ZG 76 and Bf 109Es of 6/JG 77, 1435-1440; 14 victories claimed — 3 not confirmed.
6. Wellingtons of Southern flight attacked by Reinecke's Schwarm of 2/ZG 76 and Bf 109Es of 5/JG 77, 1445-1450; 6 victories claimed — 3 not confirmed.
7. Wellingtons of Northern flight attacked by Rotte of Falck/Fresia, 2/ZG 76, and Rotte 3/JGr 101, 1435-1445; 6 victories claimed — 1 not confirmed.
8. Wellingtons of Northern flight attacked by Schwarm of Gresens/Graeff/Kalinowski of 2/ZG 76, 1500; 3 victories claimed.
9. Wellingtons of Northern flight attacked by Schwarm of Uellenbeck, 2/ZG 76, 1500-1505; 2 victories claimed.

135

Oberstleutnant Carl Schumacher, Kommodore of JG 1. *(via J. Foreman)*

Westerland/Sylt (see Map page 135). They appeared again on the Heligoland set at 1143 (1343) as they turned south-east. By 1156 (1356) the formation was due north of the island, following which another turn was made to the southwards, the Wellingtons passing Heligoland on their right side, and heading for Jade Bay and the Weser estuaries where sat the great ports of Wilhelmshaven and Bremerhaven.

A combination of communications problems and frank disbelief by the fighter commanders had caused some delay in ordering interception, and the Wellingtons were able to reach the German coast at around 1210 (1410) without any hostile aircraft having been spotted. Here the Flak opened up as the bombers passed Bremerhaven and crossed the estuary, Marineflakabteilungen 214 at Cuxhaven, 244 and 264 at Wesermünd all opening fire. South of Bremerhaven the formation turned sharply and headed slightly north of west towards Wilhelmshaven and Jade Bay. Here they turned north-north-east over the western side of the Bay, before carrying out a triangular search, passing over the shipyards and Schillig Roads, without dropping any bombs, and passing Wilhelmshaven on their left side for the second time in a few minutes. Here

Marineflakabt 212, 222, 252, 262 and 272, together with gunners on *Scharnhorst* and *Gneisenau* all engaged the bombers, but without apparent result. As the Wellingtons left the immediate area and reached the first of the Frisian Islands, it seems that they split into two groups, the leading flights continuing on their course until they were just short of Heligoland before turning west-south-west, while the trailing flights turned west along the northern shorelines of the Frisians. So far as can be firmly ascertained, it was at the moment of division that the fighters first struck.

A number of I/ZG 76's recently-arrived Bf 110s were already in the air in pairs, patrolling the general area of the Frisians, and these were vectored onto the bombers, while other fighters from all the units available in the area except II(J)/TrGr 186, were scrambled. Five Bf 109Ds of 10(N)/JG 26 had got off from Jever and pursued the bombers as they left Wilhelmshaven, finding some interference from the Flak as they did so. Others from II/JG 77 were taking off from Wangerooge, and had the shortest flight to make to intercept. Thus it was that at about 1230 (1430) the 10(N)/JG 26 Bf 109Ds led by Oblt Steinhoff, and the first two Bf 109E-1s of 6/JG 77 attacked the leading section of Wellingtons as these were heading towards Heligoland. Here seven victories were claimed, two by Steinhoff, one by Uffz Heilmayr of 6/JG 77, and four by other pilots of 10(N)/JG 26 (see list of all Luftwaffe claims on pages 149-50).

At much the same time other II/JG 77 aircraft, joined by the Geschwaderkommodore, Oberstlt Schumacher, in a Bf 109E-1, with Oblt Johann Fuhrmann of 10(N)/JG 26 in a Bf 109D as his Röttenflieger, attacked the bombers which had taken the southernmost route. Behind them came more Bf 109Es of 5/JG 77 and two Schwarme of Bf 110s scrambled from Jever by 2 and 3/ZG 76. The latter Schwarm of Zerstörer attacked the rear sections of the southernmost bombers as the Bf 109s were completing their attack. The JG 77 pilots submitted ten claims here, including two each by Fw Troitzsch and Uffz Niemeyer, but lost Lt Roman Stiegler of 6 Staffel, whose aircraft was seen to crash vertically into the sea. Fw Hans Troitzsch had also been hit and wounded, and he crash-landed his 50% damaged fighter on Wangerooge.

Oberstlt Schumacher attacked a Wellington north of Wangerooge and shot both engines out; this was almost certainly N2936 of 37 Squadron which Sgt

Bf 109Es of 6/JG 77 at dispersal. *(ECPA)*

Ruse managed to crashland in shallow water on a mud flat off Spiekeroog. He and all his crew became prisoners. Meanwhile Fuhrmann made three attacks from the side on another bomber, but when these appeared to achieve no results, he threw caution to the wind and attacked from behind. His Bf 109D at once came under crossfire from the tail guns of the whole formation, and was shot down into the sea. He carried out a perfect 'ditching' but was drowned before he could be rescued.

As the Bf 109 pilots' ten minute running battle drew to a close the Schwarm of Bf 110s of 3/ZG 76 joined the fight, Fw Gröning claiming one Wellington shot down at 1240 (1440), two further claims being made a few minutes later by Oblt Gollob and Ofw Fleischmann. One of the Schwarme's aircraft was hit and slightly damaged, the pilot breaking away and returning to base. Some of the pilots of the units involved in these particular interceptions had undoubtedly attacked Wellington 'E' N2871, of 37 Squadron. As the rearmost flight of bombers, which were being led by Sqn Ldr Hue-Williams, turned westwards after passing Wilhelmshaven, this aircraft was left behind when its speed dropped sharply due to the accidental lowering of the flaps. Without the mutual support of the other five aircraft, Flg Off Lemon sought safety by diving to sea level, where the bomber was attacked by two fighters which caused considerable damage, but failed to shoot it down. However the rear gunner, Cpl Kidd, was able to claim one of the attackers shot down in return. Lemon and his crew reached base where they crash-landed, to find that theirs was the only 37 Squadron machine to get back.

Meanwhile 5/JG 77's Bf 109Es, 2/ZG 76's Bf 110s, and a lone Bf 110 flown by Lt Helmut Lent of 1/ZG 76, who had just landed at Jever from a patrol, and had at once taken off again, had flown further to the west, and had intercepted the leading part of the southerly formation, which had reached the area of Borkum. Lent arrived first, and reported seeing ten Wellingtons, attacking two which were lagging slightly. One of these was N2888 of 37 Squadron, on which he made an unsuccessful beam attack before approaching from dead astern. The bomber at once went down and force-landed on Borkum, where seconds later it burst into flames; only the pilot, Flg Off P.A. Wimberley, survived. A few minutes later Lent reached the next bomber, which tried to flee at low level over the sea. He again attacked from dead astern and reported that both engines caught fire, the bomber breaking up as it hit the water at 1250 (1450).

Immediately behind Lent came the 2/ZG 76 Scharm, led by the Gruppen-kommandeur, Hpt Reinecke. Oblt Jäger from this unit at once claimed one Wellington shot down, reporting that this crashed into the sea at 1245 (1445). The 5/JG 77 Bf 109Es had arrived at much the same time as the Bf 110s, their pilots claiming three more Wellingtons around 1250 (1450). They reported seeing 18 bombers, and it seems probable that they had counted both the Wellingtons and the pursuing Bf 110s. Following this attack, the southern formation passed out of range of the fighters as it headed for home.

Meanwhile the northern part of the British force had also come under attack again. As the bombers turned towards England just to the south of Heligoland at about 1240 (1440) a pair of 2/ZG 76 Bf 110s which had been out on a routine patrol in the hands of Hpt Wolfgang Falck and Uffz Fresia, reported seeing 15-20 bombers — probably a dozen, followed by the last of the attacking Bf 109Ds of 10(N)/JG 26. Falck attacked the right hand aircraft of the rear section twice and saw it break up in mid air. He then attacked a second, reporting that it

A Schwarm of I/ZG 76 Bf 110Cs, that in the foreground (M8 ∣ AB) flown by Hpt Wolfgang Falck, circle their airfield after takeoff. *(via J. Foreman)*

crashed after receiving many hits in one engine. However the rear gunner had hit the Messerschmitt in the right engine, and with a stream of fuel pouring out over the wing, which by a miracle did not catch fire, he turned south and managed to force-land on Wangerooge. Meanwhile Fresia had attacked the left hand aircraft of the same section initially, setting the left engine on fire and seeing it come down in the sea in flames. He then attacked the next in line and after two attacks, reported that this also crashed into the sea with the left engine on fire.

Only one Rotte from 3/JGr 101 made contact with the bombers; Oblt Dietrich Robitzsch and Oblt Rolf Kaldrack attacking the northern formation south-west of Heligoland at about 1250 (1450) just as Falck and Fresia were claiming their

Hpt Wolfgang Falck of I/ZG 76 at readiness. *(ECPA)*

second victories. Each of these new arrivals claimed one Wellington shot down, but both aircraft were then hit and damaged, both pilots having to crash-land on return to Neumünster.

As with the southern formation, so too with that to the north, the leading section also came under attack, three more patrolling Bf 110s of 2/ZG 76 led by Oblt Gresens sighting five Wellingtons west-north-west of Borkum just before 1300 (1500). While Lt Graeff and Uffz Kalinowski each reported shooting down one Wellington in flames, Gresens attacked another which seems to have been N2983 of 9 Squadron. This landed in the sea after catching fire, coming down near a steamer. It appears that this was the British trawler *Erillas*, which picked up Sgt R. Hewitt and his crew, all of whom survived except the rear gunner, LAC W. Lilley, who was drowned. Helmut Lent, having continued northwards following his two earlier successes against the head of the southern formation, arrived in time to shoot at N2983 just before it went into the sea, but made no claim as it was obviously already very badly shot-up when he attacked it.

Finally a few minutes later a further four 2/ZG 76 Bf 110s, which were heading east-south-east 30 miles north of Ameland, came up head-on to a single vic of three Wellingtons about 60 miles west of where Falck and Fresia had attacked. Lt Uellenbeck swung round and attacked from above, claiming two victories; the first crashed into the sea in flames, the second went into the water after going down to low level. Uellenbeck's aircraft was hit by return fire 33 times, and both he and Uffz Dombrowski, the gunner, were wounded, but nonetheless he was able to land back at Jever with his aircraft 15% damaged. Then the bombers had gone; the time was 1305 (1505).

The Germans were understandably jubilant. In the 30 minutes running battle, beginning north of Wilhelmshaven and continuing all the way along the Frisians to Ameland, no less than 38 claims had been made. 11 or 12 of these were subsequently disallowed, including four of 10(N)/JG 26's six, one of them Oblt Steinhoff's second claim, all three made by 5/JG 77, and two of 6/JG 77's, including Niemeyer's second. Only two of ZG 76's claims were not confirmed, these being Falck's second and Gollob's. Nevertheless, 26 or 27 British bombers for a relatively minimal loss (only two pilots actually killed) seemed a victory for the defence of major proportions.

Yet this was a larger number of aircraft than had been involved in the whole British formation — so what of Bomber Command's actual losses? These had indeed been heavy — although not of the level believed by the Luftwaffe. 11 Wellingtons had gone down during the running fight, one had come down in the sea during the return flight, and six more were so damaged that they crashed or crash-landed on reaching the English coast. Of the five survivors that landed at their bases, one or two had suffered damage of one sort or another; only the trio from 38 Squadron seems to have escaped relatively unscathed. The Germans noted that the Wellingtons burned with ease when hit — not surprising, for they had not yet been fitted with self-sealing fuel tanks or any form of armour protection. Surviving crews claimed that 12 attacking fighters — six of them Bf 110s — had been shot down; as has been demonstrated, actual losses were two Bf 109Es and one Bf 109D, with one more Bf 109E badly damaged (50%), one damaged 25% and one less than 5%, plus two Bf 110Cs damaged 15% and seven hit but suffering less than 5% damage — a ratio of claims to losses somewhat less favourable than that of the Luftwaffe's claiming in this action.

The results of the 'Battle of the Heligoland Bight' have subsequently been the cause of much controversy between British and German historians, particularly as regards the numbers of British bombers involved. As will have been noted, Luftwaffe fighter claims at this time were generally remarkably accurate, so why should there be this sudden upsurge of overclaiming? As a result much detailed investigation has been expended with regard to this day.

Much of the strength of the German argument has centred on the fact that naval observers on the ground reported a force of 54 bombers — later revised to 52 — approaching Wilhelmshaven. When coupled with the number of claims made and the 'Freya' reports, this led many — particularly Oberstlt Schumacher — to the view that a further British formation — possibly an operational training unit on a navigational exercise — was also present. The operational record book for every Wellington unit — both operational and training — has been checked, as have the individual Aircraft History Cards for all Wellingtons produced up to this time. The record books of other Bomber Command squadrons have also been checked to ensure that no other types of bomber aircraft were by chance also present. None of these official records indicate that any aircraft beyond the 22 accounted for above, took any part. As a cross-check the records of the Commonwealth War Graves Commission for airmen reported 'missing in action' were studied. These records list all men lost during the war who have no known grave. Yet in this combat, which took place largely over the sea, not one man is listed who was not a member of the crews of the 12 aircraft recorded as lost. Wrecks recovered and prisoners taken by the Germans further fail to produce any unaccounted for aircraft or men.

'Freya' was a new and largely experimental form of equipment at this time, and while an excellent radar, cannot seriously be considered infallible in 1939. As to the ground sightings — perhaps the observers counted the bombers twice over during their triangular flight over Jade Bay, which caused the formation to pass Wilhelmshaven *twice* in a short period — for this is where the report of 52 comes from. There are many examples later in the war when trained observers in England greatly overestimated the strength of German bomber formations. Indeed pilots themselves were not immune from this form of error. For example in July 1940 12 Defiants of 141 Squadron were 'bounced' and roughly handled by the experienced Jagdflieger of III/JG 51. Yet the German pilots counted "24 Defiants in that clear blue sky" — at a time when the only other Defiant unit, 264 Squadron, was many miles away in the Midlands! It needs also to be remembered firstly that the German units involved were relatively inexperienced, and that secondly the whole battle took place over the sea, only two wrecks actually being recoverable, and thereby definitely confirmable.

If the Luftwaffe claims are plotted on a map of the area (see page 135) it will be seen that they occur in groups, the largest when both Bf 109s and Bf 110s were involved at the same time. This was the first occasion on which the cannon-armed Bf 110s were engaged against British bombers in substantial numbers. While the lightly-armed Bf 109Ds and E-1s had no option but to close in, in the face of the concentrated return fire of the Wellingtons' tail turrets, the pilots of the Bf 110s quickly found that their higher speed and the longer range and hitting power of their 20mm. cannon, gave them a profound advantage. They could either open fire at a range of 600 yards (beyond the effective reach of the bombers' .303in guns) and pump shells into their quarries; alternatively, they could utilize their speed (as indeed could the Bf 109E pilots) to make beam attacks from a somewhat higher altitude. This the Wellingtons' under turrets could not cope with, and having no dorsal or side armament, the bombers were virtually defenceless to such attacks.

Further, on this occasion a multiplicity of units were taking part in the interception, all attacking together in by far the largest air battle in which the participants had so far taken part. Conditions thus prevailed where one or more pilots firing at long range would not necessarily have noticed while concentrating on their targets, an attack made from the beam by another fighter. The pilot of the latter would perhaps equally not have seen the other attacker at such a distance, each believing that it was their fire alone which had caused the bomber to go flaming down. Reports from the British survivors make it clear that for a great deal of the time, simultaneous beam attacks were being made by both Bf 110s and Bf 109s. Finally the presence of observer/gunners in the rear seats of the Bf 110s created further possibilities for human error. A gunner aware that his pilot was attacking, and seeing a bomber falling in flames nearby, would almost automatically provide confirmation of his pilot's claim, without perhaps having been able really to see every detail of what had happened. Certainly the writers have considerable evidence from other campaigns and battles to confirm that as soon as more than one unit is involved in attacking an opposing formation, the level of claims to actual losses inflicted rises in almost direct proportion to the numbers involved, and the number of units present.

Another minor mystery also arises, which has not been adequately accounted for. British reports stated that no bombs were dropped so as not to endanger civilian lives, and indeed some of the men taken prisoner confirmed to the Germans that as no ships had been seen at sea, no attacks had been made since they had express instructions not to bomb vessels in harbour. Yet the two wrecks inspected by the German authorities contained no bombs. Upon being pressed, some of the POWs apparently reported that the operation had been a "navigational and training exercise with the added purpose of demonstrating RAF striking power for propaganda reasons". This seems highly unlikely, particularly bearing in mind the armed reconnaissances already flown on 3rd and 14th, and would appear possibly to have been a 'cover story' provided for any crews falling into German hands; it seems much more probable that the two crash-landed aircraft had managed to jettison their bombs in the sea before going down.

Whatever the truths or reasons discussed above, the battle had undoubtedly been a disaster of considerable magnitude for Bomber Command — though one which was carefully fabricated into a hard-won victory by the popular press at the time. It has since been held on frequent occasions that the raid put an end to Bomber Command's daylight operations, and on its belief in the ability of tight formations of medium bombers to defend themselves adequately. Yet this does not seem to have been fully the case. Bomber Command was staggered by the scale of losses, and at last officially recognised the danger posed by cannon-armed fighters *but* the official view was that losses had been due mainly to 'straggling'! Orders were at once issued for the discontinuance of such armed reconnaissance flights — for a time. It was the intention that as soon as armour had been added and the Wellingtons' fuel tanks rendered self-sealing, the flights would recommence. The orders specifically did not refer to special strikes against warships which had actually been sighted, and on 22 December, 38 and 115 Squadrons were informed that they would have to be prepared to undertake all such 3 Group sorties until further notice, due to the recent level of losses amongst the other units.

Another deficiency noted — but not improved upon for many months — was that the standard defensive armament was simply not good enough. The .303in Browning gun had a high cyclical rate of fire, but was greatly inferior in both range and hitting power to the cannon gun. It would however not be until further grievous losses had been suffered in similar circumstances during the early days of the Norwegian invasion, that the British daylight bombing policy was really brought almost completely to a halt. The raid did result in the immediate award of a number of decorations, DFCs going to pilots Flt Lt J.P. Grant and Flg Off W.J. Macrae of 9 Squadron, while Sgt J. Ramshaw and AC1 C.R. Driver of the same unit received DFMs.

Even as the Wellingtons of Bomber Command were being so badly mauled, Coastal Command was continuing its general North Sea patrolling operations, as were the aircraft of the Küstenfligergruppen. 12 Do 18s had gone off on searches before midday on 18th, one crew of 3/KüFlGr 406 reporting being attacked by three Hudsons 95 miles east of Flamborough Head, but being able to escape into cloud without damage. It seems that these were aircraft of 220 Squadron, Flt Lt Lydall in 'O' engaging a Do 18 on which several hits were claimed. Return fire caused severe damage to the British aircraft, destroying the instrument panel.

In order to tighten up frontier patrols and for the planned offensive in the West, several new commands were set up by Order Obdl/RdL Ac 16/13, to take effect from 1 January. At Jever Oberstlt Schumacher became Jagdfliegerführer 1 (Deutsche Bucht). Similar commands were set up in Luftflotten 2 and 3, as follows:

Jagdfliegerführer 2   GenMaj Hans von Döring at Dortmund
Jagdfliegerführer 3   GenMaj Hans Klein at Wiesbaden

Following the loss of two of its Gruppen to JG 1, JG 77 moved JGr 102 to Bonn-Hangelar and I/JG 77 to Odendorf on 12th.

19/12/39

Despite the losses of 18th, operations continued over the North Sea virtually unabated. On the very next day, 19 December, 19 He 111s of I/KG 26 were out on an armed reconnaissance over the area between Norway and the Shetlands. One of the bombers encountered one of the elderly Saro London flyingboats of 240 Squadron (K6525) to the east of the Shetlands, and the two at once became engaged in combat. Fire from the bomber struck the starboard engine and fuselage, and mortally wounded the pilot, Flt Lt V.M.P. Pan. Plt Off R.E. Hunter, the second pilot, took over and landed on the sea to allow first aid to be given, but Pan died ten minutes later. Hunter therefore took off again and returned to Sullom Voe, where the flyingboat was found to be a write-off. The gunners estimated that they had obtained a few hits on the starboard engine of the attacking Heinkel, and indeed the bomber had been hit, crash-landing on return having sustained 30% damage, the port engine having been put out of action. The crew had been planning to go out on dates that evening, and had their best uniforms hanging up on hangers in the aircraft, several of which they reported, had been ruined by bullet holes!

240 Squadron Saro London, K6525, is seen from the cockpit of a I/KG 26 He 111 as the two aircraft were locked in combat on 19 December. Both suffered damage. *(via A. Thomas)*

20–21/12/39

During 20th six Blenheims each from 21 and 82 Squadrons went off early on a routine reconnaissance over the North Sea. One Bf 109E from II/JG 77 attempted to intercept but was hit by fire from the 82 Squadron formation, returning to Wangerooge with 45% damage.

Next day on 21 December another unescorted bomber formation was sent off over the North Sea. This time it comprised 24 Hampdens — three from 83 Squadron, nine from 49 Squadron and 12 from 44 Squadron — which were to search for the battlecruiser *Deutschland*, which had been reported at sea off Norway. The bombers failed to find their target, but also did not approach the German coast and thereby escaped interception — by the Luftwaffe. As they returned, their approach was reported by British coastal radar in Scotland as a big raid coming in, both the Spitfire squadrons at Drem being scrambled. The fighter pilots soon identified the formation as friendly, but unfortunately not before two 44 Squadron aircraft, which had become detached from the rest of the flight, had been attacked and shot down into the Firth of Forth (Flg Off R.J. Sansom's L4089 and Flt Lt P.F. Dingwall's L4090), by a pair of 602 Squadron pilots. Fortunately it proved possible to rescue all but one member of one of the crews.

22/12/39

There was no mistake next day (22nd), although 602 Squadron again demonstrated a sad lack of aircraft recognition expertise. Red Section was on patrol over Crail at 16,000 feet, when at 1029 they encountered two aircraft which they identified as He 115 floatplanes carrying mines beneath their wings. How Flt Lt J.D. Urie, Flg Off C.H. Maclean and Flg Off Strong made this identification is hard to reconcile with the facts — the aircraft were in fact a pair of Ju 88s from I/KG 30 on a reconnaissance over the Firth of Forth. In all other respects the reports tally however; the Spitire pilots attacked without apparent results, but Air Ministry Intelligence later reported that one of the intruders had failed to return to base, coming down in the sea. In fact one of the bombers had been hit and crashed on return, suffering 50% damage.

27/12/39
A bad month for the RAF was rounded off with two more losses on 27th. Two Blenheims from 107 Squadron took off in bitter weather to make a strategic reconnaissance over Jade Bay, the Schillig Roads and the Wilhelmshaven area generally, one air gunner suffering an attack of frostbite during the sortie. One aircraft — L8779, flown by Plt Off K. Laxton — was intercepted and shot down near Langeooge by Oberstlt Schumacher, Kommodore of JG 1, crashing into the sea off Spiekerooge Island with the loss of the crew. On this same date an Anson of Coastal Command's 269 Squadron (K6286, Plt Off A.D. McDonald) went into the sea east of the Orkneys during a patrol. Again however, the aggressive Hudson crews of 220 Squadron were in action on this date. Flt Lt Sheahan in Hudson 'N' encountered one of six 2/KüFlGr 906 Do 18s which were undertaking various reconnaissances over the area. Sheahan opened his attack, but the flyingboat was quickly joined by a second. Despite being outnumbered, the British crew thought that they had obtained hits on both Dorniers before being forced to withdraw by fuel shortage. The fire of Sheahan's gunners had been excellent and 8L+CK was hard hit, Oblt zur See Steinhart being obliged to force-land at once on the sea, one of the crew being killed during this operation. The remaining three men were rescued by the Swedish steamer *Boden*.

20/12/39
Despite the severe weather which had so restricted operations over France during most of December, the end of the month saw some slight resumption of aerial activity as the skies cleared a little on 20th. On that date a Potez 637 (No 20) of GR I/33 left Saint-Dizier to make a photo reconnaissance over the Mayence-Frankfurt sector. Over Pirmasens the aircraft was attacked by Bf 109Es of I/JG 51. The damaged French aircraft escaped at low level, but was then hit again by Flak and crashed in flames in the Landstuhl region, where the wounded crew became prisoners.

21/12/39
Another Potez 637 (No 14), this time an aircraft of GR II/33, was shot down on 21st, but on this occasion the attacker was an RAF Hurricane of 73 Squadron, the pilot of which (Flt Lt R.E. Lovett) attacked under the impression that he had intercepted a Do 17. The crew had no chance, and while the pilot managed to bale out after suffering severe wounds, also breaking a leg when he struck the tailplane, Lt Castellana and Adj Pernot were both killed by fire from the Hurricane's machine guns. The stricken Lovett, a pilot note for his 'unluckiness', visited the gravely ill pilot in hospital in an effort to make his peace. The latter treated the matter with considerable fatalism; "C'est la geurre" he told Lovett. A further Po 637 was also lost on this date when No 41 of GR I/52 crashed north of Schirmeck; Adj Le Saoûlt's crew of three were all killed, and no reason for its demise could be found.

Meanwhile 12 MS 406s from GC II/7 escorted a Potez 63-11 of GR I/55 over the lines in the Karlsruhe-Aachen area. Here they were spotted by ten Bf 109Es from the new I/JG 54's Stab and 2 Staffel, led by Maj Hans-Jürgen von Cramon-Traubadel. Four of these dived on the Moranes, whilst the remaining six went after the Potez. The German pilots were relatively inexperienced, and the reconnaissance aircraft was able to elude combat and return safely to base. The Moranes turned into those which attacked them, and the Germans broke formation at once. Von Cramon did much to save the situation. The Staffelkapitän, Hpt Paulizsch, was hit at once and wounded in the legs, baling out of his damaged aircraft north-west of Freiburg; von Cramon beat off his attacker, claiming to have shot it down. Uffz Hans Wagner's aircraft was hit in the starboard wing and flaps, but again von Cramon went to the rescue, claiming this assailant probably shot down. Von Cramon then engaged a Morane which he described as apparently being flown by a 'green' pilot, and obtained strikes on its engine, whereupon it crash-landed among some young trees; only this latter claim was confirmed.

During the melee, S/Lt Gauthier claimed one Messerschmitt shot down over Sponek, and Sgt Chef Panhard one over Achern, while a third was claimed as a probable over the Gottenheim area by S/Lt De Fraville and Sgt Lamblin. Gauthier was hit and severely wounded, crash-landing his badly-damaged aircraft on the west bank of the Rhine near Artzenhein. It seems possible that he was in fact attacked twice by von Cramon, once when attacking one of the other Bf 109s, and again when attempting to control his aircraft after suffering wounds — hence the description of a 'green' pilot, flying ineptly.

During the day two patrols of H-75As from GC II/4 were engaged over Bitsche by 12 Bf 109Es of 2/JG 53 in an inconclusive combat. The Germans recorded no claims or losses, although Sgt Coisenau claimed one Messerschmitt shot down, which he reported crashed in German lines near Riming-Lettweiler.

Despite over three months of engagements over France and the North Sea between aircraft of the various combatants, there had not yet been a single occasion on which British and German fighters had come face to face. Over France Armée de l'Air pilots had had several opportunities to pit their skill against their opposite numbers, though as often as not encountering the older models of the Messerschmitt which their H-75As and Moranes at least equalled in performance. It was never to be the RAF's luck to meet such opponents, for

One of 139 Squadron's Blenheim IVs newly-arrived in France; this is XD-M, N6227.

while aircraft of Bomber Command had on occasions fought duels with Bf 109D-equipped units, the fighters were to meet only the more potent E versions — and usually in the hands of the 'cream' of the Luftwaffe's Jagdflieger; further, as 1940 now approached the Luftwaffe was beginning to get supplies of the more heavily-armed E-3 variant, with a pair of wing-mounted 20mm cannon replacing two of the 7.9mm machine guns.

22/12/39

The first such clash finally occurred on 22 December when 11 Bf 109Es of III/ JG 53 took off in the early afternoon to cover two Do 17s of 1(F)/123 on a reconnaissance west of Saarbrücken. French DCA fire was seen north-east of Metz, and then three fighters were spotted below. These were aircraft of 73 Squadron, led by Plt Off Waller. Diving from great height to attack, Hpt Werner Mölders reported: "I shot at the aircraft on the left. It began to 'swim' immediately — I must have hit the pilot. The aircraft burned, and crashed close to a village." Initially Mölders identified his victim as an MS 406. The crash was witnessed by Oblt Wolf-Dietrich Wilcke, who reported "Shortly afterwards a second Hurricane went down in uncontrolled manoeuvres, and crashed into a forest, bursting into flames." This was probably shot down by Oblt Hans von Hahn; "I remembered the orders of 'Vati' Mölders to 'go up to the enemy and sit up straight behind the gunsight'. Then I pushed the gun button, the Hurricane went into a slight turn and just at that moment it was hit by a cannon shell under the cabin. My burst must have hit the pilot. The Hurricane tipped over, a blast of flame, and like a fiery comet the aircraft crashed down."

The Hurricanes crashed at Altroff and Homburg-Budange, Sgts R.M. Perry (N2385) and J. Winn (L1967) being killed; both had been shot through the head in the initial attacks. Plt Off Waller claimed to have shot down one of the Bf 109s, although it was thought at the time that possibly he had shot down one of the Hurricanes by mistake, since only the two wrecks were found. It is more likely that he fired at one Messerschmitt which broke away, and that he then saw one of the Hurricanes falling in flames and took it to be his victim. At any event it was an unfortunate introduction to the Messerschmitt for the Hurricane pilots.

29/12/39

The last action of note during 1939 occurred on 29 December when Flt Lt J.G. Sanders of 615 Squadron took up a Gladiator on a weather test. While so engaged he spotted a weather reconnaissance He 111 of Wekusta 26 well above and gave chase. He finally reached 23,000 feet where he was able to open fire and obtain hits on it. The Heinkel at once dived into cloud and he was unable to judge the result of his attack.

On 26 December meanwhile, Plt Off R.F. Martin of 73 Squadron had returned to his unit, having escaped without undue difficulty from his internment in Luxembourg. Allowed out for exercise on a foggy day, he had lengthened his circuit gradually each time, until he was able simply to melt way into the 'murk'. One of the captured Bf 109Es — the ex 2/JG 71 aircraft, lost by the Luftwaffe the previous month — was flown to the United Kingdom for full evaluation. Handed over to the RAF at Coulommiers, it was flown by Wg Cdr McKenna and escorted during the flight by a Hudson.

By now Fighter Command's expansion programme was bearing its first fruit.

Aside from 152 Squadron, 222, 229 and 263 Squadrons had all become operational during December, albeit with their interim equipment of Blenheim IFs and Gladiators. At the same time 242 Squadron received Blenheim IFs and Battles, while 266 Squadron took on the latter type to advance the training programme. The period had also seen numerous changes of base within the command, the most important of these involving the departure northwards of a number of 11 Group units — notably 43 and 111 Squadrons.

Outlying units — particularly the Auxilliaries — had soon moved to regular airfields, 25 and 501 Squadrons moving from Filton to Northolt and Tangmere respectively, while 610 Squadron moved from Hooton Park to Wittering and 611 Squadron from Finningley to Leconfield. With the advent of the attacks by X Fliegerkorps on Scotland and the north-east coast of England, Acklington and the Scottish airfields became of more importance for 12 and 13 Group units, 41, 46 and 609 Squadrons all being involved in moves here. Martlesham Heath also became a very important base for coastal patrol duties, 17, 25, 29 and 504 Squadrons maintaining detachments here at various times, while 56 Squadron moved there during October (though continuing to maintain detachments at the unit's home base at North Weald). The new and as-yet non-operational 264 Squadron followed in December. In the south, Rochford (as a satellite to Hornchurch), Manston and Hawkinge (as satellites to Biggin Hill) were brought fully into use, with squadrons operating from them on a rotating basis.

More of the new units were to begin receiving their main equipment early in the new year as production slowly moved into higher gear. During January 1940 242 and 253 Squadrons would receive Hurricanes, and 266 Squadron Spitfires while in February the already-established and operational 601 Squadron would exchange its Blenheim IFs for Hurricanes. These latter fighters also reached 145 and 229 Squadrons in March, while 92, 222 and 234 Squadrons got Spitfires.

The Luftwaffe too continued to expand. On 1 December II/KG 30 had become operational, joining X Fliegerkorps at Barth. Three more Kampfgruppen were established on 15th, III/KG 1 at Magdeburg-Burg, II/KG 28 at Jesau and III/KG 55 at Neudorf bei Oppeln.

**RAF Wellington bombers engaged in the
'Battle of the Heligoland Bight', 18 December, 1939**

9 Squadron

WS-	N2872	Sqn Ldr. A.J. Guthrie	Shot down
WS-H	N2939	Flg Off J.T.I. Challes	Shot down
WS-	N2941	Flg Off D.B. Allison	Shot down
WS-	N2940	Plt Off E.F. Lines	Shot down
WS-	N2983	Sgt R. Hewitt	Ditched (crew picked up by trawler 'Erillas'; one dead. Believed shot down by Oblt Gresens, 2/ZG 76)
WS-	N2971	Flg Off W.J.Macrae	Force-landed North Coates, Cat 2 Damaged (Damage to starboard wing, rear fuselage and rudder; two wounded)
WS-C	N2873	Sgt F.C. Petts	Crashed on return; Cat 3 Destroyed
WS-D	N2964	Flt Lt. J.P. Grant	Landed
WS-F	N2981	Sgt T. Purdy	Landed

38 Squadron

HD-K	N2908	Flg Off MacFadden	Landed
HD-L	N2909	Flg Off Hopkins	Landed
HD-E	N2952	Sgt Sayers	Landed

37 Squadron

LF-A	N2888	Flg Off P.A. Wimberley	Shot down (Crash-landed and burned on Borkum; believed shot down by Lt Lent, 1/ZG 76)
LF-P	N2889	Flg Off O.J.T. Lewis	Shot down
LF-B	N2904	Sqn Ldr I.V. Hue-Williams	Shot down
LF-H	N2935	Flg Off A.T. Thompson	Shot down
LF-J	N2936	Sgt H. Ruse	Shot down (Crash-landed Spiekeroog; crew POW. Believed shot down by Oberstlt Schumacher, JG 1)
LF-E	N2871	Flg Off Lemon	Crash-landed on return, Cat 3 Destroyed

149 Squadron

OJ-	N2984	Flt Lt Dugwit	Turned back early
OJ-	N2962	Plt Off J.H.C. Spiers	Shot down (seen falling in vertical dive in flames after diving beam attack by Bf110)
OJ-	N2961	Flg Off W.F. Briden	Ditched (Ran out of fuel due to loss through bullet holes in tanks. Came down in sea 40 miles from Cromer; whole crew lost)
OJ-	N2960	Wg Cdr R. Kellet	Crashed on return; Cat 2 Damaged
OJ-	N2866	Flg Off Riddlesworth	Crashed on return; Cat 2 Damaged
OJ-	N2980	Sqn Ldr Harris	Crashed on return; Cat 2 Damaged

NB all aircraft Wellington Mark IAs

**Luftwaffe Fighter claims of Jagdgeschwader 1,
18 December 1939**

Stab/JG 1

1435	Oberstlt Carl Schumacher	Wellington	N Spiekerooge

10 (Nachtjagd)/JG 26

1430	Oblt Johannes Steinhoff	Wellington	25-35 Km SSW Heligoland
1435	Oblt Johannes Steinhoff	Wellington	25-35 Km SSW Heligoland
*1430	Fw Willy Szuggar	Wellington	25-35 Km SSW Heligoland
1435	Uffz Werner Gerhardt	Wellington	25-35 Km SSW Heligoland
*1435	Uffz August Wilke	Wellington	25-35 Km SSW Heligoland
*1435	Uffz Martin Portz	Wellington	25-35 Km SSW Heligoland

Jagdgruppe 101

1450	Oblt Dietrich Robitzsch	Wellington	20 Km SW Heligoland
1450	Oblt Rolf Kaldrack	Wellington	20 Km SW Heligoland

II/JG 77

↑	Uffz Otto Niemeyer	Wellington	↑
*	Uffz Otto Niemeyer	Wellington	
	Oblt Helmut Henz	Wellington	
	Lt Georg Schirmböck	Wellington	Between N and
1430-	Oblt Anton Pointner	Wellington	NW Wangerooge
1450	Fw Hans Troitzsch	Wellington	and N of the West point of
	Fw Hans Troitzsch	Wellington	Norderney
	Oblt Franz-Heinz Lang	Wellington	
*	Oblt Wilhelm Peters	Wellington	
↓	Lt Winfried Schmidt	Wellington	↓
1430	Uffz Erwin Heilmayr	Wellington	30 Km SSW Heligoland
*1450	Oblt Berthold Jung	Wellington	20 Km NW Borkum
*1450	Ofw Droste	Wellington	20 Km NW Borkum
*1450	Uffz Holck	Wellington	20 Km NW Borkum

I/ZG 76

1435	Hpt Wolfgang Falck	Wellington	20 Km SW Heligoland
*1445	Hpt Wolfgang Falck	Wellington	20 Km SW Heligoland
1435	Uffz Heinz Fresia	Wellington	20 Km SW Heligoland
1445	Uffz Heinz Fresia	Wellington	20 Km SW Heligoland
1442	Lt Helmut Lent	Wellington	5 Km N Borkum
1450	Lt Helmut Lent	Wellington	10 Km WNW Borkum
1445	Oblt Hans Jäger	Wellington	NW Borkum
*1445	Oblt Gordon Gollob	Wellington	N Western point of Langeoog
1440	Fw Hans Gröning	Wellington	E Langeoog
1445	Ofw Georg Fleischmann	Wellington	NW Spiekerooge
1500	Oblt Walter Gresens	Wellington	25 Km NW Borkum
1500	Lt Maximilian Graeff	Wellington	25 Km WNW Borkum
1500	Uffz Ernst Kalinowski	Wellington	25 Km WNW Borkum
1500	Lt Gustav Uellenbeck	Wellington	50 Km N Ameland
1505	Lt Gustav Uellenbeck	Wellington	50 Km N Ameland

Totals

	Confirmed	Unconfirmed*
Stab/JG 1	1	–
10(N)/JG 26	3	3
JGr 101	2	–
II/JG 77	9	5
I/ZG 76	13	2
	27	10

*Marked on above list.

Chapter 6

WINTER TIGHTENS ITS GRIP

For the air forces the new year of 1940 came in more like a lamb than a lion! While the Armée de l'Air still struggled to obtain more new aircraft for its painfully slow re-equipment programme, the RAF saw the formation of no further new units, as the mass of recently-formed fighter squadrons awaited their operational equipment. The Luftwaffe continued to grow however, while further dispositions also took place. On the first day of the new year several additional radar sites were designated:

Luftflotte 2 – two units under Lt Werry on the Heinsberg/Birgden, north of Aachen
Luftflotte 3 – a third unit set up under Lt Jauk at Kandel/Schwarzwald.

The following new units were also established:

> Stab and III/KG 30 at Barth with X Fliegerdivision
> III/KG 54 at Pilsen under Gen zbV Luftflotte 4
> II/KG 76 at Wels under Gen zbV Luftflotte 4
> III/JG 3 at Jena under Gen zbV Luftflotte 4

Luftflotte 3 was strengthened on 5th by the arrival of ZG 26, which transferred to the following bases:

> Stab/ZG 26 to Crailsheim
> I/ZG 26 to Crailsheim
> II/ZG 26 to Gelnhausen
> JGr 126 to Lippstadt
> V(Z)/LG 1 to Würzberg

Stab, I and II/LG 1 moved to Luftflotte 1 to re-equip with Ju 88s.

When no further major raids on the naval bases in North Germany developed, I(J)/LG 2 was posted back to Gymnich on 13th, this time to join JG 27, while JG 77 was reinforced by I/JG 3 at Peppenhoven. Finally, at the end of the month Stab/JG 54 was to be established under the command of Maj Martin Mettig.

With Western Europe still firmly in the grip of the harshest winter for half a century there was little of note happening as the troops at the front stagnated in boredom and discomfort. Ice, snow and thick cloud kept activity in the air to a minimum, as Europe drifted into its fifth month of 'non-war'.

1/1/40

The North Sea Triangle, despite the inclement weather, remained a little more active, and on 1 January the year of 1940 was heralded in by a morning anti-shipping raid by six Ju 88s from I/KG 30. While four of the bombers attacked vessels in the Scapa Flow-Shetlands area, the remaining two were engaged by a pair of Hudsons from 220 Squadron, the crews of which identified their opponents as He 111s. It seems that Gladiator fighters from the Sullom Voe Fighter Flight also joined the combat, Flg Offs T.W. Gillen and R.A. Winter claiming two bombers shot down, while the crew of Plt Off G.W.F. Carey's Hudson 'L' also claimed one and reported hits on the second as it escaped into clouds. One Junkers did indeed crash into the sea, and was later confirmed as destroyed by the Royal Navy. The other Hudson, 'T', N7232, was badly damaged by return fire and subsequently went into the sea 20 miles off St Abb's Head. Neither Flt Lt T.H. Clarke's crew nor the German crew were found. Confirmed victories were granted both to Carey and his crew, and to one of the Gladiator pilots.

2/1/40

Next day Bomber Command sent out some of its newly-armoured Wellingtons on their first armed reconnaissance since the fateful operation of 18 December. On this occasion 17 aircraft made for the German Bight, including three from 9 Squadron, six from 38 Squadron, three from 49 Squadron, two from 99 Squadron and three from 149 Squadron. The formation had completed its reconnaissance and was on the home leg early in the afternoon of this bleak Monday, when the 149 Squadron trio were jumped by a Schwarm of Bf 110s from I/ZG 76, led by Lt Wilhelm Herget (reported by the British crews as 12-15 strong!). In a few minutes it was all over; Ofw Georg Fleischmann attacked the leader of the 'vic', firing from astern and hitting the starboard wing and tail unit. He reported that at 1512 the bomber blew up, scattering wreckage widely. Lt Sibo Habben claimed the second at 1515, firing on the starboard aircraft and setting its left wing alight, at which the pilot jettisoned the bombs into the sea before crashing in flames. Uffz Grams chased the third machine down to 2,400 feet where he reported it went into the sea pouring black smoke at 1520. In fact only two Wellingtons were lost, Flg Off A.A.T. Bullock's N2943 being seen to go into the sea out of control while Sgt J. Morricie's N2946 was last seen going down pursued by several Bf 110s subsequently crashing west of Heligoland. It seems possible that Fleischmann mistook the jettisoned bombs for falling wreckage, and that he and Habben double-claimed on Bullock's aircraft. The third Wellington N2968, returned safely to base, Plt Off Innes' crew claiming to have shot down two Messerschmitts. Two were indeed hit, each having one engine put out of action, while one of the observers (Uffz Petzold) was wounded; both aircraft were able to return safely to base however.

Over the Franco-German frontier on this date there were two minor engagements. Seven Bf 109Es from I/JG 53 were engaged by 12 H-75As from GC II/5. A burst of fire from one of the French fighters hit Oblt Hans Ohly's Messerschmitt, wounding the pilot who crash-landed near Hoppstädten and was rushed to hospital. Cne Destaillac and Lt Houze both reported firing at two Messerschmitts without obvious result, while Lt Huvet claimed to have hit both, seeing one emitting grey smoke; it seems likely therefore that it was Huvet's fire which had brought down Ohly's aircraft; Lt Walter Rupp's 'Weisse 13' returned hit by 13 bullets. Two Do 17s from 1(F)/123 undertook airfield reconnaissance in the Laon-St. Quentin and Lyons area, one of these being intercepted near Laon by MS 406s of GC III/2. The Morane pilots managed to obtain hits on the engines of this Dornier, at which the pilot wisely abandoned his sortie and evaded further attacks, returning to base. That night saw the first operational sorties by GB II/15. Two Farman 222s flown by the two Escadrille commanders, Cne Lachèvre and Santini dropped over a million leaflets on Nuremberg. The Groupe was to undertake 12 similar missions before 10 May. At the time a story circulated that epitomises the spirit of the 'Phoney War' period. One commander of a French bomber unit asked a crew who had just returned if everything had gone well. "Yes," replied the pilot, "but to speed things up we decided to drop the parcels of leaflets unopened." "Good gracious!" exclaimed the CO, "I hope you didn't hurt anyone!"

3/1/40

Next day, Tuesday 3 January, Moranes were again in action. Two Potez 63-11s were sent out on reconnaissance, one over the Lörrach-Schöpfheim area, near the Swiss border, and one to the Kandern-Mambach area, deep within German lines. The first aircraft was escorted by six Moranes from GC II/7, led by Cne Hugo, while six more from the same Groupe were led by S/Lt Gruyelle to escort the second Potez. At 1112 over Märkt three Bf 109Ds of JGr 176 which were providing top cover for a Dornier, attacked Gruyelle's flight; Sgt Planchard's aircraft was slightly damaged and he broke away to land at Colmar. Gruyelle and Sgt Martin tried to attack the Dornier, but it escaped, although they thought some damage had been inflicted. Three more Bf 109Ds attacked the other formation, Cne Hugo claiming one probably shot down over Lörrach, while Sgt Chef Jonaszick fired at another. He was sure that he had hit the pilot, for the aircraft went down in an inverted spin, and he reported that it crashed into the ground near Effringen. In fact the aircraft had been hit in the engine and force-landed near Schlinensen, 17 kilometres north-west of Lörrach, with 50% damage. On their return the French pilots reported that these Messerschmitts appeared to be faster and more powerful than any they had met before — hardly the case, as they were D models!

During the morning of this day Blenheim WV-B, L1410, of 18 Squadron took off for a reconnaissance over north-western Germany and the Westwall, with Flg Off Kempster at the controls. No sooner was the aircraft underway, than it was intercepted in error by a Hurricane, which fortunately inflicted no damage. Subsequently, as it passed over Aachen at 0930 it was attacked by a trio of Bf 109Es from I/JG 77. Fw Gotthard Goltzsche and Fw Adolf Borchers closed in, ripping the Blenheim with fire, and the stricken aircraft turned away for the Belgian frontier, where it fell out of control near Eupen. The air gunner was killed attempting to bale out, the other members of the crew successfully taking to their parachutes and being interned; the victory was credited to Goltzsche.

10/1/40

Almost a week elapsed before the weather allowed further activity, but on

18 Squadron Blenheim IV WV-B, L1410, shot down near Eupen in Belgium by Fw Gotthard Goltzsche of I/JG 77 on 3 January. *(via R. Cronin/A. Thomas)*

10 January a spell of brighter conditions began which resulted in four days' of much-increased flying during which some fierce engagements took place in both major areas of conflict. Around noon on 10th a Potez 63-11 from GR II/55 crewed by Lt Felix, Lt Boulard and Sgt Chef Chancrin set off on a photographic reconnaissance sortie over the Freiburg area. As the aircraft began its return flight at low altitude, it was attacked by six Bf 109Es of I/JG 54, two from the Stabskette and four from 1 Staffel. The Staffelkapitän, Oblt Reinhard Seiler, claimed to have shot the Potez down near Colmar at 1215, and indeed it crashed at Blotzheim, on the left bank of the Rhine, where the crew were all killed. Chancrin was believed to have shot down one of the attacking fighters in flames before his death; Lt Schütz was killed when his Messerschmitt hit the ground near Hirtzfelden during the chase, but it was considered by his comrades that this was probably due to pilot error during the low level engagement, rather than return fire.

A dozen Bf 109Es from III/JG 53 were also in action, engaging Moranes of GC III/7 over the frontier near Perl where Lt Walter Radlick fired on one French fighter and reported seeing hits, but failed to see it crash; it was nonetheless listed as the Gruppe's tenth victory. S/Lt Renaud's Morane (No 233) was disabled in this combat, and he suffered wounds; he crash-landed at once at Metz. Meanwhile 15 H-75As of GC II/5 provided escort for a Potez 63 during the early afternoon, and the pilots of these caught sight of three Messerschmitts in the St Avold area. Calmly they climbed up sun, but while doing so three more Messerschmitts were seen; these fighters were from I/JG 2, engaged in a frontier patrol over the Saarbrücken area. Cne Portalis fired at the leader, who dived away towards the ground at such a speed that the Curtiss could not catch up. S/Lt Villacèque got a shot at the right-hand wingman but this was similarly lost. Sgt Legrand enjoyed more success however, engaging the third Messerschmitt in a long dogfight. Legrand claimed that his opponent fell in flames east of Kircheimhof at 1315, but in fact Lt Joachim Seegart got his aircraft down southwest of Zweibrücken with many hits in the engine and tail, and having been wounded himself. The aircraft was classified as 65% damaged and was written

154

off. Portalis and Villacèque then spotted a lone Bf 109 which they both engaged. Leaving a thick trail of smoke, this fled over Sarrebrück into its own lines, but the French pilots were sure that it had been hard hit. In fact a few days later a blood-stained cockpit canopy was found, and their claim was then confirmed as the Groupe's 15th of the war. Their opponent was without doubt another Bf 109E of I/JG 2 which force-landed 10% damaged at Höchst am Rhein with the pilot unhurt.

A third Bf 109 was reported by French observers to have been seen falling in flames for no apparent reason, and it would appear that this was either the aircraft of Lt Claus von Bohlen und Halbach of I/JG 76, which crashed vertically into the ground near Bitberg whilst on a frontier patrol — apparently due to oxygen failure — or that of Ofw Wilhelm von Balka of I/JG 51, which crashed near Strasbourg whilst on a similar patrol in bad weather. Von Balka's engine seized and caught fire and he was obliged to bale out, but in doing so he hit the tailplane and was badly injured. On reaching the ground he was hurried to a French hospital.

On the morning of this day occurred the now-famous 'Mechlen incident'. During the winter Hitler had insisted upon the planning of a Western offensive under the codename Operation 'Gelb', based loosely on the old Schlieffen Plan of 1914. Intended originally for implementation during the latter part of 1939, the operation had already been postponed four times by bad weather, but was now set for 17 January. On 9th Maj Hellmuth Reinberger, communications officer of Fliegerführer 220 of Luftflotte 2, was ordered to attend a secret conference at the Luftflotte headquarters in Cologne next morning, bringing with him the operations plan for the Luftflotte's proposed involvement in 'Gelb'. He was based at Münster, some 80 miles distant, and that night while drinking in the bar at the local airfield he complained to an old World War I flier, Reserve Major Hoenmanns, of the bad journey he faced on the morrow. Hoenmanns offered to fly him to his destination, an offer Reinberger gladly accepted, subject to the weather being good. 10 January dawned fine, and the pair set off in a Messerschmitt Bf 108 courier aircraft, but no sooner were they well on their way than the weather closed right in. In conditions of almost nil visibility Hoenmanns strayed right of course, and suddenly the engine cut, obliging him to crash-land at once through a row of poplars. To their horror the pair soon realised that they had come down in Belgium — in fact near Mechlen, a little to the north of Maastricht.

Reinberger at once attempted to burn his documents, but his cigarette lighter failed. He was able however, to borrow some matches from a passing peasant, and was so engaged when Belgian troops arrived. With the papers only partially destroyed, the two were taken to the local gendarmerie, where Reinberger managed to get hold of the papers again and to thrust them into the stove. A few partly burned fragments were retrieved by one of the Belgians, whereupon Reinberger tried to seize a pistol from the officer's belt in order to shoot himself. Realising that the documents were obviously important, the officer passed them 'up the line', and by nightfall they were in the hands of GHQ, where the half-burned remnants clearly indicated an invasion plan based on a drive through Holland and Belgium.

During the day the German troops had begun moving up to the frontier for 'Gelb', and a furious Hitler, threatening firing squads for the unfortunate majors, determined to proceed with the operation notwithstanding. However

Pilots of GC I/5; from the left, Sgt Gérard Muselli, Sgt Chef Vuillemin, Sgt Frantisek Perina (Czech), Lt Edmond Marin la Meslée, Capt Jean-Marie Accart and Lt Marcel Rouquette. Marin la Meslée, Accart and Muselli were involved in action on 11 January.

the weather now broke again, and when news of Belgian and Dutch mobilization as a result of the incident was received, the invasion was postponed indefinitely, and subsequently considerably replanned.

As a direct result of this affair, Felmy, the Luftflotte 2 commander, was removed from his post and replaced by Albert Kesselring. Reinberger and Hoenmanns were interned, and subsequently after 10 May, were transferred to British captivity, being shipped to Canada. In 1943 Hoenmanns was repatriated due to heart trouble, returning home to face a court martial. This exonerated him completely, as he had not been aware of the documents that his passenger had been carrying.

11/1/40

On 11 January, the day following the incident, a further success was achieved by the French fighters when at 0945 Lt Edmond Marin la Meslée and S/Lt Rey of GC I/5 chased a reconnaissance Do 17P of 3(F)/11 from Koblenz/Karthausen, which they intercepted at 22,000 feet over Verdun, harrying it until they finally caused it to force-land near the border at Haucourt, close to Longwy. The crew of three, including the pilot, Ofw Hugo Erlbeck, were taken prisoner, Marin la Meslée commenting favourably on the excellent airmanship of the wounded Erlbeck. A second Do 17 was also attacked at 1100 by two more of the Groupe's H-75As flown by Cne Accart and Sgt Chef Muselli. The French considered that the aircraft had been disabled when it escaped across the Belgian frontier, and it was credited to the pair as a probable; in fact it had escaped without having sustained any damage. (Muselli was a future Dassault test pilot who won a world record in a Mirage III in June 1959, but was killed in a crash in 1970.)

12/1/40

Blenheim L8859 of 114 Squadron was despatched on a reconnaissance over the German airfields at Greimerath, near Saarbrücken, and at Losheim and Wahlen in the Merzig area during the morning of 12 January.

Plt Off G. Turner climbed to 20,000 feet for the sortie. At 1245 he was attacked from below by a Schwarm of Bf 109Es from I/JG 76, Lt Malischewski inflicting severe damage and believing that he had succeeded in shooting the intruder down. The crew of the Blenheim subsequently reported that the recently-fitted armour plate proved most effective, all surviving the attack although bullets tore the observer's flying clothes, piercing his helmet and knocking him unconscious. With one dead engine, Turner managed to nurse the crippled aircraft to a force-landing at the French airfield at Metz; the Blenheim was discovered to have been damaged beyond repair.

Do 17s carried out many sorties in the opposite direction during 12th, but while two of these were intercepted by French fighters, no losses were suffered and all regained their bases safely.

13/1/40

Next day a Do 17S-O was sent out by 1(F)/ObdL to reconnoitre Southern England, flown by Lt de Res Theodor Rosarius; the Do 17S-O was a specially-equipped adaptation of the Do 17P, only three of which were built. The condensation trail left by this aircraft, T5+FH, at 30,000 feet was spotted over Calais as it crossed the French coast on its way westwards, by a pair of H-75A pilots from GC I/4, Cne Barbier and Sgt Lemaire, as they were on patrol. Flying at such a height and at full speed, the Dornier proved a formidable opponent to catch, but as it flew west, the aircraft also dived to sea level. Cne Barbier, flying the faster of the two Curtisses, kept after it. The Dornier then turned back, with Barbier now close behind, snapping out short bursts from time to time. Finally he hit it, for the Dornier lowered its undercarriage as it approached the French coast, apparently to attempt a landing. As it touched the ground the undercarriage collapsed, and it ended up on its belly. The whole crew were captured, and the aircraft examined. The French were very impressed by the fantastic camera array, which greatly surpassed their own reconnaissance equipment in both quality and quantity.

This special reconnaissance aircraft of 1(F)/ObdL, Do 17S-0 T5+FH, flown by Lt de Res Theodor Rosarius, was intercepted returning from a sortie over England on 13 January, and shot down by two H-75As of GC I/4. It proved to contain an impressive array of cameras. *(R. Violett via C-J. Ehrengardt)*

157

Whilst the West Front had been active, so too had the North Sea zone through much of the same period. On 9 January ten He 111s of 2/KG 26 flew a late morning anti-shipping operation, covering the whole of the British east coast from the Thames Estuary to Kinnaird Head. They were followed in the afternoon by two more Heinkels from the Geschwaderstab. Aircraft from 2 Staffel sank the coastal steamer *Gowrie* (689 tons) and the freighters *Oak Grove* (1,985 tons) and *Upminster* (1,013 tons). Next day at around 0730 six more He 111s from Stab/KG 26 and 1(F)/122 had flown shipping reconnaissances between the Shetlands and the Norwegian coast, being followed at 0840 by ten He 111s from 5/KG 26 and half an hour later by ten more from 6/KG 26. One of the Stab/KG 26 aircraft was intercepted during its return flight by a patrolling Hudson of 233 Squadron, the British aircraft at once attacking and expending all its ammunition before breaking off the combat. The Heinkel was hit 20-30 times but was able, with the undercarriage shot-up, to crash-land, suffering 25% damage. During the morning 2 Group of Bomber Command despatched several formations of Blenheims for sweeps over the North Sea. One of these comprising 12 aircraft from 110 Squadron which had taken off at 1015, led by Flt Lt K.C. Doran, DFC, was intercepted around midday by four Bf 110s of I/ZG 76 near Heligoland.

Hpt Falck made the first attack on the aircraft on the extreme right, by which time the Blenheims had put their noses down to gain speed and were flying only a few feet above the sea. Falck fired and saw his chosen victim lose speed and fall back. He made several more attacks, reporting that the Blenheim blew up at 1257. Lt Helmut Fallbusch attacked the next bomber on the right and claimed that it had gone into the sea in flames at 1308, while Lt Maxmilian Graeff then attacked the next in line, reporting that it left the formation two minutes later, streaming smoke, and crashed into the sea as well. In fact only Sgt Hanne's P4859 failed to return, although Plt Off Aderne's N6213 was badly damaged, the undercarriage collapsing on landing, while Flg Off Pemberton's N6203 crashed at Manby on return and was destroyed; three more Blenheims suffered slight damage. The gunners claimed that one Bf 110 had gone into the sea, but in fact all four returned, although all suffered a little damage. 110 Squadron

He 111H of the very active I/KG 26 'Loewen' Geschwader. *(ECPA)*

158

subsequently recorded that a second fighter was understood to have force-landed in Denmark where the pilot was interned, but this was in fact a Bf 109D of JGr 101 which came down after the pilot, Uffz Melchert, became lost during a patrol.

11/1/40
Next day (11th) in the early afternoon seven He 111s from I/KG 26 again took off on anti-shipping sorties further south than on the previous day. Radar provided adequate warning and three Spitfires of 66 Squadron's Yellow Section from 'A' Flight were scrambled from Duxford. The three Sergeant-pilots, D. Stone leading, D.A.C. Hunt and M. Cameron, were vectored onto a 3 Staffel He 111H-3 (WNr 3579) flown by Lt de Res Horst Näther, which was attacking a trawler off Cromer. In clear conditions, with no wind, cloud or mist, Stone went in to attack first, but his aircraft was at once hit by a well-aimed burst of return fire, and he was forced to turn for home, force-landing on the beach as soon as he regained land. Cameron and Hunt maintained the chase, but were forced to break off and return, last seeing the Heinkel with some smoke pouring from the port engine. It was subsequently learned that one such bomber had force-landed in Denmark, where it had been destroyed by the crew, and on the strength of this a victory was credited to the trio. This was not their bomber however, for unbeknown to them their victim, which had been hard hit, had later crashed into the sea off Heligoland with the loss of all the crew. A second Heinkel from 2 Staffel (Uffz Alfred Reimer, WNr 5390) had been hit by anti-aircraft fire during an attack on shipping off the mouth of the Humber, and it was this that had come down in Denmark, where the crew had been interned. Other 2 Staffel crews sank the trawler *Croxton* and the freighter *Keynes* (1,706 tons), sailing in ballast from Southampton to Sunderland.

During the day Hudson N7262 of 224 Squadron flown by Plt Off A. Barkley, attacked three destroyers of the 4th Zerstörer Flotilla near Horn's Reef whilst on a North Sea patrol, but was shot down by their Flak defences. A patrolling Anson from 500 Squadron, MK-0, was attacked off the North German coast by six Bf 109s but managed to escape with only slight damage.

12–13/1/40
On 12th seven He 111s of 1/KG 26 operated from the Wash to Newcastle, sinking the trawlers *William Ivey* and *Valdora*; there were no interceptions. 13 January was however, to be a different story. Early on this Friday morning a lone reconnaissance He 111 from 1(F)/122, flown by Ofw Helmut Brauer, approached the Firth of Forth, but was intercepted by 602 Squadron's Red Section (Flt Lt M. Robinson; Flg Off W.H. Coverley; Flg Off C.H. Maclean). The Spitfire pilots claimed that they had inficted serious damage on the bomber before it escaped in cloud. The respite was only brief however, for 111 Squadron's Red Section had also scrambled, the three Hurricane pilots — Flt Lt Powell, Flg Off Dutton and Sgt H.L. Gunn — harrying the Heinkel until it crashed into the sea near Farne Island, some 15 miles east of Carnostie. The pilot was seen to clamber into a dinghy and a search by rescue vessels found and picked him up. There was no sign of any of the rest of the crew.

14/1/40
Next day however, whilst returning from another convoy patrol, two of

43 Squadron's Hurricanes collided and crashed, Sgts E.G.P. Mullinger and H.J. Steeley losing their lives in L2066 and L1734.

19/1/40

It was not until 19 January that any encounters again occurred, but on this date a single reconnaissance He 111 once more approached the coast of Scotland. The target area was as usual the Firth of Forth, but on this occasion the aircraft had been despatched by 1(F)/ObdL (Werk Nr 5542, Lt de Res Johann Fokuhl). Sgt J.R. Caister of 603 Squadron was on a shipping patrol alone in his Spitfire when the approach of the intruder was reported, and he at once set off to intercept, catching the Heinkel off Aberdeen at 1205. He opened fire, but due to the extreme cold several of his guns failed to operate, while those that did, achieved no obvious result. At 1235 the squadron's Red Section, comprising Flg Off J.G.E. Haig, Flg Off H.K. Macdonald and Plt Off G.K. Gilroy, scrambled after the aircraft, catching it 20 miles east of Aberdeen. They attacked, seeing the undercarriage drop down and smoke pour from the bomber, but observed no definite results. In fact the bomber fell lower and lower as it tried to reach home, finally crashing into the sea; two bodies were later recovered.

In France meanwhile the British Expeditionery Air Force had now finalised the location of the headquarters and command structure on 15th. British Air Forces in France (BAFF) under Air Marshal A.S. Barratt was headquartered at Chauny, while the subordinate commands were located, AASF under Air Vice-Marshal P.H.C. Playfair at Reims, and the Air Component under Air Vice-Marshal C.H.B. Blount at Maroeuil.

19–20/1/40

There had been little aerial activity here for some days, but on 19 January whilst on a 'patrouille a priori' over the Mulhouse area, six Moranes of GC II/7 were vectored onto intruders at 1115, flying at 20,000 feet. These turned out to be Bf 109Es of 2/JG 54 which Lt Gruyelle's section attacked over Bantzenheim. Gruyelle made repeated attacks on one Messerschmitt which it was reported landed at Strünshütte in French Alsace, where the pilot, an NCO, was made prisoner. S/Lt De Fraville attacked another Bf 109 which was on Gruyelle's tail but lost sight of this. He thought it had crash-landed in Germany, near Eschbach, but this was not confirmed. In fact it seems that Gruyelle's victim had crashed in flames rather than landed, Uffz Ernst Wagner having baled out wounded, and been taken prisoner. His was the only aircraft lost on this date. Next day a Do 17M of the Nachtkette (night flight) of 3(H)/13, returning at dawn from a nocturnal sortie, crashed east of Pforzheim, possibly as a result of damage sustained from French DCA fire. Fw Paul Auer and his crew were killed.

On 10 January the last sortie had been flown by the initial detachment of photographic reconnaissance Spitfires, which had been sent to France by the PDU. Now however a PDU (Overseas Squadron) had been formed for service on the continent. For security reasons it received the obscure Coastal Command designation 212 Squadron, and arrived in France on 18th, the first sorties being flown next day. January also marked the announcement of the first decoration for the RAF in France, when on 14th the award of the DFC to 73 Squadron's successful New Zealander, Flg Off E.J. 'Cobber' Kain, was announced.

25/1/40
Following the activities of 19th, weather again forced a five day lull until 25 January. During the early afternoon of this latter date Blenheim L1280 of 57 Squadron, flown by Plt Off J.N.O'R. Blackwood, was despatched on a strategic reconnaissance sortie over North-West Germany. Several Luftwaffe fighter units were alerted, and the bomber was shot down in flames over Delfzijil, near Duisberg, by Fw Scherer of 2/JGr 102 in a Bf 109D; the crew were killed. Several reconnaissances were made over France by the Luftwaffe, one He 111 of 3(F)/121 being intercepted and driven off by Moranes of GC I/3, although no damage was inflicted.

29/1/40
Late in the month the North Sea area again exploded into life with a number of spirited combats. Nine He 111s of 6/KG 26 were sent out after shipping early on 29th, these splitting up to search for targets. At 0905 the Hurricanes of Red Section, 43 Squadron, were scrambled, Flt Lt C.B. Hull, Plt Off H.L. North and Sgt F.R. Carey finding one of the bombers ten miles south-east of Hartlepool at about 0945. The bomber at once slipped away into cloud, the rear gunner achieving one hit on Hull's aircraft (L1744) as it went! Meanwhile at 0938 yet another Red Section — this one from 609 Squadron, which had moved to Drem — was engaged in practice flying when ordered to intercept an enemy aircraft which was bombing trawlers in the mouth of the River Tay. An He 111 was seen at 1500 feet one mile out from the estuary, above a merchant vessel, and Flt Lt D. Persse-Joynt at once led Flg Off G.D. Ayre and Flg Off Edge in a line-astern attack on the bomber as it headed for the cloud. The trio gave chase until the aircraft could no longer be seen, and although all had fired, no hits were seen. Months later on 8 May 1940 they were advised that the bomber had come down at Wick, the captured pilot apparently having volunteered this information.

This was not in fact the case, for the Heinkel had suffered only slight damage. As it headed for base however, it became engaged with a Hudson, which attacked it. This would appear to have been aircraft 'D' of 220 Squadron, flown by Sgt Culver. Culver reported being attacked by a Bf 110, LAC Creegan, the turret gunner, returning fire and believing that he had shot it down, the aircraft diving away towards the sea with smoke pouring from the port engine. Culver also fired at it with his front guns, but missed. Return fire hit the Hudson ten times, one bullet shooting the navigator's pencil out of his hand! The Heinkel was in fact hit 20 times in one engine, but still managed to regain its base, where it crash-landed. On this date a Bf 110 pilot did report attacking a Hudson near Horn's Reef, but the patrol bomber escaped in cloud. It is possible that 'D' was in fact involved with both German aircraft, and that the gunner's report became garbled in the recording — or in the memories of the returning crew.

During December 152 Squadron, which had been formed in October with 603 Squadron's old Gladiators, had become operational. In January it had moved to Acklington to re-equip with Spitfires, but while doing so continued to maintain a single operational flight of the biplanes. At 1037 on 29th Red Section (yet another!) was scrambled to cover a convoy reported under attack, Plt Off Falkson leading the trio to the area where he saw a hostile aircraft circling over two ships and at once closed on it. The bomber crew opened fire immediately, gaining hits on two of the Gladiators before escaping unscathed into cloud. This was probably an He 111 of 2/KG 26, nine of which had followed the original 6 Staffel aircraft later in the morning.

Some Heinkels got through to the Shetlands during the day, five bombs falling within 500 yards of HMS *Coventry*, whilst further south the freighter *Stanborn* (2,881 tons) was sunk off Flamborough Head. Three Heinkels had each suffered 20% damage during interceptions on this date, one of 6 Staffel south-east of Hartlepool (43 Squadron), one of 2 Staffel near Kinnaird Head, and then again near Horn's Reef (609 and 220 Squadron) and one east of the Tyne Estuary (152 Squadron).

30/1/40

Next day KG 26 launched a larger anti-shipping effort, three He 111s from the Stabsstaffel and 23 more from II Gruppe setting out for the English east coast during the later morning. The II Gruppe crews enjoyed considerable success, sinking three freighters — *Bancrest* (4,450 tons), *Giralda* (2,178 tons) and *Highwave* (1,178 tons), and the tanker *Voreda* (7,216 tons), all heavy laden. One of the Stab aircraft was intercepted by 111 Squadron's Blue Section at about 1230, but escaped in cloud over May Island before an attack could be launched. However it seems that the aircraft had suffered some damage, for it force-landed at Neumunster on return, suffering 30% damage, and the crew reported a combat off the Moray Firth. Hurricanes from 43 Squadron were scrambled at 1240, and two of these had more luck. Flt Lt Hull and Sgt Carey caught an He 111H-2 of 4 Staffel (1H+KM) flown by Fw Helmut Höfer, ten miles east of Coquet Island and shot it down into the sea; all four members of the crew were listed as missing.

A second, smaller reconnaissance was flown during the afternoon by nine He 111s of 6/KG 26, one of these being intercepted near the East Anglian coast by Hurricanes of 504 Squadron which had just moved to Martlesham Heath from their main base at Debden. Once more the Heinkel was able to slip away in cloud before the fighters could get within firing range.

After one of the many anti-shipping sorties made by KG 26, this He 111H of the Geschwader's Stabsstaffel, 1H+AA, has crash-landed on the beach on return to North Germany. *(ECPA)*

Chapter 7

THE QUIETEST MONTH

Firmly in winter's grip, the first ten days of February remained still and icy over France. In Germany Fliegerdivision 9 was ordered to be formed by the Luftwaffe Führungsstab, the main duty of this new command to be aerial mining. GenMaj Joachim Coeler, at the time FdL-West, was appointed as commanding general, with Oberstlt Hans-Armin Czech as his Chief of Staff. The new division was initially allocated KG 4, based as follows:

Stab/KG 4	Fassberg
I/KG 4	Gütersloh
II/KG 4	Fassberg
III/KG 4	Lüneberg

The production of mines was to be stepped-up with effect from April. Coeler's new units were not left undisturbed for long however, for on 10th the transfer of I/KG 4 to his command was halted while the Gruppe was diverted to Luftflotte 2 to undertake special training in the aerial re-supply of air-landed troops. On 20 February III/KG 4 — and I/KG 1, which had also been training for the mining role — relinquished their specialization in this respect to KGr 126.

3/2/40

It was over the North Sea that operations were to continue sporadically during February, notably on 3rd and 9th. On the first of these dates the weather cleared sufficiently for X Fliegerkorps to send out its bombers in some force again, to harrass British shipping in the area from the Orkneys to East Anglia. The first wave to leave the German coast comprised 14 He 111s from II/KG 26 and two Ju 88s trom I/KG 30, soon followed by ten more He 111s from I/KG 26.

Radar plots were soon being reported thick and fast, numerous fighter patrols being launched. For 43 Squadron it was to prove a very busy morning, and one which brought considerable success. Flg Off John Simpson and Flg Off J.D. Edmunds were first off at 0935 to patrol the area between Farne and Coquet Islands. Two bombers were seen attacking shipping five miles south-east of Farne Island, which were identified as He 111s. Both fighter pilots concentrated their attack on one of the pair, seeing strikes all over the bomber before it escaped in cloud, pouring black smoke. They returned claiming a probable, but this was later confirmed when the crew of a downed aircraft were picked up by a British vessel. Two possibilities arise here however; an He 111H-3 of II/KG 26 was attacked by fighters east of Farne Island and received 40 hits; this bomber force-landed on return to base, being classed as 40% damaged. One of the two I/KG 30 Ju 88s failed to return, Hpt Rosenthal and his crew being reported missing, and it seems probable that this was the crew picked up by the British ship; however German records report this aircraft as having fallen to AA gunners on English minesweepers in the Moray Firth. On balance it does seem likely that Simpson and Edmunds had attacked the Heinkel, but had received credit when the Junkers crew were rescued.

Five minutes after the first pair of Hurricanes had taken off, Blue Section (Flt Lt P. Townsend, Flg Off Folkes and Sgt J. Hallowes) followed, intercepting another He 111 of II/KG 26 fives miles east of Whitby, off the North Yorkshire coast. All three Hurricanes attacked and the stricken 4 Staffel bomber — 1H+FM (WNr 2323) — turned towards the coast, becoming the first German aircraft of the war to crash on English soil. The pilot, Fw Hermann Wilms, and the radio operator survived the crash, but the other two members of the crew were killed.

Red Section was off at 1030, Flt Lt Hull, Flg Off Carswell and Plt Off North patrolling in the Farne Island area where another II Gruppe He 111 was encountered. This was chased into cloud, but only a 'Damaged' could be claimed on this occasion; the bomber returned with 35% damage. Ten minutes later 152 Squadron's Yellow Section of Gladiators were scrambled from Acklington, Sqn Ldr Shute leading Plt Off Falkson and Sgt Shepperd to intercept a I/KG 26 Heinkel over Druridge Bay. Shute turned to port and made a quarter attack from 250 yards, moving to dead astern. Falkson repeated the manoeuvre, following which Shute again attacked from astern, closing to 50 yards. The bomber's gunners returned fire, and it disappeared into cloud heading south, pouring dense black smoke and with the undercarriage hanging down. Unseen by the attackers, the bomber crashed into Druridge Bay moments later, Lt Luther von Brüning and his crew all being killed; the success was later confirmed to the squadron by 13 Group.

Pilots of 43 Squadron active on 3 February, pose in front of one of the unit's Hurricanes. Left to right, Sgt. J. Arbuthnot, Sgt H.J.L. Hallowes, Flg Off J.W.C. Simpson, Flt Lt P.W. Townsend and Plt Off H.C. Upton. *(IWM)*

43 Squadron was off again at 1115, Yellow Section (Sgt F.R. Carey and Sgt P.G. Ottewill) intercepting another He 111 from 2/KG 26 (1H+GH) in the act of attacking shipping off Tynemouth. Both attacked at once and the bomber glided into the water with both engines stopped. Three members of Ofw Fritz Wiemer's crew were taken prisoner, a fourth dying of his wounds; one was killed during the engagement.

These were not the only interceptions however. Off the Scottish coast Anson 'F', N5203 of 608 Squadron met three Heinkels whilst on patrol, Flg Off Johnson attacking one, which escaped in cloud; this II/KG 26 aircraft returned with 35% damage, the undercarriage collapsing as it landed. Much further south another II Gruppe aircraft had a brief brush with some Hurricanes of 46 Squadron off Yarmouth, this bomber also suffering 35% damage. One Hurricane was hit by return fire and the pilot was obliged to force-land in the sea ten miles east of Brightlingsea; he was rescued safely.

As a result of the level of interceptions and the heavy cloud, the rate of success achieved by the raiders was disappointing on this occasion. II/KG 26 managed to sink the Norwegian freighter *Tempo* (629 tons) which was loaded with paper, whilst 2/KG 30 Ju 88s attacked the minesweeper HMS *Sphinx* north of Peterhead and sank this too. Coastal Command continued to suffer regular operational losses during its long oversea patrols in the poor weather conditions prevailing. On 2 February Anson N5194 of 608 Squadron had ditched off Blyth on the Northumberland coast whilst on convoy patrol, while on 5th London K6927 of 240 Squadron ditched and sank near Holyhead, Anglesey Island, whilst on an anti-submarine patrol. Another Anson, K8746 of 217 Squadron, was lost on 6th, and another crashed on 7th in bad weather. Three of the four men aboard the 217 Squadron aircraft were killed, but all the other crews were rescued safely.

9/2/40

After five more days of snow and fog, the Luftwaffe was back on 9th, eight Ju 88s of I/KG 30 and nine He 111s from II/KG 26 again setting out to harrass the east coast convoys. At 0930 a pair of Spitfires were scrambled by 602 Squadron, Sqn Ldr Farquhar and Flg Off A.M. Grant catching a 5 Staffel Heinkel flown by Uffz Helmut Mayer (1H+EN; WNr 6853) over the Firth of Forth and chasing it out to sea. Farquhar attacked and followed the bomber into cloud, where he lost it. It was hard hit however, and turned back for the coast, force-landing at North Berwick on the border. Mayer and two other members of the crew were taken prisoner, though again one later died from his wounds. The He 111 was later given the RAF serial AW177.

Slightly before this engagement, three Blenheim IVF fighters from the newly-operational 254 Squadron had taken off to patrol over fishing vessels, but two returned early with technical problems. The third, flown by Plt Off Baird, remained on station and an hour and a half later at 1100, saw an He 111 over the trawlers. Baird made after it with all speed, but it at once escaped in cloud. He spotted it again in a momentary gap and cracked off a quick burst, but with no visible results. Green Section from 603 Squadron (Flg Off Cunningham; Flg Off R.McG. Waterston; Plt Off B.G. Stapleton) were scrambled meanwhile, catching another He 111 ten miles east of Arbroath at 1137, but once more this escaped in cloud. The I/KG 30 bombers had again attacked a minesweeping flotilla near Peterhead, sinking HMS *Robert Bowen* and HMS *Fort Royal*, both converted trawlers. However one Ju 88 was hit by AA fire and damaged, subsequently crashing into the sea north-west of Sylt; a search failed to find Fw Friedrich Pfeiffer and his crew.

The final interceptions occurred when 43 Squadron launched two sections on scrambles. Off at 1155, Sqn Ldr George Lott and Sgt Peter Ottewill intercepted one Heinkel, but at once lost it in cloud. Blue Section, led by Flt Lt Peter Townsend, followed at 1215. They chased two more bombers into cloud, but could make no claims, although Townsend and Sgt Jim Hallowes each got in a burst as the bombers fled. It seems that one of the squadron's aircraft suffered engine failure during the morning, Hurricane L1744 being reported to have crashed into the sea south-east of Coquet Island. Flg Off M.K. Carswell was rescued.

The RAF's own anti-shipping aircraft were also out on this date, Hudson 'F' of 220 Squadron attacking the German submarine hunter 'B', which was incorrectly identified as a minesweeper, off the North German coast during the morning.

Eight Bf 109s intercepted, but did not close on the aircraft and Flg Off Parker was able to escape them after severe damage had been inflicted to the tail assembly, dorsal turret and radio compartment.

10–11/2/40

Next day seven He 111s of 2/KG 26 undertook an armed reconnaissance along the Scottish east coast, where they sank the minesweeper HMS *Teresa Boyle*. Another Heinkel from Stab/KG 26 was attacked east of the Orkneys by an unidentified Hudson, the pilot, Ofw Herbert Moldenhauer being badly wounded. On 11th a Blenheim I was despatched by 18 Squadron in France on a reconnaissance over North-West Germany. Three Bf 109s were seen, but only one attacked and this gave up the attempt when the Flak began firing at the British aircraft. Plt Off Hughes was able to complete his sortie and return safely.

13/2/40

A chance for the 11 Group fighters at last arrived again on 13 February when an He 111 of KGr 100 approached the Thames Estuary on reconnaissance. This aircraft, 6N+BB, was being flown by the Gruppenkommandeur, Oberstlt Joachim Stollbrock. By good fortune for the RAF, 54 Squadron's Blue Section had taken off from Rochford at 1635, and was engaged on a convoy escort patrol. When radar picked up the intruder, Sqn Ldr H.M. Pearson was ordered to intercept, leading Plt Offs B.H. Way and J.D.B.McKenzie in a search for the bomber. They caught it north-east of Manston, chasing it out to sea where it was finally shot down; this was confirmed over a month later when HMS *Brilliant* recovered some of the wreckage.

16/2/40

2 Group of Bomber Command despatched Sgt G.H. Tice on a reconnaissance in Blenheim L8759 of 21 Squadron to the Heligoland area at 0500 on 16th. Once again the 'Freya' radar gave warning of his approach, several Rotten of Bf 109Es from 4 and 5/JG 77 being scrambled to intercept. Fighters from the latter Staffel caught the aircraft near Heligoland, where it was shot down into the sea by Uffz Herbert Kutscha, all the crew being lost. During the scramble by the German fighters, a Bf 109E of II(J)/TrGr 186 crashed at Nordholz. The pilot, Uffz Hans

Spitfire KL-O, N3188, of 54 Squadron at Hornchurch early in 1940. *(C.G. Gray via A. Thomas)*

Behrmann, baled out but fell into the sea and was drowned. On the other side of the North Sea a Hurricane of 79 Squadron (L1699) failed to return from a convoy patrol, Flt Off J.J. Tarlington not being found.

Coastal Command was deeply involved during the day in a search for the German fleet auxilliary supply ship *Altmark*. This vessel had been providing supplies for the pocket battleship *Graf Spee* before the latter had been scuttled outside Montevideo harbour. Now on its way back to Germany, *Altmark* was carrying 228 British, 67 Indian and eight negro merchant seamen who had been aboard some of the vessels sunk by the raider. Patrols of Hudsons were out from 0825 onwards, 'K', 'M' and 'V' of 220 Squadron searching for eight hours. The first sighting was made at 1225 by Plt Off McNeil in 'K', the ship being seen south of Obrestad off the Norwegian coast. This was confirmed soon afterwards by Plt Off Fleetwood in 'M', and then by Flt Lt Downton in 'V. Later in the afternoon the ship was reported to have taken refuge in Jøssingfjord by a 233 Squadron Hudson, N7241, flown by Sgt Collinson. Despite the location of the vessel in neutral waters, a British destroyer raid that night put a boarding party onto *Altmark* and rescued the prisoners. This flagrant breach of Norwegian neutrality enraged Adolf Hitler, and speeded the resolve he already had developed to seek an early occupation of Norway and Denmark.

17–19/2/40

Bomber Command Blenheims were again out on 17th, a 110 Squadron machine (N6211) flown by Sgt F.J.R. Bigg, setting off at 1215 to reconnoitre Heligoland and Borkum. Again the intruder was to be intercepted, this time by Bf 110s of 2/ZG 76, and the aircraft was shot down 30 miles north of Ameland at 1610 by Hpt Wolfgang Falck.

On 18th *Scharnhorst* and *Gneisenau* again sought to break out into the North Sea to intercept convoys passing to and from Norway. On this occasion, code-named Operation 'Nordmark', they were accompanied by the cruiser *Hipper* and eight destroyers. Hudsons of 220 Squadron attacked 6 Minensuchflotilla, which was operating west of Horn's Reef in support of the break out, but without success. Next day many German coastal aircraft made sorties in co-operation with the foray, but saw nothing.

Hurricanes of 111 Squadron being refuelled from a bowser whilst on readiness at Wick in February. *(111 Squadron Records via A. Thomas)*

20/2/40

On 20th however 11 He 111s from I and II/KG 26 undertook a series of armed reconnaissances over the North Sea between the Shetlands and the Thames Estuary, but on this occasion escaped all interception. Attacks were made on ships off the Orkneys at one extreme and Yarmouth at the other, but on each occasion one crewman was wounded by return fire in each of the bombers involved. East of Copinsay Island a 5 Staffel Heinkel crew were successful in sinking HMS *Fifeshire* during an attack on the 11th Minesweeping Flotilla. The day was also marked by the loss of one of the new Saro Lerwick flyingboats of 209 Squadron, when L7253 force-landed near Lismore Island and sank. Only the body of Sgt G.A. Corby, the pilot, was found.

That night some 20 Wellingtons from 38, 99 and 149 Squadrons made a return armed reconnaissance to the Heligoland area. Heavy and accurate Flak was encountered, N2951 from 38 Squadron flown by Flg Off N. Hawxby, being shot down over Borkum, while two more bombers were badly damaged and crashed on landing.

21/2/40

Two more RAF fighters were lost on 21st; Hurricane L1729 of 43 Squadron crashing on take-off at Acklington when about to undertake a convoy patrol; Flg Off J.W.C. Simpson was injured and the aircraft was written off. Further south Flt Lt A.N. Wilson of 616 Squadron flew out of low cloud straight into the sea just off the Yorkshire coast near Hornsea.

22/2/40

Somewhat better weather on 22 February brought Luftwaffe reconnaissance aircraft over Scotland and Northern England again. Four He 111P-2s from Fernaufklärungsgruppe ObdL were sent out, and two of these were intercepted. From Scotland two Spitfires were scrambled at 1150, intercepting an aircraft from the Gruppe's 1 Staffel near St Abb's Head. One of the Spitfires was again flown by Sqn Ldr Farquhar, commanding officer of 602 Squadron; the other, L1007, was an experimental machine fitted with a pair of 20mm, Hispano cannons, which had been sent up on attachment to 602 in the hands of Plt Off G.V. Proudman of 65 Squadron.

Farquhar went in first, his fire putting both engines out of action and silencing the rear gunner. Proudman then attacked as the bomber slowly glided down towards the coast, Farquhar noting that the cannon shells were blasting complete panels off the Heinkel. When it became obvious that the crew were surrendering, the two Spitfire pilots held their fire and followed the bomber in as it performed a successful belly-landing at Coldingham, near St Abb's Head. Fearing that the crew might destroy the aircraft, Farquhar went in to land alongside, but to his considerable discomfiture, turned his Spitfire over onto its back! Lt de Res Erich Grote and his crew did indeed set fire to their aircraft (T5+ OH; WNr 1594) before coming over to aid an embarrassed and extremely annoyed Squadron Leader in escaping from his upturned cockpit!

Almost at the same moment that this combat had been taking place, three Hurricanes from 43 Squadron had been after another of the Heinkels, this one from 3 Staffel. Flt Lt Townsend, Flg Off Christie and Sgt Ayling were on patrol over Farne Island at 2,000 feet when a vapour trail was seen to the south at about 20,000 feet. At maximum boost all three climbed after it, but Christie was forced to turn away and return to base with engine trouble. The other two pressed on to make a perfect interception, Townsend shooting down the Heinkel (L2+CS; WNr 2694) into the sea east of South Shields; Oblt Hans-Werner Krüger and his crew were lost.

13 more He 111Hs of II/KG 26 had gone off on a morning armed reconnaissance up the east coast, one of these attacking a minesweeping flotilla near Cromer. Hit by return fire from the ships, it returned to Neumünster 25% damaged.

Three of 254 Squadron's fighter-Blenheims were again on fishery patrol during the morning, having taken off at 1114. An hour later an He 111J was seen 100 miles east of Flamborough Head; this was one of the newly-operational coastal Heinkels of 3/KüFlGr 806, seven of which had made a North Sea reconnaissance and were now returning individually. Sqn Ldr G.K. Fairtlough, Flt Lt Mitchell and Plt Off G.K. Taylor flying respectively L8786, L8841 and L8842, made a copy-book 'No 1 Attack' with front guns, all then expending their remaining ammunition in individual attacks. They then manoeuvred to allow their turret gunners to have a go. After some 20 minutes combat the Heinkel disappeared in some mist, but the Blenheim pilots believed that it had been badly hit and would probably not get back; they were awarded a probable. In fact the Heinkel had taken only some 10-30 hits, and reached base safely, its gunners having achieved hits on both Fairtlough's and Mitchell's aircraft during the fight.

That night six destroyers of 1 Zerstörerflotilla were despatched to undertake Operation 'Wikinger', a surface attack on British vessels in the Dogger Bank area. At 2018 the destroyer *Leberecht Maass* was reported sunk 25 miles northwest of Terschelling, while at 2050 *Max Schultz* was also reported to have gone down, possibly to a submarine. It was later discovered that eight He 111s of II/KG 26, off on an interdiction mission to attack east coast shipping, had bombed *Leberecht Maass* in error, while *Max Schultz* had hit a mine laid by the British destroyers HMS *Esk* and *Express* during the night of 9/10 January. Seven more Heinkels of KGr 100 had set off on their first night operation, but one had returned early with technical problems. Unfortunately, it was identified as a Wellington by Marine FlakAbt 216 at Borkum and was shot down, Fw Kurt Otto Späte and his crew being killed. It had been a bad night for the Germans!

Wellingtons were out over Germany next night (23/24th), one aircraft (N3004) from 99 Squadron being hit by Flak. Flg Off Williams force-landed the damaged

Following a North Sea sweep early in 1940, this Blenheim IVF fighter, QY-L of 254 Squadron, crash-landed on return to Lossiemouth. *(R.D. Cooling via A. Thomas)*

bomber near Brussels, where it was interned by the Belgian authorities.

More decorations were being announced for RAF pilots at this time for recent operations. On 21st Sgt Frank Carey of 43 Squadron received a DFM, whilst Sqn Ldr Farquhar of 602 Squadron would receive the DFC early in March, by which time he had also been promoted to the rank of Wing Commander.

24/2/40

Over the North Sea Triangle aerial activity continued as weather allowed. 2 Group, Bomber Command, was active again on 24th, a reconnaissance once more being flown. This time two Blenheims from 110 Squadron took part, Sqn Ldr K.C. Doran, DFC, leading the pair towards Heligoland, Cuxhaven and Brunsbüttel. On the way out the second aircraft was obliged to abort, but Doran continued alone. Completing his mission, Doran was heading west again when he saw five Bf 109s flying southwards — these were from 1/JG 1, and soon spotted the lone bomber. The outer fighter turned towards the Blenheim, and Doran at once turned into the attack. The other four then joined in, Doran continuing to turn into each attack, although his gunner, whose gun had suffered a severe stoppage, could reply only with single shots. By the expert handling of his aircraft however, Doran was subsequently able to escape into cloud, the Blenheim having been hit by only six bullets.

25/2/40

From their base in France, three of 18 Squadron's Blenheim Is flew a reconnaissance over North-West Germany next day, where Plt Off Monette's L1444 was hit by Flak. With the observer dead, he made direct for England, crash-landing his damaged aircraft at North Coates on the east coast. Here it was declared a total write-off.

27/2/40

At 1000 (CET) on 27 February five He 111s from I/KG 26 set off for another armed reconnaissance along the British coastline between Newcastle and the Orkneys. As they approached, Spitfires were already in the air. Red Section of 609 Squadron had just relieved Yellow Section at 1205 over a convoy code-named 'Alice' off St Abb's Head, when an He 111 was seen over the ships. The bomber at once climbed into cloud, followed by Red 1, Flt Lt D. Persse-Joynt, who then lost it and did not see it again. Flg Off G.D. Ayre and Plt Off J.R. Buchanan kept after it however, making two attacks which caused the engines to catch fire. The bomber, He 111H-3 1H+AX of 2 Staffel, flown by Oblt Ernst Heinrich, then came down in the sea, the crew of four getting into their dinghy, from which they were subsequently rescued by the Royal Navy. During the chase Buchanan's Spitfire was hit by 14 bullets from the rear gunner, but was not badly damaged.

At 1255 152 Squadron, which had become fully operational on Spitfires on 14th, sent off Blue Section to patrol over Farne Island. Here Plt Off J.S.B. Jones and Plt Off T.S. Wildblood caught another 2 Staffel He 111H-3, flown by the Staffelkapitän, Hpt Hans-Joachim Helm. Mistaking this for an He 115, they attacked 15 miles off Coquet Island and shot it down at once into the sea, the crew of five failing to survive.

Meanwhile at 1230 two more 2 Group Blenheims, this time from 82 Squadron, had taken off for another reconnaissance to the Frisian Island. Flg Off Blake in P4842, who was to cover the sector Heligoland to the Elbe, failed to return, and was subsequently reported by the German High Command to have been shot down. He had been intercepted by five Bf 109Es from II/JG 77 and brought down into the southern part of the German Bight by Oblt Jahnny, who incorrectly identified his aircraft as a Wellington.

28-29/2/40

The month ended sadly for the home-based RAF squadrons, for on 28 February whilst on a convoy patrol, Sgt A.E.A. Bruce of 611 Squadron dived into the sea near the East Dudgeon lightship in Spitfire L1051, and was reported missing. Next day (1940 was a Leap Year) Sqn Ldr F.W.C. Shute, the energetic commanding officer of 152 Squadron, took off at 1520 in one of the unit's new Spitfires (K9898) to investigate an aircraft reported down in the sea. He was heard to report: "My engine has cut and I'm landing in the sea", but he was never found.

While the North Sea area had been active intermittently throughout most of February, the Western Front had been forced by the weather conditions into the quietest month of the whole 'Phoney War' period. A number of changes in disposition were made by the RAF during the month however. Within the AASF the programme for re-equipping the Battle squadrons with Blenheims was halted, and in mid month 72 and 74 (B) Wings were disbanded, the squadrons all being absorbed into 71, 75 and 76 Wings as follows:

> 71 Wing; 105, 114, 139 and 150 Squadrons
> 75 Wing; 88, 103 and 218 Squadrons
> 76 Wing; 12, 142 and 226 Squadrons

As part of the re-organisation 103 Squadron moved to Betheniville. Meanwhile 71 Wing moved from this airfield to Chateau Faguieres, 139 Squadron moving to Plivot.

Within the Component other changes were also afoot. During the month another Lysander unit — 16 Squadron — arrived, while the Blenheim I squadrons of 70 (B) Wing, 18 and 57, began conversion to the more modern Mark IVs. The Gladiators of 607 Squadron spent much of the month on affiliation exercises with the Lysander units, while 87 Squadron moved its Hurricanes from Seclin to Le Touquet.

22–24/2/40

The AASF fighter airfield at Vassincourt was so badly affected by the weather that on 21 February 1 Squadron was obliged to send three of its Hurricanes to Rouvres for operations. Next day these three, led by Plt Off P.W.O. Mould, were sent off on patrol at 0950. An He 111 of 1(F)/123 was seen at 1030, and was intercepted, but to the pilots' chagrin most of the fighters' guns failed to fire due to the freezing conditions, and the aircraft escaped them in cloud. Further south the He 111s of KG 55 made their first operational flight — a leaflet raid over France.

23/2/40

The Armée de l'Air saw no more action than did the RAF. On 23rd a reconnaissance Mureaux 115 No 89 of GAO 553, flown by S/Lt Melchior, crash-landed near La Wantzenau in the Strasbourg area, on the left bank of the Rhine, after being hit by automatic fire from 2 Batterie, Leichteflakabt 851, the aircraft being totally destroyed by fire; one member of the crew was wounded. Next day (24th) two Moranes of GC II/7 made the only claim of the month for the Armée de l'Air when they identified an intruder over Staufen in the Kaiserstuhl area, as an He 111, chasing it in and out of cloud. It finally disappeared emitting white smoke, and was claimed as a probable. It was in fact a Do 17P of FAG 123, which escaped its two pursurers without being hit!

Again during February there had been a lot of coming and going of units within the Luftwaffe. On 1st I/ZG 2 (ex JGr 102) and III/ZG 26 (ex JGr 126) had both begun re-equipment with Bf 110Cs, while on 2nd III/KG 1 had become operational at Nordhausen, and a further 'Freya' had been installed at Wilsum, north of Lingen in the Luftflotte 2 area, under Lt Esken.

On 5th the newly-appointed Jadgfliegerführer 3 was replaced by Oberst Gerd von Massow, whilst in Luftflotte 2 five days later part of JG 26 moved to new bases, as follows:

Stab/JG 26	Dortmund
I/JG 26	Bönninghardt
II/JG 26	Dortmund
III/JG 26	Essen-Mühlheim

Three days later on 13th Stab/JG 51 moved to Bönninghardt, I/JG 26 and I/JG 20 both being transferred to its command.

On 18th the night fighter Staffeln, 10(N)/JG 2, 10(N)/JG 26 and 10(N)/LG 2, were brought together at Jever to become IV(NJ)/JG 2, coming under the control of JG 1. At the same time JGr 101, one of the last independent Jagdgruppen, left this Geschwader to re-equip with Bf 110Cs, coming under the direct control of Luftflotte 2 for the time being. I(J)/LG 2 returned to JG 1 on 28 February, moving to Stade airfield.

Finally, establishment of four more new units was ordered during the month:

> II/JG 3 at Döberitz
> III/KG 26 at Lübeck-Blankensee
> III/KG 28 at Jesau
> Zerstörerstaffel/KG 30 at Perleberg

Chapter 8

MÖLDERS' MEN IN THE ASCENDANT

As the harsh winter at last began to ameliorate slightly, and the first signs of the early spring started their tentative appearances, March was to prove a much busier month. It also saw at last the first concrete evidence of the new products of the French aviation industry which were beginning to reach units at the front and elsewhere. The first three of the excellent Bloch MB 174 reconnaissance aircraft were issued to GR II/33, while within the Aeronavale the eagerly-awaited dive-bomber escadrilles approached operational readiness. Deliveries of the American Vought V-156F had allowed both AB 1 and AB 3 to re-equip with these aircraft, AB 1 now moving from Boulogne-Alprecht airfield to Hyères on the Mediterranean coast, while AB 3 took its place at Alprecht. AB 4 began training with the first of the home-built Loire-Nieuport LN 411s.

1–2/3/40
The French-based RAF was gradually coming back to life after the long winter 'hibernation', several of the Battle squadrons of the AASF commencing night leaflet-dropping sorties over Germany during the month — 88, 103, 218 and 226 Squadrons included; 88 and 114 Squadrons both began moving to Perpignan. Within the Component, 2 Squadron began undertaking some low level reconnaissance and photographic work again with its Lysanders, as well as the affiliation exercises with the fighters. In England 206 Squadron started to exchange its Ansons for Hudsons. Within JG 1 in North Germany, I(J)/LG 1 moved to Westerland/Sylt, and II(J)/TrGr 186 to Nordholz.

Battle of 226 Squadron (K7705). *(IWM)*

KG 26 He 111s were out in strength over the North Sea again on 1st and 2nd March, although they were to escape interception on both days. Early on 1st a Heinkel of the Korpsführungkette/Fliegerkorps X with Maj Martin Harlinghausen aboard, sank a Norwegian freighter, *Vestfoss* (1,388 tons) south-east of Copinsay Island. 12 I and II/KG 26 aircraft achieved no success, but 1H+KN (WNr 6889) of 5 Staffel crashed into the sea off Westerland soon after take-off with the loss of the Staffelkapitän, Oblt Sieghard Donner and his crew. Next day Maj Harlinghausen was out again on an armed reconnaissance of the Eastern Channel, where the passenger steamer *Domala* (8,441 tons) was attacked off St Catherine's Point and very badly damaged, 98 of the people on board being killed. Three KGr 100 He 111s and 15 more from I/KG 26 on an east coast armed reconnaissance, sank the Dutch motor vesel *Elzienna* (197 tons) off Coquet Island.

Over the continent the month got off to a lively start on this date (2nd), when several sharp engagements took place. During the morning a number of Do 17s from FAG 121, 1 and 4(F)/22, and other units undertook reconnaissances over the length and breadth of the Western Front area. Two Dorniers from FAG 121 were forced to abort due to technical and weather problems, whilst a third, 7A+KM from 4(F)/121 flown by Uffz Karl-Heinz Jagielki, was intercepted over Luxeuil by two MS 406s of GC II/7 flown by Sgt Chef Doudiès and Sgt Sonntag. This was attacked at 20,000 feet and went down in a spin to crash at Harol, ten miles west of Epinal; a single parachute was seen by the French pilots. A fourth aircraft — this time from 1(F)/22 — was intercepted by Adj Chef Gras, Adj de Montgolfier and Sgt Chef Janeba of GC II/5, who identified it as a Do 215. They claimed to have probably shot it down north of Wolkingen, but in fact it evaded them with only slight damage, and escaped into Belgian airspace. Here it was intercepted by three Hurricanes of the Armée de l'Air Belge, from Escadrille 1/I of the 2ème Regiment from Schaffen, all painted with their unit's famous World War I 'Thistle' emblem on their fuselage sides. The section leader, Lt Henrard, led the trio in a tail chase in line astern, presenting the German rear gunner with an easy target. One after the other the three Hurricanes were hit; Henrard's aircraft was shot down and crashed, the pilot being killed, whilst the other two were both crippled. One force-landed at once and turned over on its back, while the third, H-23, managed to reach Schaffen, where it too force-landed, riddled with bullets. Despite all these attentions, the Dornier returned with only 5% damage!

At 1045 three 1 Squadron Hurricanes were scrambled from Vassincourt and 20 minutes later sighted a Dornier from 4(F)/11 at 24,000 feet near Metz. As they approached this intruder Plt Off 'Hilly' Brown's Hurricane (L1974) suffered a mechanical fault which caused his propellor to come completely off, and he glided down to make a 'deadstick' landing. Sgt Soper in L1843 and Plt Off J.S. Mitchell in L1971 attacked the Dornier, but the rear gunner's fire proved most accurate, the engine of Mitchell's Hurricane being hit, causing the fighter to fall away pouring thick smoke. Mitchell, obviously blinded by the smoke, was guided down by Soper, but at the crucial moment the latter lost sight of him and he crashed to his death near Fenetrange, nine miles north of Sarrebourg. No claim was submitted by Soper in respect of the Dornier, but in fact 6M+AM had been hard hit, and Oblt Adolf Leupold put it down in a very smooth crash-landing near La Petit Pierre. It seems he and his crew then resisted capture, for all of them were wounded before giving themselves up. A further Do 17P, this one from 1(F)/22, flown by Lt Karl-Wilhelm Barchfeld, was inter-

This Do 17P of 1(F)/22 was shot down near Bouzonville on 2 March by Sous Lt Robert Martin and Adj Chef Pierre Le Gloan of GC III/6. Lt Barchfeld's crew were captured.

cepted by a pair of Moranes from GC III/6 flown by Sous Lt Martin and Adj Chef Pierre Le Gloan, and was shot down, crashing near Bouzonville, about three miles west of the Franco-German border; the crew were captured.

73 Squadron was in the air at 1125, four Hurricanes being despatched to escort a French Potez 63. At the same time Moranes of GC III/3 were similarly escorting a Mureaux 117 (No 66) of GAO 509 near Saarbrücken. The Allied formations were engaged by patrols of Bf 109Es from III/JG 53 and I/JG 51. Both Schwarme attacked the Moranes/Mureaux first, Uffz Reckers of III/JG 53 shooting down the Mureaux, which Sgt Foriel crash-landed at Becourt, while Hpt Georg Mayer of 2/JG 51 hit the MS 406 flown by Sgt Chef Ribo; Ribo was mortally wounded, but managed to crash-land his damaged aircraft before he died. A second Morane was also hit, but Sgt Edouard Le Nigen crashed this whilst attempting to belly-land at Nancy on return.

The III/JG 53 pilots then attacked the Hurricanes, Oblt Mölders claiming one shot down at 1220, while Uffz Hermann Neuhoff claimed a second at 1230 and Oblt Wilcke attacked a third. The latter saw his opponent burnt, but did not observe the aircraft crash, and his claim was not confirmed. The Hurricanes were indeed hard hit, and it seems that all four force-landed, although one did come down due to technical problems, rather than combat damage. Flg Off Kain claimed a Messerschmitt shot down in flames from two he engaged, but III/JG 53 reported no loss. Kain was then forced to crash-land his badly shot-up Hurricane (L1808) at once near Metz. Sgt Sewell also force-landed at Bruhaye (in L1958) after being attacked by five Messerschmitts; it was considered that both pilots survived only because of the recently-installed armour plate behind their seats, and it seems probable that these two were the victims of Mölders and Neuhoff. Plt Off Tucker also force-landed, but it does seem likely that he was the victim of the technical fault. It had certainly been an expensive day for the AASF fighters! One RAF Spitfire PR 1B had undertaken a photographic sortie over the Ruhr during the day, where it was intercepted by three Bf 109s. It was able to outrun these with ease.

Cpl Chef Korber, a Czech pilot with GCII/3, was shot down by Hpt Werner Mölders of III/JG 53 on 3 January, and managed to crash-land his Morane 406 at Toul.

3/3/40

Next day (3rd) again proved busy over France. At 1120 three 1 Squadron Hurricanes were once more sent off to patrol over the Metz-Nancy area, where just before noon a reconnaissance He 111H of 3(F)/121 was seen at 24,000 feet. Plt Off Brown and Sgt Soper each made several attacks, and the aircraft went down in flames to force-land in a field south of Forbach. The radio operator and gunner had both been killed in the action, and one other member of the crew wounded, but this latter with the pilot, Uffz Fredy Nagel, were rescued from this area of No Mans' Land by a German infantry patrol. Mölders was out at the head of his III/JG 53 again at 1334, patrolling to the east of Metz. 12 Moranes of GC II/3 on similar duty were seen below, and the Jadgflieger were able to carry out a good 'bounce', Mölders claiming one shot down over Diedenhofen. One Morane went down damaged, the wounded pilot, Cpl Chef Korber, carrying out a belly-landing at Toul. Cne Naudy snapped of a burst at one of the Messerschmitts, claiming a probable over Boulay.

During the day in Southern England a PDU Hudson (N7334) was intercepted in error over Meopham at 1440 by three Spitfires, and was shot down. Some of the crew fortunately managed to bale out.

4/3/40

A return of inclement weather reduced operations once more, following which it was again over the North Sea that activity was experienced. On 4 March Blenheims from 107 Squadron were on anti-shipping sorties off the North-West German coast when Sgt R.S. Gunning reported seeing a U-Boat in the Schillig Roads at 1535. He got in one attack before it submerged, claiming a hit on the conning tower with a stick of four 250lb bombs before the submarine disappeared in the seething foam; it had not in fact suffered any damage at all.

6/3/40

I/KG 26 He 111s were out after shipping on 6th, two being hit and slightly damaged by fire from vessels which they attacked. Two 110 Squadron Blenheims were sent on meteorological reconnaissance flights, encountering two aircraft

On defensive duties at Catterick in March were the Blenheim IF fighters of 219 Squadron. FK-D in the foreground was L6733. *(Gp Capt H.L. Goddard via A. Thomas)*

which the crews took to be He 111s. They gave chase, only to find that their quarry were a pair of I/ZG 76 Bf 110s, which at once turned on them. By some quick manoeuvring both Blenheims made good their escape in clouds. A similar experience was suffered by a pair of 10 Squadron Whitleys which were sent out on an early evening North Sea patrol. These also chased two apparent Heinkels, only to find themselves turned upon by Bf 110s too, but these aircraft were also able to escape in cloud.

7/3/40

Three reconnaissance He 111Ps from 1(F)/ObdL were sent out towards the Scottish coast on 7 March, but just after 1300 Lt Hans Froese's T5+AH was caught near Aberdeen by five Spitfires of 603 Squadron (Flt Lt J.T. MacDonald, Flg Off B.J. Carbury, Plt Off G.K. Gilroy, Plt Off C. Robertson, Sgt J.R. Caister) and was shot down into the sea 70 miles out, only the radio operator

Newly-operational on Hurricanes in March was 145 Squadron, one of this unit's aircraft being seen at Croydon. *(B. Haines via A. Thomas)*

surviving to become a prisoner. Eight I/KG 26 Heinkels flew interdiction sorties along the east coast, in one of which a Luftwaffe war correspondent was wounded by AA fire. He 115s from KüFlGr 106 and 506 were also out over the North Sea, one of these being intercepted over some fishing vessels by Hudson 'M' of 220 Squadron, flown by Flg Off Selby, at 1328. In a brief fight the Hudson crew managed to inflict 15-20 hits on the floatplane before it escaped in cloud.

8/3/40
Next day three Ju 88s from I/KG 30 took off late in the morning and in bad weather for a reconnaissance over Scapa Flow. Cloud blanketed their target completely, and they started their return flight with nothing to report. 111 Squadron's Red Section had been scrambled however, and Flg Off R.G. Dutton caught the 2 Staffel bomber flown by Oblt Frithjof von Sicharthoff 40 miles east of the Orkneys and shot it down into the sea. Initially the aircraft was identified as an He 111 by the squadron.

11/3/40
Little was seen thereafter until 11th when 82 Squadron Blenheims were sent out towards the Frisians on anti-shipping duties. At 1215 Sqn Ldr M.V. Delap found a surfaced U-Boat — *U-31* — off Borkum and attacked at once. Two direct hits were seen and the vessel went down, a huge gout of oil rising to the surface; Kapitänleutnant Habekost and his crew were all lost.

12/3/40
During the late evening of 12th three He 115s of 3/KüFlGr 506 dropped torpedoes for the first time against shipping off the English east coast, but all missed.

16/3/40
Five days later on 16 March nine Blenheims of 21 Squadron left at 0645 to attack Flakships off Borkum, the bombers approaching the target area singly. Two were intercepted by Bf 109Es from II(J)/TrGr 186, both escaping in cloud with only slight damage. Return fire had struck one of the Messerschmitts however, and the pilot was obliged to force-land in the sea close to Borkum; his aircraft was recovered, but was an 80% write-off. Another of the unit's aircraft suffered similar damage when it force-landed at Westerland due to bad weather conditions. That evening a return raid was made on Scapa Flow by 21 He 111s from I/KG 26 and 18 Ju 88s from I/KG 30. Some 100 bombs were dropped, causing damage to the cruiser *Norfolk* and the depot ship *Iron Duke* — and causing the first British civilian casualties of the war on land, one killed and six injured. As a direct result plans were now laid for the first Bomber Command attack on German soil. During the return flight from the raid on Scapa Flow a Ju 88 of 3 Staffel became lost and the pilot, Uffz Werner Mattner, crash-landed near Cöbelen on the Danish island of Laaland, where he and his crew were interned.

17/3/40
Early next morning however, six of II/KG 26's He 111s approached the Scottish coast followed by four Ju 88s of 6/KG 30. Here the latter were intercepted by Spitfires of 603 Squadron's Red Section, which had taken off at 0845 to patrol

Uffz Werner Mattner of 3/KG 30 crash-landed his Ju 88A on the Danish island of Laaland when he became lost returning from a raid on Scapa Flow on 16 March. Note the 'Chamberlain's Umbrella in the Bombsight' emblem on the engine nascelle. *(IWM)*

Aberdeen-Peterhead. One of the Junkers was spotted at 0915 by Flt Lt G. Denholm, and then again at 0920 by Flg Off Haig. Both attacked, but it escaped in cloud and no claim was made. In fact the bomber had suffered some slight damage, and the radio operator had been wounded.

19/3/40
The RAF's reciprocal attack for the Scapa Flow raid came during the night of 19/20th, when 30 Whitleys and 20 Hampdens raided the seaplane base at Hornum/Sylt. Much damage was claimed, but little was actually achieved, most bombs falling into the sea. Whitley N1405 of 51 Squadron flown by Flt Lt Baskerville, was shot down by Flak, all the crew being lost.

20/3/40
Next day six He 111Js from 2 and 3/KüFlGr 806 were out early on reconnaissance off the southern section of the North Sea, but found nothing. One 3 Staffel aircraft was obliged to come down in the sea, Lt zur See Helmut Ostermann and his crew being picked up by a Dutch fishing trawler and interned in Holland; they were to be repatriated on 14 May 1940, after the German invasion of that country. At 0830 an He 111H of 1(F)/122 set off on a reconnaissance over the Shetlands/Bergen/Enge area, this crew spotting a convoy east of Sumburgh Head at around midday which they reported as a cruiser, three destroyers and 40 merchantmen, all heading south-west. This was a returning convoy code-named HN 20 'Alice'. On receipt of this information, Fliegerkorps X ordered off three more He 111s of 1(F)/122, 13 of I/KG 26 and 14 of II/KG 26, the two bomber formations departing about an hour apart in the course of the afternoon.

The further reconnaissance aircraft found the convoy 80 miles north-east of Kirkwall and set out a 'Knickebein' radio-guidance beam to guide in the KG 26 aircraft. Towards evening one of the 1(F)/122 crews saw another convoy — ON 20 'Maria' — north-east of Ratray Head, and nearly an hour later this was attacked by 14 KG26 Heinkels, which inflicted damage on five ships. Hurricanes of 43 Squadron were up on patrol and Sgt T.A.H. Gough found the aircraft of the 6 Staffel Kapitän, Hpt Otto Andreas, which was shot down into the sea off the Scottish coast.

Two Blackburn Skuas of 803 Squadron, Fleet Air Arm, were patrolling at 1930 when a single German aircraft was spotted by Lt W.P. Lucy as it was being pursued by three Hudsons. Losing sight of these aircraft, Lucy then saw another Heinkel attacking ships east of Copinsay Island while he was flying back to Wick. He attacked at once and fairly riddled the bomber which made off with the undercarriage down and streaming oil and smoke; he was credited with a probable. This aircraft, a 2 Staffel machine, was indeed hard hit and was obliged to crash-land near Duhnen, west of Cuxhaven, the radio operator having been killed in the action. The aircraft was classified as a complete write-off. A third Heinkel, one of the 1(F)/122 reconnaissance aircraft flown by Oblt Blievernicht, ran out of fuel during the return flight and crash-landed near Flensburg, three of the crew being killed.

Bomber Command also sent out some Blenheims on anti-shipping duties, an aircraft from 82 Squadron being chased briefly and without effect by a Bf 110 near Borkum. Two more raided Westerland airfield and a patrol boat near Borkum, but all without success. At evening Maj Harlinghausen was off again in one of Fliegerkorps X's He 111s, undertaking an armed reconnaissance southwards down the English Channel. Here he attacked the freighter *Barn Hill* (5,439 tons) south of Brighton, and sank the vessel. However she settled on a sandbank in shallow water, and most of her cargo was saved.

9/3/40

The Western Front had seen only sporadic activity in the meantime. On 9 March seven Bf 109s from I/JG 2 clashed briefly with 14 Moranes of GC III/1, which had arrived at the front to relieve GC II/5, following the departure of that unit to Cannes for a rest. Ofw Franz Jänisch claimed one victory against the French fighters, Adj Guigno being hit and wounded; he crash-landed at Metz, where his damaged Morane was written-off.

11–13/3/40

On 11th a Potez 63-11 No 22 of GR I/22 flown by Lt Maitret, was intercepted over its own airfield at Metz-Frescaty by five Bf 109Es from III/JG 53. The reconnaissance aircraft was shot down by Oblt Wolf-Dietrich Wilcke, and crash-landed with one member of the crew wounded. The Bf 109Es of III/JG 53 clashed with six Moranes near Thionville without result on 12th, while on 13th Flak gunners claimed a Mureaux 117 shot down, which reportedly crashed on French soil; no Mureaux is recorded as lost on this date, but a Potez 63-11 of GAO 548 was indeed hit by Flak near Kehl on the Rhine, one member of Lt Roussel's crew being wounded.

15-17/3/40

During the night of 15/16th 77 Squadron operated from Villeneuve, two Whitleys dropping leaflets on Warsaw and Prague. On return Flt Lt Tomlyn landed mistakenly in Germany in KN-L, N1387. Climbing out of the aircraft to speak to a passerby, he sprinted back on finding that he was talking to a German farmer, taking off again under rifle fire from approaching troops. On 16th reconnaissance aircraft were again engaged by the German Flak, Po 637 No 45 of GR I/52 being damaged near Koblenz and returning to crash-land near Nancy with one member of the crew wounded; this aircraft had to be written-off. Next day another Po 63-11 (No 590) from GAO 509 flown by Lt Royanneau was reported missing over German territory and probably also succumbed to the guns.

18/3/40

Little further occurred for some days apart from a case of 'mistaken identity' on 18th, when a Blenheim from 59 Squadron was badly damaged by a Hurricane and reduced to 'write-off' condition; the radio operator was killed. That night the AASF undertook its first night 'Nickel' sorties, with Battles of 88 and 226 Squadrons. The operation was repeated next night by 103 Squadron aircraft, Saarbrücken, Mannheim and Koblenz being the targets. The first loss on these activities was to be suffered during the night of 22/23rd when one of two 88 Squadron aircraft suffered an equipment failure at the end of a long and fruitless search for its home airfield. Flg Off D.L.R. Halliday and his crew baled out of P2247, which crashed near Pont-sur-Yonne.

22/3/40

A PDU Spitfire from 'N' Flight at Heston, was lost on 22 March — the first of these aircraft to go missing. Plt Off C.M. Wheatley took off from Heston in N3069 in the morning, heading for Germany. Since he carried no radio in his lightened aircraft it is not known what went wrong, although it was assumed that he was forced to descend below 25,000 feet to avoid leaving a vapour trail. Bf 109Es of I/JG 20 were scrambled, and the Spitfire was intercepted over Kleve by Lt Jung, who shot it down. Wheatley baled out, but his parachute failed to open; his aircraft crashed on Dutch soil, coming down on marshy ground by the River Waal.

Over the front III/JG 53 was engaged with 73 Squadron when six Bf 109Es met five Hurricanes over Bouzonville at 1410. Fw Weigelt was taken by surprise by Flt Lt R.E. Lovett, but escaped with hits in the fuselage and armour plate of his fighter; Lovett was credited with having shot the Messerschmitt down. During this fight one Hurricane was lost, but no German claim appears to have been made.

23–25/3/40

On 23rd a pair of 607 Squadron's Gladiators were in collision over Vitry-en-Artois, Flg Off N.S. Greame and Plt Off H.P.J. Radcliff both being killed in K8030 and K8000. Next day on 24th four Bf 109Es of II/JG 52 intercepted Potez 637 No 36 of GR I/52 over Zweibrücken, Ofw Griener closing on the French aircraft and shooting it down into the lines south of Rohrbach; the pilot, Adj Barbier, survived with wounds, but his observer, Sous Lt Brugnolles and the gunner were both killed. A further clash occurred next day when four Bf 109Es of III/JG 53 engaged eight Moranes of GC III/3 in a dogfight near Saarbrücken at 1520. Four more Messerschmitts from the same unit joined the fight, followed — according to the French — by two Bf 110s and then ten more Bf 109s. Oblt

Wilcke claimed one of the French fighters shot down and Adj Marias crash-landed his extensively damaged aircraft at Morhange, though he suffered no personal injury. Several other French fighters were damaged during this fight, but one got in a burst of fire which damaged one wing of Lt Riegel's Messerschmitt.

26/3/40

The RAF was again involved on 26th when at 1215 three Hurricane pilots of 73 Squadron saw anti-aircraft fire in the distance while on patrol. The gunners were firing at 16 Bf 110s of V(Z)/LG1 which were escorting a reconnaissance Do 17 over the area. Flg Off Walker and Sgt Pilkington closed on the Dornier and three of the fighters, attempting to draw the attention of the Zerstörer pilots away from Flt Lt Lovett, who managed to claim damage to one of the aircraft which he took to be the bomber. He was then attacked and driven off by some of the escort, his Hurricane being slightly damaged. He had in fact attacked one of the Messerschmitts, wounding the radio operator, Uffz Petry. This aircraft — a 13 Staffel machine — was subsequently force-landed near Mainz with 40% damage. During the return flight a second Bf 110 was also obliged to force-land due to a technical fault, damaged 15%.

Three more Hurricanes were off at 1340, climbing to 20,000 feet. Over Saarlautern four Bf 109Es of III/JG 53 were engaged, Flg Off Kain claiming one shot down in flames, while Plt Off Perry and Sgt T.B.G. Pyne expended all their ammunition on two others. At this point a second Schwarm attacked from above, and although Kain managed to get off a burst which led him to believe that he had possibly brought a second Messerschmitt down, he was shot down in flames himself by Fw Weigelt; Kain managed to bale out of L1766 unscathed. It seems likely that it was fire from his fighter which had struck the engine of one of the Messerschmitts during his first attack, and this landed at Trier/Euren with 15% damage. Perry was subsequently also credited with one Messerschmitt shot down, and Pyne with one probable.

Another three Hurricanes took off at 1450 and these also met Bf 109s,

Some of 73 Squadron's most notable pilots of spring 1940; left to right. Fl Lt R.E. Lovett, Flg Off E.J. Kain, Flg Off N. Orton and Sgt T.B.G. Pyne. *(IWM)*

attacking a reported nine, Flg Off N. Orton claiming two shot down, one of which was seen to fall out of control by Flg Off Walker. Their opponents were in fact eight aircraft from III/JG 53, and Orton's fire had indeed hit two of these, both of which were struck in wings, fuselage and fuel tanks, and landed at Trier where both were classified as damaged 40%. Orton's own aircraft was damaged, by Hpt Mölders (who mistook the Hurricane for a Morane on this occasion), who claimed to have shot it down, but the remaining Messerschmitts then departed.

During the day GC III/1 reported flying an escort mission to a Potez between the Saar and the Moselle. 26 Bf 110s were met in two groups — possibly the same aircraft as were engaged by the 73 Squadron Hurricanes — but nothing resulted from brief skirmishing. Two Moranes were damaged by Flak. Over the border in Germany two Bf 109Es of 4/JG 52 collided while being scrambled to intercept an incursion, Fw Walter Hoops being killed in the crash.

29/3/40

73 Squadron was engaged again three days later on 29 March. At 0815 a formation of six Do 17s passed over the unit's base, heading into France at 20,000 feet. Three Hurricanes were scrambled at 0835 to intercept when they returned, Plt Off Perry and Flg Off Brotchie attacking one Dornier and both obtaining hits on it which forced it down low. The combat was noted by a Bf 109E pilot who was passing above at a great height, and Oblt Otto Boenigk, Staffelkapitän of 9/JG 53, at once rolled into a dive to the rescue. Travelling at tremendous speed, he shot down Perry's aircraft with a single burst and was away before Brotchie had even seen him, Perry crashing to his death near Epernay. So swift had been the attack indeed, that Brotchie thought his fellow pilot had been shot down by return fire from the Dornier — an aircraft of 2(F)/22, which now escaped.

1 Squadron sent up three Hurricanes at 0910, these chasing an aircraft spotted amongst AA bursts over Metz, but losing it. They then saw two more Bf 109Es of III/JG 53's 9 Staffel 1,000 feet above them and climbed to engage these, getting beneath their tails. A general dogfight began during which Flg Off Paul Richey managed to obtain hits on one of the fighters, and this made off leaving a thick black smoke trail. The wounded pilot, Lt Joseph Volk, subsequently crash-landed in German territory near Saarbrücken, his aircraft being classified as damaged 40%.

Three more of 1 Squadron's Hurricanes were sent off over Metz at 1400, climbing up to 25,000 feet. 30 minutes after take off they spotted nine Bf 110s of V(Z)/LG 1 away to the east, and at once headed for these. The Zerstörer had climbed to great height to undertake a test of their armament at altitude; however, they engaged the Hurricanes in a dogfight in which the British pilots found these new opponents fast and manoeuvreable, but still easily out-manoeuvred by the Hurricane.

Flt Lt P.R. Walker attacked one, seeing hits, but was attacked by another and had to take evasive action. Flg Off Stratton, seeing Walker's first opponent in trouble, with black smoke issuing from one engine went after it, hitting it again and seeing smoke now from both engines, one of which had almost stopped. They were down to 2,000 feet now, and Stratton was out of ammunition, as was Walker; the Bf 110 was last seen gliding eastwards trailing a banner of black smoke. Sgt 'Taffy' Clowes had attacked two Messerschmitts in quick succession, seeing both fall apparently out of control. Subsequently it was

A French Potez 25toe biplane has collided with PZ-E, a Blenheim of 53 Squadron. To the rear can just be seen the nose of a Potez 540 bomber. *(53 Squadron Records via A. Thomas)*

confirmed that Walker and Stratton's victim, an aircraft of 14 Staffel flown by Fw Friedrich Lindemann, had crashed in Allied territory. Lindemann baled out near Bitsche to become a prisoner, while his observer, Uffz Kurt Radeck, was killed. Clowes was credited with two 'believed shot down', but in fact V(Z)/LG 1 suffered only the one loss. The Gruppe's leading pilot, Oblt Methfessel, claimed two of the attacking British fighters shot down in return; 1 Squadron suffered no damage at all to any of its aircraft.

During the day the Luftwaffe lost a further fighter when Lt Leopold Margarth of 8/JG 53 ran out of fuel. He crash-landed, damaging his aircraft seriously and injuring himself in so doing. It was on this date that Cne Antoine de Saint-Exupery, the famous French airman-poet, made the first operational flight in one of GR II/33's new Bloch MB 174s, covering the Neufchateau-Montmedy region.

31/3/40

The last day of March was to see a major defeat for the French fighters. 11 MS 406s from GC III/7 had taken off for a patrol and were flying in four 'patrouilles' near Morhange. Cne Lacombe, leader of the top cover found his '02' oxygen mask not working, and fearing suffocation, made a sudden dive to about 13,000 feet to the thicker air, where he could attempt to carry out repairs. Unfortunately the whole patrouille followed, and during this unplanned and very ill-advised manoeuvre, 20 Bf 109Es of II/JG 53 appeared, chose their moment to attack from the most favourable position, then hit the French like thunderbolts. Completely disorganized, the latter had no time to react and in seconds seven of the Moranes had been hit and the Messerschmitts were away. Adj René Chavet in No 971 went down in flames near Gros Tenquin and was killed; Sous Lt Rupied (No 811) baled out, wounded, while his blazing aircraft also crashed south of Gros Tenquin; Sgt Maurice L'Hopital-Navarre baled out of No 176 near Renning, wounded in one foot; Sgt Chef René Morlot's No 177 was badly shot-up, but he managed to crash-land at Metz-Frescaty. Three more Moranes were badly damaged, Sous Lt Renaud being wounded and crash-landing No 212 in a field, while Sgt Chef Bedrich Dvorak (Czech) was slightly wounded in No 229, and Sgt Jean Bodin unhurt in No 806, both managing to regain their base, where Bodin crash-landed. Six victories were credited to the II/JG 53 pilots,

Oblt Heinz Bretnutz (centre) of II/JG 53, who claimed two of GC III/7's Morane 406s shot down on 31 March.

two of them going to Oblt Heinz Bretnütz, another Legion Condor veteran; one each went to Hpt von Maltzahn, Lt Gerhard Michalski, Fw Albrecht Baun and Uffz Werner Kaufmann.

22–23/3/40

Following the Bomber Command raid on Hornum during the night of 19/20 March, the bombers were active over the North Sea area for several more days. During the late afternoon of 22nd three Hampdens from 50 Squadron undertook an armed reconnaissance during which they were intercepted by — and evaded — a Bf 110. On 23rd a Hurricane of 32 Squadron (N2531) on patrol off Folkestone, crashed into the sea without obvious cause; Flg Off L.G. Bowler was lost. That night Wellingtons were out over the Frisians, dropping leaflets; two of these failed to return, P2515 of 37 Squadron being shot down by Flak near Delmenhorst, where Plt Off P.F. Templeman, the pilot, and one other member of the crew was killed; four others survived as prisoners. 149 Squadron's P9225, lost and short of fuel, tried to land near Dunkirk, but was driven off by heavy fire from the French DCA. The aircraft was subseqently abandoned by the crew over Holland, and crashed near Hondeschoote. Sgt Wilson and his crew were interned, but were later repatriated.

24/3/40

With daylight on 24th Blenheims from 110 Squadron repeated the attack on Hornum seaplane base without particular effect, while that night three Hampdens of 44 Squadron set out to reconnoitre the Elbe Estuary and Kellerfjord. At 0035 Sgt S.A. Williams in L4102 sent out an SOS requesting a position fix, but was not heard from again; it was presumed that the aircraft had crashed into the North Sea during the return flight when fuel ran out.

On 27 March five Blenheims from 107 Squadron were off at 1150 on an anti-shipping sweep, reporting attacks on a destroyer and other vessels. Two more aircraft from the unit were sent on reconnaissances over Sylt, Hornum and List. Flg Off J.D. Murphy met much Flak and several fighters in the Hornum area, but managed to escape in clouds. F/Sgt D.W.G. Nicholls was not so lucky; his aircraft, L8747, was last seen entering clouds with fighters on its tail. It was shot down into the sea 20 miles west of Westerland by a Bf 109E from II/JG 77 flown by Uffz Kurt Opolski.

That night seven Whitley Vs from 77 Squadron were sent over the Ruhr on another leaflet raid. N1351 flown by Flg Off Boardman was shot down by Flak, crashing near Gerolstein, west of Koblenz; four of the five crew were captured. Flg Off Geach's N1357 (KN-H) was intercepted as it returned at 0630 by a Dutch Fokker G-la twin-engined fighter of the 3ᵉ JAVA, flown by Lt P. Noonan, and was shot down by it into the Dutch territory that it was overflying, coming down near Parnis. One member of the crew was killed, the other four being interned.

28–29/3/40

After undertaking their initial operational sorties, the He 111Js of 2 and 3/KüFlGr 806 had moved from Ütersen/Wenzendorf on 21st. On 28th however it was the bombers of X Fliegerkorps which were out for the first intercepted Luftwaffe anti-shipping flights for some days, three He 111s from the Korps-führungskette reconnoitring the Orkneys and Shetlands. Unfortunately for these intruders, 43 Squadron had moved up to Wick, on Scotland's northern coastline only two days earlier, being joined there on the morning of this very day by 605 Squadron.

Two sections from 605 Squadron were already in the air on patrol during the morning when the approach of the Heinkels was reported. At once Sqn Ldr Lott led 'A' Flight of 43 Squadron off to intercept, leaving the ground at about 1230. One of the intruders was seen almost at once in good visibility at 10,000 feet by Sgt Ottewill, 15 miles offshore. Ottewill got in a good burst and attacks were then made by Flt Lt Hull, Sgt Carey and Sgt T.A.H. Gough, following which the disabled aircraft turned for the coast with its fuselage on fire, losing altitude as it went. At this point 605 Squadron's Red and Yellow Sections appeared on the scene, unaware of 43 Squadron's presence. Red Leader, Flg Off G.R. Edge, dived down after the Heinkel, but as he did so Yellow Leader (Flg Off P.G. Leeson) saw the bomber entering cloud at 6,000 feet and at the same time was fired on — possibly by the gunners, but possibly by some of the pursuing fighters. He at once loosed off two short bursts, following the aircraft through the cloud into the clear, where he emptied the remainder of his ammunition into it. Now at 3,000 feet, the stricken bomber, well ablaze, fell into the sea eight miles east of Wick, and about ten miles offshore; this was P4+BA of the Korpsführungskette/FlgKps X. Oblt Horst Gollmann and his crew were all lost. The victory was subsequently credited jointly to the two squadrons.

That same day 803 Squadron reported a Skua missing from a patrol in the Orkneys area, the crew not being found. Widespread operations were being undertaken during the day by the Oberkommando der Marine Do 18s and He 115s; one Dornier M2+GK of 2/KüFlGr 106 force-landed 175 miles north-west of Hornum with the loss of Lt zur See Karl-Friedrich Bölck and his crew; it was believed that the aircraft might have been damaged in combat with a Hudson, but no Coastal Command report corresponding to this has been found. The possibility remains therefore that the missing Dornier and Skua had been engaged in combat with each other. An He 115, S4+FH of 1/KüFlGr 506, while returning from a search for the missing flyingboat, crashed at Lista at night, Ofw Paul Gregarek and his crew all being killed.

That same evening, 29th, ten Ju 88s from II/KG 30 were out on anti-shipping sorties off the English coast. The Staffelkapitän of 6 Staffel, Oblt Rudolf Quadt, attacked a convoy south-east of Sunderland, but 4D+AP was hit by AA fire from the vessels and crashed into Cresswell Bay with the loss of all aboard. Another Do 18 had gone out to look for Bölck's missing aircraft, but this 2/KüFlGr 906 aircraft was also obliged to force-land, the crew being picked up safely by *U-30*.

31/3/40

On 31st a Do 17Z-2 of Wekusta 26 undertook a sortie over the English Midlands, but was intercepted over the eastern end of the English Channel by Red Section of 54 Squadron at 1225; Flg Off Max Pearson (Red 3) attacked from astern, apparently unseen, firing all his ammunition in two long bursts, the first of which immediately silenced the rear gunner. The Dornier reared up violently, stalled, and dived vertically towards the sea off Orfordness from a height of about 7000 feet, black smoke pouring from the starboard engine. At low level the aircraft pulled out of its dive and flew away eastwards, still trailing smoke. The leader of the pair of Spitfires failed to spot the Dornier, and Pearson did not see it crash, so was credited with an unconfirmed victory. The aircraft nonetheless failed to return, Uffz de Res Gerhard Hertel and his crew being reported missing.

At the start of the month the Luftwaffe ObdL had ordered the formation of three more new units, III/JG 52 at Straussberg and I/KG 3 at Magdeburg-Burg, both in the Luftflotte 1 area, and III/KG 2 with Luftflotte 3 at Illesheim. In preparation for Operation 'Weserübung', the forthcoming invasion of Scandinavia, a unit known as Chef AW was set up to train a number of newly-formed transport units for their role in this; these were:

Stab Lufttransportchef Land
Kampfgruppe zbV 101, 102, 103, 104, 105, 106, 107 and 108.

JG 2 was strengthened on 11 March by the arrival of I/ZG 26 at Langendiebach (near Hanau), while I/ZG 1, reinforced by 12(N)/JG 2, moved to Marx to join JG 1. Three days later II/JG 2 moved to Nordholz to join this Geschwader also, which now had:

Stab/JG 1	Jever
II(J)/TrGr 186	Wangerooge
II/JG 77	Westerland
I(J)/LG 2	Neumünster
I/ZG 1	Marx
II/JG 2	Nordholz

At Marx also, the newly-formed KGr 126 was to be reinforced by 7, 8 and 9/ KG 26, the Staffeln of III/KG 26, which had itself been formed from I/KG 28.

On 15 March III/JG 2 had been formed at Magdeburg-Burg, and would move to join JG 2 at Frankfurt-Rebstock on 10 April. I/JG 51 moved under Jagdge-schwader 51's control at Krefeld on 22nd, while on 31st a weather reconnais-sance unit, Wekusta 51, was re-equipped with four He 111s, two Do 17s and a Ju 52/3m at Langendiebach. At the same time Stab and I/JG 27 moved from Krefeld to München-Gladbach, while I/KG 4, its training complete, moved from Gütersloh to Perleberg to join Fliegerdivision 9.

By now those Luftwaffe units picked to take part in the forthcoming actions over Scandinavia had received their operational orders for Operation 'Weserübung', and were preparing for this new venture.

Chapter 9

NO CALM BEFORE THE STORM

The improving weather was to make April an active month on both fronts, although it would soon be dominated by events in Scandinavia, as will be related in the second section of the book. From the first day of the month, a Sunday, engagements were occurring frequently. On this April morning nine Blenheim IVs from 82 Squadron were despatched on an armed reconnaissance to the German Bight, seeking targets of opportunity. Leaving the airfield at Bodney — to which they had been detached — at 1100, the formation was just attacking a patrol boat flotilla 95 miles west of Amrum, off the Danish coast, when Bf 109Es of 5(J)/TrGr 186 intercepted them, Lt Otto Hintze shooting down Blenheim P8867 (Fl Off G. Harries) at 1415 — at last the first victory for this Gruppe which had seen so many fruitless scrambles during the past few weeks. Later that same afternoon nine Blenheims from 15 Squadron on a similar reconnaissance encountered a single Ju 88, which they attacked and claimed damaged.

2/4/40
Next morning ten He 115s of 3/KüFlGr 506 were sent out on reconnaissance sorties over the south-western region of the North Sea. Operating in pairs, the floatplanes spread out to carry out their task in the face of deteriorating weather conditions and thunderstorms. Off the English coast two Hurricanes of 504 Squadron's Red Section had taken off at 0542 on patrol, and were warned of 'bandits' approaching from the east. Around this time (0620) three more Hurricanes of Blue Section were scrambled to provide patrol cover for a coastal convoy.

After spending about 15 minutes over the ships at 1,500 feet, the latter trio were vectored towards the South Knock Lightship, where the two Red Section fighters were found orbiting. The five Hurricanes were then joined by three Spitfires, but after five minutes these departed, followed at 0715 by the Red Section pair, which were now low on fuel. After a further five minutes two unidentified aircraft were seen approaching, and Flt Lt Royce ordered Blue Section to close up, leading them towards the intruders. These were quickly seen to be He 115s, which at once dived to sea level and headed away east at full power. The Hurricanes went into line astern formation and attacked, making several firing passes which silenced the rear gunners. By now fuel was running short for these Hurricanes too, and two of them were forced to turn for home. Flg Off D. Phillips continued the chase alone for another ten minutes, closing to within 100 yards and continuing to fire until a burst from a gun in one of the Heinkels hit his aircraft and damaged it seriously; he was also wounded in the leg. Phillips was then obliged to force-land in the sea at once, but was subsequently rescued.

Both floatplanes had been hit however, one having had its floats riddled, while the other suffered damage to both engines and the rear gunner was wounded. This latter machine, S4+EL, attempted a force-landing when both engines failed, but crashed and sank. Due to the damaged floats, the other Heinkel was unable to land and pick up the survivors, who were seen swimming; Oblt zur See Erwin Birking and his crew were later picked up safely by another aircraft from their unit. British Intelligence subsequently confirmed the loss of the downed aircraft, and on 9 April credit for this victory was given to Flg Off Phillips.

Much later on 2nd ten Ju 88s from Stab and II/KG 30 made an evening attack on Scapa Flow. One of the Geschwaderstab aircraft was damaged by the AA defences and subsequently crashed into the sea some 200 kilometres off the coast, Oblt Bülow and his crew being lost. A second bomber from 4 Staffel crashed at Bederkesa, 15 miles north-east of Bremerhaven, whilst trying to reach Bremen in fog and low cloud. Hpt Fritz Koch, the Staffelkapitän, and all three members of his crew were killed.

Fighter Command lost two more aircraft during the day, one of 152 Squadron's remaining Gladiators, N5646, crashing into the sea, whilst Hurricane L1799 of 151 Squadron suffered a similar fate off the east coast somewhat further south. Whilst the biplane pilot was rescued, Plt Off H.C.F. Fenton, the pilot of the Hurricane, was not.

3/4/40

During the morning of 3rd several reconnaissance He 111s from 1(F)/122 were sent out to search the area between the Orkneys and the Firth of Forth, and at 1240 one of these reported the presence of a convoy to the east of Peterhead. One of the Heinkels had been intercepted off Kinnaird Head at 0950 by an 803 Squadron Skua, but no damage could be inflicted; three more inconclusive engagements were reported by the Navy pilots some 40 minutes later. A further interception was made by a Gladiator from the Sumburgh Flight, but with no better success.

Even before the convoy had been sighted, II/KG 26 had despatched 14 He 111s on an armed reconnaissance between Peterhead and Flamborough Head, the approach of the first of these being plotted on the British radar around noon. At 1220 Flg Off E.N. Ryder of 41 Squadron scrambled in Spitfire N3114 to investigate a 'bandit' off Whitby, soon finding an He 111H-2 which he at once attacked. The bomber, 1H+AC, which was being flown by the II/KG 26 Gruppenkommandeur, Oberstlt Hans Hefele, put up a fierce barrage of return fire, but Ryder closed in resolutely and saw his bullets striking the starboard engine, which promptly blew up. The crippled bomber sank towards the water and was successfully ditched; all the crew were later rescued, two of them having been wounded, and became prisoners. Ryder had problems of his own however, for the last burst of fire from the rear gunner had disabled the Spitfire, and he too was obliged to come down in the sea. Before he could get out of his cockpit, the fighter sank like a stone. He watched the green water rapidly darkening, and "...when it turned black, I knew it was time to get out!" Fighting his way free, he rose to the surface where he was picked up by the fishing boat *Alaska*. His report of his "Green-to-black" escape was subsequently to become an RAF classic.

Spitfires of 41 Squadron on Catterick airfield early in 1940. *(Gp Capt H.L. Goddard via A. Thomas)*

One more of II/KG 26's Heinkels was damaged by fire from the convoy, which it had found and attacked, and it returned with one man wounded. Eight He 115s of 2/KüFlGr 506 had also gone off early on reconnaissance in the Shetlands-Bergen area, where at 0955 one of them found convoy ON 24 60 miles north-west of Bergen. Following this report five more He 111s of Stab/KG 26 which were already airborne, were directed to this target, while 11 more from KGr 100 were ordered off, followed by two waves of four Ju 88s from 5/KG 30 and 21 He 111s from I/KG 26; by 1250 all 36 aircraft were in the air.

On the previous day four Sunderland flyingboats from 204 Squadron had been sent up to Sullom Voe in the Shetlands on detachment, and during 3 April 'F' (N9046) was sent off to provide escort for the convoy. Flt Lt Frank Phillips and his crew had been on station for some four hours when the German bombers began appearing from the east and neared the ships. Heavy AA fire forced the first to arrive to sheer away, and in so doing two of KG 30's Ju 88s sighted the Sunderland and began circling it, firing from long range. According to the British crew, four more then appeared and all six attacked the flyingboat, which Phillips took down to low level. Since only four Ju 88s were present on this raid, it is surmised that two of the attackers may have been Heinkels — or that the Sunderland crew overestimated the number of their attackers. Indeed according to the German account of this combat, only two Ju 88s actually made the attack. Whatever the numbers, the result was not in doubt. Oblt Karl Overweg, Staffelkapitän of 5 Staffel, made a fast approach from astern, but as he closed to 100 yards' range Cpl W.G. Lillie, the tail gunner, opened fire with his quadruple Brownings and sent the bomber straight into the sea. Plt Off Armitage, the second pilot, then co-ordinated the fire from the turret and the two waist gun positions, and the second Junkers was hard hit, limping off in the direction of Norway with smoke pouring from one engine. It crash-landed on Norwegian soil where it burnt out, the crew of Uffz Willi Erkens being interned at Stavanger.

The big flyingboat had itself suffered damage during these attacks, and headed for base. As it went other bombers attempted to bomb it from 1,500 feet, but none of the Heinkels ventured near the deadly 'sting' in the tail, and it got away without further damage. Phillips was later awarded the DFC for this action, while Cpl Lillie received the DFM. The results for Fliegerkorps X were again disappointing; only two small trawlers, *Gospen* and *Sansonnet* were sunk, both by aircraft of I/KG 26. FdlOst also lost an He 111J of 1/KüFlGr 806 when

M7+CH developed an engine fire while on reconnaissance over the Kattegat. Oblt zur See Werner Beck ditched the aircraft near Sansö Island and the crew paddled their dinghy for seven hours before reaching the sanctuary of this haven.

4–6/4/40

It was the turn of the RAF to send out bombers again on 4 April, six Blenheims of 82 Squadron heading for Wilhelmshaven where reconnaissance had earlier spotted two warships. In bad weather the bombers failed to reach their target, while fighters from I/ZG 76 and II(J)/TrGr 186 scrambled to intercept them, but failed to do so; Uffz August Wilcke of the latter unit, lost in the murk, crashed off Wangerooge and was killed.

Nine more Blenheims, this time from 21 Squadron, were sent out after the same target next day, but these also failed to find their objective, attacking instead the base at Norderney. Here Flak inflicted slight damage on two of the attackers. Further reconnaissance on 6 April would confirm a build-up of warships in Wilhelmshaven which was taking place in readiness for the invasion of Norway. Thereafter all operations over the North Sea area were to become involved with the preparation for and execution of this undertaking, and will therefore more properly be dealt with in the next chapter.

1/4/40

While the North trembled on the brink of major action, over the Franco-German border area April had got off to a brisk start. On 1st — All Fools' Day — the usual trio of Hurricanes were off at 1140, despatched by 1 Squadron to patrol over the Thionville-Boulay area at 22,000 feet. From this height the pilots saw some 4,000 feet higher, a formation of nine Bf 110s from I/ZG 26, which were providing escort for a Do 17 of 3(F)/11, and which were surrounded by AA bursts. Flt Lt Prosser Hanks led Flg Off Clisby and Plt Off Mould up in a steep climb to engage, but the Zerstörer crews spotted them, fanned out and dived to the attack. Hanks engaged one head-on, his Hurricane receiving cannon shells in the wing and cockpit, and he was forced to break away and make an emergency landing on 73 Squadron's airfield at Rouvres-Etain. Mould and Clisby became engaged in a dogfight during which each believed he had shot down one of the Messerschmitts, and indeed BAFF recorded that three were thought to have been shot down in total, one by each pilot. In fact only one Bf 110 was hit (35% damage), Ofw Eugen Blass being wounded; all returned to their base.

73 Squadron was not to be successful on this date, three of this unit's Hurricanes intercepting a new Ju 88D reconnaissance aircraft of 1(F)/123 near Charleville without effect. The French had more luck however, reporting several sharp clashes. Ten MS 406s of GC I/2 engaged eight Bf 109Es of II/JG 52 south-west of Pirmasens, and in a brief fracas inflicted severe damage on one Messerschmitt which was landed by the pilot to be classified as 50% damaged. This was the first combat of the war for I/2; the successful pilot had been Sgt Gloanec who had attacked four Messerschmitts and believed that he had hit one of them when 50 kilometres inside German territory. He did not stop to check his

victim's fate however, heading for home with all speed at low altitude.

Near Longwy five H-7As from GC I/5 caught a Do 215 flown by Oblt Erich Marquardt of 3(F)/ObdL, which was badly damaged (35%), but escaped with two of the crew wounded, one Curtiss being claimed shot down by the rear gunner. S/Lt Lefol and Sgt Girou had expended some 1,200 rounds on the Dornier before it made good its escape over Trier. Lt Boitelot attempted to close, but his H-75A was hit and slightly damaged, causing him to break away. This was undoubtedly the fighter claimed by the German gunner. Adj Salmand was also sent off to give a hand, but found himself faced by a reported two Dorniers, nine Bf 109s and two Bf 110s. Attacking over the Carignan area, he saw no results; he had in fact been engaged with the same 3(F)/ObdL aircraft.

A second reconnaissance Dornier from 4(F)/11 was not so fortunate as the first; it was intercepted at 1210 over Ligny forest, to the east of Sedan by two Moranes of GC II/2 (Adj Chef Renaudie and Sgt de La Gasnerie) and two Potez 631s of ECMJ 1/16 (Lt Cormouls and Adj Blanchard). It fled and appeared to escape, but had been hard hit and crashed at La Fourche au Bouleau, seven miles from Sedan, where its wreckage was found a few days later; it was then credited as a confirmed victory. Two members of Uffz Helmut Gerhard Altmann's crew had been killed, but one survived as a prisoner.

Soon afterwards at 1330 more GC II/2 Moranes flown by Lt de Rohan-Chabot and Sgt Chef De Muyser, attacked a lone He 111 east of Mézierès, while at 25,000 feet. Apparently badly damaged, the bomber dived to 1,500 feet and flew across the Belgian border. No Luftwaffe loss is recorded on this date for such an aircraft, but the French note that the wreckage was found at Monthermé, and was credited to II/2 as another confirmed victory.

That night an Amiot 143 of GB I/38 on a reconnaissance over the Remagen-Cologne area was forced to land near Diekirch in Luxembourg, where the crew were interned after they had burned their aircraft.

2/4/40

Dorniers again appeared over France on 2 April, six Moranes of GC I/2 catching a 4(F)/121 aircraft while on a free chase over Saverne. Two more Moranes from GC II/3 and two from III/3 joined the chase, but none of these late arrivals were to receive any credit for this combat. Adj Bruckert of I/2 closed to point-blank range and opened fire, his bullets being seen to hit the aircraft. Return fire then struck his Morane and it began to stream thick black smoke. Blinded by this, he crashed into a tree whilst attempting an emergency landing near Erstein, 15 miles south-west of Strasbourg, and was killed instantly. The Dornier was subsequently credited to him as a probable; it crash-landed near Lahr, 25% damaged.

Another Dornier from the same unit then appeared, this time with an escort of nine Bf 110s from V(Z)/LG 1. The Moranes from all three Groupes were still in the air, and intercepted over the Lunéville area. Here Adj Le Martelot of I/2 and Lt Bissoudre of II/3 each claimed one Messerschmitt shot down, one aircraft from 15 Staffel crewed by Lt Hans Busching and Uffz Heinz Arndt falling in flames east of Lunéville. Even as Le Martelot watched the burning Zerstörer fall, he was himself shot down by Oblt Werner Methfessel, the Morane being totally destroyed when the badly-wounded pilot attempted to force-land it on Lunéville airfield. Although it seems probable that Le Martelot had been mainly responsible for the demise of the Bf 110, it was credited as a

Adj Emile Le Martelot of GC I/2 was hit and badly wounded by fire from Oblt Werner Methfessel's V(Z)/LG 1 Bf 110 as he watched another Messerschmitt which he had just attacked, go down on 2 April. This was the result of his force-landing at Lunéville.

shared victory between himself, Bissoudre and another pilot of II/3.

Meanwhile Cne Naudy of II/3 led a triple patrol to intercept an aircraft identified as a Do 215 over Metz, flying towards the Saar. Naudy was the only pilot to get within firing range, and with only his 20mm cannon working, was credited with shooting down the Dornier. The aircraft, which it was believed had crashed south-east of Zweibrücken, was in fact a Do 17P of 3(F)/123 which had been returning from a sortie over Reims when attacked. It force-landed at Mannheim, 30% damaged, and with the radio operator wounded.

Five patrolling Hurricanes from 1 Squadron, aloft in the St Avold area, chased

Lt Maurice Bissoudre of GC II/3 with the wreckage of a V(Z)/LG 1 Bf 110 shot down by himself and Adj Le Martelot of GC I/2 on 2 April.

195

Flg Off J.I. 'Iggie' Kilmartin of 1 Squadron. *(IWM)*

a lone Do 17, but failed to catch it. Overhead a Schwarm of Bf 109Es from III/JG 53, which had been led off at 1125 by Hpt Mölders, spotted the unsuspecting British fighters and dived on them. Mölders poured fire into Plt Off C.D. Palmer's aircraft, hitting the cockpit areas and reserve fuel tank, which blew up. Palmer at once rolled the Hurricane over and dropped out, landing just inside No Mans' Land, 500 yards from the German outposts; he was rescued by a French patrol. Meanwhile a dogfight had developed, during which Flg Offs Kilmartin and Clisby each claimed Messerschmitts shot down; no losses were actually suffered by the German unit.

7/4/40

A few quiet days followed, but the fighters were once again engaged on 7th. At 0815 a pair of Morane pilots from GC III/6 caught sight of a lone Dornier northeast of Laon at 23,000 feet. Much time was spent in trying to catch the bomber, which was only marginally slower than the fighters; meanwhile three more Moranes from GC III/2 joined the chase. By now the Dornier was down to 13,000 feet, but the first two Moranes had exhausted their ammunition in vain at long range, and had run low on fuel. The III/2 fighters reported obtaining repeated hits on the Dornier, but it vanished in a dive, leaving a trail of thick black smoke. One MS 406 had been hit by the rear gunner, and Sgt Chef Pizon, the pilot of this, was obliged to make an emergency landing as a result. The Dornier, an aircraft of 1(F)/123, returned to its airfield only 5-10% damaged, and with one engine stopped; it landed safely.

73 Squadron's 'B' Flight patrolled over the Thionville area during the mid morning period, the six Hurricanes meeting two formations of Bf 109Es, totalling 16 in number. These fighters were from I and II/JG 53, and engaged the Hurricanes in a brisk dogfight during which Plt Off P.V. Ayerst shot down 'Weisse 4' of 4/JG 53, flown by Fw Erwin Weiss, who was killed when he crashed near Ham-sur-Varberg. A second Messerschmitt was claimed probably destroyed by Sgt Campbell, when it vanished eastwards leaving a trail of smoke. Flg Off Brotchie's Hurricane was shot up and he baled out wounded in the leg by shrapnel; his aircraft was shot down by Hpt Wolfgang Lippert of I/JG 53, who identified it as a Spitfire.

A little later six Bf 109Es from I/JG 54 were 'jumped' over the lines to the west of Strasbourg by a dozen Moranes of GC I/2. One Messerschmitt was lost, Lt Paul Stolte becoming a prisoner after being shot down by Cne Hyvernaud, while a second was claimed as a probable by Cne Patureau-Miraud. The German pilots were able on this occasion to fight back, and Cne Vidal's Morane was shot down by Oblt Reinhard Seiler; Vidal attempted to bale out, but his parachute caught on the tail of his aircraft and he crashed to his death with the Morane near Marmoutier, west of Saverne.

Shortly after this engagement a patrol of Bf 109Es from II/JG 53 appeared over the area again, waiting to provide cover for a returning reconnaissance aircraft. 15 Moranes of GC III/3 were out providing escort to a GR I/36 Potez when they were warned by radio of enemy aircraft, and diverted towards these — probably the German reconnaissance aircraft. It was quite a rare event for the French ground control to work effectively in this way, so it came as no surprise to the Morane pilots that the arrival overhead of the patrolling Messerschmitts had not been noticed from the ground, and these fell upon the French formation. S/Lt Bevillard's aircraft was hit by several bullets and he broke away. Deprived of his wingmen in the confusion, Cne Andre Richard tried to collect them together over Gros Tenquin, but was caught unawares by the Messerschmitts and his aircraft was disabled by the first burst from Fw Stefan Litjens' guns. Richard attempted a crash-landing on rough ground near Morhange, but the aircraft burst into flames. Probably unconsious inside, he made no attempt to get out, and died in the burning wreck.

Somewhat later in the afternoon Hpt Hannes Gentzen led I/ZG 2's new Bf 110Cs on an escort to a reconnaissance machine over north-west France. They encountered a formation of French fighters over Longuyon, where three H-75As of GC I/5 were providing top cover for MS 406s of GC III/6. The French pilots waded in at once, Lt Michel Dorance shooting down one of the big fighters over Stonne, where Fw Kurt Müller and his gunner, Gefr Herbert Penkert, crashed to their death, while Sous Lt Francois Warnier claimed a second over Beaumont-en-Argonne, as the fight spread over the Argonne Forest. This was Lt Johannes Kiel's machine, from which the wounded pilot baled out to become a prisoner; his gunner, Uffz Werner Ehm, did not get out and perished in the crash. For the Germans the only success was claimed by Gentzen, who reported shooting down one Curtiss. Adj Chef Salmand was killed when his H-75A exploded on hitting the ground near Beaumont-en-Argonne, although the French reported that he had died because his '02' mask had failed. In fact possibly

Lt Michel Dorance (centre) victor over one of the I/ZG 2 Bf 110s shot down by GC I/5 on 7 April, and soon to become one of the Armée de l'Air's highest scorers.

the failure diverted his attention, allowing Gentzen to make his attack. This was Gentzen's ninth victory of the war and his first with the Bf 110; at this stage he was still just ahead of Mölders in terms of victories since September 1939, the latter pilot now having claimed eight. Johannes Kiel would be freed after the capitulation of France in June 1940, and was later to be credited with 25-30 aerial victories and 62 aircraft destroyed on the ground — mainly in Russia.

During the afternoon six H-75As from GC I/4 were involved in an inconclusive engagement with a 1(F)/122 Do 17. More successful were 16 Moranes, 12 from GC II/7, reinforced by four from GC I/6, which were providing cover for three Potez 63-11s of GR I/52 over the Fribourg area. A Ju 52/3m of the Fliegerkompanie Des Luftnachrichtenregiment ObdL, equipped with special radio equipment for eavesdropping on the French aerial navigation system, had been sent out in conditions of thick cloud on such a mission. At 1620 the Junkers was spotted by the Moranes which were returning to base early, having had to break off their mission due to bad weather. They at once attacked the transport over Lure, all making several passes which riddled the unfortunate aircraft, which then crashed in flames south-east of Mercourt. Nine bodies were found in the wreckage as well as numerous radio sets and ten machine guns. The French investigation team were puzzled to find stencilling inside the cabin in Spanish — obviously left over from the Spanish Civil War.

German Flak gunners claimed a Mureaux 117 shot down near Kehl during the day, but this was again a Potez 63-11, this one from GR II/36. It was indeed damaged when near Weissenburg, but the pilot managed to crash-land in French territory.

8/4/40
Weather had caused the trio of Potez 63-11s sent out on the afternoon of 7th to abort their mission, and in consequence three more were despatched over the

same area next day, this time covered by 14 Moranes from GC II/7. Once again poor visibility over the target caused the mission to be aborted, but at 1112, as they headed for home, Cne Hugo was ordered to take his fighters over the Colmar area, where a combat was reported. Nothing was to be seen here, but suddenly, after some 20 minutes in the locality, seven Bf 109Es of I/JG 76 dived on the Moranes. Sgt Bret's aircraft was badly hit and he crash-landed in open country near Bessoncourt. No claim appears to have been submitted by the German pilots on this occasion.

9–10/4/40

The following day came news of the German occupation of Denmark and the invasion of Norway; for 24 hours the world seemed to 'hold its breath'. The only event of note over the Western Front occurred when Bf 109s of II/JG 51 flew a sweep over French territory. Over Kehl one was hit by DCA fire and returned to force-land at Baden-Baden, 70% damaged. 10 April saw a return to normality however, the day being marked by two interceptions of German reconnaissance aircraft. On the first such occasion two H-75As from GC I/4 engaged one of 3(F)/121's Ju 88As without effect but the second appeared more fruitful. During the afternoon an He 111 of Wekusta 26 flew a weather reconnaissance over the Channel. Returning via Berck-sur-Mer on the Normandy coast, it was intercepted near Cap Griz Nez by Plt Off J.R. Cock of 87 Squadron, who had scrambled in his Hurricane from Le Touquet, and claimed to have shot it down into the sea; in fact the aircraft escaped in cloud and returned to Marx airfield, undamaged. During the day a reconnaissance Spitfire, P9396, which was on the strength of 212 Squadron, was reported missing; its fate is not known.

11/4/40

More such interceptions followed on 11th, this time with rather more success for the Allied units. In the morning three Do 17s from 5(F)/122 made sorties, but one flown by Oblt Max Guse was caught over Montmedy at 0700 by a composite formation comprising two H-75As of GC I/5 (S/Lt Boitelot and Sgt Chef Tallent), two Moranes from GC III/6 (Sgt Chef Boymond and Lt Stenou) and one from GC III/7 (Adj Delarue). The reconnaissance aircraft crashed at Wez-Thuisy, about 15 miles from Reims, and was credited to all five pilots jointly. A second Dornier from the same Staffel which had broken off its sortie due to bad weather was intercepted by Moranes from GC II/6 near St Quentin, but escaped with only slight damage. An He 111 of 2(F)/121, flown by Oblt Bruno Wühlisch became lost while on a sortie over the Sedan-Laon-Charleville area, wandering as far as Paris. This aircraft was attacked over Reims at 0755 by three Moranes of GC III/6, Lt Vuillemin seeing the bomber some 1,000 feet higher than himself, flying north. He attacked from below, followed by Sgt Chef Pimont. Meanwhile Sgt Chef Maigret climbed above and attacked, the Heinkel crashing in flames in a forest north-west of Amifontaine; one member of the crew survived to become a prisoner. The only other action reported on this date was an inconclusive skirmish between 12 Bf 109Es of JG 53 and a Hurricane patrol.

Two Blenheims of 57 Squadron took off from Rosieres-en-Santerre to undertake a reconnaissance of roads and railways in the Kleve/München Gladbach area, but L9181 crashed as it left the ground, one member of the crew being killed. The other aircraft proceeded alone, and was intercepted by a Bf 109 of

One of the new Bloch MB 174 reconnaissance aircraft received by GR II/33 at Orconte in March.

1/JG 21, but escaped by climbing into cloud.

Several remarkably quiet days followed, with only occasional engagements to note.

14–18/4/40

During 14 April a Blenheim of 57 Squadron — L9465 — was intercepted over Emmerich at 1745 while on a reconnaissance, and was shot down in flames by Oblt Arnold Lignitz of I/JG 20, Flg Off H.G. Graham-Hogg and his crew being killed when the aircraft crashed near Babberik on Dutch soil. Two days later it was the turn of I/JG 3 to make a similar interception; on this occasion Lts Helmut Rau and Walter Fiel caught one of the new Bloch MB 174s (No 16) as it was returning from a photographic sortie over the Aachen-Cologne area in the hands of Cne Maurice Laux of GR II/33. The German pilot identified the aircraft as a Potez 63 — not surprisingly, due to its close similarity in appearance; they claimed it shot down, but reported that they were unable to observe the crash. In fact the aircraft fell near Longlier, about a mile north-east of Neufchateau on Belgian soil, only the badly burned pilot surviving. Two Bf 109s were lost on this date, one of I/JG 26 crashing and burning after a collision over Wesel with another of the Gruppe's aircraft; the pilot managed to bale out unhurt. A I/JG 27 aircraft became lost and force-landed near Siegen, suffering 65% damage. Two days later other Messerschmitts of 8/JG 3 undertook a scramble, but as they returned to base one Bf 109D came out of cloud too low and crashed into the ground, Uffz Gottfried Dietrich being killed. A Bf 109E of III/JG 26 force-landed near Recklinghausen and burnt out, the pilot escaping unhurt.

19–20/4/40

Poor weather continued to limit activity until 19 April, on which date an Hs 126 of 2(H)/13 was attacked south of Neubreisach whilst on a reconnaissance for 16 Armée. The assailants, Moranes from GC II/7, shot down the Henschel; both Lt Wilhelm Hellmann, the observer, and the pilot, Gefr Hermann Meisner, managed to bale out over German territory even though they had both been wounded. The aircraft was credited to Cne Hugo, Adj Chef Ponteins and Sgts Passemard and Catois. Cne Hugo was also to be credited with a victory over a Do 17 in the Biensen area on this date, shared with Sgt Planchard. A patrouille from GC II/7 also chased a reconnaissance Ju 88 of 4(F)/121 fruitlessly, although

Adj Chef Valentin claimed the aircraft as a probable. Another of these fast aircraft was to be less fortunate next morning when Flg Off 'Iggie' Kilmartin of 1 Squadron was scrambled at 0945 after a high flying aircraft between Chalons and Reims. The Junkers — again from 4(F)/121 — was reconnoitring the St Dizier-Beaune-Romilly area when Kilmartin's Hurricane appeared, and a long chase began which took the two aircraft down from 26,000 feet to ground level. Return fire struck the engine of the Hurricane and Kilmartin was obliged to break away and force-land. It appeared that his shooting had been accurate however, and the German machine crash-landed shortly afterwards near Macon, north of Lyons, where Oblt Klaus Pritzel and his crew were captured. It seems however that it had not succumbed to his fire alone, for Adj Amouroux of GC III/9 in a Bloch MB 152 had engaged a lone Ju 88 over Ozolle, which it was believed had already been damaged at high level over Haute-Saone by anti-aircraft fire. He claimed this shot down for the Bloch's first victory of the war.

Meanwhile four other 1 Squadron Hurricanes had taken off to patrol over Metz and these encountered an He 111 escorted by four Bf 109Es of III/JG 2 at 23,000 feet. The Hurricane pilots at once attacked, Flt Lt Prosser Hanks claiming to have shot down the Heinkel, which he reported landed in Allied territory. The AASF recorded that this aircraft had come down at Macon and the crew had been taken prisoner, but this was clearly confused with the 4(F)/121 Ju 88. No other Luftwaffe loss has been found to account for this. Three fighters were also claimed, one each by Sgt F.G. Berry and Sgt Albonico, while Plt Off Mould claimed an 'He 113', credited as a probable. These were all seen diving steeply towards Germany, pouring black smoke, and none were confirmed; it was obviously the usual story of the Daimler-Benz engine's thick exhaust smoke trail.

A second four-aircraft patrol from the British unit was also in action, engaging nine Bf 109Es of 7/JG 53 near the frontier over the Sierck-les-Bains area. In the brief combat which followed two Messerschmitts were lost; Lt Sievers was shot down by Flt Lt P.R. Walker, crashing to his death near Thionville, while Flg Off 'Hilly' Brown claimed another which he reported fell on German soil. Flg Off Billy Drake attacked three, seeing one going down apparently out of control — probably Sievers' aircraft — before chasing another into Germany, where he reported that it crashed into a hill. This aircraft in fact crash-landed near Gau-Bickelheim, east of Bad Kreuznach, 50% damaged.

French fighters also engaged their German counterparts on several occasions during the day, the initial fracas occurring over the Belfort area at 0655 when five Moranes of GC II/7 took on six Bf 109Es of 2/JG 54 in a short but fierce dogfight. Sgt Boillot shot down the Messerschmitt flown by Lt Helmüt Hoch, and this aircraft blew up, crashing in flames at La Chapelle-sous-Chaux. In achieving this victory, Boillot expended 37 20mm shells and 210 7.5mm bullets!

During the late morning Hpt Mölders led his pilots of III/JG 53 on a Freie Jagd patrol over the Zweibrücken area. 23 H-75As of GC II/4 were on similar duty, providing top cover for a Potez 63 of GR II/36, and inevitably the two formations clashed, the top section of H-75As meeting the Messerschmitts at about 28-30,000 feet. The experienced Germans in their faster aircraft enjoyed the edge, and in moments two of the French fighters had gone down. With bullets in the engine and oil tank of his Curtiss (No 136), Adj Chef Cruchant crashed in No Mans' Land near Bliesbrück; he was badly wounded. It seems probable that he had been shot down by Mölders himself, but gunners of a

Flg Off Billy Drake of 1 Squadron, who claimed two Bf 109Es shot down on 20 April. *(IWM)*

20mm flak battery of I/Flakregt 4 had also opened up on the French fighters, and seeing Cruchant's aircraft come down, claimed this shot down themselves.

Two Schwarme of Bf 109Es from 1/JG 2 were also out on patrol in the Saarbrücken area, and these also attacked the French formation. Oblt Otto Bertram shot down another H-75A, No 189, in which Sgt Chef Casenobe crash-landed at Xaffevillers. The Messerschmitts also engaged the Potez, but experienced fierce resistance from the gunner. Uffz Kurt Geisler's aircraft was hit when to the west of Saarlautern, and the pilot was wounded; he landed at Bassenheim, his Messerschmitt having suffered 10% damage. A second Bf 109E was also hit and suffered 25% damage.

Elsewhere on this very active day a 'patrouille double' of Moranes from GC II/3 intercepted a reconnoitring He 111 of Stab/KG1 — V4+DA − near Mauberge, chasing this to the Franco-Belgian-Dutch border, where they shot it down. It fell near Maastricht, but crash-landed in Dutch territory west of Sittard. One man was killed, but the rest of Lt de Res Paul Lehmann's crew were interned. Credit for the victory went to Sous Lt Troyes, Sous Lt Codet, Sgt Chef Vié, Sgt Loi and Adj Poincenot. Whilst on a patrol over the frontier, Lt Paul Kranz of 4/JG 52 suffered fuel supply problems which caused him to force-land near Landau. The aircraft turned over on the rough ground and the pilot was injured. The German fighters also enjoyed other successes however, four Bf 109Es of II/JG 51 intercepting Bloch MB 174 No 31 of GR I/52 near Strasbourg. This aircraft was shot down in flames north of Schirmeck, 30 miles inside German territory, by Hpt Horst Tietzen; the crew of three (Sous Lt Fevrier; Laneure and Adj Chef Mougel) were all killed.

As night fell both sides continued to take advantage of the improved weather, and soon many aircraft were in the air again. Bombers from KG 1, KG 2, KG 51, KG 53, KG 55 and 4(F)/121 flew sorties to drop leaflets and undertake reconnaissances over French territory. One Do 17Z-3, U5+BD of Stab III/KG 2, strayed into Switzerland and force-landed at Basle, where Lt Horst von der

Oblt Otto Bertram of 1/JG 2 shot down Sgt Chef Casenobe's H-75A at Xaffevillers on 20 April. *(ECPA)*

Groeben and his crew were interned. They and their aircraft were returned to Germany on 9 May 1940. From the Allied side Battles of 75 Wing, AASF, were also off to drop leaflets, but one of these, an aircraft of 218 Squadron (P2201), was intercepted over the Kreilsheim area by a Bf 109D night fighter of IV(N)/ JG 2, flown by Ofw Schmale, and was shot down; this was the first night fighter victory of the war for the German fighters. Only the pilot, Plt Off H.D. 'Hank' Wordle, survived to become a prisoner. (Some two years later, after many adventures, he escaped from the infamous Colditz Castle with Capt Y.R. 'Pat' Reid and Airey Neave — see 'The Colditz Story').

21/4/40

The better weather continued next day, bringing the opposing forces into several conflicts once more. The first of these occurred when six Hurricanes of 73 Squadron set off at 1005 to provide indirect support for a French Mureaux on reconnaissance, nine H-75As of GC II/5 acting as top cover. Bf 109Es of 1/JG 53 were engaged by the Hurricanes, two claims being submitted by the British pilots, plus a probable and two damaged; (Sqn Ldr J.W. More one and one damaged; Flg Off G. Paul one; Plt Off R.A. Marchand one probable and one damaged). No losses were suffered by JG 53 on this occasion, but Oblt Hans-Karl Mayer was able to claim one Hurricane shot down in return. His fire had hit Plt Off P.B. Waller's aircraft causing considerable damage and slightly wounding the pilot; Waller force-landed. Whilst this fight was in progress, a covering Schwarm from the same German unit engaged the H-75As at higher altitude, but no claims resulted on either side.

73 Squadron was up again in the afternoon, six Hurricanes initially engaging two Schwarme of 1/JG 2 Messerschmitts and one from 2/JG 76 in the Merzig area. At once a wide-ranging dogfight commenced which cost the Germans two Messerschmitts, one of them at least shot down by Flg Off Orton. One Bf 109E-1 of 2/JG 76 went down in flames, Fw Leopold Wyhidal being killed, while a similar aircraft of 1/JG 2 was hard hit and Ofw Werner Höppner baled out. He had however been mortally wounded, and was dead when found. As the Hurricanes reformed, four Bf 110s of I/ZG 1 escorted by five Bf 109Es of Stab/ JG 76 were seen, and the Hurricane pilots at once got 'stuck in' to the Zerstörer, Orton and Flt Lt Lovett each claiming one shot down, while claims for probables were made by Plt Offs R.F. Martin and D.S. Scott, and by Sgts L.S. Pilkington. Orton and Plt Off B.E. Tucker each claimed one more damaged. Two Bf 110s were actually lost, both from 1 Staffel; Fw Siegfried Fischer's aircraft crashed north-west of Merzig in German territory, the pilot being killed, although the badly wounded gunner, Uffz Ernst Mayer, was able to bale out. Lt Hans Nocher, who had also been badly wounded, managed to force-land at Hermes-keil, south-east of Trier, his gunner, Uffz Alois Kirchof, also having been wounded; their aircraft was totally destroyed.

During the day two of GC I/5's H-75As intercepted a Do 17 of 1(F)/123 near Stenay; S/Lt Warnier and Sgt Chef Tallent chased the Dornier for some way, firing off 1,500 rounds at it as it lost altitude steadily. Finally it escaped over the Belgian frontier, but was later reported to have crashed on Belgian soil, and was credited as confirmed. This was not in fact the case, for the aircraft actually landed safely at Ansbach with 10% damage.

On this date one of the RAF's unarmed reconnaissance Spitfires of 212 Squadron was off over Germany in the hands of Flg Off Cecil Milne. This aircraft (PR 1A N3071) was intercepted over Böblingen at around noon by a

Oblt Josef Fözö of II/JG 51 grew a beard which he swore to keep until the unit achieved its first victory. By April 1940, it had gone! *(H. Illner)*

patrol of Bf 109Es sent up by II/JG 51, as Milne later recounted: "Six Messerschmitts approached under my 'contrail' but I did not see them as I was busy photographing. The leader put a cannon shell into my engine which rapidly failed. While it lasted I tried to get back to France, suffering further attack on the way. 30 miles from the frontier, at a few thouand feet, the engine gave out so I baled out between attacks, after putting the Spitfire in a dive to destroy its equipment. Landed in a village and was immediately arrested." The Spitfire crashed into an orchard in the village of Grossbettlingen, south-west of Nürtingen, near Stuttgart. Credit for shooting down Milne's aircraft went to Ofw Johann Illner, although it was apparently also claimed by Fw Hans John; the pilot was actually taken prisoner by two of the JG 51 pilots involved in the interception, Oblt Josef Fözö and Lt Erich Hohagen — both later to become famous 'Experten'. It is probable that they collected Milne from the village where he had landed and been secured by the local police.

22/4/40
At this time 1 Squadron was expressing its distaste for the personal publicity some members of 73 Squadron had been receiving in the press — notably Flg Off 'Cobber' Kain. Following the recent combats nearly all the unit's original pilots had been in action, and "It is most commendable that the Squadron has worked so well and made it a Squadron 'SHOW' without any publicized individuality." recorded the unit's Operational Record Book. The squadron was eager to keep pace with its rival nonetheless, but while a patrol of four 1 Squadron pilots spotted two Staffeln of Bf 109Es from I/JG 77 near Metz on 22nd, they were unable to catch them.

The French fighters had a little more luck on this date however. Early in the morning a trio of GC I/5 H-75As (Adj Chef Bouvard, S/Lt Rouquette and Sgt Chef Morel) intercepted another Do 17, this time from 3(F)/11, which they claimed to have shot down. This aircraft actually did come down in Belgium, crashing near Leglise with the mortally wounded radio operator still aboard;

Ofw Johann Illner at dispersal with his Bf 109E; the tailfin of his II/JG 51 Bf 109E carries two victory bars denoting the two claims he made on consecutive days in April 1940. *(H. Illner)*

Oblt Wolfgang Kratzmann and his observer had managed to bale out and were interned.

23/4/40
On 23rd 13 Curtisses from GC II/5 provided cover for a Potez 63-11 over the Differten-Hitzbach area soon after midday. A Do 17P of 1(H)/13 was seen flying over the border near Sarrebrück, heading for Pont-à-Mousson, with an escort of 12 Bf 109Es provided by I/JG 52. Five H-75As were led by S/Lt Villacèque to intercept the Dornier, while Lt Houzé led five more after the Messerschmitts, action beginning to the east of Metz. Lt Ruchoux and S/Lt Klan both attacked Bf 109s, which got away over the border, Klan's victim last being seen on fire near Bouzonville. The Dornier was hit in the starboard engine by Sgt Salès, but he too had to turn back and let it go. Adj Chef Delannoy's aircraft was hit several times, and that flown by S/Lt Jaske was struck by anti-aircraft fire occasioning a force-landing in open country near Pont-à-Mousson.

Subsequently Klan was credited with a confirmed victory, his Bf 109 having been seen to crash near Tromborn; this was probably the aircraft of Ofw Franz Essl of 2/JG 52, who crash-landed in German territory, wounded and with his

Flg Off Cecil Milne (left) with Lt Erich Hohagen (centre) and Oblt Josef Fözö of JG 51. *(via J. Foreman)*

Curtiss H-75As of GC I/5 at Suippes. In the foreground is a four-gun A-1 version, while beyond it is a six-gun A-2.

aircraft 55% damaged. A second Messerschmitt was credited to Ruchoux as a probable, while the Dornier was also credited in this category to Villacèque, Salès, Portalis, Jaske, Sgt Audrain and Sgt Hanzlicek. It was believed to have been brought down over the Saar within German lines, but had in fact only been damaged 20%.

During the morning two sections of Hurricanes had been sent up by 73 Squadron to patrol over the front. Flg Off Kain spotted an aircraft reported as a Bf 110, and attacked this, claiming to have damaged it. However the rest of the formation was badly bounced by Bf 109Es of III/JG 53, Sgt C.N.S. Campbell being hit and wounded, and being obliged to bale out of N2391 at once — probably shot down by Hpt Mölders. Sgt T.B.G. Pyne's aircraft (P2576) was also hit — almost certainly by Fw Franz Gawlick, Mölders' Rottenflieger on this date — and he had to carry out a force-landing near Sierck-les-Bains, 15 miles west of Merzig, having been wounded in the shoulder. It seems possible that Kain's target was in fact a decoy Bf 109 from III/JG 53, since one of these aircraft was hit hard; the pilot, who had been slightly wounded crash-landed on return to Hoppstädten airfield, his aircraft damaged 50%. That night the Germans lost a Do 17 of III/KG 2 flown by Lt Günter Karsten, which failed to return from a sortie over France, crashing at Avenay a d Marne. The crew were killed, but the reason for their loss was not ascertained.

24/4/40

Thereafter activity declined once again for the remainder of the month. During the morning of 24th I/Flakregt 75 claimed damage to a Potez 63-11 near Saarburg, while a second of these was claimed shot down by Flak near Baden-Baden, reportedly falling in French territory. That same afternoon another claim was made by the Flak defences, when the gunners of 2/Leichtflakabt 851 shot down Mureaux 117 No 83 of GAO 548, which crashed south of Kehl. Lt Roussel was killed, but Sgt Chef Wibaux baled out after being seriously wounded.

25/4/40

Next day a Do 17 of 4(F)/121 force-landed south of Tournai in Belgium due to engine failure, Oblt Peter Döring and his crew being interned. Two of them

Flg Off 'Cobber' Kain (centre) with Flg Off J.E. Scoular (left) and Sgt C.N.S. Campbell of 73 Squadron, April 1940. *(IWM)*

were later to turn up as POWs in Canada, but the third man was never accounted for. On 30th a further Potez 63-11 was claimed by the Luftwaffe; this aircraft flew into the area off Völkingen during the evening, four Bf 109Es from 3/JG 2 being scrambled from Bassenheim to intercept. They caught the intruder near Merzig where it was claimed shot down jointly by Lts Helmut Wick, Rudi Pflanz and Haunschild at 1917. These pilots reported that it fell in French territory east of Merzig; it was credited as a Staffel victory, rather than to the individual pilots. A Blenheim of 57 Squadron (L8875) undertaking a reconnaissance over Western Germany, was obliged to force-land in Belgium, where Sgt A.W.S. Thomas and his crew were interned.

April had seen a number of changes in the RAF's Order of Battle and equipment, but not in the case of the Luftwaffe, which was now virtually ready for the forthcoming offensive. In France the Air Component had been joined by 16 Squadron with Lysanders, while 98 Squadron joined the AASF, not as an operational squadron, but as a training unit for Fairey Battle crews. Flying over from Finningley, it had established itself at Bougan by mid month. Having undertaken no operational flying at all since its arrival in France some months earlier, 59 Squadron was at last ordered to begin reconnaissance duties over Western Germany when 52 Wing took over these operations from 70 Wing. The first Blenheim was despatched by the squadron on such a sortie on 30 April.

Amongst the fighter squadrons, 85 had moved to Lille-Seclin and 607 to Abbeville. On 27 April 615 Squadron moved from Poix to Abbeville where it at once began converting 'A' Flight from Gladiators to Hurricanes. So swiftly was conversion undertaken that by 9 May this flight was able to move to Le Touquet with its new aircraft to undertake Channel patrols, while 'B' Flight began a similar conversion.

On 2 May 1 Squadron received four new Hurricanes with constant-speed airscrews — a great improvement on the older fixed pitch and adjustable types in use at the time. Next day six of this unit's pilots inspected one of the captured airworthy Bf 109Es at Amiens, and Flg Off Brown was able to fly it in a mock combat with a Hurricane flown by Prosser Hanks. It was discovered that the

A mixed bag at Poix. To the upper left is a 59 Squadron Blenheim (TR-Z), while closer at left is an Armée de l'Air H-75A. To the right, beyond the interesting collection of camouflaged RAF vehicles, is a Miles Magister trainer and liaison aircraft, believed to belong to 53 Squadron. *(53 Squadron Records via A. Thomas)*

Gladiator IIs of 615 Squadron in April; KW-T is K7938 and KW-R is N2304. *(via L. Hunt/ A. Thomas)*

Hurricane was definitely more manoeuvreable, and was slightly faster at ground level. At any altitude above this however, the Messerschmitt had the edge so far as speed was concerned. It also enjoyed an excellent view to the rear. On 4 May Brown flew the aircraft across the Channel to Boscombe Down for full RAF evaluation; he was escorted by three Blenheims and a Hudson.

In England meanwhile the expansion of Fighter Command continued as fast as possible. During April 245 and 253 Squadrons became operational on Hurricanes, while 64 Squadron at last converted to Spitfires. At Turnhouse 141 Squadron became the second unit to receive Defiants. At the start of May three more units became operational, 145 Squadron with Hurricanes, 92 and 234 Squadrons with Spitfires — all by 9th of the month. Meanwhile three more new units began formation; these were 238 and 249 Squadrons which were to have Hurricanes, and 252 Squadron which was to be another coastal Blenheim fighter unit. The only change in Bomber Command's operational line-up occurred on 4 April when the RNZAF Heavy Bomber Flight with No 3 Group at Feltwell became a full squadron, being given the number 75, previously allocated to one of the Wellington OTU squadrons.

At the start of May the French re-equipment programme was still very far

Newly-operational in April, one of 253 Squadron's Hurricanes is seen at Northolt with Plt Off John Greenwood at the controls. *(J.B. Greenwood via A. Thomas)*

from complete. More Bloch 152 units were now available, but there was still not a single unit of Dewoitine 520s at the front. Amongst the bombers the situation was still grave. Only ten groupes were on an immediate war footing, and six of these still employed old Farman 221 and 222s, and Amiot 143s. Two groupes of Breguet 693s and two of LeO 451s were ready, while others were at least nearing operational status. A further groupe had completed re-equipment with LeOs and two groupes of the new Martin 167F attack bombers had just moved to north-western France from North Africa. Three more assault groupes were well-advanced on their training with Breguet 691s, 693s and Potez 633s, while five groupes were currently exchanging Bloch 210s for LeO 451s with all speed.

To bolster up the weak Armée de l'Air striking arm, the Aeronavale now had four dive-bomber units — two with Vought V-156Fs and two with LN 401s and 411s — at land bases, while five units of the modern Late 298 floatplanes, each with ten aircraft, were operational, three at Cherbourg and Boulogne, the others on the Mediterranean coast.

At the beginning of May the Air Component despatched six Lysanders of 2 Squadron and a dozen Hurricanes of 87 Squadron to Senon, near Metz, to co-operate with the Expeditionary Force's 51st Highland Division. The rest of 87 Squadron joined 85 at Lille-Seclin. 26 Squadron moved its Lysanders to Dieppe, while the first six aircraft of this type from 614 Squadron arrived in France, going initially to Amiens.

There had been little further change within the Luftwaffe amongst the units not involved over Scandinavia during the month. On 1 April Stab/ZG 2 had begun forming at Darmstadt-Griesheim, Wekusta/X Fliegerkorps has been established at Hamburg-Fuhlsbüttel, as had II/KG 51 at München-Reim. II/ZG 1 had moved to Gütersloh on 10th, under the direct command of Luftflotte 2. Within this air fleet on 1 May, Stab I/KG 40 and 2/KG 40 were established, while all 'Freya' units except those under Lt Diehl's command, were transferred to the west for the defence of Berlin.

1/(F) 124 was placed under the command of FAG/ObdL on 6 May to raise the High Command's reconnaissance Gruppe to five Staffeln strength, whilst on 8th, ready for the new offensive, several new transport units were formed. These were Stab KGzbV 2, KGrzbV 9, 11, 12 and 172, and 17/KGrzbV 172. All was now in place for the assault.

3–4/5/40

During this period reconnaissance activities by both sides continued uninterrupted. Late on 3 May Blenheim L9329 of 53 Squadron took off on a night reconnaissance in the hands of Plt Off J.L.G. Butterworth. It failed to return, crashing near Nornisgründe/Schwarzwald with the death of all the crew. The cause of the crash was not determined. Next day a Potez 63-11 of GR I/55 was also lost, crashing near Villingen. Once again the crew failed to survive, and no cause for this loss has been discovered. That night six He 111 of III/KG 27 flew a reconnaissance over Lille, Bethune and Arras, but as they returned in the early dawn, they strayed over Dutch territory in the Vlieland area. Here they were intercepted by Fokker D XXI fighters, but were able to escape without damage.

Many Allied airfields were reconnoitred by the Luftwaffe on 8 May, one Do 17 of 3(F)/123 being intercepted near Dijon by five Moranes of GC III/7. Lt Costey and Sgt Dehaus fired at the Dornier, but it disappeared in cloud, returning to base slightly damaged. Next day two He 111s of 2(F)/122 flew a reconnaissance over the Thames Estuary, where one was intercepted by three patrolling Hurricanes of 56 Squadron. These gave chase to what they identified as a 'Ju 88', but it escaped them. The Heinkel's gunners identified the fighters as 'four Spitfires' and claimed one shot down in flames. No loss or damage was actually suffered by either side.

Over France during the morning of 9 May Hurricanes of 87 Squadron were undertaking patrols from their new base at Senon. Two of these fighters headed for the Maginot Line area in the hands of Plt Off Dunn and Sgt G.L. Nowell. Here a Bf 110 of II/ZG 1 was seen over Longwy, and was attacked by both pilots, who reported that it went down pouring smoke. The Messerschmitt was indeed badly hlt (80%) and crash-landed near Merzig, the crew unhurt. As the Hurricanes returned, Dunn spotted two Do 17s — aircraft of Stab/KG 2 — near the Lille-Seclin area. He attacked one of these (U5+A), but the radiator of his aircraft was at once hit by the fire from the rear gunner and he was obliged to force-land immediately without observing the result of his attack; thrown forward on landing, he suffered a cut head. Again his fire had been accurate however, and the bomber was damaged, crash-landing near Hamburg on return. The crew were unhurt, but the aircraft was a total write-off.

A Ju 88 of 1(F)/123 was involved during the morning in a series of airfield reconnaissances over Chartres-Etampes-Tours, but it was hit by DCA and force-landed near Azy, north-east of Bourges, Lt Franz Oswald and his crew becoming prisoners. Meanwhile a Do 17P of 4(F)/121 was on similar duty, covering Sezanne-Romilly-Troyes, but this was attacked south of Vitry-le-Francois by three MS 406s of GC II/7, and was damaged by their fire. The Dornier then escaped into cloud, returning 15% damaged, with the radio operator wounded.

That evening all Allied units were put on full alert and immediate readiness. An imminent German offensive was correctly anticipated. In the early hours of the next morning one of the most fateful and significant military campaigns of history was to be unleashed, which would transform the whole face of Europe and alter the power bases of the world in an incredibly brief time; the waiting was over — the Battle of France and the Low Countries was about to commence.

On the eve of the 'Blitzkrieg', Luftwaffe fighters had claimed a total of 160 or so victories since September 1939. 73 of these claims had been made by the pilots of JG 53, 71 of them having been confirmed. This unit had lost 15 pilots killed to all causes; however at least 24 aircraft had been shot down or damaged in combat, with nine of their pilots dead, five wounded and one a prisoner. The French fighters had claimed 70 confirmed victories and a number of probables. The Curtiss H-75A equipped units had gained the bulk of these — some 40 — with GC II/5 and II/4 the two most successful units. Amongst the Morane 406 groupes, GC II/7 had emerged top-scorer with ten and one shared.

PART TWO

THE SCANDINAVIAN ADVENTURE

Chapter 1

INVASION

Following the seven months of desultory air actions over the North Sea Triangle area, it was here that the first major escalation of the war was to occur. From the very beginning of the war the Scandinavian nations had been the source of much soul-searching amongst the leaders of Britain and France for a number of reasons, principally concerned with iron ore. Sweden is possessed of vast quantities of high-grade ore of the greatest possible value to the industrialised nations of Western Europe, and particularly to nations at war. The very geographical position of Sweden on the Baltic, a sea under complete German domination at its western end at this stage of the war, made it impossible for the Allies to purchase all, or even a major proportion of the country's output, which went in vast amounts straight to the blast furnaces of the Ruhr, Germany's industrial heartland. Indeed, no less than two thirds of German industry's total consumption of iron ore was imported from Sweden.

There are two main areas of Sweden where ore is mined, one near Stockholm, in the southern part of the country, the other in the far north. Supplies from the former provided no problems, being shipped direct across the Southern Baltic to Kiel, Rostock and Lübeck. In the north however, an area of steep and rugged mountains, and extreme climatic conditions, outlet was more complicated. A single-track railway led to the small port of Luleå on the northern shore of the Baltic, but here ice put an end to all traffic for six months of the year, from December to May. For the winter period therefore, the rail track had been continued westward through the mountains into Northern Norway, and the all-weather port of Narvik. From here the ore was shipped through Norwegian coastal waters of the North Sea, south to the Skagerrak, and thence eastwards into the Baltic, or alternatively, continuing southwards to Hamburg and Wilhelmshaven.

When war broke out between the third Scandinavian country, Finland, and her giant neighbour the Soviet Union, in November 1939, the possibility of a Russian occupation of that country, bringing the Red Army within a few miles of the Swedish ore fields, did not enamour the Allied governments. Indeed, no more did the continued supply of ore to the Germans, but the new situation did appear to offer a chance to do something to improve things, albeit in a rather roundabout way. Previously any idea of an invasion to occupy the ore fields had been discounted, since quite apart from the effect on neutral opinion, it would undoubtedly have provoked a violent German reaction in an area where all the advantages would be theirs.

From November 1939 however there was a strong body of opinion in both

MAP 4: LANDINGS ON AND KEY LOCATIONS IN SOUTH NORWAY

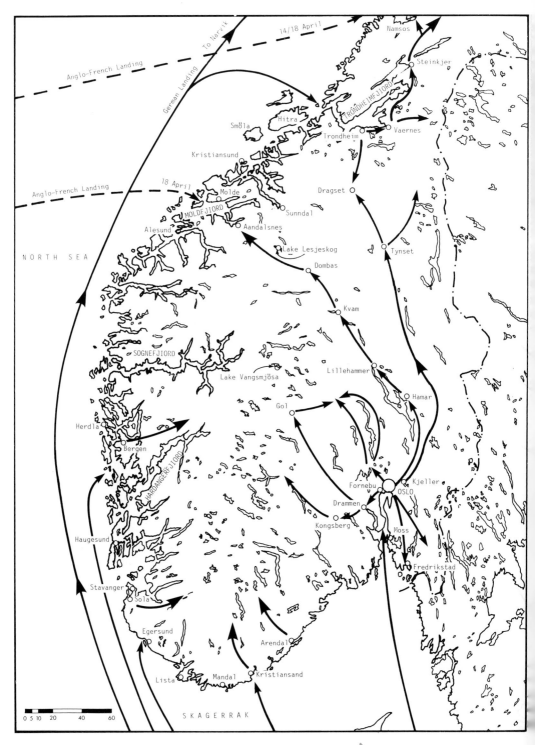

Namsos

14/18 April

Steinkjer

Anglo-French Landing

To Narvik

German Landing

TRONDHEIMFJORD

Smøla

Hitra

Vaernes

Trondheim

Kristiansund

Dragset

Anglo-French Landing

18 April

Molde

MOLDEFJORD

Sunndal

Alesund

Aandalsnes

Tynset

Lake Lesjeskog

NORTH SEA

Dombas

Kvam

SOGNEFJORD

Lillehammer

Lake Vangsmjøsa

Hamar

Gol

Herdla

Bergen

HARDANGERFJORD

Fornebu

Kjeller

Drammen

OSLO

Haugesund

Kongsberg

Moss

Stavanger

Sola

Fredrikstad

Egersund

Arendal

Lista

Mandal

Kristiansand

0 5 10   20   40   60

SKAGERRAK

MAP 5: LANDINGS ON AND KEY LOCATIONS IN NORTH NORWAY

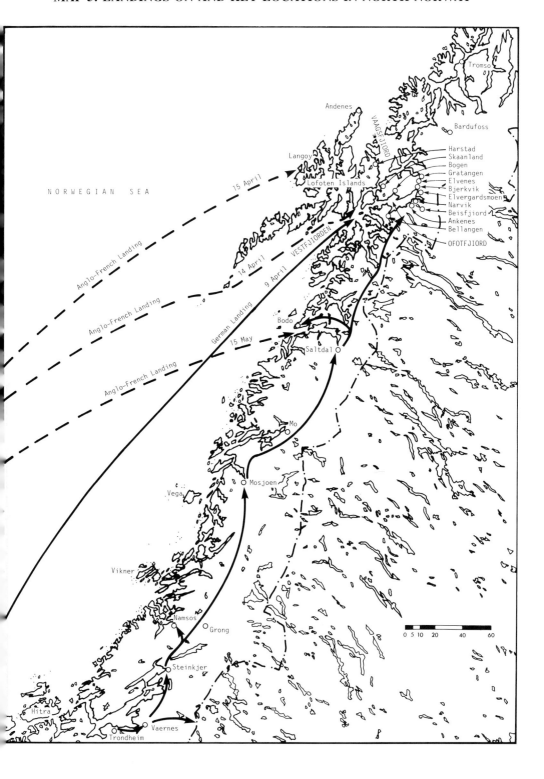

France and Britain which favoured the sending of assistance to the gallant Finns, who had put up such a stout resistance. Much of this pressure came from Winston Churchill, then First Lord of the Admiralty. A plan was therefore mooted to despatch a force to Norway and Sweden under cover of helping the Finns, and with the agreement of the Scandinavian governments, which could then put a stop to the flow of ore.

Not surprisingly, the Norwegian and Swedish governments had no desire to lose their lucrative export market, or to risk a German occupation of their territory, and effectively put an end to Allied plans. A suggestion that the Royal Navy should mine Norwegian territorial waters to interrupt the traffic from Narvik met no more favourable response, but by this time Allied intentions had thoroughly alarmed the German government. Announcements by the British and French governments of their intention to send aid to the Finns had by mid-December 1939 resolved Adolf Hitler on the necessity of gaining control of Norway. Initially he hoped to do this by assisting the Norwegian Nazi, Vidkun Quisling, to seize power. The British counter-violation of Norwegian coastal waters during February 1940 to capture the supply ship *Altmark* and free the prisoners aboard her, had further highlighted the undesirability of allowing Norway to remain an unoccupied neutral.

By February 1940 it had become clear that Finland could not hold out much longer, and requests were again made that Allied troops be allowed to pass through Norway and Sweden to go to her aid. Once again a refusal was forth-coming, and at the same time the Scandinavians made clear their insistence that the export of ore to Germany should continue. The British government once more considered the laying of mines, despite the fact that only about one third of the total quantities exported passed through Narvik. After considering the proposal fully, the Cabinet decided against this however.

Even as the British deliberations were taking place, in Germany action was being planned to safeguard the flow of Swedish ore, a directive being issued on 1 March 1940 for the preparation of a combined operation under the codename Operation 'Weserübung' (Weser Exercise) to occupy Norway and Denmark, but leave Sweden free. By this time Quisling had shown his inability to gain power, but his influence and supporters would assist in full a German occu-pation. In the event this influence was to prove extremely limited and of very little practical help to the Germans, either during the invasion or in their subsequent occupation of the country. On 13 March the war in Finland ended, while on 26th the date of the proposed invasion was set for the next full moon period — early April — and preparations were swiftly put in hand, strong naval units and air forces being concentrated in North Germany for support of the army units involved.

For this operation the Luftwaffe greatly strengthened Generalleutnant Geissler's X Fliegerkorps, and by early April he had a powerful force assembled ready for action. The Order of Battle may be seen overleaf. The units available could of course, be further supported by elements of Luftflotte 2 as necessary.

5/4/40

The French were by now keen to take action in Norwegian waters, feeling that a positive move would be welcomed, but the British were not convinced. As a compromise, notes were despatched to the Swedish and Norwegian govern-ments on 5 April, informing them that their interpretation of neutrality was

LUFTWAFFE ORDER OF BATTLE OVER SCANDINAVIA, APRIL 1940

Unit	Base	Commander	Number Aircraft Available	Type
X FLIEGERKORPS	Hamburg	GenLt Hans Geissler Chief of Staff — Maj i G. Martin Harlinghausen Ia — Maj i G. Christian		
Korpsführungs- kette	Hamburg- Fuhlsbüttel		2	He 111H
Korpstransport- staffel	Hamburg- Fuhlsbüttel		2	Ju 52/3m
Wetterkette X Flgkps	Hamburg- Fuhlsbüttel		3	He 111H
1(F)/122	Hamburg- Fuhlsbüttel	Hpt Caesar	8	He 111H
1(F)/120	Lübeck-Blankensee and Kiel-Holtenau	Maj Schub	5 / 3	Do 17P / He 111H
I/StG 1	Kiel-Holtenau	Hpt Hozzel	39	Ju 87R
II/JG 77	Husum	Hpt Hentschel	38	Bf 109E
I/ZG 76 and 3/ZG 1	Westerland	Hpt Reinecke	32	Bf 110C
	Westerland	Oblt Ehle	10	Bf110C
I/ZG 1 (less 3 Staffel)	Barth	Hpt Falck	22	Bf 110C
2(H)/10	Flensburg		9	Hs 126B
Kampfgeschwader 26		Oberstlt Fuchs		
Stabsstaffel	Lübeck-Blankensee		5	He 111H
I/KG 26	Marx	Oberstlt Alefeld	36	He 111H
II/KG 26	Lübeck-Blankensee	Hpt Vetter	36	He 111H
III/KG 26	Lübeck-Blankensee	Maj von Lossberg	26	He 111H
KGr 100	Nordholz	Hpt von Casimir	27	He 111H
Kampfgeschwader 30		Oberstlt Loebel	1	He 111P
Stabsstaffel	Westerland		1	Ju 88A
I/KG 30 (less 1 Staffel)	Westerland	Hpt Doench	25	Ju 88A
II/KG 30	Westerland	Hpt Kinkelbein	30	Ju 88A
III/KG 30	Westerland	Hpt Mahrenholtz	13	Ju 88A
Zerst Staffel/KG 30	Westerland	Oblt Bönsch	6	Ju 88C-2
Kampfgeschwader 4		Oberstlt Fiebig		
Stabsstaffel	Fassberg	Hpt Altvater	6	He 111P
I/KG 4	Perleberg	Oberstlt Rath	36	He 111P
II/KG 4	Fassberg	Oberstlt Freiherr von Massenbach	36	He 111P
III/KG 4	Lüneburg	Maj Neudörffer	17 / 20	He 111P / Ju 88A
Küstenfliegergruppe 506		Maj Minner		
1/KüFlGr 506	List/Sylt	Hpt Wiesand	11	He 115B
2/KüFlGr 506	List/Sylt	Hpt von Zetschwitz	12	He 115C

1/KüFlGr 506	List/Sylt	Hpt von Schrötter	12	He 115B/C
Lufttransportchef Land		Oberstlt von Gablenz		
Kampfgeschwader zbV 1				
Stabsschwarme	Ütersen		3	Ju 52/3m
I/KGzbV 1	Ütersen	Maj Witt	53	Ju 52/3m
II/KGzbV 1	Schleswig, Stade	Oberstlt Drewes	53	Ju 52/3m
III/KGzbV 1	Ütersen, Hagenow	Hpt Zeidler	53	Ju 52/3m
IV/KGzbV 1	Hagenow	Maj Beckmann	53	Ju 52/3m
KGrzbV 101	Neumünster	Oberstlt Mundt	53	Ju 52/3m
KGzrbV 102	Oldenburg	Oberst Baur de Betaz	53	Ju 52/3m
KGrzbV 103	Schleswig	Hpt Wagner	53	Ju 52/3m
KGrzbV 104	Stade	Hpt von Jena	53	Ju 52/3m
KGrzbV 105	Holtenau	Maj Dannenberg	8	Fw 200B/C
			11	Ju 90
			1	Ju G-38
KGrzbV 106	Ütersen	Maj Stolt	53	Ju 52/3m
KGrzbV 107	Fuhlsbüttel		53	Ju 52/3m
Lufttransportchef See		Maj Lessing	14	He 59
KGrzbV 108	Rantum, Hörnum	Hpt Förster	13	Ju 52/See

LUFTWAFFE GROUND ORGANISATION

Luft-Nachrichten-Verbände (Intelligence and Information Units)
Luftgau-Stab zbV 300 (for Denmark)   GenLt Andrae
6 Flugmeldekompanie (mot) LgNRgt3
Luftgau-Stab zbV 200 (for Norway)   GenLt Süssman
Part of I/LgNRgt 3 on the steamer *Neidenfels*

Flakverbände (Anti-aircraft units)

With X Fliegerkorps	I/Flakregiment 32	
	II/Flakregiment 33	
	I/Flakregiment 611	
Under Gruppe XXXI	I/Regiment Gen Göring	
	I/Flakregiment 8	
	I/Flakregiment 18	

Fallschirmjägerverbände (Paratroops)
I/Fallschirmjäger Regiment 1
    (four Companies)   Hpt Erich Walther

damaging to Allied interests. It was now agreed with the French that mines should be laid by the Royal Navy, and that if this caused a German invasion of Southern Norway, Allied ground forces should be despatched to occupy Narvik, Trondheim and Bergen, and to demolish harbour facilities at Stavanger. A Swedish reply was sent swiftly, stating that the Allied attitude brought their countries near to war, but no reply had been received from the Norwegians when the situation was overtaken by events.

At the same time as the Allied governments were making known to the Swedes and Norwegians their displeasure at the latters' attitudes to neutrality, the first German supply vessels disguised as merchantmen, were already at sea having sailed on 3 April to reach Danish and Norwegian waters before hostilities commenced. As mentioned in the last chapter, a careful watch on the Germans was already being kept by the RAF in an effort to spot any reaction to the Allied pressures on the Scandinavian governments, and on 6 April two high-flying unarmed reconnaissance Spitfires of the PDU brought back from the port of Wilhelmshaven evidence of the presence of the warships *Admiral Hipper, Scharnhorst* and *Gneisenau*, as well as many other vessels. That evening the main German forces set sail and during the night the cruiser *Hipper* was spotted by a Hampden of 83 Squadron to the north of Heligoland. At once the search was on, Hudsons of Coastal Command being sent out to find the ships on 7 April, while another PR Spitfire, piloted by Flt Lt M.V. Longbottom, flew to Kiel, where large concentrations of shipping were seen, together with many aircraft on nearby airfields; a substantial proportion of these were noted to be Ju 52/3m transports.

As Hudsons of 220 Squadron spread out on their search, 18 Do 18s of KüFlGr 406 had been sent out to reconnoitre the area Peterhead-Shetland-north of Bergen to ascertain whether any opposition to the German sortie was developing, while six He 111Js from KüFlGr 806 provided direct escort to the warships. One Hudson crew reported an inconclusive encounter with a Do 18 (K6+CK of 2/406), while another became engaged in a fight with K6+JK of this unit, both being damaged, while one member of the German crew was wounded. However during the first hours of daylight another of the Hudsons, flown by Flg Off Bruce, came upon the *Hipper* and her attendant destroyers off Jutland. Although driven off by Flak, he was able to radio their position and raise the alarm, reporting one cruiser and six destroyers in position 55° 30' N, 07° 37' E. Six Bf 109s of II/JG 77 were scrambled, but failed to locate the intruder.

At 1045 a dozen Blenheim IVs from 107 Squadron and six from 82 Squadron set off from Wattisham, led by Wg Cdr Basil Embry, their target being *Admiral Hipper* and six destroyers; they found instead a fleet of 17 vessels including *Scharnhorst* and *Gneisenau*, and at once attacked, though no hits were scored. The German noted near-misses close by *Hipper* and the destroyers *Paul Jacobi* and *Friedrich Eckoldt*. Close behind the Blenheims came 24 Wellingtons, 12 each from 9 and 115 Squadrons, which had left their base at 1105. Although these bombers were able to catch fleeting glimpses of ships through low clouds, the weather prevented a definite sighting, and they were forced to return with their bombs still aboard. As they made for home, 'A' Flight of 115 Squadron fell behind, and was suddenly attacked by a pair of Bf 110s from I/ZG 1, three or four of these aircraft having been spotted in the distance. While the gunners aboard the Wellingtons thought one of the big fighters had been shot down by them, N2949 and P2524, piloted by Plt Offs Wickenkamp and Gayford respectively, fell flaming into the sea, shot down by Lt Lindemann and Uffz Dünsing; the three other bombers were all hit and had their fuel tanks pierced in every case. P9226 (Sqn Ldr Marwood-Elton), P9236 (Flg Off Wells) and P9227 (Flg Off Barber) were all damaged Cat 2; the two latter aircraft had to be returned to the manufacturers for repairs. Marwood-Elton was slightly wounded. On this occasion the gunners had somewhat under-estimated the effect of their fire, which had been quite devastating. Lt Lindemann's Bf 110 fell into the sea with the loss of both members of the crew, whilst Uffz Dünsing's aircraft suffered severe damage to one engine and the landing gear.

The Royal Air Force was not well-placed to operate over Norway in April 1940, all but the southernmost parts of that country being beyond the range of the majority of aircraft available. The heavy bombers of Bomber Command could reach the area from their bases in the Midlands, but it was not practicable to move more than one or two squadrons to the north of Scotland for operations further afield for a variety of reasons — lack of suitable bases being not the least among these. Further, while it was contemplated sending formations of Wellingtons and Hampdens out unescorted in daylight once more, the slower Whitleys could not be risked in this manner, although they possessed the longest range of any bomber then in service with the RAF. They could operate only by night, when targets in Norway would be extremely difficult to find. An added hazard was the very short period of darkness pertaining in the far North during the spring, so that if careful timing was not observed, the bombers would find themselves still within range of hostile fighters when dawn came.

The most keenly-felt deficiency in RAF equipment at this time was for an effective long-range fighter; the only aircraft available in this category was still the fighter version of the Blenheim — an aircraft which left much to be desired performancewise when faced with modern German types like the Bf 110, Ju 88 or Bf 109E. It was clear that for any sustained operations, unless airfields in Norway itself were swiftly to become available, the bulk of the operations in the air would have to be borne by the patrol-bombers of Coastal Command. This Command was still in the midst of its programme of re-equipment, exchanging elderly London and Stranraer flying-boats, Anson patrol bombers and Vickers Vildebeest torpedo-bombers, for Sunderlands, Lerwicks (the latter soon to prove a disappointing failure), Hudsons and Bristol Beauforts.

In early April 1940 Coastal Command could muster in Scotland and the North of England the following units:-

204 Squadron at Sullom Voe in the Shetland Islands; this unit was equipped with Sunderlands and had just arrived from Mount Batten. It was to be reinforced during the month by detachments from 210 and 228 Squadrons, also with Sunderlands, which were based at Pembroke Dock, and which sent aircraft up to Invergordon and Sullom Voe.

240 Squadron was also at Sullom Voe, flying Saro London IIs; these elderly biplane flyingboats could not operate with safety within range of German shore-based aircraft.

201 Squadron at Invergordon was also equipped with London IIs, but was about to convert to Sunderlands.

209 Squadron at Oban was operating Stranraers and Lerwicks, converting slowly to the latter as they became available.

220 Squadron was at Thornaby in North Yorkshire with Hudsons.

224 Squadron was at Leuchars with Hudsons.

233 Squadron was at Leuchars with Hudsons.

254 Squadron had arrived at Lossiemouth on 5 April with Blenheim IVFs for long-range fighter operations.

With the exception of 254 Squadron, these units were normally involved in the escort of shipping convoys, patrols against German U-Boats, and so far as the Hudsons were concerned, searches for and attacks on German surface vessels of all types. The defence of the great naval base at Scapa Flow was in the hands of four Fighter Command units. At Drem were 29 and 111 Squadrons, while 43 and 605 Squadrons were at Wick. 29 Squadron was flying Blenheim IFs, and had also arrived only on 5 April to provide some fighter cover for convoys; the other three units were of course, all equipped with Hurricanes.

The units of Bomber Command which would operate in the area during the next weeks were as follows:

2 Group (Blenheim IVs)
Wattisham; 107 and 110 Squadrons

3 Group (Wellingtons)
Honington; 9 Squadron
Feltwell; 37 and 75 Squadrons
Marham; 38 and 115 Squadrons
Newmarket; 99 Squadron
Mildenhall; 149 Squadron

4 Group (Whitleys)
Dishforth; 51 and 102 Squadrons
Linton-on-Ouse; 58 Squadron
Driffield; 77 Squadron

5 Group (Hampdens)
Waddington; 44 and 50 Squadrons
Scampton; 49 and 83 Squadrons
Hemswell; 61 Squadron

The Fleet Air Arm was in no better position; four squadrons were stationed at Hatston in the Orkneys, three of them — 800, 801 and 803 — being equipped with Blackburn Skua fighter-dive-bombers which could just about reach Southern Norway, but lacked the range to remain for any time on patrol there. The fourth squadron, 804, was flying Sea Gladiators, which were suitable only for local defence. The only aircraft carrier readily available, HMS *Furious*, was undergoing a refit in the Clyde, while *Ark Royal* was at Gibraltar training, and *Glorious* was in the Mediterranean.

At the time of the alarm, the Norwegian air forces, both Army and Navy, were like so many other European air forces, in the throes of re-equipment and modernization. For the Army the following aircraft had been ordered: from Italy, four Caproni Ca 310 and 15 Ca 312bis light twin-engined bombing aircraft; only the four Ca 310s had so far been delivered; from the United States, 24 Curtiss Hawk 75A-6 fighters (ordered August/September 1939) and Hawk 75A-8s (ordered February/March 1940), plus 36 Northrop-Douglas DB 8A-5 attack-bombers (ordered March 1940); 19 of the Hawk 75A-6s had been delivered, but these were still in the process of being removed from their crates and erected; none were in service, or indeed in operational condition. The other five from this order were still at sea on their way, and would not arrive in time. From Germany ten Focke-Wulf Fw 44 Stieglitz trainers were due for delivery at the time, but none actually arrived.

For the Navy 12 Heinkel He 115A-2 twin-engined floatplane reconnaissance-bombers had been ordered and six delivered from Germany (designated He 115N — *Norwegen* — in Germany), and six more He 115N–IIs had been ordered in November 1939. None of the latter, nor any of 24 Northrop N-3PB single-engined floatplanes ordered from the United States, had arrived.

Of equipment on hand, most was old; 22 Fokker C-VD and 18 C-VE two-seat reconnaissance-bomber biplanes made up the bulk of the operational

Gladiators of the Norwegian Fighter Wing at Oslo/Fornebu airfield. *(via B. Olsen)*

strength of the Haerens Flygevåpen (Army Air Service), together with a dozen Gloster Gladiators. Six Gladiators Is had been built for Norway and delivered in August 1937, these aircraft carrying an armament of four Colt .303in machine guns. Six more to Mark II standards had been ordered, but had not been delivered, and eventually six RAF Gladiator IIs, N5919-5924, had been diverted to Norway. Training was undertaken mainly in DH Tiger Moths and C-Vs. Available for operations at dusk on 8 April 1940 were the following aircraft:

Oslo/Fornebu;   Ten Gladiators (seven serviceable) of the Fighter Wing (Jagevingen).

Oslo/Kjeller;   Five C-VDs (three under overhaul) and five Tiger Moths (one unserviceable) of the Speidevingen (Reconnaissance Wing) under Capt Ole Reistad.

Nine C-VDs (one unserviceable) plus 15 Tiger Moths (15 serviceable) of the Flygeskolen (Flying School).

Four C-VEs of the Bombevingen (Bomber Wing).

Norwegian DH Tiger Moths. *(via B. Olsen)*

Three of the four Caproni Ca 310 bombers of the Norwegian Bomber Wing at Stavanger/Sola; aircraft 505 is in the foreground. *(Arveng Collection via B. Olsen)*

Stavanger/Sola;   Four C-VEs and three Ca 310s (one unserviceable), plus two Tiger Moths of the Bombeveingen (Bomber Wing).
                         Two C-VDs of the Speidevingen.
Trondheim/Vaernes;   Nine C-Vs and one Tiger Moth.

Northern Norway — Hålogaland Flygeavdeling (Air Corps)
Seida, Tana Valley;   Three C-VDs and one Tiger Moth.
Banak;   Three C-VDs.

Marinens Flygevåpen (Naval Air Service) equipment comprised largely home-designed and built Høver MF 11 reconnaissance-bomber-torpedo biplane float-planes, 14 of which were serviceable, together with six very elderly Douglas DT-2B and 2C aircraft, designated for similar duties. Apart from the He 115A-2s, there was a single Junkers Ju 52/3m, (No 400) ex-Norwegian Air Lines LN-DAI *Hauken*, which had been modified for use as a bomber; this aircraft was under-going overhaul at the time. These aircraft were based as follows:

Heinkel He 115A of the Norwegian Marinens Flygevåpen. *(via B. Olsen)*

Southern Norway

Horten;	Five MF11s, two DT-2Cs and one MF 10 trainer. (1 Flyavdeling)
Kristiansand;	Three MF 11s and one MF 10 of 1 Flyavdeling (1 Wing).
Flatøen, near Bergen;	Four MF 11s (one unserviceable), two He 115As and three DT-2Cs (none serviceable) of the 2 Flyavdeling (2 Wing).
Sola/Hafrsfjord;	Two MF11s on detachment from 2 Flg avd, and one He 115A on detachment from 1 Flg avd.
Aunøy, near Hitra;	One MF11 on detachment from 2 Flg avd, and one Ar 196 (of which more later).

Northern Norway

Skatøra, near Tromsø;	Three He 115As of 3 Flg avd.
Vadsø;	Two MF 11s of 3 Flg avd.

Høver MF 11s in flight. *(via B. Olsen)*

Most airfields were situated in the south of the country, Kjeller and Forenbu being in the vicinity of Oslo, the capital, while Sola was at Stavanger on the south-west coast. The Naval Air Service base at Kristiansand was situated approximately midway between these two former localities. Vaernes was somewhat further north, in the vicinity of Trondheim where the country becomes much narrower; in the far north, near Narvik, there was one substantial airfield at Bardufoss.

The Danish air forces were even smaller than those of Norway. The most modern aircraft on hand were of Fokker manufacture, including a special Danish version of the D XXI fighter with a pair of 20mm. Madsen cannon underwing, and the C–VE biplane reconnaissance bomber. Ten older C-VBs were still in service as trainers, and 20 more were stored in hangars at various airfields. Other types were a variety of British-built machines — most elderly,

Høver MF 10 floatplane trainer of the Marinens Flygevåpen. *(via B. Olsen)*

apart from a few Fairey P 4/34 monoplane bombers — a development of the RAF's Battle. Units and equipment were as follows:-

Army Aviation Troops (Haerens Flyvertropper)
Jutland Command

2 Fighter Eskadrille	8 Fokker D XXI
2 Reconnaissance Eskadrille	4 Fokker C-VE

Seeland Command

1 Fighter Eskadrille	16 Gloster Gauntlet IIJ
1 Reconnaissance Eskadrille	8 Fokker C-VE
	4 Fairey P 4/34
1 Bomber Eskadrille	4 Fokker C-VE
	3 Fairey P 4/34

Naval Air Service

Fighter Luftflotille	4 Gloster Gauntlet
	6 Hawker Nimrod
	6 Bristol Bulldog II
Reconnaissance Luftflotille	16 Heinkel He 8 floatplanes
Bomber Luftflotille	10 Hawker Dantorp torpedo-bomber biplanes

Still unaware of the imminence of the German invasion, Royal Navy vessels had at last begun their minelaying operations in the early hours of 8 April, one force sowing in Vestfjorden on the approaches to Narvik while another sailed for Stadhavet. In Britain troops went aboard transports and cruisers, ready to sail at once to forestall any German move once the minelaying was completed.

During 7 April the Admiralty had received intelligence reports indicating that the Germans were preparing an expeditionary force due to land at Narvik next day. This information was passed to the Norwegian authorities, unfortunately with a rider commenting that not too much reliance should be placed on its authenticity. Despite this element of doubt, the sighting of major units of the

German Navy at sea indicated that something was afoot, and to avoid any clash with a more powerful force, the southernmost of the two minelaying groups was ordered to return to base by C in C, Home Fleet, its task incomplete. At dawn the northern group followed, having finished the sowing of the minefield in Vestfjorden. At the same time the troops aboard the cruisers were disembarked swiftly in case it should be necessary for the vessels to sortie at short notice in any major naval action.

8/4/40

At 0600 on 8th three Sunderland flyingboats from 204 Squadron were ordered from Sullom Voe on reconnaissance, but weather was very bad, with rain and heavy cloud. Aircraft 'B', N9047 (Flt Lt E.L. Hyde), finally spotted a group of vessels which were identified as a battlecruiser, two cruisers and two destroyers. However the aircraft was hit by Flak and drew clear, subsequently reporting the sighting, indicating that the ships were heading west. This report was disbelieved initially. In fact however, he had been quite right, for the vessels had arrived off Trondheim 24 hours early, and were zig-zagging to fill time. When sighted, the vessels were indeed heading west on one leg of this manoeuvre. This report gave the impression that the Germans were heading out into the Atlantic however, and the Home Fleet was ordered out to position itself across their path.

The force spotted by the Sunderland was actually composed of the cruiser *Hipper* and four destroyers — the force attacked by the Blenheims on the previous day — and these vessels were soon met again. The southern of the two minelaying forces missed seeing a convoy bound for Narvik, but the destroyer *Glowworm*, out on the flank alone was suddenly attacked by two German destroyers and then by *Hipper*. Badly damaged, the British vessel hid in her own smokescreen to escape further damage, and then deliberately rammed *Admiral Hipper*, sinking immediately afterwards. The damaged German cruiser then made for Trondheim; her Arado Ar 196A catapult floatplane was flown off on reconnaissance, to see if more British warships were in the vicinity. Running short of fuel, the pilot landed at Lyngstad inside Kristiansund at about 1950; this little port is situated just to the south of Trondheim, and should not be confused with Kristiansand, which is much farther to the south. The aircraft was at once seized by the Norwegian Naval Air Service, and was towed into Kristiansund harbour. Lt Kaare Kjos was flown over in a 2 Flg avd MF 11 to secure it, flying it over to Aunøy. On 12 April he would fly the aircraft to Aandalsnes, where the German markings were later painted out and Norwegian colours painted on the rudder. During 8 April a British Walrus from one of the Royal Navy's cruisers also landed in Kristiansund, and was similarly interned, but next day, with the German invasion, was handed back to its crew. It joined the Ar 196 and MF 11 at Aandalsnes and on 13th the three flew up to Eidsøra in Sunndalsfjord, where they were joined by a second Walrus. The four aircraft formed the Romsdalfjord Flying Group for a few days, but on 19 April all flew to the United Kingdom.

To return to the 8th, other German convoys were heading for Bergen, Egersund, Kristiansand, Arendal and Oslo; Sunderlands and Hudsons searched all day, but due to the bad weather were able to see nothing. Meanwhile nine He 111Hs of 1(F)/122 had taken off from Hamburg/Fuhlsbüttel to reconnoitre the area east of the Shetlands. Here one of these sighted the 2nd Cruiser Squadron (Vice-Admiral Edwards-Collins) comprising the cruisers *Galatea* and

This Arado Ar 196 from the catapult of the cruiser *Hipper*, was seized by the Norwegians the day before the German attack, when it landed in Lyngstad. It was flown to Scotland on 17 April, and is seen here at Sullom Voe. *(240 Squadron Records via A. Thomas)*

Arethusa, with 11 destroyers heading north at high speed to intercept the antici-pated 'Atlantic breakout'. One of the Heinkels also encountered Sunderland KG-D, L5799, of 204 Squadron, which had taken off at 1030 flown by Flt Lt R.P.A. Harrison for a patrol. A running fight commenced which resulted in the Sunderland crashing into the sea west of Bergen with the loss of the whole crew; the victorious Heinkel crew returned to report their success, their own aircraft having suffered no damage. Meanwhile a Do 26 from the Tranzoceanstaffel/ KüFlGr 406 had spotted Vice-Admiral Whitworth's force comprising the battle-ship HMS *Renown* and nine destroyers, 280 miles west-north-west of Trond-heim. Two Hudsons of 233 Squadron reported engaging He 111s without results during their patrols, and these were almost certainly also 1(F)/122 aircraft returning to Hamburg.

During the day however, one transport, the *Rio de Janeiro*, was sunk by a Polish submarine *Orzel* (Lt Cdr Grudzinski) off Justøya, outside Lillesand, and to the north-east of Kristiansand. Aboard this vessel were Luftwaffe Flak troops, 9/Flakregt 33 losing two men while 6/Flakregt 33 lost 95, with one more wounded. Many others managed to get ashore on the Norwegian coast, where they stated that they had been told that they were going to Norway at the request of the government, to protect the country from the British. On learning this, the Norwegian government at once ordered partial mobilization, which began late on 8th. At Fornebu only five of the Fighter Wing Gladiators were fully serviceable, but a sustained effort had two more ready by early on 9th. No spark plugs were available for the other two, so these and two Tiger Moths were pulled to the edge of the airport and camouflaged. To forestall being attacked on the ground, the Reconnaissance Wing was ordered to leave Kjeller at first light on 9th, and fly to Steinsfjorden. The crews of the three serviceable Capronis at Sola were ordered to be ready to bomb Bergen. They were worried as to how their bombs would work, as in order to save cost in peacetime, they had never been allowed to practice with live missiles. As engines were warmed up, they were advised that the raid was off, but nonetheless they remained in their aircraft overnight in readiness. At Hafrsfjord the detachment from 2 Flg avd of the Naval Air Service was ordered to carry out a patrol along the coast at dawn on the 9th, which was undertaken by Lt Stansberg in F-346. At the initiative of the School Commander, the training aircraft were disposed to the frozen lake Øyeren during 8th.

As dusk crept over Scapa Flow an incoming raid appeared on the radar screens, and Hurricanes of 43 and 111 Squadrons which were at readiness at Wick and Drem respectively, were scrambled. 111 Squadron's Green Section attacked one bomber, Flg Off D.L. Bruce and Plt Off H.M. Ferris both firing without apparent results, although they were subsequently awarded a probable. The attackers were some two dozen He 111s from II/KG 26, which suffered their first loss at 2035 when Flg Off J.D. Edmunds of 43 Squadron and his wingman attacked one formation of six about 40 miles west of Copinsay. The formation broke up and Edmonds went after one 4 Staffel aircraft commanded by Oblt Alfred Donike, which was shot down into the sea, while Sgt J. Arbuthnot fired all his ammunition into another, which dived away into cloud, pouring smoke. This latter aircraft, another 4 Staffel machine flown by Fw Erich Morann, made it back across the North Sea, but crashed 12 miles west of Delmenhorst, three of the crew being killed. Three members of Donike's crew had meanwhile been picked up by a British destroyer and were transported into Scapa Flow; one man was lost.

Flt Lt Peter Townsend and Sgt Jim Hallowes from the same squadron intercepted two of 6/KG 26's Heinkels at 2110, when 30 miles east of Duncanby Head, with visibility almost gone. The bombers were by then on their way home, their bombing finished. Townsend climbed from well below, and put a good burst into Uffz Mathäus Hofer's aircraft, which streamed glycol coolant from the engines and dropped its undercarriage. A second attack followed, pressed to close range in the face of determined return fire, after which the bomber's navigation lights were switched on and it came down on the sea, all the crew being lost. Townsend returned to Wick to find the field lit up and in confusion, and he was ordered not to land. With fuel low however, he had no option but to go down, and went straight in. After landing he soon discovered the reason for all the excitement — in the middle of the airfield was a crash-landed He 111!

Hallowes had attacked this, Lt Kurt Weigel's aircraft, firing all his ammunition into it. The Heinkel then dived through cloud, appearing over the airfield which was now in darkness, but had lit the flarepath for the returning Hurricanes. For ten minutes the bomber circled with one engine stationary, then came in and made a smooth belly-landing in the centre of the flarepath. The pilot had been under the impression that he was over a seaplane base and had landed on the surface of the sea. The fuselage door opened, a dinghy was thrown out, and two members of the crew jumped out without their boots on! On investigation it was found that the fuselage was riddled with bullet holes, and two of the gunners had been killed. KG 26 believed that one of the four Heinkels lost had been brought doun by AA — not in fact the case. One Hurricane was claimed damaged by a German gunner, although no RAF aircraft were actually hit.

---

9 APRIL 1940; THE FATEFUL DAY

Denmark

As darkness fell German vessels entered Norwegian territorial waters, and in the early hours of 9 April they closed on their objectives, entering several Norwegian harbours and that of Copenhagen, capital of Denmark. The mass of air power gathered for the operation began taking off at dawn for various destinations, the first of these to be reached being those in Denmark. At dawn, 0450, Warship Group 8 (the minelayer *Hanestadt Sanzig* and icebreaker *Stettin*, carrying Maj Glein's strengthened II/IT 308) appeared in Copenhagen harbour entrance with their battleflags illuminated by searchlights. At 0518 troops began to go ashore unopposed, and after a brief exchange of fire at the Royal Palace, King Christian X ordered all resistance to the invaders to cease.

Three Ju 52/3ms from 8/KGzbV 1 had taken off at 0530, carrying paratroops of 4/FJR 1. At 0700 one platoon was dropped over Aalborg, where no resistance was met, while nine Junkers dropped 90 men around the Storströms bridge at Vordingborg, linking the Geber ferry terminal with Copenhagen. Here the defenders were caught sleeping, and were captured without resistance. This allowed III/Infantrieregiment 305 to cross from Rostock on the ferry almost at once. Immediately behind the initial dozen Ju 52/3ms came 53 more from I/KG zbV 1 with III/IR 159 aboard, escorted by Bf 110s of 2/ZG 76. These landed at Aalborg immediately after the initial paratroop drop, three of the transport being damaged in landing accidents.

At 0703 28 He 111s of I/KG 4 took off to make a 'show of strength' over the capital, appearing overhead with Bf 110 escorts from 3/ZG 1, and showering leaflets on the city, announcing the occupation of the country and of Norway. One He 111 which lagged due to engine trouble was hit by machine gun fire over the south-western edge of the city. 2/ZG 76, after seeing the transports to Aalborg, escorted one formation of bombers over Möen and Copenhagen, then flew back to land at Aalborg with their last drops of fuel. The Stab of I/ZG 76 and 3 Staffel were already there, having flown direct to the airfield independently and landed, again without opposition. Part of the KG 4 force had been escorted by the Stab of I/ZG 1 and 1 Staffel of that Gruppe, over Vaerlöse airfield. Here a single Fokker D XXI was seen taking off and was at once shot down by Hpt Wolfgang Falck. The Zerstörer then strafed anti-aircraft positions and parked aircraft, destroying ten Fokker C-VEs of 1 and 2 reconnaissance Eskadrilles, and four more D XXIs of 2 fighter Eskadrille. Lt Schmidt, Oblt Martin, Oblt Lutz and Uffz Michi were credited with the destruction of two of these aircraft each, the rest being dealt with by Oblt Streib, Oblt Müller, Lt Wandam, Uffz Dünsing and Uffz Eberlein. Two of the Bf 110s were damaged by ground fire, and one radio operator was wounded. All the D XXIs had their engines running when attacked, and had they got into the air, these nimble little fighters would have proved formidable adversaries for the heavy Bf 110s.

At Aalborg three Ju 52/3ms of KGzbV 1, escorted by Bf 110s of 2/ZG 76, dropped paratroops of 4/FJR 1, these securing the East and West airfields at this city without a fight. 53 more Ju 52/3ms followed with III/IR 159 aboard to occupy these airfields, followed by 1/ZG 1, 3/ZG 1 and 2/ZG 76; 2/ZG 1 arrived in the afternoon. ZG 1 was to secure the aerial corridors to Stavanger and Oslo in Norway. By evening I/Flakregt 19 had taken over defence of the airfields and the great airlift began, 139 Ju 52/3ms of KGzbV 1 and KGrzbV 101 bringing in the ground party of I/ZG 76, ammunition and fuel.

During the morning reports had been received that Esbjerg airfield had already been occupied, and at once the Bf 109s of II/JG 77 moved there, joined by I/Flakregt 8, which came overland from Germany.

NORWAY — THE EVENTS OF THE MORNING

Kristiansand

Meanwhile in Norway considerably more resistance was being encountered, though of a distinctly variable nature, dependant upon location. At Arendal the torpedoboat *Greif* entered harbour at 0850 and put ashore part of Aufklärungsabt 169 (the reconnaissance battalion of the 69th Infantry Division), which occupied the harbour and town without a fight. Egersund fell with similar ease when more Aufklärungsabt 169 troops went ashore at 0530 from the ships of a minesweeping flotilla. At Kristiansand at the same time, Warship Group 4 was delayed by a thick fog which prevented entry until 0623. At 0632 the 210mm battery at Odderöya opened fire and Kpt zur See Rieve withdrew, calling for air support. Seven He 111s of 7/KG 4 had been ordered to patrol over this area, and these opened Luftwaffe involvement with an attack on the battery, but without success. An Ar 196B from the cruiser *Karlsruhe* also made bombing attacks with a similar lack of success.

Just before the landings had begun a Høver MF 11 floatplane (F-328) from the Norwegian Navy's 1 Flg avd had been sent off on a dawn coastal reconnaissance, flown by Sub Lt Knut Oscar. 15 minutes after taking off the crew spotted warships off Oksöy and reported by radio, landing in Topdalsfjord. Here the floatplane was attacked by German aircraft, the gunner returning fire. An RAF Blenheim was later to repeat the attack, but this too, missed. Meanwhile the unit's other two MF 11s were sent off at 0500 to bomb the warships which were by then shelling Kristiansand fortress, but these were attacked by one of the KG 4 He 111s and had to flee. It was now impossible for them to return to their base, so they sought a safe landingplace elsewhere, landing at Mosby at 0830 under fire from Naval troops who took them to be Germans. The unit's MF 10 (F-204) was flown out to a small fjord west of Lillesand where it was destroyed by its pilot next day.

After a call for further air support had been made by the Germans, 16 He 111s of 2 and 3/KG 26 from Marx, bombed at 1000, silencing the Odderöya and Gleodden batteries, and blowing up the ammunition dump at the former site. One aircraft of 2 Staffel, with the Staffelkäpitan, Maj Schaeper aboard, was hit by AA fire and ditched in the sea, the crew subsequently being rescued by German mineseeper *M 1*. Following these raids, part of MarineArtlAbt 302 was landed by torpedo- and S-boats, storming and capturing the Odderöya battery.

Bergen

At Bergen a German naval group led by the cruiser *Köln*, sailed into the harbour, troops landing at strategically important points on the run-up to the town, capturing the coastal fortresses and other military installations. At once Norwegian batteries opened fire and the cruiser *Königsberg* was damaged. Here too Norwegian Naval aircraft were in evidence. Naval 2 Flg avd at Flatøen had been ordered to provide a dawn patrol over the Bergen area, MF 11 F-346 taking off at 0342, followed at 0415 by He 115 F-52. Both crews spotted a large German fleet offshore, and attempted to attack. Lt Einar Svenning could not get the MF 11 into position to drop his bombs, while Lt Hans Bugge in the Heinkel was able to bomb *Köln* and *Königsberg* as they headed for Bergen. The bombs missed, and heavy Flak drove the aircraft away, both floatplanes landing back

Marinens Flygevåpen He 115A taxying out for take-off. *(via B. Olsen)*

at Flatøen by 0615. Shortly afterwards the aircraft here were evacuated, F-52 and MF 11 F-312 heading for Norheimsund where they later formed the Hardangerfjord flygruppe. He 115 F-58 flew to Eivindvik, and MF 11s F-310 and -316 ended up at Balestrand, becoming the Sognefjord flygruppe. Meanwhile, He 111Ps from 9/KG 4 had set out early, and after refuelling at Westerland-Sylt, arrived overhead at 0706 to attack the Kvarven and Sandviken batteries, relieving the pressure on the landing forces. One Heinkel (5J+HT, flown by Lt Gerhard Haarnagel) was hit by ground fire and crashed on the Norwegian coast; one man survived and was captured. Several He 59s of KGrzbV 108 then ferried troops of IR 159 up to Bergen, but one crashed on the coast, two members of Fw Gerhard Hauck's crew and six soldiers being killed, and three men injured.

Trondheim
At Trondheim *Admiral Hipper* led Warship Group 2 into the harbour, where the vessels came under fire from the Hysnes battery. Two salvoes from the cruiser's aft turrets were sufficient to silence these guns.

Hipper flew off her two remaining Ar 196B floatplanes to reconnoitre the surrounding area and to support the assault troops by bombing the coastal batteries. Soon after midday two He 115s from KüFlGr 506, one flown by Maj Minner, the Kommandeur, landed at Trondheim, followed 90 minutes later by eight more of these aircraft from 1 Staffel and six from 2 Staffel. One floatplane was hit by fire from the ground and Hpt Lienhart Wiesand, Staffelkapitän of 1 Staffel was killed, although the aircraft managed to land safely.

At Trondheim the port was soon in German hands, and when this news was radioed back by *Hipper*, a Focke-Wulf Fw 200 of KGrzbV 105 undertook a reconnaissance over the area to determine whether conditions were suitable for the groundcrew party of KüFlGr 506 to be flown in at once. These were seen to be so, and that afternoon the latter arrived in five Fw 200s and the lone Junkers G-38. Flak equipment was also brought in by air, while floatplane transports from KGrzbV 108 landed Alpine troops in a number of fjords down the coast.

As soon as it had become obvious that Trondheim could not be held, the Norwegian Army aircraft at Vaernes airfield were ordered to leave. All flew initially to Lake Selbusjøen, where the Tiger Moth was left for communications duties. The C-Vs then flew on to Lake Aursunden to join other surviving Army Air Service elements.

Narvik

After an initial burst of gunfire from ten German destroyers against units of the Norwegian Navy, GenLt Dietl was able to negotiate a handover of the town without further resistance, a force of 2,000 troops being landed. It was subsequently believed that Col Sundlo, the local commander of the garrison, was a Quisling sympathiser. The Hålogaland Air Corps was ordered to Bardufoss at 0430 to take part in the fight to retake Narvik, but was unable to operate during the day due to severe snowstorms. These also kept the Naval aircraft at Vadsø and Skattora out of the air.

Oslo

The most determined resistance was shown at Oslo. Here the shore batteries at Fort Oscarsborg engaged a warship flotilla sailing up the fjord, the cruiser *Blücher*, flagship of the force, being sunk at 0723 by shells and shore-launched torpedoes, while the *Lützow* was damaged. At daybreak the German ambassador had demanded an immediate surrender, but as this was not forthcoming, operations continued. Three hours later demonstration flights similar to those made over Copenhagen, were undertaken by He 111s of III/KG 26, which headed up the Oslo fjord where they met Gladiator fighters — of which more later. At the same time waves of troop-carrying aircraft approached from the same direction.

First of the transports off were 29 Ju 52/3ms of II/KG zbV 1, led by Oberstlt Drewes, which carried the paratroops of 1 and 2/FJR 1 towards the Oslo/Fornebu airfield. Over Oslofjord the formation ran into fog, in which an aircraft of 5 Staffel (WNr 6570) disappeared. It had been shot down by a pair of Gladiators, as will be recounted later, and crashed north of Oslofjord with the loss of Fw Albert Meier, his crew and 12 members of 2/FJR 1. As a result at 0820 this formation turned back, and returned to Aalborg. A second wave of 53 transports were on their way 20 minutes behind the leaders. These were from KGrzbV 103, carrying the men of II/IR 234. Despite the return of the paratroop carrying aircraft, the battalion commander refused to recall this formation, and when Generalleutnant Geissler ordered a return, Hpt Wagner, the formation leader, chose not to hear this. KGrzbV 103 was being controlled by Luftransportche Land, rather than direct by Fliegerkorps X, and when the latter came on the radio, Wagner believed it to be an enemy deception. The transports ploughed on into the fog, which soon began to clear.

At the same time eight Bf 110s of 1/ZG 76 led by Oblt Werner Hansen were also arriving over Oslo after finding their way through the fog. They were at maximum range, and there was no possibility of their being able to return, and they were quickly involved in combat with Norwegian fighters. Each side gave an account of this battle, but these differed considerably in detail, and it is therefore necessary to recount the events that followed as each of the participants saw them. Oblt Hansen subsequently reported:

'... the Staffel was ordered to defend the dropping of paratroops (at about 0845) and the landing of airborne troops. At about 0837, the Staffel sighted a squadron of Gloster Gladiator single-seat fighters 15 km south of Oslo, in in a strength of approximately eight aircraft. The Gloster squadron flew about 500m higher, coming down upon us from the sun. 1 Staffel at once turned towards the single-seat fighters, who because of the cloud layer, had apparently not seen us. We passed beneath and behind the Gloster squadron, then gained height to be able to make a surprise attack from the sun. The fighter squadron must have seen us however, since as we turned to engage them, in a second they had closed on us. We at once climbed, and attacked them headon. A section of the Gloster aircraft broke downwards, the others climbed. Due to the great manoeuvreability of the biplanes, several fighters succeeded in getting behind Bf 110s, but these were immediately fired on by other Bf 110s. After taking hits the fighters dived into the clouds and vanished, so that results could not be confirmed of the first dogfight. Evidence was given by Norwegian civilians that during the battle one Gloster was shot down in flames (this was claimed by Uffz Mütscherle and his gunner, Gefr Lorey at 0838), and two more made force-landings due to motor damage.

'At 0845, the Staffel reformed and proceeded to cover the dropping of the Fallschirmjäger of Stab, 1 and 2 Fallschirmjäger Regiment 1 over Fornebu. As the Staffel reached the scene, at 0850, no transports could be seen. Instead three Gloster Gladiators were sighted five km to the north-west, which were attacked by two Rotten of Bf 110s. One was shot down by Lt Lent, and another, after being hit by the fire of Fw Jänicke disappeared in a northerly direction. He was unable to follow, petrol shortage making an early landing necessary. The third Gloster disappeared into the clouds after taking some hits. During these dogfights, the Staffelkapitän flew with the rest of the Staffel, to the airfield, where it became clear that fuel shortage would force them to land. On the runway stood two single-seat fighters that, it was later confirmed, had just landed with motor damage, and these were set on fire (by strafing).'

It is now necessary to look at these events as seen through the eyes of the Norwegian Gladiator pilots. The morning had found seven of the ten available Gladiators serviceable, while the unit had ten officers and sergeants available to fly them, three of them under training. At 0500 2/Lt Finn Thorsager and Lt Arve Braathen were sent off after the noise of aircraft engines was heard overhead. Thorsager in Gladiator 433 spotted an aircraft with twin rudders about one kilometre away, which he identified as a Do 17; it was almost certainly a Bf 110. He attacked four or five times before it disappeared into cloud. Lt. Braathen in 425 saw a large aircraft, but was unable to catch it. Both pilots then returned to Fornebu. Lt Dag Krohn (423) and Sgts Kristian Fredrik Schye (427) and Per Waaler (429) were sent off just before 0600, but found nothing and returned about 50 minutes later. Just after 0700 five Gladiators took off as Luftwaffe aircraft began approaching in force. Lt Rolf Thorbjørn Tradin (429) led, followed by Lt Krohn (423), 2/Lt Thorsager (433) and Sgts Waaler (425) and Schye (427). Passing over the fjord leading to Oslo, they saw below the stricken *Blücher* burning, but were then ordered over the radio by the commander of the Wing, Capt Erling Munthe Dahl, to patrol over Nesodden. Over Steilene at 5,500 feet, they saw a large formation reckoned to be more than 70 strong, composed of bombers and transports, some 2,000 feet below, and the Gladiators dived to attack.

The aircraft they had spotted were undoubtedly the leading Ju 52/3ms of II/ KGzbV 1, followed by those of KGrzbV 103. Meanwhile two more Gladiators had taken off, flown by Lt Arve Braathen (413) and Sgt Oskar Albert Lütken

(419). Lt Tradin attacked Fw Meier's Junkers. as already recounted, seeing hits on the starboard wing and engine. Smoke poured from the aircraft and it rolled over on its back, spinning down apparently to crash at Torgskjaer, outside Høvik. He then attacked a second aircraft, but it escaped in cloud. During these attacks three of Tradin's guns ceased operating, and now as he completed his attack the fourth also jammed. He returned to Fornebu where he could see two Gladiators on the field, but Capt Dahl warned him that an attack was underway, and he departed to seek a landing elsewhere.

Sgt Waaler had also attacked an aircraft which he identified as a Heinkel, which started to go down before he lost sight of it. Capt Dahl reported that he saw this machine spin and crash near the airfield. In the thick of a dogfight, Waaler ran out of ammunition and turned for base. His engine began to give problems however and started to cut as he went in to land. On the field he found Sgt Lütken's aircraft, which had suffered engine failure just after take off, and had landed again straight away. Re-arming of Waaler's fighter began at once, but at that point the Bf 110s of 1/ZG 76 came in to strafe, and he was forced to leap from the cockpit and into a trench. Looking out, he saw both Gladiators in flames.

Sgt Schye also attacked what he took to be a bomber, but was unable to continue due to ice forming on the windscreen of his Gladiator (No 427). He then saw what he identified as a Dornier 17 — almost certainly Mütscherle's Bf 110 − 1000 feet below him over Kolsås, and gave chase. The aircraft crash-landed at Vøyen with both engines dead after he had attacked. He was then attacked by three aircraft which he identified as He 111s, but which were undoubtedly Bf 110s; he avoided two but the third got onto his tail and he was hit in the left upper arm by two shells. He tried to crash-land his damaged fighter on Lake Daelivannet, east of Kolsås, but could not get his flaps down and overshot, hitting a high-voltage cable; this broke, but he crashed at Braatenjordet. Schye got out of his aircraft and was taken to hospital.

Gladiator 427 crash-landed near Valler station by Sgt Per Schye on 9 April, after being hit by Bf 110s of 1/ZG 76. (*Arveng Collection via B. Olsen*)

Finn Thorsager had sprayed all his fire generally at the many aircraft seen, and after exhausting his ammunition landed on a small frozen lake, Lyseren, 12 miles east of Oslo, taxiing the aircraft onto firm ground. From here he was driven by car to Oslo where he rejoined the Fighter Wing. The Gladiator was left where it stood, and while it is thought that the Germans subsequently recovered parts of it, some ten years later a local farmer told Thorsager that he still had some pieces of the aircraft.

Lt Krohn (in 421) meanwhile attacked an estimated 150 aircraft of several types — identified as He 111s, Do 17s, Bf 110s and Ju 52s. He claimed a Heinkel shot down south-west of Fornebu, and then a 'Do 17', which went down steeply over Nesodden after he had obtained hits on the cockpit area. Two Bf 110s then attacked him, but he escaped these in clouds, subsequently attacking another 'bomber' and believing that he had put the rear gunner out of action. Returning to Fornebu, he strafed some Ju 52/3ms on the ground here, then flew off and landed on the north-eastern bay of Tyrifjord, where he found Rolf Tradin and his Gladiator. (In 1978 members of the Norwegian Aviation Historical Society dug up the remains of the aircraft that Krohn had shot down at Nesodden, establishing beyond doubt that it had been a Bf 110; the crew had been killed.)

The last of the pilots in the air, Lt Braathen, attacked one aircraft which he forced to jettison its bombs near Brönnöya, although the Gladiator's Mercury engine was running rough. He then encountered more aircraft over Høvik and chased one for a long way. This finally began to lose height with the starboard engine smoking, but he was then attacked from head-on by a Bf 110 and had to break away. He landed on Lake Bogstad, but the wheels of his fighter went through the top layer of ice and stuck firm. The engine refused to produce enough power to pull the aircraft free and he had to abandon it.

As the Bf 110s had dived on Fornebu to strafe Waaler's and Lütken's Gladiators — both of which were destroyed by Oblt Hansen — heavy fire was experienced from six fixed and two free-standing gun positions. The Messerschmitts turned on the latter first, silencing them with cannon fire; they then attacked two of the fixed sites. One Bf 110 — that flown by Uffz Helmut Mütscherle — had

The wrecks of the Gladiators flown by Sgts Waaler and Lütken of the Norwegian Fighter Wing, both destroyed by fire from Oblt Hansen's 1/ZG 76 Bf 110 as they were being refuelled at Oslo/ Fornebu on 9 April. *(Bundesarchiv)*

already crash-landed near Vøyen as a result of damage suffered during the fight with the Gladiator, and this was totally destroyed, Mütscherle and Gefr Karl Lorey being taken prisoner; this Bf 110 was the victim of Sgt Schye. According to Oblt Hansen the Messerschmitt flown by Lt Erhard Kort and Uffz Heinrich Bockheimer was brought down by a direct AA hit, the crew being killed, but as will have been seen from the details of the Gladiator pilots' claims, it would

Lt Helmut Lent's 1/ZG 76 Bf 110 (note white victory bars high on the right fin), crash-landed on the edge of Oslo/Fornebu airfield. A Junkers Ju 52/3m passes overhead as it approaches to land. *(Bundesarchiv)*

in fact seem to have fallen to Dag Krohn. Five more Bf 110s were damaged during the attacks on the airfield defences, three having bullets in their radiators while two had their radio equipment hit.

At this juncture the Ju 52/3ms of Hpt Wagner's KGrzbV 103 burst through the fog at 0905 to see the two Gladiators burning on the ground. The first Junkers, in which Wagner himself was flying as a passenger, went in to land, but finding the aircraft under fire, the pilot took off again after it had been hit 52 times by machine gun bullets. One of these struck and killed Richard Wagner. At that moment five of the Messerschmitts also came in to land on their last vestigies of fuel, whilst the sixth gave cover by attacking the gunposts again. Lt Lent, with one engine dead, overshot and crashed, his aircraft being practically written off.

The vulnerable Junkers suffered quite heavily to the fire from the ground; one crashed and two crash-landed on the airfield due to damage, with the loss of three dead and three wounded, while three more crashed whilst landing under fire, but without injuries being sustained; three more were damaged 25-55% by fire. The Zerstörer on the ground had been taxied to the corners of the airfield from where the gunners could provide some cover for the landing aircraft.

Hansen jumped from his fighter and sprinted out to reach the first of the landed transports and explain the situation to the troops, who had fully expected to find the base in the hands of the paratroops. He pointed out the Norwegian defensive positions, but unknown to the Germans, these had been abandoned as soon as the Bf 110s had begun landing, and when the soldiers advanced it was to find them deserted, or in the process of being abandoned. The Norwegians had been ordered by Capt Dahl to withdraw to Fort Akershus. A stream of Ju 52/3ms then began landing one after the other in one long line.

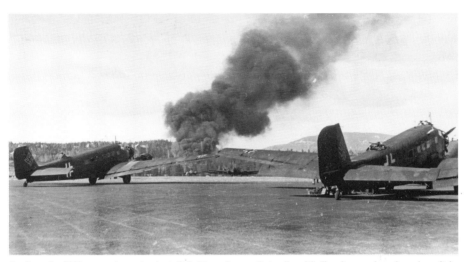

Junkers Ju 52/3ms newly-arrived at Oslo/Fornebu on 9 April, with fire from a burning aircraft in the background. *(Bundesarchiv)*

Minutes later a single aircraft came in carrying the maintenance crews of 1/ZG 76 under Hpt Flakowski, with supplies of ammunition, and these swiftly set about preparing the undamaged Bf 110s for further operations. Then the two or three transports from II/KGzbV 1, which had become lost in fog, also found Fornebu and landed, about 30 minutes behind schedule. Meanwhile a radio message was received by X Fliegerkorps from a ship in Oslo harbour, stating that Ju 52/3ms had landed at Fornebu. The Chief of Staff, Maj Harlinghausen, at once gave the order for the take-of of all reserve transport Gruppen, while the commander of the transport units, Oberstlt von Gablenz (Director of Deutsche Lufthansa) set out immediately for Oslo.

It will be recalled that 28 He 111s of III/KG 26 had also set out for Oslo, but had been delayed in cloud, finally arriving over Oslo half an hour behind the Bf 110s and the first of the transports. These bombers had attacked the Horten Naval base and bombed the fort at Bolcerne. One aircraft of 9 Staffel failed to return, force-landing south of the city; one man was killed and two wounded, but all the survivors reached Fornebu airfield on foot later in the day.

While it has proved less than easy to resolve the differences between the accounts of the two sides due to the faulty recognition of German aircraft types by the Norwegian pilots, it is likely that Thorsager's first claim against a Heinkel may well have been the same Ju 52/3m that had been attacked by Tradin. There is little doubt that Krohn's 'Do 17' was Kort's Bf 110, as already mentioned; it may be that Sgt Waaler had also attacked this aircraft. His own Gladiator had probably been damaged by Mütscherle's fire, causing him to force-land. When Schye was 'jumped' by another Messerschmitt after shooting down Mütscherle's aircraft, it is likely that he fell victim to Helmut Lent, who was certainly credited with this victory as his fifth of the war.

According to the Norwegian authorities, eight Ju 52/3ms and seven Bf 110s were believed shot down and crashed near the airport, with four other aircraft down further away. Many of these had obviously been claimed by the ground gunners, since the fighters had, as can be seen, claimed only three 'He 111s' and two Bf 110s. As indicated, the Luftwaffe had lost two Bf 110s and a Ju 52/3m in combat, six Ju 52/3ms, one Bf 110 and one He 111 being brought down by ground fire.

Notwithstanding the differences, the fact remains that German forces were firmly in control of Fornebu, now held by 350 men of II/IR 324, 80 Fallschirm-jäger, and the crews of 1/ZG 76. While the remaining Norwegians at the airfield were disarmed and the defences secured, Hpt Spiller, the Luftwaffe Attache in Oslo, arrived and ordered Hansen to report the capture of the base. One of the Ju 52/3ms was used to radio 'Fornebu in our hands'. By a remarkable piece of luck and the swift and decisive action of a few aircrew of 1/ZG 76, a complete shambles had been transformed into a triumph.

Resistance in the Oslo area continued however, and the raid by the III/KG 26 Heinkels was soon followed by one made by 24 more of these aircraft from KGr 100. These bombed Holmenkollen and the other Oslo airfield at Kjeller, where one Fokker C-VD and the Tiger Moth were destroyed on the ground. It was well for the Norwegians that the Reconnaissance Wing had left Kjeller early that morning, escaping this attack. During the 8th, the aircraft of the Flying School at this base had been ordered away by the commanding officer, Capt Normann. Nine C-VDs and 14 Tiger Moths headed for the frozen lake Øyeren. From here on 10th they flew north to Glomma, where one aircraft was abandoned due to engine trouble. A further move followed to Bolsted Farm, south of Rena, via Lake Ossjøen, which was reached that evening. Capt Normann was unable to establish any contact here with other Nor-wegian forces, and on 15 April he would decide to evacuate the school to Sweden.

From Horten five MF 11s (F-304, -306, -308, -334 and -338), one DT-2 (F-84) and one MF 10 (F-202) escaped, taxying in poor weather to Vindfangerbukta Bay near Drøbak. Two of the MF 11s (F-306 and -334) and the DT 2 flew away from the bay next morning, but the latter got lost in cloud and landed north of Tønsberg; on 13th it was taxied to Asgaardstrand and abandoned. F-334 eventu-ally arrived in Eidfjord on 21st, after stops at Nordsjø and Møsvann. F-306 crashed while landing at Vangsmjøsa on 16th. Another DT 2 also taxied away, but was to be caught two days later while still under tow, and sunk by a German whaler. The MF 10 and the remaining MF 11s at Vindfangerbukta were recovered by the Germans late in April.

Meanwhile the attack by KGr 100 was followed by one launched by dive-bombers. At 1059 22 Ju 87Rs from Hpt Hozzel's I/St.G 1 took off from Kiel/Holtenau and attacked the fortress at Oscarsborg. The stubborn resistance by the Norwegians led to calls for further air support from the attacking troops, and from 1745 successive waves of bombers from I/KG 26 (29 He 111s) and II/KG 4 (24 He 111s) were employed against the defences at Kaholmen, Drøbäk and Oscarsborg. By nightfall Oslo itself was in German hands.

During the afternoon 159 Ju 52/3ms from KGrzbV 101, 102, 105, 107, and

Although of poor quality, this interesting photograph shows a Do 18 flyingboat of KüFlGr 406 (K6+K*) at right, with a captured Norwegian Høver MF 10 floatplane at left. *(via B.Olsen)*

Høver MF 11 F-308 at Horten, was evacuated with other aircraft of the unit by taxying along the coast to Drøbak overnight. Ice formed here by dawn and the aircraft had to be abandoned as a result on 11 April; with others, it was subsequently captured. *(via B. Olsen)*

II/KGzbV 1 landed at Fornebu, carrying part of IR 324, the rest of 1 and 2/FJR 1, Luftwaffe ground staff and supplies of petrol. One crashed in the sea on its way to Oslo and one on return, while two more crash-landed back in Germany; five more suffered damage.

Stavanger

At the same time as the initial attack on Fornebu had been underway, other units were undertaking similar activities over Stavanger/Sola airfield, although on a more limited scale. Ju 52/3ms of KGzbV 1 took off in two formations for the area. Of the first 13 away, one suffered the failure of an engine and crashed into two other Junkers of KGrzbV 104, both of which were damaged. The following 12 led by Hpt Günther Capito got away safely, these two dozen transports

Høver MF 11 F-324 after capture, with a Luftwaffe He 115 in the background. *(Bundesarchiv)*

carrying 3/FJR 1 to the area. Making their way separately to provide support over the target, were the eight Bf 110s of Oblt Gordon Gollob's 3/ZG 76. Fog, with heavy cloud above, broke up the formation seriously, and Gollob with three other Bf 110 pilots turned back, only Ofw Fleischmann and Fw Gröning continuing. Two more of the Messerschmitts were not seen again, Lt Sibo Habben and Uffz Gerhard Grams colliding in the murk and falling into the sea. All four members of the crews were lost, patrol boats later recovering wreckage and items of clothing, but little else.

At Sola the Norwegian Bomber Wing had despatched an early patrol, which had seen two German ships but been ordered not to attack these. At 0900 three of the four Caproni Ca 310s and six Fokker C-Vs (four from the Wing and the two Reconnaissance Wing aircraft) were being readied for take off for Kjeller, when the two Bf 110s appeared, coming down to strafe. They were closely followed by eight He 111Ps of 8/KG 4. As this happened the radio operator in Lt Jacquets' Caproni (probably No 505) was listening to transmissions from naval units in battle. Jacquets was ready for take off, but a bomb fell alongside, smashing the perspex in all the nose and cockpit glazing, and damaging one engine. Undeterred, he got the aircraft rolling, but it was then hit by fire from a strafing aircraft and began to burn. The gunner manned the turret and fired at the attacking bombers until the Caproni had to be abandoned. Meanwhile the other two Capronis and six Fokkers got off and climbed desperately through the German formation, managing to get away unscathed. During this attack the two 3/ZG 76 crews reported finding two Fokker C-VEs about to take off and strafed these, claiming both burned. No mention was made of the Ca 310! A few minutes later the Ju52/3ms of 7/KG zbV 1 burst from the clouds, short of one more aircraft which had turned back and landed at Aalborg. They had reached Stavanger at 0920 where 131 paratroops under Oblt Freiherr von Brandis leapt from their transports. They were fired on as they landed, but the Bf 110s gave them supporting fire before landing themselves with their fuel exhausted. The airfield was swiftly taken. At this point one of the Ca 310s flown by Lt Steen, returned to bomb the German aircraft on the ground. Due to his lack of

Caproni Ca 310 501 running up its engines at Stavanger; 505 in the background. *(via B. Olsen)*

experience however, the safety pins had not been removed from the fuses, and the bombs fell harmlessly to the ground. The little bomber was then attacked by an He 111 and a fierce fight followed during which the Caproni was badly damaged. Ater three hours struggling to keep it in the air, Steen crash-landed near Opstad, where the crew burned the aircraft. The third Caproni, flown by the Bomber Wing commander, Lt Halfdan Hansen, landed at Kjevik, and later Brumunddal. Of the six C-Vs, one crashed due to fuel shortage at Efteløt, in Sandsvaer, but the others subsequently joined the Reconnaissance Wing at Steinsfjorden.

Soon after the initial action at Sola, 51 Ju 52/3ms of Maj von Jena's KGrzbV 104, and 53 more from Maj Stolt's KGrzbV 106 brought in troop reinforcements of I and II/IR 193 together with Flak equipment, from Stade and Ütersen; one of the latter aircraft (PP+AX, WNr 6458) crashed into the sea west of Jutland en route, Uffz Herbert Krieg, his crew, and 11 members of II/IR 193 being lost. One of the KGrzbV 104 aircraft was to ditch during the return flight to Stade, but the crew were rescued. Subsequently nine KGrzbV 101 aircraft brought in aviation fuel while during the evening five Ju 90s and two Fw 200s delivered the groundcrew of I/Stukageschwader 1 and part of 4/Flakregt 33, with 20mm guns. 1 Seetransportstaffel brought in 6, 7 and 9/Flakregt 33. They were followed by 22 Ju 87Rs of I/StG 1 (one of which crash-landed and was badly damaged), four Bf 110s of 3/ZG 76 and ten He 115Cs of KüF1Gr 106.

Meanwhile bombers from 8/KG 4 had managed to attack and destroy the 735 ton Norwegian destroyer *Æger* in Amøyfjorden, close to Stavanger. When an MF 11 flown by Lt Stansberg from Hafrsfjord appeared over Sola on a reconnaissance, it was to see four unidentified aircraft in the air, a U-Boat and several German merchant vessels off shore. Stansberg passed low over Sola and was able to see that it was in German hands, and he returned to land at Haugesund to report.

During the battle over Oslo, several Norwegian Gladiators had landed away from base. Later in the morning Lts Krohn and Tradin took off from Tyrisfjord and flew to Hamar, landing here on Lake Mjösa. Unfortunately the wheels of Tradin's aircraft went through the ice, and like that flown by Braathen at Lake Bogstad, it was trapped immoveably. It had to be abandoned, and was later captured by the Germans. In the afternoon Krohn took off again alone, flying to Brumunddal, where the remains of the Bomber Wing had arrived from Sola. Here however, he was ordered to drain the oil from his aircraft as this was needed for the surviving Caproni, and the Gladiator had to be left behind. It

Lt Dag Krohn (right) with Gladiator 423 on the ice of Lake Mjösa during the afternoon of 9 April. *(via S. Stenersen)*

was collected later in the month and flown to Vangsmjösa to join what had become Group 'R'; it was then the sole surviving airworthy Norwegian fighter. The Caproni was also flown up to Vangsmjösa, but here it was crashed on the lake shore and abandoned.

ALLIED REACTION — THE WAR AT SEA

As soon as news of the German moves reached the United Kingdom, aircraft were sent out to try and find what was going on, while the Home Fleet was warned to anticipate early action, and began heading for the Norwegian coast. Luftwaffe coastal aircraft were also being despatched over the North Sea on the lookout for Anglo-French attempts to interfere with the invasion by sea or air. At 0520 eight Do 18s from KüFlGr 406 left Hornum to sweep the area west of Sylt, followed between 0603 and 0659 by eight He 115s of 1/KüFlGr 106, ten from 1/KüFlGr 506, and ten more from 2/KüFlGr 506, which covered the sea area between Bergen and the Orkneys. At about the same time three Hudsons of 233 Squadron left British soil in the opposite direction, followed by more of these aircraft from 220 and 224 Squadrons.

It was a British aircraft which made the first sighting, one of the 224 Squadron Hudsons spotting four destroyers south of Haugesund at 0800. Nearly an hour later He 115 S4+CK of 2/506 reported seeing three cruisers and 15 destroyers to the south-west of Bergen, heading east; the British Home Fleet was obviously out, and the alarm was raised. This was confirmed 15 minutes later at 0910 when S4+DK from the same unit found British heavy units north-west of Bergen.

Shortly after these sightings came the first combats when two of the 233 Squadron aircraft encountered He 115s south-west of Obrestad. Flg Off Williams in N7259 attacked one, claiming damage to the starboard engine, while Flg Off Vercoe in N7224 reported fighting another floatplane for 30 minutes before it escaped in cloud, showing signs of damage. It seems both had probably engaged the same aircraft, for only M2+DH of 1/KüFlGr 106 was hit. As the aircraft landed at Stavanger one damaged float filled with water and the aircraft sank.

Meanwhile between 0925 and 0930 several more sightings were reported by German aircraft, and intelligence decided that three British flotillas were at sea. One of these consisting of two battleships or battlecruisers, six cruisers and a strong destroyer escort was believed to be north-west of Bergen; a second comprising two battleships was to the west of the port, and a third, of nine cruisers and 11 destroyers, was thought to be to the west-south-west. In fact only two flotillas were at sea; the main strength of the Home Fleet — four battleships, three heavy cruisers, seven light cruisers and 14 destroyers — was approaching the Bergen area under the command of Admiral Forbes, while to the north-west lay a force of four light cruisers and seven destroyers — Admiral Layton's detached force.

Somewhat behind the reconnaissance Hudsons came Sunderland 'C', N9044, in the hands of Wg Cdr Davis, commanding officer of 204 Squadron. He headed for Trondheim during the later part of the morning. In this area at 1330 the Sunderland was engaged by two aircraft. The first of these — one of the Ar 196Bs from *Hipper's* catapults — was able to achieve no result during a brief skirmish. An He 115B of 2/506 then attacked, being identified by the flyingboat crew as a Blohm und Voss Ha 140. This proved faster and more manoeuvreable than the Sunderland, getting on its tail and inflicting damage which caused Davis to turn for home. The gunners were able to gain hits on the German floatplane however, and it withdrew pouring smoke from the port engine. Flt Lt Hyde climbed into the inside of the wing of the Sunderland where he managed to plug holes in the fuel cells with plasticine, and the aircraft got back to base without further event. The Heinkel had been hit far harder than the British crew realised; with the starboard wing and engine in flames it force-landed in Trond-heim fjord where the crew were able to escape before it burnt out and sank.

Following the reconnaissance reports received from the coastal aircraft of the approach of the Home Fleet units to Bergen, X Fliegerkorps' 'naval' bombers, which had been held in reserve for just such an eventuality, were ordered off. At much the same time British reconnaissances spotted the cruisers *Köln* and *Königsberg* in Bergen harbour, the light cruiser *Karlsruhe* in Kristiansand, and *Admiral Hipper* at Trondheim. The RAF too ordered raids to be mounted by Bomber Command. From 1430 to 1600 therefore, 41 He 111s of I and II/KG 26 and 47 Ju 88s from the three Gruppen of KG 30 headed out west after the British vessels, following 22 Ju 87Rs of I/StG 1 which left Kiel/Holtenau at 1350. Due to the distance from the coast that the British ships were still at, the dive-bombers were forced to turn back, but in doing so they found a Norwegian destroyer, which had just sunk the German freighter *Roda*. Hpt Hozzel led the Stukas down to sink the warship before heading back for the Norwegian coast, where they landed at Stavanger/Sola. In the meantime at 1510 British bombers had taken off towards the east, 12 Wellingtons from 9 and 115 Squadrons heading for Bergen, followed at 1600 by 12 Hampdens from 50 Squadron.

The first German bombers to make contact with the British warships were part of the KG 30 force, the Ju 88s attacking at 1530 to start the biggest air-sea engagement of the war to date. They claimed to have gained two hits on a heavy cruiser and one on a light cruiser; in fact they sank the destroyer *Gurkha*, and inflicted slight damage on the cruisers *Southampton* and *Galatea*. Shortly after this initial attack, the remaining Ju 88s and He 111s arrived overhead,

Carefully-posed propaganda photograph, as Norwegian female skiers watch the bombing-up of a I/StG 1 Ju 87R. The pilot sits astride the starboard wheelspat, while armourers move the 500kg bomb into position. *(Bundesarchiv)*

claiming three hits on a battleship and one on a heavy cruiser. They actually damaged the heavy cruiser *Devonshire* and the light cruisers *Sheffield* and *Glasgow* with near-misses. One bomb did strike the battleship *Rodney* but failed to penetrate the thick deck armour. The dense fire put up by the ships' AA defences proved effective on this occasion, no less than four Ju 88s being shot down into the sea. These were a Ju 88A-2 of the Stabskette III/KG 30, flown by the Gruppenkommandeur, Hpt Siegfried Mahrenholtz, which crashed into the western entrance to the Skaggerrak, a Ju 88A-1 of 4 Staffel (Fw Hans Sültmann) and two Ju 88A-2s of 3 Staffel (Ofw Ernst Fahr and Uffz Herbert Lipke), all three of which went down west-north-west of Bergen; all the crews were lost. The Ju 88A-2 was a rebuilt A-1 which had been equipped for a catapult-assisted take off to allow greater range.

The smaller British raids were achieving less success; the Wellingtons gained only near misses, while the Hampdens did no better, although they claimed one vessel sunk. At the time more German coastal aircraft were out on patrol, 13 Do 18s from 2 and 3/KüFlGr 406 and 2/KüFlGr 906 having been despatched on patrol at 1540. As the Wellingtons were on their return flight one of these flyingboats — K6+HL of 3/406 — was seen, and was attacked by one of the 9 Squadron aircraft, the gunners shooting it down. Oblt Heinrich Vlieger and his crew perished while attempting to force-land off the Norwegian coast.

During the day three Sunderlands of 210 Squadron had been ordered to Invergordon on detachment from Pembroke Dock, arriving late in the morning. At 1300 L2167 took off on reconnaissance to the Oslo area, but six hours later it was intercepted here by 1/ZG 76's two serviceable Bf 110s from Fornebu, flown by Oblt Hansen and Lt Lent. The former shot the aircraft down, aided by his gunner, Uffz Gross. The flyingboat blew up in mid air and the radio operator/air gunner was thrown clear, falling 1,500 feet without a parachute into the sea, and surviving! The rest of Flt Lt P.W.H. Kite's crew were killed.

Later in the evening *Köln* left Bergen, and *Karlsruhe* sailed from Kristiansand. 12 British submarines had been lying in wait in the Kattegat and Skagerrak since the previous day, and one of these — HMS *Truant* — caught the latter

At Sullom Voe the Sunderlands of 204 Squadron were reinforced by detachments from 201 and 210 Squadrons. Here ZM-Y, L5805, of 201 Squadron is seen on arrival. Immediately behind is one of 204 Squadron's aircraft. *(A. Thomas)*

vessel and sank her. Her catapult-mounted Arado Ar 196A floatplane from 1/Bfl 196 went down with her. Three more of these aircraft from 5/Bfl 196 had been lost when *Blücher* was sunk, together with one of the aircrew and seven servicing personnel. During the day a Do 17Z of 3/KüFlGr 606 failed to return from a reconnaissance and anti-submarine patrol over the Skaggerrak, Lt Walter Priehe and his crew being lost, while Uffz Otto Backhaus' Do 18 — 8L+CK of 2/KüFlGr 906 — crashed while landing at Hörnum after a sortie.

In England meanwhile, another Gladiator unit — 263 Squadron at Bristol's Filton airfield — was ordered to re-establish to field strength and collect Arctic scale equipment from the stores. The destination was obvious....

THE SECOND DAY; CONSOLIDATION
With morning on 10 April came confirmation that the German hold on Southern

In a hangar at Oslo/Kjeller airfield, newly-assembled and partly assembled Curtiss H-75A-6 aircraft were captured intact. *(O. Simonsen via B. Olsen)*

Curtiss H-75A-6 439 under test by the Luftwaffe at Kjeller. *(via B. Olsen)*

Norway was secure. At Oslo, Kjeller airfield was now occupied, and amongst the aircraft captured there were all the newly-delivered Curtiss Hawks. Kjevik, the little field at Kristiansand was also taken, providing a useful staging point for short-range aircraft from Germany and Denmark, while Vaernes airfield at Trondheim was captured on 10th. Hundreds of transport aircraft continued to fly in men and equipment throughout the day, while the Luftwaffe also moved in a number of operational units. Stavanger/Sola was the airfield chosen for the subsequent operations of the Ju 87Rs of 1/StG 1, which had arrived in Norway during the preceding afternoon and for the Zerstörer of Stab, 2 and 3/ZG 76, all of which were arriving from Aalborg, plus nine He 111s of 3/KG 26. At Fornebu by evening were 1/ZG 76, 1/StG 1, and three He 111s of 8/KG 26. 1/ZG 76, having flown back to Aalborg from Fornebu the previous evening, and then back to Fornebu again, would join the rest of the Gruppe at Sola next day, when Bf 109Es of II/JG 77 also moved over from Esbjerg, taking up residence at Kristiansand. All would then be in a position to intercept RAF or Royal Navy attacks on either Oslo or Bergen.

Luftwaffe officers examine one of the remaining Norwegian Gladiators at Oslo/Fornebu. *(Bundesarchiv)*

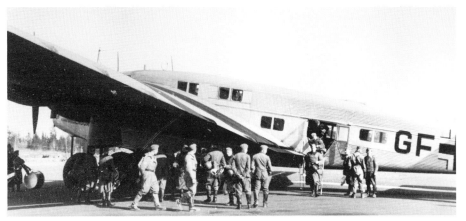

KGrzbV 105's sole Junkers G-38, 'von Hindenburg' is unloaded at Oslo/Fornebu. *(Bundesarchiv)*

A Junkers Ju 90, still resplendent in its Lufthansa paintwork, at Oslo/Fornebu. It had been pressed into service with KGrzbV 105. *(Bundesarchiv)*

A military band provides immediate entertainment to celebrate the successful seizure of Fornebu airfield. They are performing alongside KGzrbV 105's G-38. *(Bundesarchiv)*

Oslo/Fornebu airfield seen from the air on 10 April. Amidst a mass of Ju 52/3m transports (at left), some in the light colours of Lufthansa, may be seen KGrzbV 105's G-38 and one of its Ju 90s (centre). To the right are He 111 bombers. *(F. Selinger)*

For the Norwegian air forces it was a day of reorganization as stock was taken of what remained. In the south the Bomber Wing had gathered its surviving aircraft on the frozen Lake Vangsmjösa on 11th, while all aircraft equipped with skis, including those of Speidevingen (the Reconnaissance Wing), some Tiger Moths and a few civil aircraft, moved to Fefor near Hamar on 10th. Here the C-Vs were hastily camouflaged and moved to Lake Espedalsvannet the following day. The Tiger Moths and Klemm 25 LN-EAG were based a little to the north of the lake, from where they would undertake communications sorties. Further north the Hålogaland Air Corps aircraft were split up in pairs at Bardufoss, Andsvann and Moen, in Målselv. Only the naval aircraft operated during the day, all remaining serviceable machines having arrived at Skattora. A few reconnaissances were undertaken over the northern coastlines by He 115s on 11th and 12th, but nothing was seen.

Hastily-camouflaged Fokker C-VD 374 of the Norwegian Reconnaissance Wing at Fefor, following evacuation of Oslo/Kjeller airfield. *(via B. Olsen)*

Fokker C-VD 375 displays well the temporary white 'zig-zag' camouflage added to the normal dark green finish at Fefor. *(via B. Olsen)*

At dawn the Luftwaffe and the RAF again despatched their coastal reconnaissance aircraft, KüFlGr 406 sending out ten Do 18s, while Hudsons headed eastwards manned by crews from 220, 224 and 233 Squadrons. One aircraft from 220 Squadron had an inconclusive skirmish with one of the newly-arrived Bf 110s, but managed to escape undamaged. Coastal Command's morning reconnaissances reported a cruiser, 30 supply vessels and 12 seaplanes at Bergen, together with large concentrations of aircraft on the airfield here, and on that at Stavanger, where further seaplanes were also noted. Following the

Lt Edvard Omholt-Jensen, of the Norwegian Reconnaissance Wing, takes time off from cleaning the machine gun of C-VD 375 to chat to an admiring lady visitor. *(via B. Olsen)*

247

unwelcome appearance of the British Home Fleet on 9 April, ten He 111s of KGr 100 were sent out on an armed reconnaissance east and south-east of the Orkneys and Shetlands, followed by an He 111P of 3(F)/ObdL. Immediately behind this reconnaissance 'screen' came 35 He 111s of KG 26 to respond immediately to any targets spotted. As the 3(F)/ObdL aircraft approached the Scottish coast, it was intercepted by seven Hurricanes of 43 Squadron which were flying out to sea towards Ronaldshay Island, led by Sqn Ldr George Lott. Five miles east of the island, Oblt Karl Heinz's aircraft was seen and the fighters attacked this in line astern, Lott and his two flight commanders Peter Townsend and Caesar Hull, all getting in shots, as did the four other pilots. Against such opposition the bomber had no chance; shot to pieces, it flopped onto the sea and broke in half. Three men were seen swimming, but were much too far from land for there to be any chance of them being picked up before they succumbed to exposure.

The KGr 100 aircraft subsequently reached the area and reported that two convoys had been seen off the Moray Firth, and heavy naval units south of the Orkneys. These reports referred to 2 and 3 Cruiser Flotillas and a French force under Rear Admiral Derrien, which were now retiring to Scapa Flow, and at once these became the prime targets. The first attacks began when the KGr 100 aircraft found shipping off Kinnaird Head, but their bombing caused little damage. Numerous interceptions by defending fighters then followed, and some heavy fighting ensued. The first such engagement occurred during the afternoon; Plt Off I.J. Muirhead of 605 Squadron was on convoy patrol when at 1545 he spotted a German aircraft; this was a Heinkel of 1/KGr 100. Two attacks were made, but the bomber slipped away in cloud, returning with the flight engineer dead, but only minor damage to the aircraft.

Almost an hour later Flg Off Leeson from the same unit was leading Red Section out on a patrol when two He 111s were seen at 14,000 feet. The three Hurricanes climbed to the attack and one of the bombers was shot down by Leeson, Plt Off P.E. Carter and Sgt W.M.F. Moffat; two members of the crew were seen to bale out, but in fact Oblt Harald Vogel and all his crew in this 4/KG 26 aircraft survived, being rescued by a Royal Navy trawler. 111 Squadron's Green Section had been scrambled to intercept the raid on the convoy as well, but arrived only in time to see the Heinkel and parachutes going down. During the return flight a second Heinkel encountered a Blenheim when halfway across the North Sea, and was at once engaged in combat. The first shots fired by the British aircraft (of which more later) wounded the flight mechanic, and the bomber was heavily damaged (60%). It returned and landed at Stavanger, where it was subsequently written off.

Six Sea Gladiators from Hatston's 804 Squadron were sent up during the early evening and these also engaged some of the German aircraft, which were identified as one He 111 and two Do 17s. The pilots of the biplanes claimed the Heinkel shot down east of Burray by Lt Cdr J.C. Cockburn in N2266, and one other aircraft damaged by three other pilots jointly. It would appear that they actually attacked two He 111s; one 1/KGr 100 machine was badly damaged but succeeded in getting back with one wounded aboard. One of the fighters crashed on return, and was written-off. Meanwhile, following the reports of the British shipping from the 3(F)/ObdL aircraft, a heavy raid had been prepared, and this came in at dusk once again, when about 40 bombers approached, comprising 19 Heinkels of I/KG 26, followed by 19 Ju 88s from I and II/KG 30, the latter

Fleet Air Arm pilots of 804 Squadron at Hatston with one of their Sea Gladiators (N2272). Note the arrester hook beneath the fuselage and the interesting personnel emblem beneath the cockpit. *(PRO)*

briefed to bomb naval oil supplies at Scapa. Ten Hurricanes from 43, 111 and 605 Squadrons were scrambled, first off at 2005 being Yellow Section of 111. Flt Lt R.P.R. Powell, Flg Off H.M. Ferris and Sgt W.L. Dymond managed to shoot down one Heinkel, before landing again at 2115. This was an aircraft of Stab I/KG 26 flown by Fw Busacker, and commanded by the Gruppenkommandeur, 45 year-old Oberstlt Hans Alefeld, who perished with his crew. Flg Off G.R. Edge of 605 Squadron attacked three bombers, while Plt Off C.F. Currant expended all his ammunition into another, but no definite results were observed in either case. In fact the attacks of these pilots had obviously been more effective than had been realised in the dusk. One He 111 of 1/KG 26 crashed into the sea off the island of Sylt on return, Oblt Otto Houselle and two of his crew drowned, whilst another bomber of 2/KG 26 (Lt de Res Hubert Schachtbeck), which had been very badly damaged by fighters, crash-landed at Marx and was a total loss. The anti-aircraft defences claimed three bombers shot down, and it seems that on this occasion their fire had been most effective. Two Ju 88s were lost, one 2/KG 30 machine (Ofw Walter Brünn) failing to return after radioing an SOS that one engine had been lost due to a Flak hit, whilst a 4 Staffel machine flown by Lt Hans Hohendahl was also missing. German air gunners claimed one Gladiator and one Hurricane shot down during the day's various combats.

Following the morning reconnaissance by the Hudsons, such immediate action as could be taken was put in hand to attack the various targets reported. Sgt C.F. Rose lifted one of 254 Squadron's fighter Blenheims off the airfield at Lossiemouth at 1415, arriving over Stavanger at 1600. Here he identified 18 Blohm und Voss flyingboats in the harbour, 40-50 Messerschmitts and 10-20 Heinkels on the airfield (the latter probably the Ju 88Cs of Z/KG 30, the former probably I/St G 1's Ju 87Rs). Diving down to attack, he strafed the airfield first, claiming two Heinkels destroyed; he then attacked the anchorage, where he believed he had damaged at least five flyingboats. As he headed for home he

Soon to play an active part over the Norwegian coastal area are these Blenheim IVF fighters of 235 and 254 Squadrons of Coastal Command, seen here at North Coates. QY-O of the latter unit can be seen in the right foreground, with LA-F, E and G of 235 Squadron immediately beyond. *(235 Squadron via A.Thomas)*

met the He 111 from II/KG 26 which has already been mentioned, when about midway across the North Sea, and made a stern attack on this at 1820. Thinking he had killed the rear gunner and put the port engine out of action, he pulled up alongside and turned in for a beam attack, the turret gunner getting a number of hits on the bomber on this occasion. Rose finally departed without seeing any further effect from his fire, and having identified his opponent as a Ju 88. He landed at 1925 with 20-30 bullet holes in his own aircraft. During this sortie aircraft recognition certainly seems to have been one of the pilot's main problems!

The attack on the airfield had in fact destroyed a Ju 52/3m of KGrzbV 107, and damaged another 45%; a mechanic of I/ZG 76 was killed; in the harbour Rose's fire had sunk an He 59D of KGrzbV 108. Nonetheless, in one sortie Sgt Rose had been responsible for the destruction of three Luftwaffe aircraft. Most of these had flown in during the day when 18 He 59s of KGrzbV 108, with Ju 52/3ms of various transport units, brought in III/IR 193, ground staff of I/ZG 76 and KG 26, ammunition and bombs, and personnel of II and III/Flakregt 33.

Bergen
While this initial strike by a single aircraft had been quite effective, albeit in a very minor way, of much greater significance was an attack launched during the same afternoon by the Fleet Air Arm. From Hatston in the Orkneys Lt W.P. Lucy led five Skuas of 800 and 11 of 803 Squadrons to attack the shipping in Bergen harbour at maximum range. En route one of the 803 Squadron aircraft crashed into the sea with the loss of Lt B.J. Smeeton/Mdspmn F. Watkins. Arriving overhead without encountering fighter opposition, the naval aircraft unleashed a classic dive-bombing attack on the motionless vessels below. Lucy led the 15 Skuas to attack the light cruiser *Königsberg*, which was moored alongside a wharf. At 0805 the cruiser took three direct hits and two near-misses from 500lb SAP bombs, the latter causing more damage than the former. As the hull ruptured, masses of water poured in, and at 1051 the vessel sank with

Top left: Immediately after being hit by bombs from the Fleet Air Arm Skuas, a column of smoke rises skyward from *Königsberg*. Top right: Well-ablaze, the vessel begins to list to port. Middle: Seen from the other side of Bergen harbour, *Königsberg*'s list is becoming more pronounced, and the fires burn more furiously. In the foreground is one of KGrzbV 108's Ju 52/See transport floatplanes. Bottom: Suddenly the wharf appears empty! *Königsberg* has just gone down. *(IWM)*

the loss of 18 dead and 24 wounded; with her went her catapult Ar 196A of 1/ Bfl 196. This was the first major vessel ever to be sunk by air attack in time of war, this epoch-marking action being accomplished for the loss of a single Skua; the aircraft crashed at Askøy, near the port, the crew (Sub Lt Faragut/Mdspmn Owbridge) surviving unhurt. They were rescued by the Norwegians and served with the Norwegian Naval Air Service for the rest of the month. Meanwhile, one bomb which had missed the cruiser, destroyed a Ju 52/See floatplane, one of 12 such aircraft of KGrzbV 108 which, with He 59s, had brought in the remainder of 5/IR 159 and some Luftwaffe personnel.

Narvik

The far North — still beyond the effective range of Luftwaffe aircraft — offered the best opportunity for Allied involvement, and it was here that the Royal Navy struck another blow during the day. Even as the fore-mentioned actions were underway, five British destroyers slipped into Ofotfjorden under cover of mist and snow, surprising and sinking two German destroyers and eight merchant-men. Four larger German destroyers then appeared from Ballangen, and in the action which followed *Hardy* and *Hunter* were sunk, *Hotspur* and *Hostile* damaged. Led by the undamaged *Havoc* they made for the open sea, getting clear without further loss. Half an hour later, close to the mouth of the fjord, they met the *Rauenfels*, a large German transport steamer which was carrying to the area a battery of 150mm guns and their ammunition, two batteries of 88mm Flak artillery and a battery of 37mm automatic Flak, the two latter batteries belonging to I/Flakregt 32. On sighting the British warships the captain at once ordered that the ship should be abandoned, and the 48 men under his command took to three lifeboats. *Havoc* opened fire and *Rauenfels* began to burn; this destroyer took aboard the Captain and 18 men from one of the boats. *Hostile* then fired two salvoes at the stricken merchantman and she blew up. The other two German boats reached the shore, where the 29 men aboard were taken prisoner by Norwegian troops. The commander of the British flotilla, Capt B.A. Warburton-Lee, had been killed aboard *Hardy* during the fight, and was awarded a posthumous Victoria Cross — the second of the campaign — for one also went to the captain of the destroyer *Glowworm* for his ramming attack on *Admiral Hipper*.

During various reconnaissance and bombing attacks on 10th, two He 111s were damaged in accidents and one 7/KG 26 aircraft crashed into the sea off the Norwegian coast for no obvious reason. 113 various Ju 52/3ms flew into Fornebu with III/IR 307, the balance of the Divisional Staff of 163 Infantry Division, Stab/IR 324 and elements of IR 159. One transport crashed on arrival, and one failed to arrive back at Schleswig, while seven more suffered damage to one cause or another. At Fornebu now were ten He 111s of 8/KG 26 and parts of I/ZG 76 and 1/StG 1.

During the day the aircraft carrier *Furious* joined the fleet at sea, having completed her refit only days previously. Her air group still comprised only 816 and 818 Squadrons, her departure having been so hurried that no fighter unit could be onloaded in time. Thus for the first two weeks, urgently-needed fighter cover for the Home Fleet and Expeditionary Force was still not forthcoming.

11/4/40

At dawn on 11 April the vessel launched the first air strike of the war by carrier−

borne aircraft, 18 Swordfish from 816 and 818 Squadrons taking off to attack suspected cruisers in Trondheimsfjord — later to be the scene of much Fleet Air Arm effort. Lack of knowledge of the area had led to the wrong depth settings to the torpedoes, and most grounded in shallow water, no hits being obtained. No cruisers had been found in any event, but the destroyers *Bruno Heinemann*, *Paul Jacobi* and *Theodor Riedel* were there, together with the submarine *U-30* and a number of transports. Two Swordfish returned to the area later in the morning to bomb these, but missed. This inauspicious result was somewhat ameliorated when HM Submarine *Spearfish* (Lt Cdr J.H. Forbes) managed to torpedo the cruiser *Lützow* as she was making for Kiel, severely damaging the rudder and propellors; the damaged cruiser returned to Oslo.

Whilst this first air strike was underway, the Coastal Command units were once again out on reconnaissance, Hudsons from 220, 224 and 233 Squadrons all being away at first light. On the other side of the North Sea 3/KüFlGr 406 sent off five Do 18s at 0421, and three more at 0600. At 0645 a 220 Squadron Hudson spotted the cruiser *Köln*, accompanied by two destroyers and two E-Boats to the west of Lista. The searches continued, and at 0810 Hudson N7217 of 224 Squadron, flown by Plt Off Wood, came into contact with Do 18 8L+ EK east of Kinnaird Head. Wood managed to make a stern attack and the flyingboat crashed into the sea, the British crew watching as their opposite numbers clambered into their dinghy. Lt zur See Helmut Kühl and his crew were later picked up and made prisoner by a Royal Navy vessel. Flt Lt McLaren of 233 Squadron was not so lucky. He also encountered one of the Dorniers in N7243, getting on its tail and seeing hits. The 'boat proved to be remarkably nimble however, out-turning the Hudson and inflicting damage to it. The navigator, Plt Off A.E. Evans, was hit, and as he was bleeding profusely, McLaren abandoned the fight and turned for home. Evans was beyond help however, and died shortly afterwards.

201 Squadron despatched one of the remaining Londons on a special search for the German troopship *Levante*, but nothing could be found. Following this sortie the squadron was stood down to complete re-equipment, before undertaking further active operations.

254 Squadron's Blenheim fighters were also operating throughout the second

Do 18 8L+EK of 3/KüFlGr 406 in the water immediately after having been shot down by Plt Off Wood's 224 Squadron Hudson on 11 April. *(IWM)*

half of the day. Shortly after 1330, two set off to strafe Hardangerfjord. Here at 1740 Do 18 K6+AH of 1/406 was caught in the air and attacked; both Blenheims were hit by return fire and were forced to break off, leaving their opponent with both engines apparently on fire — the Dornier had in fact suffered only 6% damage. 45 minutes after this pair had left England, a third Blenheim took off for Stavanger. Here 80 aircraft were counted on the airfield and 18 flyingboats in the harbour, but six Bf 110s were seen taking off and the pilot headed away north towards Bergen. At 1800 he encountered a Ju 88, a short engagement following during which both aircraft were damaged.

Meanwhile ten He 111s from III/KG 26 had taken off on an armed reconnaissance, finding the carrier *Furious*, accompanied by three battleships, three heavy cruisers and many destroyers, to the north-west of Trondheim. At 1700 the Heinkels attacked through a heavy anti-aircraft barrage; one hit on the carrier was claimed, but none was actually achieved, although two bombs did strike the destroyer *Eclipse*.

At 1515 another of 224 Squadron's Hudsons had set course for the Bergen area, Flg Off Bullock in N7305 sighting the MV *Theseus*, and attacking with three 250lb bombs — all of which missed. He then engaged another of the tough Do 18s, and in the fight which ensued believed that he had killed the rear gunner, although the Hudson's radio operator suffered slight wounds. The Dornier, M2+IK of 2/106, returned having suffered 25% damage, and with its own radio operator wounded.

Heinkel He 111H of KG 26 (left) newly-arrived at Stavanger/Sola, with one of the abandoned Caproni Ca 310s (507) of the Norwegian Bomber Wing. *(Bundesarchiv)*

Bomber Command had still played only a minor part, but the problem was that only Stavanger/Sola was within range of the Hampdens and Wellingtons, at a distance of some 450 miles from their bases. Only Whitleys could reach Fornebu or Vaernes, and these airfields would be hard to find at night. At around 1800 the first raid against a target on Norwegian soil by the Command was at last laid on, six Wellingtons of 115 Squadron being led to the Sola area by two Blenheims from 254 Squadron. These Blenheims strafed first, damaging a Do 17P of 1(F)/120 on the airfield; this was the only real damage suffered during the attack, although the bomber crews claimed hits on four Ju 88s. A fierce barrage of defensive fire was put up by 9/Flakregiment 33 and P9271 was hit three times, F/Sgt Powell, the pilot, and another member of the crew being

Powell got the aircraft back to base and carried out a crash-landing; he was later awarded the DFM. A second Wellington, P9235 flown by Flg Off Scott, was also hit, and the navigator was wounded. Two Bf 110s were scrambled after the bombers, but could not catch them.

During the day more Bf 110s of 2/ZG 76 arrived at Sola, accompanied by Z Staffel/KG 30 with Ju 88Cs, 3/KG 30 and three Do 17Ps of 1(F)/120. One Bf 110 and one Ju 88C crashed on landing and both were severely damaged. Three Ju 52/3ms brought in 7/LgNachRegt 3.

A KG 4 He 111P and an He 111H of 8/KG 26 (1H+ES) have crash-landed and run off the edge of Oslo/Fornebu airfield; Ju 52/3m in the background. *(Bundesarchiv)*

Apart from engaging the somewhat sporadic British attacks, the Luftwaffe continued operations against the Norwegian Army during 11 April. Three He 111s of 6/KG 4 bombed troops to the north of Kristiansand at Evjemoen, while 15 more from 1 and 2/KG 4 bombed traffic around Oslo, particularly in the area between Frederikstad and Rakkestad. 11 more He 111s from II/KG 26 raided Nybergsund on the Swedish frontier, where the Norwegian General Staff was believed to be, while an Fw 200 of 1/KG 40 reconnoitred the Trondheim area, seeing no activity. Six Do 17Ps of 1(F)/120 flew reconnaissances during the early afternoon, two returning damaged by anti-aircraft fire — in one case German!

Arrival of German reinforcements continued, 89 Ju 52/3ms carrying the ground organisation of II/JG 77 to Kjevik airfield, while 258 more flew into Oslo/Fornebu with I/IR 236, PioneerBatt 234, ground staff of KG 26, spares, ammunition and weapons. One aircraft brought in a group of radio specialists. Two transports were lost during these operations, and six were damaged.

Following reconnaissance over the Kiel-Oslo route, German shipping was ordered to be attacked at night by RAF Bomber Command, 13 Whitleys of 10, 77 and 102 Squadrons being despatched to the Skaggerrak and Kattegat, while 20 Hampdens from 49,83 and 61 Squadrons operated over the southern Kattegat and Baltic. Ten north-bound ships were found and bombed, and it was believed that one vessel, the *Robert Ley*, had been sunk; in fact this ship was not lost. Whitley N1347 of 77 Squadron came down in the sea 60 miles off Wick, Flg Off G.E. Saddington and his crew being lost.

Lines of Ju 52/3m transports prepare to carry reinforcements north to Norway. *(Bundesarchiv)*

A DAY OF DISASTER FOR THE BOMBERS

Early on 12 April Hudsons discovered the battlecruisers *Scharnhorst* and *Gneisenau* (the latter damaged by the battleship *Rodney* on 9 April) heading back towards Germany in company with *Hipper*. These vessels were sighted to the west of Lista at 0645 by a Hudson of 224 Squadron. Bomber Command was ordered to launch a strike at once, whilst more Hudsons attempted to keep the warships under surveillance. One of the searching aircraft, N7258 from 233 Squadron, had taken off at 0728 in the hands of Plt Off G.J.D. Yorke, and this aircraft failed to return. It had fallen as the first victim of the campaign for the Bf 109E pilots of II/JG 77 from Kristiansand, shot down by Ofw Robert Menge into the sea south-west of the port. Another Hudson was more fortunate, finding the vessels off Horn's Reef and maintaining contact for an hour before losing them at 1015.

First off of the attacking force were seven Hampdens of 44 Squadron and five of 50 Squadron, which departed from Waddington from 0815 onwards, while 12 more Hampdens of 61 and 144 Squadrons set off from Hemswell. The latter formation, unable to find any targets, turned back; the former, led by Sqn Ldr

A Hudson of 233 Squadron leaves the British coast for a patrol. *(IWM)*

D.C.F. Good of 50 Squadron, having also found no vessels at sea in the bad weather prevailing, headed instead to attack two naval vessels in Kristiansand harbour.

As they made their bombing run the weather cleared and the Bf 109Es of II/ JG 77 struck. At 1215 the fourth section of bombers was seen to be in heavy Flak bursts, and two bombers were observed to fall in flames. These were L4083 (Flg Off M.W. Donaldson) and L4073 (Sgt G.M. Wild) of 50 Squadron. At that moment the fighters were seen making a beam attack, and within seconds the third bomber of the section, L4081 (Plt Off M. Thomas), and two more from the 44 Squadron part of the formation — L4099 (Flg Off W.G. Taylor) and P1173 (Flg Off H.W. Robson) — were all shot down in flames. Taylor's aircraft had apparently been hit by Flak, and was lagging when caught by the fighters.

For 25 minutes the Messerschmitts kept after the remaining Hampdens and when they finally broke off due to shortage of fuel and ammunition, all the bombers had been damaged, two of them badly. In Sqn Ldr Good's L4168, air gunner Cpl J. Wallace shot down one Bf 109, for which he was later awarded a DFM. P4290 (Plt Off F.E. Eustace) of 44 Squadron was attacked by two Bf 109s and badly damaged, but one of the attackers was eventually shot down by cross fire from another Hampden. L4074 (Plt Off M.G. Homer) from the same unit was also repeatedly attacked, receiving cannon shells in the right wing, left engine and through the astro-hatch. Sgt E. Apperson, the rear gunner, put a burst into one fighter and saw flames from the engine — this was later confirmed to bring the credited score to two destroyed and two seriously damaged.

Four of the bombers crashed into the sea south-west of Kristiansand, while Flg Off Donaldson's aircraft crash-landed on a nearby island, where three of the four crew were captured — the only survivors from the five aircraft. As the bombers limped home Plt Off J.B. Bull's L4064, another 50 Squadron aircraft, came down in the sea 120 miles east of Newcastle, the crew being lost, while 44 Squadron's L4091 crash-landed at Acklington, the crew unhurt. Only five made it back to Waddington, where Sqn Ldr Good was the first to land at 1555. The Germans had pressed home their attacks closer than was wise, or indeed necessary with their cannon armament, and the Hampdens' gunners' return fire had been more effective than they had realised. Claims by the German pilots totalled six Hampdens but Ofw Erich Herfeld and Uffz Kurt Opolski of 5 Staffel, together with Oblt Wilhelm Ruthammer and Ofw Hermann Stierle of 6 Staffel were all shot down and killed; a fifth Bf 109 ditched near Kristiansand, the pilot being rescued by a German ship. Herfeld and Opolski were amongst those known to have shot down bombers and they were posthumously credited with one apiece. Two more were credited to Ofw Robert Menge and one to Ofw Hans-Jacob Arnoldy, a sixth victory remaining unaccounted for, believed shot down by another of the dead pilots.

While this epic air battle had been raging, more bombers were on their way. After the departure of the Hampdens, Wellingtons followed in substantial numbers. Nine aircraft from 9 Squadron, which was now operating from Lossie-mouth under Coastal Command control, led the way. They were followed by 11 from 37 and 75 Squadrons, 12 more from 38 and 149 Squadrons, and 12 from 115 Squadron.

As the bombers approached the Norwegian coast the Zerstörer were scrambled, ten Bf 110Cs and three Ju 88Cs taking off. The latter, from Z/KG 30, made contact first, and it seems that these fighters intercepted 149 Squadron,

Bf 109E fighters of II/JG 77 line the taxiway at Kristiansand airfield in April 1940. A pair of Ju 52/3m transports prepare to take off. *(Bib für Zeit)*

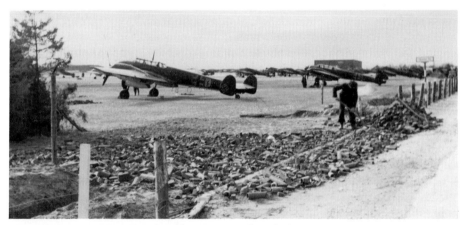

Bf 110 Zerstörer of I/ZG 76 at Oslo/Fornebu. *(Bundesarchiv)*

which was lagging behind 38 Squadron. A number of attacks from astern were made as a result of which two bombers were seen to turn back and make for the coast, still under attack; Sgt G.E. Good in P9266 and Sgt H.J. Wheeler in P9246 and their crews were not seen again; they had crashed into the sea south-west of Sola, shot down by Ofw Martin Jeschke (at 1645) and Uffz Peter Lauffs (at 1650).

The remaining four closed up as the big fighters made a number of beam attacks, which damaged two more of their number, although only slightly. From Sqn Ldr Collett's crew, AC 1 Francis claimed a Bf 110 shot down while it was making an astern attack, as did AC 2 Barrie in Flg Off G.P. Miers' aircraft. LAC Chapman in this latter Wellington and AC 2 Green in Flg Off H.M. Robertson's aircraft each claimed Bf 110s which were making beam attacks, but it was considered on evaluation that only two aircraft had actually been shot down, in each case by the joint fire of the claiming gunners. In fact only one Ju 88C, flown by Uffz Erwin Maus, was shot down during this fight, crashing into the sea south-west of Sola with the loss of the crew. However a second crash-landed on Sola airfield, 50% damaged.

Meanwhile the Bf 110s had arrived, and immediately after Lauffs of Z/KG 30 had claimed the second 149 Squadron machine, Lt Helmut Woltersdorf of 2/ZG 76 claimed another — almost certainly P9296 of 38 Squadron, flown by Sqn Ldr M. Nolan. The Zerstörer kept after the bombers, and at 1655 Oblt Gresens, also of 2 Staffel, claimed another, although this was not confirmed. No more Wellingtons from this formation were lost, but all the other five 38 Squadron machines were damaged, one of them (P9226) heavily.

Nearly 20 minutes later, more Wellingtons were engaged, Lt Woltersdorf claiming a second victory at 1714, while Fw Leo Schumacher, also of 2 Staffel, claimed another at 1720 and Ofw Fleischmann of 3/ZG 76 one at 1735; Schumacher's claim did not receive confirmation. Their opponents appear to have been the 9 and 115 Squadron formations, Sgt C.R. Bowen's P2520 of the former unit and Plt Off F.E. Barber's P9284 from the latter, both crashing near Stavanger, Bowen's aircraft in the sea and Barber's on land; both crews were lost.

While the Luftwaffe fighters had been fully involved with the RAF bombers, 19 Skuas from the FAA's 800, 801 and 803 Squadrons had left Hatston for a repeat attack on Bergen. This time no noteable success was achieved. Some ships were dive-bombed, but only near-miss damage was inflicted, while the lone E-Boat *S-24* was strafed; it suffered shrapnel damage and three sailors were wounded. One of 210 Squadron's Sunderlands, L5748 (Flt Lt Van Der Kiste) attacked a troopship in Hardangerfjord, but was damaged by Flak.

Meanwhile the Home Fleet had made its way northwards from Trondheim, and late on 12th reached a point 150 miles from Narvik. Here two waves of Swordfish totalling a dozen aircraft, drawn equally from 816 and 818 Squadrons were launched on a bombing strike. The second wave, led by Lt Cdr Gardner, became lost in a snowstorm, and returned later to make the first night deck landings. In the meantime the earlier wave, led by Lt Cdr Sydney Turner, had attacked the port, claiming direct hits on two destroyers. One bomb hit the destroyer *Erich Koellner*, one member of the crew being killed and five wounded, while the Norwegian fishery protection vessel *Senja* was also hit and severely damaged. A blizzard of anti-aircraft fire from I/Flakregt 32 and warship Flak shot down two 818 Squadron aircraft, but both crews were rescued by British warships. A third was set on fire, but Leading Airman J.G. Skeats, although wounded, managed to dowse the flames — a feat for which he subsequently received the DSM. A further 818 Squadron aircraft — U-3K — had its port wheel shot off, but landed safely. Less fortunate was one of 816 Squadron's machines which went over the side during the night landing. This raised the number of British aircraft lost over and around Norway during the day to 17.

On this date an invasion force had sailed for the Narvik area from Britain, under the command of Maj Gen P.J. Macksey. It was intended to put ashore at Harstad, a fishing port on an island in Vaagsfjord, 55 miles by sea from Narvik itself. Following a further successful destroyer foray on 13 April, Admiral of the Fleet the Earl of Cork and Orrery suggested a direct assault on Narvik be undertaken instead, but this idea was declined as the troops involved had not been trained for opposed landings. This area had seen the only offensive action undertaken by the Luftwaffe on 12 April when a lone Fw 200 from 1/KG 40 on an armed reconnaissance over the Narvik area, made an unsuccessful attack on four British destroyers.

Fairey Swordfish of 818 Squadron shot down by Flak on 12 April. *(Bib für Zeit)*

During the day an He 115B of 2/KüFlGr 506 failed to return to Trondheim from a coastal reconnaissance sortie, while over the Baltic another such aircraft from 1/KüFlGr 906 (8L+GH; Lt zur See Wolfgang Reich) flew out of cloud whilst patrolling over *Lützow*, and crashed whilst making a steep turn; one man was killed and two injured.

Reinforcement flights continued; 146 Ju 52/3ms flew into Oslo carrying III/IR 236, Stab Gruppe XXI, II/IR 236, spares, ammunition and other equipment. 19 Ju 52/3ms ferried 7/LgNachrRegt 3 to Stavanger, while nine more took further ground personnel of II/JG 77 to Kristiansand/Kjevik. 18 aircraft of KGrzbV 105 ferried aviation spares to Trondheim/Vaernes, while the motor vessel *Levante* brought in more supplies and provisions, plus the 88mm Flak guns of 4/Flakregt 33 and the 20mm weapons of 10/Flakregt 33. One of KGrzbV 105's Ju 90Bs hit an obstruction as it took off again, and crashed. Two Ju 52/3ms also crashed during the day.

One of KGrzbV 105's big Junkers Ju 90B transports comes in to land at an airfield already crowded with Ju 52/3ms and He 111s. *(Bundesarchiv)*

Equipment is prepared for loading aboard a KGrzbV 105 Ju 90B. *(Bundesarchiv)*

To improve the command structure and control of the growing Luftwaffe force in Norway, Luftflotte 5 was now established under the command of GenObst Erhard Milch.

13/4/40
On the morning of 13th in support of Admiral Whitworth's battle group, three Swordfish from 818 Squadron flew anti-submarine patrols, while ten more from 816 Squadron headed again for Narvik, led by Capt S. Burch. Their attack was not successful once more, near-misses again being all that could be achieved against the destroyers *Bernd von Arnim* and *Hermann Künne*. Gunners on the former vessel claimed one Swordish shot down, the crew being rescued by a British destroyer, while a second was claimed by the guns of the *Erich Giese* and the harbour defences jointly, the crew being reported killed.

The second aircraft crashed into Ofotfjord with the loss of Sub Lt G.R. Hampden and his gunner, while the first crashed whilst attempting to force-land off the coast at Elvenes. Sub Lt L.C. Franklin was killed, but the two other members of the crew were picked up from the side of the fjord by HMS *Punjabi*. The German gunners claimed damage to a third Swordfish, and when it was later found that Franklin's aircraft had come down at Evenes, this was believed to have been the victim, since it was thought that *Bernd von Arnim's* victim had crashed at once. This was not the case, only the two Swordfish being lost.

Meanwhile at noon a Royal Navy destroyer force led by the battleship *Warspite* entered Ofotfjord to flush out the remaining German destroyers there. *Warspite* launched her catapult Swordfish floatplane, flown by Lt Cdr W. Brown, who saw two destroyers, and then spotted the submarine *U-64* (Kaptlt Wilhelm Scholz). He attacked at once with the bombs he was carrying and obtained a direct hit, following which the vessel sank — the Fleet Air Arm's first victory over a submarine. Not finished yet, Brown and the crew of his aircraft then spotted a destroyer lying in ambush, and this was reported to, and swiftly sunk by, the naval force. During the remaining hours of daylight the surviving seven German destroyers were all sunk, the British force then withdrawing. While engaged in this hunting expedition, the ships also shot down two Ju 52/3m transports which passed overhead. How these came to be there is connected with a saga of some interest.

At 0845 that morning ten Ju 52/3ms from 3/KGrzbV 102 and two from 1/102 had taken off from Oslo/Fornebu with two officers and 58 NCOs and men of Gebirgsbatterie 2/AR 112, four 75mm mountain guns and much ammunition, and other supplies. The formation was led by Oberst Baur de Betaz, Gruppenkommandeur of KGrzbV 102, and accompanied by a Nachtrichten Ju 52/3m of Na-Flug-Kommando Käthen, which was to report on the mission.

The weather deteriorated as the aircraft flew northwards, and as a result the British warships in the Ofotfjord were not seen until too late, five of the transports being hit by anti-aircraft fire. Immediately after this, nine of the 3 Staffel aircraft and one from 1 Staffel landed on the frozen Lake Hartvigvann, five standing on their noses and two more damaging their undercarriages. Two aircraft became lost in bad weather; SE+JZ(WNr 6582) and CN+BS (WNr 6402) both came down on the ice in Gullesfjord, Fw Walter Thomas and Uffz Herbert Lochmann and their crews got to safety, and forced local Norwegians to feed and house them at gunpoint. They were later all captured and shipped to Britain.

At Lake Hartvigvann the aircraft were unloaded and put under guard, but three more Ju 52/3ms which had been supposed to fly up with fuel for the return journey did not arrive. The Nachtrichten aircraft returned to report that due to damage and deep snow, only two aircraft appeared to have any immediate chance of taking off again. The crews and gunners went into nearby Elvegaardsmoen where they found warm clothes, then returned to set up machine guns removed from the damaged aircraft for AA defence.

14/4/40
The presence of the two aircraft in Gullesfjord was reported that evening by the

After a few days in hospital recovering from his wounds, Sgt Kristian Schye of the Norwegian Fighter Wing visits the wreck of Gladiator 423 at Toppåsbråten, near Kolsås. Schye (centre) wore civilian clothes to makes the trip. *(Hoenvoll via S. Stenersen)*

local telephone exchange, and a strike was swiftly organized. At 0745 on 14th He 115As F-50, -54 and -56 from the Naval Air Service attacked. F-50 set one transport on fire, while the other was riddled with machine gun fire by both of the other floatplanes. A Fokker from the Hålogaland Air Corps found the 11 Ju 52/3ms on Lake Hartvigvann that same morning, so six Fokker C-VDs were despatched against them. Aircraft 379, 381, 383, 385, 387 and 389 set off, five armed with 50kg bombs and one with a camera, but on arrival over the target saw that a take off strip was being stamped out in the snow. Believing the workers to be innocent Norwegian civilians, the crews of the Fokkers 'buzzed' the lake twice to clear it, then attacked from 3,000 feet. Unfortunately the aircraft possessed no efficient bombsights, and the bombs fell short, doing little damage although it was believed that some transports had been hit by splinters. At 1430 No 387 returned after refuelling at Bardufoss, bombing and strafing, and claiming four badly damaged; two of the transports were destroyed in this attack.

Fokker C-VD 385 was one of the Hålogaland Air Corps aircraft which attacked the Ju 52/3ms on Lake Hartvigvann on 14th and 16 April. *(via B. Olsen)*

15/4/40

Furious was refuelling at Tromsø on 14th, so was unable to despatch her Swordfish to Lake Hartvigvann on this date, which also saw the landings at Harstad, as well as further south (of which more later). The Germans on the lake received some 1,500kg of supplies during the day, dropped by three more of the unit's Junkers, but still no fuel. During 15 April unloading of the transports continued, and when Fokker 381 flew over on reconnaissance it was noted that four of them had been drawn up on the north-east shore, while local people were again at work on flattening down the snow. Later in the day *Furious* launched nine Swordfish to undertake their first dive-bombing attacks against the aircraft on the lake. Each pilot took one aircraft as his personal target, direct hits on two being claimed, while others were believed damaged by near misses; four were then strafed. Two Ju 52/3ms were actually totally destroyed in this attack. Two of the Swordfish did not reach the lake, attacking other targets in nearby Beisfjord, of which more later. The Germans now reported that four of the aircraft on Lake Hartvigvann were a total loss as a result of the various air attacks.

16/4/40

The Norwegians now prepared for a further attack, C-Vs 381, 383 and 385 attacking a little after 0230 on 16th, claiming three of the four aircraft on the shore damaged by near misses. Work on a makeshift runway had continued throughout the night, while Oberst Baur de Betaz had requested the bombing of Bardufoss to keep the Fokkers away. Finally at 0900 on 16 April one aircraft, SE+KC, managed to get off with great difficulty — the only Junkers to escape from the lake. Even this then had further trouble, for it became lost and landed in Sweden. Following German pressure it was painted with Swedish registration SE-AKR, and flown to Germany on 2 September 1940 by a Swedish Air Force crew.

With their remaining aircraft incapable of flight, the aircrews were finally got out on 19 April by the only route open to them — by rail into Sweden. Here they were allowed to pass unhindered, sailing for Germany in due course, and finally reaching Berlin on 26th. But this was not the end of the story — these Ju 52/3ms will feature again at later date.

13/4/40

To return to 13 April however, the Luftwaffe had been far from idle despite bad weather in the South Norway area. Six He 111s of 2/KG 26 flew an abortive mission from Aalborg, via Stavanger, to raid Bardufoss airfield in the north, whilst other bombers attempted to find and bomb British naval forces known to be present offshore. First sightings came during the morning when four Heinkels of 1(F)/122 found the light cruisers *Sheffield* and *Glasgow* east of Aalesund, although these vessels were incorrectly reported as battleships. In the early afternoon six destroyers were seen north of Vigra Island, and these became the objective for 19 He 111s from 5 and 6/KG 26 and 7/LG 1, plus a second formation of six from 3/KG 26. These bombers failed to find their quarry however. Simultaneously 18 more Heinkels from I and II/KG 26 and two Ju 88s from 3/KG 30 flew armed reconnaissances. One cruiser was seen by 1/KG 26, while six destroyers were attacked by 2/KG 26, but without any success.

Neither had the weather prevented the Hudsons of Coastal Command from reaching the area — nor the Zerstörer from intercepting them. Sgt J.L. Hawken, DFM, had taken off at 0920 in N7241 of 233 Squadron to bomb Stavanger, but he did not return. During the morning three more Hudsons from 220 Squadron left for a reconnaissance along the Norwegian coast, but in the Stavanger area Flt Lt Sheahan's 'B' was attacked four times by a Bf 110 when at only 1,000 feet above the sea and was damaged. Plt Off Nicholas, the gunner, got several bursts into the attacker, seeing black smoke after which the fighter appeared to dive into the sea in flames.

No loss was reported by the Luftwaffe, but two interceptions were made. At 1115 Uffz Lauffs of Z/KG 30 claimed a Hudson east of Stavanger, but his claim was not confirmed. At 1352 Lt Helmut Fahlbusch of 3/ZG 76 claimed another Hudson south-west of Sola airfield. Although Lauffs was flying a Ju 88C rather than a Bf 110, it does seem rather more probable that he attacked Sheahan's aircraft and that Fahlbusch shot down that flown by Hawken. Another 233 Squadron Hudson, N7323 'Y', flown by Sgt R.S. Callinson, was off at 1342, also to bomb Stavanger. This aircraft was caught west of Sola by Uffz Brückner of 1/ZG 76 and was shot down at 1725.

During the afternoon four He 115s of 1/KüFlGr 106 left Stavanger for Narvik. These found *Warspite* surrounded by a heavy screen of destroyers, as they

264

The crew of an He 115 prepare for take-off. *(Bundesarchiv)*

reached their destination, but an attempt to attack was driven off by the AA barrage. They then found the destroyer *Ivanhoe* alone and attacked this vessel, but were unable to score any hits. The formation then continued to Narvik, where they landed.

89 Ju 52/3ms and 11 He 59s carried a Nachrichtenkommando (intelligence radio unit), other equipment and a large quantity of petrol to Oslo, one Junkers being destroyed in a crash just short of Aalborg. 65 more Ju 52/3ms and six Ju 90Bs flew II/IR 334, another Nachrichtenkommando and other supplies to Trondheim. During the return flight three Ju 52/See floatplanes of KGrzbV 108 force-landed by the coast, the crews becoming prisoners for a short time, while a KGrzbV 103 Ju 52/3m force-landed on the Swedish coast, the crew being briefly interned.

That night a planned British aerial mining offensive in German coastal waters commenced. The magnetic mines, each of 1,400lb weight, were dropped by parachute, ideally in water with a depth of about 30 feet, from a height of 350-1,000 feet. 15 Hampdens took off to lay such mines in the Great and Little Belts, off Kiel and the Danish coast, but Flt Lt R.J. Cosgrave and his crew failed to return, L4065 of 50 Squadron disappearing into the North Sea off Mablethorpe.

14/4/40
This day saw not only the arrival of British troops at Harstad, but also a landing at Namsos, 75 miles north of Trondheim. This latter port was still held only by about 2,000 German troops so there appeared to be a chance for an Allied success here before the Germans could spread their hold to all of Central Norway.

Early in the morning three Wellingtons of 115 Squadron raided Stavanger, while later in the day six Hudsons from 224 Squadron also set out for this target, three actually finding the airfield where their bombs destroyed a Bf 110 of 2/ZG 76. Other Bf 110s attempted to take off while the raid was in progress, one 3 Staffel machine crashing shortly after getting into the air. Claims for two Hudsons were submitted by II/Flakregt 33, although none in fact seem to have been lost on this occasion. Flakregt 33's elements at Bergen were also very active, claiming two Skuas shot down when 15 of these aircraft from 800 and 803 Squadrons returned to this target from Hatston and Sumburgh to attack the port again in the early morning. Only one was lost however, Capt E.D. McIver, RM, and his gunner being reported missing. The others sank the troopship *Bärenfels*, which was in the process of being unloaded, and damaged three more vessels. A strafing attack on moored seaplanes brought claims for one flyingboat destroyed and two floatplanes damaged; an He 115 of 1/KüFlGr 106 was indeed written off.

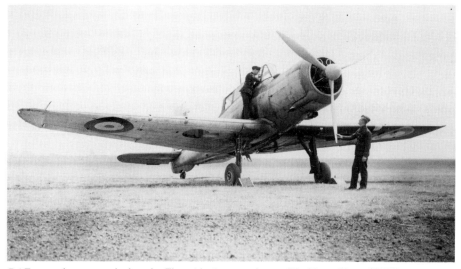

RAF ground crew attached to the Fleet Air Arm, work on a Blackburn Skua. *(IWM)*

An attempt by KGrzbV 103 Ju 52/3ms to ferry aviation supplies up to Narvik was halted by the weather, one aircraft becoming lost and landing in Sweden. The crew were returned after a brief internment.

Reconnaissances over the North Sea by Do 18s and He 115s were rewarded only with fleeting glimpses of British aircraft and warships, and it was not until the early evening that the German forces began to react in any strength to the reports of British landings. The Fallschirmjäger of 1/FJR 1 under Oblt Schmidt were then ordered to take Dombås by air assault, and despite having no photographs of the area and insufficient maps, the force departed Oslo in the late afternoon aboard 15 Ju 52/3ms of II/KGzbV 1, led by Oberstlt Drewes. Due to bad visibility, the Junkers had to circle for some time in order to find the dropping zone, and in so doing came under heavy fire from the ground, which shot down one 8 Staffel aircraft. Lt Erich Schiffer, two members of his crew and eight paratroops survived, but were taken prisoner by the Norwegians. For both the paratroops and the Luftwaffe aircrews the operation was a disaster. Of the remaining 14 transports, seven returned to Oslo, where an aircraft of the Stabskette crash-landed at Fornebu and was a complete write-off. Another Stabskette aircraft, plus one from 5 Staffel and one from 8 Staffel force-landed during the return journey, and in every case the aircraft was written-off, although all three crews survived unhurt. Three more landed at Trondheim with battle damage, one 5 Staffel aircraft coming down on its belly and again suffering a write-off level of damage, while two members of the crew were wounded. The last aircraft, another Stabsketten machine, force-landed in Sweden where it was interned with its crew.

The troops were to face even worse. Dropped into the gathering gloom of evening, their orders were to take Dombås and thence proceed to Aandalsnes, taking the vital road and rail bridges to prevent the Norwegian troops from Oslo linking up with any British advance from Namsos. During the first engagement after their landing, the paratroops lost their Company commander, Oblt Schmidt, who was wounded.

During 14 April the Luftwaffe lost six other aircraft. The four He 115s of 1/106 which had flown to Narvik during the previous afternoon, took off for the return flight to Trondheim. En route they overflew some British warships in Vestfjord, and two aircraft were hit by fire from these. One crashed into Ofotfjord with the loss of the pilot, (Lt zur See Joachim Vogler), the rest of the crew surviving as POWs. The second force-landed near Vega Island, Oblt zur See Baerner and his crew also being captured and shipped to England. Further south two Bf 110s of the Danish-based I/ZG 1 collided in bad weather and crashed into the North Sea. A Ju 88 of III/LG 1 and a Ju 87 of 1/StG 1 were written-off in airfield accidents.

In England some changes were made in the disposition of certain bomber squadrons. 9 Squadron now ended its attachment to Coastal Command at Lossiemouth, flying back to Honington. Its place at the former airfield was taken by the Blenheims of 107 Squadron from Wattisham. Meanwhile 115 Squadron moved its Wellingtons to Marham. That night a series of airfield raids were commenced which would amount to 200 sorties over the next week. The Hampdens continued their noctural operations, 23 mining sorties being flown, during which three losses were suffered, L4113 (Sgt V. Emanuel) and L4152 (Flg Off K.R. Sylvester) of 61 Squadron failing to return, while L4043 of 49 Squadron, flown by Sqn Ldr G. Hope, crashed on the coast at Ryhope on return.

15/4/40
Early on 15th Sqn Ldr K.C. Doran, DFC, led a pair of Blenheims of 110 Squadron off from Wattisham to reconnoitre Wilhelmshaven and the Schillig Roads. He made a shallow dive-bombing attack on a patrol vessel, his aircraft suffering hits to the starboard wing and tail from return fire, but as these were not serious he headed on to Heligoland. Nothing was seen here, but Flt Lt M.L. Morris in L8752, who had separated from him over the target area, failed to return. He had been intercepted and shot down into the sea west of St Peter by a Bf 109 of I(J)/LG 2, flown by Lt Georg Graner.

Somewhat later in the morning 11 Blenheims from 107 Squadron left their new temporary base at Lossiemouth to attack Stavanger harbour. They dived through pouring rain to bomb ten He 115s and an He 59 in Hafrsfjord, claiming two of the former sunk. Hostile aircraft were met, but were avoided in heavy clouds, although two Blenheims were damaged by Flak. No losses of German floatplanes were recorded on this date. Six Wellingtons from 38 Squadron had launched an early morning attack on Sola also, but were intercepted by Bf 109Es of II/JG 77, Lt Heinz Demes shooting down Plt Off G.L. Crosby's L4339, which crashed into the sea south-west of Stavanger; no one survived.

A little after midday Plt Off Lingwood of 220 Squadron took off in Hudson 'U' on patrol. Leaving the Lillesand area, he was attacked by two Bf 110s, which inflicted damage on the tail of his aircraft. The gunner reported that he obtained hits on the second Messerschmitt and thought that it had possibly dived into the ground. Lingwood then flew over two destroyers which opened fire on the Hudson and inficted further damage. These were *Friedrich Eckoldt* and *Bruno Heinemann*, which reported an engagement with two Hudsons between Norway and Horn's Reef. Another of 220's aircraft — 'J', N7225, flown by Flg Off F.C. Tullock — was also out on a search, but was intercepted by Uffz Helmut Eberlein of 3/ZG 1. Eberlein was part of a detachment from this unit which had moved from Aalborg to Norway for temporary duty at Oslo and Stavanger. He shot down the Hudson at 1550, the aircraft falling into the western Skaggerrak.

A Hudson from 224 Squadron followed, Plt Off Rothwell setting off at 1300 in N7287 and engaging a Do 18; fire from the latter slightly damaged the Hudson. At 2125 Plt Off L.G. Nolan-Neylan set off in N7306 of the same squadron, but failed to return. It seems that this aircraft had been spotted by the crew of a 3/KüFlGr 506 He 115, the radio operator sending a report which brought out two more of II/JG 77's Messerschmitts, the Hudson being caught and shot down by Oblt Carmann.

Once again the Luftwaffe attempted to find the British warships lurking around the rugged Norwegian coastline. Following reconnaissance sorties by He 111s from KG 4 and II/LG 1, three Ju 88s from 3/KG 30 set out in the early afternoon on a similar mission. Heavy shipping — including a battleship — was identified west of Aalesund, a cruiser north-west of Kristiansand, 27 cargo vessels near Stavanger and an aircraft carrier off Aandalsnes. This latter ship and a cruiser were subjected to an inaccurate attack by these bombers. During the day at Bergen 8/Flakregt 32 had become operational with 88mm guns, 4/Flakregt 611 with 37mm automatic Flak, and 10/Flakregt 33 with 20mm weapons.

Maj Gen Carton de Wiart, VC, arrived at Namsos in a Sunderland of 228 Squadron on 15th to find his force there already experiencing some heavy bombing raids by the Luftwaffe, principally by He 111s of III/LG 1. He pushed a spearhead southwards through the Steinkjer defile, but halted the men there to await reinforcements. Meanwhile III/LG 1 had attacked the Vigra Island radio station which was put out of action — when one of the Heinkels rammed the main aerial with its wing! The bombers returned in the late afternoon and reduced the station to rubble.

The Sunderland that had brought Carton de Wiart to Norway (N6133, flown by Wg Cdr Nicholetts) was employed during the day to provide cover for destroyers in Namsenfjord. Just before turning for home after eight of its 13 hours in the air, the flyingboat was attacked at 1810 by three Ju 88s of 3/KG 30, with two He 111s in attendance. These had arrived to bomb the ships, and took on the Sunderland with vigour. Before the big aircraft could escape many hits had been sustained, one of which wounded Lt Elliott, Carton de Wiart's adjutant. Nevertheless the flyingboat avoided destruction and was able to return without further mishap to Scapa Flow.

That day nine Whitleys of 77 Squadron and three from 102 Squadron, with one reserve aircraft, had flown up to Kinloss, from which airfield they could more effectively operate over Trondheim. As darkness fell six of these aircraft raided Stavanger airfield, where a Ju 52/3m of KGrzbV 103 was destroyed and a second damaged. The airfield surface was also badly cratered by their bombs. Aircraft of Coastal Command were also out, nine Beauforts of 22 Squadron

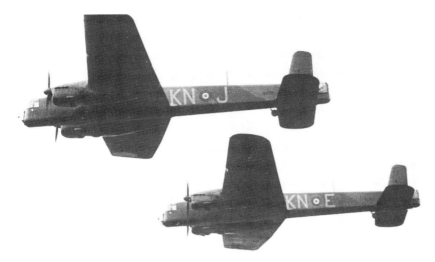

Whitley Vs KN-J, N1373, and KN-E, N1347, of 77 Squadron pass over their base at Driffield en route for Southern Norway. *(Real Photos via A. Thomas)*

undertaking mine-laying sorties in the Heligoland area. L4465 (Flg Off A.R. Fordham) failed to return, going down into the sea off Spurn Head, whilst on the way home.

The commander of the Norwegian Flying School, Capt Harald Normann, had found it difficult to make contact with his superiors. On 15th therefore he ordered the evacuation of the school's aircraft to Sweden. In poor weather only 11 aircraft reached neutral territory (four C-VDs and seven Tiger Moths), and all were immediately interned. Capt Normann himself crashed while attempting a force-landing near Elverum, but was not hurt. The remaining aircraft returned to Nordre Osen and were used for the rest of the campaign for communications and light transport duties.

In the Narvik area things were 'hotting-up' during 15th. Early morning reconnaissance by an Fw 200 of 1/KG 40 noted the presence of 16 British supply ships, five transports and a cruiser off Narvik itself, another cruiser and several destroyers also being seen in Vestfjord. A Ju 90 of KGrzbV 105 dropped ammunition and clothing to the German garrison at Narvik, whilst two Do 26 flying-boats of KGrzbV 108 flew in from Travemünde with similar supplies, landing in Beisfjord. During the day Swordfish from *Furious*, had taken off to attack the Ju 52/3ms stranded on Lake Hartvigvann as already described earlier. One of these attempted to attack one of the Do 26s on the water in Beisfjord as it passed over, but a heavy barrage of Flak was put up and this aircraft, U4B, P4167, of 816 Squadron, was shot down by gunners of I/Flakregt. 32. The pilot managed to force-land in the fjord from where the crew were rescued by the destroyer HMS *Zulu*. A second Swordfish, U4H, had the main spars of both starboard wings broken, but made it back to the carrier nonetheless.

16/4/40
Next day one Fw 200 of 1/KG 40 and three He 111s of II/KG 26 set off for an armed reconnaissance over the area, finding Admiral Layton's cruisers off Vega Island. At once 15 Heinkels were ordered off, finding the British warships still

in the area during the mid afternoon. Their attack proved unsuccessful however.

By this time the Allied plan of action was taking shape more positively. The landing at Namsos had encountered no real opposition on the ground, and appeared to be making good progress inland. Going was very slow however, in conditions of deep snow. Much to the relief of the Navy, a proposal for a direct assault up the fjords to Trondheim was now dropped and instead a further landing went ashore to the south of Trondheim at the little port of Aandalsnes on 17 April. This was situated some 95 miles from the former town, the intention being that an advance from here would sweep up in a north-easterly direction to form one arm of a pincer movement, designed to connect with the Namsos force and cut off the port from the Germans in the south. With this plan in mind Carton de Wiart's contingent was reinforced on 19th by the arrival of a French demi-brigade of Chasseurs d'Alpines, who it was assumed, would be at home in the snowclad Norwegian mountains.

While this plan of action was getting underway, efforts to disrupt German sea communications, cripple her naval power and tie down the Luftwaffe continued. During 16 April Skuas of 803 Squadron from the Orkneys again attacked Bergen, claiming the sinking of an armed trawler and damaging a U-Boat; no such damage was in fact inflicted. Luftwaffe reconnaissance aircraft were out in force, ten Do 18s from KüFlGr 406 reporting sightings of British aircraft on three occasions — almost certainly all patrolling Hudsons. At 0953 seven He 111s of KüFlGr 806 left Varrelbusch on general patrols. Over the North Sea at 1348 the crew of Hpt Hahne in M7+AK sighted and bombed a submarine, reporting a large oil slick following their attack. In the Trondheim area four II/KG 4 Heinkels reconnoitred the Namsos, Vikna Island and Indrefjord area. One of these bombers attacked and sank the Swedish steamer *Mertainen* off Hitra Island; the vessel was loaded with iron ore and bound for Newcastle from Narvik. Another aircraft made an unsuccessful attack on a group of warships which were identified as a battleship and four destroyers.

Stavanger/Sola airfield was the target for a raid despatched by Bomber Command during the morning, six Blenheims being sent off by 107 Squadron. In bad weather five aborted, but one continued, bombed accurately, totally destroying an He 111 of II/KG 26 and setting fire to a Ju 88C-2 Zerstörer of Z/KG 30, which burned out; a Ju 52/3m was 30% damaged. This airfield was also the scene of several accidents during the day as 84 Ju 52/3ms flew in urgently-needed supplies of all types. An He 111 from III/KG 26 collided with a parked Ju 52/3m of Stab/KG 26 as it landed, the transport 'hack' being destroyed and the bomber damaged. Eight Ju 52/3ms, a Ju 88 of II/KG 30 and a Do 17P of 1(F)/120 all suffered slight damage in various accidents, and in consequence Fliegerkorps X ordered all aircraft except a few bombers to have left the base by nightfall.

After leaving Sola, a Ju 52/3m of 14/KGzbV 1 crashed in bad visibility near Aana Sira, Fw Bernard Kaltöhner, his crew and 13 men of LuftnahrKomp Weimar being killed.

Nightfall on 16th brought two raids, by the Whitleys of 4 Group; five aircraft from 77 Squadron raided Trondheim/Vaernes, but one of these (N1387) crashed on return. A second raid by three aircraft of 58 Squadron on Fornebu and Kjeller airfields at Oslo was totally abortive. Sola suffered a further attack by 12 Wellingtons of 9 and 115 Squadrons, all of which returned safely.

Sola was given only a brief respite, for a few hours later — before dawn on 17th — a Hudson of 233 Squadron piloted by Flg Off Edwards, dropped flares and incendiaries over Stavanger while the cruiser *Suffolk* shelled the area for 80 minutes. One of the flares released by the Hudson hit a 'hack' Ju 52/3m of Stab/KG 30, which was burned out. As dawn crept over the area the Hudson was attacked by a Ju 88C of Z/KG 30, Ofw Jeschke identifying his opponent as a Blenheim in the gloom, and claiming to have shot it down. According to the Hudson crew however, the Zerstörer had broken away and caused them no further trouble. As the Hudson had departed, it passed a Walrus of 700 Squadron which had been launched from *Suffolk's* catapult to spot for her guns, and this aircraft was indeed shot down. It seems that in the dusky conditions this, rather than the Hudson, had been Jeschke's Blenheim! Her duty done, *Suffolk* headed away from the danger area with her escort of destroyers as the daylight spread, but the ships soon came under attack as Luftwaffe bombers searched for them.

First off were ten He 111s of I/KG 26, which departed from Sola at 0815. Four of the bombers succeeded in finding the British units as they fled at high speed, and *Suffolk* was hit twice by bombs, which did little to reduce her speed. The Heinkels were followed by Do 18s of 2/KüFlGr 106 and 1/406, ten of these flyingboats taking off between 0900 and 0930. M2+KK of 2/106 was first to make a sighting, reporting three cruisers and four destroyers heading away west. More bombers were already airborne, 28 Ju 88s of II/KG 30 having left Westerland at 1000. 12 of these found the fleeing *Suffolk*, and she was hit again.

At this point fate took a hand. As a follow-up to the shelling of Stavanger, further air attack was underway, Wg Cdr Basil Embrey having led off 12 of his 107 Squadron Blenheims to attack the same target. When en route at 1125 they saw below them *Suffolk* and four destroyers under attack by seven bombers identified as He 111s, but without doubt the KG 30 Ju 88s. "Acting like fighters", they went for the German bombers and dispersed their formation into some clouds. One brief attack on one of the Blenheims by a single Bf 109 was made, but this inflicted no damage. Having effectively prevented further damage being inflicted on the already-battered cruiser, the Blenheims continued on their way to Stavanger, climbing to 18,000 feet to deliver a high level attack on the airfield. Most bombs fell into the sea rather than on land, though one man of I/ZG 76 was killed by splinters and a second wounded. A Bf 110 from this unit's 1 Staffel hit one of the bomb craters which had been formed on the airfield as it took off, and crashed, suffering 90% damage; both members of the crew were injured.

Over the target heavy Flak was encountered, and a sustained attack was made on the bombers by Bf 110s of I/ZG 76. Lt Böhmel and Fw Johnann Schönherr each claimed one shot down as the interception commenced, a third being claimed by Lt Fahlbusch as the running fight ended 15 minutes later. All the Blenheims were badly hit, and two failed to return, L9041 (Flt Lt P.E. Warne) and N6185 (Flg Off T.V. Poltock) crashing west of Stavanger; Plt Off D.H. Keedwell crash-landed P4924 on arrival at Lossiemouth with 53 holes in his aircraft. Strangely on this occasion the German pilots failed to get confirmation for any of the three claims.

Apart from the rather ineffectual results of the Blenheims' bombs, the naval shelling had been quite effective, the real damage being inflicted by this in the harbour. Here four He 115s of 1/KüFlGr 106 and four He 59Ds of KGrzbV 108 were all destroyed. Based at Stavanger by this time were:

I/ZG 76 with 16 Bf 110s
Z/KG 30 with 4 Ju 88Cs
1(F)/120 with 2 Do 17Ps
I & II/KG 26 with 14 He 111H-4s

As the surviving Blenheims began their long journey home, *Suffolk* and her cohorts had come within range of fighter escort from the Orkneys. All afternoon Do 18s had hunted for the ships, and several were in the vicinity when the first three Skuas of 801 Squadron arrived overhead. At 1400 this comforting presence was relieved by three more of the unit's aircraft, and these soon spotted German 'shadowers', going into the attack on one at once. An He 111 was claimed damaged, while a flyingboat identified as a Do 18 or 26 was shot down. This was in fact a Do 18G K6+FH of 1/KüFlGr 406 flown by Lt zur See Max Keil; the successful pilots were the unit commander, Lt Cdr H.P. Bramwell, with Lt W.H. Martyn and Sub Lt B. Wigginton. Another Do 18, K6+HM, later landed to rescue the shot-down crew, but found that they had been drowned. This particular flyingboat was obliged to force-land on the sea a little later due to engine failure, but succeeded in taxying to Lista. A third 'boat, M2 + KK of 2/106 which had made the first sighting of *Suffolk* earlier in the day, suffered engine damage on a later sortie, force-landed at Haugesund in damaged condition, and sank; the crew got out safely and were rescued.

The Luftwaffe had not given up the hunt however; an hour later 22 He 111s from II/KG 26 again found the ships and made ineffectual attacks. 22 more Heinkels from III/KG4 found not *Suffolk*, but Admiral Layton's battle group returning to the Shetlands from the Aandalsnes area, but their attack on these vessels proved no more successful.

The day's operations had also cost the Luftwaffe a further five aircraft. Do 17Zs of 1/KüFlGr 606 bombed the Norwegian MTBs *Jo*, *Grib* and *Ravn* in Løktesundet, near Lyngør, near-misses seriously damaging *Jo*, although AA fire from *Grib* shot down one of the Dorniers, Oblt zur See Helmut Eiermann ditching north-east of Arendal; the crew were rescued. That evening the crews of the three MTBs scuttled their vessels to prevent them falling into German hands. Elsewhere, a Ju 88 of I/KG 30 crashed while attempting to land on the frozen Lake Jonsvannet on return from a sortie, and later sank when the ice melted. Three Ju 52/3ms were also lost in various crashes.

During the day two more Orkney-based Skuas from 803 Squadron operated over Bergen again, bombing the training ship *Bremse*, but missing. As darkness fell the RAF's 'heavies' returned to the area, six Wellingtons from 99 Squadron plus three apiece from 37 and 75 Squadrons, attacking Stavanger/Sola, while two Whitleys from 58 Squadron raided shipping in Oslofjord. Two Hampdens from 83 Squadron reconnoitred Aalborg, reporting 50 aircraft "wingtip to wingtip" on the airfield there. Wellington P9234 (Flg Off A.F. Smith) of 99 Squadron failed to return, a search next day by aircraft from 149 Squadron failing to find anything. 9 Fliegerdivision undertook the first Luftwaffe mining operation of 1940 against England, eight He 111s of KGr 126 and ten He 115s of 5/KüFlGr 506 laying 24 mines in the Downs and the Edinburgh Channel, in the Thames Estuary.

18/4/40

The bombers of Fliegerkorps X had their own tasks during the morning, attacks on shipping in Vaagsfjord, Tromsø and Harstad in the north, being ordered. Accordingly, eight He 111s of II/KG 26, accompanied by three Fw 200s of 1/KG 40, set out towards midday, arriving over the target area at around 1400. A total of 16 British ships were seen, including three battleships, three cruisers, eight destroyers, one carrier and a large transport. The battleship *Warspite* was first to be attacked, Heinkels bombing at 1410 and 1440, whilst a freighter off Langøy Island was also attacked. The Focke-Wulfs then found the carrier *Furious* in a fjord north of Tromsø, and gained a near miss, which caused damage to the vessel's propellors. One He 111 was hit in the hydraulic system by AA, and later belly-landed at Sola, where it was written off; the crew were unhurt.

Focke-Wulf Fw 200C reconnaissance-bomber of 1/KG 40, with He 111s in the background at a snow-covered Norwegian airfield. *(ECPA)*

Further south Namsos was the target for six Ju 88s of I/KG 30 on armed reconnaissance. Due to severe weather conditions only one was able to find anything, sighting four warships and several freighters. One of the bombers – a 3 Staffel aircraft – failed to return, force-landing south of Namsos after being hit by AA. One member of Lt Hermann Peter's crew was killed, the other three being shipped to Britain as prisoners. Coastal aircraft from both sides were out, but no engagement ensued. During the day three He 115s of 1/KüFlGr 106 attempted to get through to Narvik, but were forced back by the weather. One flown by Oblt zur See Heinz Witt crashed near Vosna Island, west of Trondheim, where the crew were killed.

At Stavanger, Sola continued to see a high rate of activity, 140 Ju 52/3ms flying in personnel for many units, including II/IR 355 and part of III/IR 355. At Oslo an He 111P of II/KG 4 rammed a group of parked KGrzbV 107 Ju 52/

3ms as it came in to land, the bomber and three of the Junkers being destroyed.

During the day the Sullom Voe Fighter Flight Gladiators achieved their second interception, Flg Off Gillen engaging a Ju 88 25 miles from his airfield, reporting that he had managed to set the starboard engine on fire.

Steadily the British air effort was being increased. On 18th 102 Squadron moved all its Whitleys up to Kinloss, while next day the Blenheims of 110 Squadron arrived at Lossiemouth to join 107 Squadron. One of the Fleet Air Arm's squadrons, No 701, moved to Harstad with its Supermarine Walrus amphibians to undertake both reconnaissance and bombing duties, while during 18th the carrier HMS *Glorious* arrived at Scapa Flow post haste from the Mediterranean, carrying aboard 802 Squadron with nine Sea Gladiators.

By night the bombers were increasing their attacks, and during the night of 18/19th three Whitleys from 77 Squadron raided the Stavanger area, losing 'B', N1352 (Plt Off R. Hall). This bomber force-landed in the sea, four of the crew being rescued by HMS *Basilisk*, although Hall himself was lost. Three more Whitleys from 102 Squadron repeated the attack two nights later while six Wellingtons from 37 Squadron made the first attack on Kristiansand airfield.

19/4/40

Early next morning six Blenheims from 107 Squadron again prepared to raid Stavanger. Due to a series of mechanical mishaps only three got off, and two of these returned when the pilots realised that the formation was incomplete. Sgt P. Chivers continued alone in P4906, and was intercepted by Fw Lothar Linke of 3/ZG 76, who shot the Blenheim down west of Stavanger. Linke reported that the Blenheim crew put up a good fight. Even with flames pouring from the aircraft when just about to crash into the sea, the pilot pulled up into a climb, opened fire and obtained hits on a second Bf 110 which was flying as Rottenflieger to Linke.

At this point the weather turned unseasonably fine and the Luftwaffe appeared in force to attack the Allied forces to the north and south of Trondheim, and to harrass the hard-pressed Norwegians who were making a long, slow fighting retreat from the Oslo area. Over Namsos a lone He 111 of 1(F)/122 appeared overhead early to discover Admiral Layton's cruisers and their accompanying destroyers present. At 0730 a He 115 of 1/KüFlGr 506 attacked one of the cruisers in Namsfjord without success. Not until late afternoon did any further attacks materialize, but another single He 111 then unsuccessfully bombed the ships in Namsfjord, followed by three Ju 87Rs from I/StG 1. The latter enjoyed no more success, but lost one of their number to anti-aircraft fire from the cruiser *Cairo*, this aircraft making a force-landing near Namsos where the crew of Lt Karl Pfeil/Ogfr Gerhard Winkels were taken prisoner.

One of 1(F)/122's Heinkels was also over Aandalsnes, spotting much shipping in the vicinity, and reporting two battleships, three cruisers, five destroyers and several supply ships. This was plainly in error, for by this time Vice-Admiral Edwards-Collins had already departed for Rosyth with the cruisers *Arethusa* and *Galatea*. Here too no attack developed until much later, one He 111 of Stab/KG 26 attacking Admiral Layton's returning force in the afternoon. During the evening another He 111 from I/KG 26, two Ju 88s of 6/KG 30 and a single Ju 87R from I/St G 1 raided Aandalsnes, but without inflicting significant damage.

20/4/40

Next day the Hardangerfjord flygruppe of the Norwegian Naval Air Service under Lt Cdr Manshaus sent out He 115A F-52 and Høver F-346 to attack German ships in Uskedal. F-52's bomb-aimer obtained a direct hit on the artillery training ship *Bremse* (attacked by 803 Squadron's Skuas on 17th) together with several near-misses but all the bombs failed to explode! German forces were now approaching Hardanger, so on 23rd Manshaus would be ordered to evacuate to Sognefjord. F-52 was flown out to this destination, but F-346 was abandoned.

The remaining elements of the Norwegian Army Air Force were now involved in further operations as the weather improved, but with the small numbers available the results were uniformly disappointing. The Luftwaffe were hitting the Norwegian ground forces hard at this time, Bf 110s strafing troops at Aalgard, while 23 He 111s of III/KG 4 were ordered to bomb this area, but recalled at the last moment as German forces had overcome resistance and occupied the Norwegian defensive positions. Resistance still continued around Oslo, however, and eight 4/KG 4 Heinkels bombed the Norwegian headquarters at Aamot. One bomber was hit by ground fire and force-landed north of Oslo; the aircraft was a write-off, but the crew survived unhurt, subsequently managing to reach advancing German ground forces. In the Dombås area meanwhile, the 162 German paratroops of 1/FJR 1, alone and without supplies or ammunition, surrendered to Norwegian forces.

Operations by Norwegian aircraft continued over the next two days. On the 20th MF 11 F-306 crashed while landing at Vangsmjøsa; of the original Horten-based aircraft, only F-334 now survived. 21 April brought no better luck for the unfortunate Norwegian aviators. Naval 1 Flg avd had flown three MF 11s to Tinnsjø, but here one had damaged its propellor and had to be abandoned. The other two, F-328 and 332, then flew on to Lake Mösvatn, where they joined the ex-Horten F-334.

21–22/4/40

A few aircraft still survived at Vangsmjösa, and at 0933 on 21 April Sgt Per Waaler took off in the last serviceable Gladiator to reconnoitre Gardermoen airfield to see if it was in use by the Luftwaffe. North-west of the airfield his engine misfired and the aircraft struck the tops of a line of trees. He managed after desperate efforts to struggle back to the lake, but the Gladiator had been very badly damaged and would never fly again. At Vangsmjösa next day the Bomber Wing recorded that an He 111 appeared overhead early in the morning to drop leaflets stating: "You will be shot if you do not surrender immediately." Thirty minutes later more Heinkels appeared and bombed the frozen lake from 3000 feet, following this with a strafing attack. The Heinkel crews had probably had their attention attracted by the Ca 310, but this was not hit during the attack. However, it was unserviceable and had to be abandoned. Three Fokker C-Vs managed to take off after the bombing but had to land at Øylo as the fabric covering on one had been badly torn. As work to repair this was underway, three dive-bombers reported as Ju 87s, attacked, two of the C-Vs being destroyed by their bombs. The remaining aircraft took off for the north next morning (23rd) at 0400, but a few minutes later went into a spin and crashed; the crew were hurt. The German account of these events differs somewhat. A lone He 111 of II/LG 1 was on reconnaissance over the fjords around Bergen when passing Vangsmjösa lake several parked aircraft were seen, and six bombs dropped which destroyed two C-VEs. As the Heinkel returned towards its base, it passed over Mösvaan Lake where another aircraft was seen and was also bombed. This was MF 11 F-332, which had just been preparing to take off as the remains of 1 Flg avd evacuated the area and made for Hardanger. F-332 burnt out completely, the wreckage later sinking when the ice broke up. The other crews had hoped to join forces with 2 Flg avd at Hardanger, but this unit had, as already mentioned departed from this base two days earlier.

19/4/40

Meanwhile during the 19th German bombers had enjoyed more success over the Narvik area. Here during the morning eight Ju 88s of 2/KG 30, which had refuelled at Trondheim en route, arrived to attack reported aircraft carriers in the area north of Narvik-Tromsø. When over Langöy Island, weather forced them to abandon the raid, but one crew sighted HMS *Warspite* in Vestfjord and released two SC 500 bombs, which missed. Three more found a convoy under the command of Rear Admiral Derrien just outside Namsfjord, escorted by the cruisers HMS *Cairo* and the French *Emile Bertin*. The latter was attacked and severely damaged, necessitating withdrawl to Scapa Flow.

At this time Fliegerkorps X took control of KG 30, 1/KG 40, II and III/LG 1 and I and II/KG 54.

20/4/40

The centre of the Luftwaffe's attacks was now Namsos however, and during 20 April raids were redoubled here. A high-flying reconnaissance by a 1(F)/120 Do 17 brought a report of much shipping in the harbour and in Namsfjord, and an attack in strength was ordered. First to arrive were 18 He 111s of I and II/KG 26 which bombed shipping at 1130 without gaining any hits. 14 more Heinkels from II and III/KG 26 then followed, with nine more from KGr 100 and three Ju 88s from 6/KG 30. These attacked defensive emplacements ashore, but the damage done was small compared with that achieved by the third wave. 24 He 111s of II and III/KG 4 arrived at 1730 to attack the harbour and town; they hit the Royal Navy submarine chaser *Rutlandshire*, an ex-trawler, which was badly damaged and abandoned by the crew, who got ashore at Namsos. The harbour jetties, railway station and town were devastated. The sole casualty to the Luftwaffe was one crewman of 5/KG 4 wounded by ground fire. However on return to Trondheim one of the KGr 100 Heinkels attempted to force-land on Lake Jonsvannet, but broke through the ice and was lost.

20 more KG 4 Heinkels and four Ju 88s of 2/KG 30 were despatched after targets around Namsos, four Heinkels finding the cruiser *Curacao* in Romsdalsfjord, although they failed to obtain any hits. At Aandalsnes the Ju 88s bombed the AA cruiser *Carlisle* with equal lack of success.

Narvik was now reinforced by Stab/IR 334, I/IR 334, DivSatb 181 InfDiv, II/GebArtRegt 112, Luftwaffe ground staff and some special equipment, carried to the area by 89 Ju 52/3ms, a Do 24 and a Bv 138. One Junkers of KGrzbV 108 sank due to an accident at the seaplane base.

Over the North Sea Hudsons of 220 Squadron skirmished with Do 18s of KüFlGr 406. The former attempted to bomb two of the low-flying German aircraft south-west of Egersund, but without success. By night six Wellingtons of 37 Squadron raided Kjevik airfield at Kristiansand, three 102 Squadron

German troops shift a sledge of provisions across Trondheim/Vaernes airfield past Junkers Ju 88A bombers of KG 30. *(Bundesarchiv)*

Whitleys attacked Trondheim, and three 83 Squadron Hampdens bombed Aalborg. All returned to base, though two of the latter received slight Flak damage.

That night both sides undertook minelaying operations, 24 Hampdens managing to put down only 11 mines in the Weser-Ems estuaries due to bad weather, while 11 He 111s and 11 He 115s dropped 26 off Ramsgate, the North Foreland and the Kings Channel of the Thames.

21/4/40
The Luftwaffe bombers were back over Namsos and Aandalsnes next day, 24 He 111s of I/KG 4 raiding the former town where they bombed the railway station and surrounding area. They were followed at 1430 by 17 more He 111Ps of II/KG 54, which now joined in the assault, raiding shipping in Namsfjord. One bomber from 5 Staffel (Uffz Günter Golz) violated Swedish airspace and was fired on by both the destroyer *Nordenskjöld* and by a fighter (either a J-6A Jaktfalk or J-8A Gloster Gladiator). Golz was obliged to force-land the damaged aircraft on Swedish soil, where he and his crew were interned. Two more 4 Staffel aircraft became lost in bad weather, Lt Alfred Kiefer force-landing B3+CM on a beach on Gotland Island, while Lt Hans Shute landed B3+JM on this same island, both these crews also being interned. A single Fw 200 of 1/KG 40 flown by Oblt Beckhaus on an evening reconnaissance over the Narvik area also failed to return, probably also due to bad weather.

At Aandalsnes six II/KG 30 Ju 88s were out on an anti-shipping strike, one of these sinking the anti-submarine trawlers *Penn* and *Hercules II*. They were followed during the early afternoon by 18 He 111s of II/LG 1 and five Heinkels plus four Ju 88s of III/LG 1, which attacked the Dombås-Verma railway line and the Aalesund radio station. With no air support and little anti-aircraft artillery ashore, the Allied troops were in a bad position now, and de Wiart signalled the War Office prophetically: "I see little chance of carrying out decisive, or indeed any operations, unless enemy air activity is considerably restricted."

While eight He 111s of II/KG 54 supported the advance of Kampfgruppe Fischer up both sides of Lake Mjösa, 78 Ju 52/3ms again visited Narvik, transporting II/IR 359 and the rest of Stab 181 InfDiv and II/GebArtRegt 112.

A patrolling Hudson of 224 Squadron was engaged during the day when Plt Off Rothwell attacked a Do 18. The flyingboat was forced down onto the water, but taxied away, and the Hudson crew, out of ammunition, were forced to return to base.

Feverish efforts were being made in the United Kingdom to provide just the support General de Wiart required. On 20 April the 18 Gladiators of 263 Squadron had flown from Filton to Scapa Flow via Sealand, while next day *Glorious* was joined at the anchorage by HMS *Ark Royal*, which had also sped to the area from Gibraltar. During the day 263's Gladiators were flown aboard *Glorious* by Sea Gladiator pilots of 802 and 804 Squadrons; one Gladiator (N5624) suffered engine failure as it approached the ship, and fell into the sea. Plt Off C.D. Gordon-Wilson's dead body was recovered, and to make good the loss of the aircraft, a Sea Gladiator was handed over by the Navy.

22/4/40

Glorious sailed on 22 April carrying 263 Squadron's 18 aircraft, 18 Sea Gladiators of 802 and 804 Squadrons, and 12 Skuas of 803 Squadron from the Orkneys. Fighters, fighters and more fighters was clearly the order of the day, and when *Ark Royal* followed, she had taken aboard 800 and 801 Squadrons from Hatston; each unit had nine Skuas, while the former also had two Blackburn Rocs and the latter three more of these ill-conceived turret fighters. The ship's complement of air power was completed by 12 Swordfish of 810 Squadron, 11 more of 820 Squadron, and a single Walrus. With Hatston almost empty of Skuas, 254 Squadron (no longer maintaining its detachment at Lossiemouth since the arrival of the bomber squadrons there) moved its fighter Blenheims here from Bircham Newton.

In Norway an RAF advance party had arrived at Aandalsnes just before midnight on 22nd under the command of Wg Cdr Keens. Initial exploration for a suitable airfield was undertaken by Sqn Ldr Whitney Straight, himself a fighter pilot. He decided at once that the only possible solution in the short term was a frozen lake. His initial suggestion was to join the Norwegian Army Air Force remnants at Vangsmjösa, but this was felt to be too near the front. He chose instead Lake Lesjaskog, situated to the north of Vangsmjösa, between Dombås and Aandalsnes. Within two hours Whitney Straight had recruited 200 local people to clear a runway through the snow. The next 24 hours saw the arrival of the first party; 263 Squadron servicing equipment was unloaded and the most urgent items put into two lorries — the only local vehicles that could be found and commandeered — and rushed to the lake. By the afternoon of 24 April Lesjaskog was ready to receive its aircraft.

24/4/40

Towards the end of the afternoon of that day the Gladiators began taking off from *Glorious*, the two carriers and their escorts having arrived 150 miles off the Norwegian coast that morning. In two flights of nine each they were led to the airfield by two Skuas, landing at 1800. The conditions they found were depressing in the extreme. No facilities, no refuelling bowsers, no acid for the starter trolley batteries, and only one armourer to service and rearm all the guns — 72 of them! To cap it all the ice at one end of the lake was already beginning to melt, AND there was no form of early warning system. It did not augur well for Sqn Ldr J.W. Donaldson and his men. This first British fighter squadron to

Norwegian Air Force Tiger Moth at Alapmoen, in use for liaison duties. *(via B. Olsen)*

arrive in Norway comprised the following pilots: Flt Lt R.S. Mills, Plt Offs L.R. Jacobsen, S.R. McNamara, P.H. Purdy, M.A. Bentley, Carpenter, Wyatt-Smith, Hughes, McKenzie, Richards, Craig-Adams and Hogg, and Sgts H.H. Kitchener, B.E.P. Whall, Russell, Milligan and Forrest.

With 263 Squadron and the carriers in the area, the Allies now had something approaching an adequate fighter force — on paper. Already the situation had deteriorated alarmingly however. As soon as the troops at Aandalsnes were ashore and moving inland the Norwegians had made strong representations that they be turned south instead of north, to secure the Dombås rail junction to the south of which the main bulk of the Norwegian troops were fighting the major German advance northwards. With little equipment and the troops very inexperienced, the British fared badly in the face of repeated air attacks and harsh ground conditions. A second brigade was quickly landed at Aandalsnes and rushed down to help them.

Even as the threat to Trondheim from the south was thus eased, German forces sailed up the fjord north of the port, landing at the little town of Steinkjer to take the Namsos column in the flank. Two heavy air attacks here rendered the position untenable for the British, and by 23rd de Wiart had decided that unless air superiority was established at once there could be no alternative but evacuation. Already his forces had ceased any further forward movement and were on the defensive.

22/4/40

With so little opposition of any sort, the Luftwaffe operated almost without loss, and only when it ventured over units of the Royal Navy or French warships did it sustain any casualties. More units were joining the fighting, bringing the bomber force available to formidable size. On 22 April Namsos suffered day-long rolling attacks by almost all the available Luftwaffe bomber units; KG 4 sent 26 He 111Ps to attack the reserve lines at Namsos, the harbour and shipping targets, 22.5 tons of bombs being dropped; one bomber crashed on take off from Aalborg. The roads south of Aandalsnes, ships in Molde and Romsdalsfjords and disembarking troops were attacked between 0620 and 2300 by 34 He 111s of KG 4, 26, LG 1 and KGr 100, plus 19 Ju 88s of KG 30 and LG 1; 37.5 tons of high explosive and incendiaries were dropped. One Ju 88 of 9/KG 30 was shot down by AA from the escort vessel *Pelican*, diving into Moldefjord with the loss of Fw Hans Ramming's crew. An He 111 suffered an engine failure as it returned, belly-landing at base and suffering 80% damage, while another from 1(F)/122 was so badly shot-up that it was written off after crashing at Stormene on return. A reconnoitring He 115 from 1/KüFlGr 106 was obliged to ditch in Limingen north-east of Namsos, the crew burning their aircraft before surrendering to British forces.

From Stavanger, Bf 110s of I/ZG 76 undertook ground strafing sorties near Birkjedal, while 78 Ju 52/3ms and four He 59s brought I/IR 388, PzJägAbt 222 and 4/GebArtRegt 112 to Trondheim/Vaernes.

He 59 transport floatplane of KGrzbV 108 at Trondheim, 22 April. *(Bib für Zeit)*

The RAF's retaliation was weak. Five Hudsons from 224 and 233 Squadrons raided Bergen, but damage was slight. Another 224 Squadron aircraft flown by Flt Lt Wright carried out a reconnaissance to Kristiansand. Three Ju 88s and two Do 18s were seen, but three Skuas then arrived and the rest of the patrol was uneventful. Sgt Arden of the same unit saw an He 59 when patrolling in the Stadlandet-Haugesund area; he chased it to Haugesund where it was last seen going down in a glide off the jetty. A single Blenheim of 110 Squadron flown by Sqn Ldr Doran failed to reach Stavanger and returned early. In the north *Furious* attempted to maintain the pressure on the Narvik defenders, four Swordfish of 816 Squadron being launched on an armed reconnaissance. One of these was shot down into Ofotsfjord by the vigilant gunners of I/Flakregt 32, Lt C.R.D. Messenger/LAC T.G. Cutler being lost. Next day the same German unit claimed another Swordfish — reportedly from 818 Squadron on this occasion — in the same area, the crew being rescued by a destroyer.

21–22/4/40

RAF Bomber Command continued to do all in its power to restrict Luftwaffe activities, but in so doing sustained higher casualties than its opposite numbers. Realising that Aalborg was one of the main staging bases on the way to Norway, the Command sent three Wellingtons of 149 Squadron to attack this airfield. These flew over in formation during the evening of 21st, bombing singly as darkness fell. Flg Off F.T. Knight went in low in P9218, only to be shot down by the guns of ReserveFlakabteilung 603 and I/Flakregt 19; Knight force-landed west of Augesund on the coast, he and his crew being made prisoners. 36 Hampdens undertook minelaying sorties, eight crews placing their mines in the Elbe estuary, 17 in the Little and Great Belts. L4088 of 44 Squadron force-landed near Heiligendamm, north-west of Rostock, where Flt Lt F.G. Dutton and his crew were captured.

The following night, 22/23 April, it was the turn of the Whitleys again, two of these aircraft from 77 Squadron bombing the frozen Lake Jonsvannet at Trondheim in case the Luftwaffe were using it, while two from 58 Squadron bombed Oslo/Fornebu, damaging four Hs 126s of 2(H)/10. Six more from 51 Squadron raided Aalborg, Kjeller and Fornebu airfields; at Aalborg Res Flakabt 603 was again successful, shooting down K9043 (Flg Off J.R. Birch) which crashed in Limfjorden. That same night six 816 Squadron Swordfish, land-based in eastern England, laid mines north-east of Schiermonnikoog in the central Frisian Islands. Six Whitleys from 102 Squadron attacked Lake Jonsvannet again on 23/24 April, while three from 58 Squadron, two from 10 Squadron and one from 51 Squadron all raided Aalborg. Here Res Flakabt 603 shot down the lone 51 Squadron aircraft, K9048, which Flg Off Milne force-landed near Hatsund. The crew set fire to the bomber before being captured.

Henschel Hs 126 of 2(H)/10 at Oslo/Fornebu on 21 April. *(Bundesarchiv)*

23/4/40

23 April was to be the last day before the arrival of British fighter aircraft, the early morning bringing two attacks on the Aandalsnes area. 52 He 111s of KG 4, LG 1 and II/KG 54, and 25 Ju 88s from KG 30 and LG 1 attacked supply lines in the battle area, Dombås-Otta-Hjelle, and shipping targets in the Molde and Romsdalsfjords. 47.5 tons were dropped, sinking the Norwegian coastal steamer *Sigurd Jarl* in Moldefjord. One Ju 88 of 8/LG 1 was hit over the fjord by ships' AA and crash-landed on the northern bank of Romsdalsfjord; one man was killed and three captured from Uffz Ernst Röder's crew. A second Ju 88 from the same unit had crashed and burnt out on take off. I and III/KG 26 launched a sharp raid on Lake Lesjaskog during the morning, while the same

units bombed communications in the area as the cruiser *Arethusa* began unloading the first of the 263 Squadron equipment in the harbour, where three Hudsons of 224 Squadron patrolled overhead to give protection.

24/4/40

As the carriers had been approaching Norway efforts were redoubled, and 24 April was to prove one of the most active days for some time. At 0120 six 107 Squadron Blenheims set off for Stavanger, but were picked up on a newly set-up Wurzburg radar of 7/LgNachrRegt 3 when still about 25 miles out. Consequently the bomber crews found fighters waiting for them when they arrived over the airfield at low level. Here L8750 (Plt Off J.D. Murphy) was apparently shot down by Bf 110s of I/ZG 76, crashing west of Stavanger. A Dornier Do 215B reconnaissance-bomber of 1(F)/ObdL was destroyed on the ground during this attack. At this airfield Fliegerführer Stavanger had now been formed under Oberst Robert Fuchs, controlling 3(F)/ObdL, 1(F)/ObdL, 1(F)/120, 1(F)/122, I/ZG 76, Z/KG 30, part of II/JG 77, 2/KG 30 and 1/KüFlGr 106.

Dornier Do 215B reconnaissance aircraft of FAG/ObdL newly-arrived in Norway, takes off from Stavanger/Sola past parked Ju 52/3ms. *(Bib für Zeit)*

Dawn brought widespread patrols by Do 18s of the Küstenfliegergruppen over the North Sea. At Leuchars 220 Squadron had formed a special 'Battle Flight' of three Hudsons, and these took off at 0430 to give support to three French destroyers in the Skagerrak; these were *L'Indompable*, *Le Malin*, and *Le Triomphant*, under the command of Cne Bartles. The Hudsons were followed at 0500 by N7283 of 224 Squadron (Flg Off H.L.M. Bullock) on anti-submarine patrol, and at 0635 by three more Hudsons from 233 Squadron which were also proceeding on escort duty. 220 Squadron's 'Battle Flight' was attacked at 0805 by two Bf 109Es of 4/JG 77 flown by Lt Demes and Ofw Arnoldy, and aircraft N7289 'L', (Sgt W.A. Peachey) was hit at once. With the port engine on fire, Peachey tried to land alongside one of the destroyers while the dorsal turret gunner continued to engage the attackers, but the Hudson fell out of control and crashed into the water. One member of the crew tried to bale out, but his parachute caught fire. At this moment N7286, 'Z', (Plt Off M.C. Petrie) was attacked and was last seen diving towards the sea trailing black smoke. At this, 'N' took evasive action at low level and escaped. Demes and Arnoldy were each credited with one Hudson shot down.

Less than half an hour later the three aircraft from 233 Squadron, flown by Flt Lt Butler, Flg Off Edwards and Plt Off Matson, were also attacked by two Bf 109s, and two were damaged, two members of the crew in one of these aircraft being wounded.

They may well have met the same pair of Messerschmitts as the earlier formation, and owed their survival to the Germans by then being short of fuel and ammunition. Around the same time the 224 Squadron Hudson flown by Bullock was also lost, shot down west of Bergen by Hpt Günther Reinecke, Gruppenkommandeur of I/ZG 76. Meanwhile at 1000 the French ships were spotted by Do 18 K6+AH of KüFlGr 406, being seen steering south-west. They were later found again by three He 111Js of 2/KüFlGr 806 as they were approaching the Firth of Forth, but a bombing attack achieved no success.

During the day snowstorms put a halt to aerial activities over the Namsos area, and during the morning the southern battle area was similarly affected. In the afternoon however, 24 He 111s from KG 4, 26 and LG 1, a single Fw 200 of I/KG 40 and a Ju 88 from LG 1 attacked targets in the Aandalsnes-Lesjaskog-Dombås-Otta-Kvam and Ringebu area, 19.5 tons of bombs being dropped.

As already mentioned, *Glorious* and *Ark Royal* had arrived off the coast on this date, but during the morning a snowstorm prevented aircraft being launched. The weather improved in the afternoon and 12 Skuas were sent off from *Ark* over Trondheim. Six aircraft from 803 Squadron climbed to 8,000 feet and split into two sections to patrol. At 1755 each section saw an He 111, and both were claimed shot down, all three aircraft of each section participating in each case. These were both aircraft of KG 4; 5J+AT of 9 Staffel, with the Staffelkapitän, Hpt Schumann, and the Gruppenkommandeur of III Gruppe, Maj Ernst Kusserow, aboard, belly-landed south-east of Romsdalsfjord, all five men aboard getting out unhurt and managing to reach German-held territory. A second Heinkel of 4 Staffel fell in flames north of Dombås; one member of Oblt Wolfgang Richter's crew managed to bale out, and was rescued by German troops. Another aircraft, reported as a Do 17, was seen at 1820 and was attacked by Lt Lucy and Lt Christian. The latter pilot was out of ammunition from the earlier combat, so his rear gunner engaged the aircraft with his Lewis gun until he too had no ammunition left. This would appear in fact to have been another He 111 of 9/KG 4, which was badly damaged; it got back to Oslo/Fornebu, but was written-off after landing. Two Skuas were hit and lightly damaged during these engagements, the gunner of a 3/KG 4 aircraft claiming to have shot one down; in fact all returned to the ship. Here two were so low on fuel that they had to land in the water, but only one crew was picked up safely; Sub Lt S. Lyver and Pty Off C.L. Smeathers were lost.

The crews and aircraft involved in this first carrier fighter clash over Norway were:

8F Lt W.P. Lucy/Lt M.L.E. Hanson
8G Lt A.B.B. Fraser-Harris/
    L/A G.S. Russell
8H Lt J.M. Christian/
    N/A S.G. Wright

8P Lt L.A. Harris, RM/
    Pty Off K.G. Baldwin
8Q Lt C.H. Filmer/N/A Pickering
8C Sub Lt I.H. Easton/N/A Hayman

During the past 48 hours the Trondheim area had been further reinforced, 120 Ju 52/3m sorties bringing in various units and 4/Flakregt 33. There were no

He 111 of III/KG 54 (apparently 5J+JT) believed to be the aircraft which crash-landed at Oslo/Fornebu after being attacked by Skuas on 24 April.

bomber operations that night, but seven 815 Squadron Swordfish laid mines in the Ems estuary, operating under the control of RAF Coastal Command.

25/4/40

After the initial success on 24th, major carrier group activity was planned for the next day. At 0300 Ark Royal's two Swordfish squadrons took off for Trondheim; one Swordfish crashed on take off but the crew were unhurt. The seven remaining 810 Squadron aircraft headed for Vaernes airfield, while 820 Squadron's six made for Lake Jonsvannet with orders to attack Vaernes instead if they found no aircraft there. This was indeed the case, and all 13 attacked Vaernes in the face of considerable light Flak, each dropping four 250lb and eight 20lb bombs. Three hangars were destroyed, some small buildings hit and one or two large aircraft claimed destroyed. Three Swordfish force-landed on the way back to the ship due to Flak damage sustained.

Immediately behind the Swordfish came the Skuas. At 0315 five 803 Squadron aircraft from *Glorious* had set off, and these dive-bombed floatplanes in the Trondheim roads which were riding at anchor. One Skua flown by Lt Fraser-Harris force-landed in Størnfjord. Three more led by Lt Brokensha followed at 0415, dive-bombing two oilers and setting these alight. Seven Skuas from 801 Squadron and two from 800 Squadron left *Ark Royal* at 0420, each with a 250lb and eight 20lb bombs. No warships were seen at Trondheim, so they attacked two 5,000 ton merchant vessels instead, dropping their 20 pounders on some floatplanes. Three of the 801 Squadron pilots then attacked a Ju 88 on the ground, two strafing while the third bombed. The bomber was obviously preparing to take off, for the gunner opened fire from the stationary aircraft. A burst of fire appeared to kill him, and the aircraft was thought to have been badly damaged.

Following this attack, one 801 Squadron Skua force-landed on the Lake Lesjaskog airstrip, while a second crashed into the sea, apparently out of fuel, Pty Off L.M. Lloyd and Lt A.A. Pardoe being lost. Two more of the unit's aircraft subsequently also force-landed on Lesjaskog due to fuel shortages.

Meanwhile a further three Skuas from *Glorious*'s 803 Squadron were off at 0430 led by Lt G.R. Collingham. They got lost on the way, arriving late and bombing a ship at Trondheim. During the return flight the third aircraft became separated and while orbitting in an effort to find this, the other two spotted an He 115 of 2/506. Collingham attacked it at once, but his port guns jammed, although he was able to silence the rear gunner with only those in the starboard wing working. The floatplane climbed for cloud and reached it, but was beginning to emit smoke. Seconds later it fell out of the cloud and crashed into trees on a mountainside near Størdalsøren, on the south-west bank of Trondheims-fjord; the crew baled out and were rescued by German troops. Collingham now did not have enough fuel left to return to the carrier, so force-landed on a sandspit. He taxied along this until all his fuel had gone, but some French soldiers then appeared and helped pull the aircraft to safety. It could not be recovered however and later had to be destroyed.

Lt G.R. Collingham of 803 Squadron was obliged to land this Skua (L3048) on a sandspit, where he was aided by these French Chasseurs d'Alpines. The aircraft later had to be destroyed. *(ECPA)*

The final launch was made at 0445, when three 800 Squadron Skuas — 6F, G and H — left *Ark*, intercepting another He 115 but losing it in cloud. They then chased a big, four-engined aircraft identified as a Ju 89 — probably one of KGrzbV 105's Ju 90s — but could not catch this.

Altogether 34 aircraft had taken part in the morning's operations. Norwegian sources later reported that six seaplanes had been destroyed or damaged beyond repair, and five aircraft destroyed at Vaernes. Four Swordfish and two Skuas were down in the sea, and four more Skuas were in Norway — mainly due to fuel shortages — while two more were unserviceable aboard ship. Actual German losses included seven Ju 87Rs of 1/StG 1 which were newly-arrived at Vaernes, together with a Ju 52/3m of KGrzbV 107, two He 115s of 2/KüFlGr 506 and two of 1/506, one of the latter having been sunk and one destroyed by machine gun fire; three more of these floatplanes were damaged. Despite these actions, 42 Ju 52/3ms had managed to fly in more ground troops to Vaernes during the day.

Just as the last section of Skuas was taking off, so too were the first pair of Gladiators airborne from Lake Lesjaskog. Delayed by frozen carburettors and controls, these were all that could initially be got into the air — and these were up two hours later than planned. They flew south to patrol over Dombås, and within 15 minutes had claimed an He 115 floatplane shot down here according to reports, although no Luftwaffe loss has been identified, and no names of claiming pilots discovered; it is possible that this first report is confused with the claim for the He 115 shot down at much the same time by the Skuas. While they were away a lone He 111 bombed the lake, this initial attack destroying four Gladiators and injuring three pilots, Sqn Ldr Donaldson amongst them; he suffered from severe concussion. The attacker was one of a pair from Stab/LG 1, which reported seeing 15 biplanes and several other aircraft on the ground. One of these Heinkels was hit by AA fire, one member of the crew being wounded.

Gladiators of 263 Squadron on Lake Lesjaskog, prior to the Luftwaffe air attacks. *(IWM)*

It was the start of a nightmare day, for two hours after the initial attack, Ju 88s, He 111s and Bf 110s began appearing in three's at regular intervals, keeping up the attack for eight endless hours. At 0700 the first of 19 He 111s from II/LG 1 headed for the lake. This attack would appear to have left four Gladiators on fire, together with four Skuas of 803 Squadron which had landed there during the day after leading the RAF fighters in from the carrier, and two more 801 Squadron aircraft which had landed that morning following the attack on Trondheim.

With the primitive facilities available however, it was taking an hour and a

Efforts have been made to camouflage this 263 Squadron Gladiator, and the Fleet Air Arm Skua behind it, with foliage. *(IWM)*

half or more to rearm and refuel the Gladiators, and it was only by dint of the most strenuous efforts that two were ready by 0900 and six more an hour later. At the earlier time Flt Lt Mills took off and patrolled for 30 minutes overhead, allowing six more Gladiators to get off undisturbed. These then provided cover for the army at the front while their fuel lasted, and also spotted for the artillery. During this patrol Mills engaged six II/LG 1 He 111s near a lake and was credited with shooting one down. This aircraft, an He 111H of 4 Staffel, actually limped back to Stavanger/Sola, but as it approached to land, both engines failed and it crashed into the sea; the crew were all rescued. During this attack a 7 Staffel bomber and one from 6/KG 54 were both reported damaged by AA fire and fighters, two crewmen being wounded.

Sgt Forrest was on patrol at 1100 when his aircraft suffered an engine failure and he was obliged to force-land near Lesjaskog. Almost at once a German aircraft appeared and finished the Gladiator off. An hour later Plt Off McNamara in N5579 headed a section of Gladiators which intercepted an early afternoon attack by 12 He 111s of II/LG 1 and six Ju 88s of III/LG 1. McNamara led his section in a deflection pass on a 4/LG 1 Heinkel flown by Uffz Helmut Nolte, which force-landed near Lesjaskog in full view of everyone on the ground, and burnt out. One member of the crew was killed and three were taken prisoner. By now however, 263 Squadron had already lost half of its aircraft.

From Scotland meanwhile a Blenheim from 110 Squadron had flown a reconnaissance to Stavanger during which Flg Off G.R. Gratton was forced to turn back by bad weather. He then saw a Do 18 — K6+DK of 2/406 — dropped his bombs on it and then attacked with guns. The flyingboat was last seen retreating south-east with one engine apparently stopped. Some time after the attack, the crew of the flyingboat radioed an SOS and then landed on the sea 70 miles south-east of the Shetlands. A second Dornier, K6+CK, was accompanying it, and indeed reported also being attacked by Gratton's Blenheim, though the latter's report made no mention of a second 'boat. The crew of K6+DK were rescued by *U-17*, the flyingboat then being destroyed by the submarine.

Believed to be the 4/LG 1 He 111 shot down near Lesjaskog by Plt Off Macnamara of 263 Squadron on 25 April. *(IWM)*

Following receipt of a reconnaissance report from a Norwegian Naval He 115 crew, six more 110 Squadron Blenheims set out soon after midday to bomb transport vessels in Granvinsfjord. Three attacked targets here, two bombed a ship at Ulvik and one could find no worthwhile targets. The second pair were apparently attacked by aircraft which were not identified, and one — flown by Plt Off R.J. Hill — then became engaged in an inconclusive fight with Bf 110s of I/ZG 76 some 100 miles out to sea. During this fight Hill was wounded in the hand, but the crew reported that one of their attackers was believed to have been shot down and crashed in the sea, while a second was forced down on the water. No losses were actually suffered by I/ZG 76, which also made no claims on this occasion. The ship attacked at Ulvik was the *Haardraade*, which was set on fire and sank in Hardangerfjord that night. During the return flight the Blenheims came across Do 18 K6+CK of 2/406, still on its way back from its long patrol around the Shetlands area, and the crew of this reported that these Blenheims also attacked it. Blenheim N6214 (Sgt W. Priestly), which had attacked the Ulvik ship with Hill, failed to return; it is possible that this aircraft suffered damage in combat with the Do 18, and came down in the sea later.

At Lesjaskog four more frozen-up Gladiators were destroyed by air attack at 1305, but two others then got off, flown by Sqn Ldr Donaldson (in N5633) and Flt Lt Mills; over the next two and a half hours these two would engage in six major combats over the lake. Firstly at 1400 both pilots attacked a Heinkel of Stab/LG 1 and brought it down to crash-land south of Vinstra, near Dombås. Fw Hans Gutt's crew set fire to the aircraft, in which the badly injured wireless operator had shot himself; the survivors were subsequently captured, and the wreckage of this bomber was later inspected by British troops. Both pilots then attacked another Heinkel from 6/LG 1, which was damaged, but made it back to Fornebu with two wounded aboard.

Late in the afternoon a Schwarm of Bf 110s from I/ZG 76 and a Schwarm of

Ju 88Cs of Z/KG 30, escorted Ju 88As of 2/KG 30 over the Dombås/Aandalsnes area. The Zerstörer crews reported seeing three Gladiators in the air, but these escaped down a fjord. They then strafed the lake airfield at Lesjaskog, Lt Riegel of I/ZG 76 and Obgfr Richard of Z/KG 30 claiming four Gladiators destroyed between them. Donaldson and Mills were both airborne again during the evening, as the last five serviceable Gladiators were withdrawn from Lesjaskog north to a temporary landing ground which had been prepared at Setnesmoen, just outside Aandalsnes. Donaldson was scrambled, and near the new base found an He 111 of II/LG 1 which had been attacking a steamer near Aandalsnes. This was believed to have been shot down into a ravine, but actually the very badly damaged bomber was almost able to reach Oslo/Fornebu before the engines failed and the crew baled out. Mills was up for a third time before twilight, having a running fight with a Ju 88, but he had to make a force-landing having used up all his fuel and ammunition. As he was examining the fighter for damage, bombers appeared and destroyed it.

Effects of German strafing; two burnt-out Gladiators on Lake Lesjaskog. An undamaged aircraft is just visible behind the wreck in the immediate foreground. *(IWM)*

The fighter Blenheims of 254 Squadron, which had resumed sorties over Norway during the previous day, undertook patrols over further Allied troop landings which were being made in Romsdalsfjord. Pairs of aircraft carried out this duty and one of these spotted an aircraft identified as an He 111 at 1616. Flt Lt Mitchell in R3628 and Plt Off Illingworth in L9406 attacked, but after five bursts Mitchell's guns jammed as the bomber dived from 7,000 feet to sea level. Illingworth kept after it and shot it down; their victim would in fact seem to have been a Ju 88 of 7/LG 1, reported shot down by Blenheims near Stadlandet when Junkers and Heinkel bombers from III/LG 1 were attacking the shipping. Ofw Friedrich Katzmaier and his crew were captured by the Norwegians, and were later shipped to the UK. During the attack the anti-submarine trawler *Bradman* was damaged and beached, the Norwegian motor torpedo boat *Trygg* was sunk, and two more anti-submarine trawlers, *Larwood* and *Hammond*, were both hit and damaged.

During the day two reconnaissance He 111s from 1 (F)/122 had taken off from Stavanger for a long reconnaissance over the Shetlands. They found the battleship *Warspite* 100 miles north-west of Stavanger, heading towards the coast, and three Ju 88s from 2/KG 30 were sent out to attack, launching an unsuccessful raid on the ship. One of the Heinkels flown by Oblt Gerhard Buer failed to return from the reconnaissance; it was thought that this aircraft had possibly fallen victim to the warship's AA fire.

Throughout the day 56 He 111s of KG 26 and 54, and 18 Ju 88s of KG 30 and LG 1 had attacked Lesjaskog or had undertaken raids in support of the ground forces, or against shipping targets, dropping between them 54.5 tons of bombs. On the lake airfield, where Bf 110s of I/ZG 76 had also strafed, five Skuas of 801 and 803 Squadrons and 13 Gladiators of 263 Squadron had been destroyed. The latter were N5588, 5589, 5628, 5632, 5634, 5635, 5639, 5641, 5647, 5680, 5714, 5720, and 5915. In the course of these actions, four bombers and an He 115 had apparently been claimed by the Gladiators, and one bomber by the fighter Blenheims, against an actual known Luftwaffe loss of five bombers, plus one more badly damaged.

With darkness, Bomber Command's aircraft approached the area on what was to prove a rather costly night. Four Whitleys of 102 Squadron attacked shipping in Oslofjord and also bombed Fornebu airfield. A small oil tank near Vallöy (Tönsberg harbour) was set on fire, and at Valmö, south of Horten, several more such tanks caught fire, but this was the limit of the damage. Four more Whitleys drawn equally from 78 and 102 Squadrons, attacked Aalborg airfield. N1383 of 102 Squadron was hit by fire from ResFlakabt 603 and crashed five miles north of the city, near Vadum, only one member of Flg Off O.G. Horrigan's crew surviving.

28 Hampdens also set out to mine Kiel Bay and the area of the Little and Great Belts. All but two aborted due to bad weather, but while German Flak crews at Lübeck and Kiel saw no visible effect for their fire, three Hampdens failed to return, all from 49 Squadron. L4040 (Flg Off D. White) was shot down in flames near Hörnum/Sylt by Ofw Hermann Förster of IV(N)/JG 2 in a Bf 109D for one of the first two victories of the war for Luftwaffe night fighters. L4092 (Flg Off P.W. Rowan-Robinson) and P1319 (Plt Off A.H. Benson) both failed to return, both probably going down into the North Sea.

26/4/40

Early next morning (26 April) two Gladiators were quickly readied for flight and took off on patrol. No sooner were they in the air than the engine of Plt Off Craig-Adams' aircraft (N5633) suffered a piston rod seizure and he baled out safely. At 1000 large numbers of bombers began appearing overhead in what was to be a six hour attack on Aandalsnes. Two Gladiators again got off, but no oxygen was available, and the pilots could not reach the bombers in consequence, as these were flying at some 25,000 feet. These were part of a force of 46 He 111s from KG 4, 26, 54 and LG 1 which were attacking road and rail targets in the Vinstra-Dovre-Dombås-Aandalsnes areas. In the afternoon the main targets were the harbour at Aandalsnes and Lesjaskog airfield, where Gladiator N5909 was destroyed.

At the same time however six 801 Squadron Skuas were launched from *Ark Royal* to patrol over the little port, and these were soon in action. Three He 111s from 5/KG 4 and three from 4/KG 54 had been despatched on armed reconnaissance over the Otta-Loma Grotli area. Both formations were spotted at about 1145, and the KG 4 trio were intercepted over Lesjaskog, one being attacked by Lt (A) W.H. Martyn in 7C. Martyn's fire hit and mortally wounded Fw Willy Stock, the belly gunner, and also struck the starboard engine. Lt Cdr

The wreck of He 111P 5J+CN of 5/KG 4, seen many years after the end of the war.

H.P. Bramwell in 7A then attacked, and it was thought that he put paid to the other engine. In fact it seems that this had already been hit by a splinter from an AA shell, and lacked sufficient power to keep the aircraft in the air. With the bomber sinking rapidly, and with insufficient power to avoid crashing into a mountain now looming ahead, Fw Richard Gumbrecht put the Heinkel — 5J+CN — down on its belly in the snow. The three survivors, Ofw Günther Hölscher, Richard Gumbrecht and Fw Karl Stolz, climbed out as the Skuas thundered overhead. A second Heinkel was attacked by 7B (Sub Lt (A) Wigginton) and this was last seen losing height and pouring smoke, being claimed as a probable.

The trio of survivors set out in deep snow, hoping to reach German forces at Kvam, but after four days they were captured and were later transferred to England, spending the rest of the war as prisoners in Canada. The Heinkel remained on the mountainside for many years in a remarkably undamaged condition, although stripped of removeable items by souvenir hunters, and of paint by the weather. Finally it was recovered by enthusiasts and was restored in 1979. In August of that year the three Germans and two of the surviving Fleet Air Arm Skua crews met at Gardermoen for the roll-out of the aircraft.

As the KG 4/801 Squadron combat had been taking place, *Glorious* was launching three more Skuas from 803 Squadron, and somewhat later at 1308 these also intercepted He 111s, part of a force of ten from II/LG 1, 14 from III/LG 1 and 11 from I/KG 26, which were undertaking a concentrated attack on Aandalsnes and Lesjaskog, where they claimed one Gladiator destroyed on the ground. The bomber crews reported having seen the two other Gladiators which had got into the air, attempting to catch them, but without success. Three of the I/KG 26 bombers were attacked over Storfjord by the three 803 Squadron Skuas, which were flown by Lt Lucy in 7F, Lt Filmer in 7Q and Lt Christian in 7H. The windscreen of 7F was at once covered in a film of oil and Lucy had to break away to clean it before returning to the fight. Filmer meanwhile made an individual attack, damaging one bomber, but 7Q was then seen diving away leaving a slight trail of smoke. He force-landed in Norway with the aircraft damaged and the observer/gunner, Pty Off K.G. Baldwin, dead. Lucy and Christian resumed the attack from the beam, but the bombers then began to draw away from them, one seeming to drop out of formation as they went. In fact two Heinkels of 2 Staffel had been damaged, though neither was very badly hit. In one, one member of the crew was killed, and in the other two were wounded. The Skua pilots then attacked an aircraft identified as a Do 17, before sighting another He 111 below, this time L1+KT of 9/LG 1. Several passes were made on this latter, and it lost height pouring smoke; the undercarriage came down and the stricken aircraft finally 'pancaked' into the eastern end of Romsdalsfjord sinking after three minutes. Some members of the crew were seen swimming to the shore as the two Skuas, both of which had been damaged during the fight, headed back for their carrier. Lt Cahl and his crew of four were all reported missing; in fact two were to die in hospital, one to remain as a prisoner and one to be freed later by German troops.

Although Filmer had been brought down by fire from the I/KG 26 aircraft, the only claim submitted was by 5/KG 54, a gunner of this unit claiming one Skua shot down. This may have resulted from a combat during the mid after-noon period, when three 800 Squadron Skuas attacked one of two He 111s which were bombing HMS *Flamingo*. No obvious effects of this interception were seen, but return fire wounded Pty Off J. Hadley in 6C. Meanwhile at Setnes-moen the last serviceable Gladiator had taken off and had managed to intercept one Heinkel, which was claimed damaged. On landing, operations by 263 Squadron ceased, for no fuel was left. In two days 49 sorties had been made, resulting in 37 interceptions and claims for six aircraft shot down, with numerous others damaged.

The final engagement of the day occurred during the evening when six Skuas of 800 Squadron launched from *Ark Royal* two hours earlier, attacked an He 115 of 1/KüFlGr 506 and undertook a running battle with it. Lts Finch-Noyes, Cunningham, Spurway and J.A. Rooper all exhausted their ammunition before the floatplane escaped, apparently very badly damaged and streaming fuel from both floats. It had only suffered damage of less than 5% however, although the radio operator was wounded. Further south during the day three He 111s of 2/LG 1, escorted by two Bf 110s from 3/ZG 76 attacked and sank the Norwegian destroyer *Garm* near Bergen.

27/4/40
There is little doubt that, but for the weight of Luftwaffe bombing, the Allied forces at Namsos and Aandalsnes could have held on for much longer. With the virtual destruction of 263 Squadron in such a short period however, Lt Gen Massey, Commander in Chief of the Expeditionary Force, decided that Central Norway would have to be abandoned and the Allied fortunes pinned on the north. Consequently during 27 April withdrawal was planned. The Blenheim fighters at Hatston would join the carrier units in covering the evacuation, although their endurance would allow them to remain on station for only one hour. It was hoped initially that it might be possible for them to land and refuel at Setnesmoen, but the bombing here had put this landing ground effectively out of action. Bomber Command was ordered to step up its attacks on Sola and Fornebu airfields during the period of the evacuation, in an effort to reduce the Luftwaffe's activities.

Meanwhile in the north reinforcements of French Alpine troops, Foreign Legionnaires and Polish infantry began arriving at Harstad for the proposed capture of Narvik. The abandonment of the Trondheim area would leave the Luftwaffe free to operate from Vaernes airfield however, this base being in range of Narvik, so an urgent search for possible fighter airfields was begun. The Norwegian Air Force bases at Bardufoss and Banak offered themselves, whilst undeveloped ground at Skaanland also appeared promising.

Over Aandalsnes the Fleet Air Arm redoubled its efforts to provide air cover on 27 April, and combats were frequent throughout the day. In the morning two Do 215s of 1(F)/ObdL and an He 111 of 1(F)/122 undertook reconnaissances to the north, spotting the warships of Admiral Wells' force, including the carriers identified as *Ark Royal* and *Eagle*. *Glorious*'s Sea Gladiators got their first chance against the Luftwaffe at 0935, when three 804 Squadron aircraft and one from 802 Squadron were scrambled, catching the 1(F)/122 Heinkel ten minutes later. The intruder was low over the water some 20 miles from the fleet. Lt R.M. Smeeton led the section down to attack, the Heinkel making off at top speed and gradually drawing away from the biplanes, although it was seen to touch the wave-tops three times. The bomber had been badly damaged, and force-landed well to the north-west of Trondheim, 65% damaged, the crew claiming that they had shot down one of the Sea Gladiators.

During an afternoon reconnaissance by three Do 215Bs of FAG/ObdL, a cruiser and seven other ships were spotted about 150 miles north-east of Trondheim, and a transport 185 miles north-west of Namsos. A little to the south of these were three destroyers and two more transports. Following these reports five He 111s of I/KG 26 took off at 1755, followed in several waves by 32 Ju 88s of KG 30, and from Narvik six He 111s were diverted from a formation of ten of II/KG 26. The weather was bad however, and most crews diverted to targets in the Aandalsnes area on the return flight.

The main target for the German bombers remained the southern arm of the British pincer movement on Trondheim however. 61 Heinkels from KG 26, 54 and LG 1, and 34 Ju 88s of KG 30 attacked Aandalsnes town and harbour, shipping in Molde and Romsdalsfjord, and ground targets to the south, dropping 81.5 tons. In Moldefjord the Norwegian MV *Nyhaus* was sunk by a KG 30 Ju 88, while the British tanker *Delius* and the escort vessel HMS *Black Swan* were both damaged.

Four waves of bombers were sent out from 1200 onwards, the first comprising six He 111s from 4/KG 54. These were followed at 1300 by 18 He 111s from III/KG 26, which were intercepted by three 800 Squadron Skuas. The fighters had taken off soon after midday and caught a Heinkel of 9/KG 26 bombing a cruiser off Aandalsnes. The bomber, 1H+CT, commanded by Lt Hans Schopis, force-landed south of Grotli after attack by 6A (Capt R.J. Partridge, RM), 6B (Lt E. Taylour) and 6C (Sub Lt B.H. Hurle-Hobbs), Partridge putting his damaged Skua (L2940) down on a frozen lake nearby. Four more Skuas from 803 Squadron were also up, having taken off from *Glorious*, but as this carrier was now ordered to withdraw to refuel, the pilots were advised to land on *Ark Royal* on termination of their patrol. Lt Lucy in 7H and Pty Off A.G. Johnson in 7L caught another Heinkel — an aircraft of 7/KG 26 — and forced it down on a hillside near Romsdalsfjord before coming aboard *Ark* at 1435. The crew of the bomber tried to make their way to German-held territory but only two got through; the aircraft commander, Oblt Hans-Ludwig Steinback, and the observer were captured by British troops.

At 1515 five Skuas, three of 800 Squadron and two from 801 were off on patrol as a larger bombing force approached. Six Heinkels of II/KG 26 and 26 Ju 88s from I, II and III/KG 30, were followed by 13 more Heinkels of KGr 100. The Skuas intercepted two Ju 88s which were dive-bombing a convoy entering Aandalsnes harbour an hour later; both made off to the south with engines apparently on fire (but probably pouring black exhaust smoke). Two 'Do 17s' were then driven off, before a large, ragged formation of 15 He 111s were seen approaching (obviously the KGr 100 aircraft). All five Skuas attacked, and one Heinkel turned for home with an engine on fire. By now all ammunition had been expended and the Skuas returned, one crew reporting that during the fight they had been attacked by a Ju 88. After debriefing Lt Cdr Bramwell and Sub Lt Wigginton were credited with a Ju 88 shot down, while a probable was given to three 800 Squadron crews. Subsequent interrogation of a prisoner of war appeared to indicate that four He 111s had been shot down in this combat, and these were all credited to the Skuas. Actual losses had not been of this magnitude in the attack, and it seems likely that the prisoner meant that four He 111s had been lost up to this point during the day which would indeed seem to be the case. In fact the evasive manoeuvres of the KG 30 Ju 88s seem to have given the impression of their demise, for this unit lost no aircraft and suffered slight damage to only one. The Heinkel initially credited as a probable to the 800 Squadron men — Finch-Noyes, Marks and Gallagher — was an aircraft of 2/KGr 100, which had been badly damaged before lack of fuel had caused the Skua pilots to break away. Ofw Richard Hensel attempted to get his bomber back to Stavanger, but the damage was too severe, and he subsequently force-landed near Hoyanger on Sognefjord. Here the crew set fire to the aircraft before becoming prisoners.

Meanwhile other KGr 100 aircraft reported attacking a Sunderland flying-boat. This was N9025 of 228 Squadron, which Flt Lt Craven had just flown over to Aandalsnes to fly out a party of RAF personnel. He was proceeding up Moldefjord at very low level when three aircraft identified as Ju 88s, attacked, attempting to hit the flyingboat with their bombs. This attempt failed, the missiles exploding 50 yards astern, but Craven then had to land, and while on the water the aircraft was attacked by 12 more bombers. Only minor splinter damage was inflicted, but at 1725 Craven was forced to take off again as his engines were beginning to overheat, since he had kept these running to enable him to take evasive action on the water as the attacks were made. As soon as the Sunderland rose into the air it was attacked by a Bf 110. This was engaged by the rear turret and midships gun positions, and was claimed shot down, confirmation of this being forthcoming by the ground party the aircraft had come to pick up, who had observed the whole proceedings.

While the fighting over Aandalsnes was still in progress meanwhile, *Ark Royal* had launched a further trio of 801 Squadron aircraft, and at 1735 these attacked a single He 111 of 2/KGr 100. Fire from the gunners struck Skua 7L (Lt (A) W.C.A. Church/Sub Lt (A) D.G. Willis) which burst into flames; the engine broke completely off the aircraft and it dived vertically into the sea, the crew being killed. The other two Skua pilots, Lt R.C. Hay, RM, and P/O H. Kimber, then shot down the Heinkel, which fell into the sea near Aalesund; Uffz Kurt Rippka and his crew were picked up by a British warship.

A further raid brought ten He 111s of II/LG 1 to the area, but as these began the return flight to Southern Norway, two 4 Staffel aircraft were intercepted over Lesjaskog by three more Skuas from 801 Squadron — 7F (Lt R.L. Strange), 7G (Sub Lt (A) P.E. Marsh) and 7H (Mdspmn (A) G.C. Baldwin). This trio attacked the rearmost of the pair, and with smoke pouring from the port engine, it went down into a forest, Fw Werner Schulz and his crew being captured by the Norwegians and shipped to Britain. With evening, two more He 111s of 2/KG 26 appeared over the port, these reporting that they were engaged by two Blenheims which inflicted severe damage on one Heinkel, three members of the crew being wounded.

After being forced to land during the first afternoon combat, Partridge and Lt Bostock found a little shed nearby where they sought shelter for the night. Inside were the crew of the Heinkel which they had brought down! The British pair wisely indicated that they had come from a shot-down Wellington. Next day Partridge and Uffz Hauck set out together to try and find help for the German observer, who had been wounded. They were discovered by a Norwegian patrol, who shot Hauck before the situation became clear. The rest of the Heinkel crew were then taken prisoner, and the two British airmen were assisted in returning to their carrier. That evening the last three Gladiators of 263 Squadron — N5579, 5723 and 5725 — were destroyed by the unit's ground personnel, who then embarked on the French freighter *Cap Blanc*, where they joined the pilots.

British 'Tommies', including a Military Policeman (left) with French Hotchkiss H-35 light tanks in a Norwegian village. *(IWM)*

28/4/40

The ground commanders at Namsos and Aandalsnes were ordered to begin their withdrawals on 28th. To reduce interference with the evacuation, *Ark Royal* launched her air group on another dawn raid on Vaernes airfield. At 0305 six Swordfish each from 810 and 820 Squadrons took off with four 250lb, four 20lb and four 25lb incendiary bombs apiece. 820 attacked at 0432, obtaining hits on huts and barrack blocks, while 810 came in ten minutes later, Lt Godfrey-Fawssett destroying the last hangar — he had been responsible for the destruction of another during the previous attack. Intense flak was encountered and several aircraft were hit, but all returned safely.

Meanwhile six Skuas, drawn equally from 800 and 801 Squadron, set off to attack the slipway and floatplanes at Trondheim. Merchant ships were seen at anchor and dive-bombed with 250 pounders. Hits were observed, but 6M was damaged by Flak and force-landed at Aandalsnes. The attack had destroyed five He 115Bs of KüFlGr 506, two of 1 Staffel and three of 2 Staffel.

During the morning 11 Ju 87Rs of StG 1, 12 He 111s of KG 26 and LG 1, and 16 Ju 88s of KG 30 attacked shipping in the fjord at Aalesund and Aandalsnes, and the harbour at the latter town. The RN anti-submarine trawler *Siretoco* was sunk by the Stukas, while KG 30 sank the small Norwegian coaster *Brand IV*. Meanwhile however, another pair of He 111s from 2/LG 1 on reconnaissance over the coastal zone, spotted the carrier and reported its presence. These bombers were intercepted by three Rocs which were scrambled after them (7P, Lt R.C. Hay, RM/N/A S. Bass; 7Q, Sub Lt (A) J.E.H. Myers/N/A P. Bolton; 7R, Mdspmn (A) G.C. Baldwin/L/A S. Smailes), but could only drive them off, reporting that they had seen one of the bombers shot down by AA fire. On receipt of the sighting report ten more Heinkels of II/KG 26 were sent off to attack.

At 1105 three of the visiting 803 Squadron aircraft were flown off, followed by three Skuas from 800 Squadron, which were to provide escort for a convoy codenamed TM 1. At 1218 the first trio saw a Ju 88 bombing a sloop and Lt Lucy at once attacked with a short burst, followed by Sub Lt Brokensha, whose fire missed the German aircraft. Pty Off Johnson then got in a solid attack, and the bomber was reported to have crashed; it was credited to Lucy and Johnson jointly. Half an hour later these same pilots saw eight Heinkels of 4/KG 26 approaching, and three of these were attacked by them, Lucy and Brokensha hitting both engines of the Staffelkapitän's aircraft (Hpt Eberhard Schnoor von Carolsfeld). The bomber was put down in the sea near Molde and the crew got out into their dinghy, save one man who had been killed during the fighters' attack; they were picked up and made prisoners. The three Skuas then chased the other seven out to sea, breaking up their formation. Several jettisoned their bombs and two were seen with engines on fire, one being credited to Brokensha as a 'damaged', the other to Johnson's gunner as a probable.

These fleeing bombers were now met by the 800 Squadron trio. All three pilots, Finch-Noyes, Taylour and Marks, shot down Fw Karl Pfluger's aircraft, and this fell into the sea in flames; there were no survivors. By now the KG 30 and LG 1 bombers were in the area, attacking the shipping in the Molde region. Lucy, Johnson and Brokensha attacked one Ju 88, but lost it, but Finch-Noyes and Taylour each claimed one of these bombers damaged in head-on attacks, while Finch-Noyes' gunner, Cunningham, claimed damage to an He 111. Marks also claimed that he had set one engine of another bomber alight. With all ammunition gone the 800 Squadron crews then made five dummy attacks on incoming bombers, succeeding in breaking up their attacks. In all these latter engagements the German aircraft actually escaped undamaged, and one Skua was claimed shot down by KG 30 gunners. One LG 1 He 111 was slightly damaged by AA fire.

Close behind these bombers came a third wave of 13 more Heinkels of III/KG 26, which arrived at about 1350. The 803 Squadron Skuas still had ammunition and fuel left, so Lucy and Brokensha at once attacked three of them and shot down an 8 Staffel aircraft which Uffz Hans Liesske managed to force-land in a valley near Sunndalsfjord, with two of the crew dead. Liesske and the observer then set fire to the aircraft before being captured by Norwegian troops. The other pair of Heinkels jettisoned their bombs and fled, following which the Skuas returned singly to the ship.

Later in the afternoon the original pair of 2/LG 1 'snoopers' returned. The three Rocs, having been refuelled, took off after them but returned empty-handed two hours later. At this stage *Ark Royal* retired out to sea for two days to rest her tired aircrews and allow maintenance to be carried out to the depleted stock of aircraft. 89 Ju 52/3ms now reinforced Narvik with army troops, equipment for 1/StG 1 and mountain guns for ArtRegt 112; four He 59s brought ammunition.

29/4/40
With the carriers not available to continue giving cover on 29 April, it was the fighter Blenheims of 254 Squadron which had to try and fill the gap. Three of these set off early for Aandalsnes, arriving overhead around 0930 and at once giving chase to a Ju 88, which outdistanced them. Two He 111s were then seen, but a Bf 110 appeared and all three turned on this, firing at it during a three minute engagement in which all used up their stock of ammunition. The Messerschmitt was last seen in a spin, but one Blenheim had suffered a puncture in its oil system to the port engine, and as a result at 1045 the propellor came loose and fell off. This aircraft, R3628, crash-landed near Scatsa and was damaged beyond repair; the crew were unhurt. Three more Blenheims arrived to replace the patrol meanwhile, and at 1155 an He 111 was seen near Molde, just after this town had been bombed again. This aircraft could not be caught, but 20 minutes later a Ju 88 was intercepted and severe damage to this was claimed.

From Trondheim 21 He 111s of KG 26 took off to attack Namsos town and harbour, while south of this area 56 more from KG 4, KGr 100 and LG 1, and 24 Ju 88s from both KG 30 and LG 1, attacked targets in the Kristiansund-Stören-Dombås-Aandalsnes area again. A Norwegian vessel, *Orland*, was sunk off Midsund in Moldefjord by an LG 1 Ju 88, while an anti-submarine trawler, HMS *Cape Celyuskin*, was damaged so badly in Romsdalsfjord by an aircraft of KGr 100, that it had to be abandoned a few days later. Air supply of Trondheim continued, costing two more Ju 52/3ms that collided whilst landing back at Fornebu, while from Bergen five He 111s of 4/KG 26 undertook armed reconnaisances along the coast between this port and Aalesund. The freighter *Begonia* was discovered in Aurlandsfjord, near Flaam, and was sunk.

During the day MF 11 floatplane F-328 from the Naval 2 Flg avd attacked a German troopship at Granvin and troops at Vikingnes in Hardangerfjord, but the small bombs dropped did no damage. He 115 F-52 had flown out 15 minutes earlier to bomb a cruiser at Stavanger, but suffered engine failure over the target and had to retire; both aircraft then returned to Olden in Nordfjord. The Norwegian Military Headquarters now decided that in future the remaining Navy and Army aircraft would co-operate and work together.

Bomber Command's resumed offensive against the airfields was now underway, but once again it was not proving cheap. At night on 29/30 April six Whitleys from 102 Squadron attacked shipping at Olso, and the adjacent Fornebu airfield. Flg Off K.H.P. Murphey's DY-C, N1421, was shot down by I/Flakregt 611, and crashed at Sylling, near Drammen. The other five dropped 40 250lb bombs on the airfield.

With morning on 30th the ever-active Maj i G Martin Harlinghausen of Fliegerkorps X was out undertaking a reconnaissance in one of 2/KüFlGr 506's He 115s, covering the coastal area between Trondheim and Namsos. He discovered worthwhile targets in Namsfjord, and 11 Ju 87Rs of 3/StG 1 were despatched to attack. The first Kette of three trapped and sank the anti-submarine trawler HMS *Jardine*; the next Kette sank the similar *Warwickshire*, while the third found the escort vessel *Bittern*, which was badly damaged by Oblt Elmo Schäfer's bombs; she was finally sent down that evening by a torpedo fired from HMS *Juno* when it was clear that she was beyond repair. An evening sortie by 12 more Stukas met with no success.

Meanwhile another of KüFlGr 506's aircraft had undertaken an early reconnaissance sortie over Aandalsnes, following which a strong force of bombers was sent out. 65 He 111s from KG 4, 54, KGr 100 and LG 1, eight Ju 87s from I/StG 1 and three Ju 88Cs from Z/KG 30 dropped 65.5 tons of bombs on shipping between Aalesund and Aandalsnes, on the town and harbour, on targets in Moldefjord and on Setnesmoen airfield. AA fire damaged one He 111 of 5/LG 1, which crash-landed on its home base in Schleswig on return, 70% damaged and with three of Oblt Wilger Schacht's crew wounded. One of the Zerstörer Ju 88Cs sustained damage to its undercarriage and crash-landed at Stavanger on return, where it became a write-off.

Ju 87Rs of I/StG 1, which began taking a full part in the fighting over Central Norway in late April. A Ju 52/3m may be seen immediately behind this pair of Stukas. *(Bundesarchiv)*

In an effort to reduce the high level of Luftwaffe activity prior to the imminent evacution of Namsos and Aandalsnes, the RAF was ordered to renew attacks on all German airfields within range, by day and night. Consequently, at 1630 six Blenheims from 110 Squadron set off to bomb Stavanger/Sola. An hour later four Wellingtons of 37 Squadron from Feltwell followed them, followed in their turn at 1800 by six from 99 Squadron and three from 9 Squadron, and then by three from 115 Squadron at 1815. As the last Wellingtons were setting out, the Blenheims attacked, not seeing the results of their bombing as they were intercepted by Bf 109Es of II/JG 77, four of which had taken off at 1825 for this purpose. The first of these fighters to approach was reported to be shot down, being seen to fall into the sea, but no German loss was recorded and the surviving crews may well have seen one of their own formation going down. The Messerschmitts pressed home their attack in a running fight, Oblt Henz and his wingman sighting one bomber at 15,000 feet over the airfield and climbing to recognise it as a Blenheim. This was F/Sgt R. Abbott's N6202, which banked and dropped its bombs as the crew spotted the fighters, making off at top speed. Fw Sawallisch attacked first from behind, and Helmut Henz then made three such attacks. After the third the bomber's port engine was hit by cannon shells and began to burn. The aircraft, now at low level in its efforts to escape its tormentors, dived into the sea from an altitude of only about 30 feet at 1835; two members of the crew were seen swimming, and were later rescued by the emergency rescue service.

Meanwhile the second Rotte, Lt Demes and Fw Harbach, had undertaken a similar chase, during which Harbach exhausted all his ammunition in nine fruitless attacks. Demes then attacked with cannon and set both engines on fire, and the aircraft dived steeply into the sea from 300 feet at 1854, and sank at once, no survivors being seen. They had shot down Sqn Ldr K.C. Doran, DFC in L9242; Doran, it will be recalled, had led the first bombing attack of the war on Wilhelmshaven on 4 September 1939, for which he had been one of the first two pilots of the war to receive the DFC. The attack on Sola achieved the destruction of a single Do 215B of 3(F)/ObdL.

At 1930, shortly before the first 37 Squadron Wellingtons reached Sola, Fliegerührer Stavanger announced that an estimated 80 RAF aircraft were attacking Bergen, and all available Bf 110s of I/ZG 76 were scrambled and led off south by Hpt Reinecke. Thus when the Wellingtons appeared two hours after the Blenheims' attack, with the light still good, there were available for interception only four Bf 109s of 4/JG 77 and two Bf 110s of 2/ZG 76, all of which were in the air. One Rotte of Bf 109s (Lt Heinz Demes and Fw Erwin Sawallisch) and the Bf 110s (Lt Helmut Woltersdorf and Lt Dietrich Knoetzsch), made several attacks as the bombers dived in pairs on the target, shooting down the first pair. Demes and Sawallisch made a number of beam attacks, Sawallisch's fire hitting one which burst into flames and exploded low over the water. He then witnessed the second bomber being shot down by a Bf 110 — Knoetzsch and Woltersdorf both claiming Wellingtons at 2040 and 2045 respectively; they had double-claimed. These two bombers, P9213 (Sqn Ldr R.L. Bradford) and P9215 (Flg Off G.V. Gordon) were last seen by the rest of the British formation, diving away westwards with all six fighters in pursuit; it was noted that both had their retractable ventral 'dustbin' turrets down and neither were seen again. Both had gone into the sea, Gordon's aircraft west, and Bradford's south-west of Stavanger.

The second pair of 37 Squadron Wellingtons had dived to sea level, keeping their underturrets retracted to allow more speed and manoeuvreability. Flg Off Warner's aircraft had failed to release its bombs and had fallen behind, and it was this that Demes and Sawallisch now attacked. The rear gunner concentrated his fire on the starboard Bf 109 — Demes' aircraft — which had approached to close range. At 200 yards Demes climbed slightly and his fighter was hit, swinging away and crashing straight into the sea in flames. Following this success, Warner managed to catch up with the leading Wellington, flown by Sgt Fletcher. At 2110 they were attacked by a Bf 110, which kept after them persistently for about 30 minutes making ten astern and beam attacks. The rear gunners kept up a steady fire at it but finally one of the front gunners got in a good burst, reporting he had knocked pieces of it, hereupon it turned for the coast which was now some 70 miles away, and headed east.

It seems that the I/ZG 76 Bf 110s which had headed south, had returned in time to join in the latter part of the interception, for Lt Kamp of 3 Staffel claimed a Wellington at 2053, while Lt Woltersdorf made a further claim at

2100. This latter may relate to one of the 115 Squadron aircraft, R3154, which was damaged, and which Flg Off E.J.T Clarke subsequently crashed in bad visibility on return near Lastingham in Yorkshire. A 99 Squadron machine may also have been hit, for F/Sgt J.W.L.G. Brent's P9276 crashed in the Wash; this aircraft was later found in 18 inches of water with all the crew dead. However it seems that at least three Bf 110s were also hit; two of these crash-landed at Sola, one 1 Staffel aircraft catching fire and burning out. In the second Lt Helmut Fahlbusch of 3 Staffel was killed and his gunner, Fw Georg Scharfe, was injured. Another 3 Staffel aircraft turned over, Ofw Georg Fleischmann and Ogfr Hans-Dietrich Mierke both being hurt, while the Gruppenkommandeur, Hpt Günther Reinecke, crashed into the sea south-west of Stavanger, he and Gefr Enno Gruschwitz being lost.

It had been quite an expensive engagement in the air for the Luftwaffe, but on the ground the results of the 13 Wellingtons' attack had been limited to a single Do 17 of 1(F)/120 destroyed and one damaged (in addition to the Do 215B already destroyed by the Blenheims), one Bf 110 damaged, one of the groundcrew killed and three Flak gunners wounded — a poor return for the loss of four Wellingtons and two Blenheims! For their part in this engagement Flg Off Warner received a DFC and his rear gunner, AC 1 Waterfall — victor over Demes — a DFM.

It is interesting to examine the assessment of the British bombers made by II/JG 77 following these engagements with their still-new cannon-armed E-3 aircraft. 'The defence of the Bristol Blenheim to the rear is weak,' the report concluded, 'and need not be considered. The speed in a dive is very inferior to the Bf 109 Emil. The high effectiveness of the B-ammunition (7.9mm) was apparent through the stripping off of the fabric and metal parts, but it did not succeed in setting the aircraft on fire. By comparison, one hit with cannon ammunition was sufficient to explode one motor in flames. The Blenheim flew easily, turning away from the attack in a defensive curve, and continued away. The known strength of the Vickers Wellington defence was seen to be inferior, although attacks were only made from the side. It was established in not only this air battle, but in the following night attack on the airfield that the Wellington had one 20mm cannon to the rear as well as the front — the rear turret possibly mounted two cannon.' The latter statements were quite incorrect however, for the Wellington carried only two .303in machine guns in each of the nose and tail turrets at this time.

As the Wellingtons made their way homewards through the dark, more bombers were on their way north-eastwards. Even as the combat had been at its height 12 Whitleys from 58, 77 and 102 Squadron headed for Stavanger/Sola airfield, while six from 51 Squadron and seven more from 102 Squadron made for Oslo/Fornebu, followed by five Hampdens drawn from 44 and 50 Squadrons. Over Stavanger Whitley N1465 of 58 Squadron (F/Sgt C.R. Heayes) was shot down by II/Flakregt 33, crashing into the sea. A second Whitley from 51 Squadron (K9039) flew into a hill near Slaidburn, Yorkshire, on return from Oslo, while a 61 Squadron Hampden (L4119) crashed at Croxton, Leicestershire, in bad visibility on the way back from Aalborg, the crew being killed. The Fornebu attack achieved some substantial success however; eight Ju 52/3ms of the transport Gruppen were destroyed by fire and two more were shattered by the explosions of delayed-action bombs. Another 27 of these aircraft were damaged.

In the opposite direction 12 He 111s from KGr 126 undertook the fourth mining operation by 9 Fliegerdivision, laying 11 mines in the Tyne estuary and ten in the Humber. T1+AL of 3 Staffel strayed way off course and was hit by AA over the north Essex coast, crashing into Clacton-on-Sea where four houses were destroyed and 50 others damaged. Civilian casualties amounted to five dead and 144 injured. A Hurricane of 504 Squadron (L1947) had been scrambled to attempt an interception of the minelayers, but this crashed at Bungay in Suffolk, where Sqn Ldr R.H. Watson was killed.

The Norwegians had also been active during 30th, and with some success. However during the morning another German raid on Setnesmoen landing ground destroyed the C-Vs and had killed and wounded a number of Army Air Force aircrew, and set the final seal on the impracticability of further use of this field. Later in the day three Ju 88Cs of Z/KG 30 escorted five Ju 88As of 2/G 30 to attack the airfield again, Zerstörer pilots Lt Pack, Ofw Hermann and Uffz Wiesmann strafing and each claiming one Fokker C-V of the Reconnaissance Wing destroyed on the ground. Pack would later become one of the first German night fighters to be shot down in combat, while Kurt Hermann became a successful long-range night fighter pilot, credited with nine victories. Late in the evening two MF 11s bombed two ex-Norwegian minelayers which had been taken over by the Germans. Their bombs did no damage and the crews returned to base to report their lack of success, whereupon He 115A F-58 was sent out. This aircraft made two attacks on the minelayer *Uller*, damaging her so badly that her captain ran her ashore. Here F-58's gunners strafed her, setting the ship alight, and causing the mines which remained aboard to explode.

1/5/40
Next day, as the evacuation reached its last stages, 2 Flg avd was ordered to withdraw too. Two He 115As and three MF 11s still survived, F-58 and MFs F-312 and -334 flying northwards to Tromsø, while F-52 and F-328 headed for Scotland. The Heinkel, flown by Lt Offerdal, reached Invergordon safely, but the MF 11 was believed to have been shot down by British AA guns in error, the crew being killed. F-52 carried with it the Skua crew, Faragut and Owbridge, who had been flying with the Norwegians since being shot down on 10 April.

By now — May Day — the evacuation was nearing completion, but the airfield attacks by the RAF continued. Following the raids of the previous evening and night, three Hudsons from 269 Squadron, which had just completed re-equipment with these aircraft, undertook the unit's first mission against the Germans in Norway, led by Flg Off Hayley-Bell. Taking off at 0500, the three reconnaissance-bombers appeared over Stavanger a little over three hours later. As they approached they saw below them Lt Georg Schirmböck of 4/JG 77 taking off in his Bf 109E 'Weisse 10' (White 10). The latter gave chase and at 0823 shot down Hudson N7278 'A', (Sgt K. Bell) south-west of Stavanger. Meanwhile three Blenheim fighters from 254 Squadron had departed from Hatston at 0400 for Romsdalsfjord to provide cover for the shipping there. At 0705 a single He 111 was seen and attacked by all three. It managed to dive away after the third pass, and as all ammunition had by this time been exhausted, no further pursuit was made.

The carriers were now operational again, the Home Fleet returning in three groups to provide escort for the departing convoys. *Glorious* now carried an air group composed entirely of fighters — nine Sea Gadiators of 802 Squadron, ten of 804 and a dozen Skuas of 803. Early in the morning four Do 17Ps of 1(F)/120

A pair of 269 Squadron Hudsons, UA-R and C, low over the North Sea. *(IWM)*

left Trondheim, one of these finding Vice-Admiral Wells' force, including two aircraft carriers, one heavy and two light cruisers, at about 0700. The aircraft was at once intercepted by two of 804 Squadron's Sea Gladiators, and was damaged. The alarm had been given however, and at once two waves of Ju 87Rs from I/St G 1 were led in the direction of the force by two He 115s of 2/KüF1Gr 506. Bf 109Ds of 11(N)/JG 2 (which had just arrived in Norway) gave escort to the limit of their range, but were unable to reach the ships. Six Ju 87s attacked *Glorious* unsuccessfully, but the second group of seven were driven off by a patrol of Sea Gladiators. He 111s of I/LG 1 from Stavanger then bombed, but missed.

The Sea Gladiators reported the next engagement at 1540, some 70 minutes after three 804 Squadron aircraft had taken off. Now an He 111 was seen well ahead at 16,000 feet, the section climbing after it. Two pilots got in a short burst from almost a stalling position beneath, but the bomber escaped. Another was seen at 1600, but could not be caught. These were probably reconnaissance machines of 1(F)/122, looking for Admiral Cunningham's force.

Red Section took off at 1630 to relieve Blue Section, Lt R.H.P. Carver leading the trio of fighters after a single raider which was spotted at low altitude. Having chased this away, they climbed back up to 18,000 feet and at 1750 were

Bf 109Ds of 11(N)/JG 2, newly-arrived at Trondheim/Vaernes at the start of May. *(Bundesarchiv)*

A bomb-laden Ju 87R of I/StG 1 taxies out for a sortie from Trondheim/Vaernes. *(Bundesarchiv)*

ordered to intercept another intruder at sea level. This time an He 115 floatplane was seen about 20 feet above the waves, and during a long, fruitless chase, all ammunition was expended. This floatplane would seem to have been an aircraft of 2/506, which had just led a further six Ju 87Rs of 2/StG 1 to the area, and at this stage the Sea Gladiators were called back to the ship to try and aid in heading off the incoming raid by the Stukas.

Other fighters were already up, 802 Squadron's Blue Section of two Sea Gladiators led by Lt J.F. Marmont, having been scrambled at 1800, followed at 1815 by another three 804 Squadron machines. Marmont's section had gone off initially to chase another shadower — an He 115 which once again escaped. The three 804 Squadron aircraft were by then engaged with the incoming Ju 87s, and seeing them so involved, Marmont and his wingman hurled themselves into the fray and shot down one dive-bomber at 16,000 feet over the fleet at 1825. This 2 Staffel aircraft crashed into the sea west of Namsos, Ofw Erich Stahl and Uffz Friedrich Gott being picked up by a British destroyer. The 804 pilots had first seen six Ju 87s approaching at 1823, in an open V formation, and had rolled onto their tails, each pilot attacking one of the Stukas until it went into its bombing dive. At this point they broke off, leaving them to the ships' pompoms. One pilot then engaged another Ju 87 at low level, but no decisive damage could be inflicted.

During the raid one bomb missed *Ark Royal* by only 30 feet but no serious damage was inflicted. Oblt Böhne of I/StG 1 claimed this as a hit on *Glorious*. Two hours later another Do 17P of 1(F)/120 appeared overhead when the group was west of Namsos, and this too was slightly damaged by intercepting Sea Gladiators. During the afternoon searching He 111s from 1(F)/122 had found Vice-Admiral Cunningham's group west of Namsos, and Vice-Admiral Edwards-Collins' group further south, near the coast. The former group, comprising two heavy and one light cruisers, five destroyers and three other vessels, was attacked by 12 He 111s of II/KG 26, but suffered no damage. The bombers were intercepted by patrolling Skuas, but these were not able to gain any success on this occasion. Lt Brokensha of 803 Squadron was shot down by the fleet's AA by mistake during the day. Unhurt, he and his gunner were rescued by HMS *Nubian*.

Meanwhile Edwards-Collins' force was attacked by 18 Ju 88s of II/KG 30, none of which was able to achieve any hits. 17 He 111Ps of II/KG 4 attacked

Namsos town and railway station, and rail lines between Grong, Namsos and Trondheim. 13 more Heinkels from KGr 100 raided shipping off Aandalsnes and 19 from II/LG 1 bombed targets at Molde, Aandalsnes and Aalesund. Fighter Blenheims of 254 Squadron had also been active over Romsdalsfjord again during the day, but had only been able to record inconclusive engagements with a Ju 88 and an He 111.

That night five 9/LG 1 He 111s attempted without success to bomb warships near Otteröya and in Romsdalsfjord, but one bomber came under heavy fire from Admiral Layton's battlegroup and fell in flames in Freanafjord, Lt Franz Schäfer and his crew being killed.

Minelayers were again out, 9 Fliegerdivision sending 16 He 111s of KGr 126 and seven He 115s of 3/KüFlGr 506 to lay 16 mines in the Tyne estuary, 12 in the Humber and six in the harbour entrance at Middlesborough. In return 12 Hampdens dropped seven mines in the Elbe estuary, whilst three more aircraft undertook similar duties elsewhere.

By now the evacuation was all but complete. The last troops had been taken off at Aandalsnes during the night of 30 April/1 May, all the ships from here reaching the UK safely. On 2nd nine He 111s of II/LG 1 made attacks in Ketten strength (three aircraft) against the harbour and town perimeter of Stadlandet, and also against unloading areas at Salangen and Laberget, refuelling at Trondheim en route. One crew attacked the Norwegian passenger vessel *Dronning Maud*, and damaged her so badly that she had to be abandoned. This vessel was serving with the Norwegian Army Medical Corps and carried prominent Red Cross markings; casualties aboard were high. The same bomber then attacked the village of Gratangen, destroying several houses and killing two civilians.

The next night the evacuation of Namsos was also completed, and the carriers then set course for Scapa Flow, both arriving there by 3 May. The final flurry occurred during 3rd when reconnoitring He 115s from KüFlGr 506 discovered Vice-Admiral Cunningham's Battle Group of eight cruisers and ten destroyers escorting a convoy 70 miles out from Follfjord. Seven He 111s from KGr 100, now at Vaernes, and six Ju 87Rs of I/StG 1 went out first, all attacking without success. An hour later 14 more Ju 87Rs were led to the scene by Hpt Hozzell, and these obtained a hit on the forward magazine of the French destroyer *Bison*, 108 members of her crew being killed. Survivors were taken off and the stricken vessel was then sunk by HMS *Afridi*. Soon after midday four more Ju 87s appeared overhead as *Afridi* and two other destroyers followed the rest of the force, and this time it was *Afridi* herself which was sunk; 49 seamen and 14 soldiers who were aboard were killed. A final raid during the afternoon by 15 more Stukas found the anti-submarine vessels *Aston Villa*, *Gaul* and *St Goran*, all of which were damaged by near-misses.

With the conclusion of these operations came rewards for some of the Luftwaffe participants. On 4 May Maj Martin Harlinghausen became the first bomber pilot to be awarded the Ritterkreuz (Knights' Cross of the Iron Cross) for his outstanding contribution to the operations of X Fliegerkorps. Four days later a similar award was made to Hpt Paul-Werner Hozzell, commander of I/StG 1. One of the first four Stukaflieger to receive this honour, Hozzell had already flown with distinction in Poland in September 1939. Both men were to continue distinguished careers over the coming years, which would bring them further honours and promotions.

At this time too, Luftflotte 5 relinquished control of KG 4, KG 30, KG 54 (the two latter units to Luftflotte 2) and LG 1. I/ZG 1 also departed, although a single Staffel from I(J)/LG 2 moved to Aalborg partly to replace this unit. At the same time 2/ZG 76 was despatched from Norway to this airfield to bring the defences here back to a reasonable level. 5 and 6/JG 77 moved up to Trondheim/Vaernes.

1–4/5/40

Meanwhile, Bomber Command's attacks on Sola and Fornebu continued for a little longer, but were already being run down now that the immediate emergency was over. Three Whitleys of 77 Squadron and two of 102 Squadron were over the latter airfield during the night of 1/2 May, where one Hs 126 of 2(H)/10 and a Ju 52/3m of KGrzbV 106 were destroyed on the ground. Oslo Flak defences claimed one bomber shot down, but all returned. Next night six 58 Squadron Whitleys struck at Stavanger. On 4 May however, 77 and 102 Squadrons left Kinloss to return to Driffield, while the Blenheims of 107 and 110 Squadrons had already flown back to Wattisham on 2nd and 3rd.

The Hampdens continued their mining activities for the time being, these having a dual role in relation not only to the Norwegian operations, but also to the passage of German naval units to and from the Atlantic generally. During April 107 mines had been laid by these aircraft, all by parachute from a mean height of 500 feet. The cost so far had been seven aircraft. Latterly however, they had been meeting a new adversary in the unaccustomed form of the night fighter. I/ZG 1 at Aalborg had been little-engaged in action recently, but the constant presence by night of Bomber Command Whitleys over their base had caused the formation within the Gruppe of a night fighter flight, prior to the unit's withdrawal from Denmark. During the night of 30 April/1 May Fw Thier reported encountering a Wellington on one of these early flights, but lost sight of it again after making three attacks. The following night two of 50 Squadron's Hampdens attacked Aalborg airfield, and the crew of one of these (flown by Plt Off Stenner) reported meeting two Bf 110s, which managed to damage the bomber slightly before the gunners drove them off. 24 hours later Flg Off Jacklin and his crew from the same unit saw three Bf 110s with their navigation lights on over the Husum area, when the British aircraft was involved in a minelaying sortie. On this occasion the pilot was able to escape from these fighters in cloud.

As the Norwegian ground forces retreated steadily northwards, the only aerial action overhead, apart from the Luftwaffe's persistent bombing attacks, remained the activities of the surviving Norwegian aircraft, which were limited to reconnaissance flights, and to the bombing and strafing of German troops in support of the front line forces. On 4 May 13 He 111s of KGr 100 were despatched on a raid on the Narvik area, where the destroyer *Thunderbolt* was attacked, and the Polish destroyer *Grom* was sunk with the loss of 65 of her crew. Two Fokker C-Vs had taken off from Bardufoss and bombed targets east of Laeigastind and around a location referred to as Lake 780, when they were spotted by some of the Heinkel crews, and one attacked them. One Fokker made good its escape, but the other, C-VD 389, crewed by Lts Eggen and Kyllingmark, was forced to stay and fight it out with the bomber. During the first attack by the German aircraft, the C-V suffered a few holes in the wings, while Kyllingmark managed to obtain hits on the Heinkel with his rear gun, but without obvious damage resulting. After a ten minute dogfight, Eggen made off down a valley, flying at low level in the hope that the bigger Heinkel could not follow.

It did follow however, flying some 600 feet higher, and when the Fokker was obliged to climb at the head of the valley, put in another attack during which the biplane was shot down. Both the Norwegians were badly wounded, but survived. Subsequently Kyllingmark would twice become a Minister in postwar Conservative governments.

Following a long break in reinforcement operations, a Do 26V of KGrzbV 108 carried ammunition and post for GebPzjgAbt 48 to Beisfjord. During the afternoon nine Ju 87Rs of I/StG 1 undertook an armed reconnaissance of the Namsos area with considerable effect. Four Norwegian steamers were discovered in Namsfjord, and all were sunk. These were *Blaafjeld* bound for Rochester and *Sekstant* bound for London, both loaded with timber, *Pan* and the passenger vessel *Aafjorfd*.

8/5/40

On 8 May the remaining five C-Vs and five Tiger Moths in Central Norway, which had been operating as Group R under Capt Ole Reistad, were flown north to join the Hålogaland Air Corps, bringing with them an impressed Klemm L-25 (ex LN-EAG). These proved a welcome reinforcement, for one more of the Hålogaland C-Vs had crashed while landing from a bombing trip on the previous day, and the unit had been down to only two serviceable Fokkers and one Tiger Moth.

All hope now rested in the north.

Chapter 2

THE SECOND PHASE

While the Allied forces were withdrawing from Central Norway and Bomber Command was returning its squadrons to their permanent bases further south, the units in the Narvik area to the north were steadily being built up. On 29 April a landing had been made at Bodø, well to the south of Harstad, where it was hoped that an advanced airfield could be set up to act as a fighter base for operations against Luftwaffe aircraft heading towards the main battle area from Trondheim. A further landing at nearby Mosjøen followed on 2 May, intended as a diversion, while on 4th a small force landed at Mo.

Air support for this distant area could not be provided from the United Kingdom direct, hence the departure of Bomber Command, but interdiction against German lines of communication would be possible, and in this role Coastal Command would play an important part. In the Narvik area the main support would be provided by Fighter Command, and by the ubiquitous carriers of the Royal Navy. Indeed on 4 May HMS *Ark Royal* departed Scapa Flow to support continued operations in the area, carrying the following air group:

800 Squadron	12 Skua IIs
803 Squadron	11 Skua IIs
810 Squadron	10 Swordfish Is
820 Squadron	11 Swordfish Is

Meanwhile, 22 Squadron moved to Lossiemouth with 12 of its new Beauforts for anti-shipping activities around Stavanger, while on 2 May a Sunderland from 204 Squadron was detached to Tromsø, where the remaining Norwegian Naval Air Service aircraft were now situated. Strength of the latter force here now stood at five He 115s — two of which were captured Luftwaffe aircraft — and two MF 11s.

Tromsø was now the seat of the Norwegian government, the King and his Ministers having been transferred there from Molde on the cruiser HMS *Glasgow* on 29 April. The Germans were also preparing for further action in the far north, and as Trondheim became a more secure base, more units moved to Vaernes at the start of May, fighter cover for the area now including the whole of II/JG 77 and the Z-Staffel/KG 30.

In Britain meanwhile 46 Squadron at Digby was ordered to despatch three Hawker Hurricane fighters to Prestwick, so that Naval pilots might make test landings on an aircraft carrier, prior to taking the unit over to Norway. At the same time the unit began moving to Greenock on the Clyde. In Scotland 263

Squadron was also together again at Turnhouse, where on 7 May 18 new Gladiator IIs were issued. On the same day the main ground echelon went aboard SS *Chroby* and set sail for Harstad, arriving there four days later.

In Norway work had already begun on preparation of the airfields at Bardufoss, Elvenes, Banak and Skaanland to make these suitable for RAF operational use. In each case local volunteers were called for over the radio, and many hundreds came forward — about 1000 at Bardufoss and 120 at Banak. Snow five feet in depth had to be cleared, and then ice on the surface broken or dynamited away to allow runways to be drained, levelled and lengthened. Taxiways into nearby woods were formed at Bardufoss, and blast pens for the aircraft sited therein, as well as shelters for the men. Within three weeks, by dint of incredible efforts, all were ready. Banak, situated 200 miles north-east of Narvik, was intended for Blenheims of 40 Squadron, but work stopped here on 22 May; the two other fields were both suitable for fighters. Bardufoss was about equi-distant from Narvik and Harstad, being of the order of 50 miles from each, while Skaanland was a mere 15 miles from Harstad and 25 from Narvik.

Meanwhile an RAF Component for the North-Western Expeditionary Force ('Force X') had been formed at Uxbridge late in April under Grp Capt M. Moore, ostensibly to direct and control air operations in both Northern and Central Norway. By the time it was ready to sail (7 May) only the north remained. In the same situation was Lt Gen Claude Auchinleck, newly-appointed as Commander of Allied Forces in Norway, who also headed out to take over his new command at this time.

3/5/40

During this period of relative quiet, while redeployment took place, some Coastal Command activity over the North Sea area continued. On 3 May two Hudsons from 206 Squadron made a reconnaissance to the Elbe Estuary, near Norderney. In this ever-dangerous area they were attacked by two Bf 109s of II(J)/TrGr 186, which concentrated their attack on Plt Off Keen's N7319. The Hudson was badly damaged, but regained its base airfield where the pilot carried out a crash-landing. The turret gunner, LAC Ernest Townsend, had been killed, but it was claimed that he had first shot down the leading Messerschmitt into the sea. No loss was actually suffered by the intercepting fighters.

5–7/5/40

Two days later fighter Blenheims of 235 Squadron from Bircham Newton carried out a coastal reconnaissance near Wilhelmshaven, and these were attacked by a trio of Bf 109s — part of a force of seven which had been scrambled by II(J)/TrGr 186. At 1720 Ofw Reinhold Schmetzer and Uffz Herbert Kaiser reported intercepting two Blenheims and claimed both shot down. In fact only one of 235 Squadron's aircraft was hit, and this was able to return on one engine. On Tuesday, 7 May, II(J)/TrGr 186 claimed a further success when six of 22 Squadron's Beauforts were sent off to bomb a cruiser of the *Nürenberg* class, which had been reported between the islands of Norderney and Juist. One Beaufort returned early with technical trouble, but the other five were reported by 'Freya' radar, six Bf 109Es scrambling to intercept. Flg Off S.P. Woollatt in OA-G, L4464, was shot down by Uffz Herbert Kaiser, the aircraft crashing into the sea off the Frisians with the loss of all the crew, while 'C', L4518, the aircraft flown by the formation leader, Wg Cdr H.M. Mellor, was badly damaged by Lt Hans-Wilhelm Schopper, one of the gunners being slightly wounded; this machine crashed on landing and was written off.

Meanwhile other events of note had been taking place in the area. On 5th two Arado Ar 196 floatplanes of 5/Bf1 196 at Aalborg had taken off at 0230 for a pre-dawn reconnaissance over the Kattegat at low level. Here Lt zur See Günther Mehrens in 6W+IN spotted the conning tower of the large British submarine *Seal* moving slowly east. *Seal* had been engaged in laying mines, but had hit one herself and suffered severe damage. The Captain, Lt Cdr Rupert Lonsdale, was now trying to make for neutral Sweden.

Mehrens fired a burst from his aircraft's wing-mounted 20mm cannons at the conning tower, and flashed out 'K', the international code for 'Heave-to immediately' on his signal lamp. When the submarine failed to halt, he climbed to 3000 feet and dived to drop his 50kg bombs, repeating this attack a second time. Lonsdale replied from the conning tower with a twin-Lewis anti-aircraft machine gun mounting, but the second Arado floatplane, 6W+EN, then appeared, and Lt zur See Karl Schmidt also bombed, achieving a near miss, the shock wave from which halted *Seal's* engines.

There was now little option but to surrender, and Lonsdale ordered a white flag to be hoisted. Schmidt at once landed alongside and shouted for Lonsdale to swim across to him, which the latter did. Climbing onto the float, Lonsdale protested that he was in Swedish territorial waters, but Schmidt ordered him aboard and flew him to Aalborg. Mehrens meanwhile had returned, leading He 115 8L+CH of 1/KüFlGr 906 (Lt zur See Broili) to the scene, and both now landed. A dinghy was inflated and Broili's observer paddled to the submarine to prevent documents being burned. At that point a Swedish Air Force Ju 86 patrol bomber approached, and Mehrens was obliged to scramble and fend off this aircraft as it attempted to attack the submarine. The submarine hunter *UJ-22* (formerly the fishing vessel *Franken*), which was on anti-submarine patrol nearby, arrived at this point and was able to put a tow on *Seal*, which was then taken to Friederikshaven, Denmark.

This was not the only German success on this spring Sunday. On the previous day Short Empire 'C' Class flyingboats had arrived at Harstad, carrying amongst their passengers, Admiral Lister. These two aircraft, 'Cabot' and 'Caribou', had been impressed with their crews into the RAF from Imperial Airways on the outbreak of war, and issued with the serials V3137 and V3138. Initially they served with the Special Duty Flight at Invergordon, undertaking ASV (Air to Surface Vessel) radar trials. For RAF service the 'boats were each fitted with seven hand-held Vickers 'K' machine guns and dummy tail turrets. In April 1940, with the outbreak of fighting in Norway, the pair were converted as special transports, forming C Flight of 19 Group; they had been engaged in flying radar sets and crews to Harstad in the hands of Flt Lts Stone and Long (both ex-Imperial Airways Captains). Now on 5 May they flew down to Bodø, but shortly after landing they were spotted by two Do 17s of 1(F)/120, which reported them as 'Sunderlands'. The two reconnaissance aircraft dived to bomb and strafe the 'boats, as Gordon Stone got 'Cabot's' engines started. The aircraft was attacked eight times whilst taxying, and ran aground in soft mud. 'Caribou' meanwhile would not start, and five of Long's crew were wounded. The fuel tanks were holed in this attack, shortly after which the aircraft was bombed and burnt out. Both crews in two motor boats managed to tow 'Cabot' several miles up the coast to shelter under some steep cliffs, but here next day it was again discovered by 1(F)/120, and was destroyed by a lone Do 17 which bombed it with incendiaries. The crews were returned to Britain by ship later.

Even as the Dorniers first saw the flyingboats at Bodø on 5 May, other aircraft from their unit and an Fw 200 from 1/KG 40, were reporting the presence of heavy units of the British Home Fleet in Ofotfjord. The fleet had indeed again sailed from Scapa Flow to provide support for the army, and would arrive off Narvik on 6th. At once bombers were ordered off from the Luftwaffe's new bases in southern and central Norway, and throughout the day on Sunday 50 sorties were to be made over the area by He 111s from I and III/KG 26 and KGr 100. One of the III Gruppe aircraft was hit by AA fire over Harstad and crashed in Trondheimsfjord on return, the crew baling out safely. Bad weather prevented further raids on 6 May, but during that day *Ark Royal* joined the vessels in the area, her fighters beginning patrol activity before the end of the day, aided by a type 79Z radar set aboard the cruiser HMS *Curlew*, which could detect raiders up to 90 miles away, and to a height of 20,000 feet. Near Elvenes on this date an He 111 of 1/KGr 100 was brought down by AA and other ground fire, force-landing south of Holtåsen; Fw Oswald Lochbrunner and his crew managed to make their way through the lines on foot to reach German Alpine troops.

Ark Royal's Skuas first engaged German aircraft over the new area of operations during the afternoon of the next day, 7 May, when five Heinkels from 5/KG 26 arrived to attack, following an earlier reconnaissance by four aircraft from the Geschwader's III Gruppe. Two 801 Squadron aircraft had taken off at 1330 (7K, L3030, Lt(A) T.E. Gray and 7L, L2878, Mdspmn D.T.R. Martin), followed at 1450 by two from 803 Squadron (Lt Lucy and Lt G.F. Russell, the latter in 8G, L2918). At 1630 both pairs attacked four He 111s (apparently the III Gruppe aircraft) over Ofotfjord, two of which had just completed their bombing. The other pair jettisoned, and the bombers pulled close together, their formation-keeping and return fire being reported as much better than with those aircraft previously encountered over the Trondheim area. Lt Russell's aircraft was hit, and he lost the tip of one finger to a bullet, force-landing in Ofotfjord where he and his gunner were picked up by a destroyer. Meanwhile, the 801 Squadron pair claimed one Heinkel shot down, this last being seen in a vertical dive south of Ofotfjord. This 8/KG 26 aircraft in fact managed to limp back to Trondheim and crash-land on Vaernes airfield, where some 100 bullet holes were counted in it. A second bomber returned to claim one Skua shot down — obviously Russell's aircraft.

8/5/40

Next day the Luftwaffe was out in force looking for the carrier, but was unable to find her in clouds and mist. Four He 111s of I/KG 26 were first to arrive early in the morning, and while not able to attack the ships, did see a single Norwegian Fokker C-VE on artillery observation duties, which was claimed shot down by one of the crews. Further attacks by 13 Heinkels of KG 26 and six escorting Z/KG 30 Ju 88Cs, making their first bomber support sorties over Narvik, gained no success at all.

By now there had been some considerable reorganisation of the Luftwaffe air transport force, much of which had departed to take part in operations due to take place over Holland and Belgium. KGrzbV 101, 104, 105 and 106 had all

He 111H (1H+GK) of 2/KG 26 in flight over Norway. *(Bib für Zeit)*

gone to Luftflotte 2, while 102 and 103 had been disbanded. Only KrzbV 107 and 108 now remained in Norway. Do 26 flyingboats from the latter unit had made single sorties up to Beisfjord and Narvik on 5th and 7th, but now on 8th the first attempt at a larger air-supply operation to the latter location was also carried out when two Do 24s and five Do 26s carried 103 men of 3/Geb Jag Regt 138 (under Oblt Ploder) up from Trondheim during the early afternoon. The flyingboats followed the Heinkels and Ju 88 Zerstörer to Rombaksfjord, but so bad was the weather that the two Do 24s and two of the Do 26s turned back and returned to Trondheim. One Do 26 landed at Rombaksfjord, but a second which attempted to come down here, was fired on by warships and took off again at once, landing instead in Beisfjord. The fifth Do 26, P5+BH, was engaged by three Skuas of 803 Squadron as it approached the Narvik area alone; the Skuas formed one of two flights which had taken off on patrol, and were flown by Lt L.A. Harris, RM, Sub Lt P.N. Charlton and Pty Off A.G. Johnson. The flyingboat was intercepted at 1615, and was last seen diving away south of Ofotfjord, the pilots believing that they had disabled it. The Dornier had indeed been hard hit, and with three of its four engines out of action it escaped in bad visibility and force-landed by the east bank of the entrance to Vestfjord. Here

Do 24V-1 flyingboat TJ+HR, seen in Ofotfjord in May whilst serving with KGrzvV 108. *(F. Selinger)*

311

Oblt de Res Siegfried Schack and his crew destroyed the aircraft. They, Hpt Joachim Fehling who was acting as observer, and the 17 men of 3/GJR 138 who had been their passengers, became prisoners eight days later.

Meanwhile at 1630 Mdspmn A.S. Griffiths, one of the pilots of the other trio of Skuas, attacked and claimed damage to both a Ju 88 and an He 111; the other two crews were unable to spot the bombers due to thick cloud. Skua L2916 suffered an oil pump failure and Sub Lt P.N. Charlton was obliged to ditch in Ofotfjord, he and his gunner being rescued by a destroyer.

One of the pre-production Do 26V flyingboats of the TransozeanStaffel, incorporated into KGrv6V 108 in May 1940. *(ECPA)*

9–10/5/40

At 0800 on 9 May three 800 Squadron Skuas took off to escort a bombing mission by Swordfish against a bridge at Nordalen and the Hundalen area. The Skuas strafed the ten abandoned Ju 52/3ms on Lake Hartvigvann, which had already been disabled during the attacks in mid-April. One Skua crew became lost and had to make a force-landing, subsequently walking to safety. As soon as the remaining aircraft had landed back aboard, *Ark Royal* withdrew from the area out to sea due to the very adverse weather conditions then prevailing.

Luftwaffe reconnaissance aircraft meantime sought to find just how much of the Home Fleet was at sea, camera-equipped aircraft heading for the base at Scapa Flow. One flight of Hurricanes from 605 Squadron were already in the air on an exercise over Dunnet Head when they were ordered to investigate a suspicious aircraft approaching Wick from the north-west. There was a thick layer of cloud over the locality, and as they patrolled above this, a pair of Hurricanes from 43 Squadron were scrambled to patrol beneath the cloud.

The 43 Squadron aircraft had only just got airborne at 1110, when they heard in their earphones the "Tally-ho!" of the 605 men, who had spotted a Do 17Z of the Wekusta ObdL at their own altitude. Flg Off G.R. Edge attacked this intruder, closing to 50 yards astern, but it then went into cloud. Despite this, Flg Off Austin followed it in; it had obviously been hit, for both Hurricanes were covered in oil. Edge was then able to get in a second attack and the Dornier went down out of control after he had fired 2000 rounds. The aircraft crashed and burst into flames, which leapt 150 feet up into the sky. One warrant officer had managed to bale out, but when a rescue launch reached him he was found to be dead from strangulation by his own parachute lines; the rest of Ofw Alfred Fally's crew were all lost.

Thinking that they would now have no opportunity to engage in combat, the two 43 Squadron pilots, Flt Lt John Simpson, who only two hours before had been promoted to lead 'A' Flight on the posting of Flt Lt Caesar Hull to 263 Squadron, and Sgt Peter Ottewill, headed out to sea in somewhat disgruntled mood. Just before turning back, Simpson suddenly spotted a Dornier flying just below the cloudbase, about 4 miles out to sea. He fired a burst with full deflection, but from too long a range; despite this, he was able to close before the aircraft could disappear into cloud, and with his next burst blew the nose right off. He thought he must have killed the pilot, and watched as the aircraft, burning furiously, crashed into the sea and exploded. Three members of the crew jumped out at about 800 feet, hitting the water almost at once. Despite these reports, only the one loss has been found, and it has to be assumed that both squadrons had attacked the same aircraft at much the same time.

On the other side of the North Sea more action soon followed. At 1550 three Hudsons from 224 Squadron went out to cover Force RZ, a flotilla comprising the cruiser *Birmingham* and seven destroyers (including *Kelly* and *Bulldog*), which was operating in the area. These aircraft reported a number of inconclusive fights with Do 18 flyingboats. More Hudsons, this time from 220 Squadron, followed at 1715, these reporting sighting three destroyers, four minelayers and an MTB. Sgt Sprowston in 'N' then saw a Do 18 on the water and strafed this, leaving it in sinking condition. Plt Off Horden in 'A', while escorting the three destroyers, claimed to have shot down a Do 18 which landed on the sea, the crew getting out onto the sponsons and raising their hands. Flt Lt Sheahan flew low over this aircraft, but was fired on and his Hudson was hit by one cannon shell. Whether all three pilots had actually engaged the same flyingboat is not clear, but seems likely. 15 Do 18s of 2/KüFlGr 406 and 2/KüFlGr 106 had been operating over the area during the afternoon, M2+EK of 2/106 being attacked by a Hudson at 1953, and force-landing after receiving hits. It was subsequently found by the crew of M2+HK, who landed their aircraft alongside. M2+EK was sunk, and the crew taken off safely. It seems probable that this was the aircraft first attacked by Horden and then by Sprowston. Later in the afternoon K6+FK of 3/406 was attacked inconclusively by one Hudson, and then by another half an hour later, this latter assailant attempting to bomb the 'boat.

During the day a newly-formed Fleet Air Arm squadron, 806, arrived at Hatston equipped with Skuas. At once, at 1610 eight of these aircraft took off, escorted by six Blenheim IVFs of 254 Squadron to resume the attacks on Bergen that had ceased when the other Skuas had gone aboard the aircraft carriers. The Skuas went in first and dropped 500lb bombs, claiming three hits on the training ship *Bremse*. The Blenheims then followed, each dropping eight 20lb bombs. L9482 (Flt Lt A.C. Heath) was seen to go into a spin and crashed into the harbour, the aircraft having been hit by Flak. Nevertheless it was considered that much damage had been caused by this attack, and two transports were thought to have been sunk. In fact they had sunk the patrol boat *Jungingen*, three of the crew being killed and eight wounded. One Skua crashed while landing back at Hatston. The last sorties over the area were undertaken by five

Beauforts of 22 Squadron, which left to lay mines at 1940. Four were forced to turn back by bad weather, but the fifth, L4453 (Flt Lt C.M. Lester) was lost when it crashed into the North Sea.

On 9 May 804 Squadron left *Glorious* to allow more Skuas and some Swordfish to be taken on board. Three slightly damaged Sea Gladiators were then flown to Campbelltown but the other six landed on *Furious* to become that carrier's fighter complement. *Glorious* then sailed to Greenock to take on board the Hurricanes of 46 Squadron. On 10 May these aircraft were taxied through fields to Blackburn's wharf at Abbotsinch, where they were hoisted onto lighters and sailed 20 miles down the Clyde to where the carrier was moored. Eight were transported in this manner during the day, ten more following next day. 17 pilots accompanied the aircraft, while the groundcrews had gone aboard the MV *Batory* for transport to Norway.

Hurricane of 46 Squadron about to be hoisted aboard HMS *Glorious* on the Clyde on 10 May. *(Via A. Thomas)*

11/5/40

The 263 Squadron advanced ground party reached Harstad on 11 May, moving from here to Bardufoss. The rest of the squadron followed on the *Sobiesti*, while on 12 May the 18 Gladiators were flown onto *Furious* by 804 Squadron pilots. The Squadron's own pilots — much the same men as before, but joined now by Flt Lt C.B. Hull from 43 Squadron, Flt Lt A. Williams (ex 222 Squadron), Plt Off J.L. Wilkie (ex 266 Squadron) — Flg Off H.T. Grant-Ede (ex 111 Squadron) and Plt Off J. Falkson (ex 152 Squadron), went aboard the carrier. Flg Off W. Riley (ex 610 Squadron) and Plt Off Parnall were under orders to join the unit in Norway.

14/5/40

Glorious and *Furious* sailed at 2030 on 14 May with an escort of four destroyers. En route one of the original 263 Squadron pilots, Plt Off Wyatt-Smith, suffered considerably from shrapnel wounds in his legs, which he had received during the evacuation from Aandalsnes in *Delius*, and his place was taken by a FAA volunteer from 802 Squadron, Lt Anthony Lydekker.

Even as the carriers began taking aboard these reinforcements came news of the most momentous events of the war — the unleashing of the German 'Blitzkrieg' against France and the Low Countries. In an instant the whole balance of the war had swung southwards. No longer was Norway the most active theatre of hostilities; overnight it had become a mere sideshow, and quickly it was realised that no further reinforcement was likely to be forthcoming — for either side. Certainly it put an end to any further operations over Southern Norway by Bomber Command for the time being, all efforts of that force now being directed over the main conflict and beyond.

The revised and reduced forces available to Luftflotte 5 for continued operations over Narvik and for the defence of the Norwegian coastal areas, Oslo and of Denmark were now disposed as set below.

LUFTWAFFE ORDER OF BATTLE FOR OPERATIONS OVER SCANDINAVIA, 10 MAY 1940

Unit	Base	Commander	Aircraft on Strength	Service-able	Type
LUFTFLOTTE 5	Oslo	Gen der Flg Hans-Jürgen Stumpff			
Fliegerführer Stavanger	Stavanger	Maj i G Martin Harlinghausen			
3(F)/ObdL	Stavanger-Sola	Oblt Werner Rosenberger	8	7	He 111P
			12	10	Do 215B
1(F)/122	Stavanger-Sola	Hpt Edgar Caesar	6	4	He 111H
			6	4	Ju 88A
1 & 3/ZG 76	Stavanger-Sola	Hpt Werner Restemeyer	25	16	Bf 110C
4/JG 77	Stavanger-Sola	Oblt Helmut Henz	12	8	Bf 109E
1/KüFlGr 506	Stavanger-Sola	Hpt von Schrötter	8	3	He 115B
Fliegerführer Trondheim	Trondheim	Oberst Robert Fuchs			
1(F)/120	Trondheim-Vaernes	Maj Günther Schub	5	3	Do 17P
			3	0	He 111H
Kampfgeschwader 26		Oberst Robert Fuchs			
Stabsstaffel	Trondheim-Vaernes		6	5	He 111H
I/KG 26	Trondheim-Vaernes	Maj Gerhard Schaeper	36	27	He 111H
III/KG 26	Trondheim-Vaernes	Hpt Victor von Lossberg	33	26	He 111H
KGr 100	Trondheim-Vaernes	Hpt Artur von Casimir	27	13	He 111H
I/StG 1	Trondheim-Vaernes	Hpt Paul-Werner Hozzel	39	27	Ju 87R

LUFTWAFFE ORDER OF BATTLE FOR OPERATIONS OVER SCANDINAVIA, 10 MAY 1940 (Continued)

Unit	Base	Commander	Aircraft on Strength	Service-able	Type
Z-Staffel/KG 30	Trondheim-Vaernes	Oblt Herbert Bönsch	15	5	Ju 88C
11(N)/JG 2	Trondheim-Vaernes	Oblt Bär	11	6	Bf 109D
Küstenfliegergruppe 506	Trondheim--See	Maj Minner			
1/KüFlGr 506	Trondheim-See	Oblt Peukert (temporarily)	8	3	He 115C
2/KüFlGr 506	Trondheim-See	Hpt von Zetschwitz	9	4	He 115C
X Fliegerkorps	Oslo	GenLt Hans Geissler			
Korpsführungskette	Aalborg-West		1	1	He 111H
Korpstransportstaffel	Aalborg-West		1	0	Ju 52/3m
Wetterkette X	Oslo-Fornebu		3	3	He 111H
2(H)/10	Oslo-Fornebu	Hpt Jäger	9	8	Hs 126B
II/KG 26	Aalborg-West	Hpt Martin Vetter	36	7	He 111H
I/KG 40	Copenhagen	Hpt Edgar Petersen	4	2	Fw 200C
2/ZG 76	Aalborg-West	Oblt Gustav Uellenbeck	11	7	Bf 110C
5 & 6/JG 77	Kristiansand-Kjevik	Hpt Karl Hentschel	28	20	Bf 109E
KGrzbV 107	Aalborg and Oslo-Fornebu		48	35	Ju 52/3m
KGrzbV 108	Hörnum,		5	4	Ju 52/See
	Aalborg		11	8	Ju 52/3m
	and	Hpt Förster	13	8	He 59D
	Bergen		4	2	Do 26V
			2	1	Do 24
			2	1	Bv 138A

10/5/40

For the time being however, operations continued much as before. Early on 10 May two Hudsons from 233 Squadron and three from 220 Squadron again operated over Force RZ. Both squadrons reported engagements with Do 18s, and it seems that these were again one and the same combat. Plt Off Culver in 'X' and Plt Off Horden in 'A' of 220 Squadron reported seeing flames and smoke coming from the engines of their opponent, while the two crews of 233 Squadron reported that the flyingboat which they had attacked escaped trailing white vapour and brown smoke from its engines. It seems that their opponent was Do 18 K6+CH of 1/KüFlGr 406, which crash-landed in the sea 140 miles south-west of Egersund at 0700 following a fight with Hudsons. When a British warship appeared, the crew sunk their aircraft; three were picked up, one of whom died on board from his wounds, but of Oblt zur See Wüsthoff, the pilot, there was no sign. At the conclusion of these sorties 220 Squadron moved to Bircham Newton to take part in operations over the northern sector of the English Channel area.

Early in the afternoon of 10th three Skuas from 801 Squadron on a patrol over the fleet, chased an He 115 over Harstad, losing the aircraft in cloud. An hour later they were relieved by three 803 Squadron aircraft, and these chased an He 111 into clouds. During the day Narvik was heavily bombed by 23 He 111s from I and III/KG 26, escorted by Z/KG 30. One Zerstörer Ju 88C of the latter unit suffered engine failure on return and force-landed in the Mo area where Uffz Alfred Weimann and his crew were captured, subsequently being shipped to the UK.

11/5/40

Early next day three 254 Squadron Blenheim fighters, each carrying eight 25lb incendiary bombs, and six 806 Squadron Skuas, again raided Bergen. Cloud covered the target, but the Skuas managed to dive-bomb seven oil tanks at Florvaag on the island of Strusshamn from 8000 feet, claiming to have set two of these on fire. The Blenheims then added their incendiaries to the conflagration, and strafed the area generally. In fact all seven tanks were destroyed, burning for nearly a week. It proved impossible to extinguish the blaze and 19,000 litres of oil and petrol were lost.

During the afternoon an He 111J from 3/KüFlGr 806 discovered Force RZ, and at once eight more aircraft from this unit took off to attack. M7+AK was slightly damaged by AA fire, while M7+BK (Lt zur See Heinz Brücker) was attacked by an escorting Hudson of 224 Squadron. The British crew claimed hits on one of two Heinkels seen, but observed no results. The damage was critical however, and the aircraft — from the Gruppe's 2 Staffel — went into the sea, from where the crew were subsequently rescued by a British destroyer.

Over Northern Norway German positions at Vassdalsfjellet and on Hill 697, both near Lake Hartvigvann, were bombed by Norwegian Army C-Vs and Navy He 115s during the night of 11/12 May, while I/Flakregt 32 at Narvik claimed a Skua shot down, although no loss is recorded.

Air reinforcement was continuing for the German forces at Narvik, two Do 24s having landed in Rombaks and Beisfjords on 10th, bringing an officer and 30 men of 3/GJR 138, while on 11th seven Ju 52/See floatplanes brought in Oblt Rudolf and 66 more men of this unit to Hemnes Island in Ranafjord. One of these aircraft damaged a float on landing, and sank as a result. On 12th two Do 26Vs set off, but only one reached Beisfjord with Hpt Schreiner and 13 more GJR 138 troops, and a 200 Watt transmitter. During 11th however, a Do 17P of 1(F)/120 reconnoitred for a suitable landing zone for paratroops to be dropped to the east of Narvik, and on 14th such troops jumped from six KGrzbV 108 Ju 52/3ms, escorted by three Ju 88Cs of Z/KG 30. Lt Becker and 65 men of I/FJR 1 landed without opposition, weapons and supplies being dropped by an accompanying Fw 200B.

12/5/40

Before this occurred, *Ark Royal's* Skuas had been operating again on 12 May,

Mooring a Do 26V of KGrzbV 108. *(ECPA)*

when three 800 Squadron aircraft on patrol from 0405 in poor weather conditions, chased an He 111 and a Do 17. No claims were made but an He 111 of 1(F)/122, flown by the Staffelkapitän, Hpt Edgar Caesar, on a dawn reconnaissance flew into a mountain; the crew were later found dead by German troops. Further south Bergen was again visited by three Blenheim fighters and six Skuas from Hatston, merchant ships being the target on this occasion, although no hits were registered. While no engagement was recorded by the British, I/ZG 76 noted that a Bf 110 flown by Uffz Herbert Jacobi, intercepted Blenheims over Bergen, where it was surprised by one such aircraft and was badly hit; it crash-landed on Sola airfield with the radio operator wounded.

On the other side of the Skagerrak a Hudson from 206 Squadron (N7353) flown by Plt Off I.C. Gray, failed to return from a reconnaissance of the German North Sea coast, on which it had departed at 0445. It had been intercpted by Bf 109Es of II(J)/TrGr 186 and shot down into the sea north of Borkum by Oblt Peter Emmerich. Force RZ was again attacked by He 111Js from KüFlGr 806 without success, and one of the Heinkels fought a patrolling Hudson, though this time inconclusively. Eight more He 111Hs from II/KG 26 later repeated the attack.

14/5/40
In the early hours of 14 May British and French troops began an opposed landing near Narvik, soon linking with Norwegian and Polish forces approaching from the north. The assault was supported by Skuas from *Ark Royal*. Six He 59s of KGrzbV 108 on a supply flight to Hennesøy in the Bodø area, lost one of their number (flown by Uffz Richard Hesse) to ground fire, which caused him to ditch north of Trondheim; one member of the crew survived and returned later.

An early reconnaissance had brought sightings of British warships in Ofotfjord, Vestfjord, and off Harstad, and 23 He 111s had been despatched by KG 26 to attack. All that could be found however, was a Norwegian fishing vessel, *Folden*, north-west of Harstad, and this was hit, later being abandoned. The bombers at Trondheim were reinforced during the day by the arrival of 12 Ju 88A-1s of 6/KG 30, now returned to Norway.

Ju 52/3m D9+RC of KGrzbV 102 at Lake Hartvigvann, sinks through the ice as the thaw gets underway, after being stranded on the lake for a month.

Later in the day the Skuas began a new series of attacks on Lake Hartvigvann, three 801 Squadron aircraft taking off at 1100 to strafe the derelict Ju 52/3ms here. An hour and a half later three bomb-carrying 803 Squadron aircraft headed for the same area to break up the ice on the lake by dive-bombing. Having completed this task, they then saw several He 111s of KG 26 at 17,000 feet and chased these for some time. Lt W.P. Lucy in 8F, L2925, and Lt T.E. Gray in 8S, L2918, inflicted damage on one and then chased another down to low level, seeing their fire hitting this too; an aircraft of the Stabskette II/KG 26 was hit and later crash-landed at Vaernes, its hydraulics shot up, suffering 30% damage. As the Skuas attacked the second bomber, Lucy's aircraft became the target for cross fire from this and another Heinkel, and suddenly it exploded at only 60 feet above the sea off Tranöy. Gray at once flew off to seek aid, leading HMS *Whirlwind* to the area. Here Lucy's body was found, but of his observer, Lt M.C.E. Hanson, DSC, there was no trace. Now out of fuel, Gray force-landed at Andøya. Lucy was a sad loss — the most successful of the Skua pilots to date, he had been credited with taking part in the shooting down of at least six Luftwaffe bombers; he had of course, also led the successful strike which sank *Königsberg*, for which he had been awarded the DSO.

Two more 803 Squadron Skuas returned to Lake Hartvigvann at 1535, again bombing the ice which was now reported to be melting. Seven more II/KG 26 He 111s had also arrived over the Harstad and Narvik area to attack shipping at this time, and two of these were encountered by Lt L.A. Harris, RM, and Pty Off Johnson, who identified them as an He 111 and a Ju 88. Harris claimed damage to the latter, the undercarriage of which dropped down, while Johnson fired at the former, although his own aircraft was hit. He was wounded in the shoulder and his gunner received some splinters in his face. Two 5 Staffel Heinkels were indeed hit, one suffering 30% damage while the other was left in more serious condition, Fw Karl Grube force-landing it near Fauske after his crew had baled out. They were captured by Norwegian troops and shipped to the UK.

15/5/40

Bad weather on 15th prevented much action, although a few bombing attacks were undertaken by *Ark Royal*'s air group, which now mustered 12 serviceable Swordfish and 18 Skuas. Nine 806 Squadron Skuas and three Blenheims from Hatston failed to get to Bergen; during the day 254 Squadron moved from Hatston back to Sumburgh. The Luftwaffe was out during the morning; very early, six He 111s from I/KG 26 attacked the destroyer *Wolverine* and the troop transport *Chrobry* (a converted Polish passenger vessel), which had brought over part of the RAF contingent to Harstad. The latter was hit and sunk with the loss of important cargo, including three tanks of the 3rd Hussars; Lt Col Faulkner, commanding officer of the 1st Battalion Irish Guards, was also lost with five of his Staff officers. Some two hours later another Heinkel from this unit damaged the destroyer *Somali*, which had to retire to Scapa Flow for repairs. Somewhat later six III/KG 26 Heinkels attacked shipping in the Narvik area, but one was obliged to force-land on Alsten Island due to engine failure, and was destroyed. Lt Willi Meier's crew had sent off an SOS, and a rescue He 59N (D-AKUK) was sent off by Seenotstaffel 2, flown by Oblt Wilhelm Brange. This failed to return, and was later found off Sandnesjoen, 50% damaged; the crew had been captured and sent to Britain.

KGrzbV 108 Ju 52/3m transports prepare to fly paratroops up to Narvik in early May. *(Bib für Zeit)*

During the day three KGrzbV 108 Ju 52/3ms, escorted by three Ju 88Cs, dropped a further 22 paratroops from I/FJR 1 over Björnfjell. In the morning six Swordfish of 810 Squadron had attacked the Nordalen bridge again, and Björnfjell railway station where the Marine Abt, an infantry unit formed from destroyer crews left in Narvik after their vessels had been sunk, suffered two dead and eight wounded in the raid.

Further south an Hs 126B-1 of 2(H)/10 on a reconnaissance over the Mo area, was engaged by British Bofors gunners of 166 Light AA Battery, and was badly damaged. The crew baled out and Fw Fritz Mahn, the pilot, was captured and shipped to the UK. Lt Manfred von Redecker, the observer, had been wounded, and was later to be liberated by German forces.

16/5/40

Improved conditions on 16 May saw a more active day in the air as *Ark Royal's* tireless Skua crews were up again maintaining their regular patrols. At 0710 eight He 111s of KGr 100, followed at 0910 by 11 more from II/KG 26, were escorted to the Narvik area by two Bf 110s of I/ZG 76, flown by Hpt Restemeyer and Lt Lent, and two Ju 88Cs of Z/KG 30. The Messerschmitt pilots reported an inconclusive fight with four Skuas, whilst Oblt Bönsch of Z/KG 30 claimed an aircraft which he identified as a 'Blackburn Roc' to the south-east of Narvik at 1300. It seems that they had been engaged with two 803 Squadron Skuas, which had taken off at 1150 and had spotted two aircraft near Narvik which the crews identified as Do 17s (probably the two Bf 110s). These were bounced by the Skuas, which were in turn attacked by two more German aircraft, identified as being apparently of the same type, but almost certainly the two Ju 88Cs. Against these the Skua pilots found themselves quite outclassed, and in the dogfight which followed Lt Harris was forced down in Rombaksfjord, from where he and his gunner were rescued by HMS *Matabele*. The other Skua pilot, Pty Off Glover tried to draw the aggressive twin-engined machines over the British warships, where it was thought that one had been hit by both the ships' pom-poms and fire from Glover's gunner, and had been shot down. The action lasted a full 30 minutes.

Very active over Northern Norway during May and June were the He 111Hs of KGr 100, three of which are seen here at Trondheim/Vaernes. *(Bundesarchiv)*

As the Germans withdrew, the crew of one of the Heinkels spotted the aircraft carrier, a battleship and two heavy cruisers, and at once all available bombers were sent off to attack, the force despatched comprising 18 He 111s of I, II and III/KG 26 and eight Ju 88s from 6/KG 30. Three more 803 Squadron Skuas were off at 1330, and at 1415 reported engaging six Ju 88s over Ofotfjord. A tremendous dogfight followed, during which the German aircraft dived, steep-climbed, turned, and in one case spun at 1000 feet. Sub Lt R.A. Eaton in 8B, L3010, claimed one Ju 88 which he saw crash into Ofotfjord, while Mdspmn A.S. Griffiths in 8C, L2961, claimed a second which he reported crashed on a mountainside south of the fjord. 6/KG 30 did indeed lose two aircraft to fighters, Hpt Günther Noll's aircraft crashing in Narvik Bay, while Lt Heinrich Diemeyer force-landed south of Ofotfjord. An He 111 of II/KG 26 was also lost in combat, ditching in Bogen Bay. Of the 12 crew involved, two were killed, one reported missing, four were captured and five returned.

To complicate matters however, three 800 Squadron Skuas began a patrol at 1650, and these also claimed a Ju 88 shot down. After attacking an He 111 which escaped them, the trio became split up and two returned to Harstad where they saw a single bomber identified as a Ju 88. Both attacked and Mdspmn(A) R.W. Kearsley forced it down in a crash-landing on the surface of Bogenfjord, the crew of five being seen to swim ashore. From the location, it seems clear that this aircraft was actually Diemeyer's Heinkel. The British pair then claimed damage to another He 111 before returning to the carrier, where they discovered that the missing member of their formation had also inflicted damage on a Heinkel before it escaped him.

During the afternoon six more of Z/KG 30's Ju 88Cs had taken off to escort eight of KGrzbV 108's Ju 52/3ms to drop an officer and 75 men of I/FJR 1 over Björnfell. The escort spotted Allied troops being landed in Herjangsfjord, and several fishing vessels here as well, and dived to attack. These aircraft may have become involved with the 800 Squadron Skuas, and it seems that during this action Uffz Lauffs claimed one or two victories (identified either as a Roc and a Skua *or* as a Roc or a Skua). Unfortunately the time of this claim was not recorded, and it remains possible that he had in fact been Bönsch's wingman during the earlier engagement.

KGrzbV 108 lost one aircraft on this date when Bf 138A-0, NG+UD, crashed while attempting to force-land between Hemnes and Mo. One member of Uffz Helmut Schuster's crew was killed and two were captured, one by the Norwegians; the latter was subsequently released after the close of hostilities.

Further down the coast nine Skuas from Hatston had again bombed Bergen during the midday period, claiming six oil tanks bombed and destroyed. That night six Hudsons drawn equally from 224 and 269 Squadrons bombed Stavanger/Sola airfield — the first raid here in some days.

Bv 138A of KGrzbV 108. *(F. Selinger)*

322

An early reconnaissance over the Narvik area by one of 1/KG 40's long-ranging Fw 200s found several warships in Ofotfjord, Vaagsfjord and Harstad. Further south the crew released their bombs on the Norwegian steamer *Torgtind*, which sank in Aldrasundet, Helgeland. A radioed message then brought a rolling attack on the vessels that had been spotted, by five Ju 88s from 6/KG 30 and 18 He 111s of KG 26, most of the bombers operating in pairs. During the sub-Arctic dawn three 800 Squadron Skuas from *Ark Royal* again intercepted an He 111 which was believed to have been damaged; this may have been one of the KG 26 aircraft, the unit reporting that one crewman of 3 Staffel was wounded whilst operating over Narvik during the day.

This particular combat brought to a close the period during which the carrier had single-handed provided the bulk of air support over the Narvik operations. Since 4 May three Ju 88s, an He 111, a Do 17 and a Do 26 were believed to have been shot down, while six He 111s and three Ju 88s were considered to have suffered damage. In the same period nine Skuas had been lost to all causes, one of which had crashed on the deck while landing. Amongst the crews, three men had been wounded, but only Lucy and Hanson had lost their lives.

As the carrier departed for Tromsø to refuel, *Glorious* and *Furious* arrived, carrying the two RAF fighter squadrons as well as their own Sea Gladiators, nine Swordfish of 816 Squadron and six more Walrus amphibians for 701 Squadron. They joined the Home Fleet west of the Lofoten Islands. Initially however the airfields ashore were not quite ready to receive the RAF aircraft, and for the time being these stayed aboard. The ground parties were also now arriving, that of 46 Squadron reaching Harstad on 17th and moving on to Skaanland next day, while 263 Squadron's contingent together with seven reserve pilots, disembarked from *Sobiesti* on 17th, moving on to Bardufoss three days later. On 18th, whilst on an anti-submarine patrol around the fleet, one of 816 Squadron's Swordfish crashed into the sea, Sub Lt H.D. Mourilyon and N/A1 R. Parkinson being lost.

At Bardufoss the RAF men found the remaining Norwegian Army Air Service elements operating with their last three or four Fokker C-Vs. The clearance of

Still operating around Narvik in May were a few Fokker C-VDs of the Hålogaland Air Corps, 325 being one of them. *(via B. Olsen)*

snow from Bardufoss for the British, and the thaw generally had led to these aircraft having their skis replaced by wheels. These were in short supply however, and two C-Vs had to be fitted with car wheels instead. All non-serviceable Fokkers had now been cannibalized, useable parts being employed for maintenance and repair, which was undertaken at Alapmoen. At this latter base the remaining Tiger Moths were still being used for training.

From Scotland and the Orkneys operations over Southern Norway continued on a limited scale. A morning reconnaissance by Coastal Command discovered a German convoy off Egersund on 17th, and at once nine Hudsons were despatched by 269 Squadron to attack, but no hits were gained. One Hudson encountered one of three He 111Js of 3/KüFlGr 806 which were on escort duty, but this made off when the British aircraft attempted to close. During the day three of 254 Squadron's Blenheim IVFs flew over to reconnoitre the coast from Nordfjord southwards; near Bergen a Bf 110 — one of a Rotte from I/ZG 76 — appeared and attacked 'D', which could not retaliate due to the Messerschmitt's greater speed. After its initial pass, the Zerstörer got onto the tail of Blenheim 'C', and the pilot of 'D' took the opportunity to dive away to a height of 300 feet, to continue the reconnaissance. 'C' was now in some trouble, unable to shake off the attacker, but at this point Sgt F.D. Mottram in 'G' saw his chance. Dropping height, he then climbed steeply to come up underneath the Messerschmitt and put a good burst into its underside as it passed overhead. At once it went straight into a steep dive and appeared to crash into the side of a mountain. No smoke or fire was seen, and it was presumed that Mottram's burst had hit the pilot, but no definite confirmation of such a loss is available.

Elsewhere, over the Baltic the Küstenflieger lost several aircraft during the day. One Ar 196 of 5/Bfl 196 (6W+RN) spun out of a steep turn whilst returning from a sortie, and crashed into the sea east of Niddingen with the loss of the crew. A second aircraft from the same unit was damaged by gunfire from a German patrol boat, and force-landed at Läesö-Rinne with one man wounded. More unusual, an unidentified type reportedly on anti-submarine patrol, carrying the civilian registration G-AR00, was attacked and shot down during the afternoon by Swedish fighters, force-landing in the sea.

That night six Swordfish from a new land-based Fleet Air Arm squadron, 823, which had just arrived at Hatston, carried out the unit's first airborne minelaying operation in the Haugesund area.

18/5/40

18 May proved to be a somewhat quieter day. One of a pair of reconnaissance He 111s from 1(F)/122 engaged a Walrus which had been launched from the catapult on HMS *Devonshire* over Malangen, and shot it down. This aircraft, P5647, fell into the fjord, Lt R.W. Benson-Dare and one member of his crew being killed, although the observer survived. The reconnaissance crews reported sighting British warships again, and once more three Ju 88s from 6/ KG 30 and eight He 111s of II/KG 26 were sent out to attack. No hits were seen, but in fact one bomb had struck the battleship *Resolution* and penetrated three decks without exploding. The vessel at once left for Scapa Flow for repairs. One of the reconnaissance Heinkels also attacked the Norwegian coastal steamer *Sirius* in Solberfjord, off Senja, the vessel being sunk with the loss of seven of the crew.

At noon two Blohm und Voss Bv 138A-1 flyingboats, serving with KGrzbV

108, left Trondheim to carry 15 troops of 2/GJR 138 to Beisfjord. They were spotted by British troops as they landed, and were subsequently strafed by four Skuas of 800 Squadron from *Ark Royal*, both being so badly damaged that they had to be abandoned. Four Ju 52/3ms from the same German unit dropped a further 16 paratroops of I/FJR 1, with stores and weapons.

19/5/40
Next morning at 0210 three 254 Squadron Blenheims were off to have a look at Vaernes airfield. Here at 0450 they counted some 200 aircraft on the ground, identified as 50 Bf 109s and 150 Ju 88s; several of the Messerschmitts were strafed. Further south three Hudsons of 206 Squadron reconnoitred the Heligoland area. 55 miles north-west of Heligoland itself, one was intercepted and shot down by Oblt Wulf of 6(J)/TrGr 186.

Following the report of the 254 Squadron crews, a larger raid on Vaernes was laid on for the short period of darkness, one Blenheim taking off at 2040 to lead five Hudsons from 233 Squadron and two from 224 Squadron to bomb the airfield. The Blenheim crew released a parachute flare overhead at exactly midnight, the Hudsons following close behind in line astern, each dropping three 250lb bombs and a number of incendiaries from 8000 feet. Several large fires were seen, but one Hudson was damaged by Flak. The attack had been quite ineffective however, only three bombs hitting the airfield where a single He 111 suffered slight splinter damage.

20/5/40
Next day an He 111 of 1(F)/122 again appeared over Narvik, but only just escaped interception by three fighters — believed to have been Sea Gladiators — by diving into cloud. The crew reported two transport vessels in Beisfjord, and later reconnaissances also noted other shipping here, so 14 Heinkels from KG 26 and KGr 100, and six KG 30 Ju 88s were sent off, escorted this time by eight Bf 110s of I/ZG 76 and four Ju 88Cs of Z/KG 30. Heinkels of III/KG 26 bombed the freighter *Pembroke Coast* in Harstad harbour and the vessel, carrying petrol, provisions and military supplies, was set on fire; she had to be sunk by British warships next day, after her crew had been taken off safely. A second ship, the Norwegian freighter *Deneb*, was also set ablaze, and two of her crew were killed. As she was also carrying petrol, she was towed out to sea by a destroyer and sunk with gunfire. One of 701 Squadron's Walrus amphibians was sunk at its moorings.

Despite heavy fire, two Do 26Vs landed in Rombaksfjord, bringing in 16 men of 3/GJR 138, a 37mm gun and Hpt Kless, the Flieger-Verbindungs Offizier (Luftwaffe Liaison Officer) for Kampfgruppe Dietl. Three Ju 52/3ms dropped weapons and supplies over Narvik, escorted by three Bf 110s and a lone Ju 88C. On the return flight the latter suffered engine failure and force-landed north of Namsos, two of the crew being captured, while the gunner escaped and reached German lines.

21/5/40
At last on 21 May Bardufoss was ready to receive 263 Squadron, but Skaanland was still not fit, and would not now be so until 26th at the earliest. *Glorious* therefore returned to Scapa Flow with the Hurricanes still aboard. Meanwhile two sections of Gladiators, each led by a Swordfish, took off from *Furious* in

bad weather. At this stage driving sleet prevented the take off of any further aircraft, and indeed one section successfully landed back on board again. The other pair set off behind their guiding Swordfish, but overcast and mist now extended down to the water in Torskenfjord, and all three aircraft flew into the mountain at Torsken. Flt Lt Mills in N5693 was injured, but Plt Off W.P. Richards in N5697 was killed. Later in the day conditions improved and all the remaining Gladiators got off in sections over the next two days, landing at Bardufoss under an 'umbrella' provided by trios of Skuas from 800 and 803 Squadrons, operating from the newly-returned *Ark Royal*.

This improvement also permitted eight II/KG 26 He 111s, escorted by four Bf 110s, to search for shipping around Harstad and Narvik. One crew found and sank the British anti-submarine trawler *Cape Passero* in Bogen Bay, four of the vessel's crew being lost.

Already on 21st however the decision had been taken that the defence of France and England was obviously the paramount consideration, and in the light of the disastrous situation in France, Norway would have to be abandoned. Firstly, the capture of Narvik should be completed and the port facilities demolished, but immediately thereafter withdrawal would take place.

22/5/40

Gladiators undertook more than 30 sorties on 22 May — more than had been accomplished in the whole of the first expedition — but only three raiders were seen, and actions against these were generally inconclusive. Finally eight He 111s of II/KG 26, which had set out on an armed reconnaissance at 1025, escorted by two Bf 110s, appeared and sank the anti-submarine trawler HMS *Melbourne* in Gratangsbotn. Plt Off M.A. Craig-Adams in N5698 attacked a 5 Staffel aircraft flown by Fw Karl-Heinz Hess, east of Salangen; those on the ground heard machine gun fire, and then both aircraft crashed, all four members of the German crew baling out. Craig-Adams was found still strapped in his cockpit, dead, only a few yards from the wreckage of the Heinkel in the mountains. It was presumed that he had collided with, or deliberately rammed the bomber; however Luftwaffe records noted a claim for one British fighter shot down in combat, so he may well have been hit by fire from an accompanying bomber. While two members of the Heinkel's crew were captured, two escaped, reporting that their aircraft had been hit by AA just before the Gladiator arrived on the scene; a second bomber crashed on return to Vaernes, 45% damaged.

Three He 59s of 1/KüFlGr 706 flew up to Mo during the day, refuelled, then flew inland to the Swedish frontier, before turning west and approaching Rombaksfjord from the east. Here they took off again five minutes later, one aircraft suffering engine failure and force-landing. The crew scuttled the aircraft, and were then picked up by the other two Heinkels, which had landed again alongside. During raids on Fauske, Bodø and Harstad by II/KG 26, the coastal steamer *Bjarkøy* was sunk in Gratangsbotn with the loss of some French soldiers who were aboard.

23/5/40

By the next day (23rd) 263 Squadron had 14 Gladiators serviceable. During the afternoon Sgt B.E.P. Whall attacked an aircraft which he identified as a Do 17, and engaged in a 25 mile chase. He claimed that he was eventually able to shoot it down, and it was believed to have crashed west of Harstad at 1645. Whall then had to bale out as his aircraft (N5719) had exhausted all its fuel during the combat. No confirmation of this particular engagement has been discovered, and the identity of Whall's opponent remains unknown; certainly no German aircraft were lost on this date. Due to the Gladiator's limited firepower it was now decided that in future not less than two would operate at any one time, although this resulted in the overall number of patrols being reduced. German aircraft had appeared over the area in strength during the day, following the usual reconnaissance by a 1(F)/122 Heinkel and a 1/KG 40 Fw 200. Two battle-ships, four cruisers, seven destroyers and 16 transports had been identified in the Tromsø-Harstad-Ofotfjord-Skaanland area, and all available bombers were sent out, including eight He 111s from KGr 100, six from I/KG 26, and three Ju 88s from 6/KG 30; none reported any combat.

Seven Ju 52/3ms escorted by Bf 110s and Ju 88Cs dropped Oblt Schwaiger and 65 men of 1/GJR 137 near Narvik during the day. These troops had under-taken a ten day concentrated course in parachuting, and managed to get down with only two men slightly injured.

24/5/40
Next day around midday five more Ju 52/3ms of KGrzbV 108 carrying 55 more members of 2/GJR 137 arrived over Bjornfjell from Trondheim, escorting Bf 110s of I/ZG 76 breaking away to undertake a 'Frei Jagd' against ground targets. Approaching Bardufoss, they were fired on by anti-aircraft guns and broke away, circling nearby. Flg Off Grant-Ede was scrambled in one of the Gladiators, and attacked one, but this broke off and dived away. He then attacked the second but his wing guns failed, and he dived for base as the other three Messerschmitts also broke off and departed. Grant-Ede was given credit for a Messerschmitt damaged, but Lt Loobes of 3/ZG 76 must have thought he had shot the Gladiator down when it dived away for safety, for he claimed the fighter destroyed at 1310. It is possible that Grant-Ede's fire had indeed been effective, for one Bf 110 of 3 Staffel force-landed on a small frozen lake near Thysfjord with one engine shot up in combat, and was destroyed. The crew were later rescued by German troops. It is alternatively possible however that this may have been the aircraft reportedly attacked by Sgt Whall on the previous day — for identification of a Bf 110 as a Do 17 was a frequently-repeated error — although the times appear not to tally.

Prior to this action, the usual early morning reconnaissance by 1(F)/122 had brought eight He 111s of KGr 100 on a fruitless anti-shipping operation, during which one of the bombers was hit by AA fire, carrying out a force-landing near Mo. During the afternoon an He 111 of Stabsstaffel/KG 26 and four more from I Gruppe operated over Narvik, the former aircraft straying over Bardufoss where it was intercepted at an altitude of 500 feet by Flg Off Grant-Ede and Flg Off Riley. Ede attacked first from the beam, then half-rolled into a stern attack and silenced the upper gunner. Riley followed with a stern quarter attack which put the starboard engine out of action. At that moment Flt Lt Caesar Hull arrived, at the end of his own patrol, and got in a burst which stopped the other engine. The aircraft then force-landed near Storholmen, Oblt Paul Hartmut's crew being captured; two were later shipped to Britain, while two, captured by the Norwegians, would subsequently be released. During this fight

Gladiator II of 263 Squadron at Bardufoss. *(RAF Museum)*

Grant-Ede's Gladiator was slightly damaged by return fire.

While Ju 87s of I/StG 1 sank a Norwegian armed trawler, *Ingrid*, in Bodø harbour during the day, other air attacks at Rognan sent down the coastal steamer *Skjerstad* as she was evacuating British troops.

Around midday a Do 26V landed in Rombaksfjord bringing in special munitions and eight men of 6/GJR 138. Shortly after midnight two more of these flyingboats would land to deliver Lt May and 14 further men from this unit.

On 23rd, 2/Lt Lian and ten men of the Norwegian Army Air Force had reached Lake Hartvigvann from Bardufoss to see if any of the damaged Ju 52/3ms could be made flyable. By the application of much hard work three had been sufficiently repaired by the evening of 24 May, but at that point an attack was made on the lake by British fighters, reportedly from Bardufoss, and the three repaired aircraft were all destroyed, the Norwegian officer also being wounded. No record of such a strafe can be found in the annals of 263 Squadron, but it is possible that the unit might have been too embarrassed by such a mistake to record it. The attackers may however have been Hurricanes, eight of which had arrived at Bardufoss half an hour earlier.

The carriers had by now reached Scapa Flow on their return from Norway, and here on 23rd the Sea Gladiators of 804 Squadron from *Furious* went ashore to provide the air defence of the Orkneys once more, flying in to Hatston again. From this base the Skuas of 806 Squadron, their raids on Bergen having been accomplished without a single loss, returned south to Worthy Down next day. The other squadron at Hatston, the Swordfish-equipped 823 Squadron, now went aboard *Glorious*, which during 24th sailed again for Norway slipping out of harbour under the cover of a thick fog.

25/5/40

The RAF Gladiator pilots were now really beginning to get into their stride, and to make up for their disastrous first sojourn in Norway. New opponents were encountered on 25 May, the first when Flg Off Grant-Ede was returning from an early patrol in N5705 at 0900 on this morning. He became separated from his wingman and spotted a four-engined aircraft which he identified as a Ju 90 flying at 15,000 feet ten miles to the north of Harstad. This was in fact an Fw 200 of 1/KG 40 on reconnaissance. He fired two short bursts at long range, and to his surprise the aircraft went down at once and crash-landed in the sea near Dyrøy Island. The pilot, Oblt Schöpke, and one or two other members of the crew were captured by British troops, but three men escaped and reached German lines, reporting that they had been attacked by *four* Gladiators!

Following the morning reconnaissance by an He 111 of 1(F)/122, six more such aircraft from KGr 100 and three Ju 88s of 5/KG 30 took off to attack a reported naval target. One Ju 88 bombed the RN Special Service vessel *Mashroba* off Harstad; she was badly damaged and beached.

At 1030 Grant-Ede was again in the air, spotting another large aircraft, which he once more identified as a Ju 90, this time to the south-east of Harstad. He approached initially from astern and down-sun, but this time his opponent was not to succumb so easily. His first attack silenced the rear gunner and he then made four more attacks, concentrating on one of the engines on each occasion, and leaving the big aircraft powerless after his fifth attack. It then crashed in flames on Finnöy Island, to the south of Narvik. Much later in the day Plt Off Purdy and Sgt Kitchener took off at 2034, and discovered yet another big aircraft — again believed to be a Ju 90 — apparently attacking a destroyer near Harstad. Purdy dived from the rear quarter for his first attack, then swung away to approach from dead astern, silencing the rear gunner and setting the aircraft alight. It crashed into a fjord some five miles from the destroyer that had been its target.

So what were the two latter 'four-engined aircraft' claimed by 263 Squadron on this date? Luftwaffe records show that KGrzbV 108 lost two Bv 138s, which were recorded as missing due to enemy action. But would the British pilots on two separate occasions recognise a three-engined, twin-boom flyingboat as a four-engined aircraft to be confused with the Ju 90 transport/airliner? There is another possibility. Three prototype Blohm and Voss Ha 139 floatplanes were also used during the Norwegian campaign, presumably by the same unit. These aircraft were four-engined, twin tailplane monoplanes of generally similar configuration to the Ju 90, apart from the floats with which they were fitted. There is no mention of the ultimate fate of these aircraft, only three of which were built. Did some clerk or staff officer unaware of the existence of the Blohm und Voss 139, decide that a misprint had been made and that Blohm und Voss 138 was the correct designation, knowing that the (more numerous) latter aircraft were indeed in use by KGrzbV 108? Perhaps posterity will cast some further light on this small mystery. However it remains a remarkable coincidence that three such large aircraft should all be shot down by biplane fighters in a single day so early in the war.

Meanwhile during the day 99 troops from 1 and 3/GJR 136 were parachuted in from ten KGrzbV 108 Ju 52/3ms, seven more such aircraft from III/KGzbV 1 following next day to drop Hpt Walther and 80 men of I/FJR 1.

26/5/40

26 May was to prove an even busier day — and no less successful for the Gladiators. At 1030 Flt Lt Williams and Sgt Milligan were off, catching an aircraft which they identified as a Ju 88, which was bombing the new airstrip at Skaanland; this was literally cut to pieces. They began with simultaneous attacks

Bv 138A taxies up a fjord past a Dornier Do 24 (right background). *(F. Selinger)*

from above, having overhauled the bomber by cutting across its turn. During the first attack the port engine caught fire, and in the subsequent pass the port wing broke off and the starboard wing disintegrated, the stricken aircraft falling into the sea and bursting into flames. Their victim was in fact an elderly Do 17F of 1(F)/123, which Fw Anton Schairer had just flown up to Trondheim because 1(F)/120 was short of aircraft and personnel. Sent off immediately to Narvik, Schairer and his crew were all lost as the aircraft crashed near Skaanland.

Six He 111s of 2/KG 26 and five of 2/KGr 100 undertook anti-shipping sorties around Harstad with great success during the day. Aircraft from the latter unit attacked the RN trawler *Loch Shin* which was badly damaged by a near-miss and subsequently capsized as attempts were being made to beach her. The crew of one of the KG 26 aircraft believed that they had gained a hit on the stern of a transport; they had in fact near-missed the fully laden tanker *Oleander*, which had to be beached and would later be blown up prior to the Allied evacuation. Fw Paul Wierbitsky's KGr 100 crew spotted a C-Class cruiser off Skaanland and reported a direct hit, followed by black smoke and a large oil slick. They had inflicted severe damage on HMS *Curlew*, which sank within hours. The loss of this radar-equipped vessel was a great blow to the British force, and was to inhibit the air defence potential until a replacement could arrive.

Two pairs of Gladiators were sent off at 1500 to intercept these attacks, Plt Offs Purdy and Bentley first attacking one bomber at 2000 feet to the south-east of Harstad, which they identified as a Do 17 — time factors make it impossible that this was the 1(F)/123 Dornier, incorrectly identified and shot down earlier in the day. Both pilots made beam attacks, Bentley then chasing it down very low into a valley 20 miles south of Narvik. It was later confirmed to have crashed into a hillside, but this does not seem to have been the case, for no loss had actually been suffered. Purdy meanwhile had broken away to attack five more aircraft identified as Dorniers, which were bombing shipping at Harstad from 12,000 feet. He made an astern attack on the third bomber in the formation, firing from 250 yards and seeing the port engine emit white smoke. The bomber broke formation and turned south, losing height. At this, the rest of the formation split up and headed away southwards. It was reported that the 'Dornier' he had attacked was later found crashed to the south-west of Harstad. Again there is no confirmation of this from Luftwaffe records, and it is possible that the aircraft which had been found was in fact the Bf 110 lost two days earlier by I/ZG 76.

While this was going on, Flg Off Riley and Plt Off Parnall attacked five He 111s at 10,000 feet over Harstad, having already chased one such bomber away 30 minutes earlier. Riley pressed home a beam attack on the second aircraft, then repeated this but was hit and wounded. Parnall had attacked the No 4 bomber, silencing the gunner. This aircraft disappeared into low cloud over the mountains south of Bardu. Both these bombers were later reported to have crashed, and the latter's wreck was said to have been found near Bogen. Again these would seem to be mistaken confirmations of other wrecks, for the only casualties suffered by the Luftwaffe in these attacks amounted to one Heinkel from each Gruppe damaged, each with one member of the crew wounded. More He 111s from 2/KG 26 then attacked Bardufoss, destroying two Gladiators on the ground here. A third fighter went into a bomb crater while landing, and was written off.

Earlier in the day at 1300 three Gladiators had been detached to Bodø to provide cover for troops retreating northwards in the face of the German advance. Flt Lt Caesar Hull, Plt Off Jack Falkson and Lt Tony Lydekker were the chosen trio. En route they engaged in an inconclusive combat with one of the KGr 100 Heinkels on its way to Bardufoss, but on landing at their new airfield their aircraft all stuck fast in the mud. They managed to get the Gladiators to drier ground, where they began refuelling from four gallon tins. This arduous task was by no means complete when an He 111 of 1(F)/122 was seen overhead, and all three leapt into their cockpits to take off.

Lydekker got off safely, but the mud clung to the wheels of the two following Gladiators, and while Hull just managed to get into the air, Falkson crashed in N5705. Lydekker's aircraft had not yet been refuelled however, and he had little petrol left so Hull ordered him to land again and went after the Heinkel single-handed, finding it at only 600 feet and delivering three attacks. The bomber turned south, streaming smoke from the fuselage and engines, and at this point Hull broke away to attack a Ju 52/3m which he had just spotted. The Heinkel had been critically hit, and Lt Ulrich Meyer crash-landed the burning aircraft south of Mo. He and his crew were rescued by German troops. Meanwhile Hull disposed of his second opponent, an aircraft of KGrzbV 108, very rapidly; the crew managed to bale out of the blazing aircraft near Saltdalen. Still with ammunition left, he chased a second He 111 without success, and then attacked two more Ju 52/3ms, this time aircraft of III/KGzbV 1. One escaped in cloud, but the other went flaming down after six men had baled out; eight more paratroops of I/FJR 1 were killed in the crash. While he thought the other transport had got away, it was in fact also hard hit, and was already on fire. The pilot managed to reach German-held territory, where he force-landed. Crew and paratroops aboard all got out safely, but the aircraft burnt out completely. Hull had engaged yet another He 111 meantime, and drove this off, like the first with smoke pouring from it. Down now to only one nose gun still operating, he returned to Bodø where he found that during his absence wooden snow boards had been laid over the worst of the soft patches. Although he claimed only two definite and one probable victories, he had in fact shot down no less than four aircraft in the one combat!

By now it was almost time to abandon Bodø. Mosjöen had been evacuated on 10 May and Mo on 18th. During the night the two surviving Gladiators would be in the air again to cover ships leaving this last outpost south of Narvik. That same evening *Glorious* arrived again off the coast with six Hurricanes ranged on deck, but there was some initial doubt as to whether there was sufficient wind or enough deck length for a safe take off. The commanding officer of 46 Squadron, Sqn Ldr K.B.B. Cross, made the first attempt however, and got into the air without difficulty. At once the others followed, and this first flight landed at Skaanland at 2130, although one Hurricane nosed over on a patch of soft ground. The second flight followed, but the first of these to go in also nosed over, and the rest flew off to land at Bardufoss instead. During the evening three He 111s of KGr 100 bombed Bardufoss, damaging two Gladiators. Sgt Mason took off in pursuit, but the bombers escaped into cloud.

27/5/40
Early on the morning of 27th a pair of Blenheim fighters of 254 Squadron from Sumburgh flew a reconnaissance to Stavanger, leaving their base at 0530. One pilot reported that over the target area a Bf 109 tried to intercept without success; he then dived down and strafed 20 more of these fighters on the ground. II/JG 77 recorded that Hpt Franz-Heinz Lang, Staffelkapitän of 6 Staffel, scrambled alone and claimed one Blenheim shot down, but was himself hit and wounded by return fire, which damaged his Messerschmitt 8%. While this was undoubtedly the interceptor reported by the returning pilot, it seems that Lange had also attacked R3624, which failed to return, Plt Off E.H. Alexander and his crew being lost when this aircraft crashed into the sea near Stavanger.

In the north 46 Squadron undertook its first scramble at 0720 when three Hurricanes led by Sqn Ldr Cross went off from Skaanland after three He 111s. These turned away, and as the fighters had been ordered to attack only if Skaanland itself was attacked, they returned to base. Once again one struck a soft patch whilst landing, and crashed. Following this third mishap, a move to Bardufoss was requested, and that evening the squadron transferred there with a strength of 15 serviceable aircraft.

At Bodø meanwhile things were going wrong. At 0800 a formation of 11 Ju 87Rs from I/StG 1, escorted by three Bf 110s from I/ZG 76, appeared overhead and began dive-bombing radio masts at Bodøsjøen, only 800 yards from the landing ground. Tony Lydekker took off at once, but Hull and a fitter were forced to leave his Gladiator for a few minutes and shelter from the bombing. With the initial attack over they managed to get the fighter started and Hull took off, at once catching Fw Kurt Zube's Stuka at the bottom of its dive; he caused it to fall in a gentle glide into the sea, where two Bf 110s circled the wreckage. Zube and his gunner were picked up safely by German troops.

As Hull completed his attack, another Ju 87 went past and shot up his aircraft, smashing the windscreen. At the same moment he was attacked from behind by one of the escorts, flown by Lt Helmut Lent, and the Gladiator was hard hit. Hull managed to get back to the airfield at 200 feet, but was then attacked again by the Bf 110 and crashed at Bodøhalvøya, wounded in the head and knee; Lent logged his victory at 0820. Lydekker meanwhile was being attacked by most of the remaining Luftwaffe aircraft, his aircraft being badly shot up and himself wounded in the neck and shoulders. Unable to land at Bodø as three Stukas

Ju 87R of I/StG 1 en route to attack a target in Northern Norway — possibly Bodø. *(Bib für Zeit)*

were circling overhead, he set course for Bardufoss at low level, where he eventually landed with his Gladiator a complete write-off. A second claim for a Gladiator was put in by Oblt Jäger, shared with his gunner Stabsing Thönes, and timed at 0825, but this was not confirmed. Watchers on the ground at Bodø reported that the Gladiators had shot down at least three aircraft, Hull and Lydekker each having got at least one apiece. This was not in fact the case, for only one Ju 87R had been lost. That evening He 111s appeared overhead and wrecked Bodø town, while 13 Ju 87Rs finished off the runway. In Bodø 15 people were killed and 420 houses destroyed, rendering 3700 civilians homeless.

From Bardufoss at 0900 Sgt Milligan of 263 Squadron took off on patrol, attacking two He 111s at 6000 feet between the airfield and Narvik. He was in turn attacked by a third bomber, so turned his attention to this and made four passes at it. Pouring smoke it dived into a valley in low cloud, and as with so many other aircraft which were not seen to crash during the combat, was later confirmed by the Norwegians to have crashed. Once more however, no such loss is recorded by the Luftwaffe. During the day four Ju 52/3ms from KGzbV 1 dropped 46 more members of I/FJR 1.

The Allies were now virtually ready for the assault on Narvik itself, French and Norwegian troops being firmly established along the sides of Rombaks-fjorden to the north of the peninsula on which Narvik stands. They were only just in time.

28/5/40
As they began the attack, I/StG 1 Ju 87Rs made their first appearance over the area, operating from a strip at Mosjöen, 200 miles to the south. By evening however, Narvik was in Allied hands and work of demolition of the port facilities began at once. This was to prove very effective, and no iron ore cargoes would leave here until January 1941.

Reconnaissance by a 1/KG 40 Fw 200 and a 1(F)/122 He 111 early that morning had indicated that the British were about to stage a new landing in Ofotfjord, and immediate orders were issued for Kampfgruppe Narvik to receive further air support from Fliegerführer Trondheim. From 0430 on 28th six Ju 88s of II/KG 30 had begun appearing over the area, followed at 0500 by 18 He 111s of KG 26 and eight from KGr 100.

Against these new incursions the British fighters at Bardufoss continued to enjoy successes throughout the day, the two squadrons flying a total of 95 sorties. It seems that it was the Heinkels which were first intercepted, for on an early patrol Flt Lt Williams of 263 Squadron in Gladiator N5681 caught one such bomber attacking a cruiser in Ofotfjord and forced it to leave pouring smoke from both engines; he was obliged to break off due to fuel shortage, but was credited with a confirmed victory as the aircraft had been seen to be on fire. On this occasion the aircraft — an He 111H-4 of Stab/KG 26 — did indeed go down. Oblt Streng's aircraft had been badly damaged by the Gladiator, and force-landed at Saltdal, south of Bodø, during the return flight; the crew were rescued by German troops. A second Heinkel from the Stabsstaffel commanded by Ofw Hackner, was hit by AA fire from British warships over Rombaken, and force-landed south of Bjornfjell where it burnt out; the crew survived and managed to break through to the German lines on foot. One of the KGr 100 aircraft from that unit's 2 Staffel was similarly hit and force-landed near Ankenes. Two members of Fw Kurt Ebert's crew were killed and two were pulled out of the wreckage in an injured condition by Norwegians. Somewhat later Flg Off Lydall drew first blood for the Hurricanes when he caught a Ju 88 of 6/KG 30 over the same fjord and shot it down. Fw Ernst Alf ditched the bomber in Beisfjord; one member of the crew was killed, but the other three were picked up by a British destroyer.

One of the few Do 26V flyingboats to survive the Norwegian Campaign, P5+DH was the V-4 aircraft, and served with KGrzbV 108. *(F. Selinger)*

During the middle part of the day four Bf 110s of I/ZG 76 arrived overhead, strafing a small Norwegian vessel, which reportedly blew up. They were followed by Heinkels of KG 26 and KGr 100 on their second sorties of the day, this time to attack targets ashore, but no further interceptions were made. During the morning two of KGrzbV 108's Do 26Vs flew up to Rombaksfjord carrying a 75mm mountain gun of Geb Art Abt 112, together with its crew. The artillery piece was manhandled ashore with great difficulty. Shortly after 1900 that evening two more Do 26s landed, carrying three more of these weapons. This pair, the first and third protoypes, V-1 (P5+AH) and V-3 (P5+CH), were spotted being unloaded by three patrolling Hurricane pilots; Flt Lt P.G. Jameson, Flg Off Knight and Plt Off Johnson dived at nearly 90° to attack, setting both on fire. They then circled and watched as the Germans struggled to get equipment out of the wrecked aircraft and to the shore. The trio finally landed at 2200. One of the Do 26 pilots who was badly wounded, was Hans Modrow, who later became a successful night fighter pilot, ending the war with the Knights' Cross and 34 victories; the other flyingboat pilot was killed.

During the day the carriers enjoyed their first success for some days when three Sea Gladiators of 802 Squadron from *Glorious* (Lt G.H. Feeny, Lt G.D.D'E. Lyver and Lt D.H.H. Ogilvie) were scrambled after a 'shadower'. Six He 115s of KüFlGr 506 had been sent out on reconnaissances, one of these from 2 Staffel, flown by Fw Fritz Stahl, radioing that he had found a carrier 520 kilometres off Vestfjord. The aircraft was not heard from again — it had been shot down by the trio of Sea Gladiators. Other coastal aircraft, this time five He 59s of 1/KüFlGr 706, were led by Hpt Beitzke from Trondheim via Mo, to Narvik. Flying up Vestfjord at low level to Tjeldsund, they laid five mines here before returning to their base.

29/5/40

At Bardufoss Flt Lt Jameson was on the ground less than three hours, taking off again into the Arctic twilight at 0040 on 29 May with Plt Off J.F. Drummond on a defensive patrol. At about 0300 they encountered a trio of German aircraft which they identified as two Ju 88s and an He 111; these were in fact a Kette of three Heinkels from 2/KG 26 which had taken off before midnight on a weather and armed reconnaissance of the Narvik area. Jameson attacked Oblt Hans-Ludwig von Plato's aircraft, identifying it as a Ju 88, and it crashed on the bank of a fjord south of Narvik, all the crew being killed. Drummond attacked Oblt Egon Schmidt's aircraft, which was correctly identified, and it was reported that this too had fallen into a fjord, but not before the gunner, Uffz Neusüss, had hit Drummond's Hurricane and set it on fire; the pilot baled out safely and was picked up by HMS *Firedrake*. In fact Schmidt managed to force-land in Swedish territory to the east of Narvik, where three of the crew were interned; Neusüss had been killed in the exchange of fire with Drummond.

The survivor of the trio returned to report having found a carrier in Tjeldsund, and at once six He 111s of I/KG 26 were sent off. They found no vessel, so instead attacked Bardufoss airfield. With the Hurricanes patrolling, the Gladiators were free to give some support to the army, and during the day many strafing attacks were carried out by these fighters. At 1100 however, when three of the KG 26 Heinkels attacked the airfield from only 2000 feet, Sgt Milligan was scrambled at once, and was able to catch Uffz Paul Richter's bomber over Narvik. This aircraft had climbed steadily to 15,000 feet, but here Milligan was able to close to 250 yards and fire for 10-15 seconds. Many pieces flew off, but before he could see any results his engine began to malfunction — possibly having ingested debris from the Heinkel — and he had to break away. Richter had to belly-land his 1 Staffel machine near Ankenes, where the whole crew were captured and shipped to the UK.

During the mid afternoon Plt Off Banks of 46 Squadron encountered another of 1/KG 40's big Fw 200s (this one flown by Lt Otto Freytag and commanded by Oblt Günther Thiel) as it was bombing Tromsø. At once attacking the aircraft which he tentatively identified as a Ju 89, Banks shot it down on Dyrøy Island,

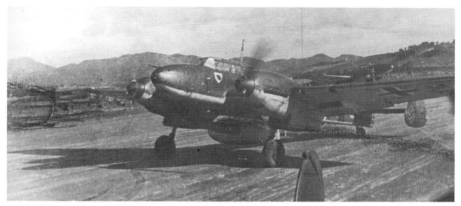
A Bf 110 of 2/ZG 76 fitted with a long-range tank beneath the fuselage for the long flight up to the Narvik area. *(via J. Foreman)*

all six men aboard being killed. The Sheriff of Langhamn later confirmed that the wreckage had been found, and that six bodies had been recovered.

As evening arrived a big force of 26 Luftwaffe bombers approached Vestfjorden from the south, comprising four Ju 88s from 6/KG 30, eight He 111s from I/KG 26 and 11 from KGr 100, escorted by four I/ZG 76 Bf 110s. Their target was again warships at Narvik. As the target area was reached, the formation split up into sections of five each. Nine Hurricanes were up on patrol and in the subsequent actions three bombers were claimed shot down. Flg Off J.W. Lydall attacked one KGr 100 Heinkel flown by Oblt Wolfgang Metzke, aboard which was the Gruppenkommandeur, Hpt Artur von Casimir. Crippled by Lydall's fire, the aircraft crash-landed on the south bank of Beisfjord, about five miles from Andenes Point. Metzke and von Casimir were both taken prisoner, having survived the attack unhurt. One member of the crew had been killed and two others wounded, but the latter pair were rescued by German troops. The two prisoners claimed that their crew had shot down a Spitfire, and indeed Lydall's Hurricane, L1816, had fallen and he had been killed.

Plt Off Banks was also shot down (in L1794) and killed during this engagement, but it was believed that he had brought down a Ju 88 before his demise. This was wishful thinking however; he had in fact joined Lydall in attacking the KGr 100 Heinkels, and had been shot down by them — one of two 'Spitfires' claimed by the Luftwaffe during the day. Another Ju 88 was credited to F/Sgt Shackley, who used one of the very first operational camera guns to record his success, filming continually as the aircraft went down to crash. His victim was not in fact a Ju 88, but an escorting Bf 110 of Stab I/ZG 76, which crashed west of Skaanland. Oblt Hans Jäger, the Gruppenadjutant, and Uffz Helmut Feick both managed to bale out, being shipped out as prisoners.

30–31/5/40
On 29th 12 Ju 52/3ms in two flights, one in the early morning and one at night, had dropped 125 more paratroops of I/FJR 1, 57 more being dropped next day by another four transports, together with four grenade launchers; three Fw 200s of 1/KG 40 dropped ammunition and other supplies. Following successful reconnaissances on 30th, two Ju 88s of 6/KG 30 and 31 He 111s of KG 26 took off in pairs and trios, dropping a total of 36.1 tons of bombs on Narvik, on troops nearby and on various road targets. Despite these incursions, few interceptions

were made during this and the next two days, the RAF fighters concentrating their efforts in support of the army at the front. On 30th for instance 263 Squadron undertook further strafes, Flt Lt Williams and Flg Offs Grant-Ede, Vickery and Dermott between them making 22 sorties to attack staff cars, stations, troops and strongpoints, whilst they also found a German HQ at Hundalen. Vickery's aircraft was hit by Flak and returned with an interplane strut and some flying wires gone, and a large hole in the port upper wing. Flg Off Jacobsen single-handed attacked a convoy of six lorries on a road north of Beisfjord, destroying two and inflicting many casualties. Next day two Gladiators escorted two Norwegian Navy He 115s and two Army C-Vs to attack forces at Rundfjell, but during the day *Ark Royal* and *Glorious* sailed from Scapa Flow again, preparatory to covering the Allied withdrawal from Norway. They would join the Home Fleet off the Lofotens on 2 June, this time carrying aboard:

Ark Royal	*Glorious*
800 Squadron — 12 Skua II	802 Squadron 9 Sea Gladiator
803 Squadron — 12 Skua II	823 Squadron 9 Swordfish I
810 Squadron — 10 Swordfish I	
820 Squadron — 12 Swordfish I	

To the south Coastal Command continued to operate, two Hudsons of 269 Squadron making a reconnaissance of the Norwegian coast during the late morning of 30 May. Aircraft 'F', N7335, (Sgt A. Townsend) failed to return, intercepted and shot down by Fw Robert Menge of 4/JG 77 to the west of Stavanger. On this same day a Ju 52/3m of KGrzbV 107 (Uffz Gerhard Werkmeister) flying from Stavanger to Trondheim with equipment and three personnel of 11(N)/JG 2 aboard, was reported intercepted and shot down by a British aircraft; all aboard were lost. It is possible that the transport was shot down by the crew of Townsend's Hudson before their own demise, but it is also possible that the Junkers may have fallen to Blenheim fighter 'B' of 254 Squadron, the pilot of this aircraft reporting shooting down an He 111 in the same area, but on 1 June. No such loss of any German aircraft in the area on the latter date exists, and it may be therefore that the combat had been recorded two days late. At Stavanger the Luftwaffe was reinforced by the arrival of 16 Do 18 flyingboats of 2 and 3/KüFlGr 406, plus a single Do 17 of 3/KüFlGr 606.

2/6/40

On 2 June the Luftwaffe launched a major attack on the Narvik area, wave after wave of bombers and Stukas, escorted by Bf 110s, attacking the base facilities and shipping at Harstad. The two RAF fighter squadrons flew 75 sorties during the day engaging in 24 combats and claiming at least nine German aircraft shot down. Many of these actions took place in view of the troops, and Lt Gen Claude Auchinleck was sufficiently impressed to send a message of thanks. The evacuation of Narvik was now due to begin on 3rd, and be completed in five days. The main duty of the fighters would be to provide the necessary air cover.

It was midday on 2 June before German attacks of a sustained nature got underway. Thereafter action was almost continuous throughout the afternoon. The first wave comprised eight Ju 87Rs of I/StG 1, four Ju 88As of 6/KG 30 and 11 He 111s of II/KG 26 and KGr 100. Because of the variety of take off times and tasks allocated to the various formations, it was not possible to provide fighter escorts for each, so instead two Schwarme of Bf 110Ds (eight aircraft in all) from I/ZG 76 were despatched to make independent sweeps over Narvik in indirect support. A second wave followed, including six more Ju 87Rs from 2/StG 1, 12 He 111s of I/KG 26, plus six more from KGr 100. Two Hurricanes were off from Bardufoss at 1230 to patrol over Narvik, where Plt Off Drummond and Sgt Taylor saw two of 2/StG 1's Ju 87s attacking a destroyer. Giving chase, they attacked one each, Taylor sending his down to crash near Fagernes, where it smashed onto rocky ground, killing Lt Klaus Küber and his gunner. Drummond's victim crash-landed to the south-east of Narvik, the pilot, Fw Hans Ott, being wounded. The gunner, Sonderführer Brack, member of a war correspondent unit, continued firing at Drummond's Hurricane even after the dive-bomber had hit the ground! Both crewmen were captured by the Norwegians but were repatriated later.

Two more Hurricanes were in the air at 1320, Flg Off Frost and Sgt Tyrer also intercepting a Ju 87 near Skaanland and chasing it into cloud in a damaged condition. Uffz Fritz Klose, the gunner, had been wounded, but a bullet from his machine gun hit the windscreen of Frost's aircraft, and this was splintered. A further pair, F/Sgt Shackley and Plt Off Bunker, took off at 1415, engaging five Bf 110s over Narvik without success. On seeing the British fighters the Messerschmitts went into a defensive circle. Each time one of the Hurricanes attempted to join the circle it was to find two Bf 110s immediately on its tail. Finally the Zerstörer broke away south, easily outpacing their opponents.

It was now the turn of the Gladiators. Plt Off Jacobsen in N5681 and Plt Off J.L. Wilkie in N5893 had followed the last two Hurricanes off in order to patrol between Narvik and the Swedish border. Here they met two aircraft which were identified as Ju 88s, and a co-ordinated attack was made on one of these. Wilkie followed up Jacobsen's initial attack with a stern chase but was shot down and did not return. Their opponents were in fact Bf 110s of I/ZG 76, and had proved too much for the Gladiators, Wilkie being shot down and killed east of Rombaksfjorden by Lt Lent of this unit. Jacobsen meanwhile had chased Lent's Rottenflieger into clouds, then turning his attack on the other aircraft, which went down vertically into more cloud. Just missing a mountain top, Jacobsen passed over the border into Swedish airspace, then spotted several He 111s circling in line astern over Björnfjell. He at once attacked one aircraft from 250 yards, at which point his wing guns ran out of ammunition. The bomber pulled up sharply, stalled and crashed. There seems little doubt that his victim was a Do 215B reconnaissance-bomber of 4(F)/ObdL. Attacked by the fighter and with the engines shot out, this aircraft force-landed on the eastern side of the frontier where Franz Reichardt and his crew were interned, although all returned later. Reichardt reported that they had also been fired on and hit by Swedish frontier AA defences.

Single-handed Jacobsen then made a head-on attack on four aircraft identified as a Ju 88 and three Heinkels. He pulled over these and pressed home an attack on one Heinkel closing from 250 to 50 yards and firing a three second burst from his nose guns. The bomber dived towards the ground apparently out of control. He then found himself surrounded by two 'Ju 88s' and six He 111s, which attacked him with cannon and heavy machine guns. He had in fact become engaged with elements of the second Schwarme of Bf 110s. The Gladiator's oil cooler was hit, the windscreen coated in oil and a flying wire shot away. To avoid colliding with any of these attackers he turned sharply onto the tail of one Heinkel and fired almost blindly. His victim rocked violently and both engines stopped just as his last remaining bullets left his guns. With fuel almost gone, he evaded the remaining aircraft at low level and flew back to base. Fw Neureiter of I/ZG 76 and his gunner, Stabsing Thönes, claimed the Gladiator shot down over Lakselvdal at 1450. Later it was reported that three He 111s had been found crashed near the Swedish border, and these were credited to Jacobsen, while it was felt that he might well have accounted for two further aircraft.

This was not the case however, for no Heinkels were lost or seriously damaged during these engagements. It does seem however that one of the aircraft attacked by Jacobsen during the later hectic stages of his sortie may have been a Ju 52/3m of KGrzbV 107. Six of these had appeared over Björnfjell to drop 45 more troops of I/FJR 1, but one was chased over the Swedish frontier by a British fighter. Here it was also fired on by the Swedish defences; the two-man crew was killed, but six of the ten paratroopers were able to bale out. It was believed by the Germans that, despite the fighter attack, the aircraft had in fact been shot clown by the Swedes, and a sharp note of protest was delivered in Stockholm. The strong possibility exists nonetheless, that Jacobsen played at least a contributory part in the Junkers' demise.

Finally, at 1500 Flt Lt Williams (in N5905) and Sgt Kitchener took off in another pair of Gladiators, intercepting the 12 He 111s of I/KG 26 at 4000 feet to the south of Narvik. Picking the last four bombers, which were flying in line astern, the two fighter pilots made a number of simultaneous beam and astern attacks on the rear Heinkel in the formation, whereupon this aircraft caught fire and force-landed south-east of Narvik, near Beisfjord. Ofw Otto Poser and his crew from 1 Staffel were captured and sent off to eventual captivity in Canada. The next bomber in line went down in a steep dive after a similar attack, while after seven more firing passes the two leading aircraft of the Schwarm went down in dives, in both cases with both engines apparently out of action. None had actually suffered any serious damage however.

A formation identified as comprising at least six 'Do 17s' was then seen, although it seems likely that these were the KGr 100 Heinkels; they jettisoned their bombs and fled. Continuing their patrol the two Gladiators then encountered a pair of Ju 87Rs of 2/StG 1 and made simultaneous attacks on these. One, flown by the Staffelkapitän, Oblt Heinz Böhne, was seen to have its port long-range underwing tank on fire, and this crashed into the mountains. The bodies of Bohne and his gunner were later recovered from the wreckage by the Germans. Meanwhile Kitchener was after the other, getting in a full deflection shot at it as it crossed his sights. It disappeared into cloud, apparently trailing white smoke from its engine; it was not hard hit however, and returned safely to its base. At that moment Williams met another He 111, and attacked from 50 yards astern. The bomber dived beyond the vertical and could not be followed. As in Jacobsen's case, confirmation came readily, with reports that three He 111s and a Ju 87 had all crashed near Beisfjord, the two pilots being credited with four destroyed and three probables as a result of this series of combats. In fact the only German casualties had been the one He 111 and the one Ju 87. There was one further German loss however, for one of the I/ZG 76 Bf 110s stayed too long over the area and ran out of fuel during the return flight. The pilot carried out a force-landing north of Trondheim, his aircraft suffering 30% damage as a result.

Following this hectic aerial fighting, mist and low cloud put an effective end to most Luftwaffe bombing attacks during the next few days. Despite this bad weather, an He 111 of 1(F)/122 attempted a reconnaissance over Vestfjord and Narvik, but was obliged to force-land near the Lofotens when it ran out of fuel. Lt Günter Wentz and his crew were rescued unhurt by a German ASR aircraft. To the south Luftflotte 5 was reinforced when the whole of KG 30 was transferred to its command, and II(J)/TrGr 186, fresh from action over Holland during the opening days of the 'Blitzkrieg', moved to Oslo/Gardermöen via Aalborg, arriving on 4th. However KGr 100 was now transferred to Luftflotte 2 for special operations over England.

3–4/6/40

On 3 June the Allied evacuation of Narvik began under cover of the adverse weather. *Ark Royal* now detached *Glorious*, escorted by HMS *Highlander*, to Tromsø to refuel, and herself began a series of anti-submarine and fighter patrols during the evening, when the weather cleared a little. Next day two of her Skuas managed to bomb a jetty at Sörfjord, but no other activity of note took place over the area.

During 4 June three 254 Squadron fighter Blenheims flew an offensive reconnaissance along the southern coastline. The aircraft took off at 1030, arriving over Fedje at 1140, and flying by way of Fensfjorden, Bergen and Voss. South of Bergen at 1245 the trio lost contact in cloud. One flew direct to Stavanger where 14 Dorniers, 20 Heinkels and 12 Bf 110s were counted on the airfield at Sola. Six of the latter were seen taking off, so the crew headed for home. The other two Blenheims completed the reconnaissance to Lista via Stavanger and then also turned west for base. When only 57 nautical miles from Sumburgh Flt Lt Mitchell in R3629 saw a Do 18 and at once attacked, forcing it down onto the sea. Following the return to base of this Blenheim, three more were sent to the scene, finding the Dornier abandoned with a dead man sprawled out of the forward cockpit with one of the wingfloats (sponsons) under water. The aircraft was 8L+LK of 2/KüFlGr 906, and the dead man was Lt de Res Hans Weinlig, who had been shot through the head; the rest of the crew had got away in their dinghy, and were later picked up by a German vessel. The RAF sent out a High Speed Launch to salvage the flyingboat, but the crew of this could not find it. Next day another Blenheim found it again, now capsized and with a mine floating in the water some 400 yards from it.

5/6/40

Glorious, her fuel supplies replenished, rejoined *Ark Royal* off the Narvik area on 5th. During the day Sqn Ldr Cross was flown out to her in one of 701 Squadron's Walruses to discuss the fate of 46 Squadron's Hurricanes. He had been ordered to organize the destruction of these on completion of the evacuation, in the belief that they could not fly aboard the carrier. Cross believed that they could, and agreed with the Captain to arrange a test landing.

During the day, at this late stage, two Norwegian Navy MF 11s (F-310 and -346) which had flown to Scotland earlier in the campaign, flew over to North Norway to rejoin 2 Flg avd. The He 115A F-52, was still in the Northern Isles and would not return before the fighting ended. A Hudson — 'S' N7255, of 233 Squadron, flown by Flg Off J. Dunn — failed to return from a patrol on this date, but the reason for this loss has not been discovered. The possibility exists however that it had been attacked in error by Flg Off Gillen of the Sullom Voe Fighter Flight, who claimed a Do 17 probably shot down eight miles north of Lerwick during the day.

6/6/40

Noting the withdrawal of the Allies from Narvik, the German Navy had put the battlecruisers *Scharnhorst* and *Gneisenau* to sea, supported by the cruiser *Hipper*, to seek out and destroy as much as possible of the retreating Allied shipping. As they headed out past Trondheim, 11 He 115s undertook reconnaissances in support, from which one aircraft of 3/KüFlGr 506 flown by Uffz Willi Rohs failed to return.

6 June saw considerable air support for the remaining Allied troops still fighting in the Narvik area. Two Hurricanes escorted five of 701 Squadron's Walruses to bomb in the neighbourhood of Sørfold, while Swordfish from *Glorious* bombed the Sildvik railway station, and a striking force of Skuas from *Ark Royal* hit German troops in the Fauske area. Later in the day Swordfish from this latter carrier undertook reconnaissance sorties in support of the French contingent, and dropped some bombs. *Glorious* again withdrew out to sea to conserve fuel. At night the Norwegians undertook their last aerial operations, a pair of He 115s (F-58 and -64) bombing positions at Storfjell, while Fokker C-V 371 flown by Lt Kyllingmark bombed Hill 623. Altogether the Håloga-land Air Corps had undertaken 148 offensive missions during the fighting over Northern Norway, dropping 120 10kg and 95 50kg bombs. Five of the six C-VDs on strength on 9 April had been lost, but five more had arrived from the south on 10th May. With darkness, three 1/KüFlGr 706 He 59s undertook their third and final mining operation to Hommelvik, in the Tysfjord; two completed their task successfully, but the third returned early with an oil leak.

7/6/40

Better weather on 7 June allowed the Luftwaffe to appear over Narvik from 0400, but it was to find 46 Squadron Hurricanes up and ready waiting. Flg Off Knight and Plt Off Drummond had taken off at 0340, followed ten minutes later by Sqn Ldr Cross and Plt Off P.W. 'Pip' Lefevre. The first pair reported engaging three He 111s over Narvik, claiming one shot down each, while the latter pair reported attacking four more of these bombers over Bardufoss and shared one claimed shot down between them. However there were no German bomber operations reported during the morning due to bad weather conditions, crews awaiting the results of reconnaissances by seven Do 18s of KüFlGr 406 north-west of Stavanger and ten He 115s of KüFlGr 506 which were operating from Trondheim as far north as the Lofotens. These found the evacuation fleet. Nonetheless Cross's Hurricane was reportedly hit by return fire and made an emergency landing with a damaged oil cooler.

Much of the rest of the day was spent in preparing for withdrawal. 263 Squadron recorded that during patrols by its ten remaining Gladiators it was believed that three more bombers were shot down, but no details are available. No German losses or combats are recorded, and it seems likely that the three claims mentioned may well have been those made by 46 Squadron during the early hours, which remain unaccounted for. At 1430 four Swordfish from *Glorious*, which had now rejoined *Ark Royal* again, flew off to Bardufoss to navigate the Gadiators out to the carrier. At about 1800 another Swordfish arrived carrying the permission for three Hurricanes to attempt a fly-on. All the pilots in 46 Squadron volunteered to make the attempt, Flt Lt Jameson, Flg Off Knight and Sgt Taylor being sent off to give it a try, the rear fuselages of their aircraft ballasted with sandbags internally to keep the tails down. All three landed on successfully at 1930, and at 2035 *Glorious* despatched another Swordfish with instructions gained from this experience as to how the rest might be brought aboard.

The Luftwaffe was certainly about on this day, for three He 111s of 1(F)/122 had found the evacuation fleet again during the early afternoon, spotting as well the two carriers, the cruiser *Coventry*, and five escorting destroyers. Following this report eight Ju 88s of 6/KG 30 took off at 1500, followed by all available He 111s of I and II/KG 26. Most of these were forced to abort by the bad weather, and returned with their bombs still aboard; a few crews sought out targets in the Narvik area. Here the weather began to clear a little as the afternoon wore on, and at 1600 three Ju 88s of 4/KG 30 and three He 111s of 6/KG 26 were despatched to this area, followed two hours later by 11 more Heinkels of III/KG 26.

Meanwhile, as the evacuation of the fighters from Bardufoss was progressing, Flg Off Mee and Plt Off Drummond flew a last patrol over Narvik during which they encountered the three 6/KG 26 He 111s as these approached. The British pilots reported four Heinkels, claiming one shot down each, while Drummond claimed to have inflicted damage on the other two. Oblt Harald Linke's He 111H-3 was heavily hit and crash-landed east of Bjerkvik, where the crew set the aircraft on fire before making for the German lines. A second bomber was damaged, but landed safely at Vaernes with one wounded aboard, the aircraft having suffered 30% damage. One of the 4/KG 30 Ju 88s flew into a storm on the way back and crashed at Grong, only one member of Lt de Res Johannes Petzold's crew surviving when he baled out. One more German loss was also suffered when over the ore railway from Sweden a Ju 88C of Z/KG 30 was hit by AA whilst strafing, and crash-landed at Björnfjell.

Following their successful combat, the two Hurricane pilots landed between 1810 and 1815. With four victories confirmed, John Drummond was certainly the most successful of the Hurricane pilots in Norway, and with the exception

Hit by AA fire whilst strafing, this Ju 88C-2 (4D+MH) of Z/KG 30 crash-landed near Björnfjell on 7 June.

of Caesar Hull of 263 Squadron, the top-scoring RAF fighter pilot of the campaign. He was later to double his score while flying Spitfires with 92 Squadron in the Battle of Britain, but was killed when he collided with a fellow pilot whilst attacking a Do 17 on 10 October 1940.

These last combats brought the fighting over Northern Norway to an end; the Norwegian forces remaining would soon agree a ceasefire with the Germans. During this final day the Luftwaffe had claimed one victory in air combat near Narvik, although no RAF losses had been sustained.

8/6/40

Now the final act began, as with the evacuation of Narvik virtually completed, the air contingent began its own evacuation. In the early hours of 8 June Swordfish led the Gladiators, Hurricanes and Walruses to *Glorious*, the ten Gladiators going aboard first, followed by a Walrus carrying Grp Capt Wood. When all were successfully aboard the five Swordfish which had led them, and the remainder of 701 Squadron's Walruses also landed and were stowed below with the other aircraft, the nine Sea Gladiators of 802 Squadron's and the balance of 823 Squadron Swordfish; then at last the remaining seven Hurricanes made their approaches and every one was landed without undue difficulty. Aboard now were the following RAF pilots:

46 Squadron	*263 Squadron*
Sqn Ldr K.B.B. Cross	Sqn Ldr J.W. Donaldson, DSO, DFC
Flt Lt C.R.D. Stewart	Flt Lt A.T. Williams, DFC
Flt Lt P.G. Jameson	Flg Off H.T. Grant-Ede, DFC
Flg Off R.M.J. Cowles	Flg Off H.F. Vickery
Flg Off P.J. Frost	Flg Off L.R. Jacobsen, DFC
Flg Off H.H. Knight	Flg Off S.R. McNamara, DFC
Flg Off M.C.F. Mee	Plt Off J. Falkson
Plt Off L.G.B. Bunker	Plt Off P.H. Purdy, DFC
Sgt E. Shackley	Plt Off M.A. Bentley
Sgt B.L. Taylor	Sgt E.F.W. Russell, MM

The remaining pilots and ground crews went aboard the MV *Arandora Star*. Pilots here included:

46 Squadron	*263 Squadron*
Plt Off J.F. Drummond	Flt Lt C.B. Hull, DFC
Plt Off P.W. Lefevre	Flt Lt R.S. Mills
Sgt E. Tyrer	Plt Off Hughes
	Sgt G.S. Milligan
	Sgt H.H. Kitchener
	Sgt B.E.P. Whall

At 0300 *Glorious* was detached with the destroyers *Ardent* and *Acasta* to head for Scapa Flow at all speed, while *Ark Royal* and the rest of the fleet remained behind to escort the slower main convoy. The achievements of the fighters during their stay had been considerable. In 13 days of flying the Gladiators had made 389 sorties, engaged in 72 combats and claimed at least 26 and possibly 35 victories. In a shorter period 46 Squadron's Hurricanes had made 249 sorties

Tiger Moth 159 of the Norwegian Air Force, seen here on floats, escaped to Finland. *(Via B. Olsen)*

including 26 interceptions, and had claimed 11 victories. The cost of the 37-46 victories claimed had totalled just two Gladiators and two Hurricanes lost in combat, plus a number of others damaged.

On departure Bardufoss airfield was demolished as far as possible, one small strip being left for the surviving Norwegian Fokkers and Tiger Moths. These at once fled on cessation of hostilities, two C-VDs (371 and 385) and one Tiger Moth (159) reaching Finland, where they were incorporated into the Finnish Air Force. One of the He 115As (F-50) and three MF 11s (F-310, -336 and -346) were also flown to Finland, while the other three surviving He 115s (F-56, -58 and -64) went to join F-52 in the Shetlands. Only one He 115 (F-62) and three MF 11s (F-312, -334 and -344) were left at Tromsø to be captured by the Germans, and none of these were airworthy. Of the four Heinkels which reached the Shetlands, two were later crashed by RAF pilots while under test, the other two being modified for clandestine agent-carrying operations. One was sent to Malta to undertake such activities until it was lost during an air raid. The other undertook one operation from Woodhaven in Scotland, but further activity was then discontinued due to fear of interception by British fighters. It was finally scrapped late in 1943 after some time in store.

Meanwhile however, a major tragedy was befalling the British, which at a stroke undid the whole success of the withdrawal of the major part of the RAF's fighter force, so gallantly commenced with such initiative. The force of German warships which had put to sea two days earlier were now to enjoy good fortune, spotting the carrier *Glorious* at 1545 escorted only by the pair of destroyers. The powerful battlecruisers *Scharnhorst* and *Gneisenau* opened fire at 1630 at a range of 20,000 yards, gaining direct hits on the bridge of the carrier with the third and subsequent salvoes. The carrier replied with her own gun armament, but was hopelessly outranged, and by 1720 was dead on the water, little more than a hulk, and sinking fast.

The sad remains of Fokker C-VE 337, abandoned at Lake Dovrevann. *(via B. Olsen)*

The two destroyers did their brave and suicidal best to protect their charge, but were both sunk during the next 45 minutes — but not before *Acasta* had launched a torpedo strike which gained a hit abreast *Scharnhorst*'s after turret, inflicting serious damage. From the three British vessels 1,519 lost their lives, including 1,207 from the carrier alone; 41 of the latter were RAF ground personnel, and 18 were pilots. Sqn Ldr Cross and Flt Lt Jameson from 46 Squadron managed to get aboard a Carley float with 61 seamen, but 25 of the latter died of exposure and exhaustion before the 38 survivors, the two RAF men amongst them, were finally picked up by a passing fishing vessel.

The main convoy escaped interception by the German vessels, which withdrew after the action, *Scharnhorst* making for Trondheim to undertake emergency repairs. Air attacks continued however, eight He 111s of III/KG 26 being sent out after shipping targets reported west of Andöya Island. On return, one crash-landed at Vaernes, suffering 80% damage.

9/6/40

Next day an Fw 200C of 1/KG 40 attacked the troop transport *Vandyk* 30 miles north of Andöya Island, the vessel being set on fire and having to be abandoned. Seven aboard were killed, and 161 were captured by German forces. In the afternoon an He 115 of 1/KüFlGr 506 spotted a flotilla of warships some 360 miles west of the southern entrance of Saltfjord and at the same latitude as Bodø. The floatplane was intercepted by two Skuas from *Ark Royal* and pursued some 100 miles eastwards, landing at Trondheim with two wounded aboard, but only 5% damaged.

Six Ju 88s of 6/KG 30 and 13 He 111s of II/KG 26 then set off to attack, three of the Junkers dive bombing the carrier without effect during the mid-afternoon period. Late in the evening the Heinkels attacked, but six of these were intercepted by a section of Skuas from 800 Squadron, reinforced by three 803 Squadron aircraft. The latter trio (Lt Gibson, Sub Lt Bartlett, Pty Off (A) A.W. Theobald) shot down a 5 Staffel aircraft flown by Oblt Kurt Böcking, while those from 800 Squadron claimed one damaged. Half an hour later at 2355 six more Skuas from the two squadrons chased another Heinkel, but this aircraft managed to escape. Following this, a similar force of Ju 88s and He 111s took off again, but was recalled. During the return flight two of the Heinkel crews of II/KG 26 discovered Norwegian vessels heading for Thorshaven in the Faroes, and attacked, sinking the freighters *Ariadne* (in which nine were killed) and *Prinz Olav*.

10/6/40

Next day, as the convoy reached home waters, Luftwaffe reconnaissances seeking the ships continued. Whilst on an early patrol a Sunderland from 204 Squadron in the hands of Wg Cdr Davis, engaged an aircraft identified as a Do 215 north-east of Muckle Flugga. This was in fact Do 17Z 7T+BL from 2/ KüFlGr 606, which attacked the Sunderland, gaining hits; it broke off when it was itself hit by return fire. The observer, Lt zur See Gerhard Prikker, was mortally wounded, dying soon after the aircraft landed, while a second member of the crew received slight wounds. During the afternoon six He 115s were sent out from Trondheim by 2/KüFlGr 506, these finding a convoy of warships including a battleship and two heavy cruisers. Overhead were a Sunderland and several Skuas from 803 Squadron, three of which (Lt Cdr Casson, Sub Lt Brokensha and Pty Off Ridler) attacked the leading floatplane. The British pilots claimed a possibly damaged, but in fact the floatplane suffered 40-50 hits which caused the pilot to make a force-landing on the sea near Trondheim on return. The crew got out just before the aircraft sank and they were later rescued.

Already on 9th Gen Otto Ruge, commander of the Norwegian forces in Northern Norway, had made contact with the Germans. On 10th a 24 hour ceasefire was agreed to allow capitulation negotiations to take place. Following these negotiations, fighting between the Norwegian 6th Division and the German forces under GenLt Dietl came to an end. A similar situation was achieved following communication between the German Gruppe XXI commander, Gen von Falkenhorst and the Norwegian High Command. Operation 'Weserübung' had been satisfactorily brought to a conclusion.

In a final gesture of defiance retreating Norwegian troops destroyed the last four Ju 52/3ms of 3/KGrzbV 102 and one of 1 Staffel, still stranded on Lake Hartvigvann. Further south, KGrzbV 107 was now disbanded, part of its personnel being posted to KGrzbV 108, the remainder returning to Germany.

Following the conclusion of operations in Norway, all British commanders, Maj Gen Paget from Aandalsnes, Maj Gen de Wiart from Namsos and Lt Gen Auchinleck from Narvik, were unanimous in their judgement that the predominant factor had been the performance of the Luftwaffe, both in attack and in its air supply role. Gen Jodl of the OKW, reported to the Führer that in his opinion (which agreed fully with that of his opponents) the Luftwaffe had indeed proved the decisive factor in the success of 'Weserübung' and the subsequent campaign.

Chapter 3

AFTERMATH

The ending of the campaign in Norway in no way resulted in a commensurate conclusion to the aerial activity over the area, which continued unabated. For several more weeks many of the same units which had been locked in combat with each other since April were to continue to clash regularly. These clashes would carry on until August, after which nearly all the Luftwaffe units involved were to be moved elsewhere. For this reason a brief account of these further operations is included here so that the activities of those whose names have become familiar in these pages may be followed to the point where they departed the skies over Norway and the North Sea triangle. It may he said that certain of these activities — particularly those of August — relate more accurately to the Battle of Britain; they are included here purely in the interests of continuity and should properly be dealt with in more detail in some future full account of the activities of the high summer of 1940.

11/6/40
Aerial reconnaissance from England swiftly revealed that *Scharnhorst*, following the damage she had suffered whilst sinking *Glorious* on 8 June, had gone into Trondheim harbour to effect repairs. Poor weather prevailed on 11th, but nonetheless at 1130 Wg Cdr Pearce led 12 Hudsons of 269 Squadron off from Sumburgh for a formation attack on the vessel. This was carried out around 1430, hits being claimed by the bomb aimers, but interception occurred while still over the target, and in addition considerable Flak was encountered at the same time.

Four Bf 109Es from II/JG 77 and a single Bf 110 — M8+HH of 3/ZG 76 — flown by Lt Kamp, were scrambled and attacked. Lt Schirmböck and Ofw Arnoldy each claimed one Hudson shot down, and a third claim was submitted by Lt Kamp, while the Flak defences also claimed to have brought down one of the bombers. 269 Squadron reported being attacked by five Bf 109s, noting that Hudson 'G', N7361 (Sgt E.B. Lascelles) was believed to have been shot down by the fighters, and 'P', P5131 (Sgt G.W. Robson) by the Flak.

12/6/40
The bad weather continued to prevail during 12 June, and little activity was undertaken during the day. By now however the period of the midnight sun was at its height, and there was little darkness at all at Trondheim. A large combined raid on *Scharnhorst* was now in preparation as *Ark Royal*, escorted by two battleships and a screen of destroyers, sailed towards the area.

Five Hudsons from 224 Squadron set out at 2055, their target the Bergen area; all returned safely six hours later. Meanwhile at 2230 Oblt Walter of 1/ZG 76 caught Blenheim IVF 'N' R3627, of 254 Squadron, which was being flown by Sgt R.W. Brown on a reconnaissance to Trondheim, and shot this down west of Romsdalsfjord. A few minutes after the recorded time of this combat, five more Blenheim fighters took off, their mission to provide escort for the Skuas which were being bombed-up on *Ark Royal*.

Five more Hudsons of 233 Squadron took off at 2115 to repeat the earlier attack on Bergen, while seven Beauforts from 22 Squadron, which had moved nine of its aircraft up to Wick during the day, made for Vaernes.

13/6/40

Two minutes after midnight *Ark Royal* began launching 15 Skuas from 800 and 803 Squadrons, all weighed down with the unusually heavy load represented by a 500lb semi-armour piercing bomb beneath their bellies. RAF support was still anticipated, the Blenheim fighters having made radio contact with the carrier as early as 2257, but in the event they were too late to escort the dive-bombers in to the target zone. Now things really began to go wrong. It had been intended that the Beauforts should bomb Vaernes airfield just ahead of the arrival of the Skuas, thereby keeping the German fighters on the ground. Unfortunately, the bombers lost formation in bad visibility, three returning to base while only four attacked at about 0150. On the ground five men were killed and 27 wounded, but material damage was slight, and the Bf 109Es of 4/JG 77 and Bf 110s of 3/ZG 76 were scrambled after them. The Beauforts could not be caught, but the result was that when the unescorted Skuas arrived over Trondheimsfjorden at 0200 on 13 June it was to find a considerable force of fighters already in the air and waiting for them. Within about ten minutes it was all over. Scarcely a match for the fighters opposing them when not trammelled with bombloads, in their laden condition the Skuas were almost helpless. Gallantly they pressed on, those that survived making their dives on *Scharnhorst*. The results failed to reward the effort; only one bomb struck the warship and by a cruel quirk of fate this failed to explode. The sacrifice had been in vain, and the cost was desperately high. Only seven Skuas — less than half the force despatched — returned to the carrier. Amongst those lost were several of the splendid crews who had played such an effective part in the earlier fighting over the Trondheim area and Narvik. At last at about 0210 the Blenheim fighters of 254 Squadron arrived, but could do nothing to help, and were able only to escort the seven survivors back to their ship.

The two German units involved each claimed four victories. Oblt Gordon Gollob of 3/ZG 76, later to become the first pilot to claim 150 victories, shot down one Skua at 0200, while Ofw Hans-Jacob Arnoldy of II/JG 77 claimed another two minutes later. Lt Krzywon of 3/ZG 76 in M8+BL, claimed another at 0205, while at 0206 others were claimed by Lt Köhler and Ofw Herbet Schob of this unit. Schob had gained six victories in Spain and then two over Poland in September 1939 with I(Z)/LG 1; he would later become a Ritterkreuzträger with 28 victories. Of II/JG 77's other three victories, two were credited to Fw Robert Menge and one to Fw Erwin Sawallisch. One more claim for a probable was submitted for the Flak batteries.

The Skua crews taking part were:

800 Squadron
6A Capt R.J. Partridge, RM/Lt R.S. Bostock*
6K Lt K.V.V. Spurway/Pty Off R.F. Hort
6C Pty Off H.A. Monk/Pty Off H.G. Cunningham*
6G Midspmn L.H. Gallagher/Pty Off W. Crawford*
6H Mdspmn D.T.R. Martin/L/A W.J. Tremler*

803 Squadron
7A Lt Cdr J. Casson/Lt R.E. Fanshawe*
7B Sub Lt G.W. Brokensha/L/A F. Coston
7C Pty Off T.F. Ridler/N/A H.T. Chatterley
7F Lt C.H. Filmer/Midspmn(A) T.A. McKee*
7G Midspmn(A) A.S. Griffiths/N/A F.P. Dooley
7L Sub Lt J.A. Harris/N/A G.R. Stevenson*
7P Lt D.C.E.F. Gibson/Sub Lt M.P. Gordon-Smith
7Q Sub Lt R.E. Bartlett/N/A L.G. Richards*
7R Pty Off H. Gardiner/N/A H. Pickering

(Those noted * were shot down; of the 16 personnel in these aircraft only Capt Partridge, RM, survived as a POW.)

It was the end of the dive-bomber as far as the Royal Navy was concerned. The lesson learned on this disastrous morning, coupled with the evidence so soon to come of the vulnerability of the Luftwaffe's Stuka to fighter attack, turned the face of the Admiralty resolutely against this class of aircraft. Despite the later outstanding success of American and Japanese carrier-borne dive-bombers in the Pacific, no such aircraft would ever again be ordered for the Fleet Air Arm. British carrier groups included only fighters and torpedo-bombers for the rest of the war once the remaining Skuas had been relegated from first line duties early in 1941.

14/6/40
It was by no means the end of British attacks on German seapower in Norway however. Only 24 hours later a force of four Hudsons from 269 Squadron and six Beauforts from 42 Squadron — newly-converted to the aircraft, and just beginning operations — approached Bergen. Although the formation had become split up on the way, the attack was made on shipping in the harbour here, all aircraft returning safely. Earlier in the day a pair of reconnoitring Blenheims had both suffered slight damage in a brush with two Bf 109Es of II/JG 77 off Trondheim. Hudson 'Q' of 224 Squadron (Plt Off R.C. Wood) was lost to the north-west of Stavanger, apparently falling victim to Flak gunners.

15/6/40
The Blenheims were back on 15th, two of 254 Squadron's fighter aircraft making a further reconnaissance of the Trondheim area, having left the Orkneys at 0945. At 1245 they were intercepted by Lts Bender and Helmut Lent of 1/ZG 76, and 'F', L9408, (Plt Off P.C. Gaylord) was shot down by the former west of Smöla Island; the aircraft was last seen by the other crew climbing into clouds over the harbour. During the day eight of 22 Squadron's Beauforts attacked an oil tanker in Sognefjorden and other vessels near Bergen, while three Hudsons from 233 Squadron swept in to attack Sola airfield. Several Rotten of Bf 109Es of 5/JG

77 were scrambled, Ofw Anton Hackl single-handed shooting down two of the bombers for his initial victories, while the third fell to Flakgruppe Stavanger. 'U' (Plt Off R.B. Asquith-Ellis), 'V' (Plt Off C.S. Greenaway) and 'W' (Plt Off N. Ewart) all failed to return; these three Hudsons were N7217, 7270 and 7279.

16–20/6/40
254 Squadron was active again on 16 June, four Blenheims escorting Hudsons and Beauforts to Trondheim on a morning raid. A repeat attack next day was called off due to bad weather. On 20th one of the squadron's Blenheims engaged in a combat with an He 115 west of Smöla, but was hit by return fire and arrived back at base with the pilot wounded. During the day Hudson N7287 of 233 Squadron was reported missing from a sortie, but reconnaissance discovered *Scharnhorst* at sea again, and heading south; a series of strikes was at once laid on for the next day.

21/6/40
Early on 21st therefore a pair of Sunderlands from 204 Squadron took off to shadow the ship and report on its position; they were accompanied by an escort of three fighter Blenheims. On the way the Blenheims — again from 254 Squadron — broke away to attack an He 115 — inconclusively as it turned out. As the Sunderlands approached five Swordfish were seen flying east — part of a force of six drawn from 821 and 823 Squadrons at Hatston, which were undertaking the Royal Navy's first land-based torpedo attack of the war. Immediately after this sighting, the flyingboats came upon the battlecruiser with an escort of seven destroyers. As the crews of the Sunderlands watched, the elderly biplanes went in to attack with torpedoes, gaining no hits and losing two of their number as they turned away.

While the shadowing continued a biplane floatplane identified as an He 60 (and probably catapulted from *Scharnhorst*'s deck) kept a similar check on the British flyingboats. Climbing above them, the German crew then attempted to bomb the big aircraft. Help was obviously being radioed for, as an hour later three Bf 109s, soon followed by a fourth, appeared on the scene and attacked. After a 15 minute exchange of fire it was claimed that one of the attackers went into the sea in flames, while 'A', N9028 (Flt Lt Phillips) returned to base in a damaged condition.

Subsequently Hudsons from 233 Squadron attacked the battlecruiser, 'X', N7246 (Sqn Ldr D.Y. Feeny) being shot down in flames. It was then the turn of 42 Squadron's Beauforts. The unit was still hardly operational at this stage, and was not considered to have had sufficient training for torpedoes to be used. The aircraft were loaded with two 500lb bombs apiece therefore — these having little chance of penetrating the armoured decks of the big warship — and at 1420 on 21st nine aircraft took off from Sumburgh. The formation made landfall near Bergen at 1600, finding the ships 15 miles to the north of the port. Three Bf 109s of II/JG 77 were patrolling overhead and these at once attacked the Beauforts, which they identified incorrectly as 'Herefords'. Two hits were claimed on *Scharnhorst*'s stern and one on the bows, but these did little damage and the ship steamed on. The Messerschmitts swiftly shot down the second and third aircraft in the leading sub-flight, L4501 (Plt Off Rigg) and L4486 (Flg Off Seagrim) last being seen disappearing eastwards. Two Bf 109s then concentrated on the second sub-flight, attacking for five minutes following which L9810 (Flg

Off Barrie-Smith) dived into the sea in flames after the starboard engine had caught fire.

During the initial attack on the leading sub-flight, the gunner in Sqn Ldr Smith's aircraft, LAC Begbie, claimed one Bf 109 shot down in flames. The pilot of another Beaufort got in a shot with his fixed forward-firing gun and claimed that he had hit another Messerschmitt, damaging its engine. II/JG 77 made three claims during this engagement, one each by Lt Horst Carganico, Fw Robert Menge and Ofw Anton Hackl, but no Messerschmitts were reported lost. However on 22nd Lt Struckmann of 5 Staffel was reported killed, and it is possible that he was in fact lost in one of the air fights on this date. One further loss was suffered by the RAF on 21st when Hudson 'P', N7359 (Flt Lt Williamson) of 224 Squadron failed to return from an escort sortie.

The Luftwaffe now revised its fighter dispositions in Norway, Z/KG 30 returning to Germany on 16 June, while during 21st I/ZG 76 began transferring a Staffel at a time to Stavanger, where the unit was joined by the Bf 109Es of II(J)/TrGr 186. II/JG 77 also moved to Stavanger on 22nd, although 5 Staffel was detached to Kjevik again.

23–23/6/40

Another claim for a Blenheim shot down was made on 23 June, this time by Lt Bender of 1/ZG 76, who claimed one of these aircraft west of Smöla at 1020. Again no loss was found. Next day however three fighter Blenheims from 254 Squadron were on an early morning anti-shipping patrol; one aircraft was forced to return early but the other two continued. Suddenly the leader, Flt Lt Jolliff in 'J', L9409, saw a ship through a gap in the clouds and dived through to attack; he was not seen again, and one victory was claimed by II/JG 77 in the vicinity of Stavanger. A second Blenheim, 'Q', R3826 flown by Sgt Hughes of the same squadron, was also reported missing, but it seems possible that this may in fact have been the aircraft claimed by Bender of 1/ZG 76, recorded a day late.

25–27/6/40

It was not a good time for 254 Squadron; again on 25 June a trio of Blenheim fighters were off on a reconnaissance of the Stavanger-Bergen area. Near Stavanger Bf 109Es of II/JG 77 attacked, R3622 (Plt Off A.J. Hill) and N3604 (F/Sgt P.G. Corey) both being shot down, one of them falling to Ofw Arnoldy, the other to an unidentified pilot. The German unit enjoyed yet more success two days later when Ofw Hackl of 5 Staffel caught two Hudsons from 269 Squadron which were making a special reconnaissance of the Norwegian coast. Hackl shot down Plt Off P.N. Trolove's 'C', N7330, but was himself wounded during the combat. Anton Hackl was to remain in action throughout the rest of the war after he had recovered from his wounds. Ultimately he became a Major with 192 confirmed victories and with the Swords and Oakleaves to the Knights' Cross.

As June drew to a close the pace of action over the Norwegian coastal belt at last fell off, and for some days there were no encounters of note. As it was by now clear that the German aircraft carrier *Graf Zeppelin* would not be ready for action for months — if at all — II(J)/TrGr 186 ceased to he held even on paper for ultimate inclusion in the ship's complement, and at the start of July this Gruppe was renumbered III/JG 77.

6/7/40

Not until 6 July was further action to take place in the air, but on that date Uffz Zickler of 3/ZG 76 intercepted a Blenheim fighter of 254 Squadron to the west of Stavanger at 1050, and shot it down in flames. P6950 (Plt Off Patterson) had been escorting British warships which were operating off the Norwegian coast when it fell foul of the Bf 110. On similar duties during the day, Sgt Tubbs was obliged to ditch L8842, he and his crew being rescued from the sea by the destroyer *Cossack*. A Hudson was apparently claimed shot down by pilots of II/JG 77, but no details are available and no loss of one of these aircraft has been discovered.

9/7/40

Late in June two Blenheim squadrons from 2 Group, Bomber Command, were again despatched to Scotland to provide an air striking force in the event of any German attempt to launch an invasion from Norway. These units were 21 and 57 Squadrons, which set up base at Lossiemouth. Here they were attached to Coastal Command for daily operations. On 9 July six Blenheims from each Squadron set off to bomb Stavanger/Sola airfield, making an attack which destroyed one Do 215B of AufklGr/ObdL on the ground there, and damaged two more. II/JG 77 and 2/ZG 76 had been scrambled on the approach of the bombers, and after gaining height, attacked as they were leaving the target area. Six claims were made by the Bf 109E pilots, including two by Lt Horst Carganico (later a leading 'Experte' with 60 victories) and two by Fw Menge, while two Bf 110 crews claimed six more. Uffz Freisa claimed one at 1005, then Fw Schumacher two more at 1008 and 1015. Fresia then claimed a fourth at 1035, and two more ten minutes later; these last two claims were not confirmed. Five 21 Squadron aircraft were lost, as were two from 57 Squadron. The remaining five were all damaged, R3608 (Flt Lt Hird) of 57 Squadron force-landing at Wick with one propeller shot off. Plt Off Rodgers landed R3914 of 21 Squadron — the sole survivor of that unit's formation — in a badly shot-up condition with both other members of the crew wounded. They did however claim to have shot down one Bf 109; this would seem to have been the aircraft of Uffz Gerhard Weber of 5/JG 77, who was killed when he attempted to crash-land in the sea during the fight. Missing British aircraft were:

21 Squadron	**57 Squadron**
R3732 Wg Cdr R.C. Bennett	R3750 Flg Off R.A. Hopkinson
R3822 Sgt W.A. Hamlyn	R3847 Sgt F.G. Mills
R8872 Sgt T.W. Hartley	
N3619 Sgt R.W. Rawson — aircraft 'K'	
R3876 Sgt C.D. Stevens	

A little later Sunderland 'Y', N6133, of 201 Squadron (Flt Lt J.D. Middleton) was intercepted while on patrol off Norway by Oblt Gollob of 3/ZG 76, and was shot down by him at 1447 about 90 miles south-west of Sumburgh. At 1720 Gollob, together with Ofw Schob and Oblt Böhmel of the same Staffel, caught a patrolling Hudson, 'J', N7377, of 233 Squadron (Plt Off L.J.E. Ewing), and shot this down also. Whether they were still returning from the sortie during which the Sunderland was shot down, or had taken off again, is not certain.

Another Hudson was lost next day when 'P' of 220 Squadron was shot down over the North Sea, one member of the crew being killed. On 21 July two more Hudsons, 'X', N7305 (Plt Off C.I. Marison) of 224 Squadron and 'Z', N7241 (Plt Off W. Laverick) of 233 Squadron both failed to return from an attack on a tanker and five escorting ships off the Norwegian coast; both were shot down at 1345 west of Hestholmen by Lt Eckardt and Uffz Ladwein of 2/ZG 76. On that same date Oblt Lorenz Weber of III/JG 77's 8 Staffel was reported missing over the sea near Linaesö Island after he had shot down a Sunderland. His victim would seem to have been 'A', N9028, of 204 Squadron flown by Wg Cdr E.S.C. Davies, OBE, DFC, which failed to return from a reconnaissance over the Trondheim area. Something over a week later 233 Squadron lost a further Hudson when Plt Off Paton failed to return; it was reported that he crashed at Trondheim, presumably shot down by the Flak defences. Next day the unit suffered a further loss when Hudson 'O', N7224 (Plt Off J.M. Horan) failed to return from an attack on a merchant vessel in the North Sea. This aircraft fell to Ofw Arnoldy of II/JG 77 (his sixth victory), while Fw Menge of the same unit claimed a Blenheim. This was R3895 of 114 Squadron flown by Sqn Ldr Kennedy, who was leading an attack on Aalborg airfield, Denmark; a second Blenheim was damaged during this raid.

August 1940

During August attention was diverted south as the Luftwaffe assault on England got fully underway. III/JG 77 left Norway at the end of July, but the other fighter units remained for the time being, I/ZG 76 to escort the bombers of KG 26 and KG 30 against targets in northern Great Britain when the time was ripe, II/JG 77 and IV/JG 2 to provide local defence. I/ZG 76 continued to aid in this latter duty, as on 7 August when the newly-promoted Fw Ladwein of 2 Staffel intercepted and shot down Hudson 'F', N7282, of 224 Squadron (Flg Off R.B. Forbes) which was on a reconnaissance sortie; the bomber went down to the west of Bergen at 1404.

A big engagement occurred on 13 August when two Blenheim squadrons of Bomber Command's 2 Group were ordered to raid Aalborg airfield again. One of the units taking part was 82 Squadron, which sent off 12 aircraft in two flights — a full strength raid. On the way across the North Sea Sgt Baron was obliged to turn back early due to fuel shortage, but the remaining 11 ran into defences that were fully prepared for them. It seems that either the German attacked both squadrons, or that they took each flight of 82 Squadron to be a full formation; two waves of bombers were reported, the first of 12 bombers and the second of 11. 11 of the first batch were claimed shot down, six by fighters and five by Flak, while from the second wave five more were claimed by fighters. There may well have been an element of double claiming between the fighters and the Flak on this occasion, but in fact all 11 aircraft of 82 Squadron were lost, while no losses were recorded in respect of the second unit taking part. Amongst the 11 claims made by the German fighters, which all appear to have been Bf 109Es of II/JG 77, four were credited to Fw Menge, two to Ofw Rudolf Schmidt, one each to Lts Carganico and von Müller-Riensburg and one to Oblt Friedrich, Staffelkapitän of 6 Staffel. This was the second time that 82 Squadron had been wiped out in this manner, the previous occasion having been over France during May. Losses were as follows:

T1934 Wg Cdr Lart	R3829 Sqn Ldr Wardell
T1827 Sqn Ldr Jones	R3802 Flt Lt Ellen
R3800 Flt Lt Syms	R1933 Plt Off Parfitt
R2913 Plt Off Wigley	R3904 Plt Off Newland
R3821 Plt Off Hale	T1889 Sgt Oates
R2772 Sgt Blair	

This combat raised Robert Menge's personal score to 14, and made him by far the most successful fighter pilot of the whole campaign over Norway and Denmark. He had previously served in Spain where he had been credited with three victories. Commissioned, he joined JG 26 later in the year, and flew in 1941 as Rottenflieger to the Geschwader Kommodore, Oberstlt Adolf Galland on occasions. Here he would gain two more victories to raise his total to 19 before being shot down and killed over France on 14 June 1941 by the great RAF fighter pilot, Sqn Ldr (then) 'Jamie' Rankin.

15/8/40

Two days after the great slaughter of the Blenheims the tables were completely turned. Assuming that all British fighter reserves had been drawn to the south, the units of Luftflotte 5 in Norway now launched their well-known attack on Northern England, 63 He 111Hs of I and III/KG 26 and 21 escorting Bf 110Ds of I/ZG 76, all from Stavanger, and 50 KG 30 Ju 88s from Aalborg, heading for Newcastle and Driffield respectively. As is now well-recorded history, both raids were intercepted by British fighters in some strength, and very serious losses were inflicted on the Luftwaffe units. Attacked by two squadrons of Spitfires and two of Hurricanes, the northerly formation lost one He 111 of I/KG 26 and seven of III Gruppe, while I/ZG 76 lost seven Bf 110s, including those flown by the Gruppenkommandeur, Hpt Restemeyer, the Adjutant, Oblt Loobes, and one of the more successful pilots, Lt Köhler. The hard-pressed Messerschmitts did what they could, and some rather wild claiming followed, 12 British fighters being believed to have been shot down. Actually one Hurricane crash-landed and a second was damaged.

Further south the Ju 88s were successful in carrying out their bombing of Driffield airfield where ten Whitleys were destroyed on the ground, but seven of the attacking bombers were brought down and three more damaged. Of those lost, two I Gruppe aircraft were Ju 88C Zerstörer.

After this disastrous start, Luftflotte 5 played no further part in the Battle of Britain, its bomber units leaving early in 1941 for the Mediterranean area. The fighters stayed an even shorter time, I/ZG 76 returning to Germany at the end of August to become part of the new night fighter force; IV/JG 2 had already left in June for the same reason, and in the event both units would provide crews for the new II/NJG 1. Meanwhile II/JG 77 moved to the Channel Coast at the start of November, this move following the arrival at Stavanger of Stab and III/ZG 76 as replacement fighter garrison. The southern coastline of Norway remained a dangerous place for the RAF however, 18 Group of Coastal Command losing six Blenheim fighters, 11 Hudsons and three Beauforts in this area between 20 August and the end of 1940. One of these, a Hudson of 224 Squadron (N7268), fell to Ofw Sawallisch of II/JG 77 on 8 September as his sixth or seventh victory of the war.

APPENDIX

EAGLES FULLY FLEDGED

As the eight months of the 'Phoney War' ended with the explosion of action as the Germans launched their attack through Holland and Belgium on 10 May 1940, it is probably true to say that of the forces involved, other than those operating in and around Norway, only the fighter pilots of the combatant nations, together with a few aerial reconnaissance crews, had properly been 'blooded' in action. Many of those whose names have appeared in these pages were to build illustrious reputations as the war progressed. Others shone brightly for a time and were then snuffed out like candles in a storm. Many feature in other titles within this series.

Before leaving the scene at the outbreak of the 'real' war therefore, perhaps it is opportune to consider what became of the more noteable of those 'Fledgling Eagles' who had enjoyed the opportunity offered by the 'Phoney War' to test their wings. Of those mentioned in this book, their subsequent involvement in the war is listed below by unit and alphabetically within each unit:

1. THE LUFTWAFFE
I/Jagdgeschwader 1
Adolph, Walter   Served in JG 27, then JG 26; 25 victories (one in Spain); Knights' Cross; KIA 18 September 1941.

I/Jagdgeschwader 2
Bertram, Otto   21 victories (nine in Spain); Knights' Cross; withdrawn from action in October 1940 as a 'last son' after his brothers were KIA.

Pflanz, Rudì   52 victories; Knights' Cross; KIA 31 July 1942.

Wick, Helmut   56 victories; top-scorer of the Luftwaffe at the time of his death in action on 28 November 1940 as Kommodore JG 2; Knights' Cross with Oakleaves.

IV/Jagdgeschwader 2
Förster, Hermann   13 victories; North Africa with I/JG 27 later. KIA December 1941.

Schmale, Willi   9-12 victories; Served in NJG3.

I/Jagdgeschwader 20
Jung, Harald   20 victories; JG 51 later.

Lignitz, Arnold   25 victories; Hauptmann in JG 54; Knights' Cross; KIA 30 September 1941.

I/Jagdgeschwader 26
Bürschgens, Joseph   10 victories; POW 1 September 1940.

Handrick, Gotthard	Probably five in Spain and five in Russia with JG 77; Kommodore JG26 during the Battle of Britain.

II/Jageschwader 26

Müncheberg, Joachim	135 Victories; Knights' Cross with Swords and Oakleaves; Kommodore JG 77 in the Mediterranean 1942/43; KIA 23 March 1943.

10(N)/Jagdgeschwader 26

Gerhardt, Werner	13 victories; Oberfeldwebel in II/JG 26 later. KIA 19 August 1942
Steinhoff, Johannes	178 victories; Knights' Cross with Oakleaves; JG 52 in Russia, then Kommodore JG 77 after Müncheberg; badly burned in Me 262 crash in final days of the war. Inspector-General of German Air Force in NATO.
Szuggar, Willy	9 victories (four in Spain); JG 52 in Russia.

I/Jagdgeschwader 51

Bär, Heinz	221 victories; Knights' Cross with Swords and Oakleaves; flew on many fronts; one of top-scorers on Me 262 jets.
Joppien, Hermann-Friedrich	70 victories; Knights' Cross and Oakleaves; one of top-scorers of Battle of Britain; KIA 25 August 1941 in Russia.
Pitcairn, Douglas	4 victories; Major later.

II/Jagdgeschwader 51 (previously I/JG71)

Fözö, Josef	27 victories (three in Spain); Knights' Cross; injured in accident as Major on 11 July 1941. Injured again 31 May 1942.
Hohagen, Erich	56 victories; Knights' Cross. Later JG2, 27 and JV 44.
Illner, Johann	7 victories; POW 5 November 1940.
John, Hans	8 victories; KIA 28 October 1940 as an Oberfeldwebel.
Tietzen, Horst	27 victories (seven in Spain); Knights' Cross; KIA 18 August 1940.

I/Jagdgeschwader 52

Berthel, Hans	6 victories; POW in England 15 September 1940.

I/Jagdgeschwader 53

Balfanz, Wilfred	8 victories; KIA 24 June 1941 as an Oberleutnant in Russia with I/JG 53.
Claus, Georg (also III/JG 53)	17 victories; KIA over England 11 November 1940 as an Oberleutnant.
Kornatz, Hans	36 victories; service in the Mediterranean and on the Russian fronts.
Lippert, Wolfgang	30 victories (five in Spain); Knights' Cross; Kommandeur of II/JG 27; died of wounds as POW in North Africa, 28 November 1941.
Mix, Dr Erich (also III/JG 2)	5 victories (2 World War I, 3 World War II); Kommodore JG 1 later.
Mölders, Werner (also III/JG 53)	115 victories (15 in Spain); Knights' Cross with Swords and Diamond Oakleaves; top-scorer during most of 1940; first pilot to reach 100 victories;

	Inspector of Day Fighters in 1941; Killed in flying accident 22 November 1941.
Ohly, Hans	15 victories; Staffelkapitän 1 Staffel in September 1940; later in III/JG3.
Pingle, Rolf-Peter	28 victories (six in Spain); Knights' Cross; Kommandeur I/JG 26 later; POW in England 10th July 1941.
Prestele, Ignatz	about 21 victories; Kommandeur I/JG 2 later; KIA as Hauptmann 4 May 1942.
Wurmheller, Josef	102 victories; Knights' Cross with Swords and Oakleaves; Kommandeur III/JG 2 later; 93 victories in the West; KIA 22 June 1944, colliding with wingman.

II/Jagdgeschwader 53

Bretnutz, Heinz	35 victories (two in Spain); Knights' Cross; died of wounds in Russia, 27 June 1941 as Hauptmann.
Litjens, Stefen	38 victories; Knights' Cross; lost right eye in Russia September 1941, but continued to fly; wounded 23 March 1944 and no further action.
Von Maltzahn, Günther Freiherr	68 victories; Knights' Cross with Oakleaves; Kommodore of JG 53 later, then Jäfü Italien 1943-44 as Oberst.
Mayer, Hans-Karl	39+ victories (eight in Spain); Knights' Cross; one of top-scorers of Battle of Britain; KIA 17 October 1940.
Michalski, Gerhard	73 victories; Knights' Cross with Oakleaves; top-scorer over Malta in 1942; Kommodore JG 4 1944-45.
Schulze-Blanck, Günther	4 victories; KIA 9 September 1940.

III/Jagdgeschwader 53

Claus, Georg	See above under I/JG 53.
Von Hahn, Hans	34 victories; Knights' Cross; Kommandeur of Gruppen in JG 1 and JG 3 later as Major.
Mölders, Werner	See above under I/JG 53.
Neuhoff, Hermann	40 victories; Knights' Cross; shot down over Malta and POW, 10 April 1942.
Stoll, Jakob	14 victories at least by autumn 1940 when Staffelkapitän 9 Staffel. KIA 17 September 1940.
Wilcke, Wolf-Dietrich	162 victories; Knights' Cross with Swords and Oakleaves; Kommodore JG 3, KIA 23 March 1944.

I/Jagdgeschwader 54

Seiler, Reinhard	109 victories (nine in Spain); Knights' Cross with Oakleaves; badly wounded as a Major.
Stolte, Paule	43 victories, JG 3 later; KIA as Hauptmann, 18 October 1943.

I/Jagdgeschwader 71 (became II/JG 51 in November 1939)

Fözö, Josef	See above under II/JG 51.
Leie, Erich	118 victories; Knights' Cross; JG 51, JG 2 and JG 77 later; KIA 7 March 1945.

I/Jagdgeschwader 76 (later II/JG 54)

Stotz, Max — 189 victories; Knights' Cross with Oakleaves; JG 54 in the East later; KIA 19 August 1943.

II/Jagdgeschwader 77

Arnoldy, Hans-Jacob — 7 victories; KIA in Greece 15 April 1941.

Von Bülow, Harry — 6 victories in World War I; Knights' Cross; Kommodore of JG 2 later.

Carganico, Horst — 60 victories; Knights' Cross; Major in JG 5; killed in landing accident 27 May 1944.

Hackl, Anton — 192 victories; Knights' Cross with Swords and Oakleaves; Kommodore of several units; served in Russia, Africa and the West.

Kutscha, Herbert — 47 victories; Knights' Cross.

Menge, Robert — 19 victories (four in Spain); Leutnant in JG 26 later; KIA 14 June 1941.

Sawallisch, Erwin — 36 victories (three in Spain); served with JG 27 in North Africa; killed in flying accident 19 August 1942.

Schmidt, Winfried — 19 victories; Knights' Cross; JG 3 later; badly wounded.

III/Jagdgeschwader 77 (previously II(J)/Trägergruppe 186)

Emmerich, Peter — 6 victories; JG 51 later.

Kaiser, Herbert — 68 victories; Knights' Cross.

Schopper, Hans — 17 victories, badly wounded later.

Jagdgruppe 101

Kaldrack, Rolf — 21 victories; Knights' Cross with Oakleaves; Zerstörer pilot in Russia; KIA 3 February 1942.

Jagdgruppe 102 (I/ZG 2)

Gentzen, Hannes — 18 victories; killed in flying accident 26 May 1940.

Groth, Erich — 12 victories; Knights' Cross; Kommandeur II/ZG 76; KIA 11 August 1941.

Kiel, Johannes — 25-30 victories, plus 62 on the ground; Knights' Cross; KIA as Hauptmann 29 January 1944.

Scherer, Walter — 10 victories, POW in England 25 September 1940.

Jagdgruppe 126 (III/ZG 26)

Haugk, Helmut — 18 victories; Knights' Cross.

Schalk, Johann — 15 victories; Knights' Cross; Kommandeur III/ZG 26; night fighter later.

Jagdgruppe 152

Elstermann, Willi — 9 victories; night fighter later as Hauptmann.

Grasser, Hartmann — 103 victories; Knights' Cross with Oakleaves; JG 51 in Russia and Africa.

Wiggers, Hans — 13 victories; Hauptmann in JG 51 later; KIA 11 September 1940.

I/Zerstörergeschwader 1

Ehle, Walter — 38 victories; Knights' Cross; night fighter later; KIA as Major 17 November 1943.

Huth, Joachim-Friedrich — Knights' Cross as Kommandeur.

Lutz, Martin — Knights' Cross; Hauptmann in ErpGr 210; KIA 27 September 1940.

Streib, Werner	68 victories; Knights' Cross with Swords and Oakleaves; night fighter and one of top-scorers at night; Inspector of Night Fighters in 1944.
Wandam, Siegfried	10 victories; night fighter later; KIA as Hauptmann, 4 July 1943.

I/Zerstörergeschwader 26

Specht, Günther	39 victories; Knights' Cross; Kommodore JG 11 later; KIA 1 January 1945.

I/Zerstörergeschwader 76

Eckardt, Reinhold	22 victories; Knights' Cross; night fighter later; KIA 30 July 1942.
Fahlbusch, Fritz	6 victories; KIA 30 April 1940.
Falck, Wolfgang	8 victories; also served in I/ZG 1; Kommodore of NJG 1 as Oberst.
Fleischmann, Georg	5 victories; KIA 30 April 1940.
Fresia, Heinz	6 victories at least.
Gollob, Gordon	150 victories; Knights' Cross with Swords and Oakleaves; first fighter pilot to 150 victories with JG 3; Inspector of Day Fighters as Oberst in 1945.
Herget, Wilhelm	72 victories; Knights' Cross with Oakleaves; night fighter later; 14 by day on Zerstörer.
Kamp, Hans-Karl	24 victories; night fighter later; KIA as Hauptmann 31 December 1944.
Lent, Helmut	113 victories; Knights' Cross with Swords and Diamond Oakleaves; for long was top-scoring night fighter — 105 by night; died of injuries from flying accident, 7 October 1944.
Linke, Lothar	27 victories; Knights' Cross; night fighter later; KIA 13/14 May 1943.
Schob, Herbert	28 victories (six in Spain); Knights' Cross; Hauptmann later.
Schumacher, Leo	23 victories; Knights' Cross.
Woltersdorf, Helmut	24 victories; night fighter later; KIA 1/2 June 1942.

Z/Kampfgeschwader 30

Lauffs, Peter	12 victories; night fighter later; KIFA 27 January 1942 in Mediterranean.

V(Z)/Lehrgeschwader 1

Methfessel, Werner	8 victories at least; KIA 17 May 1940.

I(J)/Lehrgeschwader 2

Trübenbach, Hans	9 victories; Kommodore JG 52 later.

I/Stukageschwader 1

Hozzel, Paul-Werner	France and Battle of Britain 1940, Mediterranean early 1941 — led attack on HMS *Illustrious* on 10 January 1941, Kommodore StG 2 1941-43 in Russia; Oak Leaves to Knights' Cross in 1943. Senior Staff position thereafter. POW in East until 1956.

X Fliegerkorps

Harlinghausen, Martin	First bomber pilot to receive Oak Leaves, 1941; aged 38 in 1940. Served in the Mediterranean and

then Brittany. GenMaj in December 1942, and commanded II Fliegerkorps; then General in Germany. GenLt in Bundeswehr in 1957.

2. ROYAL AIR FORCE
1 Squadron

Brown, Mark Henry	Canadian, received DFC and Bar; claimed 17-20 victories, some shared and others unconfirmed. Became Wing Commander and killed by Italian AA fire over Sicily, 12 November 1941.
Clisby, Leslie Redford	Australian; reportedly had claimed 16 by 15 May 1940 when killed in action, awarded DFC.
Clowes, Arthur Victor	DFC, DFM; Squadron Leader later, and served in North Africa. Had claimed 12 and one shared by end of 1940.
Drake, Billy	DSO, DFC and Bar, 20+ victories. 128 Squadron in West Africa 1941; 112 Squadron in North Africa 1942, then Wing Leader. RAF after the war.
Hanks, Peter Prosser	DSO, DFC; 14 victories. Commanded 257 Squadron, then Wing Leader on Malta 1942. Group Captain later.
Kilmartin, John Ignatius	DFC. 43 Squadron in Battle of Britain; 15 or 16 victories. Later commanded 602,313 and 245 Squadrons before becoming Wing Commander.
Mould, Peter William Olber	DFC and Bar; 11 victories. Commanded 185 Squadron on Malta; missing 1 October 1941.
Plinston, George Hugo Formby	DFC, 7 victories. 242 Squadron in France in June 1940, then North Africa in 1942.
Richey, Paul Henry Mills	DFC and Bar; 8 or 9 victories. 609 Squadron 1941, then commanded 74 Squadron. Wing Commander 1942, and Burma later.
Soper, Francis Joseph	DFC, DFM; 14-16 victories. Commissioned later and commanded 257 Squadron; missing 5 October 1941.
Stratton, William Hector	DFC and Bar. New Zealander; 2 victories. Served in Middle East later.
Walker, Peter Russell	DSO, DFC; 8 or 9 victories, all in France. Commanded 253 Squadron later, then Wing Commander.

41 Squadron

Blatchford, Howard Peter	Canadian; DFC; 7 victories — some shared. 257 Squadron 1940; Wing Leader, Digby later. Killed 3 May 1943.
Ryder, Edgar Norman	DFC and Bar. Later commanded 56 Squadron, then Wing Leader, Kenley. 6 victories, then POW October 1941.

43 Squadron

Carey, Frank Reginald	DFC and two Bars; DFM; 16-18 victories by end of 1940, 2 or 3 in Burma. 3 Squadron in France, 1940, then returned to 43 Squadron. Commanded 135

	Squadron 1941-2, then Wing Commander in Burma-India,
Christie, George Patterson	Canadian; DFC and Bar; 7 victories. PR pilot April-July 1940, then 242 Squadron. Killed in flying accident.
Hallowes, Herbert James Lampriere	DFC, DFM and Bar. Commissioned late in 1940. 21 victories, including two shared. 122 Squadron 1942, then commanded 165, 504 and 222 Squadrons.
Hull, Caesar Barrand	See 263 Squadron.
North, Harold Leslie	New Zealander, DFC — 7 or 8 victories. 7 June 1940 shot down and badly burned. Killed 1 May 1942.
Ottewill, Peter G.	Five and two shared victories when shot down and badly wounded in France on 7 June, 1940; too badly wounded to fly again.
Simpson, John William Charles	DFC and Bar, 13 victories. Later commanded 245 Squadron.
Townsend, Peter Wooldridge	DSO, DFC and Bar. 10 and three shared victories. Commanded 85 Squadron, becoming a night fighter. Commanded 605 Squadron in 1942 as Wing Commander, Royal Equerry after war, and famous as personality, broadcaster and writer.

46 Squadron

Cross, K.B.B.	Survived sinking of HMS *Glorious*; subsequently became fighter commander; commanded RAF fighters in Tunisia in 1942/43.
Drummond, John Fraser	DFC; did not return on *Glorious*; four and one shared victories with 92 Squadron in Battle of Britain; killed in action on 10 October 1940.
Jameson, Patric Geraint	New Zealander, DSO, DFC and Bar. Survived sinking of HMS *Glorious*; later commanded 266 and 485 Squadrons, then led Norwegian Spitfire Wing. 9 victories.
Lefevre, Peter William	DFC; did not return on HMS *Glorious*. Continued to fly with 46 Squadron in Battle of Britain, then Malta. Flight commander in 126 Squadron, then commanded 266 Squadron on Typhoons in 1943. Nine and four shared victories. Killed by Flak 6 February 1944.

54 Squadron

Way, Basil Hugh	Became flight commander; three and three shared victories; killed in action 25th July 1940.

56 Squadron

Soden, Ian Scovill	DSO; five and one shared victories in France; killed in flying accident 18 May 1940.

72 Squadron

Elsdon, Thomas Arthur Francis	DFC; eight victories in Battle of Britain; flight commander in 257 Squadron, then commander 136 Squadron and to Burma, where Wing Commander.

Son also a Wing Commander, lost in Tornado during Gulf War 1991.

Sheen, Desmond Frederick Burt — Australian, DFC and Bar. Four and two shared victories. Later commanded the squadron.

73 Squadron

Ayerst, Peter V — DFC; one victory in Battle of Britain while with OTU; long service in several theatres with 33, 238 and other squadrons.

Kain, Edgar James — New Zealander, DFC. Top-scorer of RAF in Battle of France, with final total of 17. Killed in flying accident, June 1940.

Lovett, Reginald Eric — DFC; five victories; killed in action 7 September 1940.

Martin, Richard Frewen — DFC; 7-8 victories in Battle of Britain and North Africa. Flew Tomahawks in 250 Squadron in 1942. Test pilot with Gloster Aircraft later.

Orton, Newell — DFC and Bar; 15 victories over France, then wounded. Flight commander 242 Squadron, then commanded 54 Squadron in 1941; two more victories, then killed in action 17 September 1941.

Paul, Harold George — five victories in France, May/June 1940.

Scoular, John Evelyn — DFC; 12 in France, then three more in East and North Africa. Commanded 250 Squadron on first Tomahawks in 1941.

74 Squadron

Malan, Adolph Gysbert — South African; DSO and Bar, DFC and Bar. Became squadron commander, and by 1941 was Fighter Command's top-scorer as Wing Leader, Biggin Hill, with 32 victories. Group Captain later in the war.

79 Squadron

Davies, James William Elias — American, DFC; five and two shared; missing in action as a flight commander, 27 June 1940.

85 Squadron

Atcherley, D.F.W. — later noteable as fighter commander.

Lee, Richard Hugh Anthony — DSO, DFC; about nine victories. Killed in action 18 August 1940.

87 Squadron

Cock, John Reynolds — Australian; DFC; eight and one shared.

David, William David — DFC and Bar; 11 in France, then flew in Battle of Britain, joining 213 Squadron. Night fighter later; about 20 victories.

Nowell, Gareth Leofric — DFM and Bar; 12, including one with 32 Squadron. Wounded. Commissioned later and to 124 Squadron; two more victories in 1943. Also served in 616 Squadron.

Voase-Jeff, Robert — DFC and Bar; five victories. Killed in action 11 August 1940.

111 Squadron

Broadhurst, Harry — DSO and Bar; DFC and Bar; Wing Commander,

	then Group Captain. 11 more victories by 1942, then to North Africa, rising to command Western Desert Air Force. Later commanded 2nd Tactical Air Force; Air Chief Marshal in 1957.
Bruce, David Campbell	six and two shared; killed in action 4 September 1940.
Dutton, Roy Gilbert	DFC and Bar; to 145 Squadron as flight commander; 17 and three shared. Commanded 452, 19 and 141 Squadrons, the latter as a night fighter.
Dymond, William Lawrence	DFM; 11 and one shared; killed in action 2 September 1940.
Ferriss, Henry Michael	DFC; 10-12 victories; killed 16 August 1940 in collision with Do 17.
Powell, Robert Peter Reginald	DFC and Bar. Later commanded 111 and 121 Squadrons, then led Hornchurch Wing. Seven and two shared victories.

151 Squadron

Donaldson, Edward Mortlock	brother of J.W. Donaldson of 263 Squadron. DSO; ten victories; gunnery instructor later. Gained first world air speed record in a jet aircraft after the war. Air Correspondent of 'Daily Telegraph' for many years.

263 Squadron

Carpenter, John Michael Vowles	DFC and Bar; 222 Squadron in Battle of Britain, then 126 Squadron on Malta. Eight or nine victories; commanded 72 Squadron in Italy later.
Hull, Caesar Barrand	Southern Rhodesian; DFC, back to 43 Squadron as commanding officer in England. 12 and three shared victories; killed in action 7 September 1940.
Riley, William	DFC; flight commander in 302 Squadron, then on Beaufighters in 252 and 272 Squadrons, and commander of 227 Squadrons, all in Mediterranean area. Seven and two shared victories; killed in flying accident, 16 July 1942.
Whall, Basil Ewart Patrick	nine and two shared; died of injuries from flying accident, 7 October 1940

504 Squadron

Beamish, Francis Victor	DSO and Bar, DFC; 8-11 victories. Long-serving officer, aged 37 in 1940. Commanded North Weald, June 1940, but flew on operations until missing in action 25 March 1942.

602 Squadron

Farquhar, Andrew Douglas	DFC; two and two shared victories; later Wing Commander Flying, Hornchurch.
Johnstone, Alexander Vallance Riddell	DFC; six and one shared; later Wing Leader on Malta in 1943.
McKellar, Archie Ashmore	DFC and Bar; to 605 Squadron as flight commander and one of top-scorers of Battle of Britain with about 20 victories; killed in action 1 November 1940.

603 Squadron

Boulter, John Clifford	DFC; five victories; killed in flying accident 17 February 1941.
Carbury, Brian John George	New Zealander; DFC and Bar; 14 and two shared, including five on 31 August 1940.
Denholm, George Lovell	DFC; three and three shared; commanded squadron, and later led 605 Squadron.
Gilroy, George Kemp	DSO, DFC and Bar; commander of 609 Squadron in 1941, then Wing Leader in Tunisia. 24 victories, ten of them shared,
Morton, James Storrs	DFC and Bar; six and three shared, then two more as a night fighter. Wing Commander later.
Stapleton, Basil Gerald	South African; DFC; later flight commander in 257 Squadron, then commanded 247 Squadron on Typhoons; six and two shared victories.

605 Squadron

Currant, Christopher Frederick	DSO, DFC and Bar; ten and five shared; commanded 501 Squadron, then Wing Commander.
Edge, Gerald Richmond	DFC; several victories; commanded 253 Squadron later, then returned to lead 605.
Muirhead, Ian James	DFC; six and one shared; killed in action 15 October 1940.

607 Squadron

Sample, John	DFC; five victories. Commanded 137 Squadron on Whirlwinds; killed in flying accident, 28 October 1941.

615 Squadron

Sanders, James Gilbert	DFC; nine or ten victories; night fighter later.

OTHER UNITS

57 Squadron

Day, Harry M.A.	famous escaper in prisoner of war camps; known as 'Wings' Day,

77 Squadron

Raphael, Gordon Learmonth	Canadian; DFC May 1940. Converted to night fighting, serving in 96 Squadron, then 85 Squadron. Bar to DFC summer 1941. Seven victories by 1943, and DSO. Later shot down two V-ls in a Mosquito; killed in a flying accident 10 April 1945

107 Squadron

Embrey, Basil	shot down in France and captured; escaped and got back to England; became very senior officer in 2nd Tactical Air Force, and led many daylight bombing raids.

269 Squadron

Hayley-Bell, Dennis	DFC; remustered as night fighter; commanded 68 Squadron in 1944; several victories.

3. FLEET AIR ARM

Baldwin, George C	DSC; later gained first victory of the war in a Seafire over French North Africa in 807 Squadron. Com-

	manded squadron, then 4th Naval Wing in Mediterranean and Italy, 1943-5.
Carver, R.H.P.	DSC; led 885 Squadron in the Mediterranean in 1942; led 3rd Naval Wing in Western Europe, 1944.
Charlton, Philip Noel	DFC, DSC; flew Hurricanes in North Africa late in 1941; shot down three Ju 87s on 20 November 1941. Later commanded 1834 Squadron on Corsairs in the Pacific.
Hay, Ronald C	DSO, DSC and Bar; flew Fulmars in the Mediterranean in 1941 convoy battles, then Wing Leader of HMS *Victorious*' Corsair Wing in the Pacific; two and seven shared victories; Royal Marine; Lieutenant Colonel by end of war.

4. ARMEE DE L'AIR
GC I/2

Patureau-Miraud, Raoul	four-six victories, two shared; shot down and killed by Flak, 17 June 1940.
Williame, Robert	eight victories, four of them shared in the Battle of France, plus two probables; six on 8 June 1940 (two shared and two probables) in two combats; killed in flying accident, 31 October 1940.

GC III/2

Moret, Antoine	eight victories, five of them shared.
Romey, Maurice	five and three probables, most of them shared.

GC II/3

Codet, Marcel	five and three probables, most shared.
Loi, Martin	four and one probable, then one with GC III/6 later.

GC III/3

Le Nigen, Edouard	12 and one probable in May-June 1940, the first eight on MS 406s, the rest on D 520s; eight were shared. Killed 25 July 1940.

GC III/6

Le Gloan, Pierre	11 and one probable (seven shared) by the end of the Battle of France, many of them against the Italians, flying a D 520; five and two probables against the British in Syria; final credit 18 and two probables; killed in a flying accident in September 1943, in North Africa.
Martin, Robert	five victories; killed
Steunou, Marcel	two in summer 1940, six by the end of the war, three of them shared.

GC II/7

Boíllot, Pierre	seven and one probable, several of them shared.
Doudies, Jean	five and two probables, mainly shared.
Gauthier, Gabriel	flew P-40Fs in GC II/5 'Lafayette' with the Allies in Tunisia in 1943; 11 victories, at least seven of them shared. Flew Vampires with GC I/2 in 1950.

Gruyelle, Michel	gained victories over Corsica in a Spitfire in 1943.
Hugo, Henri	six and two probables, mainly shared.
Lamblin, Jacques	several victories, including a number of probables.
Planchard, Rene	several victories, including a number of probables.
Valentin, Georges	seven and two probables, most of them shared; one against the RAF in November 1940; later flew Spitfires in 1943 as commander of an escadrille in GC I/7; killed 8 September 1944.

GC III/7

Littolf, Albert	six shared in 1940, then six and one shared with the RAF in North Africa in 1941, and the Normandie Niemen unit in Russia; killed in action in Russia on 16 July 1943.

GC I/4

Lemaire, Georges	two British aircraft at Dakar, September 1940, then nine (four shared) in Russia with Normandie Niemen.

GC II/4

Baptizet, Georges	nine and four probables, most shared.
Casenoble, Jean	seven and two probables, most shared; killed.
de la Chapelle, Antoine	seven victories, five of them shared.
Plubeau, Camille	14 and three or four probables, about half of them shared; flew briefly against the US Navy at Casablanca, November 1942.
Tesseraud, Georges	eight and three probables; flew against US Navy in November 1942; shot down and wounded 9 November. Later shot down Ju 88 in P-39 of GC I/5 in April 1944
Villey, Pierre	five, three shared, and one probable.

GC I/5

Accart, Jean	12, all shared, and four probables, including seven in two days in May 1940; wounded. Flew with RAF later. Senior officer after war.
Boitelot, Hubert	five victories, four of them shared.
Dorance, Michel	14 and three probables, most shared. Killed later.
Marin la Meslee, Eduard	16, 12 of them shared, and four probables; top-scorer of Armée de l'Air in 1940. Flew P-47s later and killed by Flak, 2 February 1945.
Morel, Francois	ten and two probables in ten days — most shared; shot down and killed on parachute, 18 May 1940.
Muselli, Gerard	six and four probables, all shared; test pilot with Dassault in 1970s.
Rey, Jean	nine victories, seven of them shared.
Rouquette, Marcel	eight and six probables, most shared; killed.
Tallent, Maurice	11, all shared, and one probable.
Warnier, Francois	eight and two probables, most shared.

GC II/5

Houzé, Pierre	five victories; shot down and baled out 6 June 1940. Joined infantry rearguard, but killed in action with them two days later.

Huvet, Robert	eight victories, five of them shared; later two more shared US Navy F4Fs on 8 November 1942, then shot down and killed.
Lefol, Georges	11, most shared, and one or two probables.
Legrand, Andre	eight and two probables; later one British aircraft off Oran in July 1940 and one F4F at Casablanca on 8 November 1942.
Portalis, Gerard	three and one probable.
Ruchoux, Georges	five victories, including a Fleet Air Arm Fulmar shared off Casablanca on 8 May 1942. Wounded by US Navy aircraft on 8 November 1942.
Salès, Edouard	seven and two probables, several of them shared.
Villaceque, Pierre	five and two probables; later an F4F on 8 November 1942. Flew P-40Fs with the Allies in Tunisia in 1943.

GCN II/13

Pouyade, Pierre	one probable in 1940. Later commanded Normandie Niemen Regiment, where six victories (four shared). General after war.

INDEX

I Personnel — a) British Commonwealth

Thompson, Plt Off K.G.S. 114 Sqn. 86
Thynne, Sqn Ldr B.S. 601 Sqn. 38
Tice, Sgt G.H. 21 Sqn. 166
Tilney, Lt Cdr G.A. 712 Sqn. 41
Tomlyn, Flt Lt. 77 Sqn. 181
Torrington-Leech, Flg Off. 9 Sqn. 51
Torry, Lt Cdr G.N. 800 Sqn. 41
Townsend, Sgt A.A. 269 Sqn. 337
Townsend, Flt Lt P.W. 43 Sqn. 164, *164*, 166, 169, 226, 248, 361
Townsend, L.A.C.E. 206 Sqn. 308
Tremler, J/A W.J. 800 Sqn. 349
Trolove, Plt Off P.N. 269 Sqn. 351
Tubbs, Sgt. 254 Sqn. 352
Tucker, Plt Off B.E. 73 Sqn. 176, 204
Tullock, Flg Off F.C.L. 220 Sqn. 268
Turner, F/Sgt A.J. 9 Sqn. 51
Turner, Plt Off G. 114 Sqn. 156, 157
Turner, Lt Cdr S. 81? Sqn. 259
Tyrer, Sgt E. 46 Sqn. 338, 343

Upton, Plt Off H.C. 43 Sqn. *164*
Urie, Flt Lt J.D. 602 Sqn. 144

Van Der Kiste, Flt Lt. 210 Sqn. 259
Vercoe, Flg Off. 233 Sqn. 240
Vickery, Flg Off H.F. 263 Sqn. 337, 343
Vickers, Sgt J.H. 88 Sqn. 71
Vipan, Flg Off. 88 Sqn. 71
Voase-Jeff, Flt Lt R. 87 Sqn. 100, *100*, *101*, 362

Walker, Plt Off P.E.W. 77 Sqn. 94

Walker, Flt Lt P.R. 1 Sqn. *120*, 184, 185, 201, 360
Walker, Flg Off. 73 Sqn. 183, 184
Wallace, Capt J.. DFM. 50 Sqn. 257
Waller, Flg Off P.B. 73 Sqn. 147, 204
Walmersley, Flt Lt A.L. 244 Sqn. 84
Walter, Wg Cdr C. 17 Sqn, 67(F) Wing. 38, 108
Warburton-Lee, Capt B.A.W., VC. HMS *Hardy*. 252
Wardell, Sqn Ldr. 82 Sqn. 354
Waring, Sqn Ldr H. 42 Sqn. 39
Warne, Flt Lt P.E. 107 Sqn. 271
Warner, Flg Off, DFC., 37 Sqn. 299, 300
Waterfall, AC1, DFM., 37 Sqn. 300
Waterston, Flg Off R.McG. 603 Sqn. 165
Watkins, Mdspmn F. 803 Sqn. 250
Watkins, Lt Cdr R.D. 823 Sqn. 41
Watson, Sgt R.H. 504 Sqn. 301
Way, Plt Off B.H. 54 Sqn. 166, 361
Webb, Lt Cdr A.S. 714 Sqn. 41
Webb, Flg Off P.A. 602 Sqn. 89
Wells, Vice-Admiral. 293, 302
Wells, Flg Off. 115 Sqn. 217
Whall, Sgt B.E.P. 263 Sqn. 279, 326, 327, 343, 363
Wheatley, Flt Lt C.M. PDU. 182
Wheeler, Sgt H.J. 149 Sqn. 258
White, Flg Off D. 49 Sqn. 290
Whitley, Plt Off W.H.R. 607 Sqn. 90
Whitworth, Vice-Admiral. 225, 260
Wiart, de Maj Gen Carton, VC. (See under Carton de Wiart)
Wickenkamp, Plt Off E.A. 115 Sqn. 217
Wigginton, Sub Lt B. 801 Sqn. 272, 291, 294
Wigglesworth, Wg Cdr C.G., AFC. 209 Sqn. 39

Wigley, Plt Off. 82 Sqn. 354
Wild, Sgt G.M. 50 Sqn. 257
Wildblood, Plt Off T.S. 152 Sqn. 171
Wilkie, Plt Off J.L. 263 Sqn. 314, 338
Williams, Flt Lt A.N.T., DFC. 263 Sqn. 314, 329, 334, 337, 339, 34
Williams, Flg Off R. 77 Sqn. 56, 87
Williams, F/Sgt R.J. 99 Sqn. 130
Williams, Sgt S.A. 44 Sqn. 186
Williams, Flg Off. 233 Sqn. 240
Williams, Plt Off. 99 Sqn. 169
Williamson, Flt Lt. 224 Sqn. 351
Willis, Sub Lt(A) D.G. 801 Sqn. 294
Willoughby de Broke, Sqn Ldr Lord. 605 Sqn. 38
Wilson, Flt Lt A.N. 616 Sqn. 168
Wilson, Sgt. 149 Sqn. 186
Wimberley, Flg Off P.A. 37 Sqn. 138, 149
Winn, Sgt J. 73 Sqn. 120, 147
Winter, Flg Off R.A. Sullom Voe Ftr Flt. 152
Womersley, Flt Lt A.L. 224 Sqn.
Wood, Plt Off N.C. 263 Sqn. 253, *253*, 349
Wood, Grp Capt. 343
Woollatt, Flg Off S.P. 22 Sqn. 308
Wordle, Plt Off H.D. 218 Sqn. 204
Wright, AVM A.C. 1 Group, Bomber Command. 36
Wright, Flt Lt A. 224 Sqn. 130, 280
Wright, N/A S.G. 803 Sqn. 283
Wyatt-Smith, Plt Off P. 263 Sqn. 279, 314

Yorke, Plt Off G.J.D. 233 Sqn. 256

I Personnel — b) French

Accart, Cne Jean-Marie. GC I/5. 119, *156*, 156, 366
Achiantre, Sgt. GAO 505. 63
Amarre, S/Lt. GR II/52. 70
Angiolini, S/Lt. GC II/5. *164*
Aouach, Cne Paul. GB I/31. 83
Armouroux, Asp Georges. GC III/9. 201
Audrain, Sgt Paul. GC II/5. 119, 208
Augereau, Gal FA 109. 35

Baize, S/Lt. GC I/3. 63
Baptizet, S/Lt Georges. GC II/4. 69, 72, 366
Barbey, Sgt. GC III/2. 107
Barbier, Cne Bernard. GC I/4. 157
Barbier, Adj. GR I/52. 182
Bardin, S/Lt Michel. GC II/2. 96
Belèze, Cne. GR II/52. 87
Bellefin, Sgt Chef André. GC III/3. 116
Berenger, Lt. GB I/31. 58
Bernard, Adj. GR II/33. 101
Barnard, Lt. GAO I/520. 68
Bertaux, Lt. GB I/31. 105
Beson, Gal Groupe de Armée No 3. 34
Bevillard, S/Lt Louis. GC III/3. 197
Billotte, Gal Groupe de Armée No 1. 34
Bissoudre, Cne Maurice. GC III/3. 119, 194, *195*, 195
Blanchard, Adj Marcel. ECMI 1/16. 194
Blanchard, Gal 7eme Armée. 35
Bodin, Sgt Jean, GC III/7. 185
Boillot, Sgt Pierre. GC II/7. 201, 365
Boitelot, S/L Hubert. GC I/5. 75, 194, 199, 366
Bonal, Lt. GOA 507. 62
Borne, Cdt André. GC I/4. 28
Bouhy, Sgt Jean. GC II/5. 103, 119
Boulard, S/Lt. GR II/55. 154
Bouvard, Adj Chef Louis. GC I/5. 205
Bouvry, Sgt Chef. GR I/14. 56
Boymond, Sgt Chef Emile. GC III/6. 199
Brard, Adj. GR I/52. 71
Bremond d'Ars, Sgt Pierre de. GC II/6. 116
Bret, Sgt Emile. GC I/7. 199
Bruckert, Adj Henri. GC I/2. 194
Brugnolles, Lt. GR I/52. 182

Cadoux, Cne. GR II/22. 105
Canonne, Gal FA 101. 35
Capdeville, S/Lt. GR I/22. 60
Cappoen, Lt. GAO I/520. *58*, 59
Casenobe, Sgt Chef Jean. GC II/4. 54, 114, 202, *203*, 366
Catois, Sgt. GC II/7. 200
Castellana, Lt. GR II/33. 145
Challe, Cne Bernard. GC I/3. 67
Chambe, Gal FA 107. 35
Chancrin, Sgt Chef Jean. GR II/55. 154
de la Chapelle, Sgt Antoine. GC II/4. 67, 72, 74, 107, 366
Chaussant, Sgt. GC I/3. 67
Chavet, Adj René. GC III/7. 185
Claude, Cne Pierre. GC I/6. 69, 70
Codet, S/L Marcel. GC II/3. 202, 365
Collin, Cdt Pierre. GC I/8. 28
Combette, Adj Antonin. GC I/3. 67, 116
Corap, Gal IXeme Armée. 35
Cormouls, Lt Henri. ECMJ 1/16. 194
Costey, Lt Paul. GC III/7. 212
Crémont, Cdt Louis. GC III/7. 28
Cruchant, Adj Chef Robert. GC II/4. 54, 82, 201, 202
Cuffaut, S/Lt Leon. GC II/6. 116

Dalliere, Cdt Henri. Esc B 5. 111
Dardaine, Adj Henri. GC II/4. 67
Daru, Cdt Marie. GC I/2. 28
Davier, Lt. GAO 553. 55
De Fraville, S/Lt Robert. GC II/7. 146, 160
Dehaus, Sgt GC II/7. 212
Delannoy, Adj Chef. GC II/5. 206
Delarue, S/Lt Raphaël. GC III/7. 115, 199
Delozanne, Cne. GB II/31. 57
De Muyser, Sgt Chef Guy. GC II/2. 194,
Derrien, Admiral. 248, 276
Destaillac, Cne Raymond. GC II/5. 96, 152
Dorance, Lt Michel. GC I/5. 197, *198*, 366
Doudiès, Sgt Chef Jean. GC II/7. 175, 365
Ducasse, Lt. GAO I/520. 88
Duclos, Sgt. GC III/2. 63
Dugoujon, Adj Jean. GC II/5. 103
Dumas, Cpl Chef. GR I/52. 58, 81
Duperret, S/Lt Gabriel. GC II/4. 67
Duriex, Cdt André. GC II/7. 28
Dvorak, Sgt Bedrich (Czech). GC III/7. 185

Enselen, Lt Col. 31eme Escadre. 58

Escarden, Gal 1ere DAe. 34
Escudier, Cne Georges. Esc 5/2. 28
Evano, Cne. GR II/55. 71

Fantanet, Cdt Raymond. GC II/6. 28
Felix, Lt. GR II/55. 154
Ferran, Lt de Vass. AC 1. 32
Fevrier, S/Lt. GR I/52. 81, 87, 202
Fion, Cne. GR I/14. 56
Folliot, Lt de Vass. AC 2. 32
Foriel, Sgt. GAO 509. 176
Frebillot, Cne. GR I/14. 57

Garnier, Sgt Jean. GC I/3. 66
Gasnerie, Sgt de la. GC II/2. 194
Gauthier, S/Lt Gabriel. GC II/7. 115, 146, 365
Genty, Adj Pierre. GC II/5. 62, 75
George, Adj Chef. GAO 553. 72
Gerard, Cne Roger. GC I/3. 66, 66, 67
Gillat, Adj Chef. GAO I/506. 102
Gibon-Guilhem. Cdt. GC II/8. 28
Giraud, Adj Chef. GR I/55. 71
Giraud, Gal VIIeme Armée. 35
Gloanec, Sgt Louis. GC I/2. 193
Girou, Sgt. GC I/5. 194
Gossart, Lt. GAO II/506. 102
Gras, Adj Chef Georges. GC II/5. *104*, 175
Gruyelle, S/Lt Michel. GC II/7. 115, 153, 160, 366
Guerin, Adj. GR II/33. 97
Guieu, Lt Regis. GC II/4. 75
Guigno, Adj. GC II/5. 181
Guillaume, Sgt Jean. GC III/7. 116

Halle, Asp. GR II/52. 55
Hanzlicek, Sgt Otto. (Czech). GC II/5. 208
Hautiere, Lt. GAO 553. 85
Havet, Sgt. GC I/3. 116
Hebrard, Gal 6eme DAe. 34
Heme, Sgt Lucien. GC II/5. 72
Heurtaux, Cdt André. GC I/4. 28
Hirschauer, Lt Jean-Louis. GC I/4. 117
Hocqueviller, Cne. GR III/3. 105
Houzé, Lt Pierre. GC II/5. 102, 103, *103*, *104*, 152, 206, 366
Hugo, Cne Henri. GC II/7. 153, 199, 200, 366
Hugues, Cdt. GC II/5. 28
Huntziger, Gal IIeme Armée. 35
Huvet, Cne Robert. GC II/5. 62, 75, 153, 367

Israel, Lt. GR II/33. 67, 68

Jacquin, Sgt Chef. GC II/7. 116
Janeba, Sgt Chef Josef (Czech). GC I/5. 175
Jaske, S/Lt Josef (Czech). GC II/5. 206, 208
Jonaszik, Sgt Chef Raoul. GC II/7. 153

Kerangueven, Cne. GC III/2. 107
Klan, S/Lt Jan (Czech). GC II/5. 206
Körber, Cpl Chef Karel (Czech). GC II/3. 177, *177*

Lachaux, Adj Francois. GC II/5. 62, 75
Lachèvre, Cne. GB II/15. 153
Lacombe, Cne Georges. GC III/7. 185
Lacombe, Lt Gaston. GC I/3. 58, 116
Laemmel, Lt. GR I/33. 87
Lahayer, Sgt. GAO I/520. *58*
Laluée, Asp. GAO 553. 85
Lambert, Lt. GAO 2/508. 72
Lamblin, Sgt Chef Jacques. GC II/7. 115, 146, 366
Lancrenon, Lt Claude. GC III/7. 117
Laneure. GR I/52. 202
Lapadie, Lt. GAO 553, 72
Laux, Cne Maurice. GR II/33. 200
Le Bideau, Cne. GC III/3. 28
Lechat, Lt. GC II/2. 96
Lefol, S/Lt Georges. GC I/5, GC I/5. 103, *104*, 194, 367
Le Gloan, Sgt Chef Pierre. GC III/6. 119, *119*, 176, 176, 365
Legrand, Sgt André. GC II/5. 62, 102, 103, 154, 367
Leleu, Lt. GAO 1/506. 58
Lemaire, Sgt Georges. GC I/4. 157, 366
Le Martelot, Adj Emile. GC I/2. 194, 195, *195*
Lemoine, Adj Chef. GC I/5. 75
Le Nigen, Sgt Edouard. GC III/3. 176, 365
Leonard, Cne. GAO 507. 63
Lepreux, Sgt Edouard. GC I/5. 75
Lequeu, Lt.GAO 2/508. 72
Le Restif, S/Lt. GC I/5. 75
Leroy, Lt. GR I/22. 60
Le Saoült, Adj. GR I/52. 145
L'Hopital-Navarre, Sgt Maurice. GC III/7. 185
Littolf, Adj Albert. GC III/7. 117, 146, 367

Loi, Sgt Martin. GC I/3. 202, 365

Magniez, Sgt. GC II/5. 75
Maigret, Sgt Chef. GR III/6. 199
Maitret, Lt. GR I/22. 181
Marias, Adj Michel. GC III/7A. 74, *74*, 183
Marie, Adj Chef. GR II/22. 105
Marin la Meslee, Lt Edmond. GC I/5. 156, *156*, 366
Martellière, Cpl. GR I/14. 57
Martin, S/Lt Robert. GC III/6. 119, 176, *176*, 365
Martin, Sgt René. GC II/7. 153
Melchior, S/Lt. GAO 553. 172
Mercy, Adj Chef. GR II/52. 74
Michel, Cdt René. GC II/2. 28
Mioche, Lt Col. Groupement de Chasse 23. 120, 121
Moll, S/Lt. GAO 1/506. 58
Montgolfier, Adj Paul de. GC II/5. 103, 114, 119, 175
Moreau, Sgt Chef. GR II/33. 97
Morel, Sgt Chef François. GC I/5. 205, 366
Moret, Adj Antoine. GC II/2. 96, 365
Morlat, Cdt Jules. GC I/3. 28
Morlot, Sgt Chef René. GC III/7. 185
Mougel, Adj Chef. GR I/52. 202
Murtin, Cdt Jacques. GC I/5. 28
Muselli, Sgt Chef Gérard. GC I/5. 156, *156*, 366

Naudy, Cne André. GC II/3. 177, 195

Octave, Sgt Chef. GC I/3. 67

Pallier, Cdt Gabriel. GC I/1. 28
Panhard, Sgt René. GC II/7. 146
Pape, Cne Joël. GC I/3. 85
Pas, Cdt Deschamps de. GC I/7. 28
Passemard, Sgt. GC II/7. 200
Patrou, Lt Pierre. GC III/3. 74
Patureau-Miraud, Cne Marcel. GC I/2. 197, 365
Pechaud, Sgt. GC II/5. 62
Perina, Sgt Frantisek (Czech). GC I/5. *156*
Pernot, Adj. GR II/33. 145
Petit, S/Lt. GAO I/520. 68
Piaccentini, Sgt Chef. GAO 553. 55
Pilatre-Jacquin, Sgt Chef. GC III/7. 87
Pimont, Sgt Cyhef. GC III/6. 199
Pizon, Sgt Chef René. GC III/2. 196
Place, Cne de. GC III/6. 28
Planchard, Sgt Henri. GC II/7. 153, 200, 366
Plubeau, Adj Camille. GC II/4. 67, 74, 97, 107, 116, *116*, 366
Poincenot, Adj Pierre. GC II/3. 202
Ponteins, Adj Chef. GC II/7. 200
Portalis, Cne Gerard. GC II/5. 154, 155, 208, 367
Potier, Lt Lucien. GC I/3. 67
Potié, Lt. GAO I/520. 59
Pouyade, Cne Pierre. GCN II/13. 28, 367
Pretelot, Gal Groupe d'Armée No 2. 34

Queguinier, Sgt Roger. GC II/7. 62
Quenet, Cne. GC II/2. 87, *87*

Renaud, S/Lt. GC III/7. 154, 185
Renaudie, Adj Chef Marcel. GC II/2. 194
Restif, Lt (See Le Restif)
Rey, Lt Jean. GC I/5. 156, 366
Reyne, Cne Elie. GC I/5. 96
Ribo, Sgt Chef Jules. GC III/3. 176
Richard, Cne André. GC II/2. 194
Risacher, Cdt Louis. ERC I/561, GC II/10. 29
Robert, Adj. GR II/33. 68, 101
Robillon, Cdt Edmond. GC I/1. 28
Rohan-Chabot, Lt Henri de. GC II/2. 194
Romey, Adj Maurice. GC III/2. 63, 64, 365
Ronzet, Cdt Guy. ERC I/561, GC II/10. 29
Roques, Gal FA 102. 35
Rossignol, Cne. GAO 3/551. 59
Rouquette, S/Lt Marcel. GC I/5. *156*, 205, 366
Roussel, Lt. GAO 548. 60, 181, 208
Rousseau-Dumarcet, Cdt Louis. GC I/9. 28
Royanneau, Lt. GAO 509. 182
Ruchoux, Lt Georges. GC II/5. 206, 208, 367
Rupied, S/Lt. GC III/7. 185
Rupert, Adj. GAO II/506. 102

Sagan, Lt. GR II/33. 117
Saillard, Sgt Pierre. GC I/4. 114, 116
Saint-Exupery, Cne Antoine de. GR II/33. 185
Salès, Sgt Edouard. GC II/5. 102, 103, *104*, 105, 114, 208, 367
Salmand, Adj Chef. GC I/5. 62, 194, 197
Salva, Lt. GC I/3. 67
Santini, Cne. GB II/15. 153
Saron, Adj. GR I/22. 60

370

Saudry, Adj. GR II/52. 72
Schmidt, Lt. GAO I/506. 102
Schneider, Cne. GR I/33. 62
Senne, Adj Chef. GAO507. 62
Sonntag, Sgt Leon. GC II/7. 175
Steunou, Lt Marcel. GC III/6. 199, 365
Strub, Sgt Chef. GR I/33. 105
Sueur, Lt. 3/GAO 551. 59

Tacquart, Sgt. GAO 1/520. 59
Tallent, Sgt Chef Maurice. GC I/5. 199, 204, 366
Tesseraud, Adj Georges. GC II/4. 67, 69, 72, 366
Têtu, Gal Cdt FA de C NE. 35
Thibaudet, Cdt André. GC I/3. 28
Thiebault. Adj. GR I/14. 57

Thierry. GC I/3. 116
Tissier, Lt. GR II/52. 68, 70
Tourné, Sgt Robert. GC II/3. 119
Treillard, Cne Jean. GCN I/13. 28
Tremolet, Lt René. GC II/5. 103, *104*, 114
Trévis, Adj. GR I/33. 105
Tricaud, Cdt Georges. GC I/6. 28
Troyes, S/Lt Aimé. GC II/3. 202

Valentin, Adj Chef Georges. GC II/7. 115, 200, 366
Valin, G^{al} 3eme DAe. 34
Verge, Sgt Chef. GR II/52. 87
Verry, S/Lt Pierre. GC I/4. 68
Vidal, Cne. GC I/2. 197.

Vié, Sgt Chef Henri. GC II/3. 202
Viguier, Cdt Armand. ERC 562, GC III/9. 29
Villacèque, S/Lt Pierre. GC II/5. 154, 155, 206, 208, 367
Villey, Adj Pierre. GC II/4. 54, 75, 114, 366
Vinchon. GC I/3. 116
Vuillemin, Gal Armée de l'Air C in C. 34
Vuillemin, Sgt Chef. GC I/5. *156*
Vuillemin, Lt. GC III/6. 199

Warnier, S/Lt Francois. GC I/5. 62, 197, 204, 366
Waryn. Sgt. GR I/33. 105
Weis, Lt André. GC I/4. 117
Wibaux, Sgt Chef. GAO 548. 208
Williame, Cne Robert. GC I/2. 199

I Personnel — c) German

Adolph, Oblt Walter. I/JG 1. 81, 355
Ahlefeld, Oberstlt Hans. I/KG 26. 24, 215, 249
Alf, Fw Ernst. 6/KG 30. 334
Altmann, Uffz Helmut-Gerhard. 4(F)/11. 194
Altvater, Hpt. Stab/KG 4. 215
Andrae, Genlt. Luftgaustab zbV 300. 216
Andreas, Hpt Otto. II.KG 26. 181
Arndt, Uffz Heinz. V(Z)/LG 1. 194
Arnoldy, Lt Hans-Jacob. II.JG 77. 257, 282, 347, 348, 351, 353, 358
Auer, Fw Paul. 3(H)/13. 160
Augustin, Oberstlt. II/KG 77. 21
Awater, Oblt Gustav-Adolf. 1(F)/122. 92

Bascilla, Oblt. 11(NJ)/LG 2. 16
Babekull, Maj. III/KG zbV 172. 24
Backhaus, Uffz Otto. 2/KüFlGr 906. 243
Baerner, Oblt z S Hermann. 1/KüFlGr 106. 267
Baier, Oberst. LG 2. 22
Balc, Maj. I.KG 77. 21
Balfanz, Lt Wilfried, 1.JG 53. 60, 356
Balka, Ofw Wilhelm von. 1/JG 51. 155
Bär, Fw Heinz. I/JG 51. 68, *69*, 356
Bär, Oblt. 11(NJ)/JG 26. 316
Barchfeld, Lt Karl-Wilhelm. 1(F)/22. 175, *176*
Bartels, Maj. 2/KüFlGr 406. 18
Baun, Fw Albrecht. II/JG 53. 186
Baur de Betaz, Oberst. KG zbV 102. 216, 262, 264
Beck, Oblt z S Werner. 1/KüFlGr 806. 192
Becker, Lt. I/FJR 1. 317
Beckhaus, Oblt August. 1/KG 40. 277
Beckmann, Maj. IV/KG zbV 1. 216
Behnke, Lt Kurt. 5(F)/122. 119
Behrendt, Oberst. KG 27. 19
Behrmann, Uffz Hans. II(J)/TrGr 186. 166-7
Beitzke, Hpt. 1/KüFlGr 706. 335
Belghaus, Fw de Res Ferdinand. 1/KüFlGr 406. 122
Bender, Lt. I/ZG 76. 349, 351
Berchem, Maj von. 3(F)/11. 22
Berg, Maj Frhr von. I/JG 51. 17
Bergemann, Hpt. 3/KüFlGr 406. 18
Berthel, Lt Hans. I/JG 52. 83, *83*, 356
Bertram, Oblt Otto. I/JG 2. 202, *203*, 355
Bezner, Uffz Heinrich. I/JG 53. 56. 58. 59
Bieneck, GenMaj. Herresgruppe C. 18
Birking, Oblt z S Erwin. 3/KüFlGr 506. 191
Bischoff, Oberstlt. 2/KüFlGr 106. 18
Blankmeier, Oblt Hans. 1(F)/22. 107
Blass, Ofw Eugen. I/ZG 26. 193
Blattner, Hpt. 4(St)/TrGr 186. 20
Blievernicht, Oblt Hans. 1(F)/122. 181
Blumensaat, Hpt. 10(N)/JG 2. 20
Bock, Oblt z S Bernhard. 3/KüFlGr 106. 128
Bockheimer, Uffz Heinrich. I/ZG 76. 233
Bodien, Uffz Willy. 4(H)/22. 82
Boenigk, Oblt Otto. III/JG 53. 184
Boettger, Lt z S Bruno. 1/KüFlGr 106. 106
Bogatsch, GenMaj. Befhl der Hflgerbd. 18
Bohlen-Halbach, Lt Claus von. I/JG 76. 155
Böhmel, Oblt. I/ZG 76. 271, 352
Böhne, Oblt Heinz. I/StG 1. 303, 339
Bölck, Lt z S Karl-Friedrich. KüFlGr 106. 187
Bönsch, Oblt Herbert. Z/KG 30. 215, 316, 322
Borchers, Fw Adolf. I/JG 77. 153
Bormann, Maj. III(K)/LG 1. 20
Börner, Maj. 9(H)/LG 1. 23
Borsikow, Hpt. 3(F)/31. 23
Borth, Oblt. JGr 152. 67
Bothmer, Oblt von. JGr 152. 58
Bottcher, Oblt Helmut. 4(F)/121. 115
Brack, SonderFührer. I/StG 1. 338
Brandhuber, Lt. I/JG 53. 62
Brandis, Oblt Frhr von. I/FJR 1. 238
Branger, Oblt de Res Wilhelm. Seenotst 2. 320
Braun, Maj von. III/KG 53. 17
Brauer, Ofw Helmut. 1(F)/122. 159
Braukmeier, Fw Friedrich. II/JG 77. 131
Bretnutz, Oblt Heinz. II/JG 53. 75, 186, *186*, 357
Broili, Lt z S. 1/KüFlGr 906. 309
Bruch, GenMaj Wilhelm. Cdr FdL Ost. 18
Brücker, Lt z S Heinz. KüFlGr 806. 317
Brückner, Uffz. I/ZG 76. 264
Brüning, Lt Luther von. I/KG 26. 164
Brünn, Ofw Walter. 2/KG 30. 249
Buer, Oblt Gerhard. 1(F)/122. 290
Bülow, Hpt Harry von. II/JG 77. 134, 358
Bülow, Oblt Hermann. II/KG 30. 191
Burk, Lt z S Ulrich. 2/KüFlGr 406. 122
Bürschgens, Lt Joseph. 2/JG 26. 72, 355
Busacker, Fw. I/KG 26. 249
Busch, Hpt. 1/KüFlGr 506. 22
Busching, Lt Hans. V(Z)/LG 1. 194

Caesar, Hpt Edgar. 1(F)/122. 215, 315, 318
Cahl, Lt. III/LG 1. 292
Capito, Hpt Günther. 7/KG zbV 1. 237
Carganico, Lt Horst. II/JG 77. 351, 352, 353, 358
Carmann, Oblt. II/JG 77. 268
Carnier, Lt. II/JG 53. 101
Carolsfeld, Hpt Eberhard Schnoor von. II/KG 26. 296
Casimir, Hpt Artur von. Stab/KG r 100. 215, 315, 336
Chamier-Glisczinski, Oberst von. KG 3. 20
Christ, Maj. KG zbV 9. 24
Claus, Lt Georg. I/JG 53, III/JG 53. 59, 117, 356, 357
Clemens, Oblt z S Giesbert. 3/KüFlGr 106. 128
Coeler, GenMaj Joachim. Führer der Seeluftstrkr West. 163

Cohrs, Lt z S. 3/KüFlGr 406.
Conrad, Oberst. KG zbV 2. 24
Cramon-Traubadel, Maj Hans-Jürgen von. 1, 2/JG 70, I/JG 54. 146.
Cucuel, Oblt. 4(H)/21. 23
Czech, Oberstlt Armin. FdL West. 163
Czikowski. Fw Walter. II/JG 53. 75

Dalwigk zu Lichtenfels, Hpt Friedrich-Karl, Frhr von. I/StG 77. 21
Dannenberg, Maj. KG zbV 105. 216
Demes, Lt Heinz. II/JG 77. 78, 267, 282, 299
Dessloch, GenMaj. FlgDiv 6. 17
Dickoré, Hpt Friedrich-Karl. I/ZG 26. 78, 125
Diebel, Uffz Erich. 1(H)/23. 95
Diehl, Lt. 'Freya'. 211
Diemayer, Lt Heinrich. 6/KG 30. 322
Dietl, GenLt. 230, 346
Dietrich, Uffz Gottfried. 8/JG 3. 200
Dinort, Maj Oskar. I/StG 2. 21
Dobratz, Maj. II/LG 1. 20
Doensch, Hpt Fritz. I/KG 30. 90, 215
Dombrowski, Uffz. I/ZG 76. 140
Domke, Lt Helmut. I/KG 51. 112
Donike, Oblt Alfred. 4/KG 26. 226
Donner, Oblt Sieghar. 5/KG 26. 175
Döring, GenMaj Hans von. Stab/ZG 26. 16, 143
Döring, Oblt Peter. 4(F)/121. 208
Dressler, Fw Siegfried. 3(F)/22. 118
Drewes, Oberstlt. II/KG zbV 1. 24, 216, 230, 266
Droste, Ofw. II/JG 77. 150
Drum, Oberst. 18
Dubois, Reg Rat Dr. Wekusta 76. 21
Dünsing, Uffz Fritz. I/ZG 1. 217, 218, 227

Eberlein, Uffz Helmut. I/ZG 1. 227, 268
Ebert, Fw Kurt. 2/KG r 100. 334
Eckardt, Lt Reinhold. I/ZG 76. 353, 359
Edric, Uffz. II/JG 77. 117
Ehle, Oblt Walter. I/ZG 1. 215, 358
Ehm, Uffz Werner, I/ZG 2, 197
Eiermann, Oblt z S Helmut. 1/KüFlGr 606. 272
Elstermann, Lt Horst. JGr 152. 67, 68, 358
Emmerich, Oblt Peter. II(J)/TrGr 186. 318, 358
Erdmann, Oberstlt. II/KG 4. 21
Erkens. Uffz Willi. II/KG 30. 192
Eschwege, Hpt Siegfried von. I/JG 51. 115
Erlbeck, Ofw Hugo. 3(F)/11. 156
Esken, Lt. 172
Essl, Ofw Franz. I/JG 52. 206
Evers, Oberstlt. III/KG 4. 21

Faber, Fw Klaus. I/JG 1. 72
Fahlbusch, Lt Helmut. I/ZG 76. 158, 264, 271, 300, 359
Fahr, Ofw Ernst. 3/KG 30. 242
Falck, Hpt Wolfgang. 135, 138, 139, *139*, 158, 167, 215, 227, 359
Falke, Lt Hans. 2/ZG 76. 51
Falkenhorst, Gen von. Gruppe XXI. 346
Fally, Ofw Alfred. Wekusta/ObdL. 313
Fehling, Hpt Joachim. 3/KüFlGr 506, KG zbV 108. 22, 312
Feick, Uffz Helmut. Stab I/ZG 76. 336
Felmy, Gen der Flg. Kdr, Luftflotte 2. 16, 156
Fick, Fw Alfred. 1/KG 26. 129
Fiebig, Oberst. KG 4. 21, 215
Fiel, Lt Walter. I/JG 3. 200
Filips, Maj. 4(H)/23. 23
Fink, Oberst. KG 2. 20
Fischer, Fw Siegfried. I/ZG 1. 204
Fischer-See, Hpt. 2(H)/21. 23
Fisser, Oberst Dr. KG 51. 17
Flakowski. Hpt. 1/KG zbV 103. 235
Flämig, Oblt Walter. 1/KG 30. 90
Fleischmann, Ofw Georg. I/ZG 76. 138, 152, 238, 259, 300, 359
Fokohl, Lt de Res Johann. Luftwaffe LehrDiv. 20, 160
Förster, Ofw Hermann. IV(N)/JG 2. 290, 355
Förster, GenLt. Luftwaffe LehrDiv. 20
Förster, Hpt. KG zbV 108. 216, 316
Fözö, Oblt Josef. 2/JG 71, II/JG 51. 17, 205, *205*, *207*, 356, 357
Franke, Gefr Karl. I/KG 30. 77
Franke, Oblt Friedrich-Wilhelm. Stab/KG 53. 120
Frankemberger, Uffz Arno. 4(F)/122. 118
Frantzius, Maj von. 1(H)/10. 22
Freese, Fw Fritz-Georg. 3/KüFlGr 506. 128
Fresia, Uffz Heinz. I/ZG 76. 135, 138, 139, 150, 352, 359
Freund, Uffz. I/JG 53. 62
Freytag, Lt Otto. 1/KG 40. 335
Friedrich, Oblt. II/JG 77. 353
Froese, Lt Hans. 1(F)/ObdL. 178
Fröhlich, Oberstlt. KG 76. 21
Fuchs, Oberst. Robert. Flgfhr Stavanger. 215, 282, 315
Fuchs, Uffz Wilhelm. I/ZG 76. 128
Fuhrmann, Oblt Johann. 10(J)/LG 2. 137, 138

Gablenz, Oberstlt von. Kdr Tranport Aircraft. 24, 216, 235
Gawlich, Fw Franz. III/JG 53. 105, 208
Geisler, Uffz Kurt. I/JG 2. 202
Geissler, GenLt Ferdinand. Kdr FlgDiv 10, X FlgKps. 214, 215, 230, 316
Geller, Lt Christof, I/JG 52. 115
Gentzen, Hpt Hannes. JGr 102, I/ZG 2. 15, 22, 102, *102*, 103, *103*, 197, 198, 358
Gerhardt, Uffz Werner. 10(N)/JG 26. 149, 356
Gerlach, Oberst von. Aufklgr 41. 23
Giehl, Fw Fritz. JGr 102. 103
Glimkermann, Fw de Res Hans. 1/KüFlGr 406. 122
Gollmann, Oblt Horst. Kpskette/X FlgKps. 187

Gollob, Oblt Gordon. I/ZG 76. 135, 138, 140, 150, 238, 348, 352, 359
Goltzsche, Ofw Gotthard. I/JG 77. 153, *154*
Golz, Uffz Günter. II/KG 54. 277
Gott, Uffz Friedrich. 2/StG 1. 303
Graber, Ofw Helmuth. 3(F)/121. 115
Grabmann, Maj Walter. I(SchwJ)/LG 1, V(Z)/LG 1. 20
Graeff, Lt Maximilian. I/ZG 76. 135, 140, 150, 158
Grams, Uffz Gerhard. I/ZG 26, 152, 238
Graner, Lt Georg. I(J)/LG 2. 267
Grasser, Lt Hartman. JGr 152. 59, 67, *68*, 358
Grauert, GenLt Ulrich. Kdr, FlgDiv 1. 19
Graumnitz, Oberstlt. I/KG 27. 19
Grauschwitz, Gfr Enno. I/ZG 76. 300
Gregarek, Ofw Paul. 1/KüFlGr 506. 188
Greim, GenMaj Robert Ritter von. Kdr, FlgDiv 5. 17
Gresens, Oblt Walter. I/ZG 76. 135, 140, 148, 150
Griener, Ofw Aly. II/JG 52. 182
Grimmling, Ofw Walter. I/JG 53. 56, 57, *57*, *58*
Groeben, Lt Horst von der. Satb III/KG 2. 202-4
Gröning, Fw Hans. I/ZG 76. 138, 150, 238
Gross, Uffz. I/ZG 76. 242
Grote, Lt de Res Erich. 1(F)/ObdL. 169
Groth, Oblt Erich. JGr 102. 358
Grube, Fw Karl. 5/KG 26. 320
Gumbrecht, Fw Richard. 5/KG 4. 291
Guse, Oblt Max. 5(F)/122. 199
Gutbrod, Lt Paul. II/JG 52. 55
Güth, Lt. JGr 176. 70, *70*
Gutt, Fw Hans. Stab/LG 1. 288

Haarbach, Fw. II/JG 77. 299
Haack, Hpt. 2(H)/41. 23
Haarnagel, Lt Gerhard. III/KG 4. 229
Habben, Lt Sibo. I/ZG 76. 152, 238
Habekost, Kaptlt. U-31. 179
Habermann, Lt. 4(F)/121
Hackl, Ofw Anton. II/JG 77. 350, 351, 358
Hackner, Ofw. Stab/KG 26. 234
Hagen, Lt Lothar. JGr 152. 67
Hagen, Maj. 5, 6.(J)/TrGr 186. 16
Hahn, Oblt Hans von. III/JG 53. 147, 357
Hahne, Hpt. KüFlGr 806. 270
Halbach, Lt Heinz. II/JG 77. 133
Handrick, Maj Gotthardt. I/JG 26. 16, 356
Hansen, Oblt Werner. I/ZG 76. 230, 233, *233*, 234, 236, 242
Harlinghausen, Maj i.G. Martin. Chief of Staff, X Flgkps. 175, 181, 215, 235, 298, 304, 315, 359
Hartmut, Oblt Paul. Stab/KG 26. 327
Hartwig, Hpt. 2/KüFlGr 506. 18
Hauck, Fw Gerhard. 1/KG zbV 108. 229
Hauck, Uffz. III/KG 26. 295
Haufer, Hpt. 2(H)/11. 23
Haugk, Uffz Helmut. III/ZG 26. 78, 358
Haunschild, Lt. I/JG 2. 20-9
Hefele, Oberstlt Hans. II/KG 26. 191
Heilingbrunner, GenMaj. Luftgaukdo XII. 17
Heilmayr, Uffz Erwin. II/JG 77. 137, 150
Heimbs, Lt Karl-Wilhelm. I/JG 53. 72, 75
Heinrich, Oblt Ernst. I/KG 26. 171
Heinz, Oblt Karl. 3(F)/ObdL. 248
Held, Fw Alfred. II/JG 77. 51
Helleben, Oberstlt. Stab/KüFlGr 306. 18
Hellge, Fw. 6/JG 53. 69
Hellmann, Lt Wilhelm. 2(H)/13. 200
Hellwig, Uffz. I/JG 52. 117
Helm, Hpt Hans-Joachim. I/KG 26. 171
Hennings, Uffz Hans. JGr 102. 103
Hensel, Ofw Richard. KG r 100. 294
Hentschel, Hpt Karl. II/JG 77. 215, 316
Henz, Oblt Helmut. II/JG 77. 72, 150, 298, 299, 315
Herfeld, Ofw Erich. II/JG 77. 257
Herget, Lt Wilhelm. I/ZG 76. 152, 359
Hermann, Ofw Kurt. Z/KG 30. 301
Hertel, Uffz de Res Gerhard. Wekusta 26. 188
Hess, Fw Karl-Heinz. 5/KG 26. 326
Hesse, Uffz Richard. KG zbV 108. 318
Hesselbach, Gefr. JGr 152. 67
Heyn, Hpt. 1/KG zbV 306. 22, 306
Heyna, Hpt. 1/KG 55. 22
Hien, Ofw Willibald. I/JG 53. 74
Hier, Fw Karl. I/JG 76. 116
Hilbradt, Lt Klaus. I/JG 53. 75, 82
Hintze, Lt Otto. 5(J)/TrGr 186. 190
Hirschauer, GenMaj. Luftygaukdo XVII. 22
Hitler, Adolf. Führer. 48, 155, 167, 214, 346
Hoch, Lt Helmut. I/JG 54. 201
Hoenmanns, Maj. 155, 156
Höfer, Fw Helmut. II/KG 26. 162
Höfer, Uffz Mathäus. II/KG26. 226
Hoffmann, Ofw Franz. I/ZG 76. 128
Hoffmann, Lt Wilhelm. I/JG 53. 58, 75
Hohagen, Lt Erich. II/JG 51. 205, *207*, 356
Hohendahl, Lt Hans. 4/KG 30. 249
Höhne, Maj. I/KG 54. 16
Holck, Uffz. II/JG 77. 150
Hölscher, Ofw Günther. 5/KG 4. 291
Hoops, Fw Walter. II/JG 52. 184
Höppner, Ofw Werner. I/JG 2. 204
Horn, Maj. 3/KüFlGr 106. 18
Hornkuhl, Lt z S. 2/KüFlGr 506. 84, *84*
Hornstein, Hpt von. I/KG zbV 2. 24
Houselle, Oblt Otto. I/KG 26. 249
Houwald, Maj Ottheinrich von. I/JG 3. 20
Hozzel, Hpt Paul-Werner. I/StG 1. 20, 215, 236, 241, 304, 315, 359

372

Schumacher, Oberst Karl. II/JG 77, Stab/JG 1. 16, 134, 135, 137, 141, 143, 145, 149
Schumacher, Fw Leo. I/ZG 76. 259, 352, 359
Schumann, Oblt August-Wilhelm. 4/JG 52. 70
Schumann. Hpt. III/KG 4. 283
Schuster, Uffz Helmut. KGzbV 108. 322
Schütz, Lt S. 154
Schwartzkopf. Oberst Günther. StG 77. 21
Seegart, Lt Joachim. I/JG 2. 154
Seeliger, Hpt. II(J)/TrGr 186. 80, 134
Seiffert, Hpt. 3(F)/22. 63
Seiler, Oblt Reinhard. I/JG 54. 154, 197, 357
Seufert, Fw Bernhard. II/JG 53.
Seywald, Oberst. KG 77. 21
Shute, Lt Hans. II/KG 54. 277
Sicharthoff, Oblt Frithjof von. I/KG 30. 179
Sicking, Ofw Oskar. I/JG 51. 69
Sieburg, Maj. KG 26. 19
Siegel, Hpt Walter. I/StG 76. 21
Sievers, Lt. III/JG 53. 201
Späte, Fw Kurt Otto. KGr 100. 169
Specht, Oblt Günther. I/ZG 26. 78, 126, 127, 359
Sperrle, Gen der Flg Hugo. Kdr. Luftflotte 3. 17
Sperrling, Oberst. 1 Armee. 18
Spielvogel, Maj. II/(St)/LG 2. 22
Spiller, Hpt. Air Attache, Oslo. 236
Stahl, Ofw Erich. 2/StG 1. 303
Stahl, Fw Fritz.KüFlGr 506. 335
Stahl, Oberst. KG 53. 17
Stein, Maj. 2(H)/23. 23
Stein, Hpt. 3/KüFlGr 706. 18
Steinback, Oblt Hans-Ludwig. III/KG 26. 293
Steinhart, Oblt z S. 2/KüFlGr 906. 145
Steinhoff, Oblt Johannes. 10(N)/JG 26. 134, 137, 140, 149, 356
Stiegler, Lt Roman. II/JG 77. 137
Stierle, Ofw Hermann. III/JG 77. 257
Stiltfried und Rattonitz, Hpt Graf von. Stab/KG 54. 16
Stock, Fw Willy. II/KG 4. 290
Stockhausen, Oblt. 1(F)/124. 22
Stoeckl, Oberst. III/KG 51. 17
Stoll, Lt Jakob. III/JG 53. 102, 105, 357
Stollbrock, Oberstlt Joachim. KGr 100. 166
Stolt, Maj. KGzbV 106. 216, 239
Stolte, Lt Paul. I/JG 54. 197, 357
Stolz, Fw Karl. 5/KG 4. 291
Storp, Oblt Siegfried. I/KG 30. 77, 90
Stotz, Lt Max. I/JG 76. 101, 358
Streib, Oblt Werner. I/ZG 1. 227, 359
Streng, Oblt. Stab/KG 26. 334
Struckmann, Lt Edgar. II/JG 77. 133, 351
Student, GenMaj Karl. FlgDiv 7. 24

Stumm, Wachtmeister. Flak. 62, 63
Stumpff, Gen der Flg Hans-Jürgen. Luftflotte 5. 315
Stutterheim, Oberst von. III/KG 77. 21
Sültmann, Fw Hans. 4/KG 30. 242
Süssmann, GenLt. KG 55, Luftgaustab zbV 200. 22, 216
Szuggar, Fw Willy. 10(N)/JG 26. 149, 356

Their, Fw. I/ZG 1. 305
Thiel, Oblt Günther. 1/KG 40. 335
Thiel, Oblt Werner. 3(F)/22. 114
Thiet, Oberstlt. 2(H)/10. 22
Thomas, Fw Walter. 3/KGzbV 102. 262
Thönes, Stabsing. I/ZG 76. 333, 339
Tietzen, Hpt Horst. II/JG51. 202, 356
Topper, Oblt z S Franz. 2/KüFlGr 406. 85
Troitsch, Fw Hans. II/JG 53. 75, 86
Trübenbach, Maj Hans. I(J)/LG 2. 20, 359

Uellenbeck, Oblt Gustav. I/ZG 76. 135, 140, 150, 316
Uhl, Uffz Fritz. I/JG 53. 75

Vetter, Hpt Martin. I/KG 26. 77, 215, 316
Vieck, Oberstlt Karl. I/JG 2. 20
Vitzthun, Oblt. JGr 152. 72
Vlieger, Oblt Heinrich. 3/KüFlGr 406. 242
Vogel, Oblt Harald. II/KG 26. 248
Vogel, Oblt Richard. JG 53. 72, 75
Vogler, Lt z S Joachin. KüFlGr 106. 267
Voigt, Lt Günther. JGr 102. 103
Volk, Lt Josef. III/JG 53. 184
Vollbracht, Maj Friedrich. II/ZG 26. 17
Vollmer, Ofw Ernst. II/JG 53. 75, 86
Vrancken, Lt Werner. 2(F)/123. 112

Waber, GenMaj. Luftgaukdo VIII. 22
Wagner, Ernst. 160
Wagner, Uffz Hans. I/KG 26. 146
Wagner, Hpt Richard. KGzbV 103. 216, 230, 234
Wagnere, Ofw Hans. 3(F)/22. 105
Walter, Oblt. I/ZG 76. 348
Walther, Hpt Erich. I/FJR 1. 216, 329
Wandam, Lt Siegfried. I/ZG 1. 227, 359
Wappenhaus, Hpt. 1(F)/122. 16
Wärnet, Hpt. 1(H)/21. 23
Weber, Uffz Gerhard. II/JG 77. 352
Weber, Oblt Lorenz. III/JG 77. 353
Weigel, Lt Kurt. II/KG 26. 226
Weimann, Uffz Alfred. Z/KG 30. 317
Weinlig, Lt de Res Hans. 2/KüFlGr 906. 340
Weise, GenLt. Luftgaukdo III. 20
Weiss, Fw Erwin. II/JG 53. 197

Weissmann, GenMaj Dr. Luftgaukdo XII. 17
Weigelt, Fw. III/JG 53. 182, 183
Weitkus, Oberstlt Paul. II/KG 2. 20
Wendland, Lt. Ln Regt (Ver) Kothen. 129
Wendt, Uffz. 4(F)/122. 93
Wentz, Lt Günter. 1(F)/122. 340
Wenz, Maj. 2(F)/121. 20
Werry, Lt. 'Freya'. 151
Wibel, Hpt. 5/Bflst 196. 22
Wichartz, Lt Franz. Stab/KG 4. 117
Wick, Lt Helmut. I/JG 2. 116, 209, 355
Wiemer, Ofw Fritz. I/KG 26. 165
Wierbitsky, Fw Paul. KGr 100. 330
Wiesand, Hpt Lienhart. 1/KüFlGr 506. 18, 215, 229
Wiesmann, Uffz. Z/KG 30. 301
Wiggers, Oblt Hans. JGr I.52. 61, 358
Wilcke, Uffz August. II(J)/TrGr 186. 149
Wilcke, Uffz August. 10(N)/JG 26. 193
Wilcke, Hpt Wolf-Dietrich. III/JG 53. 105, 147, 176, 181, 182-3, 357
Wild, Oberstlt von. II/KG 26. 164
Wilms, Fw Hermann. II/KG 26. 164
Wimmer, GenLt.Luftwaffenkdo Ostpreus. 20
Winkels, Ogfr Gerhard. I/StG 1. 274
Winkler, Uffz Martin. 1/JG 53. 62
Winter, Oblt. Stabst/KG 2. 120
Winterer, Hpt. 4/JGr 101. 84
Winterfeld, Maj von. 2(H)/41. 23
Witt, Oblt z S Heinz. 1/KüFlGr 106. 273
Witt, Maj. 1/KGzbV 1. 24, 216
Wittmann, Hpt. Stab/KG 53. 17
Wodke, Oblt z S Emil. KüFlGr 506. 128
Woldenga, Maj Berhard. I/JG 1. 20
Wolf, Maj. 10(F)/LG 2. 16
Wolff, GenMaj. Luftgaukdo XI. 16
Woltersdorf, Lt Helmut. I/ZG 76. 259, 299, 359
Woyna, Oblt. Wekusta 1. 19
Wulf, Oblt. II(J)/TrGr 186. 325
Wühlisch, Oblt Bruno von. 2(F)/121. 199
Wühlisch, Oberst. Luftflotte 2. 16
Wurmheller, Uffz Josef. I/JG 53, 73, 356
Wüsthoff, Oblt z S. 1/KüFlGr 406. 317

Zach, Oberstlt. III/KG 76. 21
Zeidler, Hpt. III/KGzbV 1. 24, 216
Zenetti, GenMaj. Luftgaukdo VII. 17
Zetschwitz, Hpt von. 2/KüFlGr 506. 215, 316
Zickler, Uffz. 3/ZG 76. 352
Zock, Oberst. 3 Armee. Aufklgr 10. 22.
Zube, Fw Kurt. I/StG 1. 332

I Personnel — d) Other Nationalities

Alaffe, Capt Roger (Belgian). 5e Escadrille. 55
Boussa, Capt Lucien (Belgian). 5e Escadrille. 55, 56
Braathen, Lt Arve (Norwegian). Fighter Wing. 231, 233
Bugga, Lt Hans (Norwegian). Naval Air Force. 228

Christian X, King. (Danish). 227

Dahl, Capt Erling Muthe (Norwegian). Fighter Wing. 231, 232, 234

Eggen, Lt. (Norwegian). Halögaland Air Corps. 305

Genot, Adj Albert (Belgian). 5² Escadrille. 55
Grudzinski, Lt Cdr (Polish). 'Orzel'. 225

Hansen, Lt Halfdan (Norwegian). Bomber Wing. 239
Henrard, Lt (Belgian). 1/I/2nd Regiment. 175

Jacquet, Lt (Norwegian). Bomber Wing. 238
Jottard, Alexis (Belgian). 4²Escadrille. 56

Kjos, Lt Kaare (Norwegian). Naval Air Force. 224
Krohn, Lt Dag (Norwegian). Fighter Wing. 231, 233, 234, 235, 239, 240
Kyllingmark, Lt (Norwegian). Halögaland Air Corps. 305, 306

Leroy du Vivier, Daniel (Belgian). 4²Escadrille. 55, 56
Lütken, Sgt Oskar Albert (Norwegian). Fighter Wing. 231, 232, 233, 233

Manshaus, Lt Cdr (Norwegian). Naval 2 Wing. 275
Michotte, Marcel (Belgian). 4²Escadrille. 55

Noonan, Lt P. (Dutch). 3²JAVA. 187
Normann, Capt Harald. (Norwegian). Flying School. 236, 239

Offenberg, S/Lt Jean (Belgian). 4²Escadrille. 56
Offerdal, Lt (Norwegian). Naval Air Force. 301
Oscar, Lt Knut (Norwegian). Naval 1 Flying Group. 228
d'Oultrement, Count Gaston (Belgian). 55
Omholt-Jensen, Lt Edvard (Norwegian). Reconnaissance Wing. 247

Quisling, Vidkun (Norwegian). Leader, Norwegian Nazi Party. 214

Reistad, Capt Ole (Norwegian). Reconnaissance Wing. 306
Ruge, Gen Otto (Norwegian). Commander, Forces Northern Norway. 346

Schuye, Sgt Kristian Frederik (Norwegian). Fighter Wing. 231, 232, 232, 233, 235, 262
Stansberg, Lt (Norwegian). Naval Air Force. 226, 239
Steen, Lt (Norwegian). Bomber Wing. 238, 239
Sundlo, Col (Norwegian). Cdr at Narvik. 230
Svenning, Lt Einar (Norwegian). Naval Air Force. 238

Thorsager, 2/Lt Finn (Norwegian). Fighter Wing. 231, 232, 233, 235
Tradin, Lt Rolf Thorbjørn (Norwegian). Fighter Wing. 231, 232, 235, 239

Waaler, Sgt Per (Norwegian). Fighter Wing. 231, 232, 233, 235, 275

II Units — i) British

a) Air Force

Royal Air Force Order of Battle, 3 September 1939. 36-41

Commands

Army Co-operation Command. 80
Bomber Command. 35, 45, 51, 81. 94, 121, 127, 132, 133, 134, 140, 147, 152, 158, 166, 170, 179, 186, 210, 218-19, 254, 255, 256, 290, 292, 305, 307, 315. 352, 353
Fighter Command. 35, 42, 43, 53, 80, 84, 91, 93, 94, 121, 147, 210, 307
Coastal Command. 43, 54, 80, 88, 93, 106, 165, 218, 247, 264, 267, 324, 354
Air Component, British Expeditionary Force. 45, 46, 81, 94, 108, 109, 124, 124, 160, 172, 209
Advanced Air Striking Force. 45, 46, 94, 108, 109, 124, 160, 172, 174, 201, 209

Groups

1 (Bomber). 35, 45, 46
2 (Bomber). 35, 45, 46, 95, 124, 158, 166, 170, 171, 219, 352, 353
3 (Bomber). 35, 142, 210, 219
4 (Bomber). 35, 53, 219, 270
5 (Bomber). 36, 219
6 (Bomber). 36
11 (Fighter). 42, 166
12 (Fighter). 42, 148
12 (Fighter). 43, 88, 148, 164
15 (Coastal). 43, 44
16 (Coastal). 44
18 (Coastal). 44, 354
19 (Coastal). 309
22 (Army Co-operation). 35, 43

Wings

50 (Army Co-operation). 46, 94, 108
51 (Army Co-operation). 46, 108
52 (Nucleus). 108, 209
60 (Fighter). 46, 47, 94
61 (Fighter). 94, 125
62 (Fighter). 109
67 (Fighter). 108
70 (Bomber). 46, 94, 172, 209
71 (Bomber). 46, 171, 172
72 (Bomber). 46, 171
74 (Bomber). 46, 109, 171
75 (Bomber). 46, 171
76 (Bomber). 46, 171
79 (Bomber). 46
81 (Bomber). 46
82 (Bomber). 46
83 (Bomber). 46

Squadrons

1 (Fighter). 43, 46, 47, 76, 94, 96, 97, 97, 108, 118, 119, 120, 175, 177, 184, 193, 195, 196, 201, 202, 205, 209, 360
2 (Army Co-operation). 46, 81, 82, 174
4 (Army Co-operation). 46, 76, 82
9 (Bomber). 50, 51, 134, 140, 143, 148, 152, 217, 219, 241, 259, 267, 270, 298
10 (Bomber). 78, 81, 133, 178, 255
12 (Bomber). 46, 124, 171
13 (Army Co-operation). 46, 76, 82
15 (Bomber). 36, 46, 124, 190
16 (Army Co-operation). 172
17 (Fighter). 148.
18 (Bomber). 35, 43, 46, 76, 94, 95, 101, 104, 108, 153, 154, 166, 170, 172
21 (Bomber). 144, 166, 179, 193, 352
22 (Coastal). 268, 307, 308, 314, 348, 349
24 (Communications). 109
25 (Fighter). 121, 122, 148
26 (Army Co-operation). 46, 82, 82, 125
29 (Fighter). 148, 219
32 (Fighter). 186, 362
37 (Bomber). 134, 137, 138, 1349, 186, 219, 257, 272, 274, 276, 298, 299
38 (Bomber). 125, 126, 126, 134, 140, 142, 149, 152, 168, 219, 257, 258, 259, 267
40 (Bomber). 46, 124,
41 (Fighter). 90, 148, 191, 192, 360
42 (Coastal). 44, 349, 350
43 (Fighter). 148, 160, 161, 162, 163, 164, 165, 166, 168, 169, 170, 181, 187, 219, 226, 248, 249, 312, 313, 314, 360, 363
44 (Bomber). 144, 186, 219, 256, 257, 281, 300
46 (Fighter). 91, 92, 93, 109, 133, 148, 165, 307, 314, 314, 323, 332, 335, 340, 341, 342, 343, 361
48 (Bomber). 49, 50, 144, 152, 219, 255, 267, 290
50 (Bomber). 219, 241, 256, 257, 265, 300, 305
51 (Bomber). 78, 94, 180, 219, 281, 300
53 (Reconnaissance). 46, 47, 72, 82, 94, 108, 211
54 (Fighter). 166, 167, 188, 361, 362
56 (Fighter). 53, 111, 113, 148, 212, 360
57 (Reconnaissance). 35, 43, 46, 76, 86, 87, 94, 95, 101, 104, 108, 112, 161, 172, 199, 200, 209, 352, 364
58 (Bomber). 49, 219, 272, 281, 300, 305
59 (Reconnaissance). 46, 82, 108, 182, 209, 209
61 (Bomber). 219, 255, 256, 267, 300
64 (Fighter). 210
65 (Fighter). 168
66 (Fighter). 159
72 (Fighter). 84, 91, 92, 128, 129, 361, 363
73 (Fighter). 46, 47, 76, 94, 95, 96, 97, 103, 107, 108, 118, 118, 119, 120, 120, 145, 147, 160, 176, 182, 183, 183, 184, 193, 197, 204, 205, 208, 208, 362
74 (Fighter). 53, 113, 360, 362
75 (Bomber-ex-RNZAF Heavy Bomber Flight). 210, 219, 257, 272
77 (Bomber). 55, 56, 87, 94, 107, 129, 181, 187, 219, 255, 268, 269, 270, 274, 281, 300, 305, 364
78 (Bomber). 290
79 (Fighter). 113, 167, 362,
81 (Communications). 109
82 (Bomber). 144, 171, 179, 181, 190, 193, 217, 353
83 (Bomber). 49, 50, 144, 217, 219, 255, 272, 277
85 (Fighter). 46, 47, 76, 108, 113, 121, 124, 124, 125, 209, 361, 362, 364
87 (Fighter). 46, 47, 76, 99, 100, 107, 108, 124, 172, 199, 212, 362
88 (Bomber). 61, 61, 71, 76, 171, 174, 182
92 (Fighter). 79, 148, 210, 343, 361

b) Royal Navy

II Units — ii) French

a) Armée de l'Air

Armées Aèriènnes

Zones d'Operations Aèriènnes

I/KG 26. 53, 85, 90, 121, 128, 129, 133, 143, *144*, 158, 159, 163, 168, 171, 175, 177, 179, 180, 192, 236, 241, 248, 249, 264, 271, 272, 274, 276, 281, 291, 292, 293, 310, 317, 320, 321, 327, 335, 336, 338, 339, 342, 354
1/KG 26. 77, 78, 159, 249, 264, 335, 339
2/KG 26. 78, 81, 121, 158, 159, 162, 165, 166, 171, 181, 228, 249, 264, 292, 296, 311, 330, 331, 335
3/KG 26. 81, 159, 228, 244, 264
II/KG 26. 162, 163, 164, 165, 168, 169, 175, 179, 180, 191, 192, 226, 241, 250, 255, 264, 269, 270, 272, 273, 276, 293, 294, 296, 303, 310, 318, 319, 321, 322, 324, 326, 337, 342, 345, 346
4/KG 26. 162, 226, 297
5/KG 26. 158, 165, 168, 175, 264, 310, 326
6/KG 26. 133, 158, 161, 162, 181, 226, 264, 342
III/KG 26. 173, 188, 230, 235, 236, 259, 270, 276, 281, 293, 296, 310, 317, 320, 321, 325, 342, 345, 354
7/KG 26. 188, 252, 293
8/KG 26. 188, 244, 252, *253*, 310
9/KG 26. 188, 293
Kampfgeschwader 27. 13
2/KG 27. 112
III/KG 27. 211
I/KG 28. 188
II/KG 28. 13, 148
III/KG 28. 173
Kampfgeschwader 30. 129, 241, *277*, 279, 281, 290, 293, 296, 297, 340
Stab/KG 30. 77, 85, 88, 90, 111, 121, 144, 152, 163, 164, 165, 179, 222, 272, 273, 294, 354
2/KG 30. 165, 179, 249, 276, 282, 289, 301
3/KG 30. 179, 180, 242, 255, 264, 268, 273
II/KG 30. 148, 188, 191, 248, 270, 271, 277, 294, 303, 333
4/KG 30. 191, 242, 249, 342
5/KG 30. 192, 328
6/KG 30. 179, 188, 274, 276, 319, 321, 323, 324, 327, 334, 336, 337, 342, 345
III/KG 30. 151, 242, 294
9/KG 30. 280
Z/KG 30 (see under Zerstörer)
I/KG 40. 211, *283*
1/KG 40. 255, 259, 269, 273, 273, 276, 277, 310, 323, 327, 329, 333, 335, 345
2/KG 40. 211
Stab/KG 51. 104, 202
II/KG 51. 80, 211
III/KG 51. 104, 112
Stab/KG 53. 120, *120*, 202
Stab/KG 54. 290, 293, 298, 304
I/KG54. 13, 276
II/KG54. 276, 277, 281
4/KG54. 277, 290, 293
5/KG54. 277, 292
6/KG54. 287
III/KG55. 80, 151, *284*
Stab/KG55. 172, 202
I/KG55. 13
II/KG55. 13
III/KG55. 80, 148
II/KG76. 151
III/KG76. 80
Kampfgruppe 100. 99, 166, 169, 175, 192, 236, 248, 276, 279, 294, 297, 298, 304, 305, 310, 321, *321*, 325, 327, 329, 330, 331, 332, 333, 334, 336, 337, 338, 339, 340
1/KGr 100. 248, 310
2/KGr 100. 294, 330, 314
Kampfgruppe 126. 163, 188, 272, 300, 304
3/KGr 126. 301

Lehr (Operational Test)

Lehrgeschwader 1. 99, 279, 281, 283, 290, 293, 296, 297, 298, 305
Stab/LG 1. 286, 288
I/LG 1. 99, 151, 301
2/LG 1. 296, 297
II/LG 1. 85, 99, 268, 275, 276, 277, 286, 287, 289, 291, 294, 304
4/LG 1. 287, *288*, 294
5/LG 1. 298
6/LG 1. 288
III/LG 1. 81, 85, 267, 268, 276, 277, 287, 289, 291
7/LG 1. 264, 289
8/LG 1. 281
9/LG 1. 292, 304
V(Z)/LG 1. 80, 115, 121, 151, 183, 184, 185, 194, *195*, 348, 359
13(Z)/LG 1. 80
Stab/LG 2. 99
II(Schlacht)/LG 2. 13
8(F)/LG 2. 81
10(N)/LG 2. 172

Träger (Carrier Units)

Trägergruppe 186. 12, 133
II(J)/TrGr 186. 80, 99, 217, 131, 134, 137, 166, 174, 179, 188, 193, 307, 318, 340, 351, 358
4(Stuka)/TrGr 186. 80
5(J)/TrGr 186. 190
6(J)/TrGr 186. 325

Stuka (Dive Bomber)

Stab/StG 1. 99
I/StG 1. 236, 239, 241, *242*, 249, 274, 296, 298, *298*, 303, 304, 306, 327, 333, 333, *333*, 337, 359
1/StG 1. 244, 252, 267, 286, 297
2/StG 1. 303, 338, 339
3/StG 1. 298
Stab/StG 2. 81, 359

Aufklärer (Reconnaissance)

2(H)/10. 281, *281*, 305, 320
3(F)/11. 156, 183, 205
4(F)/11. 175, 194
1(H)/13. 96, 206
2(H)/13. 200
3(H)/13. 160
1(F)/22. 107, 175, *176*
3(F)/22. 63, 64, 105, 114, *114*, 118
4(F)/22. 82, 95, 97, 175
1(H)/23. 85, 95
4(H)/23. 96

1(F)/120. 254, 255, 270, 272, 276, 282, 300, 301, 303, 309, 310, 317, 330
Fernaufklärungsgruppe 121. 175
2(F)/121. 81, 199
3(F)/121. 115, 161, 177, 199
4(F)/121. 107, 115, 175, 194, 200, 201, 202, 208, 212
Fernaufklärungsgruppe 122. 121, 128
1(F)/122. 92, 112, 121, 128, 158, 159, 180, 181, 191, 198, 224, 225, 264, 274, 280, 282, 289, 293, 302, 303, 318, 324, 325, 327, 329, 331, 333, 340, 342
2(F)/122. 84, 90, 100, *100*, 118, 212
3(F)/122. 112
4(F)/122. 77, 93, 118, 119
5(F)/122. 119, 199
Fernaufklärungsgruppe 123. 172
1(F)/123. 86, 107, 119, 147, 153, 172, 193, 197, 204, 212, 330
2(F)/123. 70, 96, *97*, 112
3(F)/123. 195, 212
1(F)/124. 211
Fernaufklärungsgruppe ObdL. 80, 90, 211, *282*, 293, 352
Stab FAG/ObdL. 80, 81, 168
1(F)/ObdL. 53, 81, 113, 157, *157*, 160, 168, 178, 282, 293
2(F)/ObdL. 81
3(F)/ObdL. 81, 169, 194, 248, 282, 299
4(F)/ObdL. 81, 338
Fliegerkompanie des Luftnachrichtenregt ObdL. 198

Transport

Stab Lufttransportchef Land. 188
KGzbV 1. 237, 333
I/ 227
II/KGzbV 1. 230, 231. 235, 236, 266
5/KGzbV 1. 230, 266
III/KGzbV 1. 329, 331
7/KGzbV 1. 238
8/KGzbV 1. 227, 266
14/KGzbV 1. 270
Stab/KGzbV 2. 211
KGzbV 9. 211
KGzbV 11. 211
KGzbV 12. 211
KGzbV 101. 188, 227, 236, 239, 310
KGzbV 102. 188, 236, 262, 311, *319*
1/KGzbV 102. 262, 346
3/KGzbV 102. 262, 346
KGzbV 103. 188, 230, 231, 234, 265, 266, 268, 311
KGzbV 104. 188, 237, 239, 310
KGzbV 105. 188, 229, 236, 245, *246*, 260, *260*, 261, 269, 285, 310
KGzbV 106. 188, 239, 305, 310
KGzbV 107. 188, 236, 250, 273, 286, 311, 337, 339, 346
KGzbV 108. 188, 229, 250, 251, 252, 267, 272, 276, *280*, 306, *311*, 311, *312*, *318*, 319, 320, *320*, 322, *322*, 327, 329, 331, 334, *334*, 346
KGzbV 172. 211
17/KGzbV 172. 211
Tranzoeanstaffel. 225

Küstenflieger (Coastal)

Details of changes in unit designation 25 October 1939. 97-98
Stab/KüFlGr 106. 179, 239
1/KüFlGr 106. 52, 59, 106, 112, 121, 240, 264, 266, 267, 272, 273, 280, 282
2/KüFlGr 106. 51, 59, 112, 123, 187, 254, 271, 272, 313
3/KüFlGr 106. 77, 121, 122, 128
3/KüFlGr 306. 77
Küstenfliegergruppe 406. 283, 341
Stab/KüFlGr 406. 122, 217, 225, *237*, 240, 247, 270, 276
1/KüFlGr 406. 61, 77, 90, *91*, 106, 122, 128, 254, 271, 272, 316
2/KüFlGr 406. 84, 85, 122, 217, 242, 287, 288, 313, 337
3/KüFlGr 406. 77, 85, 106, 130, 143, 242, *253*, 253, 337
6/KüFlGr 406. 111
Stab/KüFlGr 506. 179, 229, 296, 298, 304, 335, 341
1/KüFlGr 506. 188, 229, 240, 274, 286, 292, 296, 345
2/KüFlGr 506. 53, 77, 78, 84, *84*, 192, 229, 240, 2451, 260, 285, 286, 296, 298, 302, 346
3/KüFlGr 506. 128, 179, 190, 268, 304, 341
4/KüFlGr 506. 272
Küstenfliegergruppe 606. 99
1/KüFlGr 606. 272
2/KüFlGr 606. 54, 61, 77, 90, 346
3/KüFlGr 606. 243, 337
1/KüFlGr 706. 326, 335, 341
3/KüFlGr 706. 85
Küstenfliegergruppe 806. 217
1/KüFlGr 806. 192
2/KüFlGr 806. 180, 1897, 283, 317
3/KüFlGr 806. 169, 180, 187, 317, 324
1/KüFlGr 906. *91*, 260
2/KüFlGr 906. 106, 128, 145, 188, 242, 243, 340
3/KüFlGr 906. 113, 121, 128
1/BFl 196. 243, 252, 309
5/BFl 196. 243, 309, 324

Wetterkundungsstaffeln (Weather Reconnaissance)

Wekusta 26. 53, 112, 123, 147, 188, 199
Wekusta 51. 189
Wekusta ObdL. 312
Wekusta X FlgKps. 211

Miscellaneous Units

Korpsführungskette/X FlgKps (see X FlgKps)
7/LgNachregt 3. 255, 260, 287
Ln Regt (Ver) Kothen. 129
Na-Flug-Kommando Köthen. 129
Na-Flug-Kommando Weimar. 270
Seenotstaffel 2. 320

Flakartillierie (Anti-Aircraft)

I/Flakregt 4. 202
I/Flakregt 8. 227
I/Flakregt 19. 227, 280
I/Flakregt 32. 32, 252, 258, 269, 280, 317
8/Flakregt 32. 268
4/Flakregt 33. 239, 260, 283
6/Flakregt 33. 225, 239

7/Flakregt 33. 239
9/Flakregt 33. 225, 239, 254
10/Flakregt 33. 260, 268
II/Flakregt 33. 250, 265, 300
III/Flakregt 33. 250, 266
I/Flakregt 611. 297
4/Flakregt 611. 268
Festungs Flakabt 32. 86
Festungs Flakabt 33. 54
Flakabt 84. 82
2/Leichtenflakabt 851. 172, 208
Res Flakabt 603. 280, 281, 290
2/Res Scheinwerfer abt 239. 105

Fallschirmjäger (Parachute Troops - Luftwaffe Command)

I/FJR 1. 317, 320, 322, 325, 329, 331, 333, 336, 339
1/FJR 1. 230, 231, 237, 266, 275
2/FJR 1. 230, 231, 257
3/FJR 1. 238
4/FJR 1. 227

b) Army

Infanterie Divisions

69. 228
163. 252
181. 276, 277

Gebirgsbatterie (Artillery)

2/AR 112. 262
4/AR 112. 280
II/AR 112. 276, 277

GebirgsPanzerJäger. (Mountain Anti-Tank)

GebPzjgAbt 48. 306
PzJagAbt 222. 280

Gebirgsjäger Regiments (Mountain Troops)

1/GJR 136. 329
3/GJR 136. 329
1/GJR 137. 327
3/GJR 137. 327
2/GJR 138. 325
3/GJR 138. 311, 312, 317, 325
6/GJR 138. 328

Infanterie Regiments

IR 159. 252
5/IR 159. 252
III/IR 159. 227, 229
II/IR 193. 239
II/IR 193. 239
II/IR 234. 230
I/IR 236. 255
II.IR 236. 260
III/IR 236. 260
III/IR 305. 227
III/IR 307. 252
II/IR 308. 227
Stab/IR 324. 252
I/IR 324. 236, 237
Stab/IR 334. 276
II/IR 334. 276
II/IR 334. 265
II/IR 355. 273
III/IR 355. 273
III/IR 359. 277
I/IR 388. 280

Miscellaneous Units

Pioneerbat. 234, 255
Stabgruppe XXI. 260, 346

c) Navy

Units

6 Minensuchflotilla. 167
Warship Group 2. 229
Warship Group 4. 228
Warship Group 8. 227
1 Zerstorerflotilla. 169
4 Zerstorerflotilla. 159

Battleships

Graf Spee (Pocket Battleship). 167
Battlecruisers
Admiral Scheer. 50
Deutschland. 105, 144
Gneisenau. 51, 85, 121, 137, 167, 217, 256, 341, 344
Scharnhorst. 51, 121, 137, 167, 217, 256, 341, 344, 345, 347, 348, 350

Cruisers

Blücher. 231, 231, 243
Emden (Light). 50
Hipper. 167, 217, 224, *225*, 229, 241, 252, 256, 341
Karlsruhe. 231, 241, 242
Köln. 85, 228, 241, 242, 253
Königsberg. 228, 241, 250, *251*
Lützow. 230, 253, 260
Nürnberg. 131, 308

III Places — *ii) France*

III Places — iii) Germany

III Places — iv) Norway

III Places — v) Other Countries

IV Codenames

i) German

ii) British